The P.C. Support Handbook

The
Configuration
and
Systems
Guide

David Dick

Dumbreck Publishing

The P.C. Support Handbook
© 1997 by Dumbreck Publishing
ISBN 0-9521484-4-7

Introduction

This fifth edition of the book reflects the rapidly changing hardware and software specifications of computer technology. Since the last edition, a whole range of new techniques and products have arrived in the areas of data communications, the Internet, local area networks and in multimedia. These topics are, of course, covered in the book's chapters.

However, we must not lose sight of the book's main objective - to provide students and technicians with a broad understanding of <u>all</u> the computer technology in use today. The new technology is very exciting but much of it has still to find its way into general use. Many organisations still use older computers and older versions of operating systems. The support technician has to work with a broad spread of equipment and the book therefore provides information on XTs as well as the Pentium range. It covers DOS use as well as Windows 95 use.

The book attempts to accurately reflect the needs of its readers and this fifth edition introduces new material that was specifically asked for by colleges, universities and support departments. The book's contents was again shaped by the wide response to our user survey thus ensuring that it meets the needs of the maximum amount of users.

There are many books on computer architecture, tweaking DOS and Windows and on repairing computer components. They are specialised books with a narrow outlook and mostly American-based. This book provides a more general approach and information for British users. The book is updated annually to keep up to date with developments, as a glance through the contents or index pages will show.

The need for skills in both hardware and software installation and maintenance is reflected in the seventeen chapters.

I hope that you will find the book a useful reference.

David Dick

CONTENTS

Computer Basics 1
  Advantages of Computers
  Components of a Microcomputer -
    system unit, monitor, keyboard,
    discs, printers, mouse
  Assembling the System
  Getting up and Running

Operating Systems & Environments
  36
  Using DOS
  Filenames and Extensions in DOS
  Directories In DOS
  Handling Files - deleting, copying, merging,
                moving, renaming, wildcards
  DOS Error Messages,
  Command Line Editing
  Environments, Menus, DOS Shell
  Windows 3.1 - Program Manager, File Manager,
        Task Manager, The Clipboard, Recorder
  Windows 95 - Start Menu, Explorer, TaskBar

Computer Video 122
  Monochrome Monitors
  Colour Monitors
  Energy Saving
  Video Standards
  Screen Drives
  Health & Safety
  Adjustments/Controls
  Alternatives To CRTs
  Graphics Cards
  VESA Video Modes Table

Batch Files 179
  Creating Batch Files
  Replaceable Parameters
  Branching & Looping
  Decision Making
  Help Pages
  For..In..Do
  Shift, Call
  User Input
  Pipes/Filters, Redirection
  Variables in Batch Files

Software/Data 19
  System / Application Software
  Processing Systems
  Licensing Agreements -
    Commercial, Public Domain, Shareware
  Copyright , Piracy
  Software Installation
  Computer Data - types, usage, sources
  Security
  Data Protection Act
  Data Organisation
  Storage Media Library

Computer Architecture 67
  Numbering Systems - binary, hex, ASCII,
    arithmetic, negative numbers, logic operations
  How the Computer Works - CPU, registers,
    fetch-execute cycle, interrupts, pre-fetching,
    pipelining, parallel processing, clock-
    multiplying, co-processors
  The Intel range of CPUs
  Assembly Language
  PC Bus Architectures
  External Ports

P.C. Configuration 149
  The Bootstrapping Process
  Commands in CONFIG.SYS
  Device Drivers
  Commands in AUTOEXEC.BAT
  Configuring a Computer System
  MSDOS Memory Management
  Multi-Configuration
  Installing DOS
  Upgrading DOS

Computer Memory 198
  Memory Usage
  The PC Memory Map
  Memory Organisation
  Memory Types
  Chip Types
  Parity
  CPU Cache Memory
  Extended Memory
  Expanded Memory

Windows Configuration 218
Windows 3.1
    Installing, Setting Windows Options
    Creating Program Groups/Items
    Windows Configuration Files
Windows 95
    Installing, Altering the setup
    Customising the Start Menu
    Device Manager, The Registry

Computer Viruses 294
Virus Definitions, File Infection Methods
Aims of Viruses, Virus Problems
Virus Detection/Prevention
Anti-Virus Products
Virus Elimination
Table of Common Viruses

Upgrading A Computer 332
Compatibility Issues -
    IRQ, DMA, I/O Address Clashes
Safety/Handling Procedures
How to upgrade:
    CPU, Motherboard, Video, Memory,
    IDE Drive, Second IDE Drive, EIDE Drive,
    SCSI Drive, Floppy Drive, UPS, Sound
    Card, Scanner, CD-ROM, Network Card,
    Serial Port, Mouse, ZIP Drive
Using Windows 95 Control Panel

Data Communications 359
Serial Port
Modems
Data Links
PC to PC Transfers
OSI and TCP/IP standards
The Internet - Administration, Getting On,
    User Addresses, E-Mail, File Transfer,
    Searches, User Groups
WWW - Browsers, URLs, Searches,
    HTML, Internet Problems
The Information Superhighway, ISDN

Multimedia 423
Applications of Multimedia
Multimedia Hardware Standards
Digitised Sound - Sound Cards
Music, MIDI
Graphic Images
Animation
Full-Motion Video
Multimedia Software
Designing a Project

Discs & Drives 245
Floppy Discs
Hard Discs
Interfaces - ESDI, IDE, EIDE, SCSI
Cache And Cache Controllers
DOS Disc Organisation - Boot Record,
Files, Directory,
Windows 95 - FAT32, Long Filenames
Initialising a Disc - Partitioning, Formatting
Backing up Files
Compression Utilities
CD ROM - Construction, CD-R, Standards
DVD
Magneto-Optical Drives

PC Support 306
System Maintenance
Problem Diagnosis - Response Time,
        Down Time, Record Keeping
Ensuring Safe Practices
Running a Help Desk
Assisting Users to access Support
System Diagnostics
Fault Finding
Health And Safety

System Selection 350
Hardware Definition
Selecting Options -CPU, Motherboard,
    Memory, Monitor, Hard Disc, BIOS,
    Floppy Disc, Miscellaneous
Technical Check List
Evaluation
Equipment Testing
Equipment Costing
Purchasing Policy
Post Delivery

Local Area Networks 397
Advantages/Features of a LAN
LAN Topologies
Network Interface Cards
Servers
LAN Media
Transmission Methods
LAN Standards
Practical Cabling Issues
Fast Networks
Software On The Network
Client/Server Software

The Support Shareware CD

A CD has been specially prepared to accompany this book.   The best programs, utilities and reference material has been included in a single CD which is designed to further assist the reader.

The CD contains hundreds of programs that are directly linked with the subjects of the book.

EXAMPLES OF THE CONTENTS

MULTIMEDIA
VidFun - multimedia viewer and image processor
Midi Jukebox
TZ Video Master - video editor

VIRUSES
F-PROT - virus scanner
Fibre - anti-virus
AVP - anti-virus encyclopaedia

PC SUPPORT
HelpScribble - help file authoring tool
TechFacts
The Hardware Book
TheRef

DATACOMMS
WebWagon - download home pages from a web site
Sitebuilder - web page creator
Internet call charge logger
HTMASC - converts web pages to text
Cel Assembler - build animated GIFs

ARCHITECTURE
W32DASM - a recommended disassembler/debugger
NASM - freeware Assembler

All the programs are included in the CD with the author's approval.

The selection includes program that run under DOS, Windows 3.1 and Windows 95.

WINDOWS
ERS32 - Emergency Recovery for Windows 95
Windows swap file monitor
Windows desktop utilities
JWALL - wallpaper manager

These are the latest versions and are distributed complete and unmodified, according to the distributor's wishes and methods.

LEGAL PROVISIONS
The price paid for the CD purchases the right to try the shareware.   Payment to the original author is required if shareware is used beyond the specified trial period.
All software is intended to be virus-free.   However, we recommend that the files be check before being installed, as new viruses are continually being developed.   Consequently, Dumbreck Publishing assume no responsibility for any consequences of using these files.

HOW TO ORDER
The CD is available in the UK for £5 per copy.   There is an additional charge of 50p for post and packing.   Two or more copies are sent post free.
Cheques should be sent to:
Dumbreck Publishing, 24 Brandon Gardens, Prestwick, KA9 1RY.
Phone/Fax : 01292-470310
E-Mail : sales@dumbreck.demon.co.uk

Computer Basics

Today, computers are used in a vast variety of applications. Almost all aspects of life, work and play are influenced by their use. Sometimes, the computer chip is even embedded inside a piece of equipment - such as a video recorder or washing machine. In these cases, the chip is dedicated to a particular function and the user is only given a small degree of control over its operations.

In industry and commerce, the computer comes in all shapes and sizes - from the hand portable carried round by the busy executive to the giant mainframe that crunches its way through millions of tax bills. The larger machines handle complex operations such as Automatic Banking, Weather Forecasting, Traffic Control, Scientific Modelling, Computer Aided Manufacturing, etc. The book is concerned with the 'microcomputer'. This is the machine that sits on the office desktop. Despite its relatively small size, it is becoming more powerful every year; it can store larger and larger programs and can run ever faster. Above all, it is programmable - it is not tied to a single program.

Typical uses of microcomputers are:

Budgeting, Payroll Processing, Word Processing, Databases, Stock Control, Project Management, Desk Top Publishing, Graphic Design, Multimedia, Electronic Music, Communication between offices and within the office, World-wide electronic mail, Internet access, etc.

ADVANTAGES OF COMPUTERS
- They can carry out repetitive and large volume tasks without fatigue.
- They are much less error prone than humans, providing an output of consistently better quality.
- They are much quicker than humans. Masses of information is always readily available.
- They are more reliable than humans, allowing for better planning and control of output.
- They can work 24 hours a day, in the dark, with minimum heating and little supervision.
- They are immune from human conditions - such as sick leave, maternity leave, strikes, etc.
- They occupy less space than humans; they don't need seats, desks, canteens, toilets, etc.
- Over a period of time, they are cheaper than humans, due to savings in wages, power and accommodation and savings through improved output and quality.

DISADVANTAGES OF COMPUTERS
However, all is not on the plus side.
- Computers can be expensive to install and maintain.
- Trained personnel are required to use the computer applications.
- Trained personnel are required to maintain the machines, the programs and the company data.
- There are problems of compatibility between computers. Files from a Unix system will not run on a PC; PC files will not run on an Amiga or Macintosh. There is no 'standard' computer, although those based around the IBM PC model account for most business and commercial use - providing a common system for exchanging data.
- There are problems of 'concurrency'. If data (eg a price list) is duplicated on several machines and changes are made, which computer holds the most up-to-date version?
- Storing masses of data on computers, particularly when computers are connected together, presents a real security problem. By law, companies have to prevent unauthorised access to their data; this may come from employees or from outsiders 'hacking' in to the system using modems.
- Any failures in the system threaten the users' activities. Where all a company's activities and data are stored on a single computer, any breakdown in that computer leaves the company unable to function.

Above all, computers are stupid! There is great truth in the phrase - "Garbage In Garbage Out". If you enter wrong information into the computer, you get incorrect results! If you place correct information in the computer, but the program is wrong - you still get incorrect results! The computer is merely a machine with no intelligence other than that programmed into it. For example, if the programmer forgets to tell a computer that no employee in the company is likely to be over 70 years old, it will happily accept an employee's age as one million. Consequently, the company's statistics are completely flawed, showing an average employee age of several thousand!

At the end of the day, computers are a tool for use by humans and cannot fully replace human common sense and experience.

WHAT IS A COMPUTER ?

There have been *'computers'* for a long part of society's history. The abacus and mechanical devices have long been used as an aid to calculation. Today's definition of computers really describes the electronic computing device. A computer is essentially an information processor that is able to perform substantial computation without intervention by human operators.

To function, a computer requires both hardware and software elements. The physical machinery involved in the computer system is called *'hardware'* and consists of components such as the processor unit, monitor, keyboard, disc drives and printer. If you can touch it, it must be hardware. The more efficient the hardware, the quicker the programs will run. Software is the programs that you buy or create for the computer. These carry out specific tasks such as word-processing or accountancy. The better designed the software, the more facilities are offered to the user.

In the microcomputer market, the IBM PC is by far the most common machine, without around 90% of the world share. The *'PC'* stands for *'personal computer'* and the machine first appeared in early 1980's. All subsequent PC machines have been built round this basic architecture. Of course, many machines in everyday use are not manufactured by IBM. They may be Compaq models or Packard Bell, etc. These are termed *'clones'* since they follow the basic architecture of the IBM model. In practice, they perform like an IBM PC in almost all respects (within the limits of copyright).

MICROCOMPUTER COMPONENTS

The main components that comprise the typical PC are:

- The main system unit
- Input devices
- Storage devices
- Output devices

The typical process for using a computer is:

1. Load a program into the computer's memory (e.g. a word-processing package). The program will initially be held on some storage device such as a floppy disc or the computer's internal hard disc. A <u>copy</u> of this program is transferred into the memory of the computer; the disc still stores the original copy. The program is then run from the version stored in memory.
2. Input any data (e.g. type in a report)
3. Process the data (e.g. spell check the report)
4. Output the data to screen or printer (e.g. print the report)
5. Save the data (on to a floppy disc or the internal disc)

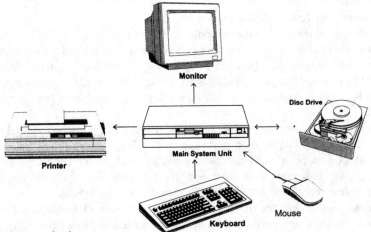

A brief description of the units is:

MAIN SYSTEM UNIT : This case houses the CPU (Central Processing Unit) chip which carries out all the computer's programming tasks.

KEYBOARD : The keyboard allows the user to type in input to the computer (e.g. commands to do things, words for a report, choices from menus, etc.).

MONITOR : This is like a TV screen and allows the facts, pictures, etc., generated by the computer to be viewed by the user.

DISC DRIVE : Stores the programs and information that the user needs.

MOUSE : A pointing device that makes some operations, such as using Windows or drawing packages, easier to use than with the keyboard.

PRINTER : Produces a permanent copy of the program's output (e.g. a letter or a graph) on to a sheet of paper.

MAIN SYSTEM UNIT

The main system box comes in a variety of shapes from tiny hand-held plastic cases for portable use to large metal tower cases for network servers and power workstations. Inside any case, there will still be a main electronic board, called the 'motherboard' that houses the CPU, memory, etc.

MOTHERBOARD

This comprises a printed circuit board, about the size of an A4 sheet of paper in the case of standard desktop computers. It has all the computer's processing chips mounted on it, either being soldered directly to the board or being plugged into sockets on the board. All the power, data and addressing information is carried between components on the copper tracks etched on to the printed circuit board. Each motherboard is designed to handle a particular computing processor, since modern processor chips have more sophisticated needs than older processors. Thus, manufacturers supplied motherboards specially made for use with 386 chips and these are of different design from motherboards intended for use with Pentium chips.

CPU (Central Processing Unit)

The main chip in any computer system is the Central Processing Unit. The speed and design of this chip largely determine the overall speed of the computer. The early PC's used a chip known as the 8088 and this was followed by the 8086, 80286, 80386SX, 80386DX, 80486SX, 80486DX, the Pentium Pro and the Pentium MMX chip. The 8086 machines ran at a speed of 4.77MHz while the Pentium Pro now runs as fast as 266MHz. Apart from their raw speed improvements, modern chips have other in-built advantages over earlier models. For example, modern computers handle data at a faster rate due to their data bus being 32 bits wide; older models only had a 16-bit bus and the earliest XT machines had only an 8-bit bus. While the older systems are no longer for sale, machines of all types and speeds are currently in use in commerce, industry and in the home.

The CPU is the heart of the computer system and is a silicon micro-chip. Its function is to interpret and execute the required instructions (see chapter on Computer Architecture).

MEMORY

To carry out its function, the computer has to temporarily store the program and data in an area where it can be used by the computer processor. This is known as the computer's 'memory' or sometimes as 'primary storage'. Memory consists of computer chips which are capable of storing information; that information may be the instructions of a program, or it may be the data that the program uses or creates. When the user wishes to run a program (e.g. a database), a copy of the program is loaded from the disc and placed in the computer memory. The program is then run from the computer memory. This makes it possible for the machine to be a typist, editor, designer, artist and many other functions. The machine, in fact, will run whatever program is currently in memory. If another program is loaded, that becomes the new function of the machine. This is what makes the computer so versatile - it is not tied to any one activity. The computer memory not only has to store the program - it also has to store the data associated with that program (e.g. letters from word-processing or records from a database).

The memory chips consist of a large number of cells, each cell having a fixed capacity for storing data and a unique location or address. This type of memory is known as RAM (Random Access Memory) and it is volatile (i.e. the program and data held in the memory is lost when the machine is switched off). This is not a problem, since the program in memory is only a copy - the original program will still be stored on disc. However, any data created (e.g. a letter or drawing) will reside in memory and will have to be permanently saved to disc before the computer is switched off.

Another type of memory is known as ROM (Read Only Memory) and this is non-volatile (i.e. the data remains after the machine has been switched off). This type of chip is used to store system programs. For more information, see the chapter on memory.

Measurement Of Capacity

Memory capacity relates to the amount of data a storage device can hold at any one time and is measured in bytes. One byte represents one character. A character can be a letter or a number, or any of the many special characters found on the keyboard including a space. There are many other characters used in the internal workings of the microcomputer that you will never see in print. For example, the 'beep' for the computer's internal loudspeaker is stored as a single character.

In computing, where operations are often considered in units of 2, the Kilo or K actually means 1,024 characters with similar definitions for the larger numbers.

Kilo is 2 to the power of 10, or 2 x 2 x 2 x 2 x 2 x 2 x 2 x 2 x 2 x 2. Tera is 2 multiplied by itself 40 times, or exactly 1,099,511,627,776.

Kb (Kilobyte)	1,024 characters
Mb (Megabyte)	1,048,576 characters
Gb (Gigabyte)	1,073,741,824 characters
Tb (Terabyte)	1,099,511,627,776 characters

A rough measure of memory requirements is:

> 1 byte can store 1 character
> 1 Kb can store a few paragraphs of text
> 1 Mb can store a reasonably-sized book

Running Out Of Memory

The ability of a microcomputer to run programs is limited by the physical capacity of the computer memory. The operating system takes up a certain amount of the available memory. All programs have to be loaded into memory before they can be used and data created by a user from a program is stored in memory before it is written to a backing store device for permanent storage.

Almost all modern machines have a nominal RAM of 640Kbytes, with the possibility of expandable user-memory on some machines. Not all of the memory is actually available to the user. The operating system takes up a chunk of RAM, the amount being dependent upon the DOS version. Sophisticated software packages such as Microsoft Excel and Microsoft Word take up large amounts of RAM and the user may create large worksheets and documents using these packages that can use up the rest of the available memory.

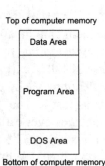

INPUT DEVICES

Input devices are used to enter or input data into the CPU. The main input device on computers is the keyboard. There is a wide range of other input devices including the mouse, optical scanners, pressure pads and other sensors, graphic tablets, touch screens, communication devices and audio and video capture cards.

OUTPUT DEVICES

Output devices convert data from the computer into forms which humans can understand or use. There are two main output devices on the microcomputer system, the monitor screen and the printer. Other output devices include graph plotters, modems, audio boards with speakers and robot arms.

BACKING STORE

This is also known as external memory or secondary storage and is used for the long-term storage of data. The bulk of information (programs and data) used by computer applications are stored on backing store and must be transferred to main memory before it can be processed by the CPU. Backing store devices include magnetic discs (removable floppy discs and built-in hard discs) and magnetic tape.

THE POWER OF THE MACHINE

The power of the machine is usually indicated by the speed of the processor; the faster the speed of the chip, the more instructions it can process in any given time.

The following measurements of time are used:

> Millisecond = 1/1,000th of a second
> Microsecond = 1/1,000,000th of a second
> Nanosecond = 1/1,000,000,000th of a second

These measurements are used to describe the time taken for the computer processor to process one unit of data, usually one byte. In recent years, this method of measurement has been replaced by estimating the number of instructions or operations able to be processed by a computer e.g. a number of MIPS or MFLOPS (representing Millions of Instructions Per Second or Millions of Floating Point Operations Per Second) which are better indications of computing power.

Different models of computer are designed to run at different speeds. The faster the machine, the higher the price. One measure of speed of a machine is the number of cycles per second it can process (measured in MHz - MegaHertz - millions of cycles per second). The slowest PC was just under 5MHz. The fastest speed is always being improved upon and is currently in the order of 233MHz, with even faster machines on the way.

The choice of machine depends very much upon its expected use. If the machine was used entirely for word processing, for example, a low speed machine would be perfectly satisfactory. Since the slowest part of the process is the typist's thinking and typing time, there is little to be gained by very fast processing in between long pauses at the keyboard. On the other hand, where there is going to be a great deal of machine processing, such as graphics calculations and other number crunching, a faster machine would become essential.

For even faster processing, the machine can be fitted with an extra chip - called a *'maths co-processor'*. It takes on the task of most of the mathematical calculations, leaving the main processor free for other tasks. Since the tasks are being shared, the whole program runs much more quickly. The chip is available as an optional extra on older machines, while it is already built into the Pentium chips.

Of course, the raw speed of the CPU is not the only factor in determining the machine's overall speed. Other factors, such as the speed of the disc and video card, the amount of RAM available, whether the machine has an efficient caching system, etc., also determine the machine's performance.

MONITORS

Most programs send the output from their calculations to a screen (apart from those such as payroll programs that send most of their output to the printer, with only a summary going to the screen). The screen is contained in unit called the *'monitor'* - sometimes also called the VDU (*'visual display unit'*).

MONITOR TYPES

Monitors are available in either monochrome (black and white, or perhaps a green or amber screen) or colour. Almost all modern applications are written to provide text and graphics in colour. Sometimes this is used to enhance the use or appeal of the product. On other occasions, such as graphic design, PCB design, etc., the use of colour would be essential. A monochrome monitor is still capable of displaying screen output from applications written for

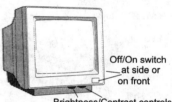

Off/On switch at side or on front

Brightness/Contrast controls

colour monitors but may merge some of the colours into similar shades of grey. A colour monitor comprises more parts and is more difficult to construct and is therefore more expensive. Screen output can vary from user messages and prompts, to displaying graphs and pie charts.

SCREEN RESOLUTION

The PC supports different degrees of screen resolution. The higher the screen resolution, the better the quality of the picture, allowing graphics to be used. The resolution of a screen is measured in 'pixels' (picture elements). Each pixel is an independent dot appearing on the screen. The resolution of a screen is given by the number of pixels in the horizontal and the vertical plane.

The most common screen resolutions are:

VGA	640 x 480
SVGA	800 x 600 or even 1024 x 768

Other standards, such as the Hercules, CGA and EGA resolutions are almost extinct as far as new sales are concerned but there is still a large number of such monitors in daily use.

The higher resolution models produce a sharper, more detailed picture but are more expensive. The highest resolution becomes a necessity where desk top publishing, CAD or other graphic applications are to be run. Microsoft Windows and Windows applications are greatly improved with higher resolution monitors; a 1024 x 768 screen will reproduce a greater number of Windows icons on the screen at any one time. The greater resolution monitors require more demanding construction and these are more expensive to buy.

All monitors have on/off switches and controls for screen brightness and contrast; some models have other, more sophisticated controls. All monitors have two connecting cables; one to connect power to the monitor and one that connects to the system unit's video output socket.

KEYBOARD

This is the main input device to the computer and is used to enter commands or data directly into the machine, for processing. On some computers, there is a lock on the main unit casing, to provide some limited security against unauthorised use.

The keyboard's main features are:

1. The computer keyboard consists of a normal typewriter layout with some additional keys incorporated, and a group of function keys (situated on the left with older models and along the top with newer models), a numeric pad on the right, and an optional group of direction keys also on the right side.
2. The keys for numeric zero (0) and alphabetic oh (O), and numeric one (1) and alphabetic 'l', the 12th letter of the alphabet (l), cannot be interchanged.
3. In normal circumstances, the screen will display whichever key is pressed. Most keys have an automatic repeat function, which means that if you hold a key down for more than a pre-determined time (say half a second), the key will start to repeat itself. So, a whole line of characters can be entered with a single press of the desired key. With Windows, the time allowed to elapse before the key auto-repeats can be altered.
4. The normal setting for the keyboard means that when you press a key that is engraved with an alphabetic character you will see a lower case letter of the screen, and a key with two engravings will show the character in the lower half of the key top. To get capital letters and the characters on the top half of the key top you must hold down one of the SHIFT keys while you press the other key. If most of your keying requires the use of capital letters, you can press the CAPS LOCK key, which remains ON until you press it again, and gives the upper case with alphabetic keys only.
5. There are many operations that need to be carried out on a microcomputer that could need a wide range of keys or commands to carry them out. Users cannot be given a giant keyboard layout as this would cause great confusion as well as occupying the entire computer desk area. Manufacturers of modern microcomputers have evolved a standard key-sequence procedure to enable these operations to be achieved while still using a standard-sized keyboard. This involves the use of the CTRL and/or the ALT keys in conjunction with one of the normal keys in the same way as the SHIFT key would be used to give capital letters. This operation is usually indicated in documents as CTRL-B, CTRL-G, etc (or ^G where ^ indicates the use of the control key)

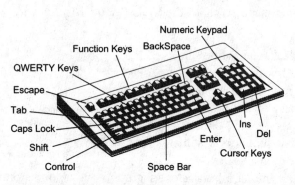

Function Keys BackSpace Numeric Keypad
QWERTY Keys
Escape
Tab
Caps Lock
Shift
Control Space Bar Enter Cursor Keys Ins Del

6. The keyboard contains an *'Enter'* key which is the key with the bent arrow on the right of the centre section of the keyboard. This MUST be pressed after a line of text or a command to tell the computer to process that line. It is sometimes also called the RETURN key.
7. The keyboard has a single cable attached to it and the plug at the end of this cable is attached to the keyboard socket on the computer main system unit. This cable takes the power from the unit to the keyboard and returns any keys pressed back to the motherboard.
8. The early computers, the XT models, had a different keyboard layout from that used on modern machines. Some keyboards have a switch that allows the unit to be used with either an XT or a modern machine. This switch is usually situated in a recess in the base of the keyboard casing.

THE CONTROL KEYS

This set of keys does not produce any printable characters; they are used to control the editing and display activities and are as follows:

Enter This key has two functions. One is to move the cursor from one line to the next, as would be expected with a typewriter carriage return key. The second function is to enter a program command. In DOS, the Enter key terminates an entry sequence and lets the machine know that the letters typed in so far constitute a command to be carried out.

Backspace This key moves the cursor to the left by one position each time it is pressed. As it travels backwards, it erases any character it passes over.

Shift This activates upper case letters and the top half value of various keys.

Caps Lock This changes the alpha keyboard between shifted and unshifted mode.

Control [CTRL] This key accesses alternate functions of other keys. Hold the Control key down and press the key with the desired function.

Del [DEL] This key removes characters from text at the cursor position.

Tab [TAB] The Tab key functions similarly to a typewriter tab key. DOS has preset positions on the line so that when the Tab key is pressed it moves to these preset positions. The tab key may also be used in a number of applications.

Ins This key activates an insert mode in which characters can be entered at the cursor position. Characters already on the line are moved to the right to make room for characters entered. If this key is not active, typing a character at the keyboard will result in that key overwriting the character at the current position of the cursor.

THE QWERTY GROUP

These are the typewriter keys and are used to write commands or type text. Their function is user-dependent; the user can type correspondence, give DOS commands, choose from menus, etc. by pressing these keys.

THE NUMERIC KEYPAD

The numeric keys along the top of the keyboard are repeated and grouped together at the right-hand side of the keyboard, known as the 'keypad'. The proximity of the numeric keys is an aid to speedy input for users who are involved in a lot of numeric data entry work. For those not involved in such work, the keypad also doubles up as a cursor movement set of keys. The Num lock key is used to activate and deactivate the number keys on the right-hand keypad. When Num Lock is engaged, key presses in the keypad group are interpreted as the entering of numbers; when Num Lock is not engaged, the same key presses are interpreted as Page Up, Page Down, and other cursor movement key operations. The application package may inform you that the Num Lock is engaged or the keyboard may have a Num Lock light which lights when in this mode.

Ctrl/Break Control and Break pressed together causes the program running to be halted.

PrtScr This key causes the information displayed on the screen to be sent to the printer.
Control and PrtScr together will cause the printer to echo everything displayed on the screen.

FUNCTION KEYS [F2]

These are marked F1 .. F10 (or up to F12 on some keyboards). They are programmed to perform different functions within different software applications. In DOS they allow the user to retrieve and edit single commands.

CURSOR KEYS [↓][↑][→][←]

[↑] The upward arrow key, inactive in DOS, moves the cursor up one line each time it is pressed. This key is program dependent.

[↓] The downward arrow key, inactive in DOS, moves the cursor down one line each time it is pressed. This key is program dependent.

[→] The cursor-right key moves the cursor one character to the right each time it is pressed. It does not delete any character it passes.

[←] The cursor-left key moves the cursor one character to the left each time it is pressed.

End The End key, inactive in normal DOS activities, is program dependent and moves the cursor to the last character in the current line or screen.

Home The Home Key, inactive in DOS, is software dependent and moves the cursor to the home position - usually the top left corner of the screen.

[PG↓] **PgDn** Inactive in DOS, the Page Down key, moves the screen up in predetermined increments.

[PG↑] **PgUp** The Page Up key moves the screen up in predetermined increments.

DISCS

Computer needs somewhere to store its programs and data, when they are not in the machine's memory. The most common storage medium is the disc system. Programs are loaded from disc to run in the computer memory, as previously mentioned. Additionally, when the program has created its data, it can store it permanently on the disc for later use.

There are two main types of disc storage medium - the hard disc and the floppy disc.

How Discs Work

The physical characteristics of all magnetic discs are similar. Thin, non-magnetic plates are coated on both sides with magnetic recording material. A special set of heads is used to both record data on the disc and to read data from the disc. The method is identical to that used for recording video tapes or audio cassettes. The only real differences are that the medium is a disc instead of a long strip; and the information being transferred is digital data, instead of audio or video information. So, the disc is a direct access device, which means that the reading/writing heads can move directly to the track and sector where the desired information is stored (unlike tape, which is a serial device, where you have to search from one end of the tape to find the information).

Hard Discs

The hard disc is supplied with all but the most basic of microcomputers and is mounted inside the machine casing. These discs hold an incredible amount of information, anything from early 10 Megabyte models to current 9,100 Mbytes and over models. It is known as a *'hard disc'* because it is made from a solid sheet of aluminium. It is then coated with ferric oxide and a number of such discs are stacked on top of each other and placed in an airtight casing. Each disc surface has its own read/write head and they are linked so that they will all move in unison. The discs spin at a constant speed. The slowest models ran at 3600 rpm (12 times faster than a floppy disc) and current models range up to 10,000rpm. Apart from their large capacities, hard discs have a much better access time than a floppy disc. A hard disc reads in data about 3.5 times faster, writes a file up to 10 times faster and finds files 15 times faster - compared to the times for a floppy disc.

The discs are mounted on a vertical shaft and are slightly separated from each other to provide space for the movement of read/write heads. The shaft revolves, spinning the discs. Data are stored as magnetised spots in concentric circles called tracks on each surface of the discs. Each disc contains several hundred tracks for the storage of data.

It is possible for the read/write heads of discs to come into contact with debris on the disc surface, causing it to *"crash"* into the surface of the disc and corrupting the data. Special devices have been developed to get over this problem. One such device is the Winchester disc drive. Winchester discs are sealed units containing the discs and the read/write unit. These types of discs are the hard discs on the microcomputer and are fast and reliable. Hard discs are fixed within the microcomputer cabinet and are therefore not very portable but are faster to access information and have a higher storage capacity than floppy discs.

Floppy Discs

These are flat discs of polyester film with and iron-oxide magnetic coating. The disc is covered with a protective jacket, and reading/writing to the disc is performed through the head access slot. Floppy discs have a capacity of 360Kb to almost 3Mb. Floppy discs are very portable and can be used by different microcomputers (provided they are of a similar type).

The construction of hard discs and floppy discs is covered in detail in the chapter on Discs and Drives.

Floppy Sizes

The floppy disc comes in two sizes - 3.5" and 5.25". Each of these discs is capable of being formatted to different capacities, dependent on their quality (i.e. whether they are double/high/quad density). At its basic format, the 5.25" disc may store 360 Kilobytes. Modern computers have drives that can handle quad density disc, providing a capacity of 1.2 Megabytes. The 3.5" disc has a basic format of 720 Kilobytes, with the high density version holding 1.4 Megabytes and a few versions storing 2.88 Megabytes.

Disc Recording Terms

Sector	Division of magnetic surface of disc into separate but continuous pie-shaped information zones by either magnetic or physical coding of disc.
Soft Sector	Sectors defined magnetically by software.
Hard Sector	Sectors defined physically by punching holes around inner/outer disc diameter.
Initialisation/Formatting	Magnetically coded pattern recorded on disc to identify each track and sector.
Double-Sided	Disc made for use on drives with two recording heads.
Single-Density	The standard density for floppy discs. No longer used.
Double-Density	Method of recording twice the amount on disc as possible with single-density. This is 360k for 5.25" discs and 720k for 3.5" discs.
High/Quadruple-Density	Method of recording four times the amount on disc as possible with single-density. This is 1.2Mb for 5.25" discs and 1.4Mb for 3.5" discs.

Care Of Disc Files

- When a 5.25" floppy disc is not in the disc drive, it must be kept in its protective envelope.
- Never touch the recording surface of a floppy disc because you will leave a small amount of grease to which dust will stick.
- Never bend a floppy disc.
- Insert a floppy disc into a disc drive carefully to avoid bending or crushing the disc.
- Keep the discs away from excesses of temperature; absolute limits are between 10º C and 50º C.
- Keep the discs away from any form of magnetic field. That includes telephones, printer motors, hi-fi speakers, etc.

PRINTERS

The printer is used to produce a paper copy (often called a *'hard copy'*) of the letters, reports, graphs, etc. produced by the program.   They have two connector cables; one for the mains supply and one to take the data from the computer to the printer. The manufacturers produce two different types of connection for printers and these are known as serial and parallel systems. These names describe how the data arrives at the printer from the computer. Serial printers accept data one bit at a time from the computer; parallel printers have more wires and receive 8 bits, i.e. one byte, at a time.   Most printers have only a serial or a parallel connection, while a few have sockets for both types.   There are different printers for different jobs.   All have different qualities as described next:

IMPACT PRINTERS

This involves an inked ribbon being struck against the paper to produce the character and these printers are available in Dot Matrix and Daisy Wheel varieties.

Dot Matrix

On a dot matrix printer, characters are formed by striking an inked ribbon with a rectangular array of needles. The dots of ink are transferred to the paper, producing a pattern that can comprise letters, numbers, or even graphics. These types of printers are relatively cheap and 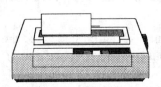 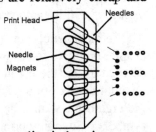 fairly fast, printing from 50 to 400 characters per second. The quality of print from a dot matrix printer is much improved if the number of dots that make up a particular character is increased. The earliest machines used a vertical row of seven print needles that printed 5 times for each character. Each character was thus formed from a 7 x 5 array of dots. The latest machines use 18 x 24 arrays of pins or 24 x 24 or 48 x 24 arrays.   These printers are commonly in use where quality is less important than cheap and quick copies and are mostly employed for internal use in an organisation.   The print head is pulled back and forward on a metal rail and the printing speed can be increased by making the head print on its reverse stroke as well as its forward stroke. This is known as *'bi-directional printing'*. Another speed improvement is achieved by *'logic seeking'* or *'short line seeking'*, where the printer electronics detects the end of a short text line and returns immediately to the left-most column.

PAPER TRANSPORT MECHANISMS

There are two methods of moving paper through the printer mechanism. These are:

Friction Feed :

This is the type of feed used in ordinary typewriters. The paper is held between the main roller and a number of small rollers; as the rollers rotate, the paper is pulled through. This has the advantage that ordinary paper can be fed into the printer; the printer can handle ordinary A4 sheets of paper or pre-printed stationary. It can also handle continuous stationery or fanfold paper but this can cause problems. Since the paper is not of consistent thickness and the rollers do not maintain a constant friction, the paper gradually is pulled through unevenly. This effect is known as *'skew'* and becomes a greater and greater problem with the length of the paper being pulled through. With single sheets, the effect of skew should be so slight as to be unnoticeable.

Tractor Feed :

This mechanism uses belt-driven pins on each side of the paper. These pins engage in holes that are punched down both edges of the paper. This ensures that the paper is pulled through evenly. When the paper is printed, the holed edges can be torn away since these areas are perforated off. The disadvantage is that it requires that specially made paper be bought. Fortunately, fanfold paper is in easy supply and there is a special version with tiny perforations, so that the final sheet looks like a normal sheet of A4.

PRINTER CHARACTERS

The characters fed to the printer by the computer are in the form of ASCII code. This stands for *'American Standard Code for Information Interchange'* and is the internationally recognised set of code for letters, numbers, punctuation marks, etc. For example, every printer recognises the number 68 as the code for upper case 'D'.
Character 32 is a space character and all the codes under 32 are printer control codes.

The most important printer codes are numbers 10, 12 and 13. Code 12 is a form feed code and if this is received by the printer, it moves the paper through the mechanism until the top of the paper is lined up with the print head position. Some printers have a 'FF' or 'TOF' button to do the same thing (the letters stand for *'Form Feed'* or *'Top Of the Form'*). A code 10 is a *'Line Feed'* code and this moves the paper up one line. A code 13 is a *'Carriage Return'* code and this moves the print head back to the left most position of the paper. When both a code 13 (CR) and a 10 (LF) are given, the printer head moves down to the start of a new line on the paper. Most applications send both the CR and LF characters but some only send the CR code, expecting the printer to supply an accompanying line feed. To cope with this, most printers have a switch to decide whether to automatically insert a line feed along with each received carriage return. The switch may be marked as CR/LF or ALF (Automatic Line Feed). Incorrect setting of this switch may lead to the printer constantly printing over the same line (since it is getting no line feeds) or printing in unwanted double spacing (since the printer is inserting an extra line feed on top of the one sent by the computer).
When the user presses the *'On Line'* button once, the printer is switched off-line and it will not accept any data from the computer. During this time, the paper can be advanced through the printer one line at a time by pressing the *'Line Feed'* button. Another press of the *'On Line'* button switches the printer back on line - i.e. it is again ready to accept data from the computer.

All the alphabetic, numeric and punctuation characters can be encompassed in a seven-bit code (see the chapter on buses for an explanation of binary numbering). So, Epson, the dominant printer manufacturer, decided to use the eighth bit of the 8-bit code to represent italic characters. IBM then brought out its own dot matrix printer, called the 'Proprinter', and decided that the extra 128 codes allowed by employing the eighth bit should be used for a range of foreign characters and various box drawing and graphic symbols. So, many printers support both modes and allow the user to switch between the Epson and the IBM character set. This is normally achieved by changing the settings of the DIP switches inside the printer casing, as per the printer manual. Windows uses the top 128 codes to solely provide the ANSI foreign character set.

Another innovation from Epson allowed the printer to print in bold characters, underlined characters, etc., while still only using an 8-bit code. This involved codes doubling up in their use. If a code was given on its own, it had a particular meaning. If, however, the same code was prefaced by a number 27 it had an entirely different meaning.   The number 27 tells the printer to treat the following number, or set of numbers, as a special case.   For example, sending 27 71 tells the printer to go into double-strike mode, while 27 72 switches off double-strike mode. Without being prefaced by the 27 character, the two numbers would tell the printer to print the characters 'G' and 'H' respectively. The number 27 is called the *'Escape code'* often shortened to *'ESC'* and Epson describes its system as the ESC/P system.   Many printers are designed to be compatible with this system.

Daisy Wheel And Thimble
These printers operate like typewriters. The typeface for each character is individually mounted on a daisy wheel or thimble. The wheel or thimble is mounted in front of the ribbon and is free to rotate from character to character to produce the desired results.   A hammer hits the character shape against the ribbon, transferring the ribbon's ink on to the paper as in ordinary typewriters.   Speeds of operation vary considerably from 12 to 14 characters per second in the earliest machines to 90 characters per second in the later machines.   These printers produce high quality output, since they are composed of whole shapes instead of collections of dots.   They are often used for external correspondence due to their high quality output.   However, they suffer from a design limitation.   The only characters that can be printed are the ones present on the daisy wheel or thimble.   This means that they are unable to produce any graphics, so charts, graphics, logos, etc. are unavailable.   Even switching to italics mode is only available if the user has a wheel with the italics version of the normal wheel set.   Even worse, to switch from normal to italics printing would involve pausing printing while one wheel was removed and the other wheel fitted.

NON-IMPACT PRINTERS
Both dot matrix and daisy wheel printers are *'impact printers'*.   As a result, this type of printer can be both noisy and slow in operation.
Non-impact printers do not use physical impact to transfer the character to the paper and there is no inked ribbon. Examples of this type of printer are laser printers, ink-jet printers and electrostatic and electro-thermal printers. Lasers are the most common high-quality printers in use, although sales of ink-jet printers are rapidly catching up.

Ink Jet Printers
An inkjet printer is also a *'non impact'* printer, preferring instead to spray dots of ink on to the paper. The ink is stored in a small plastic case about the size of a matchbox and this case also comprises the printing head. A small printed circuit board takes the signals from the computer right up to tiny holes in the ink reservoir.   The ink is attracted through the holes and carries on to strike the paper.   This produces an output that approaches the quality of the laser printer, at a fraction of the cost. It typically produces a resolution of about 300 dots per inch and is very quiet in operation. Colour inkjet models use four ink heads and mix their outputs to achieve an even greater range of colours. The inks used are the primary print colours (cyan, magenta and yellow) and black. These are known as CMYK printers.

Laser Printers
A laser printer works on a similar principle to the normal photocopier; in fact, a laser is like the second half of a photocopier. With a photocopier, the image from an inserted master is scanned and turned into a stream of digital information. This digital information is then used to modulate a laser beam on to a drum. The electrostatic charge thus built up attracts the toner powder which is eventually transferred to

the paper.   With a laser printer, the stream of digital information is supplied directly by the computer, via the printer cable.   So, the laser printer is like a cut down version of a photocopier, which explains why so many lasers are made by photocopier manufacturers.   Even other manufacturers use photocopier manufacturer's engines - such as Canon.
The resolution of a laser printer is measured in the number of dots in an inch and is normally 300 dpi, with modern versions now at 600 dpi or 1200 dpi.   They are thus capable of both high quality text and graphics.   The average laser is capable of printing either 4 pages per minute or 8 pages per minute - although high-speed models can operate at up to 200 ppm.   These speed figures describe the number of

pages that the printer can produce once the image is ready to print. In fact, the normal laser printer makes up a copy of the picture in its own internal memory, prior to starting the printing process. This time has to be added to the time for printing. So, for a single copy, the printing speed is fairly slow; if many copies are required, the image is still only built up once and the overall speed becomes closer to the printing speed. The size of the printer's memory has an influence on the final quality of print that can be handled. If the printer has only a small internal memory, say 256k or 512k, then it will not be able to store a complete A4 page of graphics. To reduce retail prices, many manufacturers produce models with small internal memories. Of course, most printers are able to have their memory size upgraded by adding extra memory boards, although this is fairly expensive.

Due to their mechanics, laser printers are very quiet in operation. There is no impact noise as the paper is not struck; there is only the sound of the motor and its roller mechanisms.

GDI PRINTERS

Another type of laser, known as GDI (Windows Graphical Device Interface) models, are produced. They are able to handle a full page of graphics without requiring a large internal memory. They work by building the image up in the computer's memory or the hard disc. Since they use little memory and simple control electronics, they are cheap. This benefit is balanced against greater strain on the computer's memory and CPU. Also, some GDI printers only work well with Windows, with printing in DOS being a problem.

PRINT QUALITY

Daisy wheel/thimble printers and laser printers produce true letter quality print. Dot matrix printers can produce almost letter quality or NLQ (near letter quality) by increasing the number of dots in the character or by passing over the same line twice. Dot matrix printers can produce faster output in draft mode. This produces a readable document fairly quickly. The printers can be switched from one level of quality to another by a hardware switch on the printer or by sending a signal through the software to the printer. Inkjet printers produce a quality which somewhat less than a laser but much better than a dot matrix.

Since daisy wheels and thimbles have a fixed set of characters, they cannot be used to print graphics. All the other printers operate on a matrix of dots, therefore the dots can be arranged to produce any graphics image (e.g. graphs, drawings, DTP).

All impact printers use ribbons - either ink impregnated fabric or one-off ribbons. With fabric ribbons, the quality can be poor at the beginning of the use of the ribbon due to overinking, while the quality also suffers at the end of the ribbon's life due to lack of ink. Laser printers and inkjet printers, on the other hand, maintain a constant quality of output, with the quality suddenly dropping off as the toner or ink reservoir runs low.

PROPORTIONAL PRINTING

The standard print size on most machines is 10 characters to an inch. It is possible to change this using either a hardware switch on the printer or by sending special codes to the printer. The number of characters printed to an inch can be increased (making the print smaller) to 12, 17 and 20 cpi. It is also possible to print expanded characters and to produce characters with proportional spacing. With proportional spacing, a character only occupies as much width of the paper as it actually needs. So, the letter 'm' uses more space than the letter 'i'. As a result, proportional spacing results in a more professional output, similar to typeset documents as seen in books.

```
This is an example of proportional spacing
This is an example of standard width printing
```

However, one problem with proportional spacing is lining up data into columns as seen in this example. Since each digit occupies a different page width (e.g. an eight is wider than a one), figures do not line up in neat columns. In this respect, a fixed-width character set produces more readable results.

```
9866 99.55 88
2311 18.11 28

9866 99.55 88
2311 18.11 28
```

The selection of pitch sizes can usually be achieved by setting the buttons on the printer front panel, as in DeskJet, or by pressing the NLQ button a prescribed number of times, as in the Mannesman Tally MT81.

ADJUSTING FONTS

The better dot-matrix printers and all laser printers allow the user to choose the shape or style of the type to be output.   The term *'typeface'* describes the shape of the letters and characters.   So, a plain unadorned character

> This is a serif typeface
> And this is sans serif

would be one typeface, while a fancy Gothic script would be another typeface.   If a typeface has feet and twirls, it is said to be a *'serif'* typeface; if it is a plain typeface, it is described as a *'sans serif'* style.   Each typeface comes in a variety of sizes, measured in *'points'*; there are 72 points to one inch.   So, a 36-point character is a half-inch character.   The collection of all the sizes of a particular typeface is called the *'fonts'*.   A half-inch character would be available in the 36-point font of a particular typestyle.   In addition to the character's outline and size, the user can usually have control over whether the character is printed in normal, bold, italic and underlined.

A printer may have its own range of pre-defined typestyles saved in its internal memory (held in ROM). These fonts may be used by switching to them via the front panel of the printer, or via software commands given to the printer.   In addition, many printers have a section of extra memory (RAM) set aside to store any other typestyles.   These extra styles are given to the printer by the computer before the printing process starts.   This process is known as *'downloading'* the fonts and such fonts are known as *'soft'* fonts.   This allows the printer to print in a whole range of new type faces, limited only by the extra fonts being held in the computer's hard disc.

PRINTER DRIVERS

Different printers expect to be fed their data from the computer in different formats. If the computer thinks that it is connected to a Hewlett Packard LaserJet when it is actually connected to an Epson dot-matrix, then a graphics printout will be unrecognisable.   Similarly, if the computer is trying to dump text to the printer as a bit-image (i.e. it is sending a graphics file) then the results will be equally disappointing. To prevent this, most packages can be configured to send out their data to a variety of printers.   The software that carries out the translation between what the application actually stores and what the printer needs, is called a *'printer driver'*.   Most packages allow many such drivers to be used. So, when a user switches from a laser to a dot-matrix the appropriate printer driver is called up.

EMULATIONS

Most software is supplied with printer drivers for the more common printers.   The most common printers of all are dot-matrix models such as the Epson FX80, inkjet printers such as the Hewlett Packard DeskJet series and laser printers such as the Hewlett Packard LaserJet series.   Virtually all software is written to include drivers for these models.   As a result, a manufacturer of a new printer model has to ensure that the machine will be able to act like one of these models - i.e. it will be able to *'emulate'* an Epson or a LaserJet.   Being able to emulate a popular printer guarantees that the printer will work with most existing software.   With a dot-matrix printer, the emulation is usually achieved by setting the DIP switches inside the printer case to make the machine work like an IBM Proprinter or an Epson FX80 model. Laser printers can be taken off-line and the emulation set via the front panel controls.

POSTSCRIPT

Dot-matrix printers and inkjet printers print in a sequence of single lines, whereas the laser composes the entire page in its internal memory before commencing printing.   This has led to the development of a programming language for printers - called *'PostScript'*.   These printers have their own CPU and the computer sends the page as a set of instructions.   These are written in ordinary text and the printer's own CPU translates them into the necessary steps to create text, graphics, etc.   This has become the standard format for high quality DTP (Desk Top Publishing) and graphics programs.

PRINTER BUFFERS

Computers send data to the printer at a much faster rate than the printer can print it out; this is because the printer is a slow mechanical device.   This would leave the user sitting waiting until the printer had finished the print job before he/she could carry on using the machine.   To increase efficiency, all printers have a block of memory built in, called the *'print buffer'*.   This is able to read a chunk of data from the computer and, if the block of memory is large enough, the entire file can be transferred to the printer in one operation.   This would immediately free the computer for other processing.   To keep the retail price down, most printers have a nominal buffer size and additions to this are regarded as extras.

PRINTER PAPER

Printers can use different types of paper. The most commonly used type of paper is continuous stationery. This is held in place and moved by tractors gripping the sprocket holes at the side of the paper. There are two basic sizes; 13 x 11 inches, which will allow a maximum of 132 standard characters per line and 66 lines on every page and 8 x 11 inches, which gives 80 character lines. This may be plain paper or specially printed paper providing office stationary or commercial facilities such as accounts. This may be single or multi-part stationary (i.e. more than one sheet with carbon backing so that several copies of the data are printed on the different copies of the sheet). Self-adhesive labels are also commonly used on continuous rolls, so that mailing labels are quickly produced.

Many printers also allow the use of single sheets of paper using a friction mechanism as on a typewriter, to hold and move the paper. Cut sheet feeders may also be supplied to guide the paper in the printer. Again, the paper may be plain or pre-printed. Some printers also allow acetate sheets to be inserted so that OHP slides (overhead projector) may be created. These use special acetate sheets that will not melt in the normal heat in a laser printer.

Adding Paper

The steps for adding paper to most tractor printers are:
- Remove the front cover flap.
- Unlock both tractors; this normally involves opening their locking levers.
- Adjust the left-most tractor to the start position of the paper; this will depend upon the width of the paper in use.
- Open both tractor flaps, normally by folding them upwards and outwards.
- Insert the paper into the left tractor, lining up the holes with the tractor pins.
- Close the left-most tractor locking lever.
- Adjust the right-most tractor to the width of the paper.
- Insert the paper into the right tractor.
- Close right-most tractor flap, ensuring the pins engage the holes in the paper.
- Adjust the right-most tractor until the paper is under a slight tension.
- Lock the right tractor lever.
- Move the bail roller lever outwards away from the paper. This is the roller that normally holds the paper against the main roller. It should be moved back so that the paper can be fed through without snarling against the roller.
- Turn the manual feed knob until the paper appears under the bail roller.
- Release the bail roller back down on to the paper, to hold the paper securely against the main roller.
- Replace the front cover flap.

The steps for adding paper to a laser printer are much simpler. If the printer has an open tray, the paper should be inserted into the tray as far as it will go. The paper should be sitting squarely in the tray and the height of the paper should not exceed the maximum specified (some printers will have a guide mark for the maximum height). Slide the paper guide to touch the left of the stack of paper. This guide ensures that the sheets are fed through without skew. However, if the guide is jammed too tightly against the paper, it prevents the free movement of the paper, causing paper jams. These instructions also apply to inkjet printers such as the Hewlett Packard DeskJet series. If the laser has a bin to hold the paper, then the bin has to be lifted out of the machine and filled with paper to no more than the maximum amount. The paper should have its edges aligned prior to inserting into the bin; the stack of paper should be held loosely and tapped on a flat surface.

POINTING DEVICES

Windows and many DOS applications now make very good use of a mouse or other pointing device for choosing menu options and drawing activities. Although the activities can be carried out using the keyboard cursor keys, it is much more cumbersome than using a mouse or other pointer.

Mouse

By far the most common pointing device is the mouse, although other devices such as trackerballs, touch screens, pens and joysticks are available. The mouse has won support through its accuracy and ease of use. The most common is the opto-mechanical type that houses a large, heavy, rubber ball which protrudes from its

base.   When the mouse is moved over a surface (preferably a *'mouse mat'* - a mat with the correct friction to optimise the ball's movement), the ball rotates inside its case. The ball movement rotates two rollers, one for vertical and one for horizontal movements. Moving the ball diagonally will rotate both rollers.   The rollers, in turn, rotate slotted wheels.   Each wheel passes through a beam of light and the wheel rotation results in pulses of light reaching a light sensor.   In this way, the hand movement results in a stream of electrical pulses being passed via the serial port to the computer.   The quicker the mouse is moved, the faster the pulse stream; the further the mouse is moved, the longer is the pulse stream. The incoming signals are used by the program to produce pointer movements on the monitor screen.

Mouse Drivers

The translation of the incoming data stream into screen activity is carried out by a special piece of software called a *'device driver'* that has to be installed before the mouse is used (See chapter on PC Configuration).   The mouse driver might be included in the AUTOEXEC.BAT file or it might be automatically installed by the application package (Windows has its own mouse device driver).   When a mouse is purchased, it will include a disc containing the device driver and probably some drawing utilities.   The most significant mouse standards are the Microsoft and the Mouse Systems standards; virtually all units conform to the Microsoft standard and many also conform to the Mouse Systems standard.

Connecting A Mouse

The mouse can be connected to the computer in the following ways:
- Using the computer's serial port as an input device.
- Using a dedicated mouse interface on the motherboard. This will have a socket into which the mouse cable can be plugged.
- Using an add-on card that plugs into a spare expansion slot.

The performance of a mouse, like all other pointing devices, is usually measured in terms of its positional accuracy and its sensitivity.   If a screen pointer is to be finely positioned, then the mouse has to have a high resolution.   If a mouse generates a greater number of output pulses for the same travel as another mouse, then the first mouse has the greater resolution.   Resolution is measured in pixels-per-inch or dots-per-inch.   The earliest Microsoft mouse had a resolution of 100dpi and later models progressed through 200dpi to 400dpi.   Thus, a mouse with 400dpi resolution provides an accuracy of .0025 inches.

The sensitivity of the mouse is a measure of the relationship between the movement of the mouse on the mat and the movement of the cursor on the screen.   There would be little benefit in having a high resolution mouse if a small hand movement resulted in a very large screen movement, since it would be extremely difficult to achieve pinpoint accuracy.   The ideal mouse will have the ability to vary its characteristics, to allow it to work at its best for a given application. A high sensitivity ratio might be useful, for example, with a spreadsheet. This may not require any greater accuracy than the relatively large area occupied by a worksheet cell. In that case, the user may prefer a high ratio, so that the cursor can traverse the screen very quickly.   For a drawing package, on the other hand, it may work best with a lower ratio. The mouse mat area might not be sufficient to map to the entire screen area. This would involve the user in having to lift and re-position the mouse, in order to traverse an entire screen.   But the very fact that the mat area acts like a window on the larger screen area, means that intricate designs can be worked on, without having to possess an ultra-steady hand.   If the mouse is able to have its resolution adjusted, then it can be set for the needs of a particular application.   Sometimes, the sensitivity adjustment can be made in software (e.g. in Windows), rather than in hardware.   In such cases, the mouse driver provides a facility to adjust sensitivity.

Another feature in most mice is control over cursor acceleration. If the mouse is moved slowly, then the software supposes that the user is making detailed movements and will maintain the normal sensitivity. If the mouse is moved quickly, the software assumes that the user wishes to traverse the screen quickly and temporarily increases the sensitivity ratio.   The ratio returns to normal when the mouse movement is slowed down. This facility can be useful for rapid movement between spreadsheet cells or for other long distance screen movements. The code to achieve this is incorporated in the mouse driver and the speed thresholds that trigger the sensitivity ratio changes can often be altered by the user, via a pop-up *'control panel'* provided by the driver.

The mouse has two, sometimes three, buttons on its casing to allow the user to click on a particular choice or lift/drop the pen while drawing. Some mouse drivers allow the buttons' functions to be transposed, so the mouse can be used more easily with left-handed operators. Finally, some drivers, such as in Windows 3.1, allow an option to leave a trail as the cursor moves, so that the cursor position can be easier identified, which is useful on portable computer screens.

TRACKERBALL

A common complaint about mice is that they take up a lot of desk space, since there has to be enough space to accommodate the mat and all the hand and arm movements involved in using the mouse. In response, manufacturers produced the trackerball, also called trackballs. These are growing in popularity. They overcome the shortage of desk space by having a stationary mouse. In fact the trackerball is really nothing other than an upturned mouse. Its design is very similar to the mouse, except that the ball is larger, to allow control by movement of the user's fingertips or palm of the hand. All the earlier points on mouse sensitivity, interfacing, compatibility, etc. apply to trackerballs. They are generally held to be less accurate than a mouse and are at their best in spreadsheet and option-choosing environments rather than design work. Keyboards are available which have a built-in trackerball. Miniature versions are produced for the portable PC market and these clip on to the computer casing.

OTHER HARDWARE ITEMS

MODEM A modem ('*modulator/demodulator*') allows a computer to communicate with another computer at great distances over the ordinary telephone network, or over specially hired lines. It translates (modulates) the 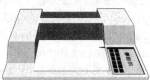 data which is held in the computer as electronic pulses into audible tones that are capable of being sent down telephone cables. The modem at the receiving end translates (demodulates) the tones back into electronic pulses for use by the receiving computer. For more details, see the chapter on data communications.

CD DISC This computer CD player works in a similar way to an ordinary CD player, except that  the data that is read is computer digital data instead of audio data. The discs used with such players can store around 640Mbytes of data, which is equivalent to about 500 high-density floppy discs. The discs are removable and not easily damaged. The only drawback is that the basic system only reads data from disc to computer. Read/write systems are available but are very expensive. For more information, see the chapter on discs and drives.

PLOTTER A plotter is a device to reproduce architectural drawings, road maps and components designed by CAD (computer aided design) systems. It uses a set of pens to draw the lines that comprise the drawings. It is capable of producing large size drawings that would not be possible with dot-matrix or laser printers.

SCANNER A scanner is a device that analyses a printed piece of work (e.g. picture, drawing or  even text) and converts the image into a file that can be further processed. A scanned file of a picture or drawing might be incorporated into desk top publishing and a scanned piece of text from a book, etc. may be converted back into ASCII text using a software package called OCR (optical character recognition).

ADD-ON CARDS When an extra device such as a modem is to be added to a system, the user can choose to fit external equipment which attaches to the computer's port connections or fit an internal board. Some other devices such as sound-producing cards are normally only available as internal boards. These boards contain all the electronics and hardware to carry out their particular function and are plugged into spare unused slots on the motherboard. These are known as the computer's '*expansion slots*'. The add-on board is fitted and the software to make it function is then installed.

ASSEMBLING THE SYSTEM

When a computer is first purchased, it arrives in several boxes. The monitor is in one box, while the system unit, keyboard, mouse, manuals and discs are usually packed separately. The monitor has its own power cable and video cable permanently connected to it in most cases, while the system unit comes as an independent component with separate cables.

The steps to assembling the system are:
- Choose a suitable location for the computer. Avoid situations of excessive heat, cold, damp, dust or vibration. Also avoid locations close to magnetic disturbance such as lift motors, power transformers, etc. A good location would be one with a flat, stable surface and good air circulation.
- Carefully unpack the components from the boxes. The contents of the boxes should then be checked against the system checklist, to see that all components have been delivered.
- Read the assembly instructions carefully to ensure that you understand the necessary steps and that any special precautions are understood.
- Gather any tools that you may require. Normally, the only tool might be a Philips screwdriver to secure connections to the system unit. Some connections use thumbscrews to make a secure connection and do not require a screwdriver - read the manual.
- Carefully connect the components together, in the order directed by the computer manual. Do not force any connections; if a plug will not easily connect to a socket, it may mean that a connector pin has become bent. It might also mean that the wrong socket is being chosen, or the plug is being inserted upside down!

A typical order of assembly is:
- Place the system unit on the surface to be used.
- Place the monitor on top of the system unit.
- Attach the video cable from the monitor to the video out socket of the system unit. Ensure that the plug and the socket are of compatible types. A CGA or EGA monitor cable has a 9-pin plug on the end of its connector cable, while a VGA or SVGA monitor has a 15-pin plug. The two are not interchangeable. A CGA or EGA monitor can only connect to a video outlet of the same type. Similarly, VGA and SVGA monitors only connect to 15-pin outlets. Note that the edges of the plugs are shaped so that they only connect one CGA / EGA   VGA / SVGA

  way round. On some connectors, the plug is secured to the system unit with metal screws and a screwdriver is required to tighten the screws. With other connectors, the plug has plastic thumbscrews that are tightened by hand.
- Connect the mains lead to the system unit. This cable has a normal 3-pin plug on one end and a connector similar to those used in electric kettles on the other end. Do not connect the mains plug to the mains at this time; simply plug the other end of the cable into the system unit mains inlet socket.
- Connect the monitor to the mains supply. Some monitor mains cables have normal 3-pin plugs and these plug directly into a mains supply. Other monitor power cables have a plug that matches a socket at the rear of the system unit. These are useful, since switching on the system unit also supplies power to the monitor. So, if the monitor power switch is left on, both units can be powered up from the system on/off switch
- Connect the keyboard to the system unit. These are 5-pin plugs and are produced in two sizes. The larger size plug has a matching socket on the system unit and can only be connected one way since the socket has a key to guide the plug. With the smaller size keyboard plug, there is also a matching

  Standard Keyboard   PS/2 Keyboard

  socket. This smaller socket size is also be the same type as used for a dedicated mouse socket. Care should be taken to plug the keyboard into the correct socket. Where the two sockets are of the same size, the system unit should clearly label them as 'KBD' and 'Mouse'.

- Connect the mouse to the system unit. The mouse may be of the type mentioned above and the same care should be taken to ensure that the plug is inserted into the correct socket. Some mouse cables connect to the system unit's serial port connector. This is either a 9-pin or 15-pin socket and is usually marked as *'Serial'*, *'COM1'* or *'RS232'*.

15-pin mouse socket   9-pin mouse socket

- Connect the printer to the system unit. The most common cable is the *'parallel'* or *'Centronics'* type 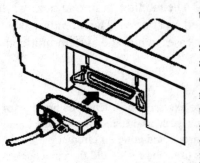 which has a 25-pin cable. The cable at the system unit side terminates in a 25-pin plug that connects to the socket marked *'Parallel'* or *'LPT1'*. The other end of the cable connects to the socket on the printer. Some printers may have a serial connector and connect to the system unit socket marked as *'COM1'*, *'Serial'* or *'RS232'*. Some system units have two serial sockets, so that the machine can connect a mouse and a printer at the same time. In these cases, the machine will be set up to recognise one of the serial outlets as a printer port and the other as a mouse port, and the manual should be checked to determine the use for each port. Finally, connect the printer to the mains supply and ensure that it is supplied with paper and is on-line.
- Check that the monitor is at an angle which affords easy and comfortable viewing and adjust this if necessary; the monitor rests on a plinth that allows the monitor angle to be altered.

GETTING UP AND RUNNING

The steps involved are:
- Connect the printer to the mains supply, switch on the printer and run a self-test. The method for doing this will vary from printer to printer and the printer manual should be consulted. With a dot-matrix printer, this usually involves holding a key depressed (such as the LF key) while the unit is switched on; when the key is released, the printer prints out a sample of its output. With a laser printer, this normally involves taking the printer off-line and carrying out a key sequence (e.g. pressing the Shift and Test buttons).
- Plug in the monitor and system unit mains connectors to the mains supply and switch on the mains at the wall sockets.
- Switch on the monitor and check that the mains indicator light illuminates.
- Switch on the system unit. The computer ON/OFF switch is located on the main body of the machine. It can be a button on the front, or a switch at the side or the rear. Before switching on, you should ensure that the floppy disc drive is empty and the gate is open. There will often be an additional switch to power the monitor, usually on the side of the monitor casing.

After being switched on, the microcomputer will take about 30 seconds to establish its operating system before it can be used. The computer checks itself to see that its main board, its memory and other key components are working. If the machine passes the self-test and the keyboard and monitor are correctly connected, the monitor screen will show the DOS prompt, which should be the C:> characters. If this is not the case, then probably your microcomputer system has been specially designed as a *'turnkey system'* i.e. instead of the operating system prompt of C:> you are presented with a *'menu'* of operations from which you can select a function. For Windows-based machines, the opening Windows options are displayed.

This first level of operation is the point at which you can safely switch the microcomputer system off. It is most important always to return to this level if you have been using another piece of software. Failure to do so can result in either or all of the following circumstances -
- loss of data through incomplete file update,
- loss of automatic backup copy of a file,
- partial update and consequential corruption of database data.

The connection between the computer and the printer can be tested by pressing the PrtScr key. This should send a copy of whatever is currently appearing on the screen to the printer. If this prints out correctly, then the printer connection is working.

If the system does not work properly, the machine manual on trouble-shooting should be consulted. If this is not successful, the chapter on fault detection should be inspected.

USING THE COMPUTER

The machine should be used in a way that protects both the operator and the machine. Protection of the <u>user</u> is outlined in the chapters on P.C. Support and Computer Video and covers ergonomics and safety. Protection of the <u>machine</u> is outlined in the chapter on P.C. Support and covers cleaning, maintenance, dust, magnetic fields and static problems.

Software/Data

SOFTWARE

Software is the program you buy, or create, for the computer. Without software, a computer is just a black box of electronic equipment that is incapable of any useful function. Software tells the computer exactly what to do and when to do it. Such programs are written in a form of code that only that particular type of computer understands. This machine specific code is called *'machine code'* and code written for an Amiga or an Atari will not run on a PC, for example. The code used by the computer is written using one of the many programming languages. The computer requires step-by-step instructions to reach a solution to a given problem. This series of instructions is known as a program.

THE DIFFERENCE BETWEEN PROGRAMS AND DATA

- Data is facts or information available for, or the result of, processing. The source of data is usually via the keyboard where an operator types information such as names and addresses, payroll information, measurements, etc.
- Programs are the instructions for processing data. Programs are created by a systems analyst and a programmer specifying and writing a set of instructions that the computer understands and which will be able to process the data supplied. Programs can be simple or complex, and usually form part of a software package bought from a *"software house"*.

Software falls into two main categories - Application software and Systems software.

Application Software

This consists of general purpose programs developed for computer users to solve specific tasks. Typical applications are Word, Excel, Access, Corel Draw and MS Project.

Systems Software

This consists of programs that enable users to make efficient use of the machine. They co-ordinate and maximise the use of the computer's circuitry. Examples of systems software are MSDOS, Windows, Netware, Unix and communication utilities.

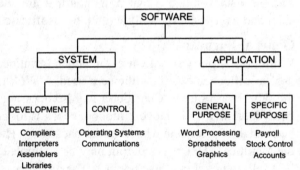

Application and System software act as interfaces between computer users and computer hardware. If this software did not exist, very few computers would be in use. As application and system software become more sophisticated, computers become easier to use.

SYSTEM SOFTWARE

System software can be divided into two categories - Control and Development Software.

Development

This software is concerned with the creation of other software; it comprises sets of software tools to allow programs to be written and tested. A knowledge of the appropriate programming language is assumed. Cobol, for example, is a commonly used language for writing stock-control and database programs, while 'C' is commonly used for creating real-time programs.

The writer can choose from the following tools:

- Editors (to enter and modify the program lines)
- Assemblers (to write in machine-specific language)
- Compilers (to turn the writer's program into a form to be saved and run by the machine)
- Interpreters (to convert the written program and run it, one line at a time without being previously compiled)
- Libraries (to store commonly used bits of program, so that the writer can include them in his/her program without having to re-write them from scratch)
- Diagnostic utilities to detect *'bugs'* - errors in the logic of the program.

Control

This software appears on all computers in one form or another. The most common control software is the computer's Operating System. This is the software that controls the machine's disc, screen, keyboard and printing activities, etc. The most commonly used system is MSDOS (Microsoft's Disc Operating System). This is described in detail in the chapter on PC Configuration. Other commonly used system software is Microsoft Windows and various Local Area Networks programs.

APPLICATION SOFTWARE

Application software can be further sub-divided into Specific Purpose and General Purpose categories.

Specific Purpose

These packages are written to carry out a prescribed set of tasks and the user has very little control over the process. Consider the use of a payroll package. The user is prompted to enter details such employee number, number of hours worked, number of night hours, etc. The program then calculates the deductions such as tax and determines the final net wage of the employee; the program then prints the employee's payslip. The role of the user is restricted to feeding the machine with the appropriate answers. A menu may allow different reports to be generated but there is no opportunity to deviate from the pre-programmed activities. Other examples of specific purpose packages are accounting packages, company budgets and stock control software. The advantages of such an approach are:

- Little training, since the program produces a series of simple tasks that are easy to carry out.
- Comprehensive error checking. All likely errors that can be made by users are predicted in advance and the program is written to prevent the user from entering erroneous information (e.g. an age of -17 or entering numbers for a person's name).

The big disadvantage is that programs that are specific to a company's needs are not available off the shelf and have to be specially written by a software house, which is a very expensive business.

General Purpose

With general purpose software, the general routines are included in the package but the user has a great deal of influence over how they are used. With these packages, the user controls the software and not the other way round. Consider a word-processing package. The program will have fixed facilities to enter data, modify it, move it around, check it for correct spelling or grammar, etc. These facilities will be available to anyone who uses the package. The difference lies in how each user takes advantage of the facilities. One user's output may be a simple company memo, while another user's output may be a best selling novel or a love poem. The differences will be even more striking between different users of graphics packages, where the flair, imagination and artistic abilities of the user are more significant than the packages' abilities.

The normal commercial sector of industry also has great use for general purpose packages such as spreadsheets (e.g. Lotus 123, Excel, Quattro) and databases (e.g. dBase, DataEase, Paradox). These packages provide basic facilities and these can be used to put together a system that can be used by ordinary operators. So, one company might tailor a spreadsheet to provide a budget program while another company might produce a sales forecasting program. Note that these packages are created without the need for a formal programming language. The person tailoring the package need only know its internal language. This means that a commercial system can be developed within the company, saving the huge costs involved in ordering a custom designed product from a software house.

PROCESSING SYSTEMS

The PC can be set up and used in a variety of ways, to meet the organisation's specific needs at any one time. Examples of different processing systems are:

Single-User, Single-Tasking Systems

This is the simplest of systems and the most common one in use. Here, a single computer is used by a single operator at a time (i.e. 'single-user'), only ever running one program at any one time (i.e. 'single-tasking'). This only requires a simple operating system and this is almost always the MSDOS product. The single-user machine has to be connected to its own range of input and output devices. If there are two machines in an office and they both need fax facilities, they both require to have fax boards fitted.

If both machines require lots of disc space, they both require to have large hard discs fitted. If both users require a particular package, it has to be installed on both machines. If they both use the same data, copies of the data have to be placed on the disc of both machines. The only shared resource might be a printer with an extra switch box that allows the printer to be connected to a number of machines, with only one being actually switched through to the printer at any one time. This system is the way in which many office machines are run and most software assumes that this is how the machine is set up. Single-user, single-tasking systems are used for a wide range of activities from word-processing, DTP (desk top publishing), small databases, spreadsheets and small company payroll and accounting. In the home, the single PC is also used for games. Specialist uses of single machines include electronic music (using a 'MIDI' interface to connect the computer to an electronic instrument) and video capture (converting images from camcorders or video players into graphics images that can be stored on disc).

Multi-Tasking Systems

This system allows a single user to run more than program at the same time. So, a user can open a database package and a word-processing package at the same time. While the word-processor is being used to type a report, the database can be compiling all the facts from the database; both programs are functioning at the same time; the word-processor is the one seen by the user and this is described as being in the *'foreground'*, while the database search is said to be operating in the *'background'*. Running Windows applications under Microsoft Windows 95 is a good example of a single-user machine being used for multi-tasking. The user can open up both the Excel spreadsheet and the Word word-processor and data from Excel can be copied over directly into a document being written in Word. Both packages can be seen on the screen at the same time, with each occupying a different area, or 'window' of the screen. Other examples of multi-taking systems are Windows NT, OS/2 Warp and UNIX.

Multi-User Systems

Each year, more and more PCs are being connected together by special cables and software, to produce *'networked'* systems. Such systems range from a few PCs wired together using Windows for Workgroups or Windows 95 software, through to many hundreds of computers linked together with highly complex LAN (local area network) software such as Netware 4 or LAN Manager or Unix systems. This provides many advantages such as:

- Sharing software resources. All the application programs can be held on a main computer, known as the *'file server'* and only a single copy is required for each program. When a computer wishes to run a program, a copy is sent from the server to the computer. Since there is only one central copy of all programs, additions and upgrades are much easier to perform.
- Sharing data resources. With copies of data being held in separate machines, the information held in each computer soon varies from that held in the other copies. If the data is held centrally, there is no need to have multiple copies in all individual machines. This means that the one central copy is the most current copy available for all users.
- Sharing hardware resources. If the printers, plotters, modems, etc. are attached to the central machine, they are available to all computers connected to the system. This means that even the most expensive piece of equipment can be made available to all computers in the organisation and results in substantial savings in duplicated equipment.
- Communications - since all the machines are interconnected, they are able to send messages to each other via 'E-Mail' (electronic mail) software.
- Added security.

Real-Time Systems

Older systems used *'batch processing'* where a collection of jobs was saved and run at the same time (usually overnight). This suited older banking and order-processing systems. Modern banking involves cash points and Point-Of-Sales outlets where a high-street transaction alters the user's bank balance as soon as transaction is completed. In real-time systems, the input is immediately accepted and processed very quickly so that further action can be taken using the results of the processing. Real-time systems use a PC to control or monitor activity that is happening in real time. Other examples are robotics, alarm systems, music sequencers and speech recognition.

On-Line Systems

On-line systems use a computer to access a larger system, such as remote banking, or access to bulletin boards and databases such as Compuserve. It is often used in conjunction with real-time activities.

LICENSING AGREEMENTS

Software can be obtained in a variety of different ways and in a variety of different pricing structures. The main channels are:

COMMERCIAL

This is the most common method of acquiring software.   Thousands of products are available with the most common programs being produced by large software houses and corporations such as Microsoft and Lotus.   These are copyrighted programs with strictly enforced licences.   The various user options are:

Single licence

A single copy is bought and is supplied with the installation discs and user manuals.   The software can only be installed on a single machine.   Each extra machine is added by purchasing another complete package.

Site Licence

A single copy of the software is bought with permission to install the software on an agreed number of computers; a 20-user licence allows 20 machines to have the software installed.   Only one or two copies of the user manuals is provided.   This is a cheaper method than purchasing a single copy for each machine.   An increase in the number of licensed users is achieved by paying for an extension to the existing licensed amount.   There is no extra software provided; the increase is purely financial.

Licence by Use

This allows the software to be installed on a large number of computers, but the licence only allows a fixed number of users to be operating the software at any one time.   A 20-user licence on these terms would allow the software to reside on 100 machines as long as there was never more than 20 operators using the package at any one time.   Increasing the users on this system is identical to the site licence arrangements.

Licence by Station

This allows a fixed number of machines to have the software installed.   If it's a single-user licence, the software must reside on a single machine; if it's a 10-user licence, then only ten machines can have the software installed.

Network Multi-Licence

If an organisation has a local area network, an individual software package for all the computers will reside as a single copy on the file server. Many single-user packages will refuse to work over a network and special network versions have to be bought.   In addition, network versions contain facilities to allow many users to read and update the same data without getting in each other's way.   If a 20-user network version of a package is bought, then only 20 operators can use the package at any one time.   There can be 30, 40 or 100 machines on the network and the package will be available at any one of the computers.   When a 21st operator attempts to access the package, the software will not be able to be accessed.   The system is extended by purchasing upgrade discs. If, for example, a 4-user upgrade was purchased for an existing 20-user system, then the disc would be run to change the maximum allowable from 20 to 24.

Licences allow the user to make a back-up copy of the installation discs and most allow the user to install the program on a machine and to sell the program provided no copies are kept.   Licences usually prohibit the renting/leasing of the program and prohibit additions/alterations to the software.   Licences often also attempt to limit the manufacturer's liability for any problems caused by use of the software.

PUBLIC DOMAIN

Often abbreviated to *'PD'*.   These programs are not copyrighted by their authors and can be distributed and used free of charge.   Users are allowed to alter any program code. This type of software is normally restricted to small programs and utilities.   These programs are largely obtained by downloading them from bulletin boards.

FREEWARE

This is similar to public domain except that the alteration of program code is not permitted.   The author retains the copyright over the program and its code.   The user is allowed to use and copy the program. It is also sometimes described as *'Bannerware'*.

SHAREWARE

These are copyrighted and usually full-working versions of programs.   The author retains all rights over the program and can alter it or withdraw it from public use if desired.   Unlike the normal commercial sector, these are freely distributed on a *'try before you buy'* basis.   This normally involves allowing the free use of the software for a limited period (typically 30 days) so that a user can evaluate the usefulness of the product for the specified purpose. If the product is satisfactory, the user has to register the program by sending the author the prescribed fee. This fee acts as a licence to use the software and may also provide a printed manual, free updates and telephone or mail support. If the product is not found to be satisfactory, the user should stop using it. These programs are obtained from bulletin boards or from shareware distributors. The user is not allowed to alter the program code.

The quality of shareware programs varies tremendously, from the insultingly bad to entirely professional products. Some products are 'clones' of well-known spreadsheet and word-processing packages, examples being As-Easy-As and Galaxy Lite respectively. Such packages provide broadly similar facilities at a fraction of the normal commercial price. In other cases, the shareware version is a cut-down equivalent to a well-known product, offering fewer facilities. However, since most users only use a small proportion of a package's facilities, this need not represent a real loss of program functionality for the user. If cost is a factor and compatibility with existing packages is not an issue, then shareware products can be a cost-effective purchase.

In America, the Association of Shareware Professionals provides a standard of writing, support and protection.

In the UK, the equivalent body is the Association of Shareware Professionals (UK) Ltd, Treble Clef House, 64 Welford Road, Wigston Magna, Leicester, LE8 1SL.

SHOVELWARE

This is not an actual licensing category but is included for completeness. The term has come to describe the habit of supplying large amounts of shareware/PD software on the one CD disc, particularly common as give-aways with computer magazines. It also covers the cramming of many illegal copies of major application packages on to one CD ROM for sale as pirate copies.

COPYRIGHT

Software, once written, can be copyrighted and protected by the UK Copyright, Designs and Patents Act of 1988. The Act was subsequently slightly amended by an EC Directive (which takes precedence) in 1992 and is now referred to as the Copyright (Computer Programs) Regulations. The criminal penalty is up to two years imprisonment and a £2,000 fine. The Act defines a computer program as a 'literary work' and the copyright applies to the program for the life of the author, plus fifty years. In the case of an employee, the copyright is owned by the employer.

SOFTWARE PIRACY

The copying of software to avoid paying the licence is widespread and is estimated to cost hundreds of millions of pounds in the UK alone; world losses are estimated to be several billion dollars.. Huge amounts of money are invested in developing software and potential income is lost through piracy. As a result, the development costs are recouped through increased retail prices to the legal purchasers. When a user opens a sealed pack of new software, he/she is deemed to have accepted the conditions printed on the envelope. This lays down whether the software is a single user/single computer licence, the restrictions on its use, etc.

It is illegal to:
- Copy copyrighted software without permission from the copyright owner.
- Copy the software's manuals and program notes, without permission from the copyright owner.
- Distribute copyrighted software without permission from the copyright owner.
- Distribute the software's manuals and program notes, without permission from the copyright owner.

Police have search warrant powers to enter premises where there is a suspected breach of the Copyright Act involving computer software and a number of highly publicised fines have been imposed on well-known public and private organisations. Maximum penalties are 6 months/£5000 in the Magistrates Court and 2 years/unlimited fines in the Crown Court. Six month jail sentences have already been given in a number of cases of selling counterfeit software. A successful prosecution has also been brought against the importation of pirate software, under the Trademarks Act.

There is now some evidence that employers are taking the issue of piracy seriously and many now have policies to prevent unlawful copying of programs or bringing unlicensed software into the workplace. In some cases, culprits face disciplinary measures up to the level of dismissal.

ANTI-PIRACY AGENCIES

One of the major groups is the Federation Against Software Theft which was formed in 1984 to combat computer piracy and is supported by the subscriptions of its around 400 members (mostly corporate users or from the computer industry). It works closely with local police forces and council Trading Standards departments. Its purpose is twofold:

- To educate and advise computer users against software piracy.
- To support software developers and law enforcement agencies in preventing and detecting computer piracy and to aid the prosecution of offenders.

A group of FAST computer auditors can descend, without warning and at any time, upon a suspected company and serve an 'Anton Piller' court order allowing a search for illegally copied software. An Anton Piller order is a court order that requires a company to allow the inspection team to search the premises and produce a permanent record of all software installed on the premises. The inspection team is usually compiled from computer experts and lawyers and their records may be used in evidence in any legal action against an offending company. The consequences of such an action are severe and include:

- The individual responsible for the installation of the software may lose his/her reputation or even his/her job. Even if that person is not personally responsible, he/she will still be held liable and will pay the price for poor control of staff.
- The offending organisation may have to delete all illegal software and purchase new packages.
- The offending organisation may have to pay for its use of the illegal software.
- The offending organisation will have to pay for all the inspection and legal costs.
- The offending organisation will suffer extremely bad publicity.

To date, FAST has not lost a single court case. They can be contacted at 2 Lake End Court, Taplow Road, Winster, Derby, Tel 01628-660377. FAST has concentrated largely on large corporations but has recently declared that it will now also focus on the SoHo (small office/home office) market. This will mainly be an educational drive with the legal drive being against those who produce and market illegal copies.

There are a number of other active agencies.

The ELSPA, the European Leisure Software Publishers Association, has its own crime unit. They pay particular attention to pirate games CDs and can be contacted at 01386-833810.

The BSA, Business Software Alliance operates internationally, specialising in combating piracy of business applications. Its members include Microsoft, Novell and Lotus. In the UK it works closely with FAST and can be contacted at 0171-491-1974; its Software Crimeline is 0800-510510.

'Intercept' is a group including major software companies such as Lotus, IBM and Microsoft. It has laid some stress on the detection and elimination of computer pornography.

Although not an enforcing agency, the British Computer Society has a number of specialist working groups in this area - the Law Specialist Group, the Technology of Software Protection Group, the Computer Security Specialist Group and the Data Protection Group. The BCS are at PO Box 1454, Station Road, Swindon, Wiltshire, SN1 1TG, Tel 01793-480269.

Novell, the major networking software supplier, has offered to legalise all unlicenced copies of its software. There will be no charge - if users say where they obtained the software. Novell's Anti-Piracy Line is on 0800-747283.

Microsoft has launched a 'Sherlock Holmes' campaign where users can call their hotline on 0345-300125 ext 1000 to confirm if their software is legal and to report dealers who are selling illegal copies. Where users have bought illegal copies unknowingly, the hotline allows them to licence with Microsoft without any legal repercussions. Microsoft provides software to large corporations under its 'Select' scheme and it now intends to invoke a clause in that contract that allows for spot-check audits of software.

SOFTWARE AUDITS

In an organisation with many PCs, keeping track of the contents of each machine's hard disc is difficult. A systematic approach has to be adopted to catalogue all the software in use on the machines in an easy form that can be compared with the software licences held by the company. The manual search through all the files on each hard disc and the collation of the results would be very time-consuming. What is required is an automated system. This is now available in the form of *'software auditing'* programs. Sophisticated programs such as PC Audit, Microsoft's 'LegalWare', Lan Auditor and CA-Netman (for local area networks) and Dr Solomon's Audit for standalone PCs can now be purchased..

SPAUDIT

FAST produced an audit pack that includes a program called SPAudit. The floppy disc is inserted in each machine in the organisation in turn and its opening screen is as shown.

The first option, *'Collect Information'*, prompts the user to input a code to uniquely identify the machine. This might be the machine's serial number, room number, or other identifying

```
              S P A u d i t                          v2.8

         Collect Information
         Quit

         Print Options

         Add Additional Products

         Information about the Developer & Publisher
Searching for  967 FileSpecs
Located    38 matching FileSpecs


     Anti-V <tm>          Published & Distributed
       Protected                   by
                                 Software
   Developed by                  Publishers          Copyright 1990, 1991
     InterWorks                  Association              InterWorks
```

code. The program then searches through the machine's hard disc cataloguing all the known programs in its list. This list identifies around 1,000 programs and the fourth menu option allows other programs to the list. This option saves the machine's program details to a file on the floppy disc.

```
              P r i n t    O p t i o n s

                              Summary
     Type of Report:         Detail by Machine ID
                              Both Summary & Detail
                        ==> This Machine Only

                              Screen
     Destination of Report:  ==> Printer        ==> Single spaced
                                                    Double spaced

     Produce Report




               Press  Esc  when finished
```

The *'Print'* option can be used to produce a report on the current machine by choosing the *'This Machine Only'* option. The *'Detail by Machine ID'* option produces report on each machine that has been catalogued so far. Each machine features in a separate part of the report.

The *'Summary'* option is the most powerful and most useful. It produces a report that combines all the facts from each machine and lists how many copies of each program were found in the company's machines. This is the list that can be compared to the company's licence provision and unlicensed use detected. The reports can be sent to the screen or the printer.

SOFTWARE INSTALLATION

Each application has its own differing step-by step routine to install software. In most cases, the installation routine is straight-forward. The package will contain a set of discs and an installation guide. The guide may be contained in the package's manual or it may be a separate booklet. The discs are clearly numbered in the sequence they will be used and the first disc is placed in the floppy drive and the user runs the install program. The name of this program will be given in the documentation or may even be printed on Disc 1. This program then takes over and carries out the installation steps; it will prompt the user when it is time to insert a new disc and it will ask the user to make certain choices. From a user point of view, the process consists of answering questions when prompted and changing the discs when instructed.

When an application is set up it will want to know certain facts about the machine on which it is being used and the user should not run the installation program until the answers are known, otherwise the installation process will have to be aborted and re-started again later. The user should compile a list before running the installation program. The most commonly needed information is:

SCREEN TYPE

The package needs to know whether it will be working with a VGA or a SVGA or other monitor and whether the display is monochrome or colour. This ensures that the package will install the correct driver software to handle the screen correctly.

TYPE OF MOUSE

The package needs to know whether the mouse is a Microsoft serial mouse, a bus mouse, or other type.

TYPE OF KEYBOARD

The package needs to know whether to expect input from an 83, 84, 86, 101 or a 102 key keyboard.

WHETHER A NETWORK IS IN USE

The package will work differently on a local area network from the way it works on a standalone machine (e.g. the network version may support file locking and record locking)

PATHS TO STORE APPLICATION

The package will store all the program files together in the one directory of the hard disc.   The installation program will have a default name for this directory (e.g. the default directory for storing Word For Windows is WINWORD while the default for Excel is simply EXCEL).   The user can alter the directory for storing program files by typing in a different path to that given as the default.

PATHS TO STORE TEMPORARY FILES

Many programs create temporary files while the application is running with a certain piece of data; when the application is exited, or the work on the data is completed, the temporary files are deleted automatically. Again, the installation routine may suggest a destination directory to store these temporary files (it may even be the same directory as that holding the main program files) and the user may alter this path.

PATHS TO STORE DATA FILES

Some installation routines may also suggest a destination directory for storing the application's data files and allow the user to enter a different sub-directory name.

FURTHER ALTERATIONS

When the installation program finishes, the new piece of software is added to the hard disc and is available for use.   In the case of Windows applications, the technician may have to set up a program item and a suitable icon to make access to the program easier.   Even these tasks may be undertaken by the installation program.

In all applications, the settings are alterable again later, should the machine see any hardware changes, for example to its monitor type.   With Windows, there are a number of additional settings that can be made outwith the installation process, such as altering the keyboard repeat rate timing, changing the sensitivity of the mouse or altering the system's memory usage.   These issues are covered later.

MAINTAINING LEGALITY

Before installing software, the support technician should confirm that the software is licensed to be installed on the particular machine.   A well-run organisation will require documentation on the installation.   The technician should fill in a report that states the date of the installation, the person who carried out the installation, the name of the package and any other relevant details.

COMPUTER DATA

All organisations require to store raw data that can be retrieved for later perusal, or can be processed in a way that brings out more generalised information.   Every time a purchase is made at a supermarket checkout, raw data is saved.   This records what items were purchased, what day and time, which branch and so on.   The Board of Directors, however, are more interested in the organising of these facts and figures in a way that tells them which items are best sellers, which store performs best, which time of day records the highest sales, etc.   In most cases, data in both its raw and processed state is valuable.   Raw data, for example, can be used to send out mailing lists - while processing the same data can produce information on the total numbers in any one town, etc.   Indeed, data and information have become commodities for trading.   Lists of affluent purchasers (eg those recorded as buying expensive cars, art, conservatories, etc) are sold on to companies for mailshot purposes.

Examples of differing producers of data and information are:

Type of Activity	Type of Data	Type of Information
Weather Centre	Temperatures; barometric readings; wind speeds	Trends in the weather; average sunshine/rainfall for a particular month.
Finance Dept	Invoices paid; income receipts	Balance over a period; main spending areas.
Opinion Polling	Purchasing preferences; voting intentions; public attitudes	Degree of success of an advertising campaign; voting and public opinion snapshots and trends.
College/University	Student details, examination results	Student numbers; proportions by sex, race, etc; total successes in each performance band.

The list could be greatly extended as almost all organisations maintains records for a wide range of purposes.   In each case above, information is the result of processing the data in some way.   Large organisations will have their own *'Management Information System'* - a department equipped to gather data and produce useful information for management at all levels.

USAGE OF INFORMATION
The three main uses of the stored information are recording, monitoring and planning as shown below:

Historical recording	Used to store for later use (eg tax returns, VAT receipts/payments, targetted mailshots, etc)
Monitoring	Used to determine comparisons and trends (eg stock control, climatic changes, stock market trends, etc)
Planning	Used to determine future action (eg build more schools/roads/houses, extend factories, etc)

The MIS Department would supply information appropriate to the level of management in the organisation as shown below:

Management Level	Responsibilities	Information Required
Top Management	Long-term strategic decisions (eg market trends, new products, expansion/contraction	Market research, comparisons with competitors.
Middle Management	Tactical decisions on a month-by-month basis.	Future orders, company targets.
Junior Management	Daily operational decisions	Daily production/staffing/stock figures.

SOURCES AND TYPES OF INFORMATION
Information can be produced from within an organisation - internal sources - or can be gathered from a variety of external sources. The general classifications of organisational information would include:

Categories	Internal Sources	External Sources
Personal	Personnel records (promotion, discipline, health, etc)	Letters of complaints/praise from the public
Employment	Training programmes, Company Research & Development results, Production figures	Market Research, Government initiatives (eg on training, grants and subsidies
Financial	Sales figures, Company accounts, VAT payments, Payroll details	Sales orders, Remittance advice, Purchase Invoices, Returned goods, VAT receipts
Legal	Data Protection Act procedures, Software audits, Criminal records, rehabilitation records	Employment legislation, Health & Safety Work legislation, Trade Union laws, Case histories

The above table outlines the main categories for commercial organisations.
Other information categories can be developed, such as:

Scientific (eg scientific formulae, periodic tables, properties of materials, test results)
Engineering (eg quality controls, tolerances, templates, computer numeric control systems)
Social (eg national census, voters rolls, music charts, club membership lists)

SOURCES OF INFORMATION
As shown above, sources of organisational information can be viewed as either internal or external with corresponding sub-categories as below:

INTERNAL
- Departments (Accounting, Sales, Purchases, Development, Maintenance, Personnel, Training)
- Individuals (suggestions box, interviews, unofficial *grapevine*)

EXTERNAL
- Other organisations (orders, invoices, returns, government agencies eg Inland Revenue, Customs & Excise, Health and Safety Executive)
- Individuals (letters from the public)
- Information providers (market research organisations)
- Service providers (on-line databases)
- Product providers (manuals, technical specifications)
- Reference publications (Government pamphlets, tax tables)
- Public records (legal case histories, balance of payments figures, Hansard)

TECHNICAL SOURCES

In the rapidly changing computer world, a constantly updated reference base is required by computer and I.T. specialists.

Such a reference base could consist of:

- Bought-in training material.
- Textbooks. These are widely available and often explore beyond the user manuals.
- Manuals. Despite being much maligned, often deservedly, manuals have an important role to play in providing the detail required on any one command or activity.
- Printouts from bulletin board on-line help sessions. There are many bulletin boards throughout the country where queries can be placed and speedy answers received; some of these are provided by software houses. This can be a valuable source, since a problem experienced in one workplace has probably also been experienced and solved somewhere else.
- User Group newsletters, magazines and notes from group meetings. For the same reason as above, membership of user groups is advisable. Most subject areas are covered and there are groups for Microsoft Application users, Windows users, Novell users, Lotus users, and many more. These are not hobbyists' clubs (although individual membership is accepted) and are usually composed of representatives from private companies, local authorities, health boards, etc.
- Notes taken during suppliers on-line help sessions. Many software and hardware suppliers run their own help desks and this issue is covered later. However, the notes taken when on the telephone to these 'hot-lines' provide a useful insight into the workings of the particular package system and should be stored for future reference. A standard form can be produced for this purpose.
- Computer magazines. Subscriptions should be arranged for a range of magazines, after careful scrutiny of their general contents. The best magazines provide cover of both hardware and software issues, although some specialise (in Unix, for example). These are mostly monthly productions. Typical contents include:
  - Product reviews, both of new hardware and new software. Hardware reviews generally provide performance bench-marks, so that different products can be compared. Software reviews provide a roundup of the packages' facilities in comparison to similar products from competitor's.
  - Technological trends. This can prove specially useful in aiding future planning of I.T. provision; planned spending on upgrades and extensions might be delayed awaiting the introduction of better systems.
  - *'How to'* articles. These cover issues as diverse as *'how to plan your network'* and *'how to create macros in Word'*. These articles tend to present ideas in a popular way and can be either basic or advanced.
  - *'How things work'* articles. Similar to the above, usually with lots of helpful illustrations and diagrams.
  - Hints and tips. These sections may be categorised under database, spreadsheet, DTP, etc. headings, or there may be general sections. Many useful small hints are given in these sections, some of which are not even documented in the DOS manual, package manual or other source.

  Over a period of time, the shelves will begin to creak with the accumulated volumes of such magazines. Finding a particular article requires a reference system to be built up. Maintaining this system is cumbersome and accessing data is slow. A more useful approach may be to simply cut out the articles and file them in cardboard wallets or boxes under appropriate headings. For example, all articles on DOS batch tips could be stored in a separate wallet, as with material on spreadsheet macros, windows tips and so on. In that way, all the material on a certain subject is easily accessed. The only overhead is the breakdown of a magazine into the wallets.
- Printouts of all help text files that are supplied with application packages and with hardware driver discs, etc. These might be README.TXT or similarly named ASCII files and they provide up-to-date additions and modifications to the manuals. They often cover known bugs and hardware clashes. There are also a number of Windows files in .WRI format. And, of course, the many help pages in Windows applications are capable of being printed out; this means that the most frequently accessed help pages can be printed out and compiled into a separate booklet or included in wallets with similar information (see paragraph on magazine articles).
- Technical information on CD-ROM as supplied by some software houses (e.g. by Lotus as part of its support deal).
- Trade papers. These are weekly or monthly publications and are either general in nature or cover specialised areas such as local area networks or data communications.

PROBLEMS OF DATA STORAGE

Where large amounts of data are stored in a single computer, a number of potential problems have to be addressed and preventative/corrective measures. The most common problems are:

- LOSS OF DATA   Preventing loss due to system breakdown or data corruption
  (see Disc Backups)
- INTEGRITY   Ensuring that data is:
  - <u>Complete</u>   (all required facts and figures are entered)
  - <u>Accurate</u>   (all entries are correct - perhaps using double entry of data and/or entry validation procedures such as range checking, format checking and the use of check digits)
  - <u>Consistent</u>   (ie a price list on one computer stores the same data as a price list on another computer)
- LEGALITY   Storing data in a legal manner (see Data Protection Act)
- SECURITY   Preventing unauthorised access to data (see Computer Misuse Act)

An organisation's Management Information Systems (MIS) Department would have overall responsibility for the above issues and would institute protective measures in consultation with the P.C. support technicians.

SECURITY

A commercial organisation is greatly concerned about the security of its data since it may contain vital information about company budgets, contract bids, sales projections, business plans, product specifications and a host of other sensitive information. Often, a company's data is more valuable than the installed hardware. Machine breakdown, fire and flood remain the biggest source of data loss and security against these is covered in the section on file backups. The chapter on viruses covers the threat to data security from that source. This section is concerned with the physical security of data from the eyes of unauthorised users. Threats to an organisation's data include fraud, commercial espionage and malicious damage. These are potentially extremely damaging and the problems are now addressed in Government legislation, known as the Computer Misuse Act of 1990.

COMPUTER MISUSE ACT

It is generally accepted that breaches of data security are still mostly perpetrated by staff within a company, rather the more publicised cases of 'hacking' from external sources. However, due to the increase in networking of PCs and the increase in remote access (i.e. accessing the company computers via a modem) the threat of data loss through hacking is increasing.

The Computer Misuse Act 1990 makes it an offence to:
- make unauthorised access to computer material.
- make unauthorised access with intent to commit or facilitate commission of other offences.
- make unauthorised modification of computer material.

Case law in June 1992 established that the Act applies equally to hacking from a remote machine and also to standalone PCs. In December 1993, case law established that the offender need not even touch the keyboard to commit the crime. One party enticed another party to copy confidential information. The court ruled that the party requesting the offence was the major offender. Using a program, erasing a file, altering a file, copying a file and even viewing a file are all offences if the action is not authorised. The New Scotland Yard Computer Crime Unit (Tel 0171-230-1176) recommends that companies have a warning message displayed at the start-up of a computer, so that the user is left is no doubt about the possible consequences of his/her actions. Any subsequent activity is then being carried out in the full knowledge of the legal position. Penalties extend up to five years imprisonment or a fine, or both. Copies of the Act are available from HMSO suppliers.

ACHIEVING SECURITY

With a local area network, the access problem is partly solved by a series of passwords and accompanying rights to view, alter and delete data in various sub-directories. These are allocated by the network supervisor in a way that prohibits unauthorised access and use of files.

For a non-networked collection of PCs, other measures must be implemented and consideration should be given to the following measures.

PHYSICAL SECURITY

A PC that stores valuable programs or data can be physically protected. This can take the simple form of situating the machine in a locked room or room with sign-in, swipe card or clearance badge access. It may also mean purchasing a machine with a removable hard disc, so that the data can be stored in the safe at night. Another option is to install a key system to the computer so that it cannot be accessed without the physical presence of the key in the mechanism. Of course, the technician has to consider that a determined attempt at industrial sabotage will not be prevented by a password or keyed system; the machine may simply be stolen and entry gained at leisure. To prevent this, the machine can be bolted to the desk or can have steel cables connected to that go round furniture and be locked. Equipment can also be fitted with an alarm system. The system might include provision to detect the proximity of a person's body (e.g. the Portable Computer Protector) or it may detect the physical movement of the computer (e.g. the Computer Guardian). It may also be fitted with an anti-tamper device so that the computer alarm cannot be disabled (e.g. the PC Theft Alarm). Other methods include computer cases with key locks so that they cannot be opened to remove hard discs and their data.

HARDWARE-BASED SECURITY

A variety of hardware devices can be used to provide security. In these cases, they are effective in preventing the casual interference with the system. They are not capable of preventing the professional thief who will steal the machine, disable the security schemes and access the data. Examples of hardware security include:

- Many computers have key switches that can be turned to disable the keyboard or even disable the power button.
- The use floppy drive locks. These are blanking plates that can be fitted into the floppy drive and locked into place with a key. This prevents the unauthorised copying of files to floppy disc. If this is used in a network where all printing is to a central location, then the opportunity for removal of data is even further reduced.
- The use of 'dongles' to prevent illegal use of a piece of software. These were popular for many packages some time ago but were withdrawn due to user hostility. These were devices that plugged into the serial or parallel port of the computer. The dongle was supplied with a particular application package and the circuitry inside ensured that the application could be run. If the dongle was removed, the application package would not run. Some of the more expensive applications, such as Autocad and Authorware still use dongles. These were very inconvenient as loss of the device meant that the package was unusable. However, they can provide an extra level of security. If the user removes the dongle while not at the machine, the application cannot be used by others. Firms, such as Data Encryption Systems Ltd and BL Computer Security, will provide dongles for programmers who are developing systems within a company. In this way, the company's own programs can be dongled and protected.

SOFTWARE-BASED SECURITY

These comprise of two approaches - detection software and prevention software. Detection software does not prevent the breach of security but allows the culprit to be traced, while prevention software stops the security breach from happening.

Examples of detection software are:

- Audit/Logging systems, where the software in each computer creates a log of all files that were opened, with dates and times; it can also log the use of floppy discs or the serial port. These are regarded with some suspicion since they are also capable of monitoring the number of keystrokes entered by a user in a given period and can hence be used for employee performance monitoring.
- Embedding of company information into application logos. When the package is installed for the first time, the user is prompted for the company name, address, etc. and this information is written into the application's .EXE file. Any subsequent installation does not prompt for fresh information and uses the previously saved data in the screen logo. This does not prevent illegal copying but makes it more conspicuous.

Examples of prevention software are:

- Password and network security mentioned previously.
- Methods that prevent unauthorised entry to company networks from modems. Authorised entry, via modems and remote access software such as Carbon Copy or PC Anywhere, requires the user to enter the correct password before allowing access to the main computer network. With patience, a hacker will eventually crack the password and be able to enter the network. An improved security

system includes a *'callback'* or *'dialback'* facility. In this case, the user phones the main system and provides a valid user name and password as normal. The system software then consults a centrally held database to see what telephone number is associated with that password. It phones back the caller and allows the user's connection. In this way, a hacker will not gain access to the system even if he/she is able to work out the correct password since the call would not be coming from the authorised phone number. This callback facility is offered in Carbon Copy for Windows.

- The screen blanker, designed to turn off the screen after a pre-set time. There would be little point in having elaborate access systems if the user walked away for lunch leaving the data visible on the screen. This system blanks off the screen and requires a password to restore normal viewing.
- Where software is being developed (either in house or by a software house) for sensitive areas, the specification should include specific security measures. These measures could include passwords, security levels and authentication (the passwords of two users being required before an operation can continue).

PASSWORD SYSTEMS BUILT IN TO THE BIOS

Some computers allow a user password to be allocated to a machine. This is stored in the CMOS and a user will not gain access to the computer unless the correct password is given. This prevents the machine from being accessed by unauthorised users but is only a crude system.

PASSWORD PROTECTION SYSTEMS

A sophisticated system is often required so that users can share the same machine. Some users will be able to see budget data but be blocked from seeing personnel data. Other users will be able to see personnel data but be blocked from viewing budget data. In other words, the machine requires selective viewing of sub-directories based on a user's password. This is available in both software implementations (such as Security Guardian, Menugen and PC Guard) and hardware implementations (using add-on cards such as PC Access Control, Sysecure, StopLock or Datalarm). Beware of systems that encrypt the data on the hard disc. This is intended to thwart the person who gains unauthorised access to data. Check that there is no possibility that the authorised user ends up unable to decipher the data in the event of a hard disc fault or security card fault.

COMPANY POLICY

The organisation should evolve a security strategy that is well known and accepted by the staff. Staff should understand the need for some of the otherwise niggling procedures, as an educated workforce is the key to data security. It follows that the evolution of the strategy identifies all possible risks; it should cover networks, standalone PCs and remote access systems; it should involve the I.T. professionals and the day-to-day users. The commitment to security has to emanate from the top down and there is evidence of increasing understanding and action from top management.

The strategy should be enshrined in a company policy that details:

- who is responsible for each level of security (who manages the network security, who carries out the backups, who controls document management, who carries out configuration management, etc.).
- who will carry out the necessary staff education.
- who will monitor the efficiency of the policy.
- what the agreed penalties are for breaches of security.
- what the recovery systems will be in the event of data loss or corruption.

The policy should outline the main points of the Copyright, Designs and Patents Act, the Computer Misuse Act, the Trademarks Act and the Data Protection Act.

DATA PROTECTION ACT

The single biggest use of computers is for the creation of databases to store masses of data. This data includes personal information on individuals - as employees, clients, patients, etc. The data also includes sensitive financial information on contracts, deadlines, specifications, etc. Since 1984, holders of such data are governed by the Data Protection Act and are legally obliged to register. EC directives are expected to further tighten UK legislation in this area. Despite its name, the Data Protection Act is more concerned with protecting people - protecting them from the effects of wrong information.

The central points of the Act are:

- Data should not be available to unauthorised viewers
- Subjects of the data should have the right to view their own data

There are, however, a few areas where the Act has exemptions, such as national security and the prevention and detection of crime.   Other exemptions include personal, household and recreational use of data and data used for calculating wages and pensions.

The eight principles of the Act are:
1.   Data must be obtained and processed fairly and legally.   The data must not be obtained through subterfuge or impersonation, for example.
2.   Data shall only be held for specified purposes.   Data users have to tell the Data Protection Registrar what uses the data is intended for.
3.   Data shall not be used or disclosed contrary to the above: e.g. data held on a customer file cannot be sold to another company for mailshots, without the knowledge and permission of the subjects.
4.   Data shall not be beyond that required for the specified purposes.   A file of customers, for example, should not contain any reference to the religion or political persuasion of the customers.
5.   Data shall be kept accurate and up-to-date.   Where circumstances change (e.g. medical records), the data must be kept in a current condition.
6.   Data shall not be kept longer than is necessary.   If data is held on patients for, say, a controlled experiment, the data on individuals should not be kept after the trial is completed; the generalised data, cropped of subject names, may be kept for reference.
7.   Individuals shall have the right to view, amend or erase data, as appropriate.
8.   Data shall be protected against unauthorised access.

RIGHTFUL ACCESS

Wherever personal details are recorded, there is scope for error.   These errors could be typing mistakes or the confusion of records (how many John Smiths live in Britain ?).   These mistakes have, in the past, resulted in patients being given medical treatment meant for others.   Individuals could also find themselves being refused employment, promotion, benefits, credit or other rights, as a result of incorrect data.   It is vital that the subjects whose data is being stored have access to their own records to check their accuracy.   This could include taking away a copy of the data. Where the information is inaccurate (e.g. wrong age), the user should be able to have it altered.   Where the information is incorrect (e.g. wrong person), the user should be able to have the data erased from the file.   The Data Protection Officer will arbitrate in any disputes between subjects and organisations holding data on them.   The subject may also apply to the courts for correction or deletion of incorrect data.

UNAUTHORISED ACCESS

It is also important that only those authorised to view the data have access to personal records.   Many bodies keep very personal data on individuals, covering areas such as health details, marital details, financial details and promotion and discipline details. It is the responsibility of the body to ensure that there are adequate measures to prevent unauthorised access.   A normal procedure would be to ask a subject to complete a request form to view their data.   This might incur a search fee of, say, £10.   When the form is submitted, the subject should be obliged to provide some proof of identity. In this way, only the actual subject will be able to see his/her own data.

COMPENSATION

Data subjects can receive compensation where incorrect data has caused them harm.   Examples of this might be from the loss of data, the use of incorrect data, or the unauthorised disclosure of data.   The results might be physical damage (the wrong medicine), financial damage (passed over for promotion) or psychological damage (ridiculed by work mates about an exotic disease, unorthodox religious or political persuasion).

The Data Protection Act of 1984 requires that users of personal data be registered with the Data Protection Registrar.
Copies of the registration pack can be obtained from
>   The Office of the Data Protection Registrar,
>   Springfield House,
>   Water Lane,
>   Wilmslow,
>   Cheshire, SK9 5AX Tel: 0625-535777

These users must instigate procedures whereby the subject can request and gain access to his/her data.

The European Union's Data Protection Directive has to be translated into a British law by the beginning of 1998 and there is a view that the enforcement of good practice enshrined in the eight principles should take precedence over the emphasis on compulsory registration.

DATA ORGANISATION

The chapter on using DOS explains how to create directories and sub-directories on a disc. This section considers the best method of storing data on a hard disc. A new hard disc is empty apart from the DOS and/or Windows directories and a few system files. The way that the rest of the disc is organised can affect the efficiency of the disc's later use.

The data on the disc should be organised in such a way that it is:

- EASILY IDENTIFIED
- EASILY BACKED UP
- EASILY DELETED
- EASILY PROTECTED

The default in most installation packages is to create a single data sub-directory in the same directory

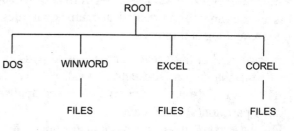

area as the main application package itself. The program files may be in one directory, while the data files may be in another directory at the same or lower level of the structure. It is common to place the data files in a sub-directory below that of the application packages. This would throw all the data files into a single sub-directory, thereby mixing together all the data files for different projects. This is convenient in the sense that all the possible data files for Word will be found in the C:\WINWORD\FILES directory. However, over time, the data will relate to many different projects and it is very easy to lose track of which files belong to which project. As a consequence, there is confusion over which files to backup, copy, or delete at the end of a project. This results in many old unused files remaining on the hard disc well past their useful life.

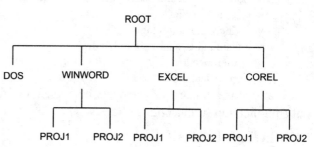

The common solution is to create different sub-directories for each project. So, for example, the application program files for Word will be in C:\WINWORD, while the documents for Project 1 will be in C:\WINWORD\PROJ1. The diagram represents a small piece of a typical hard disc's directory structure.

When the machine is used to work on a variety of projects, a number of sub-directories will be created to store these files for that particular project. So, in the example, the word-processed documents for Project 1 are in C:\WINWORD\PROJ1, while the budget calculations are in C:\EXCEL\PROJ1 and the drawings are in C:\COREL\PROJ1. This is a big improvement compared to throwing all the data files into a single sub-directory. However, it has major drawbacks for security and backup activities, since the files of a particular project are scattered across the hard disc, in many different sub-directories.

An alternative would be to completely separate program directories from data directories. In this diagram, the PROGS directory contains sub-directories for each application on the machine. Since the applications are rarely changed, this section of the structure will remain untouched apart from adding new applications or upgrading an application to a newer version. Since these files are already stored on the installation discs, there should be no need to involve this entire section of the structure in any backup strategy.

The only exception may be for an application that is heavily customised and the backup may be necessary to store the customisation details.

The DATA directory forms the starting point for all the machine's data sub-directories. The data for every application would be stored in sub-directories under the DATA directory. The important difference is that the data is not stored under the corresponding name of each application (eg all Excel files in the EXCEL directory). The structure is organised so that there is a different sub-directory for each project that the organisation is undertaking. All the data for this project is stored in the project sub-directory, regardless of the origin of the file. So, the PROJ1 sub-directory will contain all the word-processing, spreadsheet, database and graphics files relating to Project 1. Similarly, PROJ2 will only contain files relating to Project 2 and can be any mixture of file types.

This greatly simplifies backup procedures and the copying of files. With the original system, copying files was a nightmare, as the wanted files were mixed in with all other data files of the same type. The user would have to know which files related to a particular project. With the second system, the confusion was removed, since all the files of a particular project were grouped in a set of named sub-directories. This still causes problems, as a set of copy commands has to be given to fetch the files from all relevant sub-directories. The third system is straightforward, as every file for a project resides in a single directory, regardless of the format of its contents. Another benefit of the third structure is that it is uncommon for unwanted and unknown files to accumulate in project-specific directories, so disc housekeeping is improved.

A variation on the above approach is to partition the existing hard disc into two or more distinct areas (see the chapter on Discs and Drives). After partitioning, the original 'C' drive will appear as separate 'C', 'D', etc. drives. DOS, Windows and application programs can be stored on the 'C' drive, while the other partition(s) stores data.

For those computers with more than a single hard disc, there is no need for partitioning, since 'C', 'D', etc drives will already exist.

STORAGE MEDIA LIBRARY

Many organisations organise a library of commonly used media, as a common resource for use by all authorised staff. Typical library contents would include:

- computer files
- video and audio tape
- visual aids, such as OHP slides
- reference books
- specifications

The material is held centrally and can be booked out for a defined period in the same manner as booking out a publication from a council library.

COMPUTER LIBRARY

The type of material that would be found in a library of computer files might include:

SOURCE CODE

If a software house has many projects in hand, there is a very good chance that some will use similar or identical routines. Examples might be routines to validate a number or test if a date is valid. Where code is written that is liable to be re-used, the code can be saved in the library. Any writer wishing to incorporate the same facility, can simply copy the code from the library into his/her own project. This saves much development time and testing time, since the code will have been thoroughly tested before being allowed into the library.

CLIP ART

Such a collection would include the company logo, copyright-free clip art, digitised pictures and even scanned images of director's signatures. The library may also include copyrighted material as long as permission is sought before using it; copyright material, for that reason, should be stored separately from copyright-free material.

SAMPLE APPLICATIONS

Many programs include sample applications written with the package. These are designed to demonstrate what can be achieved with the package and illustrate some of the package's techniques. These tend to be large and would not normally be left on a machine's hard disc. The user would book the sample application out of the library, temporarily install it on his/her computer and delete it again when the examination was complete.

TRAINING PACKAGES

Similarly, the company may own a number of computer-based training packages. For reasons of disc space and for licensing reasons, the packages may be stored centrally and only loaned out when users have a need for them.

SHAREWARE

Some organisations, such as colleges and training institutions, may wish to loan out shareware packages to their students. Some shareware files contain source code in Pascal, C, or Basic and the examination of this code can be a valuable tool for students. Some shareware packages are clones for well-known expensive packages, and poor students may wish to register for a shareware version for home use. This aids the students in the their studies and reduces the temptation for them to make pirate copies of the institution's own packages.

WHERE TO STORE

The library may reside on a local area network server or on individual floppy discs held in a central store. If the amount of material is not substantial, the network server's hard disc will be able to accommodate it without any trouble. If, however, the material includes many digitised pictures and other large files, the only solution may be to store the data on floppy discs. Also, where there is no local area network, the floppy disc store may be the only solution. Depending upon the scale of the library, a single box of floppy discs up to drawers full of floppy discs may be required.

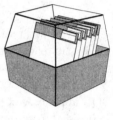

LIBRARIAN RESPONSIBILITIES

The media library has to be controlled by a responsible person, since there are legal implications to the job (i.e. storing pirate copies, insufficient licence fees, copyrighted material, etc.). The duties of the librarian would include:

MAINTAINING A MASTER SET

It is a major job to ensure that backups are kept of all material, since it is almost certain that loaned discs will, at some stage, be lost or returned with damaged, corrupted, deleted or over-written files. The master set should never be loaned out and is only used to generate another clean copy of a disc.

SECURITY

The library, and in particular the master set, must be stored in a lockfast location - preferably a separate location for both sets of discs, to reduce the chances of loss through fire or theft.

COLLECTING

The librarian must always be on the lookout for new material for the library. This may include freshly written source code procedures or it may include new files from shareware libraries. It may also involve copying files from CD-ROM shareware discs on to floppy discs.

ORDERING

The librarian will be responsible for the ordering of fresh material and ensuring that the organisation maintains the correct licence fees for the material held in the library. The librarian is also responsible for ensuring that all material held in the library can be legitimately loaned.

COLLATING

The librarian must group all material of a similar nature together. The files must be collected under defined headings, such as Pascal source code, Basic source code, C source code, disc utilities, etc. Printed catalogues should be drawn up and distributed.

KEEPING PAPERWORK

All records must be kept for inspection by auditors, FAST, etc.

BOOKING PROCEDURES

Library users should be obliged to sign out and in the material, so that a proper track can be kept of the library's stock. The signing-out sheet should incorporate a statement for the borrower to sign. This statement should include the following:

- An acceptance of the company's policy on software piracy.
- An agreement to pay for any damaged or lost discs. This will vary between organisations; a college, for example, may demand a non-returnable deposit for loans, while a large corporation may not even have such a clause.

The librarian will be responsible for checking for damages, deletions and overwrites and for pursuing overdue discs.

Operating Systems and Environments

An operating system is a set of programs to control the hardware and manage the computer's resources. The amount of files for Microsoft DOS depends on the version.   As each version is updated, new facilities are added and the number of files that make up the package increases.   DOS 6.2 comprises almost 150 files.   The main characteristics of an operating system are:

- It conceals the difficulties of handling the hardware.
- It presents the user with a relatively simple interface.
- It communicates with the user, carrying out valid commands and giving error messages when incorrect commands are attempted.
- It relieves users of DOS or software from requiring a detailed knowledge of how the computer hardware works.

With the earliest computers, users had to have a great knowledge of each item of hardware.   When DOS appeared, computers became available to ordinary users.   The user could carry out a range of activities by giving simple commands, in the knowledge that the operating system would translate the simple user command into the set of hardware tasks needed to carry it out.   The operating system could be considered as the foreman of an organisation.   When the manager (i.e. the user) gave an order for work to be carried out, the foreman took on the job of ensuring that the actual physical task was carried out.   The manager need not know where the resources are kept and what activities are involved - that is the job of the foreman.

USING THE DOS OPERATING SYSTEM

When the computer is powered up, the essential portion of MSDOS is loaded into the computer memory. The system prompt will then be displayed to the user.   This is normally in the form of showing the drive that the system is currently logged on to (i.e. currently looking at), as below:

C:\ >

The above prompt tells the user that the current logged drive is the 'C' drive, the machine's internal hard disc. This should be accompanied by a flashing line, known as the *'cursor'* and indicates that the machine is waiting for an instruction.   If the computer being used only has a floppy disc system and has to be booted up with a system disc in the floppy drive, the system prompt will display:

A:\>

Note that:

- The user cannot run any programs or perform any machine housekeeping tasks until the operating system has been loaded.
- The operating system normally checks the floppy disc drive first, so if a machine has an internal hard disc drive, no floppy should be left in the floppy drive whilst the machine is being booted.

To save memory space, only the essential and most-commonly used parts of DOS are loaded into the computer's memory when the computer is switched on.   The essential parts are required to make the computer work and the user has little control over them.   However, some of the more common commands that users require are combined into a single file and loaded into memory.   This means that these commands are quickly available to the user and these are called *'resident'* commands.   The many other utilities remain on the disc until called by the user.   If the user requires to use any of the commands (called *'transient'* or *'external'* commands), then DOS loads them into the computer's memory.   If all the possible utilities were loaded into the computer on switch on, there would not be enough memory left to do anything else!

USING COMMON DOS COMMANDS

The simplest commands comprise a single word instruction, which can be entered in upper or lower case - or even a mixture of upper or lower case.   When all of the command is typed in at the keyboard, the *'Enter'* key should be pressed.   This completes the command which is then passed to DOS to carry out. DOS will process any command until the Enter key is pressed.   The command has to be entered at the keyboard when the DOS prompt is showing. In the following examples, it is assumed that the Enter key will be pressed after entering the command. For example, to see what version of DOS is installed on the machine, the command would simply be VER, followed by pressing the Enter key. If the machine is logged to look at the 'C' drive, it can be switched to log on to the floppy drive by entering A: followed by the Enter key; logging back to the hard disc would be accomplished by typing C: followed by 'Enter'. Other simple commands are:

CLS   This clears all contents off the monitor screen and moves the prompt and cursor to the top left (i.e. home) position on the screen.

VOL   Every disc, hard disc or floppy disc, can be given an 'electronic' title, to express the general contents it contains. This title is alterable by the user (see later). The VOL command displays the disc's current label.

For more complex commands, the command is followed by various options, called *'parameters'*. For example, to delete a file from a disc, there is no point in simply telling the computer to DELETE - the computer has to be told what file to delete. Here, the parameter would be the name of the file. So, to erase a file called REPORT, the command would be

DEL REPORT

Parameters can be a single item or can be more than one item - sometimes separated by spaces, or commas, etc.

The current date and time are held inside the computer and can be viewed or altered by giving the command DATE followed by the Enter key. This will result in a display such as

Current date is Thu 16-11-96
Enter new date (dd-mm-yy)

To retain the given date, the Enter key is pressed; to alter the date, the new date is entered in the expected format, including the minus sign separators, followed by pressing Enter.

The same technique can be used to view or alter the system time, using the TIME command.

GETTING HELP

From DOS 5 onwards, on-line help has been available to the user. DOS 6 onwards has particularly useful help pages complete with examples of usage. Simply typing *'HELP'* will produce a list of topics. Typing a command followed by /? will produce assistance. Typing HELP followed by the command will produce explanations, syntax data and examples.

USING A PRINTER WITH DOS

All printers can create an exact replica of any text that appears on the screen.
This can be done in a number of ways:

- Wait until a screen of text is displayed and then send a copy of the screen to the printer. This can only display one screenful at any one time. This is achieved by pressing the PrtScr key or, on some machines, pressing the Shift and PrtScr keys together.
- Echo everything on the screen to the printer. This means that everything typed at the keyboard and all other screen output is automatically sent to the printer as well as the screen. This method can therefore handle a lot more information than the above method. Pressing the Ctrl and PrtScr keys together sets the printer echo on. To set the printer echo off again, the same two keys are pressed once again. So, the two keys toggle the printer echo off and on. (holding the keys down too long can result in the echo being turned on and then off again, giving the appearance that the action did not work).
- Redirecting output to the printer. This method sends output that was heading towards the screen to the printer instead; no output is displayed on the screen. This is achieved by placing > PRN at the end of a command. So, giving the command VER > PRN would send the DOS version number to the printer instead of the screen. This redirection can be used with many DOS commands.
- Using the PRINT command. DOS provides a specific command to print out the contents of any disc file that contains plain text. For example, to print out the file called INFO.TXT, the command would be

PRINT INFO.TXT

This command is of no use with program files, since they contain machine code instead of text and therefore display gibberish if printed out.

USING THE 'PRINT' COMMAND

As explained, the PRINT command is used to send a copy of a file's contents to a printer, with the following syntax:

PRINT C:\REPORTS\SALES.TXT

The full path must be specified if the file is not in the current directory.   Several files can be included in the one PRINT command as in the following example:

PRINT C:\REPORTS\SALES.TXT   INCOME.TXT   COSTS.TXT   C:\SUMMARY.TXT

The command provides for printing in the *'background'*.   This means that the user can carry on using other DOS commands while the printing is being done.   In fact, if the command is given several times for different files, the files are queued for printing and the system will automatically print them one after the other - while the user is doing something else.   If the PRINT command is given without any parameter, it displays a list of files that are in the print queue.

Some of the permissible parameters are:

/D:device	The computer usually has several printer ports that can be used for serial or parallel interface printers. The word 'device' in the parameter would be replaced with LPT1, LPT2 or LPT3 for parallel printers and COM1, COM2, COM3 or COM4 for serial printers. The machine's default setting is LPT1, which is also known as PRN.
/C	Removes the files listed from the print queue.
/P	Adds files to the print queue. This already happens automatically by giving the PRINT command but it can be added at the end of a command that has a /C in use. All files listed after the /C and up to the /P are deleted from the queue and all files listed after the /P are added to the queue. This is not a common situation.
/T	Removes all existing files from the print queue.
/Q:size	Sets the maximum of files allowed in the print queue, from 4 to 32, with a default of 10.
/S:size	Sets the 'scheduler' allocation between 1 to 255, the default being 8. The higher values speed up printing by slowing down other activities.

EXAMPLE:

PRINT /D:LPT1 INCOME.TXT

FILENAMES AND EXTENSIONS IN DOS

All programs and data are held on a storage device until they are ready to be used. The most common storage device is the magnetic floppy disc, although CD discs or the new memory 'flash cards' are also in use.   A file is collection of related data.   The data may be instructions to the computer (program files) or database, spreadsheet or similar information (data files).   Hard discs are likely to be storing thousands of such files at any one time.   Each file has a unique name; no two files are allowed to have exactly the same name in the same disc directory.   If a file is saved with the same name as a previous file of the same name, the new file's contents replace the old file contents.   This unique name is used by the computer to later find and load the file from anywhere on the disc.

To aid future recognition of files, there are certain conventions followed by DOS for the naming of files. Firstly, all file names may have three parts:

REPORT.DOC

File Name   Dot   File Extension

FILENAME

The FileName consists of alpha-numeric characters and certain other characters up to a maximum of eight characters and with a minimum of 1 character. So, a filename of *'G'* is valid. The filename part is compulsory and DOS will not accept a file without a name.   The file name used should express the contents of the file. A file given the name of *'HH'* or *'Z1'* may have significance when it was first saved - but will probably not convey much six months later.   More meaningful names such as *'BUDGET95'* or *'APR_MEMO'* should be used.   The Excel spreadsheet program, for example, is called EXCEL.EXE, while the DOS help program is called *'HELP.COM'*.

FILE EXTENSIONS

DOS allows a file to have up to a three-letter extension. So files called 'MEMO', 'MEMO.95' and 'MEMO.TXT' are all valid filenames. The extension can be chosen to describe the <u>format</u> of the file's contents.   The use of file extensions is optional but is recommended.

Files can have widely differing types of contents:

- The **programs** themselves; i.e. applications such as word-processors, spreadsheets and accounting packages.   Most large commercial packages, are comprised, not of a single file, but of a collection of linked files.
- The **data** used by applications; i.e. database records, spreadsheet worksheets and graphics files. These are stored in special formats used by the particular package.   Data files used in one package cannot be used in another package without converting the file format first.   It is therefore important to know the format in which data is stored.
- **Text** files that are in plain English; i.e. files that can be read via DOS.   However, most word-processors allow the text to be underlined, italicised, emboldened, etc. and involves including special codes into these files, thus making them less readable in DOS.

DOT

When a file extension is used, a dot must be used to separate the filename and extension.

PRE-DEFINED FILE EXTENSIONS

Where the user has a choice, files can be given any file extension that helps convey the file's internal format.   However, a number of file extensions are commonly used and these have to be avoided. Examples of these extensions are:

DOS EXTENSIONS

There are a number of extensions that are claimed by DOS itself.   The most important of these are the COM, EXE and BAT extensions, since any file with one of these extensions is regarded by DOS as being a program file.   This means that the program can be run by simply typing the program name, without the dot or extension, and pressing the Enter key.   For example:

    HELP.COM is a command file that is run by typing HELP then Enter.
    MSD.EXE is an executable file that is run by typing MSD then Enter.
    MYPROG.BAT is a batch file that is run by typing MYPROG then Enter.

COM and EXE files are composed of instructions, usually many thousands of instructions, in the special 'machine code' recognisable by the computer's CPU but unreadable by humans.   BAT files are also program files but are in plain English format; they are less versatile than machine code programs but are much easier to write (see chapter on batch files).   DOS also claims a number of other file extensions, such as SYS, CPI and BIN, for its own internal use.

Note that simply giving a file a COM, EXE or BAT extension does not convert that file into a program file.   If a file called REPORT.DOC contained a company report in plain English, changing the file name to REPORT.EXE would have no effect on the file's internal contents.   If the user tried to run the file by typing REPORT followed by Enter, the only result would be an error message.   Each of the three program extensions has a different meaning to DOS, since it has to handle each type differently.

WINDOWS EXTENSIONS

Microsoft Windows also claims a number of extensions to itself; these are in addition to the DOS extensions which it also uses.   Typical Windows extensions are BMP (Bit Mapped pictures) used for   creating   background   wallpaper   effects,   INI (information files) used for storing details of Windows configurations and Windows application details, and GRP (Group) used to store details of what utilities are included in the same Windows group.   Other Windows extensions include TMP,   PIF, FOT and TTF.

APPLICATION EXTENSIONS

Individual applications claim extensions for their own use.   This makes the use of a program easier, since the housekeeping is then carried out by the program itself.   If the user wishes to open up a file called REPORT, there may be various files with that same file name but different extensions.   There may be REPORT.DOC, REPORT.XLC, REPORT.DBF and so on.   The word-processing application created the text file with the extension .DOC; the user only had to choose the file name as REPORT, the application automatically added the .DOC extension.   Similarly, the Excel spreadsheet program added the .XLC extension to the worksheet saved by the user as REPORT.   The database package also automatically added the .DBF extension to the file of records that the user saved simply as REPORT. Now, when the user is in a particular application and requests to open the REPORT file, the application will know which file to open by the extension on the end.   The Spreadsheet package will ignore the other files named REPORT and only work with the file called REPORT.XLC.; the same is true of the word-processing and database packages.   The technicalities of this are hidden from the user, who need never even know that the files have been given any extensions.

There is a wide range of application extensions and some are even used by more than one application. This can confuse matters unless files of the same type are kept in their own particular compartments (see later).

Example extensions are:

ANNUAL.XLS	A worksheet created in Excel
CLIENTS.DBM	A database file created in dBase
SCREEN.HLP	A help file (common with many applications)
ADVERT.CDR	A graphics file created in Corel Draw
SALES.DOC	A word-processed file created in Word.

LANGUAGE EXTENSIONS

Many programming languages (called high-level languages) create programs by the user initially writing the instructions in an English-like format using a form of word-processor.   This text is then converted into the machine code instructions required by the computer.   This conversion can be a permanent process and the machine code instruction can be saved as a separate, independent EXE file (a process known as 'compiling') or the instructions can be simply converted and acted upon immediately, with no second file being created (a process known as 'interpreting').   In both cases, the original text is preserved, in case the writer wishes to add to or modify the instructions.   The extensions given to the text files depend upon the programming language in which they run.

Typical examples are:

GAME.BAS	The text of a Basic program
	Can be compiled or interpreted
UTIL.PAS	The text of a Pascal program to be compiled
PAYROLL.CBL	The text of a Cobol program to be compiled

OTHER EXTENSIONS

A number of other extensions are commonly in use and are regarded as a standard between packages.   In other words, every package recognises the file as being of the same format.

Examples are:

READ.ME	A text file usually included on the program disc, containing last-minute information about the release.
MEMO.TXT	A file containing plain English text.
JENNIFER.PCX	A graphics file in Paintbrush format, recognised by most word-processing, DTP and graphics packages.
MARGARET.GIF	A graphics file in Graphics Interchange Format, used regularly on bulletin boards.
STREETS.LST	A list containing related items, such as names or addresses.
NAMES.SRT	A file containing a list of items in a sorted order (e.g. names in ascending order or debts in descending order).

OBTAINING A LIST OF FILES

To obtain a list of the current files on a disc, the following command should be entered:

        DIR <Enter>

This command works with both floppy discs and hard discs and will show a list of files, giving their files' names and extensions, file sizes and the dates and times that they were created or last modified as shown:

```
            AUTOEXEC BAT        602 02/11/95    18:35
            COMMAND  COM      52925 10/03/93     6:00
            CONFIG   SYS        350 02/05/95    18:35
            MENU     BAT        572 11/10/96     7:44
```

In fact, the command only shows the files in the current directory (see later).

If the user switches to the floppy drive, by typing A: then the DIR command will display the contents of the floppy disc.   If the user switches to the hard disc, by typing C: then the DIR command displays the contents of the hard disc.   It is possible to be logged on to one drive and still see the contents of the other drive.

For example, if the user is currently logged on to the hard disc, then typing DIR A: will display the contents of the floppy disc.   When the command is completed, the user is still logged on to the hard disc and a subsequent DIR command would be of the hard disc.   This is a crucial benefit of DOS; the user can be in one part of a particular drive and still carry out operation in another part of the same disc, or even in another part of another disc. This will be looked at in more detail shortly.

The above command may not prove adequate where there are many files on a disc, since the screen can only show a portion of the files, with the rest scrolling off the top of the screen. So, DOS provides a couple of refinements to the DIR command. One of these displays the contents of the current directory one page at a time and waits until a key is pressed before displaying the next screenful. The other option is to display the file names in five columns across the screen. This option omits the file sizes, etc. but can accommodate more files on the screen at the same time, as shown:

CALC.EXE	CALC.HLP	CALENDAR.EXE	CALENDAR.HLP	CANYON.MID
CARDFILE.EXE	CARDFILE.HLP	CARS.BMP	CASTLE.BMP	CHARMAP.EXE
CHKLIST.MS	CHORD.WAV	CLIPBRD.EXE	CLIPBRD.HLP	CLOCK.EXE
CLOCK.INI	COMMDLG.DLL	CONTROL.EXE	CONTROL.HLP	CONTROL.INI
EXCEL.XLB	EXCEL4.INI	EXPAND.EXE	FLOCK.BMP	GAMES.GRP
GLOSSARY.HLP	GRAPHICS.GRP	GWS.INI	HIMEM.SYS	HONEY.BMP

If it is important to see the dates or file sizes, then the first option must be chosen. Where the user only wishes to check for the presence of a particular file on a disc, the second option is usually quicker.

DIR/P   displays the list of files one page at a time

DIR/W   displays the list of files across the width of the entire screen

These commands can be in upper or lower case or a combination of both.

VIEWING IN SORTED ORDER

When a DIR command is given, the output displays the files in the order that they were placed on the disc and this will produce a random order on the screen, for most purposes.

From DOS 5 onwards, the DIR command can be given extra 'switches' to sort the files in a particular order before displaying to the screen. The command is DIR/O: where the 'O' stands for 'Order' and the colon is optional. The command is then followed by a letter which will determine the order of the sort. The options are:

N	Sort in ascending order of filename
-N	Sort in descending order of filename
E	Sort in ascending order of extension
-E	Sort in descending order of extension
D	Sort in ascending order of date and time
-D	Sort in descending order of date and time
S	Sort in ascending order of file size
-S	Sort in descending order of file size

So, the command DIR/ON would display files in ascending alphabetical order while the command DIR/OS would display files in descending order of the file sizes.

VIEWING SELECTED FILES

A further refinement to the DIR command is to allow the user to only produce a selected subset of files. This is achieved with the /A switch and results in a listing with files that meet the following attributes:

A	Only list files where the archive bit is set
-A	Only list files where the archive bit is not set
D	Only list directories - ignore all files
-D	Only list files - ignore all directories
H	Only list hidden files
-H	Only list files that are not hidden
R	Only list files that are read-only
-R	Only list files that are not read-only
S	Only list system files
-S	Only list files that are not system files

So, the command DIR/AD would only display the directories in the current directory, while giving the command DIR/AH/S from the hard disc's root directory would display a list of all hidden files on the entire hard disc.

Other switches are /B which is the 'bare' format; this displays file and directories without any date or size information and the /L switch; this displays text in lower case.

DIRECTORIES IN DOS

A floppy disc can contain hundreds of files; a hard disc can contain tens of thousands of files.   This would make finding and operating on a file very difficult, as each file would be mixed in with the thousands of others.   It is essential, therefore, that files are stored in a logical way, so that they are easy to retrieve and manipulate.

DOS has an electronic disc filing system that is derived from an office manual filing system, where every file is kept in a filing cabinet under a different name or heading.   Files could be stored by the office department or function.

Consider, for example, searching for the discipline record of John Smith, the repair worker.   The office may have six filing cabinets but only the one labelled *'Personnel'* will need to be searched, thus removing five-sixths of the data from the search.   The Personnel filing cabinet will have three drawers and only the one labelled *'Discipline'* need be opened - the others are labelled as *'Promotion'* and *'Sick Records'* and are thus ignored in the search.   When the drawer is opened, three wallets are found, labelled as *'Clerical'*, *'Production'* and *'Maintenance'*.   Only the Maintenance wallet need be opened, again narrowing down the search.   Finally, an alphabetical search is made of the files in the Maintenance wallet, until the file of John Smith is found.   The above process provides a very speedy access to any individual file - assuming that files have been stored in a logical order in the first place.

Users of computer systems need to have the same ease of access to their computer data files as they have with their manual paper system.   This is the role of the DOS filing system.   DOS provides an electronic equivalent to the manual system.   It holds its files in different compartments (called *'directories'*) on the disc, just as the manual system holds files in different physical compartments.   If a database is in use, a directory can be created to hold the database files; if a word-processor is being used, then a directory can be created to store all word-processed files, and so on.

The creation of DOS compartments (directories) containing other compartments (sub-directories) results in a structure called the *'tree'*.

The diagram only represents a small fraction of an actual structure; a real hard disc will have dozens of directories, each containing many different files.

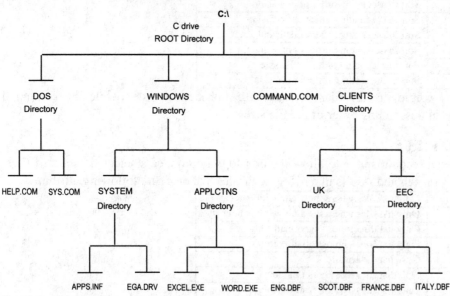

Although the structure is called a tree, it actually drawn as an inverted tree.   At the top of the structure is the ROOT directory.   This is the compartment that the user sees when the machine is first switched once (i.e. the root of the whole structure).   When the computer is first booted up and a DIR command is given, the list of files displayed will be those in the root directory.   In the example in the diagram, there will only one single file displayed - COMMAND.COM, since all the other files reside inside other compartments.

Spreading from the root directory are branches (directories and sub-directories) and leaves (the data files and program files).   Each branch of the tree (i.e. each directory) may contain leaves (i.e. files) or other branches (i.e. sub-directories).

In the example, the root directory contains one file and three sub-directories called DOS, WINDOWS and CLIENTS.   The directory names can describe the application contained within it (e.g. WINDOWS) or can describe the function or organisational structure of the company (e.g. CLIENTS).

The rules for directory construction are:
- The number of directories and their structure should mirror the needs of the organisation.
- Each directory and sub-directory should be named to clearly label its contents.
- Only the relevant files for a directory should be stored in that directory.
- Do regular housekeeping to ensure that directories are kept up-to-date. Ensure that only relevant files are being stored in each directory; move files to other directories where appropriate; remove files that are no longer used to prevent the disc becoming clogged up with old unwanted files.

DOS PATHS

To get to any file, a path is taken from the root directory, through any other directories and sub-directories until the file is reached. So, in DOS each file can be fully described in terms of its name and where it is stored.   The full file description is comprised of three parts:
- What disc is it on.
- What directory is it in.
- What the file is called.

Here are a few examples of files included in the example diagram on the preceding page:

    C:\COMMAND.COM
    C:\DOS\HELP.COM
    C:\WINDOWS\SYSTEM\APPS.INF
    C:\CLIENTS\UK\SCOT.DBF
    C:\CLIENTS\EEC\ITALY.DBF

If the same files resided on a floppy disc, filenames might be

    A:\COMMAND.COM
    A:\DOS\HELP.COM
    etc.

Since each file can be described in terms of its path as well as its name, files with the same name and extension can now exist on the same disc - as long as they are stored in separate directories.   For example, two files called REPORT.DOC could exist on the same disc in different parts of the directory structure as shown:

    C:\CLIENTS\UK\REPORT.DOC
    C:\CLIENTS\EEC\REPORT.DOC

Where this happens, the two files can have exactly the same contents or can be completely different files that happen to share the same filename and extension.

Giving the full file specification is a little laborious but can be very useful. For example, the user can be logged on to the floppy drive as the current drive and still print out a file that is sitting down in a sub-directory of the hard disc e.g.

    PRINT C:\EEC\REPORT.DOC

When the printing is over, the user is still sitting looking at the floppy drive, as before.

CHANGING DIRECTORY

In the same way that the user can switch between making the hard disc or the floppy disc the one to be currently looked at, the user will wish to control which sub-directory is the current one for any operations on that drive.   This is accomplished with the CD or CHDIR command.

MOVING DOWNWARDS..

The CD command can be used to move the user down into a lower level of the directory structure.
EXAMPLES

    CD CLIENTS

would move the user out of the current directory into the CLIENTS directory.   If a DIR command was given, only the contents of the CLIENTS directory would be displayed.

    CD UK

would move the user from the current directory, the CLIENTS directory, into the UK sub-directory. If a DIR command was given, only the contents of the UK sub-directory would be displayed.
If the user wished to go directly to the UK sub-directory, this can be achieved with the command

    CD CLIENTS\UK

These examples move the user from the current directory into a lower directory. There will be times when the user is neither in the root directory or the CLIENTS directory.

In these cases, the user can give the full path in the command and move straight to the specified directory from anywhere in the structure. Thus:

CD C:\CLIENTS\UK

will move the user into the UK directory, no matter where the user's current drive is at the time of giving the command.

If the CD command is used without any parameter it will display the drive and directory that the user is currently in.

NB: Use of this command does not switch the use from one drive to another. For example, a user may be on the A: drive and issue the command 'CD C:\CLIENTS'.   The user would remain in the A: drive but when the command 'C:' was given, the user would be in the CLIENTS directory.

MOVING BACK UP THE STRUCTURE..

If the user is in any sub-directory, DOS provides a command to move the user back up the structure:

CD..

moves the user back up one level of the structure.   So, if the user was in the EEC sub-directory, the CD.. command would move the user into the CLIENTS directory.   No matter how far down the structure the user happens to be, repeated use of the CD.. command will eventually return the user to the root directory.   There will be occasions when the user is down several layers of the structure and wishes to immediately return to the root directory, without a whole series of CD.. commands. DOS allows an immediate return to the root directory with the command CD\

CREATING NEW DIRECTORIES

The DOS structure is held on disc and can be altered at any time by the user.   The creation of a new sub-directory is very simple.   The user first has to be in the directory where the new sub-directory will branch from.   The command is simply MD or MKDIR followed by the name of the new directory.   The command can be in upper or lower case, or a mixture of both.   The new directory name can be from one to eight characters in length but should describe the contents it is intended to hold.

Some users give the directory an extension of .DIR.   This was useful in versions of DOS prior to version 5, since a DIR/W command left the user not knowing whether a particular name that was displayed was a file name or a directory name; a .DIR extension removed any doubt.   This is not necessary in DOS 5 onwards, since directories are distinguished from files in a DIR/W command by placing square brackets round directory names.

If a new sub-directory, called 'GERMANY' was to be added to the EEC sub-directory the following commands would achieve it, assuming the user was commencing from the root directory:

CD C:\CLIENTS\EEC
MD GERMANY

The same effect could also be directly achieved by the single command:

MD C:\CLIENT\EEC\GERMANY

Where an application is being shared by many users, sub-directories can be created for each individual user's initials e.g.:

MD \WINDOWS\APPLCTNS\DD
MD \WINDOWS\APPLCTNS\JD
MD \WINDOWS\APPLCTNS\RR
etc.

When a DIR command is given, the display for sub-directories is different from that for files:

```
DOS           <DIR>       08/10/95    15:49
EXCEL         <DIR>       20/10/95    19:48
MEDIAPRO      <DIR>       16/07/96    17:37
VIRUS         <DIR>       30/09/96     1:59
WINDOWS       <DIR>       08/10/96    15:50
AUTOEXEC BAT         602 02/05/95    18:35
COMMAND  COM       52925 10/03/95     6:00
CONFIG   SYS         350 02/05/95    18:35
```

A directory has no size displayed and the label <DIR> is displayed instead. When DOS creates a new directory it also creates two new sub-directories within that new directory.   These are the *'dot'* and the *'dot-dot'* directories. They are used by DOS to help navigate the system and they are not directly accessed by the user.

e.g.   Directory of C:\DOS

```
     .              <DIR>      08/10/92   15:49
     ..             <DIR>      08/10/92   15:49
     DOSSY          <DIR>      30/04/95    2:00
     4201     CPI      6404 09/04/91    5:00
     4208     CPI       720 09/04/91    5:00
```

REMOVING A DIRECTORY

As the organisation's structure changes, so the disc structure will change to reflect it.   This will involve adding new directories, as explained. It will also mean that directories will have to be removed from time to time. For example if an employee leaves, his/her personal directories should be removed and any useful files transferred to another employee's directory.

The RD or RMDIR command will remove a directory from the structure e.g.:

    RD EEC

With all DOS versions, this command only works if the EEC directory contains no files or other sub-directories and the user is currently in the directory above the EEC directory. If the user includes the path in the command - e.g. 'RD C:\EEC' - the directory will be removed without the user having to be immediately above the directory in the structure.   Similarly, a user can remove a directory from a different drive from the one currently logged to.   For example, a user can be currently logged to the C: drive and successfully give the command 'RD A:\JOHN'.   These options may not work with older versions of DOS.

DELTREE

From DOS 6 onwards, Microsoft included a utility to delete entire sections of the disc structure with a single command.   The DELTREE command can be given within a particular directory and all the files and sub-directories below that level in the structure will be deleted.   Alternatively, the command can specify a path. So, the command DELTREE C:\WINDOWS would remove all the Windows directories and subdirectories and all their contents.

The command should be used with extreme caution as it is very easy to make a mistake and eliminate large sections of the disc contents.   Consider, for example, the consequences of giving the DELTREE command from the root directory of the hard disc!   The user is asked for confirmation before proceeding, unless the /Y switch is added to the command - e.g. DELTREE /Y C:\WINDOWS

VIEWING THE STRUCTURE

DOS provides the TREE command to allow the user to view the directory structure of a hard disc or a floppy disc.   The example of using the TREE command without any parameters is shown in the left diagram below.   The first vertical line links all the directories that branch off the disc's root directory. The next vertical line is indented and shows the directories that branch off the those first-level directories.   Any other lower-level-directories would be similarly linked with other lines.   In this way, the hierarchy of the disc's structure can be easily seen.   The structure can be saved to a file by giving the command TREE > treefile and the file can be viewed or printed out later.   The structure can be directly printed by sending the output of the command to the printer with the command TREE > PRN. Since not all printers are capable of printing the graphics necessary to produce the vertical lines, TREE now has a switch to display the lines using normal characters in places of graphics characters.   The switch /A is added to the command and the right-hand diagram shows the result of giving the command TREE/A.

```
Directory PATH listing for Volume MS_DOS_6       Directory PATH listing for Volume MS_DOS_6
Volume Serial Number is 1B8F-B11C                Volume Serial Number is 1B8F-B11C
C:.                                              C:.
  ├── DOS                                        +---DOS
  ├── WINDOWS                                    +---WINDOWS
  │     ├─SYSTEM                                 |  +---SYSTEM
  │     └─APPLCTNS                               |  +---APPLCTNS
  └── CLIENTS                                    \---CLIENTS
        ├─UK                                        +---UK
        └─EEC                                       +---EEC
```

The command produces the structure from the current directory downwards; if the user is half-way down a structure, only the remaining lower section is produced; if the command is given from the root directory, the entire disc's structure is displayed.   Finally, the command allows the user to view the structure and also see what files are stored inside each sub-directory.   This can produce a very long display for a hard disc and the output for the simple structure given on page 39 would look like:

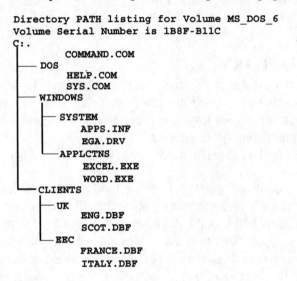

```
Directory PATH listing for Volume MS_DOS_6
Volume Serial Number is 1B8F-B11C
C:.
              COMMAND.COM
      ─── DOS
              HELP.COM
              SYS.COM
      ─── WINDOWS
           ─── SYSTEM
                  APPS.INF
                  EGA.DRV
           └──APPLCTNS
                  EXCEL.EXE
                  WORD.EXE
      └── CLIENTS
           ─── UK
                  ENG.DBF
                  SCOT.DBF
           └── EEC
                  FRANCE.DBF
                  ITALY.DBF
```

DELETING FILES

Not all files will remain on a computer's hard disc.   Normally, the programs and data that are regularly required by a user will remain on the hard disc, so that they are readily available.   Other files which are used less often can reside on floppy disc and only be loaded into memory when needed.   Additionally, many files become outdated (e.g. old correspondence, budget figures, etc.).   If they are required for future reference, they would be saved to floppy disc for archiving.   However, if the files are no longer needed, they can be removed from discs, allowing the space to be given to future files.

To delete a file, the DEL or ERASE command is used as:

DEL REPORT.DOC

This will delete the file, if the file is in the current directory.

The path can be included in the command as:

DEL C:\CLIENTS\UK\ENG.DBF

This command has a /P switch which prompts the user to confirm that the deletion should be carried out - e.g. DEL *.*/P

UNDELETING FILES

From DOS 5 onwards, a deleted file can be recovered using the UNDELETE command.   This is only possible if the deleted file is only recently deleted, as after a while the disc space used by the deleted file will be used up by a new file.   If the file is capable of being undeleted, DOS prompts for the first letter of the file to be recovered, as this gets lost after a deletion.   When the first letter is entered, the file is restored back into DOS as if nothing happened.   If a file is not able to be recovered, the user is informed of this fact.   The command UNDELETE/LIST will display a list of all the files that can be recovered in the current directory.   This is the standard system and a more secure system is available by giving the command UNDELETE/S; this saves all deleted files into a hidden directory (named 'SENTRY').   This occupies valuable disc space but makes recovery simple with the UNDELETE/DS command.

A more user-friendly version of this facility is available from within Windows (see later).

COPYING FILES

There are many occasions when a copy of a file is required:
- To send a copy of a worksheet file from the local office's hard disc to the company's head office.
- To make a copy of a program under development, so that it can be recovered in the event that the latest version fails to be an improvement.
- To make replicas of files in one directory into another directory.

The file is not actually moved to the new destination; the command creates a replica of the file in the new destination and the original file remains where it was.

The syntax of the command is:

COPY source destination

EXAMPLES

COPY COMMAND.COM A:

will copy the file COMMAND.COM from the current directly to the floppy disc; the file name on the floppy disc will be the same as that on the source disc.

COPY C:\CLIENT\EEC\ITALY.DBF A:ITALY.BAK

will copy the file ITALY.DBF from hard disc to the floppy disc and also renames the file in the floppy to ITALY.BAK

COPY C:\UTILS\COUNTER.EXE C:\DISCS*.*

will copy the file COUNTER.EXE from one directory on the hard disc to another directory on the same hard disc; the file name will remain unchanged.

COPY C:\UTILS\COUNTER.EXE

will copy the file COUNTER.EXE from the UTILS directory.   Since no destination is given, the file will be copied into whatever directory is the current directory.

With older DOS versions, a file will be copied into the target directory, automatically overwriting any file of the same name that happened to already exist in the target directory.   From DOS 6 onwards, users are prompted to decide whether to overwrite or not.   This facility can be disabled by adding the /Y parameter to the command.

MERGING FILES

Where files contain plain text, they can be merged (usually termed *'concatenation'*) into a single document using a plus sign.   The command

COPY fileA + fileB

will add the file fileB on to the end of fileA.   The file fileB remains unchanged but the fileA is now extended.   The command

COPY fileA + fileB + fileC fileD

creates a new file called fileD which contains the contents of fileC on to the end of fileB and this added to the contents of fileA.   The three files fileA, fileB and fileC remain unaltered.   If fileD already exists it is overwritten by the new contents.

MOVING FILES

From DOS 6 onwards, there is a command to move files rather than just copy them.   With the MOVE command, the nominated files are placed in the destination directory and removed from the source directory.

EXAMPLES

MOVE C:\UTILS\COUNTER.EXE C:\DISCS

will take the file COUNTER.EXE out of the UTILS directory and place it in the DISCS directory.   The command can also be used to rename an existing directory.

MOVE C:\LETTERS C:\ARCHIVE

will result in a directory called ARCHIVE which contains all the files previously stored in the directory called LETTERS; the LETTERS directory no longer exists.

Where a file of the same name exists in the destination directory, the user is asked whether the file should be overwritten.   This facility can be disabled by adding /Y parameter to the command.

RENAMING FILES

The DOS command called REN or RENAME can be used to change the name of a file; it cannot change the name of a directory.   For example

REN REPORT.DOC ANNUAL.REP

will take the file called REPORT.DOC and change its name to ANNUAL.REP.   The file's size and contents are unchanged.   The above command assumes that the file is in the current directory.   The full path name can be used, to work with files in a directory other that an the current directory -

REN C:\WORK\REPORT.DOC ANNUAL.REP

WILDCARDS

Consider having to copy 50 files with the .PAS extension from one directory to another, or having to delete 30 files with the extension .BAK from a directory, or wishing to display a list of all files in a directory with the extension .DOC.   Fifty separate COPY commands or thirty different DEL commands can be given but this is tedious and error-prone since some files might be overlooked.   What is required is a method of handling files in groups - moving a group of files, or deleting a group of files.   Similarly, it is useful to have a DIR command that only displays a desired subset (say all .DOC files) from a directory.

DOS provides this facility with the use of *'wildcards'*.   A wildcard is a character or set of character that is incorporated in COPY, DEL, DIR, etc. commands. Wildcards use the question mark (?) and asterisk (*) characters.

THE * WILDCARD

The * wildcard is used to replace a group of characters in a DOS command.   It can replace anything from zero to 8 characters

<u>EXAMPLES</u>

>   DIR *.PAS

will display only those files in the current directory that have the .PAS extension.

>   DIR BUDGET.*

will display all files with the name BUDGET, regardless of the extension.

>   DIR G*.*

will display all files that start with the letter 'G', regardless of the extension.

>   DEL A:*.PAS

will delete all files from the floppy disc with the .PAS extension.

>   COPY C:\WINWORD\FILES*.DOC A:\ARCHIVE*.BAK

will copy all the .DOC files from the WINWORD\FILES directory of the hard disc in to the ARCHIVE directory of the floppy disc, with each file having its extension changed to .BAK.

NB

There is a potential danger that has to be guarded against when using the * wildcard.   Consider the command

>   COPY C:\BUDGET.* A:*.BAK

This command will copy all files with the name BUDGET in the hard disc's root directory into the floppy disc's root directory and give them the extension .BAK.   If the C drive's root directory contained files called BUDGET.XLS, BUDGET.XLC, BUDGET.DOC and BUDGET.DBF, then they will all be copied on to the floppy disc as BUDGET.BAK.   Since only one file can have the name BUDGET.BAK the first three files will be lost and only BUDGET.DBF will be stored on the floppy disc; all other files will have been overwritten by the next file copy.

THE ? WILDCARD

The ? character is used a DOS command to replace any single character in a filename.   Unlike the * character, the ? character does not represent a group of characters. If a number of characters are to be wildcarded, then there will have to be multiple occurrences of the ? character.   The length and structure of files have to be known to use this option.   For example:

>   DIR MEM???95.DAT

will find the files MEMJAN95.DAT, MEMFEB95.DAT, MEMAPR95.DAT, etc.   Any memos written in 1993 or 1994 are ignored by this command.   The * wildcard option could not be used here, as DIR MEM*95.DAT would display all files beginning with MEM and using the DAT extension - the 95 part of the command would be ignored, since the * wildcard takes precedence and replaces the last letters of the filename.

CAUTION :

>   The user should always use the chosen wildcard with the DIR command before using it
>   with the actual command desired. For example, DEL *.DOC will delete all of a user's
>   .DOC files - but will also delete everyone else's .DOC files !   A quick check with DIR
>   *.DOC would soon reveal the inclusion of any unwanted files.

XCOPY

The COPY command has limitations, in that it a copy of multiple files will be carried out one file at a time, by copying the first file, then making a separate copy of the second file and so on.   The XCOPY command is a more efficient alternative.   It creates a buffer area using all the available memory of the machine; as many files as possible are then copied from the source into the buffer area before being transferred into the destination.   This is repeated until all the files are copied.   The benefits of the XCOPY command over the COPY command are:

- it is faster with any single file that is larger than 64k.
- it is faster for copying multiple files.
- it can copy an entire section of the source directory structure with the use of the /S switch; a replica of that section of the structure is created on the destination disc.
- it can copy a group of files that are too large for a single floppy; if the files archive bits are set with the ATTRIB command (see later) and the /M switch is used with the command.

Other permissible switches are:

/A	Only copies files with the archive bit set (does not reset the archive bit)
/D : dd-mm-yy	Only copies files that were modified on or after the given date
/E	Creates a replica of any empty sub-directories on the destination
/M	Only copies files with the archive bit set (resets the archive bit)
/Y	Overwrites any existing files without requesting confirmation
/V	Verifies that a file has been written correctly (see later)
/W	Waits for the user to start the copying process
	Produces a *'Press any key to begin copying file(s)'* message
/P	Prompts for confirmation of each file to be copied

VERIFYING COPYING

When copying files, the user may wish to know that the copying process was successful.   To achieve this, MSDOS provides a VERIFY option.   Many books state that this option ensures that the copied file is an exact replica of the original file; this is not the case.   A DOS copy comprises of copying the file from disc to memory and then from memory to disc (either a different disc or a different part of the same disc).   DOS verification checks that the newly created file is readable and that its contents are identical to the copy in <u>memory</u>. If the written version is not identical to the memory version, the user will be alerted of the error.   In most cases, this is the same as making a file-to-file check but there may be occasions when the initial copy from disc to memory resulted in a corrupted version being held in memory.   On such occasions, the corrupted version will be written to disc and verification will not be aware of any error.

Although verification slows the copying process it is a desirable activity, particularly with the creation of backup copies of files.   Since it slows down copying, the default is not to use verification.   Verification can be turned on by using the /V switch with the COPY or XCOPY commands.   Where a series of copies is to be carried out, verification can be enabled before the copies and disabled after the copies.   Typical usage would be:

```
VERIFY ON
copy ....
copy ....
VERIFY OFF
```

COPYING AN ENTIRE FLOPPY

An exact copy of a floppy disc can be made with the DISKCOPY command.   This command has the following characteristics:

- If the source disc is a system disc, the target disc will be created as a system disc
- If the target disc is not formatted, the program will format the disc
- If the source disc has clusters marked as bad, the target disc will have the same areas also marked as bad, no matter their actual condition

The syntax is DISKCOPY A: B: if both drives are of the same type.   For a single floppy drive, the command should be DISKCOPY A: A: and the discs should be swapped when requested.

NOTE: Where a machine has two discs of different types (i.e. 5.25" and 3.5" together or 720k and 1.4Mb together) the DISKCOPY command won't work. In this case, use the COMMAND XCOPY A: B: /S /E

FILE ATTRIBUTES

Every file on a disc has a set of *'attributes'*.   These are flags that indicate the current status of the file (e.g. whether it is a system file or not).
These are normally hidden from users but if the command
              ATTRIB *.*
is given, the status of all the files in the current directory will be displayed.   Each filename will be accompanied by up to four possible letters - A, R, S and H.

These attributes can also be set by the user, with the ATTRIB command and the options are:

READ

One of the attribute flags stores whether a file is able to be both read and written to (known as READ/WRITE) or can only be read (known as READ ONLY).   If a file is read-only it can still be accessed by users and can appear in directory listings, can have its data extracted and used for calculations, can have its text printed out, etc.   However, it cannot be deleted or have its contents altered. Any attempt to delete a read-only file will be disallowed and an error message will result.   Similarly, any attempt to alter the contents of a file, such as a word-processed file, would be disallowed.   This means that files can be set to prevent accidental erasure, with the command ATTRIB +R *.*   The 'R' indicates the read-only flag and the '+' indicates that the read-only is being set on.   In the example, all the files in the current directory would be set to read-only. To remove the read-only flag , the plus sign is replaced by a minus sign and the command becomes ATTRIB -R *.*   The command can also be used with individual files (e.g. ATTRIB +R REPORT.DOC) or with selective wildcards (e.g. ATTRIB +R *.EXE).

ARCHIVE

A file's archive bit can also be set by the user and is mostly used in conjunction with the BACKUP command, to control which files are selectively backed up.   The BACKUP command can make a backup copy of all files or can be set to only make a copy of files that have not been previously backed up.   The way that the BACKUP command knows whether a file has been previously backed up is via the archive flag.   When a file is created or modified, its archive bit is set to on (indicating that it should be backed up).   When a file is backed up, its archive bit is automatically set to off (indicating that it has been backed up).   A future backup process will only select the files with archive bits set on and will ignore files with archive bits set off. The user can alter the files' archive flags with commands such as ATTRIB +A *.BAK and ATTRIB -A *.BAK

HIDDEN / SYSTEM

These flags hide the file from the normal view of the user and so it does not appear in directory listings, cannot be copied and cannot be deleted.   These flags should not normally be adjusted by the user.   The commands DIR/AS/S and DIR/AH/S will list all files that are set as system and hidden files.

LABEL

The VOL command lets the user see the electronic title attached to a disc. The label also appears at the top of a DIR display. The LABEL command lets the user change the volume label.   For example :
              LABEL ADMIN
This sets the disc's title to ADMIN.   Up to 11 characters are allowed.
To remove a label from a disc, enter the command 'LABEL' with no parameter.

FORMATTING DISCS

Discs, when newly purchased, are usually not able to be used for saving users' files (some manufacturers provide discs that are pre-formatted, at an extra cost). Before the computer can read or write disc information, the discs have be formatted. The FORMAT command is used to initialise the recording surface of a disc.   This command creates compartments on the disc surface in the form of concentric tracks, each divided into different sectors.   These sectors are then able to store the users' files. It also creates information areas to track what is stored on the disc (known as the Directory and File Allocation Table areas).   Any faulty surface areas are marked as bad and are not used later. See the chapter on Disc and Drives for greater detail.

The FORMAT command does not check that there is any data already on the disc before formatting. Therefore, any previous contents of the disc will be lost forever.

CAUTION: Be very careful not to format the hard disc (drive 'C') by mistake.

When the FORMAT command is given for a floppy drive, the machine will attempt to format the disc to the highest capacity possible in that drive.

For example, the command

FORMAT A:

will try to format a 3.5" disc to 1.4Mb if it is a 1.4Mb drive, or try to format a 5.25" disc to 1.2Mb if it is 1.2Mb drive.   This is the simplest form of the command and is all that is required if the discs are at the same quality as the drive's capability.

However, if a 720k floppy is placed in a 1.4Mb drive, or a 360k floppy is placed in a 1.2Mb drive, then the machine has to be told to format the disc to a lower capacity than the drive is actually capable of. Formatting a 360k disc to 1.2Mb will result in the disc being almost useless due to the number of bad sectors; this simply means that the disc could not be set up to handle the higher capacity without many surface errors.   The only solution is to format the disc at the correct capacity.   The 3.5" tends to be a little more sturdy in this regard but still can produce surface errors.

In addition, many drives detect that a 720k disc is in the drive and will not let the user format the disc to 1.4Mb capacity.

To format a disc to the correct capacity, the FORMAT command is followed by one of these switches:

Switch	When to use
No switch	5.25" 360k discs in 360k drives
No switch	5.25" 1.2Mb discs in 1.2Mb drives
/4	5.25" 360k discs in 1.2Mb drives
/F:360	5.25" 360k discs in 1.2Mb drives
No switch	3.5" 720k discs in 720k drives
No switch	3.5" 1.4Mb discs in 1.4Mb drives
/F:720	3.5" 720k discs in 1.4Mb drives
/N:9/T:80	3.5" 720k discs in 1.4Mb drives

So the command

FORMAT A:/4

will format a 360k 5.25" disc in a 1.2Mb disc drive.

Other switches, available in later DOS versions, are:

/Q   Provides a 'quick' disc format by omitting to check for faulty disc areas. This is permissible for cleaning up discs that have already been in use and are known to be in good condition. The switch should not be used with new discs.

/U   Provides an 'unconditional' format of the disc by destroying any information currently on the disc.   This is useful to start afresh with a disc that was giving read and write error messages - although it is probably safer to replace the disc completely.

SYSTEM DISCS

Some floppy discs are required to be 'system discs'. This means that they contain the special DOS files need to make the computer boot up from that floppy.   If a floppy disc is made into a system disc (sometimes also described as a 'boot disc') it can be placed in the A drive and the computer can be switched on and set up from the floppy disc. If this facility is required the extra switch /S has to be added to the command

e.g. FORMAT A:/F:720/S

An already-formatted disc can be converted into a system disc by using the SYS command.   For example, the command

SYS A:

will copy the hidden system files IO.SYS and MSDOS.SYS and COMMAND.COM on to the floppy disc.

DOS ERROR MESSAGES

A number of errors are possible when typing in DOS commands:
- The user may make a typing error (e.g. 'DIT' instead of 'DIR')
- The user may give an incomplete command (e.g. 'DEL' without naming the file to delete)
- The user may make a logical error (e.g. 'COPY FRED FRED' is trying to copy a file onto itself)
- The user may make an incorrect hardware compatibility choice (e.g. 'FORMAT A:' when a drive is 1.4Mb capacity and the disc is only 720k capacity).
- The user may have specified a non existent file (e.g. 'DEL FRED.DOC' when the file is no longer on the disc).
- The user may omit to specify a file's path (e.g. 'COPY FRED.DOC A:' when the file FRED.DOC exists but is not in the current directory).
- The user may have left a data disc in the A: drive when the machine was switched on (so that the computer is unable to load the operating system from either the hard disc or the floppy disc).
- The user may not have set up the hardware to make the DOS command possible (e.g. issuing a PRINT command when there is no printer attached to the computer; or issuing a 'COPY *.* A:' command when there is no disc in the A: drive)

DOS is not particularly user-friendly when a mistake is made.   Part of the job of the COMMAND.COM file is the analysis of commands (called *'parsing'*).   While all the above errors are detected, the amount of help given is very limited.   DOS does not respond to errors with helpful advice; it produces cryptic messages that the user has to interpret.

The most common DOS error messages are:

Bad command or file name

This message indicates that a command has been given which is not part of COMMAND.COM or is not an external COM, EXE or BAT file in the current directory.   This error message is often due to a mis-typing of the command and the entered command should be re-checked.   If the command is found not to be a spelling error, it is likely that the program is not in the current directory or in a directory specified in the PATH statement; the command should be altered to specify the path where the program file resides.

Invalid parameter

This indicates that either too much or too little information has been specified as parameters after the command.   This error is often caused by forgetting to leave spaces between parts of the command (e.g. 'DELFRED.DOC' instead of 'DEL FRED.DOC') or breaking up an otherwise legitimate parameter with extra spaces (e.g. 'COPY FRED.DOC M ARY' instead of 'COPY FRED.DOC MARY').

File not found

This indicates that the file specified as a parameter is either mis-typed or is not in the directory given in the command.

Not ready error reading drive A

This indicates that there is no disc in the floppy drive or, in the case of 5.25" drives, the disc lever is not engaged.

Non-system disc or disc error

This usually indicates that the machine has been started up with a non-boot disc in the A: drive.

Abort, Retry, Ignore, Fail ?

This indicates that a *'critical error'* has occurred. This may indicate a hardware malfunction such as the network going down or there being no disc in the drive.   Often it indicates that part of the disc is unreadable.   With hard discs, the surface integrity should be checked with a utility; with floppy discs its often best to recover as many files as possible and replace the disc.   Choosing Abort ignores the disc operation and control is passed back to the program or application. Choosing Retry instructs the system to attempt the disc operation for another time.   Choosing Ignore ignores that particular cluster read; this may move the program on to a subsequent read operation, resulting in a loss of data.   Choosing Fail will inform the program or application that the disc operation failed.

Access Denied

This indicates that the disc is write-protected or that files have their attributes set to read-only.

COMMAND LINE EDITING

When a command is being typed at the DOS prompt, any mistakes can be corrected before pressing the Enter key by backspacing to the error and re-typing the correct syntax.   However, an error may not be spotted until the command is entered.   Having to re-type a long command for the sake of a small mistake would be laborious and can be avoided by editing facilities.   When a user enters a command, it is stored in a buffer area, allowing it to be recalled for editing.   The standard editing keys are:

f1	Copy one character from the stored previous command to the DOS prompt line. If the user pressed f1 repeatedly the entire previous command would build up in the DOS prompt line.
f2 x	Copy all the characters from the stored previous command to the command line, up to the point of the first occurrence of the specified letter x.
f3	Copy all the remaining characters from the stored previous command to the command line. So, pressing f3 after issuing a command would recall the entire command back to the prompt line.
f4 x	Copy all the characters from the stored previous command to the command line, commencing at the point of the first occurrence of the specified letter x. Put another way, this deletes all characters up to the letter x.
Ins	Allows a character to be inserted into the new command line; this does not alter the position pointed to inside the buffer.
Del	Moves the pointer in the buffer area, effectively skipping a character in the buffer.
Esc	Cancels whatever is currently in the command line; this does not alter the contents of the previously stored contents of the buffer.

EXAMPLE

Consider a previous command of COPY C:\DOA\TREE.COM   A:\DOS*.* with the DOS directory incorrectly typed in as DOA.   The user would not have to repeat the entire command. The editing sequence would be

f2 A	Places 'COPY C:\DO' into the command line
S	Adds the letter 'S' to the command (the pointer in the buffer moves along one character)
f3	Places '\TREE.COM A:\DOS*.*' into the command line

ENVIRONMENTS

Using DOS is not a user-friendly activity, since the user either requires a knowledge of the DOS commands or has to continually consult the reference manual.   To overcome this problem, there have been a number of utilities developed under the heading of *'shells'* or *'environments'*.   These utilities seek to protect the user from the need to know DOS commands. They help the user to carry out DOS functions through assistance in the form of menus and pictures.

They can be broadly categorised as:

MENUS

These range from simple menus created by users via batch files (see chapter on Batch Files) to complex, multi-level, commercial packages such as PowerMenu.   In both cases, the aim is to provide selection for the user from pre-decided choices.   Thus formatting a disc is reduced to choosing option *'D'* rather than issuing a DOS command such as FORMAT A:/N:9/T:80.   The menu options are pre-programmed by the user and are then available for all other less experienced users.   Similarly, running a particular program is reduced to pressing the letter on the keyboard which invokes it.   This is set up by the user and other users can run the package without knowing the program name or the path in which it resides.

DOS SHELL

From version 4 onwards, DOS provides its own shell program to ease the use of its own commands. This utility is called up by the command DOSSHELL and produces a screen similar to that on the next page.   This is the Shell from DOS 6 and the left-hand box displays all the directories on the disc.   The right-hand panel displays all the files that are resident in a particular sub-directory.

The shell can be mouse-operated or keyboard-operated.   When the mouse is clicked on a directory in the left panel, the files in the directory are displayed in the right panel.

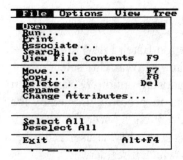

A range of file activities can be carried out using the mouse:

DELETING A FILE

Highlight the desired file in the right panel by clicking the mouse pointer on it; press the Delete key; when prompted, confirm the deletion.

MOVING A FILE

Click the pointer on the desired file in the right panel; hold the mouse button down and drag the pointer over the destination directory for the file; the file is then written to the new directory and deleted from the old directory.

COPYING A FILE

Click the pointer on the desired file in the right panel; press the f8 key; when prompted, enter the destination directory for the file duplicate; the file is then copied to the new directory leaving the original still in the old directory.

RENAMING A FILE

Click the pointer on the desired file in the right panel; choose the *'File'* option from the main menu; Choose the *'Rename'* option from the drop-down menu; when prompted, type in new file name; the file remains in its current directory but is renamed.

PRINTING A FILE

Click the pointer on the desired file in the right panel; choose the *'File'* option from the main menu; Choose the *'Print'* option from the drop-down menu.

A menu of options appears along the top of the screen and this can be accessed by pressing the f10 key.   The cursor keys can then be used to highlight the desired option from the top menu. Alternatively, the option can be directly chosen by pressing the Alt key and the first letter of the wanted choice.   For example, pressing Alt-F produces the File Menu shown.   This menu provides the activities already mentioned, plus the ability to alter file attributes, search for a particular file, run a highlighted program file, etc.

Other pull-down menus are available such as the Options menu shown.   This provides facilities to choose screen colours, the number of text lines to appear on the screen, the amount of details to be shown for each file, etc.

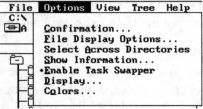

With DOS versions prior to version 4, the DOS shell was not available and a range of add-on software products was produced to carry out a similar task.   These included Xtree, Gem Desktop and PC Boss.

WINDOWS 3.1

One of the most successful and comprehensive of DOS environments has been Windows 3.1 from Microsoft.   It is known as a *'GUI'* - a graphical user interface - and it uses a range of icons (miniature pictures) to represent computing functions, so simplifying activities.   For example, if an icon of a printer was clicked by the mouse, the programs output would be sent to the printer.   In this way, it is hoped to reduce the time users spend trying to <u>understand</u> the machine and more time spent actually <u>using</u> the machine.

Microsoft Windows is a WIMP environment.   That means it uses <u>W</u>indows, <u>I</u>cons, <u>M</u>enus and <u>P</u>ointers (or <u>W</u>indows, <u>I</u>cons, <u>M</u>ouse and <u>P</u>ull-down menus).   In this respect, Windows functions in a very similar way to the DOS shell.   Like the shell, Windows allows files to be clicked on by the mouse and deleted, moved, copied, renamed, printed, etc.   However, Windows is much more than another DOS shell.
It has many additional features, such as:

- Supports multi-tasking - this means that more than one program can be running in memory at the same time.   If desired, one application can be seen on the screen while the other application is working away in the background.   Alternatively, both applications can be seen on the screen at the same time, each application occupying a different portion, or window, of the screen.
- Allows easy copying of data between programs.
- Has its own set of extra utilities, such as Paintbrush (paint program), Write (small word processor), Cardfile (small database), Terminal (for connecting the computer to a modem), Calculator, etc.
- Full on-line help system.   This includes a full hypertext system where the user can type in a search entry, find out about that item and be provided options to view items of a similar category.   So, for example, if the user is reading help on *'Copying a Help Topic Onto the Clipboard'*, the screen will display a line offering help on *'Annotating a Help Topic'*; if this line is clicked on with the mouse pointer, the user is taken a further page of information on that topic.
- Provides a set of common features and techniques for all Windows applications; this means that every application written to be used under Windows will use the same techniques (e.g. the same way to load and save files, the same way to import a picture, etc.).   This results in users being able to adapt to a new Windows application quickly, since activities learned in a previous package are re-used.   With DOS-based applications, each package would do the same job in a different way; one package would expect a particular function key, another would require a particular key combination using Alt and Ctrl keys, while yet another would expect the operation to achieved through menu options.

The Windows environment allows for extensive configuration to meet the needs of the user (e.g. screen colours, use of memory, background wallpaper, choice of printers, sensitivity of the mouse, etc.); this is covered in the chapter on Windows configuration.   Windows is able to be keyboard-operated but it is really designed for mouse operation and is certainly much easier and quicker to use with a mouse.

The Windows program is started up by the command *'WIN'* and this loads the Windows program and presents an opening screen similar to that shown.

PROGRAM MANAGER

Program Manager is the core application into which the user is taken on entering Windows (although even this is alterable). Its job is to simplify user's access to programs.   Each separate program is represented by a different icon (called a *'program item'*) and double-clicking on the icon opens and runs that program.

To save cluttering the screen with hundreds of icons, program items of a similar nature are grouped together into their own

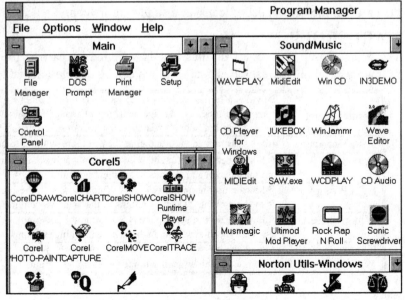

windows and the user only need open those groups that are required at any one time. In the example, Graphics Workshop, Harvard Graphics, Chartists and Gif2Icon are all separate programs but are stored in a group called *'Graphics'*.   Running one of these programs is achieved by opening the Program Group to reveal the four icons; the desired program is then run by double-clicking on the appropriate icon.

USING THE MOUSE

The Windows interface and all applications that work within Windows use the mouse in the same way. The main activities are listed below.

Point	The mouse is moved so that the screen pointer is positioned over the desired item - e.g. an icon or object.
Click	Click the left mouse button while the pointer is positioned over the desired item. This is most commonly used to select an object.
Double Click	Click the left mouse button twice while the pointer is positioned over the desired icon or object. This is most commonly used to execute an activity - e.g. open an icon or run a program.
Drag	Move the mouse while holding down the left mouse button.
Shift Click	Hold down the 'Shift' key while clicking on the desired item.
Shift Drag	Hold down the 'Shift' key while dragging the mouse.

CLOSING vs MINIMISING

When the user is finished using an application, that application can be closed by clicking on the *'File'* menu option; this produces a pull-down menu and clicking on the *'Exit'* option closes the program.   On the other hand, the user can click on the minimise button that appears in the top right-hand corner of the screen. The application is reduced to an icon, known as *'minimising'*.   This method keeps the application active, although frozen at the point at which it was minimised.   If the icon is clicked on later, the application is restored to full-screen, ready to proceed at the same stage it is was at when it was minimised.   When Windows is exited, the currently active groups are stored; when Windows is entered next time, these previously active groups are presented again.

Minimise

OPENING A PROGRAM GROUP

If a new group is needed, the user simply double-clicks on the appropriate program group icon from the ones shown on the bottom of the screen.   This will open another window on the screen; if this obscures an existing window, the screen can be re-organised by clicking on the *'Window'* option at the top of the screen. This will produce a drop-down menu and clicking on the *'Tile'* option will organise the screen so that no window obscures another.

CLOSING A PROGRAM GROUP

If a program group is no longer required, the user can close the group by clicking on the top left-hand corner of the group and clicking on the *'Close'* option from the resulting pull-down menu.   This returns the group to the bottom list of icons, as a single group icon.

MAIN GROUP

The Main Group is a set of utilities that is supplied as part of the Windows suite.   It contains the following components, each being an icon that can be double-clicked to run:

Control Panel	Provides a further window of icons to set up the mouse speed, the keyboard's repeat rate, the computer's memory management, the character fonts, screen colours, etc. These settings, when made, apply to all Windows applications from then on.
Print Manager	Allows the user to view and alter the print jobs waiting to be sent to the printer.
Clipboard	A bridge between different Windows applications, allowing text and graphics to be *'cut'* from one application and *'pasted'* to another application.
DOS Prompt	Takes the user temporarily out of Windows so that the user can run ordinary DOS commands from the prompt. The user returns to the Windows environment by typing EXIT.
Windows SetUp	Allows the user to specify the type of monitor and graphics card in use, the type of keyboard in use, the type of mouse and whether the machine is connected to a local area network.
File Manager	Allows the user to view the directory structure, directory contents and delete, move, copy and print files. This is similar to the DOS shell program.

ACCESSORIES GROUP

This group is supplied with the Windows package and contains all the handy extras such as:

Write	A simple word-processing program. Provides indenting, cut and paste, font selection, word search, etc.
Paintbrush	A basic painting program that allows the creation and editing of pictures. Provides line-drawing, box-drawing, text overlay, etc.
Terminal	A program to allow the transfer of files between two computers over the telephone network. Requires the computers to be connected to modems.
Cardfile	A simple database for storing frequently required facts - e.g. names, addresses, telephone numbers, prices, specifications. Provides search and merge facilities.
Calendar	A useful calendar utility that provides information on any day, of any month of any year. Includes an alarm facility.
Calculator	A fairly comprehensive calculator for most everyday uses; includes memory recall, the calculation of averages, standard deviation, etc.

FILE MANAGER

File Manager allows access to disc operations at file and directory level. As with DOSSHELL, there are two screen panels. The left panel is the *'directory tree window'* and it displays a graphic representation of the directory structure of the currently chosen disc drive with an icon of a folder for each directory; the right panel is the *'directory window'* and it displays icons and names representing the files and directories within a selected directory.   In the directory tree window, the currently chosen directory is highlighted.   To make a new directory the current one to be examined, the user clicks the mouse pointer on the directory name or its folder icon.

A plus sign on a folder indicates that the directory contains sub-directories that are not being currently displayed.   The terms *'expanding'* and *'collapsing'* are used to describe the display or non-display of sub-directories. In the example shown, the WINDOWS directory has been expanded and all the sub-directories at the next level are revealed.

In turn, the CORELDRAW sub-directory has been expanded, while the MSAPPS remains collapsed. When File Manager is first opened, only the top level directories are revealed; after that, information on any expanded sections is saved and the directory tree structure can be displayed in the same state that it was previously left, if the user enables the *'Save Settings on Exit'* choice from the *'Options'* Menu.

A range of file and directory activities can be carried out.   Since almost all Windows users have a mouse, this is assumed in the instructions; Windows will support keyboard operation but this makes operations slower.

The main File Manager activities are:

EXPANDING A DIRECTORY

>   Double click the mouse pointer on the desired folder; if using the keyboard, highlight the desired sub-directory with the cursor keys then press the plus key.   To expand all directories in a drive, hold down the shift key and click on the drive icon.

COLLAPSING A DIRECTORY

Double click the mouse pointer on the desired folder; if using the keyboard, highlight the desired sub-directory with the cursor keys then press the minus key.

DELETING A FILE

Highlight the desired file in the right panel by clicking the mouse pointer on it; press the Delete key; when prompted, confirm the deletion.

DELETING A DIRECTORY

Highlight the desired folder icon and press the delete key; when prompted, confirm deletion of directory and all its files and sub-directories.

CREATING A DIRECTORY

Highlight the folder into which the new directory will be added; choose the *'Create Directory'* option from the *'File'* menu; when prompted, enter the name of the new directory.

MOVING A FILE

Click the pointer on the desired file in the right panel; hold the mouse button down and drag the pointer over the destination directory for the file; the file is then written to the new directory and deleted from the old directory. To move the file to a different drive, highlight the chosen file and either press f7 or choose the *'Move'* option from the *'File'* menu; when prompted, enter the destination drive for the file.

COPYING A FILE

Click the pointer on the desired file in the right panel; press the f8 key; when prompted, enter the destination directory for the file duplicate; the file is then copied to the new directory leaving the original still in the old directory. To copy the file to a different drive, the file need only be dragged over the appropriate drive icon.

MOVING/COPYING GROUPS OF FILES

Files can be moved or copied in group at a time. If the group of files are contiguous (next to each other) in the file list, click on the first file in the desired group, hold down the 'Shift' key and click on the last file in the group. This will highlight the entire group of files which can then be moved or copied. If the desired files are not contiguous, hold down the Ctrl key while clicking on each desired file.

COPYING A DIRECTORY

Click the pointer on the desired directory in the right panel; press the f8 key; when prompted, enter the destination directory. A duplicate of the highlighted directory (including all its files and sub-directories) is then copied to the new directory leaving the originals still in the same place in the structure.

RENAMING A FILE

Click the pointer on the desired file in the right panel; choose the *'File'* option from the main menu; Choose the *'Rename'* option from the drop-down menu; when prompted, type in new file name; the file remains in its current directory but is renamed.

PRINTING A FILE

Click the pointer on the desired file in the right panel; choose the *'File'* option from the main menu; Choose the *'Print'* option from the drop-down menu.

HANDLING GROUPS OF FILES

To move, delete, or copy files as a group, highlight the first file in the desired group. Then hold down the Shift key and click on the last file in the group. This will highlight all files between the marked files and they can then be manipulated as a group.

VIEWING SUBSETS OF FILES

There are times when only a particular set of files is wished to be viewed. For example, a search for a particular .PCX file is easier if only .PCX files are shown in the file listings. This is achieved by choosing the *'View'* menu and selecting the *'By File Type'* option. This allows the entry of the desired file extension; wildcards are allowed.

FORMATTING A FLOPPY DISC

Insert the floppy disc in the drive; select the *'Format'* option from the *'Disk'* menu which will produce a dialogue box as shown. The appropriate drive letter should be chosen and the disc capacity should be set to be the same as that of the disc to be formatted. Click the *'Make a System Disk'* box, if the disc is to be formatted as a boot disc. At this stage, the user can also name the disc by typing an entry into the *'Label'* box. Clicking *'OK'* begins the formatting process.

Format Disk

Disk In: Drive A:
Capacity: 1.44 MB

OK
Cancel
Help

Options
Label: PCSUPPORT
☐ Make System Disk
☐ Quick Format

COPYING A DISC

This is identical to the DOS DISKCOPY command; it makes an exact replica of a disc on to another disc; any contents on the destination disc are lost.   Choose the *'Copy Disk'* option from the *'Disk'* menu; enter the source and destination drives being used for the copy.   The source disc is the one to be copied.   If the computer has two disc drives of the same capacity (e.g. two 1.4Mb drives) the source and destination drives can be entered as 'A' and 'B'.   Place the source disc in the nominated source drive and place the destination disc in the other drive.   If the drives are of different capacities (e.g. one 1.4Mb drive and one 1.2Mb drive) the user has to choose the same drive for source and destination and swap disc when prompted by the program.   When the *'OK'* button is clicked, the copying process begins.

TASK MANAGER

When working in Windows, there will often be a number of applications running at the same time. Some of these may have been automatically loaded at the startup of Windows (see the chapter on Windows Configuration) or they may have been loaded during the Windows session.   Some of these applications may be running in the *'background'* - i.e. the program is operating but there is no evidence on the monitor screen.   Examples of this might include the Print Manager printing documents while the user carries on with other tasks, a database sorting or searching records, etc.   On other occasions, each program may be visible in its own window on the screen, as in the example on page 41.   The active program - the one whose icons can be double-clicked - is the one whose top bar is highlighted.   In the page 41 example, Excel is the current application.

There are a number of ways to switch between applications:

- If an application has a window on the screen, click anywhere in the application's window.
- Press the ALT and ESC keys repeatedly to cycle through all the loaded applications, until the desired window is made active.
- Press the ALT and TAB keys repeatedly to cycle through active applications.   When you release the TAB keys, the currently chosen application is brought to the foreground.
- Press the CTRL and ESC keys to open the *'Task List'*.   Highlight the desired application, then select the *'Switch To'* option.   Alternatively, select the desired application, then press the ENTER key.

USING THE CLIPBOARD

A big advantage of using Windows is that information in one document can be copied or transferred into another document.   This could involve the copying or transferring of data from within the same application - e.g. copying or transferring a paragraph of text from one Word document to another Word Document.   It could also involve the copying of data from one application to a different application - e.g. copying a picture from a Word document into Paintbrush for editing.   If the machine is used in 386 Enhanced mode, it could also involve the copying of data from a non-Windows application into a Windows application.   The information being copies could be graphical, textual or data.

The stages are:

- Move to the application that contains the desired information.
- Highlight the information to be copied/transferred.
- Use the *'Copy'* or *'Cut'* option to the information from the source application. If the information is <u>cut</u>, it is removed from the source document; if it is <u>copied</u>, a replica of the information is used.   In both cases, the information will be placed in a temporary store, known as the *'Clipboard'*.
- Move to the application that is the destination for the data.
- Move the cursor to the spot in the destination document where the information is to be placed.
- Use the *'Paste'* option to place the information into the document at the cursor position.

The contents of the Clipboard can be pasted as many times as required - into different parts of the same document or into different documents.   While the machine remains in Windows and no further information cuts are carried out, the Clipboard will store the information.   This will be automatic, unless leaving an application results in a particularly large piece of information being left in the Clipboard; in that event, the user is asked to confirm that the information should remain in the Clipboard.

COPYING WINDOWS TO THE CLIPBOARD

It is also possible to copy the entire Windows screen, or any individual window on the screen, to the Clipboard.   The two options are:

- Pressing the *'Print Screen'* key while in Windows results in the entire monitor screen area being saved to the Clipboard.
- Pressing the *'Alt'* and *'PrintScreen'* keys results in the active window area being saved to the Clipboard.

SAVING THE CLIPBOARD

Windows also contains a Clipboard Viewer.   This allows the user to examine the current contents of the Clipboard.   The current contents of the Clipboard can also be given a filename and saved as a file with a .CLP extension.   These files can be recalled to the Clipboard at any time for future pasting into documents.

With Windows for Workgroups, the Clipboard Viewer also contains a *'Local ClipBook'*.   The ClipBook can store several 'pages' of information.   Any of these pages can be copied back into the Clipboard at any time.   From the Clipboard, it can be pasted into a document.   With Workgroups, it can also be shared with other users of the workgroup.   Each machine on the workgroup will have its own Local ClipBook.   This allows all the users on the workgroup to connect to other users, enter the ClipBook of another computer, and use the information in these shared pages.

RECORDER

The Accessories Group contains a utility known as the *'Recorder'*.   This allows the user to record a series of mouse movements and clicks and keystrokes.   This recording is stored as a *'Macro'* and this macro can be replayed at any time, either by:

- using a simple key sequence
- calling the macro from the *'Macro'* option in the application's menu.   Find the Macro option, highlight the desired macro and choose the *'Run'* option.

The steps to record a macro are:

- Position the cursor in the application where the macro will commence.
- Go to the Macro option in the application.
- Select the *'Record Macro'* option in the Macro menu.
- In the appropriate boxes, specify a macro name and/or a shortcut key. The macro can also be given a description if desired.
- Select the *'Start'* or *'OK'* button; this will begin recording the macro,
- Enter the required series of keystrokes and mouse actions.
- When the sequence is complete, click on the 'Stop Recorder' option.

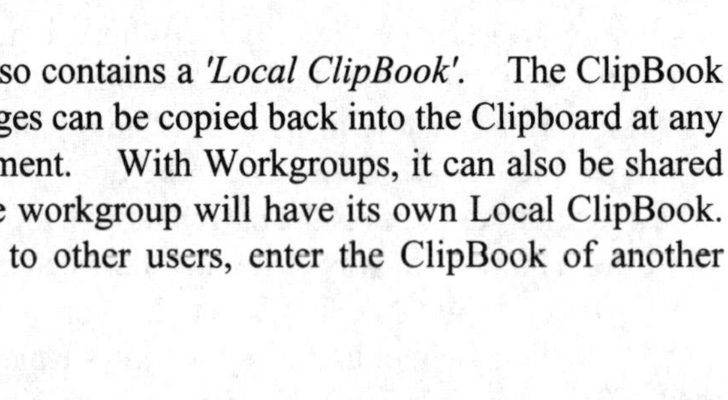

The example shown in the diagram was recorded within Word for Windows.   As the description states, the macro is designed to add a bullet and indent any paragraph.   This is a simple macro that carries out only two functions, by pressing the Ctrl-Y keys.   With spreadsheets, a long sequence of complex activities can be invoked by a single key sequence.

LEAVING WINDOWS 3.1

Choosing the *'Exit Windows'* option from the *'File'* menu of Program Manager allows the user to leave Windows; when prompted *'This will end your Windows session'*, the user clicks the *'OK'* button and all Windows files and preferences are saved and closed.

WINDOWS 95

Windows 95 is not really an *'environment'* in the sense of simply being an add-on interface to DOS. Indeed, there is no need for DOS to installed on the machine, as Windows 95 is itself a complete operating system and graphical user interface in the one package.

Windows 95 is designed to run all the old Windows 3.1 and DOS programs.   However, Windows 3.1 is unable to run programs that are specially written for Windows 95.

BENEFITS OF WINDOWS 95

- Stores and display a list of the last 15 files used on the computer, allowing simple recall of commonly used files.   Single click on any of the file names and the file name is opened inside its appropriate application.   So, if a file called 'REPORT.DOC' is clicked, the system loads Microsoft Word and then opens the REPORT.DOC file within it.
- Provides pop-up help windows.   If the user allows the mouse pointer to linger over a command button, a pop-up window displays the function of that button.
- Allows the user to allocate long filenames of up to 255 characters.   It should be understood that Windows 3.1 and DOS programs still use the old eight-dot-three naming system.   So, any files created under Windows 95 that are saved under DOS or Windows 3.1 will have their files names truncated.   A Word file called *'Consumer Report on Beef'* would probably be re-saved as *'CONSUM~1.DOC'*.
- Plays videos much more efficiently.   The improvement is dramatic and is of the order of two to three times.
- Supports plug-and-play - the system recognise p-n-p components and automatically assigns resources. Newly installed p-n-p compatible cards are automatically recognised by Windows 95.
- Provides a *'Recycle Bin'* as an improvement over Windows 3.1's undelete facility. Files that the user decides to delete appear to be deleted but are, in fact stored in their complete form and can be accessed at any time via the Recycle Bin.   The user can decide to recover a file from the Bin or can permanently empty the Bin's contents.
- Provides more extensive *'Help'* facilities .
- Adds new communications features such as The Microsoft Network, Microsoft Fax, HyperTerminal and Phone Dialler.
- Adds extensive diagnostic facilities through the provision of a *'Hardware Wizard'*.
- Easy handling of applications through an *'Add/Remove Programs'* facility.

PROBLEMS WITH WINDOWS 95

- More complex to maintain
- Still many reports of instability.   There appears to be evidence that users are waiting for Windows NT v4 and are intending to change from Windows 3.1 directly to NT, skipping over Windows 95 altogether.   Such users expect a more sophisticated and reliable product, while ensuring the benefits of the Windows 95 interface.
- More demanding hardware requirements than with Windows 3.1.
  The Hardware requirements for Windows 95 are:

	Minimum	Realistic Minimum
CPU	386DX	486/Pentium
Memory	4Mb	8Mb, preferably 16Mb.
Video card	VGA	SVGA
Bus	ISA	PCI or Local Bus
Mouse	Normal	Mouse with right-hand button

Since Windows 95 wants 4Mb of memory for its own use, even more RAM is required to provide memory for use by the applications.

Using a local bus or a PCI bus system will result in improved graphics handling.

ACCESSING PROGRAMS

With Windows 3.1, programs were accessed by double clicking on their icons within their program groups, accessed via the Program Manager.   This cumbersome method is replaced by an opening screen similar to that shown below.

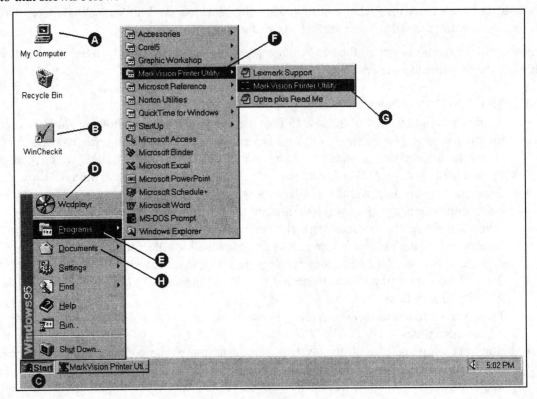

This provides a number of ways to load and run programs.

1. The icon marked **(A)** above opens a window which, like Windows 3.1's File Manager, displays all the files and sub-directories on the computer's discs.   The *'My Computer'* option extends this to provide access to the computer's printers, networking facilities and the Control Panel.

2. Icon **(B)** shows an icon for a user's application that has been placed directly on to the Windows desktop. This a *'shortcut'* to the application and the program can be run simply by clicking on the icon.   In this way, the user's most commonly used programs can be displayed as soon as Windows 95 is loaded.

3. The button **(C)** is labelled *'Start'* and clicking this button displays the menu shown on the left of the screen. The menu option **(D)** displays an application that has been placed on the start menu as an alternative means of accessing often used programs.   Clicking on the menu bar loads and runs the program.

4. One of the *'Start'* menu options is titled *'Programs'* and moving the mouse pointer over the button, marked as **(E)**, displays a menu showing all the programs available on the computer.   Clicking one of the menu options, such as item marked *'Microsoft Excel'* in the example, loads and runs that particular program.

5. In some cases, an entry in the Programs menu is not a single program but a collection of similar programs. For example, the *'Corel 5'* option contains a suite of different drawing, tracing and presentation utilities. Similarly, the menu bar option marked as **(F)** contains three supporting components.   Placing the mouse pointer on that menu option reveals another sub-menu that allows access to the sub-options.   Clicking menu bar **(G)** in the example shown runs the Lexmark printer utility.

6. Clicking option **(H)** on the *'Start'* menu reveals the last 15 documents opened by the user.   Clicking any of these documents opens the corresponding application.

7. Clicking on the file name when in Windows Explorer, the Windows 95 version of File Manager.

8. Clicking on the program name on the bottom Task Bar.

9. Using the *'Run'* option from the *'Start'* menu.   Only useful where the user knows the exact name of the file and the exact sub-directory path in which it is stored, or wishes to run a program that was recently used.

In all cases. When the application is exited the user is returned to menu screens as shown above.

Like Windows 3.1, the Windows 95 environment allows for extensive configuration to meet the needs of the user (e.g. screen colours, use of memory, background wallpaper, choice of printers, sensitivity of the mouse, etc.); this is covered in the chapter on Windows configuration.

USING THE MOUSE

The Windows interface and all applications that work within Windows use the mouse in the same way. The main activities are as listed on page 53, the main difference being that Windows 95 makes extensive use of the right mouse button.

CLOSING AND MINIMISING

When the user is finished using an application, that application can be closed by clicking on the *'File'* menu option; this produces a pull-down menu and clicking on the *'Exit'* option closes the program.   The top right-hand corner of Windows 95 applications has a set of button as shown in the diagram. Clicking the 'Close' button will also close and exit the application.   On the other hand, the user can click on the minimise button that appears on the leftmost button of that set. The application is reduced to an entry on the Task Bar at the bottom of the screen. This is known as *'minimising'* and the application remains active, frozen at the point at which it was minimised.   If the application is later clicked on the Task Bar, it is restored to full-screen, ready to proceed at the same stage it is was at when it was minimised.   The diagram shows Microsoft Word and the Lexmark Printer Utility both being held in a minimised state.

'START' MENU OPTIONS

Apart from running applications, the *'Start'* menu offers a number of useful facilities.   These are:

S̲ettings	This has three sub-options: Control Panel - Provides similar function to Windows 3.1 for setting keyboard and mouse characteristics, etc. Extra functions include adding new hardware, adding and removing software, and configuring network facilities. Printer - Provides options to add new printers, to set printer ports and to set the configuration of printers. Taskbar - Sets the options for the Taskbar and the Start Menu.
F̲ind	Searches the computers disc drives (and network drives if on a network) for specific files. Searches can be for specific names, specific contents, specific dates or specific sizes.
H̲elp	Provides comprehensive help in three ways: Contents - Help is organised in a systematic way providing information in a hierarchical fashion with the user delving deeper if he/she wants more information on a subject. Index - The user can scroll through a long list of help topics or can search by entering a word or phrase. Find - Every word used in every help file can be scrolled through or searched for.
R̲un	A pull-down menu reveals the programs that were recently loaded via the 'Run' facility. One of these can be selected or the user can click the 'Browse' option to search for a specific program to be run.
Sh̲ut Down	Provides options to close down the computer or to restart in DOS mode.

OTHER ACCESSORIES

One of the options in the *'Programs'* menu is a collection of utilities under the heading *'Accessories'*. These are supplied as standard with Windows 95 and include:

Multimedia	Three utilities - Media Player, Sound Recorder and Volume Control.
System Tools	Three disc utilities - Disc Defragmenter, Drivespace and ScanDisc.
Calculator	A more comprehensive calculator than the 3.1 version, providing scientific functions and conversion between different number bases..
Clipboard Viewer	Facilities to view, save and delete the contents of the Clipboard
HyperTerminal	An improved version of Terminal, transferring files between two computers over the telephone network. Requires the computers to be connected to modems.
Notepad	A simple word-processing program for small files, less than 64k.
Paint	A more basic version of Paintbrush, with facilities to create and edit bitmap pictures. Provides line-drawing, box-drawing, text overlay, fills, etc.
Phone Dialer	A utility allowing users with modems to place telephone calls from the keyboard or from a stored pick list.
Wordpad	An improved version of the Windows 3.1 Write word processing program

EXPLORER

Windows Explorer operates similarly to the Windows 3.1 File Manager since it allows access to disc operations at file and directory level.

As with File Manager, Explorer has two screen panels.   The left panel is the *'directory tree window'* and it displays a graphic representation of the directory structure of the currently chosen disc drive with an icon of a folder for each directory.   It also allows access to the Control Panel and the Printer utilities. The right panel is the *'directory window'* and it displays icons and names representing the files and directories within a selected directory.   In the directory tree window, the currently chosen directory is highlighted.   To make a new directory the current one to be examined, the user clicks the mouse pointer on the directory name or its folder icon.

A plus sign on a folder indicates that the directory contains sub-directories that are not being currently displayed.   The terms *'expanding'* and *'collapsing'* are used to describe the display or non-display of sub-directories. In the example shown, the GIFS_GALORE directory has been expanded and all the sub-directories at the next level are revealed.   In turn, the GIFS sub-directory has been expanded and all sub-directories within GIFS remain collapsed. The CARS sub-directory has been selected and its contents can be viewed in the right hand panel.

The main Explorer activities can be carried out using the mouse and keyboard and are:

EXPANDING A DIRECTORY
> Double click the mouse pointer on the desired folder; if using the keyboard, highlight the desired sub-directory with the cursor keys then press the plus key.

COLLAPSING A DIRECTORY
> Double click the mouse pointer on the desired folder; if using the keyboard, highlight the desired sub-directory with the cursor keys then press the minus key.

DELETING A FILE
> Highlight the desired file in the right panel by clicking the mouse pointer on it; press the Delete key; when prompted, confirm the file's transfer to the Recycle Bin.

DELETING A DIRECTORY
> Highlight the desired folder icon and press the delete key; when prompted, confirm the transfer of the directory and all its files and sub-directories to the Recycle Bin.
>
> Deleting files and directories in fact only sends them to the Recycle Bin area where they can either be recovered or permanently deleted.

UNDELETING

Since *'deleted'* files and directories are actually sent to a folder called the *'Recycle Bin'*, they are available for recovery.   Double-clicking the Recycle Bin icon on the desktop opens a window which displays all available recoverable items.   The desired files can be selected and the *'Restore'* option on the *'File'* menu will restore them to the directory from where they were deleted.   If a file came from a folder that has since been deleted, the folder is also restored.   To permanently delete a file or group of files, the file(s) should be selected and the *'Delete'* option chosen from the *'File'* menu.   The file(s) are deleted and the disc space is recovered for future use.   Choosing the *'Empty Recycle Bin'* option delete all the files currently in the Bin.

CREATING A DIRECTORY

Highlight the folder into which the new directory will be added; choose the *'New'* option from the *'File'* menu and the *'Folder'* option from the *'New'* menu.   An unnamed sub-directory will be created and it must immediately be given a name.

MOVING A FILE

Click the pointer on the desired file in the right panel so that the file is highlighted. Go to the *'Edit'* menu and choose the *'Cut'* option.   The file is now removed from the source directory. Open the directory which is the intended destination for the file.   Go to the *'Edit'* menu and choose the *'Paste'* option.   The file is now resident in the destination directory.   Note that the Windows 3.1 technique of dragging a file from the right panel to a directory in the left panel still works for data files.   For program files, it will not move the file but will place a *'shortcut'* in the destination directory.   In this way, the program can be loaded and run from the destination directory as well as from the source directory where the program file remains.

COPYING A FILE

Click the pointer on the desired file in the right panel so that the file is highlighted. Go to the *'Edit'* menu and choose the *'Copy'* option.   The file remains in the source directory.   Open the directory which is the intended destination for the file.   Go to the *'Edit'* menu and choose the *'Paste'* option.   The copy of the file is now resident in the destination directory.   Alternatively, dragging the file with the right mouse button pressed will present the user with a menu of choices as shown.   This provides for the copying or moving of a file into the destination directory.   It will also create a *'shortcut'* to a program file.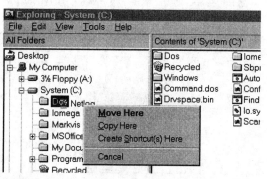

A quick way to copy a file to a floppy disc is to highlight the file and press the right mouse button; a menu opens and clicking the *'Send To'* option offers the user the opportunity to copy to the A: drive.

MOVING/COPYING GROUPS OF FILES

Files can be moved or copied in group at a time.   If the group of files are contiguous (next to each other) in the file list, click on the first file in the desired group, hold down the 'Shift' key and click on the last file in the group.   This will highlight the entire group of files which can then be moved or copied.   If the desired files are not contiguous, hold down the Ctrl key while clicking on each desired file.   An addition in Explorer is the ability click and drag a rectangle around the files to be used.   Any unwanted files within the rectangle can be deselected by holding down the Ctrl key and clicking on them.

COPYING/MOVING A DIRECTORY

The technique is identical to moving/copying files except the folder is highlighted instead of a file.

RENAMING A FILE

Click the pointer on the desired file in the right panel; choose the *'File'* option from the main menu; Choose the *'Rename'* option from the drop-down menu; when prompted, type in new file name; the file remains in its current directory but is renamed.

RENAMING A FOLDER

Click the pointer on the desired file in the <u>right</u> panel, wait a moment (so that it is not perceived as a double-click) then click again.   A box appears around the folder name and the name can be changed.

PRINTING A FILE

Click the pointer on the desired file in the right panel; choose the *'File'* option from the main menu; Choose the *'Print'* option from the drop-down menu.   The *'Print'* option will only appear on the *'File'* menu if the file is capable of being printed.

FORMATTING A FLOPPY DISC

Insert the floppy disc to be formatted in the drive. Select the floppy disc drive in the left panel and click the right mouse button. This will produce a menu from which the *'Format'* option can be selected. A 'Format' dialog box will be opened as shown on the next page.

This allows the user to set up the process to match the size of the floppy disc placed in the drive.

The user can choose to give the disc a name by typing an entry in the data entry box provided. The *'Copy system files'* option will, if checked, create a disc that is capable of starting up the computer.   These system file use up valuable disc space and the box should only be checked if a boot disc is required.

The dialog box provides for three types of formatting:

Type	Purpose
Quick (erase)	Can only be used with discs that were previously formatted. Saves time by not checking for errors on the disc surface.
Full	Checks for surface errors and marks them as bad sectors.
Copy System Files Only	Does not actually format the disc. It turns a working disc into a boot disc.

When the options are chosen, clicking the 'Start' button begins the formatting.

COPYING A DISC

This utility makes an exact replica of one disc on to another disc; any previous contents on the destination disc are lost. Insert the floppy disc to be copied in the drive. Select the floppy disc drive in the left panel and click the right mouse button. This will produce a menu from which the *'Copy Disc'* option can be selected. A 'Copy Disc' dialog box will be opened as shown.

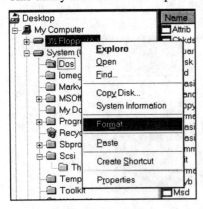

If the machine has a single floppy drive, that drive letter will be highlighted in both windows.   Where a machine has several floppy drives, they will appear in both windows and the user can choose the source and destination drives for the copy.

Clicking the *'Start'* button initiates the copying process.

Where two different drives are involved, the user only has to wait until the process is completed. Where the user nominates the same drive as both the source and destination drives, the program prompts for the switching of the discs when required.

TASKBAR

When working in Windows, there will often be a number of applications running at the same time. Some of these may have been automatically loaded at the startup of Windows (see the chapter on Windows Configuration) or they may have been loaded during the Windows session.   Each time an application is loaded, it is added as a button to the Taskbar and when the application is closed the button is removed from the Taskbar.   The Taskbar usually sits along the bottom of the screen and the buttons show every application that is currently open.   Switching between applications only requires the appropriate button on the Taskbar to be clicked.

Windows 95 provides additional access since pressing the CTRL and ESC keys brings up the *'Start'* menu, superimposed over the current application window.

LEAVING WINDOWS 95

Choosing the 'Shut Down' option from the *'Start'* menu displays a dialog box that allows the user to leave Windows 95 in one of three ways:

Option	Function
Shut down the computer	Saves data or changes to applications before closing down.
Restart the computer	Closes down then restarts so that any new settings may take effect.
Restart the computer in MS-DOS mode	Allows the user to have a prolonged DOS session.

Computer Architecture

THE BASIC SYSTEM

A computer comprises of various elements - CPU, memory, and a range of Input/Output connections to devices such as discs, keyboard, monitor and mouse. Almost all of a computer's operations are concerned with the movement of data between these elements (e.g. reading a program from disc into memory, reading spreadsheet data, recalculating results and storing them back to memory). Some of these data transfers are purely internal to the computer, as in the case of spreadsheet updating. Other data transfers are to outside peripherals via cards plugged into expansion slots on the computer motherboard, as in the case of printing a spreadsheet.

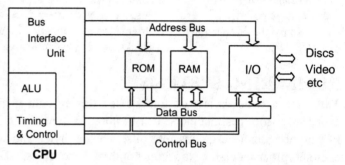

The diagram shows a simplified view of a computer system. The address bus and data bus link all the memory and input/output devices to the CPU and the main components are:

ADDRESS BUS

Each memory location has a unique address number. The CPU has to be able to read or write data to any of these addresses. The CPU accesses a memory location by putting the desired address number, in binary format, on to the Address Bus. Devices such as the parallel and serial ports are part of this addressing system.

DATA BUS

When the appropriate memory location is accessed, the CPU can either fetch data from it or write data into it; such data is transferred along the Data Bus.

NOTES:
- Some of the memory will be in the form of **ROM** (Read Only Memory). This is a chip with program coding permanently burned into it. Its contents are not lost if the machine power is switched off. Some, or all, of the system/video/disc BIOS will be stored in ROM form.
- Information never flows into the CPU from the Address Bus. The Address Bus is only used to allow the CPU to access various peripheral chips.
- Since ROM can not be written to, data only flows on to the data Bus from the ROM chip - and never in the opposite direction.
- Since RAM can either be read or written, there is a need to allow data to flow between memory and the CPU in either direction (only one direction at a time!).
- The I/O expansion bus also has to be capable of both receiving and transmitting data on the Data Bus (e.g. a modem has to transfer data in both directions).

CPU

In this diagram, the CPU has been expanded into three parts:
- The ALU - Carries out all the calculations and decision making tasks.
- The Bus Interface Unit - Takes the data to and from the CPU (held inside its internal *'registers'* - i.e. small memory stores) along the external Data Bus to read/write memory and devices. The Data Bus is a two-way bus as it must carry information in both directions. The Bus Interface Unit also places the required location addresses on to the Address Bus, in order that the required devices can be accessed for reading or writing.
- The Control Bus - Decodes all program instructions and dictates all the CPU's control and timing mechanisms. It contains six control signals. Many CPUs have two major control lines, one that is brought to a low voltage level to indicate that a read is taking place and one that is brought to a low voltage level to indicate a write taking place. Naturally, only one of these lines will be brought low at any one time. The PC range of processors, the xxx86 range, treats memory and I/O devices differently and therefore has separate control lines for each. The PC's main control lines are:

MEMR	goes low to indicate a read of memory
MEMW	goes low to indicate a write to memory
IOR	goes low to indicate a read of an I/O device
IOW	goes low to indicate a write to an I/O device

The Address Bus and the Data Bus are simply the electrical paths between the CPU and the other chips. They exist as the copper tracks of the computer's printed circuit board and the chips are soldered to these tracks. To allow other peripheral cards to attach to the buses, the buses connect to special sockets called *'expansion slots'.*   The cards plug in to these slots and pick up the bus connections, as well as power, from the edge connections.

All the bus connections are digital; they can only have two electrical states - either ON or OFF. This is due to the use of digital logic circuits.   This means that every piece of information - from an address location number to an alphabetic letter - has to be represented in combinations of these ONs and OFFs. There are various methods of implementing the ONs and OFFs in computer hardware.

Voltage levels	High or Low
Voltage polarity	Positive or Negative
Floppy/Hard Disc, Tape	Orientation of magnetic granules - North/South
CD Disc	Thickness of disc's reflective surface - shallow or deep

NUMBERING SYSTEMS

There are a wide variety of formats for storing data inside a computer. Integer numbers are stored differently from real numbers; text is stored differently in an IBM 370 computer compared to a normal PC, numbers can be groups into bits, nibbles, bytes and words; numbers can be described in terms of decimal, binary, octal, hexadecimal and BCD schemes.   Before looking more deeply, it is important to have an understanding of most of the numbering systems since numbers will be described in different ways in different manuals and different utility programs.

DECIMAL NUMBERING

The most common number system in everyday use is the DECIMAL (sometimes called the DENARY) system, which uses the digits from 0 through to 9. The number of different digits used in any numbering system is known as its BASE or RADIX.   So, the base of the decimal system is 10.   The value of any digit in a number depends on its position within the number.   For example, the digit 7 has a higher value in the number 273 than in the number 127.

The number 6,753 is pronounced as *'Six thousand, seven hundred and fifty-three"*

in other words,

$$6 \times 1000$$
$$7 \times 100$$
$$5 \times 10$$
$$3 \times 1$$

In school, children are taught numbers with column headings thus:

....	10000	1000	100	10	1	1/10	1/100	....
		6	7	5	3			

More mathematically, the column headings are :

....	10^4	10^3	10^2	10^1	10^0	10^{-1}	10^{-2}	....
		6	7	5	3			

It should also be noted that any number raised to the power 0 is always equal to 1.

From this, it follows that any numbering system can employ column headings with base R, as shown:

....	R^4	R^3	R^2	R^1	R^0	R^{-1}	R^{-2}	....

BINARY NUMBERING

Since each line of a bus can only have two states, the whole bus can only carry numbers based on a BINARY numbering system.   Numbers are expressed in base 2, with the column headings looking like :

....	2^4	2^3	2^2	2^1	2^0	2^{-1}	2^{-2}	....

Some people prefer to think of the numbering scheme as :

....	16	8	4	2	1	0.5	0.25	....

Every binary number is a collection of 1's and 0's.   A binary number can easily be converted to its decimal equivalent.

Consider the binary number 10100:

Note that the binary number 10100 is the same as 20 in decimal.

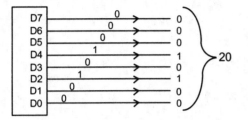

Data lines are numbered from D0 upwards, while address lines are numbered from A0 onwards.   So, an 8-bit wide data bus could carry numbers between 0 and 255 - a range of 256 different combinations (i.e. the bus has 8 lines giving 2 to the power 8 combinations).   The number 20 on an 8-bit bus would be as in the diagram.

CONVERSIONS

The above diagram shows how to convert a binary number into a decimal number.   It is also possible to convert a decimal number into its binary equivalent.   This is done by repeated division, where the decimal number is repeatedly divided by the base (in the case of binary this is 2) until the decimal number is reduced to zero.   The remainder from each division is recorded and these remainders constitute the binary number.

Consider the case of converting the decimal number 11.   Dividing by two gives five with a remainder of 1 (i.e. 11 is made up of 5 groups of 2 and 1 group of 1).   Dividing again by two gives:

```
2 | 11
2 | 5   remainder 1

    2   remainder 1
```

So, 11 = 2 groups of 4, 1 group of 2 and 1 group of 1.
This is repeated thus:

```
2 | 11
2 | 5   remainder 1     ↑
2 | 2   remainder 1     |
2 | 1   remainder 0     |
    0   remainder 1     |
```

So, 11 =   1 group of   8
             0 groups of   4
             1 group of   2
             1 group of   1

So, 11 in decimal is 1011 in binary.
Note that the remainders are read <u>upwards</u>.

HEX NUMBERING

All data is stored and moved around in binary format - no matter how the program or the user might wish to regard it or organise it. However, binary numbers can comprise very long strings of 0's and 1's when it is representing a large number.   For example, the binary number 010110011001110011001 is, in fact, the decimal number 1,468,217.   The binary version is hard to visualise; users find it hard to look at two binary numbers and know which is the largest.   As a result, binary numbers are difficult to handle and are prone to human errors.   When dealing with very large numbers, it is often convenient to express the number in base 16, instead of base 10 or base 2.   This is known as hexadecimal (often shortened to 'hex') and it is simple to convert from binary to hexadecimal. Also, the data on an 8-bit bus can be represented by just two alphanumeric characters instead of eight binary digits.   The hex system requires symbols to represent from 0 through to 15. Since 10 to 15 are outwith normal single decimal digits, the letters A to F are used to represent 10 to 15.

The table shows the relationship between binary, decimal and hex.

Binary	Decimal	Hex
0000	0	0
0001	1	1
0010	2	2
0011	3	3
0100	4	4
0101	5	5
0110	6	6
0111	7	7
1000	8	8
1001	9	9
1010	10	0A
1011	11	0B
1100	12	0C
1101	13	0D
1110	14	0E
1111	15	0F

HEX CONVERSIONS

These are carried out in the same manner as decimal to binary, except that the base used is 16 instead of two.

Examples:

Converting hex number B3 to a decimal number:

```
B3
 |
 |───────────→ 3 x 1  =    3
 └──→ B x 16  = 11 x 16  = 176
                          ─────
                           179
```

So B3 = 179.

Converting 349 to a hex number:

```
16 │ 349
16 │  21   remainder 13 ( ie D) ↑
16 │   1   remainder 5
        0  remainder 1
```

So, 349 is 15D in hex.

Large numbers can be represented quite compactly in hex. For example, the 640k memory boundary in the computer is A000. Hex is the preferred way of describing memory addresses and port locations.

NB

> Since not every occasion will see a hex number using the A to F characters, there can be confusion. For example, a 64k block of memory is 1000 in hex; this is not the same as the decimal number of one thousand. To prevent confusion, hex numbers are often followed by the letter 'h'. Thus, a 64k block would be 1000h when given in hex. Similarly, 256d and 0101b can be used to express decimal and binary numbers.

ASCII

Not all data stored in memory or carried on the computer buses will be numbers. Often it will be alphabetic characters and punctuation symbols. When the data is in alphabetic form, the *ASCII* (American Symbolic Code for Information Interchange) numbering scheme is employed. The range of alphabetic characters, numeric digits, punctuation symbols, etc. are given a unique number. For example, the letter D is represented by 68, the number 7 is represented by 55, the comma by the number 44 and so on. Upper case letters have a different code from lower case letters and the full set of printable characters uses numbers from 32 to 127. The set of numbers between 0 and 31 is non-printable; they are mainly used for control printers (the number 12, for example, provides Form Feed control character for a printer). A single byte provides 255 different numbers (0 to 255) but, since no ASCII character number is greater than 127, the codes are contained in a 7-bit sequence. IBM created an extended character set to take advantage of the codes from 128 to 255. Printers using the IBM character set can print out various box drawing and other symbols.

The range of ASCII printable codes is:

Decimal	0	1	2	3	4	5	6	7	8	9
30			space	!	"	#	$	%	&	'
40	(	)	*	+	,	-	.	/	0	1
50	2	3	4	5	6	7	8	9	:	;
60	<	=	>	?	@	A	B	C	D	E
70	F	G	H	I	J	K	L	M	N	O
80	P	Q	R	S	T	U	V	W	X	Y
90	Z	[	\	]	^		_	`	a	b	c
100	d	e	f	g	h	i	j	k	l	m
110	n	o	p	q	r	s	t	u	v	w
120	x	y	z	{			}	~	DEL		

Printer control characters include:

12	(0C in hex)	Form Feed
13	(0D in hex)	Carriage Return
10	(0A in hex)	Line Feed

An example showing different ways of representing a string of characters is given below:

ASCII	H	e	l	l	o		!
Decimal	72	101	108	108	111	32	33
Hex	48	65	6C	6C	6F	20	21
Binary	01001000	01100101	01101100	01101100	01101111	00100000	00100001

NB - The number stored in a particular location may be an instruction from a program, it may be an alphabetic character or it may simply be a number.

Consider the following examples:

"67" is stored internally as 36h 37h

67 is stored internally as 43h

"C" is stored internally as 43h

If the computer is asked to print out the contents of a particular location, it has to know whether it's meant to print the number it finds there, or the ASCII character represented by the number. This is settled by the <u>context</u> in which the print request is made. If the printer is asked to print a string of characters, it will convert the number into its ASCII equivalent before printing it; if the printer is asked to print out the numbers that it finds, the number is printed out without any conversion.

OTHER NUMBERING SCHEMES

Less common numbering schemes are in use and these include:

EBCDIC

The Extended Binary Coded Decimal Interchange Code (EBCDIC) is an 8-bit code that was introduced by IBM and ICL for their mainframe computers. It is of little interest to PC users except where data has to be converted between EBCDIC-based machines and ASCII-based PCs.

BAUDOT

This is a five-bit code that was popular for telegraphy, telex and computer-controlled radio communications systems (popular with radio amateurs). Since it a five-bit system it can only support 32 different combinations. By using two codes (called *'Letters shift'* and *'Figures shift'*) the system shifts between using the numeric codes to represent alphabetic characters and using the same numbers to represent numbers and punctuation symbols.

BCD

Where the data is only in numeric format, each individual number can be converted into its binary equivalent and handled separately. Since each individual number will only be between 0 and 9, only four bits are required to store each number.

So, the decimal number 5931 would produce a BCD equivalent of:

5	9	3	1
0101	1001	0011	0001

whereas the normal binary equivalent would be 1011100101011. This only occupies 13 bits compared to the BCD equivalent. Since each BCD number has its own collection of four bits it is often used to drive LED meters in instrumentation, monitoring and control computer systems.

OCTAL

Octal numbering works with a base of 8 and therefore uses a 3-bit system. It is little used today and is only mentioned for completeness. Conversion between decimal and Octal is similar to that already described for decimal/hex conversion, substituting 8 for 16 in the calculations.

UNITS OF MEASUREMENT

As already seen, a stream of data is nothing other than a continuous flow of binary 0's and 1's. To make sense of the stream of 0's and 1's, the system must break the stream up into manageable groups and process data a group at a time. The standard ways of organising binary information are given below:

BIT - this is the single binary digit and stores only two conditions (ON or OFF). This is the basic unit on which the system works.

NIBBLE - this is a group of four bits. It can store 16 different combinations (from 0 through to 15) and is not in common use.

BYTE - this is group of eight bits.   It can store 256 different combinations (from 0 through to 255) and is the standard method of representing a single character. The lowest order bit - the one storing the lowest value is known as the *'Least Significant Bit'* while the largest value is stored in the *'Most Significant Bit'*.

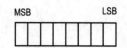

WORD - This is not an fixed amount.   A word is a group of bits which is treated by the computer as a single unit for retrieving, processing and storing.   So, if a data bus happens to be 8 bits wide, it can process 8 bits at a time; in this case, the computer's word size is a single byte.   If the data bus happened to be 16 bits wide, its word size would be 16 bits, or a double-byte.

When measuring data (either as disc capacity, memory, bus widths or as speed of transfer) it is always referred to in its binary state - e.g. One Byte, One Kilobyte, One Megabyte, etc.

Some important Data Sizes

2 raised to the power	Binary Number	Description
1	2	A single Bit
2	4	A Nibble
3	8	A Byte
4	16	
5	32	
6	64	
7	128	
8	256	The XT Data Bus
9	512	
10	1,024	A Kilobyte
11	2,048	
12	4,096	
13	8,192	
14	16,384	
15	32,768	
16	65,536	The AT Data Bus
17	131,072	
18	262,144	
19	524,288	
20	1,048,576	The XT Address Bus - 1Mbyte
21	2,097,152	
22	4,194,304	
23	8,388,608	
24	16,777,216	The AT Address Bus - 16Mbytes
25	33,554,432	
26	67,108,864	
27	134,217,728	
28	268,435,456	
29	536,870,912	
30	1,073,741,824	1GigaByte
31	2,147,483,648	
32	4,294,967,296	The 386/486 Address Bus
		/ The 386/486 Data Bus
64	18,446,744,073,709,600,000	The Pentium Data Bus

The above table shows the numbers which result from the binary numbering method.   Since each number increases by a factor of two, no number can ever be an exact thousand or an exact million.

In order to maintain the convenience of expressing size in thousands and millions, sizes have to be rounded to the binary number nearest to the wanted number.

This produces the following common expressions of size:

Amount	Calculation (2 raised to the power of n)	Actual Amount
1 kilobyte	2^{10}	1,024 bytes
1 megabyte	2^{20}	1,048,576 bytes
1 gigabyte	2^{30}	1,073,741,824 bytes

NB

This numbering system is <u>not</u> used to measure the speed of a computer's CPU.   The CPU clock speed is measured in *MegaHertz* (A MegaHertz, or MHz, being one million cycles per second).   The clock speeds quoted are the <u>actual</u> speeds - e.g. 4.77MHz means 4,770,000 pulses per second.

Computer Arithmetic

The computer constantly carries out arithmetic and comparison operations. These operations may requested by the user in an application package (eg spreadsheet calculations) or may be used by the computer system (eg for graphics and video).

Binary Addition

In denary, adding two numbers might result in a carry over between columns. In the example, adding 7 and 8 produced 15. This is another way of saying one lot of ten and 5 units. This was represented by carrying a one from the units column into the next column.

Tens	Units
	7
	8
1	5

Similarly, adding 1 and 1 in binary produces no lots of 1 and one lot of 2. Again, there was a carry from the units column into the next column. In binary addition, the calculation on any column has to take into account the possibility of a bit being carried over from a calculation on the previous column.

2^1	2^0
	1
	1
1	0

The general rule for binary addition is:

$0 + 0 = 0$
$0 + 1 = 1$
$1 + 0 = 1$
$1 + 1 = 1$ carry 1

Consider adding 6 and 7 together. Six has a binary pattern of 0110, while seven has a pattern of 0111.

Addition takes place from the lowest value upwards; this means from the right-most column through to the left-most column.

	2^3	2^2	2^1	2^0
6=	0	1	1	0
7=	0	1	1	1
result	1	1	0	1

The example of 6+7 would be processed thus:
- Adding the bits in this column (ie 0+1) produces a 1 without a carry.
- Adding the bits in this column (ie 1+1) produces a 0 with a carry into the next column.
- Adding the bits in this column, plus the carry (ie 1+1+1), produces a result of 1 plus a carry into the next column.
- Adding the bits in this column, plus the carry (ie 0+0+1), produces a result of 1 with no carry.

The final result is 1101 which is the binary pattern for 13.

It is common for arithmetic to take place on full bytes of data. For example, adding 109 and 54 produces:

```
01101101
00110110
10100011
```

However, adding 130 and 140 produces:

```
10000010
10001100
100001110
```

This calculation has produced an answer that cannot be stored in a single byte. The number of bits needed to store the result (ie 9 bits) has overflowed the size of the storage area (ie 8 bits). This final carry has to be detected and acted upon otherwise the carry is ignored and the computer thinks that 130+140=14!

Binary Subtraction

The general rule for binary subtraction is:

$0 - 0 = 0$
$1 - 0 = 1$
$1 - 1 = 0$
$0 - 1 = 1$ borrow 1

Consider subtracting 3 from 5:

	fours	twos	units
5=	1	0	1
3=	0	1	1
	0	1	0

In the right-most column, taking 1 unit from 1 unit results in 0 units.   In the 'twos' column, there is nothing in the top row to subtract the lower 1 from.   So, the 1 is borrowed from the column on its left. However, since each column increments by a factor of 2, borrowing from its left is, in fact, borrowing four - or two lots of 2.   Subtracting one lot of two from two lots of two leaves one lot of two which is placed in the middle column of the result.

Negative Numbers

The examples on the previous page used simple examples.   The example additions only used positive numbers; the subtraction example avoided negative numbers and subtracted the smaller number from the larger number to avoid a negative result.   In practice, the computer has to store and calculate negative values.

A byte has eight bits and can store a range of contents varying from all zeros (ie 0) through to all ones (ie 255), storing 256 possible different values.   However, this does not allow for negative numbers to be stored.

If the most significant bit of the byte was ignored, then the byte would store from 0 to 127 (ie seven ones).   The eighth bit can then be used to store an indicator of whether the number was positive or negative.

A zero value in the eighth bit (Most Significant Bit) indicates a positive number, while an eighth bit containing a value of one indicates a negative number.

In the first example, the MSB is 0, so the number is positive; a value of 71 in the example.

The MSB in the second example is 1 indicating a negative number.   However, the number stored is not 19 as may be expected.   The explanation lies in the way the computer works with negative values.

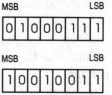

The computer, for example, need not have separate addition and subtraction operations.   The calculation of 7-3 can be represented as 7+(-3).   Both calculations are identical.   The second representation allows the computer to avoid a subtraction; it simply adds together two values - one a positive number and the other a negative number.   A subtraction problem has been converted into an addition problem.

Unfortunately, normal binary operations produce the wrong result.   The calculation of 7-3 can be represented as:

$$
\begin{array}{ll}
+7 & 00000111 \\
+(-3) & \underline{10000011} \\
\text{result} & 10001010 \quad = -10
\end{array}
$$

This has produced the wrong answer and so other methods are used for storing and manipulating negative numbers.   The most common of these is known as *'two's complement'*.

Two's Complement

With two's complement, sometimes written as 2's complement, positive numbers are represented in their normal binary conversion.

Negative values are converted using the following rules:

Decimal to 2's Complement Conversion Rules	Worked Example for value of -3
Drop the negative sign	3
Convert to binary	00000011
Invert all bits (convert all 1's to 0's and all 0's to 1's). This stage is known as converting to One's Complement.	11111100
Add 1 to the result	11111101

So, -3 is represented by 11111101.   The earlier calculation of 7-3 is now represented by:

$$
\begin{array}{ll}
+7 & 00000111 \\
+(-3) & \underline{11111101} \\
\text{result} & \underline{1}00000100 = +4
\end{array}
$$

The carry resulting from the addition is ignored, producing the correct answer of +4.

Any carry resulting from these calculations is always discarded.

If the MSB (eighth bit) is zero, the number is positive and is converted back to decimal in the normal way.

In some cases, the result of a calculation produces a negative value.
Consider the calculation 4-8.

+4	00000100	2 converted to binary
- 8	11111000	this is 8 in 2's complement
result	11111100	result has MSB set to 1

The resulting value cannot be immediately converted to a decimal number.

If the MSB is set to 1, then the following rules apply:

2's Complement to Decimal Conversion Rules	Worked Example for value of 11111100
Invert all bits (convert all 1's to 0's and all 0's to 1's).	00000011
Add 1 to the result	00000100
Convert to decimal	4
Place a minus sign in front of the number	-4

Hex Addition

Hex numbering requires a multiplier of 16 between columns, compared to multipliers of 2 and 10 for binary and decimal respectively. The carry over methods involved in the earlier examples of decimal and binary addition also apply to hex addition, except that the carry between column involves a base of 16. The least significant column stores single units with the column's contents allowed to range from zero (ie 0 lots of 1) to F (ie 15 lots of 1). The next column stores how many 16s help comprise the number stored; it can range from 0 lots of 16 to 15 lots of 16. Each subsequent column's contents increase by a factor of 16. In the table below, the columns represent 1s, 16s, 256s and 4096s - reading from right to left.

The example shows 75 and 211 being added together. 75 converted to hex is 4B while 227 converts to

	16^3	16^2	16^1	16^0
75=	0	0	4	B
211=	0	0	D	3
result	0	1	1	E

E3. The addition of the first column combines B (ie 11) and 3. This produces an answer of 14 which is E in hex. The second column adds 4 and D (ie 13). This produces and answer of 17. Since the column only stores factors of 16, there is a carry over into the next column and a remainder of 1 placed in second column.

The final result is 11Eh which is 286 in decimal.

Hex Subtraction

Hex notation is the most common way to describe memory locations and address location in computers. For example, the program necessary to drive a SCSI hard disc may be described as sitting in memory between C800h and D000h. To find out how much memory this occupies, the two hex figures should be subtracted; the difference in hex can then be converted to decimal if required.

16^3	16^2	16^1	16^0
D	0	0	0
C	8	0	0
0	8	0	0

The subtraction would be processed thus:
- The right-most column produces a 0 since 0-0 = 0.
- The second column also produces a 0 since 0-0 = 0.
- The third column subtracts 8 from 0, forcing 1 to be borrowed from last column. Borrowing one lot of 16^3 effectively means borrowing 16 lots of 16^2. 8 from 16 leaves 8 in the third column.
- Since there was a borrow from the last column, the value of D is reduced to C. Subtracting C from C leaves 0 in the last column.

This means that the memory requirements were 0800h.

This converts to hex as	0	x	1	=	0
	0	x	16	=	0
	8	x	256	=	2048
	0	x	4096	=	0
			Total	=	2048

The program occupies 2048 bytes of address space - ie 2k.

Logical Operations

Users constantly use logical operations when carrying out day-to-day activities:
- To make a word bold in Word requires both that the word be highlighted **AND** the Bold option be clicked on the Toolbar.
- DOS **OR** Windows can be used to copy files.

In the first example, <u>both</u> conditions had to be met before the third condition was met.

This can be shown with the use of a TRUTH TABLE.   A Truth Table is a table that shows the results of all possible permutations of conditions.

For the first example, it would be:

Condition A	Condition B	Result (or output)
Word not highlighted	Bold option not clicked	Word not Bold
Word not highlighted	Bold option clicked	Word not Bold
Word highlighted	Bold option not clicked	Word not Bold
Word highlighted	Bold option clicked	Word made Bold

In the second example, <u>either</u> condition being met made the third condition true.

The truth table for the second example is:

Condition A	Condition B	Result (or output)
DOS not used	Windows not used	File not copied
DOS not used	Windows used	File copied
DOS used	Windows not used	File copied

With computer circuitry, the state of particular electrical bus lines or the state of particular bits of data are used to determine the result of an action.

AND

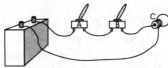

The normal way to show an electronic AND logic is the use of a battery, a lamp and two switches.   The switches are wired in series with each other.   This means that both have to be switched to light the lamp.   Its truth table is shown below, with the left table describing it fully in words while the right table shows a shortened form.:

Condition A	Condition B	Result (or output)		Switch A	Switch B	Lamp C
Switch A Off	Switch B Off	Lamp not lit		OFF	OFF	OFF
Switch A Off	Switch B On	Lamp not lit		OFF	ON	OFF
Switch A On	Switch B Off	Lamp not lit		ON	OFF	OFF
Switch A On	Switch B On	Lamp lit		ON	ON	ON

If a zero is taken as a condition being OFF (or a condition being false) while a one represents a condition being ON (or a condition being true) then the most common method showing a truth table is as shown.   The right-most column describes the expected outputs while the other columns described the variety of possible input conditions.

A	B	C
0	0	0
0	1	0
1	0	0
1	1	1

Of course, there may be more than two inputs and this would result in extra input columns.

EXAMPLE USE

All alphabetic text may require to be converted to upper case.   A lower case letter 'a' is ASCII value 97 which is 01100001 in binary, while upper case 'A' is ASCII 65 or 01000001.   In fact, the difference between the lower and upper case version of any letter is 32 and this is binary 0010000.   Subtracting 32 from the binary pattern would convert from lower to upper case.   Since all lower case letters have bit 6 set to 1, a 'mask' can be used as an AND filter to let all of the binary pattern, apart from the 6th bit (value 32), appear in the output.

example input   01100001

AND with 223   <u>11011111</u>

example output 01000001

Logical operations are 'bit-wise' operations; the condition of any output bit is purely the result of the logical operation on the corresponding input bits, independent of the result of any other bit operation. So, for example, bit 3 in the output byte was determined solely by the contents of the third bit in the two inputs - with no carry being used.

OR

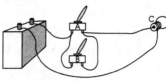

In this example, the switches are wired in parallel and switching on either of the switches will light the lamp.

This is known as an OR configuration and its truth table is as shown.

A	B	C
0	0	0
0	1	1
1	0	1
1	1	1

EXAMPLE USE

All alphabetic text may require to be converted to lower case; this is the reverse of the previous example. Since no lower case alphabet letters have the 6th bit set, 32 has to be added to the input to provide a lower case output. This is achieved by ORing the input with 32 - a binary mask of 00100000.

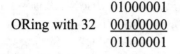

```
                    01000001
ORing with 32       00100000
                    01100001
```

NOT

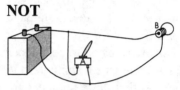

In this case, the lamp is permanently wired to the battery and will normally remain lit. If the switch is thrown it will place a short circuit across the battery/lamp and the lamp will be extinguished.

A	B
0	1
1	0

Throwing the switch reverses the normal condition (ie the lamp changes from lit to unlit) and this logic is known as a NOT. It has a simple truth table.

XOR

This is the term for and Exclusive OR, also sometimes known as EOR. The truth table shows that where there are no input conditions, there is no output; this is identical to a normal OR. The table also shows that where either of the inputs is on, the output is set to on; this also identical to a normal OR. However, if both the inputs are set, the output remains off. It only functions as an OR logic if one single input is set.

A	B	C
0	0	0
0	1	1
1	0	1
1	1	0

EXAMPLE USES

Upper case D is ASCII 68 or 01000100 as a byte in binary. If that pattern is transmitted from one computer to another computer at a distant location, the receiving end can re-transmit what it received. This will be returned (ECHOed) to the sender and the patterns can be compared. using XOR.

Pattern sent	01000100	01000100
Pattern returned	01000100	01100100
Result of XORing	00000000	00100000

In the first example, the pattern returned was identical to the pattern sent and XORing results in a byte full of zeros. In the second example, the data was corrupted during transmission and XORing produces a value which is not all zeros. Therefore, testing for a byte value of zero reports on a successful or an unsuccessful transmission of that character.

PARITY CHECKING

Sending data over distances can result in the corruption of a data byte's contents (see chapter on data communications). Since the ASCII range only requires 7 bits, the eight bit of the data byte is used to store a check value. For 'odd parity' systems the totals bits set to 1 should be an odd number, while 'even parity' systems maintain the number of bits set to zero as an even number. Where the receiving computer expects - and receives - the correct parity the output will show no error; any discrepancy will set the output to indicate that an error (ie corruption) occurred.

Expected	Actual	Error
0	0	0
0	1	1
1	0	1
1	1	0

ANIMATIONS

If any number is XORed with itself, it will produce an output of zero (eg 129 XOR 129 = 0). This can be used to switch graphics off and on.

It is also a handy way to clear the contents of a CPU register.

HOW THE COMPUTER WORKS

The CPU is the intelligence of the machine but it still needs a pre-written program to create, use and modify the user's data.   If the computer needs to compare two numbers, or add two numbers, this is carried out <u>inside</u> the CPU and the numbers have to be fetched into the CPU from the computer's memory chips.   Similarly, any program instructions have to be fetched into the CPU so that it can be acted upon. This means that CPUs work with
- programs that are stored in memory
- data that is stored in memory

The memory store can be the machine's main RAM memory or it can be the system ROM (e.g. the BIOS chip).   It cannot run programs straight from the disc - it loads the program from the disc into the machine's memory and then runs the program from the memory.   Similarly, all data - whether incoming or outgoing - will have to reside in memory at some stage.   So, programs and data from disc, tape or CD and data from keyboard, mouse, networks, sensors, etc. are all placed in memory for the CPU to access.

The program, no matter its origin, will end up as a series of instructions stored in the low-level language that the CPU understands.   This is the CPU's *'instruction set'* and will be different for different CPU variations.   Since the CPU can only process numbers, all programs and data are reduced to sequences of numbers.   The most complex Windows application is simply stored as a long set of numbers; the most beautiful graphic is similarly reduced to a stored set of numbers.   The way that these numbers are interpreted by the CPU gives the program or data its meaning.

DATA HANDLING

The normal process of a computer is a sequence of getting instructions from the program, interpreting them and acting upon them - mostly resulting in the manipulation of data.   Therefore, the CPU is constantly reading instructions from the program in memory.   It does this by fetching a copy of the instruction from the memory, along the data bus, into the CPU for interpretation.   If this instruction requires an alteration of the user's data, this altered data will need to be transmitted from the CPU on to the data bus and used to overwrite the old data held in memory.

Of course, it is imperative that the programs and data are held separately and are not allowed to overwrite each other.   To achieve this, the programs and data are stored in different areas of the machine's RAM memory. If the CPU knows where each is stored, it can get at each for reading data from, or writing data to, these specific areas.   Every individual memory location has its own unique location number, known as its *'memory address'*.   The CPU can only read from, or write to, a particular address by asking specifically for that address - that is the purpose of the address bus! Only one address number can be on the address bus at any one time and only the memory location with the same address number will respond to that address data.   So, if the number 7700 is placed on the address bus by the CPU, only location 7700 can be accessed.

CONTROLLING THE FLOW

There is one final complication.   Once a location is accessed, it needs to know whether it is supposed to dump a copy of its contents on to the data bus or whether it is meant to alter its contents to that currently on the data bus.   That is the purpose of the Control Bus.   When an address is accessed, the lines on the control bus will state whether the location is to be read or written.   These control signals are organised by the CPU and will be either *'read'* or *'write'* instructions dependent on the task required.

Examples of typical operations may be:
- reading a new instruction from the program
- reading the contents of the ROM (remember that you can't write to ROM)
- writing to a data memory location (e.g. updating a cell in a spreadsheet)
- writing to a device memory location (e.g. sending a character to the printer)
- reading from a device memory location (e.g. reading a joystick or mouse position)

The process of getting each instruction from memory, interpreting the command and carrying it out is known as the *'fetch-decode-execute cycle'*.   The following pages give a simplified version of this process but it should be noted that all computers use variations based on the system outlined.   The precise details will vary with the specific architecture of each CPU and the modern techniques used to speed up the process.

INSIDE THE CPU

The diagram shows a simplified layout of a basic XT PC's architecture. Many improvements are built upon this general framework.

The components are grouped under two headings:

BUS INTERFACE UNIT

This comprises the Instruction Queue, Control Unit and Address Segment Registers. These components move data in and out of the CPU and translates program instructions into CPU tasks. It also uses the Control Bus to control many of the computer's other components such as memory and peripheral devices.

EXECUTION UNIT

This comprises the Data Registers, the Pointer Registers, the Flags Register and the Arithmetic Logic Unit. These components carry out the

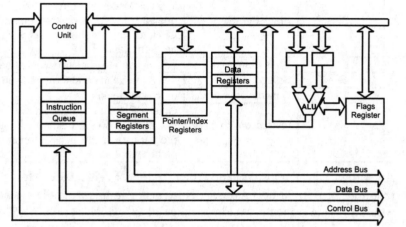

arithmetic and logic calculations and determine program flow using the pointer registers.

FETCHING INSTRUCTIONS

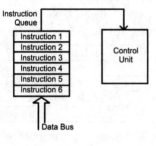

The BIU is capable of fetching a number of program instructions at a time. The Instruction Queue shown stores up to six instructions at any one time. The instructions are individually taken off the top of the queue and sent to the Control Unit where they are decoded. Since these instructions are already inside the CPU, they are more quickly available than fetching from memory via the Data Bus. This pre-fetching is a simple form of 'pipelining' and is carried out while the Execution Unit is busy executing internal instructions (eg arithmetical calculations). In this way, fetching and execution can be overlapped in time.

DECODING INSTRUCTIONS

A single machine code instruction will, in practice, require a number of operations to be carried out. For example, the instruction 'cmp dl, al' requires that the contents of two registers be compared. This translates into smaller sub-programs to fetch the contents of register dl and place it in the ALU, fetch the contents of register al and place it in the ALU, initiate the ALU comparison and set the flags register to reflect the results of the comparison. The Control Unit is responsible for decoding all instructions into sub-programs and transmitting the control signals in the correct sequence, with the required timings.

STORING DATA

The CPU has a number of internal short-term memory stores; these are used for storing values that are currently required. The number of registers used and their size varies with different CPUs. The simple model has four data registers and these are:

Description	Title	Use
AX	Accumulator	General Purpose. Also used to store values prior to, and resulting from, arithmetic operations
BX	Base	General Purpose. Also used for forming base-displacement addresses.
CX	Count	General Purpose. Often used for counting.
DX	Data	General Purpose. Also used for accessing machine and system interfaces.

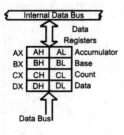

The above registers are 16 bits long and all 16 bits can be read or written to in one operation. However, to allow more flexibility, each register can be treated as two separate 8-bit registers. Thus, the AX register is 16-bit, while the lower byte is addressed as AL and the upper byte is addressed as AH.

OTHER REGISTERS

Another set of registers are designed specifically to locate data held in memory - they 'point' to required locations. These registers are:

Description	Title	Use
SP	Stack Pointer	A stack is an area of memory allocated to store data. The stack works in a LIFO manner - Last In First Out. Items are placed in the stack and peeled off later in reverse order. The Stack Pointer is used by the CPU to implement the stack but is not often manipulated by the programmer.
BP	Base Pointer	This is used to access data that has been pushed on to the stack.
SI	Source Index	They can be used to form indexed addresses
DI	Destination Index	or to point to strings.
IP	Instruction Pointer	Other CPUs refer to this as the Program Counter. The register stores the address which holds the <u>next</u> instruction to be fetched. As the program runs, the IP will continually update to reflect the flow of the program code.

An further set of registers, known as Address Segment Registers, are used to build up the addresses required for normal operations.   No register in this example system is more than 16 bits wide.   This would provide a memory address range of 2^{16} which is only 65,536 unique address locations.   Since even the oldest PC had 1Mb of addressable locations, a 16-bit register is insufficient to store all required locations.   This led to the *'segment + offset'* principle of memory addressing.   One register is used to store the upper part of the memory address (the segment) while another register is used to store the lower part of the address (the offset).   The combined registers form the required address.

The Address Segment Registers are:

Description	Title	Use
CS	Code Segment	Used with IP to form the address of the next instruction to be fetched
DS	Data Segment	Used with SI to form the address of a particular item in memory.
SS	Stack Segment	Used with SS for stack accesses.
ES	Extra Segment	Similar to DS; used for additional data accesses.

DOS runs two kinds of machine code programs. One has the extension .COM (eg FORMAT.COM) and the other uses a .EXE extension (eg ATTRIB.EXE).   With COM files, the entire program including all its data and resources fits within a single 64k segment.   When run, DOS decides which segment to use and only a single 16-bit register is required to address the entire program code.   With EXE files, which are usually of large size, the program occupies several segments and the segment+offset method using two registers is required.

THE ALU

The diagram shows the Arithmetic Logic Unit as a V-shaped object being fed by two *'operands'*.   An operand is a value about to be used for arithmetical or logical operations.   Typical activities within an ALU are:

Arithmetic	+ - * /
Logic operations	AND OR NOT XOR
Operand comparisons	Is one operand greater, smaller or equal to another operand
Operand values	Is an operand's value positive, negative or equal to zero

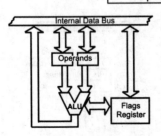

Arithmetic operations typically fetch one operand from the Accumulator and the other operand via a register.   After the arithmetic operation, the result exits the Accumulator and is placed into the Accumulator. These data movements take place via the CPU's internal busses.

The CPU also has a Flags Register (known in some other CPUs as the Status Register). This is a 16-bit register where individual bits are set (ie 1) or cleared (ie 0) to notify specific results from the ALU's operation.

FLAGS REGISTER

The Least Significant Bit, Bit 0, is set to indicate that an arithmetic operation resulted in a carry.   Bit 6 is set when a previous instruction (eg Compare or Subtract) produced a zero result.   Bit 11 is set when an overflow occurred (ie the result is too large for the register to store it).   The program can test these flags and take appropriate action (if Bit 6 is set then jump to another piece of code; if not carry on).

THE PROGRAM TO EXECUTE

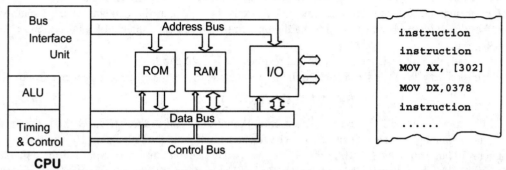

The diagram shows an extract from a program, displaying two instructions from a larger program. The first instruction is to read the contents of location 302 into register AX. This could well be reading the value from an external sensor via an add-on data acquisition card. The next instruction places the value of 0378 into register DX. This could well be setting the system up to write to the parallel printer ports, as 0378 is the normal location of the LPT1 port.

The instructions and their values in hexadecimal are:

MOV AX,[302]	A1 02 03
MOV DX, 0378	BA 78 03

Each of these instructions would be stored in different memory locations and would be in a pure hexadecimal numeric format as shown in the example below:

Location in RAM	Location Contents	Meaning of Contents
1017	??	Part of previous instruction
1018	A1	MOV into register AX the contents of the following address
1019	02	Part of address 302
1020	03	Rest of address 302
1021	BA	MOV into DX the following number
1022	78	Part of 0378
1023	03	Rest of 0378
1024	??	Part of next instruction

The addresses shown for storing the instructions are illustrative only. Note that each instruction happens to occupy three bytes of memory and that addresses are entered in reverse order - 0378 is stored as 78 followed by 03.

THE FETCH-DECODE-EXECUTE CYCLE

The steps in running the example instructions would be:

FIRST INSTRUCTION

1. The CPU's Control Unit places the value of 1018, from the Instruction Pointer, on to the Address Bus. This is the location that stores the beginning of the instruction to be fetched. Only the RAM byte at location 1018 responds to this action.

2. The Control Unit brings the MEMR control line low. This signal tells the memory chip that the contents of the location 1018 should be placed on the Data Bus. The memory chip dumps the current contents of location 1018 - i.e. the value A1 in this example - on to the Data Bus.

3. The CPU reads the value A1 off the Data Bus and restores the MEMR line to high.

4. The CPU then proceeds to read locations 1019 and 1020 in the same way. It knows that the instruction consists of three parts by decoding the first value read in. The Control Unit knows that the value A1 translates to moving a value into the AX register from a port address. It also knows that the port address is two bytes long. Therefore it knows that it has to fetch two more bytes of data to make up the entire instruction.

5. The next two reads are used to determine the address for the port read. The CPU now knows that it requires to read the contents of port location 302.

6. The CPU stores the value 1021 into the Instruction Pointer - this is the location to fetch the <u>next</u> instruction when it has finished carrying out the current instruction.

7. The value A1 is converted by the Control Unit into a sequence of control signals, both within and outside the CPU itself, under the control of the system clock.

8. The CPU places the value of 302 on to the Address Bus.   This is the location that stores the beginning of the instruction to be fetched.   Only the data acquisition card will respond to this activity.

9. The CPU brings the IOR control line low.   This tells the card that the contents of the location 302 should be placed on the Data Bus.   The card chip dumps the current contents of the location on to the Data Bus.

10. The CPU reads the value off the Data Bus and restores the IOR line to high.

11. The value read from the Data Bus is placed in the AX register.   The instruction has been carried out.

SECOND INSTRUCTION

12. The CPU places the value 1021 from the Instruction Pointer on to the Address Bus. 1021 is the location storing the beginning of the next instruction to be fetched.   Only the RAM location 1021 will respond.

13. The Control Unit brings the MEMR control line low.   This tells the memory chip that the contents of the location 1021 should be placed on the Data Bus.   The memory chip dumps the contents of location 1021 - i.e. the value BA - on to the Data Bus.

14. The CPU reads the BA value off the Data Bus and restores the MEMR line to high.

15. The CPU then proceeds to read locations 1022 and 1023 in the same way.   It knows that the instruction consists of three parts by decoding the first value read in.   The CPU knows that the value BA translates to moving a fixed value into the DX register.   It also knows that this value is two bytes long. Therefore it knows that it has to fetch two more bytes of data to make up the entire instruction.

16. The CPU stores the value 1024 into the Instruction Pointer - this is the location to fetch the <u>next</u> instruction when it has finished carrying out the current instruction.

17. These next two reads are used to determine the value to be placed in register DX. The CPU now knows that it requires to place the number 0378 into the DX register.

18. The DX register has 0378 placed in it and the second instruction is completed.

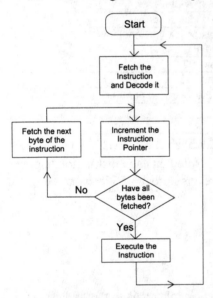

The CPU would then fetch the third instruction by reading the contents of location 1024.   The flow chart shows the sequence of events in processing an instruction.

It should be noted, however, that programs do not continually run in an unbroken sequence.   At certain parts in the program, depending upon the result of some test, the CPU may fetch an instruction from another part of the program; the instruction does not reside at the address stored in the Instruction Pointer.   It has to alter the IP to store the exact address where the new instruction is stored and the processing is known as 'branching'.

INTERRUPTS

The computer runs a program by the repeated use of the fetch-execute-decode cycle, systematically working through the program instructions.   Once a program has started there has to be provision for the user to control the flow of the program (eg by key presses or mouse clicks).   The CPU has to also be able to handle external error conditions (eg an unformatted floppy disc or a memory parity error).   If the CPU had to continually test whether the keyboard or mouse had been used, etc, a great deal of machine time would be wasted through this 'polling' of devices.   A more efficient method is to allow the CPU to proceed as normal and only interrupt the program when an event is triggered.

The program sequence can be interrupted at any point by outside events, such as:

- Those generated by the computer's own hardware (such as a user pressing a key or the computer's built-in clock being incremented).
- Those generated inside the CPU in response to an unexpected condition (eg a divide-by-zero error).
- Those generated by add-on cards connected via the expansion slots on the motherboard such as the mouse port, serial port devices, network interface cards, etc.
- Those deliberately embedded inside the software program so that it can gain access to external routines in the ROM (e.g. BIOS routines) or the RAM (e.g. user-created routines).   These are called 'software interrupts' and examples are sending a character to a parallel printer (one of interrupt 17h routines) or one of the many DOS services provided by interrupt 21h (such as reading and writing to discs, reading the built-in clock, etc.).   Examples of interrupt 21h calls are given in the chapter on batch files.

A total of 256 different routines are available and each routine has its own interrupt number from interrupt 0 up to interrupt 255.   The first 16 are allocated to hardware interrupts which means that they are designed to detect activity from hardware elements.   The first eight interrupts are allocated for system activities such as detecting mathematical overflow errors or the user pressing the PrtScr key.   The next eight interrupt numbers are allocated for the use of add-on cards (for the interfacing of modems, mice, etc.).   These are called IRQ0 through to IRQ7.

Num	Description
00	Divide Error
01	Single Step / Debugging
02	Non-Maskable Interrupt / Parity Error
03	Breakpoint / Debugging
04	Overflow
05	Print Screen
06	Reserved
07	Reserved
08	IRQ0 - Timer
09	IRQ1 - Keyboard
0A	IRQ2 - Cascade to second PIC
0B	IRQ3 - COM2
0C	IRQ4 - COM1
0D	IRQ5 - LPT2
0E	IRQ6 - Floppy Controller
0F	IRQ7 - LPT1
10	BIOS Video Interrupt / Coprocessor Error
11	BIOS Equipment Check
12	BIOS Memory Size
13	BIOS Disk Services
14	BIOS Serial I/O
15	BIOS Cassette Tape / XMS Services
16	BIOS Keyboard Services
17	BIOS Printer Services
18	BIOS ROM BASIC Startup
19	BIOS Bootstrap
1A	BIOS Clock Services
1B	BIOS Keyboard Break
1C	BIOS Clock Tick
1D	ROM Video Init Tables
1E	ROM Diskette Parameter Tables
1F	ROM Character Bitmap Table
20	DOS Terminate Program
21	DOS Service Requests

NOTE

Some confusion exists because the <u>IRQ</u> numbers that users see and set within utilities do not equate to the <u>interrupt</u> numbers within the system.   A look at the chart will show that IRQ0 is interrupt 08, IRQ1 is interrupt 09 and so on.

Note that the interrupt numbers are given in hexadecimal notation (i.e. in base 16).   Examples of the first few interrupts and their uses are shown in the table.

When an interrupt occurs, the normal program is suspended and the chosen *'interrupt service routine'* is run instead.   When the interrupt routine is completed, control is passed back to the main program which carries on from the point that it was interrupted.

MI & NMI

There are two types of interrupt that are external to the CPU:

- Those that prevent the computer program from proceeding any further. Examples of these problems are falling supply voltage in the computer or a memory parity failure. These are so serious that they can not be disabled via software - i.e. they are interrupts that are unable to be masked.   These are not normally altered by the user or technician.
- Those that denote non-fatal errors or are deliberate acts within a program (e.g. BIOS calls).   These interrupts are commonly used by application packages as it makes sense to use the existing routines provided within the BIOS chip.   These are known as maskable interrupts and allow operations that require strict timing - such as disc activities - to carry on unhindered.   In these cases, the interrupt request is only carried out when the CPU is ready to handle it.

Since there are two levels of interrupt, there is a separate physical line for each on the motherboard.

PRIORITISATION OF INTERRUPTS

It is likely that more than one interrupt will occur at any time and the CPU has to be told which ones are the most important to service.   The table shows the priorities for various interrupt conditions.   Note that the first column shows system interrupt numbers and not IRQs.   If the CPU is servicing a low priority interrupt and a higher priority interrupt is triggered, the CPU suspends the lower interrupt routine and only returns to it when the higher priority interrupt has been successfully completed.   This practice of interrupts interrupting other interrupts is called the *'nesting of interrupts'*.

Interrupt Type	Priority	Example	Source
Int 0	1	Dividing a number by 0	Inside the CPU
Int 4	1	Overflow - Calculation result too large for storage allocated	Inside the CPU
Software	1	Interrupts calls within program code	Inside the CPU
Int 2	2	NMI - Memory parity error	External to CPU
Hardware	3	MI - Keyboard, PrtScrn, etc	External to CPU
Int 1	4	Single stepping during debugging	Inside the CPU

HARDWARE INTERRUPT HANDLING

Program interrupts are handled by dedicated chips called the *'interrupt controllers'*.   These connect to the various hardware lines that require servicing.   These can be seen in the expansion slot connectors diagrams in the chapter on Architecture.   One chip will handle the lower eight interrupts while another chip will handle the IRQ lines.

The routines for handling all these interrupts are stored in the computer's memory.   This is likely to be within the machine's BIOS chip but a routine could also be stored as a TSR somewhere in the main memory area.   When an interrupt occurs the CPU has to know where the routine for that particular interrupt is stored.   This achieved by holding the addresses of all the interrupt routines in the first 1k of the conventional memory - from address 0000h to 0400h.   This is known as the *'interrupt vector table'* and each interrupt number has a corresponding 4-byte address that points to where the interrupt handling routine can be found.

The diagram shows the relationship between the various components and activities.

EXAMPLE

Here are the steps that result from the user pressing a key on the keyboard.

1. The user presses a key.
2. This activates the hardware line from the keyboard to the PIC (Programmable Interrupt Controller).
3. The PIC activates the MI line to the CPU.
4. The CPU takes a note of where it is in the main program so that it can return to that point again later.
5. The PIC places the interrupt number on the Data Bus.

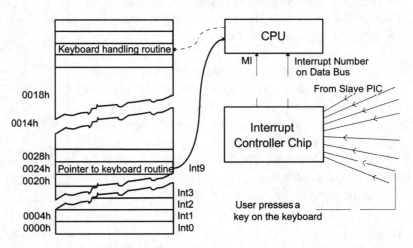

6. The CPU uses this number to fetch the address of the PrintScreen routine. Since each interrupt vector is 4 bytes long, the wanted vector is stored at an address given by multiplying the interrupt number by four.   So, in this example, the vector is stored at 9x4 = address 36 (which is 24h in hexadecimal).
7. The CPU fetches the vector from the interrupt vector table - in this case the four bytes stored from address 24h onwards.
8. The CPU runs the routine that is located at this address.
9. When the routine is completed, control is passed back to the main program.   The CPU remembers where it stops processing the main program and returns to that point for further processing.

The above sequence will be identical for any add-on cards that are using the IRQ lines.

A further eight interrupt lines are available from IRQ8 through to IRQ15. These are allocated to interrupt 70 onwards as shown in the table.   These IRQs are serviced by their own PIC.

70	IRQ8 - Real-Time Clock
71	IRQ9 - Re-directed IRQ2
72	IRQ10 - Reserved
73	IRQ11 - Reserved
74	IRQ12 - PS/2 Mouse
75	IRQ13 - Maths Processor
76	IRQ14 - Hard Disc
77	IRQ15 - Reserved

The NMI (Non Maskable Interrupt) Line is not handled through the PIC and has its own logic chips and own direct line to the CPU.

SOFTWARE INTERRUPT HANDLING

Interrupt calls that are made within a piece of software are handled in a slightly simpler fashion than that shown above.   The CPU is informed of the interrupt number by the software call, the normal operation of the program is suspended and the interrupt number is multiplied by four as in step 6 above.   It then carries out steps 7 to 9 as already explained.

NB
Practical consideration of IRQ usage is covered in the chapter on upgrading.

SPEEDING UP THE PROCESS

The example so far assumes that each new instruction is fetched from the memory <u>after</u> the previous instruction has been fully executed.   If this was the case, then the only way to increase the computer's efficiency would be to increase the rate at which the CPU was clocked through the fetch-decode-execute cycle.   This has already happened, with clock speeds being raised from the original 4.77MHz to 266MHz and beyond.   However, the laws of physics and the cost of manufacture restrict the ability to continually raise machine clock speeds.   Very fast CPUs, for, example, would require very fast address buses and data buses, since these support chips would have to be able to keep up with the demands of the CPU.   This would result in a very expensive motherboard.

In practice, other methods are used to speed up the CPU's efficiency.   These include:

- increasing the data bus width so that a larger data word is handled with each read or write, thus saving the time required to execute several reads or writes.
- pre-fetching techniques, to read several instructions at a time, saving subsequent reads.
- pipelining techniques, to decode one instruction while carrying out another, saving time.
- using two ALUs, or two or more CPUs, so that several instructions can be processed simultaneously.
- using maths co-processor, or FPUs, to carry out the number crunching while the main CPU carries out other tasks.   These are add-on chips to older CPUs, while today's chips have the FPU built in.
- clock multiplying - making the operations inside the CPU chip run faster while maintaining the existing speeds for the main buses and motherboard devices.
- introducing efficient memory caching systems, either built in to the CPU chip and/or as external secondary cache.

MEASURING PERFORMANCE

Comparison of performance between different computers requires some standard for measurement. Difference systems are in use but they all seek to measure the *'throughput'* of the computer - how much work it can get through in a given time, usually one second.

CPU STANDARDS

Since the CPU is stepped by the system clock at speeds ranging from 4MHz to 266MHz, this could be a starting point for comparison.   However, many instructions require more than one clock cycle to complete, so a 120MHz machine will not carry out 120 million instructions per second.   In addition, different CPUs may require a different number of clock cycles to carry out the same kind of activity.   So, one common measurement is the number of instructions that can be carried out in a second.   This is known as the 'MIPS' rating (<u>M</u>illions of <u>I</u>nstructions <u>P</u>er <u>S</u>econd).   Another standard notes that floating point operations (handling real numbers) are the most demanding of a computer's processing time and therefore measures 'MFLOPS' (<u>M</u>illions of <u>F</u>loating Point <u>O</u>perations <u>P</u>er <u>S</u>econd). However, these standards do not take into account the word size of the CPU.   An instruction that handles a 32-bit number will operate faster than one only handles 8-bit numbers.   This has evolved a definition of *'memory bandwidth'* that looks at the millions of memory bits accessed per second.   This standard is dependent on clock speed, the average clock cycles for instructions and the memory word length; it is therefore a more accurate reflection of machine performance.

MACHINE STANDARDS

The above measurements, though important, do not accurately measure the whole machine's performance.   A fast CPU performance can easily be marred by a slow disc system, slow memory chips or a poor graphics card. For this reason, utilities are available to produce a factor that takes into account all components of the system. Scores are produced for each component (e.g. CPU, maths co-processor, memory, video, disc) and an overall performance score. Examples of these utilities are PC Bench, PC Tools and Norton Utilities. The figures still have to be interpreted by the user. For example, a machine mostly used for graphics would require the best video and CPU performance while a machine mostly used for databases would benefit greatly from a good disc sub-system; a multimedia workstation would require all components to be top performance.

APPLICATION STANDARDS

From the user's point of view what matters is the speed in carrying out real-world applications. The time taken to perform normal application tasks is a more useful yardstick of a computer's performance than simple CPU speed or machine speed measurements.   A group of CPU chip manufacturers have developed a benchmarking system known as *'P-rating'*.   This measures the performance of a particular CPU when carrying out a range of application package activities. This measure is then compared with the performance of an Intel CPU using the same hardware and software, to give a rating.   For example, the Cyrix 5k86 processor with a clock speed of 100MHz is given a P120+ rating indicating that it performs the range of application tasks faster than an Intel 120MHz CPU.   For machines with Windows-based applications, performance measuring utilities are WinBench and WinStone.

VON NEUMANN MODEL

Computers were, and still largely remain, based around the model developed by Von Neumann in the 1940's. The main points are:

- The same memory is used for storing both input and output.
- The memory holds a 'stored program' of instruction.
- The Program Counter maintains the program flow by pointing to the next instruction.
- The CPU can adopt one of a finite range of states.
- The action taken by the CPU depends upon its current state and current input.
- The instructions are fetched and executed one at a time.

Treating each stage of the fetch-decode-execute cycle as separate sequential activities produces system bottlenecks and other approaches have been developed to increase throughput.

PRE-FETCHING & PIPELINING

As mentioned, the CPU has its own internal registers which are, in effect, fast access memory stores. These are fast because they are already internal to the CPU and don't suffer the slow fetch times associated with the addressing of external memory chips.   Unfortunately, these registers are used for holding intermediate data for calculations and comparisons.   The solution lies in providing other internal stores within the CPU, capable of providing fast access to instructions and/or data.   This is called the 'pre-fetch buffer' and Intel's 8086 began with a buffer area capable of storing six pre-fetched instruction bytes.   When the wanted instruction was read from memory, the CPU fetched the next instruction(s) at the same time.   The system was designed so that the buffer would be refilled every time it dropped to below five bytes and the CPU was not already accessing memory.

The 80386 attempted a form of 'pipelining' to speed up operations within the CPU. This system realises that while instruction 1 is being executed, instruction 2 and probably instruction 3 are already stored in the CPU.   It is able to apply the decode phase to instruction 2 while concurrently carrying out the execute phase for instruction 1.   This was a sound theory but was never fully exploited in the 386 chip.

The 486 took the pre-fetch a stage further, with its 'burst mode' approach.   The first initial access of a memory address is still relatively slow but reading the subsequent adjacent memory addresses is much faster.   This, coupled to a block of 8k of static cache ram built into the CPU, resulted in much improved processing times.   The sequence in a 486 was defined as instruction fetch, instruction decode, address generation (described by Intel as 'Decode 2'), execution and write-back (writing its results back to an internal register).   This system allowed instruction 1 to be at the write-back stage, while instruction 2 was at the execute stage and instruction 3 was at the decode stage.

SUPERSCALAR ARCHITECTURE

The Pentium moves the process even further with a 'superscalar architecture' which means that it has two separate ALUs.   Each of these pipelines is capable of processing an instruction and the resultant system is capable of processing two instructions simultaneously.   Since not all instructions have to carried out in a serial fashion, this will speed up some sections of code.   This capability would not be used where an instruction must follow another in time (e.g. the second instruction is dependent upon the output of the first instruction). The Pentium has two internal 8k caches, one for storing instructions and the other for storing data.   The two ALU pipelines, known as the U-Pipe and the V-Pipe, are supplied by pre-fetch buffers.   A new 'Branch Prediction' unit examines the instruction cache, predicts the most likely flow of instructions and feeds the pipelines accordingly.   This moves away from the original principle on which computers were designed.   This was termed the 'Von Neumann' architecture and required that all the program instructions and data be processed by a single CPU using a single data bus.

PARALLEL PROCESSING

Both pipelining and superscalar systems are elementary forms of parallel processing, in that more than one processing task is taking place at any one time.   Full parallel processing is available with the use of two or more separate CPU chips.   These communicate with each other to share tasks most effectively. This is the basis of the 'transputers' that are being developed at the supercomputer end of the market. However, PCs are already available employing two or four Pentium chips.   These are currently aimed at the network server market, so that server tasks and database engine tasks can be carried out simultaneously. Standalone dual Pentium systems offer around an 80% increase in performance.

CLOCK-MULTIPLYING

Introduced with Intel's 486 processor, modern CPUs are all clocked to run at faster speeds than the main computer bus speeds. This is termed *'clock multiplying'*. By having extra memory, known as *'cache memory'*, built in to the chip, the CPU can read ahead and pre-fetch both data and program instructions. This way, the amount of traffic between the chip and the bus is reduced by around 50%. As a consequence, the <u>internal</u> speed of the CPU can be doubled or tripled without straining the CPU/bus interface. So, for example, the overall computer system can be running at 25MHz while the CPU runs at 50MHz.

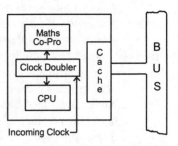

ADVANTAGES:
- The machine gives around 70% overall system performance improvement.
- The speed increase also applies to the built-in maths co-processor.
- It is a cheap system, since it still uses the standard motherboard and standard components;

DISADVANTAGES
- The chip runs very hot, requiring large heat sinks to dissipate the heat.
- There are problems when running some older software which use delay loops that will now complete sooner than anticipated, causing unexpected results.

The clock doubled range of chips are known as *'DX2'*; so, a 486DX2/66 is a 486 machine with a 33MHz clock being doubled inside the CPU to 66MHz.

Intel also produced *'clock tripled'* CPUs that are designed to treble the internal running of the CPU compared to the normal clock rate of the system. This is the *'DX4'* range and this takes a 25MHz machine and runs the CPU at 75MHz. The 100MHz model of the chip can either treble a 33MHz system or double a 50MHz system to produce the 100MHz internal clock rate.

PENTIUM SETTINGS

The technique is continued in the Pentium range. The 'clock' frequency (ie number of pulses per second) is divided in half and used to supply the timing pulses on the PCI bus. The same frequency is then multiplied by a chosen factor and clocks the internal operation of the CPU. The setting of links on jumper blocks determines the clock's working frequency; other jumpers set the multiplication factor. The chart shows a typical range of clock rates and multipliers.

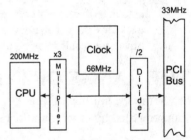

A Pentium with a 60MHz clock speed and a multiplier of 1.5 produces

CPU	Basic Clock Frequency		
Multiplier	50MHz	60MHz	66MHz
x1.5	75	90	99
x2	100	120	132
x2.5	125	150	165
x3	150	180	198

a CPU speed of 90MHz. clock speed. Similarly, a 66MHz clock speed and a multiplier of 3 produces a 200Mhz (approx) clock speed. Operations via the separate memory bus are processed at the basic clock rate. This means that a 150MHz system using 50Mz x 3 is less efficient than a system using 60MHz x 2.5.

MATHS CO-PROCESSORS

Almost all of the earlier PCs made provision for the addition of an extra chip to improve the computer's number crunching operations. The 8086 chip had the 8087 companion chip, the 80286 had the 80287, the 80386 had the 80387 and the 486SX had the 80487. The 486DX and the Pentium chips have their own maths co-processors built in to the CPU chip.

The demand for maths co-processor chips result from the design of the 80xxx series of CPU chips. The computer's main CPU is best at handling integer calculations; its speed drops dramatically when confronted with floating point (i.e. fractions) calculations. The companion chip for the 80xxx series - known as a *'maths co-processor'* - is designed to run in parallel (hence the term *'co-processing"*) with the main CPU. Mathematical tasks normally undertaken by the CPU are delegated to the co-processor. The maths co-processor chip, unlike the main CPU, does not have to be designed for a general purpose role. As a consequence, its design is tailored to carrying out its functions in the most efficient way possible. The co-processor built in to the 486DX chip, for example, has huge 80-bit registers, so that it can manipulate very large numbers with great accuracy.

This provides great potential advantages:
- The co-processor is much quicker at mathematical calculations
- The main CPU is freed to carry out other tasks
- According to the manufacturers, the combined effect is to improve speeds by up to 500%.

However, there are a number of other considerations:
- This great improvement only occurs for a <u>proportion</u> of the machine time, since the computer only spends a proportion of its time on mathematical calculations.
- Not all older applications packages can utilise the co-processor . The software has to be able to detect the presence of a maths co-processor and make use of it.
- Some applications benefit much more from the employment of a maths co-processor than others.

EXPECTED BENEFITS

<u>WORD-PROCESSING</u>   Almost nil.   The number crunching element in this package is almost non-existent. Besides, by far the slowest link in the chain is the user.   The machine spends most of its time waiting for the typist.

<u>DATABASES</u>   Usually minimal. Most database activity requires file accesses, which are very slow compared to any processing activity. The collation of figures for reports would involve some calculations including real numbers expressing currency. Even here, though, many reports tend to maintain integer counts and totals.

<u>SPREADSHEETS</u>   The degree of benefit depends on the complexity of the worksheet being processed.   If the worksheet is huge, contains many formulae and uses lots of mathematical functions, then the re-calculation of the worksheet will be greatly speeded up. For small or simple worksheets, there will be little noticeable improvement.

<u>CAD</u>   Normally, dramatic performance increases can be expected. Computer-aided design packages rely heavily on the calculation of curves, etc. and are almost all equipped to use a maths co-processor to best advantage.

<u>GRAPHICS / DTP</u>   Desk Top Publishing and other graphic-oriented applications also rely on substantial amounts of number crunching to calculate arcs, vector co-ordinates, etc.   However, many of the older packages do not recognise a maths co-processor. In these cases, the purchase and fitting of the co-processor would have no effect on the performance of that package.

THE RANGE OF INTEL CPUs

From the beginning of the PC range of computers, the main CPU has been from the Intel range, supplemented by other manufacturers with *'clones'* or improved versions of each chip in the series.

The current series consists of the following chips:

<u>8086</u>   These are no longer manufactured or sold.   Since it only had a 20-bit address bus, it was only capable of addressing 1Mb of unique addresses.   This means that it is unable to support extended memory and is completely incapable of running Windows and most modern DOS applications.   Its speed is much slower than its successors - e.g. the Pentium can be 150 times faster than the XT, when measured in MIPS.

<u>286</u>   Like the 8086, they are no longer sold, and are rarely found in current commercial use.. They are slow, running at speeds from 10MHz to 20 MHz. With a 24-bit address bus, the AT was able to address up to 16 million different address locations. To complement this, the AT had two operating modes - *'real mode'*, where it used only 8086 code and acted like a fast XT and *'protected mode'*, where it was able to access beyond the 1Mb address limit and employed its added features.   It also ran at about 4 times the MIPS rate of the XT.   Since *'real mode'* is the natural mode for normal DOS operations, the *'protected mode'* was intended for multi-tasking operations, Windows, OS/2, etc.   Unfortunately, the chip is not really powerful enough for these tasks.

<u>386</u>   Also out of production, these chips ran at speeds from 16MHz to 40 MHz and could carry out the effective multi-tasking operations (i.e. run two programs at the same time) that eluded the 286.   It was also the minimum processor for running Windows, with a machine with at least 4Mb of RAM.   It introduced substantial improvements in both memory management and an enlarged instruction set.   The chip was available in two varieties - the 386SX and the 386DX.·   The SX version had a 32-bit internal data path but had only a 16-bit path between the CPU and the computer's memory.   So, the SX model could only transfer data in 16 bit chunks at a time.   The DX model had a 32-bit data bus between the CPU and the memory chips, allowing larger data transfers and therefore faster throughput.   The ability to use external cache memory, usually about 64k, also improved performance.   The 386SL model was a low power consumption model used in portables.

486 This was the entry-level standard chip (the standard at which most people currently buy a new machine, before upgrading) although it is now superseded by the Pentium. It ran at speeds from 20MHz to 100MHz. Little change was made to the 386 instruction set, with the emphasis being placed on enhancements to improve performance. This chip was also available in SX and DX varieties. In this case, the difference lay in the fact that the SX did not have a built-in maths co-processor unlike the DX. Motherboards using the 486SX chip always had a spare maths co-processor socket to upgrade to a DX. Apart from the raw clock speed of the CPU, the 486 was faster than previous chips because it was designed to carry out the most common instructions in a single clock cycle (compared to two or three clock cycles for the 386 chip). This demonstrated a move towards the RISC philosophy ('**R**educed **I**nstruction **S**et **C**omputer'). The 486 chip also had a built-in 8k block of cache memory. This, coupled to a new *'burst mode'*, means that data was transferred at a far higher rate than the 386 system. Burst mode allowed memory transfers from consecutive memory locations to be achieved at the rate of one per clock cycle. A 486DX ran about 40% faster than a 386DX with a maths co-processor. It was also available in clock doubled (DX2) and clock tripled (DX4) models. The 100MHz DX4 ran faster than the bottom end of the Pentium range - i.e. the 60MHz and 66MHz models. Since the DX4 range used only a 3.3 volts supply, compared to the normal 5 volts, they consumed less power and created less heat, making them good choices for portables.

Pentium This chip is the current entry-level standard for computers. It is significantly faster than a 486, with a 66MHz Pentium being twice as fast as a 66MHz 486. A 250MHz model is on the way. It is effectively two CPUs in the one chip with a 256-bit internal bus and a 64 bit external data bus. On most occasions this allows two instructions to be executed in parallel and this alone greatly speeds up throughput. The chip also has the main mathematical operations (i.e. add, divide and multiply) hard-wired into the chip; its new maths co-processor is re-designed to be up to 10 times faster than the 486DX maths co-processor. All Pentium models are 'superscalar'; the basic Pentium chip has two integer processing pipelines. It also has a *'branch prediction'* facility that 90% of the time correctly predicts the flow of the program and fetches the instruction from a buffer area. The Pentium also has a specially designed high-performance Floating-Point Unit and has a 16k internal cache. It uses CISC technology with some RISC elements. 60MHz and 66MHz chips required a 5 volt supply while models from 75MHz upwards use a 3.3 volt supply for both core operations and input/output operations.

Pentium Pro This chip uses six different pipelines and 40 general-purpose registers. All the pipelines can operate simultaneously, offering greatly improved processing capability. To fully utilise this architecture, the Pro reads the incoming program instructions into an 8k instruction cache. The instructions are then turned into fixed-length RISC type *'micro-operations'* by three parallel decoders and sent to one of the free pipelines. In this way <u>parts</u> of the original instructions are being processed independently rather than sequentially. The CPU has an *'out-of-order'* approach so that instructions that that can't be immediately executed (eg waiting for data) are not placed in a pipeline where they will prevent other micro-operations from being processed. In this way, bottlenecks are minimised. The results of the micro-operations are then assembled in the correct order for use by the external software application.

For even greater speeds, the Pentium Pro has all the necessary logic on board to allow four CPUs to be connected to the same motherboard for parallel running. This is known as *'symmetric multiprocessing'* and the Pentium Pro's implementation is described as *'glueless'* since no extra logic circuitry is required to make the CPUs communicate. Examples are IBM PC Server 720 and the Dell XL 5133-4.

The chip uses 16k of internal level 1 cache in a *'unified'* mode. The Pentium uses two banks of cache - one for instructions and one for data. If the instruction cache is full the CPU can stall, even if there is spare capacity in the data cache. The Pentium Pro regards its two 8k caches as a single block of 16k that can be used dynamically for either data or instructions. This balances any changes in load and minimises CPU stalling.

There is also 256k or 512k of second level cache built into the chip. With ordinary Pentiums or other CPUs, the second level cache is a plug-in unit or is soldered to the motherboard. With the Pentium Pro, the cache is internal to the chip and directly connected to the CPU itself. This means that the cache operates at the full CPU speed while external caches may operate at only half that speed. This makes the Pro's caching much more efficient.

The Pro's design is optimised for 32-bit working and actually runs 16-bit code slower than a Pentium. For maximum results it needs to run 32-bit program code with a 32-bit operating system (eg Windows NT).

Pentium MMX This is a new version of the Pentium with 57 additional instructions in the CPU instruction set. These are multimedia and communications extensions to the CPU giving them the title *'MMX'* - multimedia extensions. The new instructions use a technique known as SIMD - Single Instruction, Multiple Data. One instruction can work on up to 8 bytes of data simultaneously. This provides very fast repetitive processing of data - ideal for video decompression, sound synthesis, multimedia, 3D rendering and other graphics-intensive activities. MMX aware programs - ie those using the new MMX instructions are expected to return a 40%

speed improvement.   It will also run existing programs 10-20% faster because of its 32k internal cache (16k for code and 16k for data). It contains a more efficient branch prediction unit   The instruction pipeline also works one level deeper - it can carry out more work in advance than a normal Pentium. MMX chips have 8 enhanced internal registers which are 64 bits wide, comprising virtual registers using the normal registers along with the Floating Point registers). It uses 2.8v for core operations and 3.3v for input/output operations. This reduces power consumption and reduces heat. This means that an MMX chip cannot be used to upgrade a motherboard that does not have a dual voltage supply on Socket 7 CPU holder.   Intel has introduced an 'Overdrive' MMX chip that only runs on 3.3v and is intended for upgrading with older, Socket 5, motherboards. In either case, the motherboard's BIOS chip needs to be MMX compatible.

PENTIUM II   Soon to be released, the Pentium II, previously known as the *'Klamath'*, is an improved Pentium Pro with MMX additions.   Its initial release is a 233MHz CPU with a 100MHz bus.   The built in second level cache is taken out of CPU and is mounted, along with CPU on a plug-in card.   This card plugs into a special connection slot known as *'Slot One'* which means that the Pentium II needs a completely re-designed motherboard. It uses a 2.9v supply to reduce heat dissipation.   The external second level cache also means that the performance is diminished.   However, the 32-bit performance, coupled with MMX capabilities, places Pentium II machines in the multimedia and graphics workstations market.

RISC vs CISC   The main approaches to CPU design are CISC and RISC processors.   CISC (Complex Instruction Set Computer) processors provide a comprehensive instruction set and a wide range of address modes.   The more complex instructions can replace a number of more simple instructions, making programming easier.   The subcommands within the instruction may be of different lengths and the processor has to act to provide the required processing space for each subcommand. This takes time and these complex instructions often take more clock cycles to complete compared to a group of simpler instructions, lowering overall throughput.   RISC (Reduced Instruction Set Computer) processors perform a more basic set of instructions, each of uniform length.   Each instruction is highly optimised and this reduces the number of clock cycles for an operation.   When combined with caching and pipelining, RISC processors sometimes appear to execute an instruction in zero clock cycles.   Hybrid CPUs, combining elements of CISC and RISC and term CRISC chips.

Alternatives to Intel

This domination of Intel chips is being constantly challenged as other designs threaten the Intel line.

One threat comes from the Apple Corporation, normally associated with the Macintosh range of computers. Until now, the Macintosh has been successful in universities and the printing, graphics and design areas but has been unable to break through as a serious competitor for the normal commercial market.   In a change of emphasis, Apple has designed the PowerPC. This is be able to run normal DOS and Windows applications as well as running normal Macintosh software. This makes the machine a very versatile unit. In addition, the PowerPC 603, 604 and 620 chip use RISC technology and will run faster than a Pentium.

Also competing is the Cyrix M2 chip. This CPU is MMX equipped and has 64k of internal cache to be faster than the Pentium II.   It supports a 75MHz bus compared to Intel's 66MHz to increase performance

The AMD K6, is a RISC chip that that also supports MMX and integrates a 64k cache. Unlike the Pentium II, the K6 fits a standard Pentium motherboard Socket 7 CPU connector.

In response, Intel plans a new CPU - currently titled *'Deschutes'*, which appears to be based on a Pentium II with a lower supply voltage and speeds around 300MHz.

Summary of P.C. Processors

	8086/88 the 'XT'	80286 the 'AT'	80386	80486	Pentium	Pentium Pro	MMX
Introduced	1978	1982	1985	1989	1993	1995	1996
Number of Pins	40	68	132	168	273	387	273
Transistors	29,000	120,000	275,000	1.2m	3.1m	5.5m	4.5m
Data Bus Size	8088 8 bit 8086 16 bit	16 bit	32 bit	32 bit	64 bit	64 bit	64 bit
Address Bus Size	20 bit	24 bit	SX 24 bit DX 32 bit	32 bit	32 bit	36 bit	32 bit
Addressable Memory	1Mb	16Mb	SX 16Mb DX 4Gb	4Gb	4Gb	64Gb	4Gb
Clock Speed (MHz)	4.77 / 8	10/12/16/20	SX16/20/25/33 DX 33/40	SX 20/25 DX 33/50 DX2 50/66 DX4 100	60/233	150/266	166/200
Performance (in MIPS)	0.75	2.66	11.4	54	112	300	182

ASSEMBLY LANGUAGE

All computer programs are loaded from their backing store (eg disc, tape, CD) and placed in memory. The program instructions are then fetched by the CPU for decoding and execution (see the earlier explanation of the fetch-decode-execution cycle). These could be instructions for an applications package such as Excel or Corel Draw, or could be the instructions for carrying out systems operations under DOS or Windows. Program instructions, of all types, are stored in binary format (eg 1001110001010001). Each binary pattern is unique for a particular CPU instruction and the decoder's job is to turn the incoming binary pattern into the set of control signals required to carry out that instruction. A different instruction would have a different binary number and would be decoded as a different set of control signals. Since these are instructions to run the computer, they are known as 'machine code'. They are in binary but are represented to writers in hex format for easier understanding. This complex process is hidden from the computer user.

From a programmers point of view, writing programs purely in binary would be both very tedious and error-prone. That is the motive for the development of the range of computing languages that are available. All languages, from ancient old COBOL to modern JAVA, provide the programmer with easier ways to write programs. These programs are later turned into the binary patterns that will be stored on file and later used by the computer. Programmers have to learn the particular syntax of a language and get used to the methods used for converting their work into executable programs.

HIGH LEVEL LANGUAGES

With high level languages, programmers do not need to know how the CPU works. The program is written as a script file with a line of text for each stage of the application's activity. The script file is saved, usually as ASCII characters, and can be reloaded later and amended just like any other text file.

When the program is ready to test, the language instructions have to be converted into their machine code equivalents and run.

Two methods of conversion are used:

INTERPRETERS

This looks at the script file and takes each line at a time. The instruction in the first line is immediately converted to machine code and run. When the activity is completed, the next line of text is read and similarly converted to machine code and run. The program is run using only the original text file; there is no additional file such as an EXE or COM file.

Examples of interpreted systems are:

BATCH FILES

All batch files, including the AUTOEXEC.BAT that sets up the computer on bootup, have their lines interpreted and acted upon one at a time. Although simple, batch files can be very powerful. The following line in a batch file

            COPY A:*.DOC C:\

could produce hundreds of reads from a floppy drive and hundreds of write operations to the hard disc. Each read involves accessing the floppy, reading the file name, checking its extension and perhaps copying the files contents into memory. This one batch file line may result in thousands of CPU activities.

CONFIGURATION FILES

The DOS CONFIG.SYS file and all Windows INI files are used to set up the machine to particular hardware and software requirements. The files are written in English-like commands (eg BUFFERS = 10 or sCurrency = £) and the interpreter converts them into the corresponding memory configuration, etc.

EARLY VERSIONS OF BASIC

The programming language called 'Basic' was very popular in the earlier days of computing, particularly in schools and colleges and among those looking for a gentle introduction into programming. An example line might be:

            INPUT age%

which would result in the CPU waiting for keyboard input, checking that a numeric value was entered and placing the value into a memory storage area.

Later versions of Basic allowed the program to create executable versions (ie compiled versions).

COMPILERS

With compilers, the entire script file is converted into another separate file containing machine code instructions corresponding to the script commands.   The resulting files are usually EXE or COM files, but could be DLL or SYS files.   The script is known as the *'source code'* while the compiled output is known as the *'object code'*.

The chart shows that the programmer creates a script file and uses the facilities of the programming environment to convert the script into a binary file equivalent.   If the writer has made a syntax error (ie used incorrect syntax) then the conversion stage will report an error.   The writer can then edit the script file and try again.   If the conversion process was successful, a compiled version of the program will and exist and can be run.

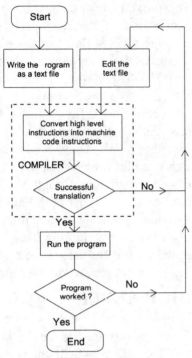

The compiler only tests whether the syntax of the input file is correct (eg the correct order of items, the correct usage of punctuation).   The program may still be logically incorrect (eg adding tax to a wage packet instead of deducting it).   If the compiled version is run and found to be incorrect, the programmer can recall the text version, edit and re-compile the program.

Languages such as Pascal, Cobol and C use compilers to convert to executable formats.   A line in Pascal such as

Writeln('Dumbreck');

would instruction the CPU to place the text string on the computer screen and produce a carriage return and line feed (ie place the cursor at the start of the next line).   Again, a single line instruction is translated into several differing CPU instructions. This is defined as a *'one to many language'*.

LOW LEVEL LANGUAGES

High level languages benefit from their ease of use but suffer varying degrees of speed loss, mainly due to their use of general purpose routines.   For example, the Pascal *'Writeln'* routine may be asked to display text as in the above example; it may also be asked to display the contents of a variable (eg Writeln(age) or even a mixture of text and variable values (eg 'Writeln('My name is ',name,' and my age is ', age);.   This produces a routine that is bulkier and slower than a routine dedicated to a single activity. Low level languages require that the programmer has a detailed knowledge of the workings of the particular CPU that the program is being written for (code for a PC will not run on a Macintosh or an

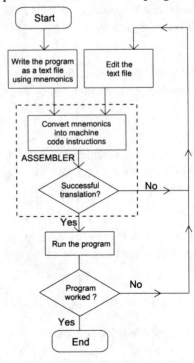

Amiga).   The number and size of registers, the methods employed and the available range of machine code instructions can be exploited by the knowledgeable programmer to produce to produce code that runs at the fastest possible rate.   This positions low level programmers in the software markets requiring instant responses. Examples include defence, production lines (eg process control and robotics) and embedded systems (eg modems, Point-of-Sale terminals).   Low level programming produces more compact and faster programs.

The text file is written using *'mnemonics'* - small commands giving explicit CPU instructions.   For example:

MOV AL,8

will place the value of 8 into the al register.

This makes the simple assembler a *'one to one language'*, with one CPU instruction per text line.   The more developed assemblers are also *'one to many'* since they allow the use of *'macros'* where a single text line substitutes a pre-written collection of instructions. The macro code substitutes for the macro line prior to the assembly process.   Some assemblers also support *'many to many'* through the use of IF-THEN-ELSE and DO-WHILE constructs.

The charts below show the relationship between the source code (the programmers text), its conversion to object code (ie machine code) and its storage in memory.

High level instruction	Low Level equivalent	Machine Code equivalent	Binary output after conversion
write('A')	MOV DL,41	B2 41	10110010 01000001
	MOV AH,02	B4 02	10110100 00000010
	INT 21	CD 21	11001101 00100001
	INT 20	CD 20	11001101 00100000

The first column shows a single Pascal instruction which displays the upper case letter A on the screen. The second column shows the equivalent commands in assembler mnemonics. The third column shows the conversion into machine code expressed in hex. The last column shows the actual storage in binary as it will be saved to disc as a file.

A compiler takes the single instruction from the first column and creates the binary output seen in the fourth column. An assembler takes the four instructions shown in the second column and creates the same binary output. The hex shown in the third column is only used where the programmer wishes to view a file or a register's contents.

The second table shows the program as it would be stored in memory, assuming it was placed in address 20000 upwards. The binary for B2 is placed in address 20000, the binary for 41 is placed in address 20001, and so on.

Memory Address	Contents
20007	00100000
20006	11001101
20005	00100001
20004	11001101
20003	00000010
20002	10110100
20001	01000001
20000	10110010

INSTRUCTION SETS

Each CPU has a different design, different electronic wiring inside the chip and differing sets of instructions to control the chip's operations. The Intel range of chips for the PC uses the existing core of instruction throughout its range. The commands for the earliest chips such as the 8086 are still to be found in the most modern chips such as the Pentium range. Newer chips provide additional facilities but the basic commands will work with any PC. That explains why so much existing software will run on all machines while new software is written specifically to take advantage of the additional facilities of the Pentium or the MMX.

Instructions are grouped round functions and examples are:

- data transfer
- arithmetic operations
- interrupt instructions

SAVING DEVELOPMENT TIME

Writing in assembly language can be quite a slow and intricate task. Methods have evolved to speed up the development of machine code programs.

These include using:

- LABELS   The program often jumps to particular chunks of coding, depending upon the result of some activity (eg jumping to a piece of code to display an error message if something goes wrong, or returning to an earlier point in a loop). If the programmer can always refer to the start of that coding as a label written in English, then programming becomes faster and less error prone than referring to actual address locations. For example, jumping to a label called hiscore is more understandable than jumping to address 1234h. To indicate that the text is to be regarded as a label, a colon finishes off the word - ie the line would be written as   hiscore:
  When the program is assembled, the assembler places the correct address in place of the label.
- CONSTANTS The ASCII values for Line Feed and Form Feed are 0Ah and 0Ch. Programming can be simplified by using the letters 'LF' and 'FF' in place of the ASCII codes.
- VARIABLES   Similarly, variables can be set up to store values or text string such as 'Hello'.
- FUNCTION CALLS   DOS has a wide range of built-in facilities that it uses for its own functions such as reading the keyboard, writing to screen and printer, etc. The programmer can tap into these existing routines and save re-inventing the wheel. These are explained more fully later.
- SCRIPT LIBRARIES   Many activities, such as checking if a date is valid (eg no 30th Feb or no 13th month) are common to many programs. Once the piece of code is written and tested, it can be stored for use with other programs. When another program is being developed, the text can simply be inserted into the new program script at the appropriate point.

- OBJECT LIBRARIES   A collection of similar routines (eg screen handling routines, modem routines, etc) can be combined in a single assembled object file. This produces a set of pre-written routines that are already in machine code format. This *'library'* of routines is then *'linked'* to the programmer's code to create a standalone EXE file.
- MACROS   There are activities that a program might wish to carry out many times in different parts of the program. Examples might be string-handling routines, serial port operations and disc activities. It is inefficient and error-prone to insert the same code in all of these places; if the code needs altering then every occurrence of the code has to be found and altered. A better way is define the set of instructions only once, at the beginning of the program. The set of instructions (known as the *'macro'*) is named by the programmer and every time the code needs to be used only the macro name needs to be inserted in the code. When the program is assembled, the full code is inserted each time the macro name is found in the program. If the macro is changed and the program is re-assembled, all the occurrences of the code are automatically updated.

CREATING SMALL PROGRAMS

The chart on page 92 shows the process of turning a single script file into a single-segment COM file. This is adequate for a variety of small utilities that are under 64k in size.   This process, using fully featured assemblers such as MASM or TASM, can handle labels, script libraries, DOS function calls and user-defined macros.   Running the object code through a linker (see below) will convert the program into an EXE file.

CREATING LARGE PROGRAMS

Writing a large program in assembler is similar to writing a program in any procedural language such as Pascal.   The stages of program design are:

1. Produce a precise specification of the program's needs.
2. Break the overall problem down into a set of smaller tasks; if necessary a task can be broken down into smaller sub-tasks.
3. Write the program for each task as an independent module.
4. Bring the modules together with any external modules from libraries.
5. Test and debug the program
6. Document the program.

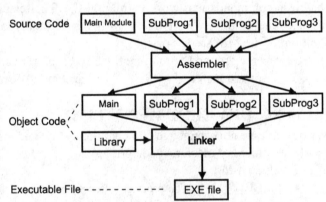

The chart shows a collection of source code modules being converted into their machine code equivalents and then merged with any library code to produce a single EXE file.

If the program is less than 64k in size, the final EXE file can be converted to a COM file using the EXE2BIN program provided with DOS.

ASSEMBLER TOOLS

The most commonly known assemblers for the Intel range of CPUs are:

- MASM from Microsoft
- TASM, bundled with Turbo Pascal
- A86 (shareware)
- NASM (freeware)
- DEBUG, bundled with MSDOS

DEBUG is supplied with DOS; with Windows 95 it is not automatically installed but can be found on the installation CD). It does not support all the time-saving elements such as labels, macros, constants, variables, etc. It does, however, support the DOS function calls and is very useful for creating small programs.

Since different tools may be available to different readers, the examples in this chapter use DEBUG since it available to all DOS users. It does not provide all the improvements provided by the other assemblers but these are also outlined in the appropriate places.

SCRIPT SYNTAX

With a number of important exceptions, lines in a program script make use of four components which are shown in the example line of code below:

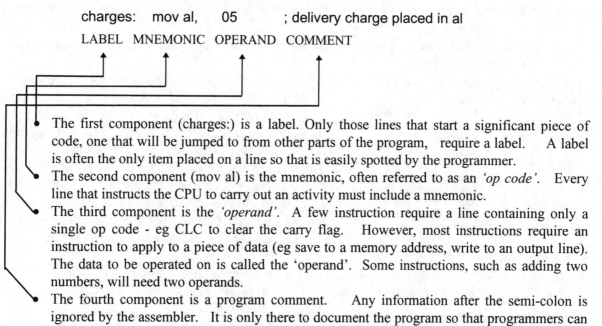

charges: mov al,   05   ; delivery charge placed in al

LABEL MNEMONIC OPERAND COMMENT

- The first component (charges:) is a label. Only those lines that start a significant piece of code, one that will be jumped to from other parts of the program, require a label. A label is often the only item placed on a line so that is easily spotted by the programmer.
- The second component (mov al) is the mnemonic, often referred to as an *'op code'*. Every line that instructs the CPU to carry out an activity must include a mnemonic.
- The third component is the *'operand'*. A few instruction require a line containing only a single op code - eg CLC to clear the carry flag. However, most instructions require an instruction to apply to a piece of data (eg save to a memory address, write to an output line). The data to be operated on is called the 'operand'. Some instructions, such as adding two numbers, will need two operands.
- The fourth component is a program comment. Any information after the semi-colon is ignored by the assembler. It is only there to document the program so that programmers can explain the purpose of a particular line or group of lines. Comments can be included in a line along with other components or can be placed on their own in a line.

There are variations on this basic layout, such as defining macros, assembler directives, etc.

DOS INTERRUPTS

Before exploring the instruction set commands, the readily-available functions provided by DOS are examined. These functions are loaded into the system when the computer boots up and can be called from a machine code program. DOS provides 256 interrupt functions - from interrupt 0 (INT 0) through to interrupt 255 (INT FF). Some of these, like INT 0 (Program Termination) or INT 5 (PrntScrn) are single purpose functions. Other interrupt calls provide many other functions; these are chosen by setting registers before initiating the interrupt call. These are demonstrated in the following examples.

First example

A machine code routine to write all the text from the screen to the printer (ie the DOS PrntScrn command) could be written after some time - but it already exists in DOS and can be called by a single instruction. Placing the instruction *'INT 05'* in a program will interrupt the flow of the machine code program, call up the function to print the current screen contents, and then return to continue through the rest of the program. The code calling PrtScrn can be inserted within an existing program or can be written as a single instruction program for testing.

Using DEBUG

DEBUG is not as powerful as fully-featured assemblers but it has the advantage of coming bundled with DOS. The script in the left column is entered as a text file using a plain ASCII editor such as EDIT. The heart of the program is only the fourth line. The surrounding code is common to all DEBUG scripts and is used to instruct the compiler how large to make the file, what to name the file

Data to enter	Meaning
RCX	Set the file size to 16 bytes
10	ie (10h)
N SCRNPRT.COM	Name the file
A	Assemble the following code
INT 05	Print the Screen
<Enter>	Signals end of code
W	Write a COM file
Q	Exit DEBUG

and instructions to assemble the code, create a COM file and leave the assembler program. Note that values are expressed in hex.

When completed, the script should be saved with the extension .DBG and fed into the assembler using the following command at the DOS prompt:

DEBUG < FILENAME.DBG

This produces a runnable COM file. A file saved as TEST.DBG would be compiled as TEST.COM.

Second Example

Many INT calls support multiple functions, depending on the values of their registers prior to initiating the interrupt call.

- INT 10, for example, has over 100 differing video-related functions. Options range from setting video modes to reading light pens.
- INT 13 provides a range of about 50 disc functions with various reading, writing, formatting and verifying functions.

The most widely used of all is the INT 21 which has a huge range of options for handling the keyboard, the screen output, the serial port, disc operations and much more. For example, calling INT 21 with the AH register set to 2 and a numeric value in register DL will display the ASCII equivalent of that value on the monitor screen.

Data to enter	Meaning
RCX	Set the file size to 16 bytes
10	
N PRINTX.COM	Name the file
A	Assemble the following code
MOV DL, 58	Place 88d in register DL
MOV AH, 02	Choose the display option
INT 21	Call the DOS INT 21 routine
<Enter>	Signals end of code
W	Write a COM file
Q	Exit DEBUG

The small program shows 88, the ASCII value for an upper case X, being placed in the DL register. Calling INT 21 with AH=2 chooses the 'display a character to the screen' routine and that routine uses the value held in DL for conversion to an ASCII character. An 'X' is displayed.

Third example

Another INT 21 option allows the program to wait for the user to press the keyboard. The ASCII value resulting from the keypress is placed in register AL. This is initiated by placing the value of 8 in register AH prior to calling INT 21.

Data to enter	Meaning
RCX	Set the file size to 16 bytes
10	
N PRNKEY.COM	Name the file
A	Assemble the following code
MOV AH, 08	Choose a keyboard read
INT 21	Read keyboard value into AL
MOV DL, AL	Copy ASCII value to DL
MOV AH, 02	Choose the display option
INT 21	Call the DOS INT 21 routine
MOV AH, 4C	Set for program termination
INT 21	Call the DOS INT 21 routine
<Enter>	Signals end of code
W	Write a COM file
Q	Exit DEBUG

The script shows instruction 5 through to 11 as the body of the program. Instructions 5 and 6 result in AL holding the keypress result. The character of the key pressed is not displayed (echoed) on the screen. If the 5th line were changed to MOV AH, 01 then the character would be both read into the Al register and also displayed on the screen. Instruction 7 copies the value from AL into DL. Instructions 8 and 9 display the ASCII value on the screen. Instructions 10 and 11 demonstrate another DOS function - that of terminating the machine code program and returning control back to COMMAND.COM. Program termination used to carried out by calling INT 20 but this is no longer recommended by Microsoft. The preferred method is to call INT 21 with register AH set to 4C. This method has the added advantages of returning an exit code in AL (handy for batch file programmers) and of closing any open files.

VIEWING A COM FILE

DEBUG provides many other useful features in addition to assembling machine code. It can display and alter the contents of the CPU's registers, trace through a program's execution and display a COM file in its original mnemonic form. The DEBUG command is followed by the name of the file to be examined.

DEBUG PRNKEY.COM

A hyphen is displayed; this indicates that DEBUG has loaded the file and is waiting for a command. Entering the command 'U 100 L 10' means 'Unassemble the file from location **100** with a **L**ength of **10**h bytes being displayed'. Since the first 256 bytes (ie 100h) of a COM file contain the file header, the program always starts at location 100h.

The screen output is as shown with the first column displaying the address location, the second column displaying the hex values and the third column displaying the values as assembler mnemonics. It can be seen that B4 is the hex code for MOV AH, while CD is the hex code for INT.

So B4 is stored in address 100h while 08 is stored in 101h, and so on.

```
-U 100 L 10
220F:100    B4 08    MOV AH, 08
220F:102    CD 21    INT 21
220F:104    88 C2    MOV DL, AL
220F:106    B4 02    MOV AH, 02
220F:108    CD 21    INT 21
220F:10A    B4 4C    MOV AH, 4C
220F:10C    CD 21    INT 21
```

Utilities such as Borland's Turbo Debugger provide much more advanced facilities such as opening windows to keep a watch on the value of expressions and program variables as the program runs.

DATA TRANSFER

The most used command for transferring data is MOV and its syntax is

MOV destination, source

A copy of the data in the source is placed in the destination. The data in the source remains unaltered and no flags are changed by using this instruction.

The instruction has the following formats:

Format	Examples		Explanation
Register Addressing	mov ax, bx	mov dl, al	The data is copied from one register into another
Immediate Addressing	mov al, 07	mov ax, 0B23	The first example shows that the data to be transferred is included in the instruction. The second example names the actual source address within the instruction. Note that these can be both 8-bit or 16-bit operations depending on where the whole register or just the upper or lower byte is used.
Direct Addressing	mov al, addloc	move 553B, al	The first example shows al being given a copy of the contents of the address held in the variable addloc. (ie determine the address held as addloc, go to that memory address, get its contents and copy it into al). The second example shows the contents of al being placed into the memory address 553Bh.
Indirect Addressing	move al,[bx]	mov al,[addloc]	In these examples, bx and addloc are not the addresses where the data is stored. They are 'pointers' - they store the addresses of the memory locations which hold the actual data. The first example shows al being given a copy of the contents of the address held in the register bx. (ie fetch the address stored in bx, go to that memory address, get its contents and copy it into al). The second example shows al being given a copy of the contents of the memory address held in addloc.
Indexed Addressing	mov dx, bx[si]	mov al, list[si]	The Intel series use a Source Index register to form indexed addresses. This is very useful where a set of values are held in memory and have to be sequentially fetched and processed. The data could be a set of modem commands, a printer control sequence or a series of characters comprising a text message. In each case, the data has to be fetched one byte at a time starting at the first memory address holding the data sequence. After each byte is processed the pointer points to the next piece of data to be processed. The first example shows register dx being fed data stored at the memory location held in bx+si. As si is incremented, the data is sequentially addressed and fed to to dx. The second example shows al being supplied with data from list (the label for an address). The contents of al will first contain the contents of list+0, then list+1, list+2 and so on, as the SI register is incremented This addressing method need not be used solely for reading data in a sequential manner. If the fifth byte in the series is required to be accessed, SI is set to 4 (since the first item would be si=0). This allows random access to the data.

The use of labels to replace actual addresses is also known as 'implied addressing'.
The second example on the last page used immediate addressing (ie MOV DL, 58 and MOV AH, 02).
The third example also used register addressing (ie MOV DL, AL).

BRANCHING

As in high level programming, the flow of code is not entirely sequential. Instructions are not normally carried out in strict order - starting at the beginning and finishing at the end.   One some occasions a part of a program may never be called (eg code for sounding an alarm) or may be called several times (eg code to print three copies of a text).   These *'jumps'* to sections of code have two formats:

Unconditional

The jump to a new address is carried out without any reference to the condition of flags in the flags register. For example JMP 1234 or JMP addloc. The sample code is the earlier PRNKEY program with an additional line JMP 100 which passes control back to address 100h (the start of the program code).   The program endlessly waits for keyboard input and displays the ASCI value to the screen.   The code provides no way to end the program and the user has to press Ctrl-C (the Ctrl and C keys pressed at the same time) to end the program.

Data to enter	Meaning
RCX	Set the file size to 16 bytes
10	
N PRNKEY.COM	Name the file
A	Assemble the following code
MOV AH, 08	Choose a keyboard read
INT 21	Read keyboard value into AL
MOV DL, AL	Copy ASCII value to DL
MOV AH, 02	Choose the display option
INT 21	Call the DOS INT 21 routine
JMP 100	Loop back to start of program
<Enter>	Signals end of code
W	Write a COM file
Q	Exit DEBUG

For those assemblers that support labels, the coding is much easier to understand.
Text descriptions are used to replace absolute addresses making reading and debugging much easier.   In addition, extra instructions can be added without having to recalculate absolute addresses for jumps (as would be required with DEBUG).

```
Loop:
MOV AH, 08
INT 21
MOV DL, AL
MOV AH, 02
INT 21
JMP loop
```

Conditional

Conditional jumps are performed by:
* testing for a particular condition
* jumping dependent upon the result of the test

The contents of the Flags Register (eg carry flag, zero flag or overflow flag) are set after arithmetic or logical operations are carried out.   So, the program flow can be altered by testing the condition of flags. For example, program execution might jump to an error message if an overflow is detected.
The most common conditional jumps are:

Test	Purpose
JZ	Make the jump if the zero flag is set
JNZ	Make the jump if the zero flat is clear
JC	Make the jump if the carry flag is set

The example program shows the CMP instruction being used. Its syntax is
CMP destination, source
It will set the zero flag if both operands are identical and the carry flag is set if the value in the source is greater than the destination value.

The program shown reads and displays all keyboard entries until an upper case A is entered.   After reading the keyboard, the ASCII value found is placed in register AL. The value in AL is then compared with 41h, the value of an upper case A.   If AL also contains 41h, the zero flag is set; otherwise it remains clear.
If the zero flag is set, the JZ 110 instruction moves the pointer to address 110h. Since the starting address is 100h,

Data to enter	Meaning
RCX	Set the file size to 32 bytes
20	
N PRKEY2.COM	Name the file
A	Assemble the following code
MOV AH, 08	Choose a keyboard read
INT 21	Read keyboard value into AL
CMP AL, 41	Is key upper-case A?
JZ 110	If 'A' then go to end program
MOV DL, AL	Copy ASCII value to DL
MOV AH, 02	Choose the display option
INT 21	Call the DOS INT 21 routine
JMP 100	Loop back to start of program
MOV AH, 4C	Set for program termination
INT 21	Call the DOS INT 21 routine
<Enter>	Signals end of code
W	Write a COM file
Q	Exit DEBUG

```
Loop:
MOV AH, 08
INT 21
CMP AL, 41
JZ close
MOV DL, AL
MOV AH, 02
INT 21
JMP loop
close:
MOV AH, 4C
INT 21
```

this is 17 bytes into the program and points at the MOV AH, 4C instruction. The program continues its execution from this point and runs the termination code.
If the two operands are not equal (ie the keyboard entry was not an upper case A), the zero flag is not set.   In this case, the program does not branch to address 110h and execution moves on to the next instruction (MOV DL, AL).
As before, the use of labels would make the program more legible and less error-prone.

ARITHMETIC

ADD

The syntax for this instruction is

ADD destination, source

The destination and source operands are added together and the result is placed in the destination operand. If the result is too big to fit in the destination, the carry flag is set. The example program reads in upper case characters, converts them to lower case and displays them; the program terminates when a lower case x is entered.

This is similar to the last example, with the addition of the ADD DL, 20 instruction. This adds 20h on to the ASCII value read, since the difference between upper and lower case ASCII characters is 32 (eg 'A' is 65 while 'a' is 97).

Data to enter	Meaning
RCX	Set the file size to 32 bytes
20	
N ADDON.COM	Name the file
A	Assemble the following code
MOV AH, 08	Choose a keyboard read
INT 21	Read keyboard value into AL
ADD AL, A0	Add 160 to register AL
JC 10C	If carry, jump to end program
MOV DL, AL	Copy new ASCII value to DL
JMP 10E	Jump to display code
MOV DL, 43	Place 'C' in DL
MOV AH, 02	Call the DOS INT 21 routine
INT 21	Loop back to start of program
MOV AH, 4C	Set for program termination
INT 21	Call the DOS INT 21 routine
<Enter>	Signals end of code
W	Write a COM file
Q	Exit DEBUG

Data to enter	Meaning
RCX	Set the file size to 32 bytes
20	
N LOWER.COM	Name the file
A	Assemble the following code
MOV AH, 08	Choose a keyboard read
INT 21	Read keyboard value into AL
CMP AL, 78	Is key lower case 'x'?
JZ 112	If so, jump to end program
ADD AL, 20	Add 32 on to register AL
MOV DL, AL	Copy new ASCII value to DL
MOV AH, 02	Choose the display option
INT 21	Call the DOS INT 21 routine
JMP 100	Loop back to start of program
MOV AH, 4C	Set for program termination
INT 21	Call the DOS INT 21 routine
<Enter>	Signals end of code
W	Write a COM file
Q	Exit DEBUG

The next program demonstrates the JC instruction. Like the above program, it reads keyboard characters, adds to the ASCII value and displays them.

This program adds 160 (ie A0h) on to the ASCII value read. If the total of the ASCII value and 160 can be contained in AL (ie a value no greater than 255), the updated ASCII value is displayed. This will produce odd characters on the screen since the values will be outside the normal alphanumeric range of characters.

If the total is greater than 255, the carry flag will be set and the JC 10C instruction will detect this carry situation and display a 'C' on the screen

SUB

The syntax for this instruction is

SUB destination, source

The destination and source operands are added together and the result is placed in the destination operand. If the source operand is a greater value than the destination operand, the carry flag is set.

The example program is the opposite of the earlier LOWER.COM program. It accepts keyboard input and subtracts 32 from the ASCII value to convert it to its upper case equivalent. It than displays the character on the screen. The program is terminated by entering a lower case 'x'.

INC/DEC

The INC instruction has a syntax of

INC operand

Data to enter	Meaning
RCX	Set the file size to 32 bytes
20	
N UPCASE.COM	Name the file
A	Assemble the following code
MOV AH, 08	Choose a keyboard read
INT 21	Read keyboard value into AL
CMP AL, 78	Is key lower case 'X'?
JZ 112	If so, jump to end program
SUB AL, 20	Subtract 32 from register AL
MOV DL, AL	Copy new ASCII value to DL
MOV AH, 02	Choose the display option
INT 21	Call the DOS INT 21 routine
JMP 100	Loop back to start of program
MOV AH, 4C	Set for program termination
INT 21	Call the DOS INT 21 routine
<Enter>	Signals end of code
W	Write a COM file
Q	Exit DEBUG

and adds one to the existing value of the operand. The operand can be the contents of a memory address or can be a register (excluding segment registers).

The DEC instruction has the opposite effect - that of reducing an operand's value by one.

NB

These differ from *'ADD operand, 1'* or *'SUB operand, 1'* in that INC and DEC commands to not alter the carry flag.

MUL

This instruction expects one of the operands to be placed in the AL register prior to being called. Its syntax is

> MUL source

where source is the second operand; this could be the contents of a register (eg MUL DL) or the contents of a memory address (eg MUL addloc).

Data to enter	Meaning
RCX	Set the file size to 16 bytes
10	
N MUL.COM	Name the file
A	Assemble the following code
MOV AL, 08	Place 8 in AL
MUL 09	Multiply AL by 9
MOV DL, AL	Copy value to DL
MOV AH, 02	Choose the display option
INT 21	Call the DOS INT 21 routine
MOV AH, 4C	Set for program termination
INT 21	Call the DOS INT 21 routine
<Enter>	Signals end of code
W	Write a COM file
Q	Exit DEBUG

If the source operand is a byte, (eg MUL 2F) then the result is placed in AX.

If the source operand is a double byte (eg MUL 14E7) then the lower 16 bits of the result are placed in AX and the 16 most significant bits are placed in the DX register.

The example program shows 8 being multiplied by 9. This produces 72 which is the ASCII code for an upper case 'H'.

Changing the values for the commencing value in AL or changing the multiplier will produce different output results.

DIV

First a quick refresher on terminology.   Consider the division of 22 by 4 below

> 22/4

The 22 is the dividend while the 4 is the divisor.   It will produce an answer of 5 with a remainder of 2; the 5 is referred to as the quotient.

The assembler instruction can handle single or double-byte operations.

Its syntax is

> DIV source

where the source is a single register byte (eg DIV DL) or a double memory byte (eg DIV addloc).

With single byte divisions, the dividend is placed in AX and the divisor is another single byte register.   The quotient is placed in AL while the remainder is placed in AH.

With double byte divisions, the dividend is placed in DX:AX (ie LSBs in AX) and the divisor is placed in another double byte register. The quotient is placed in AX while the remainder is placed in DL.

The example program divides 242 by 3.   Being byte operations, only the AX and DL registers are involved. The remainder is ignored by the program with the quotient being placed in AL and transferred to DL for display. Since the quotient is 80d it will display an upper case 'P'.

Data to enter	Meaning
RCX	Set the file size to 16 bytes
10	
N DIVR.COM	Name the file
A	Assemble the following code
MOV DL, 3	Place 3 in AL (ie divisor)
MOV AX, F2	Place 242 in AX (ie dividend)
DIV DL	Divide AX by DL
MOV DL, AL	Copy quotient to DL
MOV AH, 02	Choose the display option
INT 21	Call the DOS INT 21 routine
MOV AH, 4C	Set for program termination
INT 21	Call the DOS INT 21 routine
<Enter>	Signals end of code
W	Write a COM file
Q	Exit DEBUG

DB

All programs need to produce text for menus, error messages, prompts, etc.   This can be achieved using the DB instruction.   This stands for 'Define Byte' and allows the programmer to insert variables or strings of characters into the program.   The assembler recognises the DB directive, places the text into the program but does not attempt to convert the characters into machine code instructions.

Examples are:

Entry			Meaning
total	DB	3	A numerical variable is created with a value of 2
mark	DB	"Y"	A text variable has "Y" as its commencing value
msg	DB	"Here is a string of characters"	A string is defined with the label msg

All assemblers support the use of DB but DEBUG does not allow labels and the last entry would be simply entered as

> DB   "Here is a long string of characters"

STRING WRITING (1)

This example program demonstrates two techniques - the use of DB and indexed addressing.

The text string "Dumbreck Publishing" is declared at the end of the code using a DB directive. The string is nineteen characters in length and, when assembled, commences at location 114h. Register CL is used as a counter and is given an initial value of 13h (the length of the string).

The program uses *indexed addressing*; The instruction MOV DX, 114[SI] will, on the first run through the loop, place the contents of location 114 (ie 114+0) into DX for displaying. On the next circuit of the loop, DX is given the contents of location 115 (ie 114+1).

In each circuit of the loop, the offset is incremented to point at the next character - while the counter is decremented. When the counter is zero, the loop is exited and the program is terminated.

Data to enter	Meaning
RCX	Set the file size to 48 bytes
30	
N IDX.COM	Name the file
A	Assemble the following code
MOV CL, 13	Set the counter to 19d
MOV SI, 00	Set offset to zero
MOV DX, 114[SI]	Fetch a text character
MOV AH, 02	Choose the display option
INT 21	Call the DOS INT 21 routine
INC SI	Add 1 to offset
DEC CL	Decrement the counter
JNZ 105	Loop if counter not empty
MOV AH, 4C	Set for program termination
INT 21	Call the DOS INT 21 routine
DB "Dumbreck Publishing"	
<Enter>	Signals end of code
W	Write a COM file
Q	Exit DEBUG

STRING WRITING (2)

Data to enter	Meaning
RCX	Set the file size to 32 bytes
20	
N DBS.COM	Name the file
A	Assemble the following code
MOV AH, 09	Choose 'display string' option
MOV DX, 10B	Point to start of string
INT 21	Call the DOS INT 21 routine
MOV AH, 4C	Set for program termination
INT 21	Call the DOS INT 21 routine
DB "Dumbreck Publishing$"	
<Enter>	Signals end of code
W	Write a COM file
Q	Exit DEBUG

MSDOS provides a function that is dedicated to displaying text strings. DX is set to point at the start of the string while AH is given the value of 9.

Calling INT 21 will display the string.

Unlike the previous example, the routine has no counter to tell it when the end of the string is reached. Instead, this routine requires that a dollar sign be placed at the end of the text string. When the routine fetches the dollar character, it does not display it; the character is used to terminate the display routine.

LOGIC OPERATIONS

Pages 76 and 77 explained the functions of various logical operations and gave practical uses for each. These can now be re-examined as assembler routines.

AND

The program reads in a keyboard value. If the key read is lower case, then it will not have bit 6 set, whereas all upper case characters have bit 6 set. This is because the difference between the lower and upper case ASCII value of any letter is 32 and 32 is the equivalent of setting bit 6 in the binary pattern. So, subtracting 32 from the ASCII value converts it from lower to upper case. This achieved by AND, DF since DF is the hex for 223. This provides a *'mask'* which allows all of the binary pattern, apart from the 6th bit (value 32), to appear in the output.

```
        example input   01100001
        AND with 223    11011111
        example output  01000001
```

Data to enter	Meaning
RCX	Set the file size to 32 bytes
20	
N ANDS.COM	Name the file
A	Assemble the following code
MOV AH, 08	Choose a keyboard read
INT 21	Read keyboard value into AL
AND AL, DF	Filter out bit 6 (ie subtract 32)
CMP AL, 58	Has 'X' been entered?
JZ 112	If so, jump to end program
MOV DL, AL	Copy ACSII value into DL
MOV AH, 02	Choose the display option
INT 21	Call the DOS INT 21 routine
JMP 100	Loop back to start of program
MOV AH, 4C	Set for program termination
INT 21	Call the DOS INT 21 routine
<Enter>	Signals end of code
W	Write a COM file
Q	Exit DEBUG

Since upper case characters have the sixth bit set to zero, the ANDing process leaves the value unaffected. All typing, whether upper or lower case, is displayed in lower case.

This technique is widely used and has many applications. For example, Novell uses this technique with its Maximum Rights Mask and Inherited Rights Mask to enforce group and user securities on its LAN operating system.

OR

This program performs the opposite function to the previous example. All alphabetic text entered at the keyboard is displayed in lower case, whether the user types in upper or lower case.

Lower case entries are left untouched and upper case entries are converted to lower case.

Since no lower case alphabetic characters have their 6th bit set, 32 has to be added to the input value to provide a lower case output. This is achieved by ORing the input with 32d. With lower case letters, the 6th bit is already set and ORing with 32d has no effect.

Upper case entries do not have the 6th bit set and the ORing with 32d ensures that the bit is set.

Data to enter	Meaning
RCX	Set the file size to 32 bytes
20	
N ORS.COM	Name the file
A	Assemble the following code
MOV AH, 08	Choose a keyboard read
INT 21	Read keyboard value into AL
OR AL, 20	Set bit 6 (ie add 32)
CMP AL, 78	Has 'x' been entered?
JZ 112	If so, jump to end program
MOV DL, AL	Copy ACSII value into DL
MOV AH, 02	Choose the display option
INT 21	Call the DOS INT 21 routine
JMP 100	Loop back to start of program
MOV AH, 4C	Set for program termination
INT 21	Call the DOS INT 21 routine
<Enter>	Signals end of code
W	Write a COM file
Q	Exit DEBUG

XOR

This example program continually accepts keyboard input and displays it on the screen, until the space bar is pressed. The coding is identical to earlier examples with the exception of the following lines:

Data to enter	Meaning
RCX	Set the file size to 32 bytes
20	
N XORS.COM	Name the file
A	Assemble the following code
MOV AH, 08	Choose a keyboard read
INT 21	Read keyboard value into AL
XOR AL, 20	Was space bar pressed?
JZ 110	If so, jump to end program
MOV DL, AL	Copy ACSII value into DL
MOV AH, 02	Choose the display option
INT 21	Call the DOS INT 21 routine
JMP 100	Loop back to start of program
MOV AH, 4C	Set for program termination
INT 21	Call the DOS INT 21 routine
<Enter>	Signals end of code
W	Write a COM file
Q	Exit DEBUG

XOR AL, 20

JZ 110

The ASCII value for a space is 32d (20h). The keyboard input value, held in AL, is XORed with 20h.

If the keyboard input is the space bar, then:

Input value	00100000
ASCII for space	00100000
Result of XORing	00000000

Any other input from the keyboard produces a different ACSII code. For example, upper case 'A' produces:

Input value for 'A'	01000101
ASCII for space	00100000
Result of XORing	01100101

In the first case, the output result was zero. In every other case, the output will not be zero. The JZ 100 instruction tests the zero flag. If it is clear, the result of the XOR did not produce a zero and the program can continue to display the character. If the zero flag is set, the XOR produced a zero output. This means that the space bar was pressed and the program jumps to the termination sequence.

ROTATE & SHIFT INSTRUCTIONS

A number of instructions are available to alter the positions of the bits within a register or memory location.

SHL

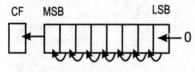

Each data bit in the location, whether a zero or a one, is shifted one bit to the left. The data in bit 0 is moved into bit1, the data in bit 1 is moved into bit 2, and so on. The bit in the most significant bit is moved into the carry flag. A zero is moved into the empty LSB.

So, if the AL register contained 10001010, the instruction

SHL AL, 1

would result in 1 (the MSB) being placed in the carry flag and the AL register's contents would be altered to 00010100. With the same commencing 10001010 in AL, the instruction

SHL AL, 2

would result in a 0 being placed in the carry flag and AL's contents would be altered to 00101000.

The contents of the carry flag after each shift can be tested using the JC test.

The example program reads in a character from the keyboard and displays its binary format as in the following example:

J=01001010

When the keyboard entry is accepted, the binary pattern 01001010 is held in the AL register. It is transferred to BL and each bit is placed into the carry flag in sequence using the

SHL BL, 1

instruction. Since bits shift to the left, the MSB is the first to be placed in the carry flag. This ensures that the bit pattern is displayed on the screen in the correct order (ie MSB through to LSB). The carry flag is tested after each shift using the

JC 11B

instruction. If the carry flag is set (ie contains a 1), the program jumps to the code that places the ASCII value for one into the display routine. If the carry flag is clear (ie contains a 0), the ASCII value for 0 is placed into the display routine.

The instruction DEC CX decrements the counter and will continually loop back for another shift/display until the counter is reduced to zero.

```
RCX                      ;set the file size to 48 bytes
30
N SHL.COM                ;name the file
A                        ;assemble the code
MOV AH,08                ;read the keyboard
INT 21
MOV BL,AL
MOV DL,AL
MOV AH,02                ;print the character
INT 21
MOV DL,3D                ;print an equals symbol
INT 21
MOV CX,8                 ;set counter to 8
SHL BL,1                 ;move bit into carry flag
JC 11B                   ;if bit is 1 jump to display 1
MOV DL,30                ;ready to display 0
JMP 11D                  ;jump to display routine
MOV DL,31                ;ready to display 1
MOV AH,02                ; display contents of DL
INT 21
DEC CX                   ;decrement the counter
JNZ 113                  ;if not yet 0 loop again
MOV AH,4C                terminate program
INT 21
<enter>
W
Q
```

SHR

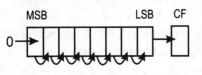

Each data bit in the location, whether a zero or a one, is shifted one bit to the right. The data in the MSB is moved into bit6, the data in bit 6 is moved into bit 5, and so on. The bit in the least significant bit is moved into the carry flag. A zero is moved into the empty MSB.

ROL

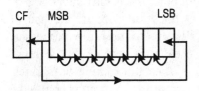

This instruction is similar to the SHL instruction except that the bit coming out of the MSB is placed in the carry flag and is also fed back into the LSB. So, the LSB is not automatically fed with a zero; it is supplied with the data from bit 7. In this way, the data in the location can be constantly rotated around.

ROR

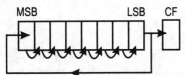

This instruction is identical to ROL except that the bits are rotated round in a rightwards direction.

The bit in bit 0 is placed both in the carry flag and is returned into the MSB, bit 7.

SUB PROGRAMS

As in high level programming, sections of program code may require to be used from different parts of the program. Sections of code to validate numbers, check dates, read or write to files, etc may be required at several points in the program. Rather than repeat the code over and over again, the code can be written once and called from those parts in the program requiring these services.

The diagram shows a main program taking a detour from its normal sequential run, to carry out instructions in a subroutine. When the sub routine code is completed, the program returns to the normal sequential flow.

Routine1 or Routine2 in the diagram could, in practice, be called many times by different parts of the program. The same routine could also be called many times over, if the program call was within a program loop.

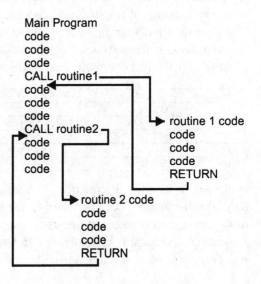

Sub program calls are completely different from the jumps discussed earlier. With jumps, the flow of the program permanently moves to the new area of code jumped to. With sub-programs, the branch to the procedure or function is purely a temporary deviation and the program always returns to the point from where the sub-program was called.

```
RCX
40
N CALLS.COM
A
MOV AH,08    ; input a character from the keyboard
INT 21
MOV BL, AL
MOV DL,AL    ; display the keyboard character
MOV AH, 02   ;      "     "     "     "
INT 21       ;      "     "     "     "
MOV DL,3D    ; display an equals symbol
INT 21       ;      "     "     "     "
MOV CX,8     ; set the counter to 8
SHL BL,1     ; move bit into carry flag (this is address 113)
JC 11C       ;
CALL 126     ;   CALL DISPLAY A ZERO
JMP 11F      ;
CALL 12D     ;   CALL DISPLAY A ONE (address 11C)
DEC CX       ; (address 11F)
JNZ 113
MOV AH,4C    ; termination routine
INT 21       ;      "        "

;=======================================
MOV DL,30    ; DISPLAY A ZERO ROUTINE (address 126)
MOV AH,02    ; the display routine
INT 21       ;   "      "      "
RET          ; return to calling code
;=======================================
MOV DL,31    ; DISPLAY A ONE ROUTINE (address 12D)
MOV AH,02    ; the display routine
INT 21       ;   "     "     "
RET          ; return to calling code

W
Q
```

The branch to the sub program is achieved with the CALL instruction. This may be a call to a label or address within the main program, or may be a separate routine from a library that will be linked in at the assembling stage. When a sub-routine finishes, control is passed back to the calling code, using the RET instruction.

In the example, calling the code in Routine1 was achieved by the instruction

CALL routine1

When the program finishes, control is passed back to the program at the point just after the call was made.

So in the example in the previous diagram, after calling Routine1 control would return to the program instruction that immediately follows the CALL instruction.

The example program is that of the previous code to display the binary pattern of a keypress.

It has been altered so that there are separate routines to print out 0 and 1 characters.

Since DEBUG does not support the use of labels, the calls are to absolute addresses. So, CALL 126 calls the routine that starts at address 126. When the routine terminates, the program returns to carry out the instruction JMP 11F.

STACK OPERATIONS

In the above program, the code leaves the program at a particular point in the code, runs one of the sub-routines and returns to the correct position in the original code. The reason it knows where to return is that it stores the return address prior to executing the sub-routine. This address is the one held in the IP (Instruction Pointer). IP always holds the address of the next instruction to be executed. This address is taken from the IP register and placed in a temporary storage area in memory, known as the 'stack'. The IP is then fed with the address of the start of the sub-routine. On termination of the sub-routine, the stored address is fetched back from the stack and placed back in the IP. The program now runs from this address. Consider the table below which is a fragment from the above program. The instruction at

Address	Contents	Meaning
115	JC 11C	
117	CALL 126	Call display a zero
11A	JMP 11F	
11C	CALL 12D	Call display a one
11F	DEC CX	

address 117 is to call the sub-routine to display a zero. The following instruction is held in address 11A. The address 11A is placed on the stack and the IP is given the address 126 (the start of the sub-routine). When the sub-routine terminates, the value 11A is taken off the stack and placed in the IP. The program then continues in its normal sequence. Similarly, the value 11F is placed on the stack prior to calling the second sub-routine. 12D is placed in the IP so that the CPU executes the code in the sub-routine. On termination, 11F is taken off the stack and placed in the IP.

In practice, the stack is in regular use and stores a range of values for differing activities such as interrupt handling, procedure and function calls and temporary data storage areas.

The most important fact about the stack is that it is a LIFO structure. This means *'Last In, First Out'* and indicates that items are placed on the stack in strict order. Items are pulled off the stack in the <u>reverse</u> order that they were stored. So, if items are placed on the stack in the order data1, data2, data3, data4, data5 - then they are removed from the stack in the order data5, data4, data3, data2, data1.

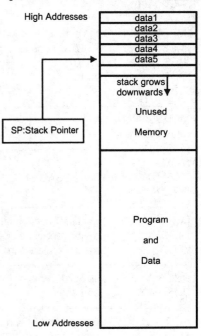

The actual addresses used by the stack are at the top of the computer's memory map and are pointed to by the Stack Pointer (SP register). This means that the <u>first</u> item on the stack is placed in the <u>highest</u> part of the stack memory and the stack pointer points at that address. When a second item is placed on the stack, it occupies the second highest position in the stack memory and the stack pointer value is reduced to point to this lower address. As the stack grows <u>up</u> in usage capacity, it grows <u>down</u> in memory and the SP holds lower and lower values.

If a program was badly written and always placed items on the stack without ever removing them, the stack would grow to a point that it would overwrite the program instructions held in memory. To prevent this, the programmer can allocate how memory to allocate for use as a stack. If this limit is reached, any further attempts to write to the stack would produce 'stack overflow' errors. It is the responsibility of the programmers to ensure that all items placed on the stack are eventually removed by the program.

Items are placed on the stack with the instruction

> PUSH operand

where the operand can be a segment register, a general purpose 16-bit register (ie AX, BX, CX, DX) or a memory location's contents. The instruction will not place an 8-bit register on the stack (eg PUSH AL is not allowed). The instruction

> POP operand

has the opposite effect to PUSH with the item last stored on the stack being placed in the operand. An example of stack operations is shown in the next example program.

NB

Since the stack is a LIFO structure, it is vital that the programmer ensure that POPs from the stack are carried out in the corresponding and opposite sequence to the PUSHes to the stack.

So, a sequence of PUSHes of AX, BX, CX, DX has to be followed by POPs of DX, CX, BX, AX. If the items are removed from the stack in the wrong order, the program will almost certainly crash.

FULLY FEATURED ASSEMBLERS

DEBUG was capable of handling all the small fragments of code from the previous pages. However, it does not handle labels, macros, variables, etc. For the last examples, the features of more developed products such as TASM are employed.

The minimum outline of a TASM script is as shown.

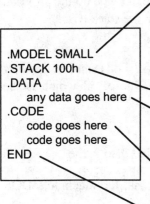

```
.MODEL SMALL
.STACK 100h
.DATA
    any data goes here
.CODE
    code goes here
    code goes here
END
```

The model can be 'small' or 'large'. The small model expects all jumps and calls to occur within a single addressing segment , usually 64k and executes quickly. The large model is for larger programs and is slower due to its use of the full SEGMENT:OPERAND operand (compared to the small model's OFFSET operand.

The STACK instruction allocates 256 bytes for stack operations.

The DATA section holds any variables and text messages and is treated as data by the assembler (ie it does not attempt to translate the data into machine instructions).

The CODE segment holds all the program instructions and numbers are entered in hex notation (ie 256 is entered as 100h). If the number is not followed by the letter 'h' it is assumed to be the decimal value one hundred.

The END is a directive, informing the assembler that the program is finished.

```
.MODEL SMALL
.STACK 100h
.DATA
  MESSAGE1   DB "Your DOS version is $"
  MESSAGE2   DB 10,13,"Time to upgrade?$"
  BESTVER    EQU 07h
.CODE
Start:
   ;----------------------------------------
   MOV AX, @DATA
   MOV DS, AX
   ;----------------------------------------
   MOV AH, 9
   MOV DX, OFFSET MESSAGE1
   INT 21h
   ;----------------------------------------
   MOV AH,30h    ; get DOS version into AX
   INT 21h       ; major version is in AL
                 ; minor version is in AH
   ;----------------------------------------
   PUSH AX       ; save AX register
   PUSH AX       ; and again
   ;----------------------------------------
   ADD AL,30h    ; convert to ASCII number
   MOV DL,AL     ; display the major
   MOV AH,02     ; version number
   INT 21h
   ;----------------------------------------
   MOV DL,2Eh
   MOV AH,2      ; print a decimal point
   INT 21h
   ;----------------------------------------
   POP AX        ; recover original AX value
   ;----------------------------------------
   ADD AH,30h    ; display the minor
   MOV DL,AH     ; version number
   MOV AH,2
   INT 21h
   ;----------------------------------------
   POP AX        ; recover original AX value
   CMP AL, BESTVER
   JE Done
   MOV AH, 9
   MOV DL, OFFSET MESSAGE2
   INT 21h
   ;----------------------------------------
   Done:
      MOV AH,4Ch ; terminate program
      INT 21h
END Start
```

TASM EXAMPLE

The example program was written using the Borland's Turbo Assembler (TASM). When run, it informs the user of the version of DOS present on the computer.

It provides a practical example of stack operations and also uses the following new features:
- EQU directive
- Labels
- Data offsets

'Labels' are used in the DATA segment. They define the labels 'MESSAGE1' and 'MESSAGE2' as containing text strings.

The data segment also contains the line

```
BESTVER   EQU   07h
```

This is an 'EQU Assembler Directive'. The label called BESTVER is defined as a constant with the value 7. The label can now be inserted throughout the program, as many times as is required. When the program is assembled, the assembler replaces every occurrence of the word BESTVER in the script with the value 7. As you can see, it adds no extra functionality to the program; it just makes the program easier to read.

The instructions

```
MOV AX, @DATA
MOX DS, AX
```

ensure that all data transfer instructions, unless otherwise directed, will refer to the current segment.

The writing of text strings is achieved by referring to the offset where the string is stored. So, the instruction

```
MOV DX, OFFSET MESSAGE1
```

loads DX with the start location for the first text message, prior to calling the 'print string' DOS routine.

Calling INT 21 with AH=30h, fetches the DOS version number (eg v4.0, v6.22, v7.0) and places the major version number in AL; the minor version number (the part after the decimal point) into AH. However, register AH is required later in the program to be set to 2 , prior to calling the 'print character' routine. This would mean that the version number would be overwritten. To prevent this, AX is pushed on to the stack, for later retrieval. In fact, AH is overwritten twice by the program and AX is therefore pushed on to the stack twice.

The instruction

```
ADD AH,30h
```

takes the decimal value stored in AH and converts it into its ASCII equivalent. For example, a major version number of 5 would have 48 (30h) added to it producing an ASCII value of 53 which is the character '5'.

The instruction

```
CMP AL, BESTVER
```

compares the machine's major version number with the value 7. If the AL value is also 7, the

```
JE Done
```

instruction exits the program. If the AL value is not 7, the user is reminded that the machine's DOS version is not the most up-to-date version.

MACROS

With EQU, a piece of data was specified once, at the start of the program. In the previous example program, it was

        BESTVER EQU 07h

The label was then included in the program in the knowledge that the assembler would replace every occurrence of the label in the script with the value associated with the label.

Macros take the process a stage further with whole segments of code being given a name and the name being included in the program code area.

When the script is being converted to object code, the assembler replaces each occurrence of the macro label with a copy of the code segment contained in the macro. Like the EQU, it adds no extra functionality but allows a faster development of the program, with less errors.

The leftmost example shows a program with the CODE section containing the program code and an area which defines all the program's procedures. Each procedure is headed by a label and finishes with a 'RET' instruction.

The rightmost example shows the same program with a number of macros. Each macro has a label followed by the word 'MACRO' and the macro code. The macro finishes with the 'ENDM' instruction.

Each macro is called by placing its label in the code. Thus, where *getdata* appears in the code the code lines of the macro will be substituted at the assembly stage.

```
Using Procedures

.MODEL SMALL
.STACK 100h
.DATA
.CODE
Start:
  code
  code
  CALL getdata
  CALL printit
  code
  code
  CALL printit
  ...
  ...
  code
  CALL getdata
  CALL printit
  code
  code
GETDATA:
  code
  RET
PRINTIT:
  code
  RET
END Start
```

```
Using Macros

.MODEL SMALL
.STACK 100h
.DATA
.CODE
  PRINTIT   MACRO
    macro code here
  ENDM
  GETDATA  MACRO
    macro code here
  ENDM
Start:
  code
  code
  GETDATA
  PRINTIT
  code
  code
  PRINTIT
  ...
  ...
  code
  GETDATA
  PRINTIT
  code
  code
END Start
```

PASSING PARAMETERS

Macros provide for the passing of parameters. Thus a macro definition of

                PRINTIT MACRO CHAROUT
                   MOV DX, CHAROUT
                   MOV AH, 02
                   INT 21h
                ENDM

will assemble the code incorporating the data in the parameter.

Thus, the following instructions are valid:

Instruction	Meaning
PRINTIT 68	Assemble as a routine to display the character with ASCII value of 68d
PRINTIT 44h	Assemble as a routine to display the character with hex value of 44h
PRINTIT 'D'	Assemble as a routine to display the character 'D'
PRINTIT 10	Assemble as a routine to produce a line feed
PRINTIT 13	Assemble as a routine to produce a carriage return

MACROS vs PROCEDURES

PROS

- Faster than procedures, since there is no time wasted making the CALL and RET operations.
- Procedures don't know what state registers were in before it was called and has to PUSH registers, carry out their code, then POP registers before closing the procedure. Since programmers insert the macro label during programming, the conditions of registers are known and set prior to calling the macro. This eliminates many unnecessary and time-consuming stack operations.

CONS

- Where the macro is called many times, the assembled program can be substantially larger than one using procedures.
- Not as easily debugged, since procedures can be easily *stepped* through with most debuggers.

COMPARISON OF PC BUS ARCHITECTURES

The following pages examine the performance characteristics of the range of personal microcomputers that have been manufactured, sold and used in the UK over the last fifteen years. All the machines discussed will still be in use for many years to come. The sales of new XT, AT, 386 and 486 ranges have dried up but there is a huge base of these machines already in use. In any case, the support technician will have to work with the whole range of machines, from the oldest XT to the newest Pentium.

As microcomputers have developed, there has been a race between the improving performance of the CPU, the memory, the peripherals - and the buses that connect them.

When considering various buses, the following questions should be asked:

- How much memory can be accessed ?
- How fast can it be accessed ?
- Is access to different components at different speeds required ?
- How much does it cost ?
- How flexible is the machine - (e.g. will cards from one machine still work in the new machine)

When examining various systems, there is no abstract 'correct answer'. The system for a user is only correct or incorrect for that user's needs. A user requiring a multi-user file server would find an old XT PC absolutely useless; a high-performance machine would be a necessity for such applications. On the other hand, a high-performance (and therefore very expensive) machine is wasted if it is only used for simple word processing since the speed of the system is only relevant for small periods (e.g. spell-checking a document); by far the greatest time sees the machine idling while the user thinks of the next word to type.

THE XT

The earliest PCs were the XT range, dating from the early 1980's and designed and manufactured by IBM. Many other companies produced *'clones'* - machines based on the architecture of the IBM XT, with only small differences to avoiding infringing IBM patents. These are often also known, more kindly, as *'PC compatibles'*

DATA BUS

The XT Data Bus was 8 bits wide (a single byte) and could therefore transfer a number between 0 and 255 at a time.

ADDRESS BUS

The Address Bus was 20 bit wide and so could access up to 1Mb of memory (1 multiplied by 2 raised to the power 20 gives over a million unique address locations)

CLOCK SPEED

Every computer has an oscillator that gives regular timed kicks to the CPU. These pulses are used to move the CPU through the individual activities that comprise each machine code instruction. Each machine code instruction can require one, two, three or four different clock pulses to ensure its completion. The XT was based on the 8088 processor and had a normal clock speed of 4.77MHz (i.e. 4.77million clock pulses per sec.)

GND	B1	A1	I/O CH CK
RESET DRV	B2	A2	D7
+5V	B3	A3	D6
IRQ 2	B4	A4	D5
-5V	B5	A5	D4
DRQ 2	B6	A6	D3
-12V	B7	A7	D2
reserved	B8	A8	D1
+12V	B9	A9	D0
GND	B10	A10	I/O CH RDY
MEMW	B11	A11	AEN
MEMR	B12	A12	A19
IOW	B13	A13	A18
IOR	B14	A14	A17
DACK 3	B15	A15	A16
DRQ 3	B16	A16	A15
DACK 1	B17	A17	A14
DRQ 1	B18	A18	A13
DACK 0	B19	A19	A12
CLK	B20	A20	A11
IRQ 7	B21	A21	A10
IRQ 6	B22	A22	A9
IRQ 5	B23	A23	A8
IRQ 4	B24	A24	A7
IRQ 3	B25	A25	A6
DACK 2	B26	A26	A5
T/C	B27	A27	A4
ALE	B28	A28	A3
+5V	B29	A29	A2
0 SC	B30	A30	A1
GND	B31	A31	A0

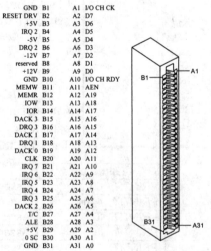

DATA RATE

The 8088 chip took four clock pulses to complete a transfer of data on the data bus. So, the data transfer rate is

bus width*clock speed/(8*clock pulses per transfer)

The wider the bus width, the more data can be transferred at a time; the greater the clock speed, the faster the transfer activities can be completed. On the other hand, some chips take more clock pulses to complete a transfer than others.

In the case of the XT, the data transfer rate is

$$8*4.77m/(8*4) = 1.2 \text{ million bytes per sec} = 1.14Mb/s$$

EXPANSION SLOT LAYOUT

The diagram shows the connector layout of the expansion slot. The slot connections carry not only the address and data lines, but also a range of power and control lines.

THE AT

The successor to the XT was the AT range of PC machines which use the 80286 chip with its improved capabilities.

DATA BUS

The width of the data bus was increased to 16 bits; this ensured greater throughput, as it could handle numbers from 0 to 64k at a time.

ADDRESS BUS

This was increased to 24 bit width. It was now capable of addressing 16Mb of memory. It was now possible to consider add-on memory (see section on extended memory). With the XT models, there was no point in adding extra memory chips above the 1Mb range, since the 8088 chip and the 20-bit address bus was unable to access the additional memory addresses.

CLOCK SPEED

The standard clock speed was increased to 8MHz, although faster machines (10MHz or 12MHz) are available. The 80286 is also able to transfer data in only two clock pulses, compared to the four required by the 8088.

DATA RATE - The data transfer rate was dramatically improved, due to the effect of greater data bus width and the improved chip design. The data transfer rate for an 8MHz system is

$$16*8m/(8*2) = 7.629Mb/s$$

However, there was a problem using the memory chips which were available at that time; their access time (the time required to read/write data to memory locations) was slower than the new improved chip and bus transfer rates.

Since the system can only run at the speed of its slowest element, the effective clock speed was reduced to that which memory could handle. This introduction of *'wait states'* was a reflection of the state of the art of chip development. With improved chips, the access time is faster and adverts talk of *'zero wait state'* systems. In practice, most ISA buses run at around 5Mb/s.

It was important that all cards currently in use with XTs would also be able to work in AT machines. Therefore, the bus layout would have to compatible - and still provide the extra data and address bus connections. This was achieved by keeping the original XT expansion bus and adding an extension section to the bus for the extra connections. In that way, XT cards would fit in the expansion slot, while AT cards would also use the slot extension.

This system is termed the *ISA* system (Industry Standard Architecture) and is the most popular PC bus.

GND	B1	A1	I/O CH CK
RESET DRV	B2	A2	D7
+5V	B3	A3	D6
IRQ 2	B4	A4	D5
-5V	B5	A5	D4
DRQ 2	B6	A6	D3
-12V	B7	A7	D2
reserved	B8	A8	D1
+12V	B9	A9	D0
GND	B10	A10	I/O CH RDY
MEMW	B11	A11	AEN
MEMR	B12	A12	A19
IOW	B13	A13	A18
IOR	B14	A14	A17
DACK 3	B15	A15	A16
DRQ 3	B16	A16	A15
DACK 1	B17	A17	A14
DRQ 1	B18	A18	A13
DACK 0	B19	A19	A12
CLK	B20	A20	A11
IRQ 7	B21	A21	A10
IRQ 6	B22	A22	A9
IRQ 5	B23	A23	A8
IRQ 4	B24	A24	A7
IRQ 3	B25	A25	A6
DACK 2	B26	A26	A5
T/C	B27	A27	A4
ALE	B28	A28	A3
+5V	B29	A29	A2
0 SC	B30	A30	A1
GND	B31	A31	A0
MEM CS 16	D1	C1	SBHE
I/O CS 16	D2	C2	A23
IRQ 10	D3	C3	A22
IRQ 11	D4	C4	A21
IRQ 12	D5	C5	A20
IRQ 13	D6	C6	A19
IRQ 14	D7	C7	A18
DACK 0	D8	C8	A17
DRQ 0	D9	C9	MEMR
DACK 5	D10	C10	MEMW
DRQ 5	D11	C11	D8
DACK 6	D12	C12	D9
DRQ 6	D13	C13	D10
DACK 7	D14	C14	D11
DRQ 7	D15	C15	D12
+5V	D16	C16	D13
MASTER	D17	C17	D14
GND	D18	C18	D15

THE 386/486

The range of micros based on the 80386/486 chip brought even better potential performance:

- DATA BUS - 32 bits wide (handling numbers from 0 to 4Gb)
- ADDRESS BUS - 32 bits wide (able to address up to 4Gb of memory)
- CLOCK SPEED - 20MHz up to 66MHz
- POTENTIAL DATA RATE = $32*66m/(8*2)$ = 132Mb/s
  (i.e. 32-bit bus, 66MHz clock, 2 clock pulses per transfer)

These demands were way beyond the capability of the normal ISA bus and alternative methods had to be found, if computers were to use this progress. To date, there have been four main responses:

1. The MCA bus
2. The EISA bus
3. A separate memory bus
4. Local bus systems - VESA and PCI

MCA

The IBM response was the introduction of the *MCA* (Micro Channel Architecture) bus with their new PS/2 range of machines in 1987. In fact, IBM introduced both 16-bit (for their 286 machines) and 32-bit versions of the bus. The design broke with tradition, both in construction and method of operation. The XT, ISA and EISA systems all use *'synchronous'* buses. In these systems, the data transfer rate of the bus is tied to the clock speed of the machine's processor. The MCA is *'asynchronous'* and runs as fast as it can in any particular situation.

ADVANTAGES:

- The standard speed for these boards was 20Mb/s, which can be specially jacked up to much greater speeds.
- The MCA add-on boards are physically much smaller than all other types of board.
- MCA buses cause less electromagnetic radiation.

DISADVANTAGES:

- Using a 16-bit board brings the machine performance back down nearer to the old ISA boards.
- IBM had strict licensing policies for MCA - even demanding back payments from any potential MCA clone-maker who had previously cloned XTs or ATs
- The technology, although still available, is largely ignored in the PC market and even IBM is dropping it from its range. MCA or PCI will be offered as options on their PC 700 server range and MCA is dropped entirely from their PC 300 desktop range.

ESYNC	B10	A10	VSYNC
GND	B9	A9	HSYNC
P5	B8	A8	BLANC
P4	B7	A7	GND
P3	B6	A6	P6
GND	B5	A5	EDCLK
P2	B4	A4	DCLK
P1	B3	A3	GND
P0	B2	A2	P7
GND	B1	A1	EVIDEO
Audio/GND	B1	A1	CD/SETUP
Audio	B2	A2	MADE 24
GND	B3	A3	GND
oscillator	B4	A4	A11
GND	B5	A5	A10
A23	B6	A6	A9
A22	B7	A7	+5V
A21	B8	A8	A8
GND	B9	A9	A7
A20	B10	A10	A6
A19	B11	A11	+5V
A18	B12	A12	A5
GND	B13	A13	A4
A17	B14	A14	A3
A16	B15	A15	+5V
A15	B16	A16	A2
GND	B17	A17	A1
A14	B18	A18	A0
A13	B19	A19	+12V
A12	B20	A20	ADL
GND	B21	A21	PREEMPT
IRQ 9	B22	A22	BURST
IRQ 3	B23	A23	-12V
IRQ 4	B24	A24	ARB 0
GND	B25	A25	ARB 1
IRQ 5	B26	A26	ARB 2
IRQ 6	B27	A27	-12V
IRQ 7	B28	A28	ARB 3
GND	B29	A29	ARB/GNT
reserved	B30	A30	TC
reserved	B31	A31	+5V
CHCK	B32	A32	S0
GND	B33	A33	S1
CMD	B34	A34	M/IO
CHRDYRTN	B35	A35	+12V
CD SFDBK	B36	A36	CD CHRDY
GND	B37	A37	D0
D1	B38	A38	D2
D3	B39	A39	+5V
D4	B40	A40	D5
GND	B41	A41	D6
CHRESET	B42	A42	D7
reserved	B43	A43	GND
reserved	B44	A44	DS 16 RIN
GND	B45	A45	REFRESH
D8	B48	A48	+5V
D9	B49	A49	D10
GND	B50	A50	D11
D12	B51	A51	D13
D14	B52	A52	+12V
D15	B53	A53	reserved
GND	B54	A54	SBHE
IORQ 10	B55	A55	CD DS 16
IORQ 11	B56	A56	+5V
IORQ 12	B57	A57	IRQ 14
GND	B58	A58	IRQ 15

EISA

The licensing demands and conditions of IBM produced a mixed response from other manufacturers. Some, like Olivetti and Research Machines, produced MCA machines under licence. Others, led by Compaq, produced their own improvement to the ISA bus. This is known as *EISA* (Extended Industry Standard Architecture).

DATA BUS - 32 bits wide (0-4Gb)

ADDRESS BUS - 32 bits wide (0-4Gb)

The bus widths, then, are identical to those of the MCA bus. The big advantage of EISA systems is their *'backward compatibility'*. Any card designed for the ISA system can still be used in an EISA bus. This involved a little ingenuity, since the EISA bus has enlarged data and address buses compared to the ISA bus.

BUS LAYOUT

The EISA expansion bus, at first glance, looks identical to an ISA bus. It is the same length and appears to have the same number of connectors on each side of the connector block. The trick in the design of the EISA bus is that it has TWO levels of connectors. The upper level is identical to the ISA bus, allowing normal ISA cards to be plugged in and used. It also has a second set of contacts which are set deeper into the expansion connection. These

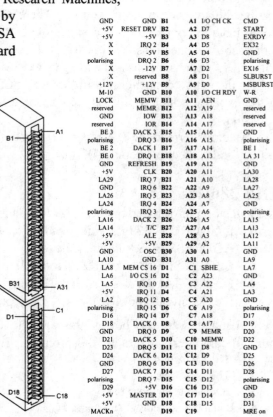

GND	GND	B1	A1	I/O CH CK	CMD
+5V	RESET DRV	B2	A2	D7	START
+5V	+5V	B3	A3	D8	EXRDY
X	IRQ 2	B4	A4	D5	EX32
X	-5V	B5	A5	D4	GND
polarising	DRQ 2	B6	A6	D3	polarising
X	-12V	B7	A7	D2	EX16
X	reserved	B8	A8	D1	SLBURST
+12V	+12V	B9	A9	D0	MSBURST
M-10	GND	B10	A10	I/O CH RDY	W-R
LOCK	MEMW	B11	A11	AEN	GND
reserved	MEMR	B12	A12	A19	reserved
GND	IOW	B13	A13	A18	reserved
reserved	IOR	B14	A14	A17	reserved
BE 3	DACK 3	B15	A15	A16	GND
polarising	DRQ 3	B16	A16	A15	polarising
BE 2	DACK 1	B17	A17	A14	BE 1
BE 0	DRQ 1	B18	A18	A13	LA 31
GND	REFRESH	B19	A19	A12	GND
+5V	CLK	B20	A20	A11	LA30
LA29	IRQ 7	B21	A21	A10	LA28
GND	IRQ 6	B22	A22	A9	LA27
LA26	IRQ 5	B23	A23	A8	LA25
LA24	IRQ 4	B24	A24	A7	GND
polarising	IRQ 3	B25	A25	A6	polarising
LA16	DACK 2	B26	A26	A5	LA15
LA14	T/C	B27	A27	A4	LA13
+5V	ALE	B28	A28	A3	LA12
+5V	+5V	B29	A29	A2	LA11
GND	OSC	B30	A30	A1	GND
LA10	GND	B31	A31	A0	LA9
LA8	MEM CS 16	D1	C1	SBHE	LA7
LA6	I/O CS 16	D2	C2	A23	GND
LA5	IRQ 10	D3	C3	A22	LA4
+5V	IRQ 11	D4	C4	A21	LA3
LA2	IRQ 12	D5	C5	A20	GND
polarising	IRQ 15	D6	C6	A19	polarising
D16	IRQ 14	D7	C7	A18	D17
D18	DACK 0	D8	C8	A17	D19
GND	DRQ 0	D9	C9	MEMR	D20
D21	DACK 5	D10	C10	MEMW	D22
D23	DRQ 5	D11	C11	D8	GND
D24	DACK 6	D12	C12	D9	D25
GND	DRQ 6	D13	C13	D10	D26
D27	DACK 7	D14	C14	D11	D28
polarising	DRQ 7	D15	C15	D12	polarising
D29	+5V	D16	C16	D13	GND
+5V	MASTER	D17	C17	D14	D30
+5V	GND	D18	C18	D15	D31
MACKn		D19	C19		MRE on

provide the extra address and data connections.

Plastic keys stop the ISA cards from penetrating to the bottom level of contacts. EISA cards have notches which match the keys. This allows the card to be pushed deeper into the connector and the cards extra connectors make contact with the lower level of bus connections.

DATA RATE

The EISA bus is synchronous and has to run at the slow speed of 8MHz, to allow it to use any slow speed ISA cards. So, the actual data transfer rate achieved is:

$$32*8m/(8*2) = 15.2Mb/s$$

An additional special data rate mode allows data to be transferred in a single clock cycle and this increases the data transfer rate to a maximum of 32Mb/s

Overall, then, the bus has to run at the speed of its slowest card. An EISA bus with an ISA card installed will only run at ISA speeds.

MCA systems, because of the IBM reputation, are the biggest sellers at the high performance end. EISA systems are common in network file servers but few manufacturers produced add-on cards apart from network cards, preventing its spread into the high performance workstation market.

SEPARATE MEMORY BUS

To maximise the computer's efficiency, it is essential that data be transferred between the processor and memory (and vice versa) as quickly as possible. When a user wishes to use a slow speed card in the computer, this should not be allowed to slow down these CPU/memory transfers. The solution from the 386 models onwards is to provide a separate high speed bus linking the processor and memory. All the communication between CPU and memory is carried over this bus. The normal ISA bus remains to handle disc, video, expansion slots, etc.

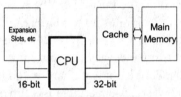

Standard 386/486 Architecture

ADVANTAGES:

- The memory chips can run as fast as the CPU will allow, while and slower speed cards are catered for on the separate slower bus. The system is running at its maximum speed.
- Now that the memory has its own separate bus, a block of even faster memory (cache memory) can be introduced between the main memory and the CPU. The cache memory is used to handle pages of memory data at a time. (see notes on memory)

LOCAL BUS SYSTEMS

Technological change left the original PC bus design lacking in terms of bus width and bus speed.

BUS WIDTH

The width of the data bus determines how much data can be transferred over a given period, This data could be memory reads/writes, disc read/writes or graphic card read/writes, along with data connected with a range of peripherals such as printers, modems, scanners, etc. The original IBM XT model had a data bus that was just 8 bits wide. The bus was common to the CPU, memory, etc. and the expansion slots used to plug in add-ons. This was increased to 16 bits for the AT model and 32 bits for the 386 and 486 machines. The bus architecture was then changed to that shown in the diagram. Although the bus between CPU and memory was increased, the data bus to the expansion slots was kept at 16-bit. This was to allow add-on cards designed for the older architectures, both 8-bit and 16-bit, to still be used on the newer machines. So graphics cards, although capable of greater throughput, are restricted to slower 16-bit data transfers. The problem also extends to disc controllers which are similarly slowed down.

BUS SPEED

The XT data bus was common to local chips and to extension boards and was clocked by the same CPU clock chip. So all chips and peripherals were clocked to run at 4.7MHz. Modern architecture may split the local and extension chips into separate buses, but the expansion bus is still separately clocked at a slower speed to allow old add-ons to be used. Even a 50MHz computer will have an expansion bus running at between 8MHz and 12MHz. Graphics cards, then, are being seriously under driven, slowing down video updates and operation of other peripheral cards. Even a fast Pentium CPU sits on a motherboard that keeps the main bus down to a theoretic maximum of 66MHz (33MHz in practice).

THE LOCAL BUS SOLUTION

All current computers use *'local bus'* architectures, where the expansion bus is 16-bit and is still clocked slowly for the benefit of slower add-on boards.   However, a *'local bus'* connects the memory, video and disc controllers to the CPU on a full 32-bit or 64-bit bus.   This bus is clocked at a much higher rate - up to that of the CPU - for maximum data transfer.   Consequently, all cards that run on the local bus outperform their equivalent ISA card versions.   Video performance, in particular, can be spectacularly speeded up but the benefits are available to disc controllers and other local bus cards.   The local bus boards still run ordinary application software and require no special operating system arrangements. Currently, the technology appears both in add-on cards and implemented on the motherboard.   There are two major variations in local bus technology - the VESA Local Bus and the Intel PCI bus.

VESA BUS

The first local bus standard is from VESA (Video Electronic Standards Association), known as the VL Bus.   This was available with a wide range of cards.   The bus is tied to the speed of the machine's CPU as the processor has to manage the timing of every card on the bus. The VESA standard provides

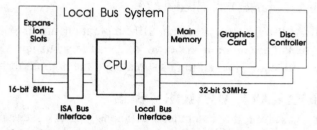

for clock rates up to 66MHz.   However, it states that plug-in cards should only be used on systems up to 40MHz.   The physical characteristics of the electrical connectors and timing problems affect performance beyond this limit.   So, local bus devices beyond 40MHz arc only an acccptable VESA standard if they are hard-wired to the motherboard, or are part of no more than two plug-in cards.   With 33MHz systems, there is a three device limit.   Practically, the VL-Bus system is optimised for 386/486 32-bit architecture at 33MHz working, although it provides the possible expansion to 64-bit bus width to accommodate the 586 chip. Video cards are now available from all major manufacturers; the Tseng ET4000 and the S3 chips, for example, appear in local bus versions.   The VESA system did not progress beyond the 486, with the PCI system taking over at Pentium level.

PCI BUS

The newest and most common system is the Intel PCI ('Peripheral Component Interconnect') Bus. Initially designed as a connection system between motherboard components, it was later developed into a full expansion bus system.   As can be seen from the diagram, the PCI bus exists as a local fast bus, separate from the slower ISA bus. A bridge controller allows the use of normal ISA cards on a normal ISA bus. In this respect it is similar to the VESA model. However, it decouples the CPU clock and data path from the bus and interfaces to it through a dedicated PCI chipset. The PCI bus is therefore independent of the machine's CPU. It works equally well with the 486, the Pentium or any future chips and is used with the DEC Alpha workstation and the PowerPC. All that is required is that each CPU have its own CPU-PCI chipset.   The chipset comprises two chips - the DPU (Data Path Unit) and CDC (Cache & Dram Controller) chips connect the PCI system to the processor's data bus and address bus respectively.

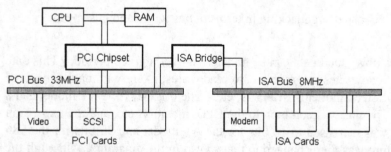

In theory, the system supports up to 10 PCI components, with each component able to talk to each other independent of the CPU.   However, the PCI-ISA bridge (a PCI-ISA chipset) counts as one of these components as do the DPU and CDC chips.   The video and SCSI adapters take up another two components.   Motherboards provide another three expansion slots. This does not add up to 10 because there is an assumed loss of signal through so many connectors; a PCI slot counts as two components.

The system is designed for a maximum operating speed of 66MHz but all current motherboards run at 33MHz, which is slower than the theoretical VESA bus maximum. However, it can easily support a 64-bit bus and this maintains the PCI system as a fast option.

With a 33MHz speed and a 32-bit bus it can produce a maximum data transfer rate of 132Mbps - identical to the VESA system's maximum.   However, since Pentiums use a 64-bit data bus, the PCI 64-bit system returns a 264Mb/sec maximum transfer rate. PCI systems are already replacing EISA systems on network servers.

Bus Type	Max Data Rate
XT	1.14Mb/s
ISA	7.629Mb/s
MCA	20Mb/s
EISA	32Mb/s
VESA	132Mb/s
PCI	132Mb/s
PCI/Pentium	264Mb/s

The PCI Bus conforms to the *'Energy Star'* requirements by running at 3.3volts, although a 5volt PCI card will be detected and still supplied with 5 volts.

All the major video card suppliers produce PCI video cards, disc controller cards, etc.

To allow the maximum flexibility, some older computer motherboards had a mix of expansion connectors - e.g. EISA with VESA, ISA with VESA, PCI with VESA, PCI with ISA and some even have ISA, VESA and PCI.   Multiple bus boards support all types of add-on cards, ISA cards plug into the ISA slots, PCI cards into PCI slots, etc.   For maximum benefit from the PCI system, as far as possible only PCI cards should be used for cards where fastest performance is required.   So, devices such as fast graphics cards, disc controllers and the new 100Mb/s network cards are best bought as PCI versions.

PCI CHIPSETS

The PCI chip has a crucial role in connecting the CPU and memory with the rest of the computer's resources.

Different chipsets provide differing facilities as shown in the current range below:

Chipset type	Features
FX	The original (ie early 1995) PCI Triton chipset of four chips. It introduced support for EDO RAM, pipeline burst cache and bus-mastered EIDE. 128Mb is the maximum RAM supported, with 64Mb being the maximum memory that can be cached. It has no ECC, USB or SDRAM support and cannot handle Concurrent PCI.
HX	Brought out in early 1996 as a business-machine chipset of two chips. It can address EDO RAM quicker than the FX but can't handle SDRAM. It provides ECC (error checking & correction) for DRAM. It supports multiple processors, USB and Concurrent PCI (regulates cards that have bus mastering to smooth out the data flow; activity on the PCI bus, CPU bus and ISA bus can be simultaneous). It caches up to 512Mb of RAM and supports MMX. It also supports EISA motherboards.
VX	Introduced along with the HX series, the four-chip VX chipset was aimed at the home user. It supports SDRAM, DIMM sockets, the USB, Concurrent PCI and MMX. Supports shared memory buffer systems (the motherboard's main memory is also used as graphics memory, to save costs). It can cache up to 64Mb of RAM. 128Mb is the maximum RAM supported. It has no ECC facility.
TX	Introduced in early 1997, this 2-chip set is the intended replacement for the VX. It supports 72-pin EDO and BEDO SIMMs and 168-pin SDRAM DIMMS, Ultra DMA-33 IDE (providing a 33Mb/s burst mode data transfer rate - ie twice that of an IDE drive). It supports Concurrent PCI and USB. It caches up to 64Mb of RAM. It is also optimised for MMX. It includes DPMA (Dynamic Power Management Architecture) support to reduce power consumption.
LX	Introduced in 1997 for the Pentium II CPUs. It supports EDO, BEDO and SDRAM, Concurrent PCI, Ultra DMA-33 and USB. It also supports the new AGP (Advanced Graphics Port) although these devices are not yet on the market.

PLUG AND PLAY
Another big benefit of the PCI system is its *'Plug and Play'* facility.

Plug and Play needs three key elements:
- The PC must support it (this is provided in all new computers).
- The adapter cards must support it (many new cards have this feature).
- The operating system must support it (Windows 95 does, NT, OS/2 and DOS don't).

PCI systems have a PCI-specific BIOS.   This provides for the auto-configuring of cards, making alterations and additions to hardware a simple process..   With all other buses, including the VESA system, the addition or swapping of cards involves ensuring that there is no clash of memory addresses, IRQs and DMA channels between the existing and the new devices (see the chapter on Upgrading). These problems are intended to be eliminated with PCI since the BIOS will maintain a list of all memory addresses, IRQs and DMAs in use and provide non-conflicting allocations for new cards.   Each of the new PCI plug-and-play cards has its own *'configuration space'* which is usually a set of memory registers which are solely devoted to storing configuration information.   The Plug and Play BIOS chip can interrogate the registers to determine the card manufacturer and type and the range of options it can handle. The cards are all capable of working with a range of different memory addresses, IRQs, etc. The BIOS determines the best use of the cards and send data to be stored in each card's configuration space detailing what the specific settings for the card will be.

With Windows 3.1, the basic plug and play services were supplemented by providing *'BIOS extensions'* (software to link the BIOS facilities and the extra facilities).   With Windows 95 the additional services are designed into the operating system.

The concept of plug and play has still to be fully realised since few users have the required combination of PnP BIOS conforming to the PPA BIOS 1.0a specification, PCI motherboard, PnP operating system (such as Windows 95 - but not NT or OS/2) or BIOS extensions and all add-on cards being of the PnP variety.   Additionally, some software still ignores best practice and by-passes some BIOS routines. True, full plug and play depends upon all the required features being present although partial benefits can be gained from a lesser specification although this will still involve some manual installation.

MULTI-TASKING
In a normal single-user, single task, system, the bus is under the control of the main processor.   The CPU is the *'master'* of the bus.   In a local area network server, however, there may be a number of *'intelligent'* cards fitted.   Any one of the these cards may be capable of being the master of the bus for a while.   In this situation, the card's chips carry out the memory data transfers, while the main CPU can carry out any non-bus processing.   This would involve multiple *'bus mastering'*.   This is not really supported by the ISA bus (both on design and speed grounds).   Both the MCA, EISA and PCI buses are designed to handle multiple bus mastering, where a system of interleaved bus transfer cycles means that a high speed bus can service several slower speed devices (e.g. network interface cards).

PCMCIA
Announced in 1990, the PCMCIA standard (Personal Computer Memory Card International Association) appeared as a standard interface for portable computer users. The standard is supported by over 500 PCMCIA members and includes all major hardware and software suppliers.   The standard aims to allow the easy connection of a range of add-ons. PCMCIA products are now referred to as *'PC Cards'*.   The PCMCIA connection is the portable's equivalent of the expansion slots on a desktop machine. Each add-on card is about the size of a credit card and the original intention was to provide the easy connection of memory chips.

MEMORY CARDS
The cards, some of which are also sometimes described as *'Flash memory'*, have a 68 pin plug at one end and connect to sockets inside palmtop and notebook computers.   Once inserted, they act like a normal bank of memory configured as a RamDisc.   When a card is withdrawn, it retains the data stored in its chips until it is required again. This also provides portability, as the card can be pulled out of one machine and inserted in another machine, just like a floppy disc.   The cards either use static RAM or EEPROM as the medium for the data storage.   A small lithium battery maintains data in the models which use Static Ram (S-Ram).   Flash RAM handles larger capacities but has some problems in ensuring that the programming voltages to set the memory contents are the same on all machines using

the PCMCIA interface. Memory cards are available in sizes from 64k to 20Mb although they are very expensive at the high capacity sizes.

The cards use an 8 or a 16-bit data bus and a 26-bit address bus to provide a maximum range of 64Mb. A 32-bit data bus version is also available. This is called the 'CardBus' and supports data rates of 100Mbps compared to 20Mbps with 16-bit cards.

PCMCIA is now used mainly as a hardware I/O standard, allowing the connection of a whole range of devices already associated with desktop PCs. These include disc drives, CD ROMs, sound cards, digital cameras, video capture cards, data acquisition cards, modems, faxes, and LAN interface cards. These connect through the PCMCIA interface and ignore any ISA, MCA or EISA bus that might be on the machine. The system dynamically assigns I/O addresses and IRQs to the cards during the boot-up or when cards are inserted. This makes PCMCIA an alternative to Plug and Play.

ADVANTAGES

- Speed. Intel claims that flash RAM has an access time that is 10,000 times faster than a hard disc.
- Software will appear in this credit-card format.
- Easy change of cards, while the computer is still running - known as 'hot plugging' or 'hot swapping'. The new card should be automatically detected and recognised by the interface, based on the information stored and supplied by the card. The functions of some of the pins on the interface will be re-mapped according to the device detected. By default, the card is assumed to be a memory card. Since the process is automatic, there is no need to re-boot the computer each time a card is changed.

DISADVANTAGE

- The range of add-ons remains much more expensive then their desktop counterparts.

PCMCIA VERSIONS

- Version 1 of the standard covers the use of the card as a memory storage device. This defines the physical thickness of the card as only 3.3mm.
- Version 2.01, announced in 1992, expanded the PCMCIA standard use to cover the connection between card and machine as the basis for designing a range of I/O (input/output) add-on cards for LAN adapters, SCSI controllers, modems, sound cards, video capture cards, etc. This card is 5mm thick.
- Extended versions of Version 1 and Version 2 standards are available. These have the same widths and thicknesses as the normal version but allow for extra long cards to be used. This allows even more complex circuitry to be mounted on the cards but means that the cards will protrude from the computer's casing by up to two inches.
- Version 3 is 10.5mm thick to allow for the inclusion of larger peripherals and small hard disc drives such as the 105Mb and 170Mb Maxtor drives and the 270Mb SyQuest drive.
- Version 4 is 16mm thick to allow for the inclusion of larger capacity hard disc drives. IBM, Western Digital and Hewlett Packard have already produced hard discs to this format, the first two being 1.8" and the HP being only 1.3". Other models are available from Maxtor and Conner.
- Version 5 is 18mm thick and was announced by Toshiba for its wireless network cards.
- Current developments centre round an enhanced specification to allow the interface to be easier used with normal desktop PCs.

STANDARDS

- PCMCIA 1.0 stated the minimum specification for early cards.
- PCMCIA 2.1 specified the interfaces used with the majority of current cards.
- PCMCIA 3.0 is the new CardBus system and supports 32-bit working, DMA and 3.3volt working (older cards require 5 volts while newer portables work on 3.3volts). Windows 95 Release 2 has built-in Cardbus card and socket services.

There is still work to be done to finalise file formats so that a card from one machine can be read by another machine. The hardware writing and reading is agreed but the format of the data interchange is still to be agreed. The device driver software has been given the title of 'enablers'. The low-level 'Socket Services', those that read the card data and link to the higher level 'Card Services', should ideally be implemented in BIOS. Intel is seeking to have its ExCA (Exchangeable Card Architecture) accepted as the standard for xxx86 machines. This has been renamed to 'QuickSwap' and may become part of the PCMCIA specification. Microsoft has introduced its own 'Flash File System' for configuring the flash RAM as a disc drive. In general, software support is lagging the development of this new hardware.

Data compression techniques, as practised on ordinary hard discs with Stacker, can be used on these ram discs to increase their effective capacity.

EXTERNAL INTERFACES

The preceding pages have covered the <u>internal</u> architecture and the available internal add-ons.   Every PC also has a number of <u>external</u> connections (known as '***ports***'), to allow the machine to communicate with the outside world.   A range of input and output devices (sometimes a device is both an input and output device) can be connected to these ports.

- Input devices include - keyboard, graphics tablet, scanner, modem, sensors, camcorders
- Output devices include - printer, monitor, plotter, modem, actuators, robots

Peripheral interfaces have a number of common characteristics:

- Data conversion - translating data from the form held inside the computer into the form required by the device (eg from computer binary to ACSII for the printer).
- Buffering - the temporary storage of data between the CPU and the peripheral (eg holding data until the modem is ready to transmit it).
- Control Signals - the transmission of control information to a device (eg moving disc drive heads).
- Status Signals - the reception of information on device readiness (eg testing if a printer is one line or out of paper).

Most interfaces are two-way devices.   A printer port, for example, has to send control information and data to a printer but it also requires status information back from the printer.   Of course, the printable data only goes in one direction (PC to printer).   With other devices, the data may flow in both directions; this is the case with a modem which must both transmit and receive data.

INTERFACE METHODS

All connections to the computer and its adapter cards use one of these interface methods:

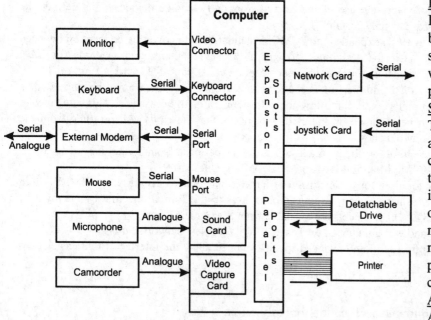

PARALLEL
Data is sent with all the byte's bits being transmitted simultaneously over a set of wires.   Used by most printers, disc drives, etc.

SERIAL
The data is transmitted one bit at a time over a single connector wire. This is slower than parallel transmission but is much cheaper (particularly over long distances). This method is used by keyboards, monochrome monitors, some printers, the mouse, and LAN cabling

ANALOGUE
Analogue signals have an infinite number of different states, as would be expected from real-world audio or video sources.   They require special adaptors to interface to the computer and examples are modems, microphones and video sources such as cameras and VCRs.

SPOOLING

A spooling system stores print jobs into temporary files from where they can be printed out at the rate that the printer can handle the data.   This saves the user waiting for a print job to finish.   The temporay files are then deleted after the printing if completed.

BUFFERING

Buffers are memory blocks used to temporarily store data until it is required.   Buffer memory areas are to be found inside printer, modems, video and network interface cards.

The computer itself also creates and uses buffer areas, usually in higher memory areas of the main system memory.   They are used for disc reads and writes and for keyboard buffering.

EXTERNAL PORTS

To facilitate the connection of external devices, PCs have a number of external ports at the rear of the machine. Normally, a PC will have at least a parallel port and a serial port, although some machines may have more. All machines will have a keyboard interface and an outlet for attaching a monitor.

PARALLEL PORT

Also known as the *'Centronics'*, *'LPT'* or *'Printer'* port. With the advent of improved ports, the conventional port is also now known as the SPP (Standard Parallel Port). In fact, the plug that fits the printer socket is a 36-pin Amphenol plug to fit the printer's Centronics socket. The plug at the computer is a normal 25-pin male D-type connector. By convention, the whole cable has been described as a Centronics cable.

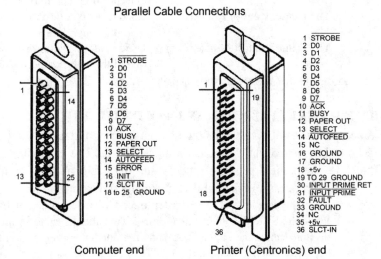

Parallel Cable Connections

Computer end   Printer (Centronics) end

In parallel transmission, the data port has eight separate wires connecting the computer to the external device.

There is a separate pin in the socket for each data wire, plus other pins for the control information. Five volts on a wire represents a logic 1, while zero volts represents logic 0. In this way, an entire byte of data can be transmitted at a time. There are problems in sending parallel transmissions over long distances. Due to the different characteristics of each wire, there will be different times taken for data to pass down each wire. So, over a long distance, the individual bits that comprise a particular byte may not all arrive at the destination at the same time - even although they were transmitted simultaneously. This effect is known as *'skew'* and is the reason that parallel transmission, although the fastest, is restricted to short cables up to two metres in length. Parallel transmission is used for the most printer cables (although it is possible to buy serial interface printers).

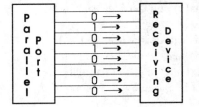

The letter 'T' being sent down a parallel cable

PORT ADDRESSES

IBM defined the first parallel port as LPT1 and the second and third, if fitted, as LPT2 and LPT3. The system can differentiate between these ports and any other devices because the hardware for LPT1, LPT2 and LPT3 (and the serial ports similarly) only responds to certain defined port address ranges.

The three possible ranges for parallel ports are:

Port	Data to Printer (output)	Printer Status (input)	Printer Control (output)
Option 1	3BC	3BD	3BE
Option 2	378	379	37A
Option 3	278	279	27A

When the computer is booted up, the address ranges above are allocated to LPT1, LPT2 and LPT3 as the defaults. The system is checked for parallel ports, any devices found are allocated to the ports and the information is stored as part of a device list stored in main memory. Plug and Play systems will dynamically allocate the port addresses. The addresses in use on any particular computer can be found using the MSDOS MSD utility. If this is not available on the machine, the DEBUG utility can be used. When this command is given, the DOS prompt changes to a minus sign prompt. When the command

d0040:0008

is entered, a set of hex numbers will appear on the screen. A typical line might be

78 03 BC 03 00 00 00 00

The first two bytes indicate that LPT1 is use and is using address 0378 (note that the bytes are displayed in reverse order) and that LPT2 is in use with address 03BC. To get back to the DOS prompt the letter 'q' has to be entered at the minus prompt. MSD looks up the printer table and displays the findings while DEBUG is used to directly access the table.

PARALLEL PORT REGISTERS

The normal computer parallel port has three registers (memory areas) to store information that will pass between the port and the printer.

The three registers are:

The Data Register	Used to send characters <u>OUT</u> to the printer. Wired through eight pins (pin 2 to pin 9)
The Printer Control Register	Used to send control information <u>OUT</u> to the printer. Wired through four active pins (pins 1,14,16,17)
The Printer Status Register	Used to store printer information coming <u>IN</u> from the printer Wired through five active pins (pins 10,11,12,13,15)

The addresses for these registers are as previously described.

THE PARALLEL PORT AS IN OUTPUT PORT

Whereas the serial port has its own chip to carry out data transmission, the parallel port requires the these tasks to be carried out by the computer's CPU.   The computer can feed data to the printer much faster than the mechanical printing process and a system of flow control (known as *'handshaking'*) must be used.   The process varies slightly but a general description is:

- Place the data in the Data Register to feed the external data lines.
- Pulse the STROBE line (pin 1) low.   This should energise the printer end which should result in the printer reading the data off the data lines and switching its own BUSY line high.
- Check the BUSY line (pin 11).   When the printer is ready to receive the next character, it will switch its BUSY line low again.
- When the BUSY line goes low, repeat the process.

In other systems, the printer informs the PC that the data is received by bringing the ACKNOWLEDGE line (pin 10) low.

The other port output lines are:

AUTOFEED (pin 14)	Tells the printer to automatically insert a Line Feed after a Carriage Return.
INIT (pin 16)	Initialises the printer on power up.
SELECT (pin 17)	Takes the printer off line. This was often used with daisywheel and golf ball head printers where the document to be printed would have special printer codes embedded in the text. When the text altered (e.g. to an italics font) the printer would be automatically taken off line to allow the operator to change print heads.

Many modern printers, particularly lasers, ignore all control signals apart from the STROBE signal.

The other port input lines are:

Paper Out (pin 12)	This line is pulled high by the printer when it runs out of paper. The printer also pulls the SELECT line (pin 13) high to tell the PC that it is on line and waiting for data.
Error (pin 15)	This line is pulled low by the printer when it detects an error such as a paper jam.

The easiest way to write to the parallel port is using the existing DOS code accessed by calling up the DOS interrupt routine 21h thus:

```
mov ah, 05h
mov dl, 0Ch
int 21h
```

THE PARALLEL PORT AS AN INPUT/OUTPUT PORT
STANDARD MODE

The Standard Mode, also known as the *'Centronics'* or *'Compatibility'* Mode, is purely an output system and does not expect any input other than status information (eg out-of-paper or paper-jam information). No user data enters the computer using this mode.

NIBBLE MODE

The Centronics interface has a number of error lines that are used to signal problems to the computer (such as shortage of paper).   If the control software is written to examine these lines, then the parallel port offers the possibility of being a two-way device.   Since the data being read into the parallel port is only four bits wide, only half a byte, i.e. a 'nibble', can be transferred at a time.   This is described as *'four bit mode'*.   Incoming data is therefore substantially slower than outgoing data and is typically 150Kbps. All parallel ports are capable of operating in this mode, since every port has these four input lines.

BYTE MODE

Four-bit working is inadequate for fast data transfer and a bi-directional parallel port was first introduced in 1987, with the IBM PS/2 range of computers. All computers after about 1993 are likely to have these improved parallel ports. Here, the eight data lines are capable of both reading and writing data, allowing the port to be an input as well as an output device. This significantly speeded up data transfers but the system was still hampered by the CPU having to carry out all the port's handshaking and flow control activities.

EPP

In 1992, the IEEE 1284 standard was brought in. This has become known as the Enhanced Parallel Port (EPP). Like the normal bi-directional ports, the EPPs are capable of either sending or receiving data on the data pins. The main advantage of the EPPs is that they do not require the CPU for flow control as the chips on the cards carry out these tasks. The EPP performance is a major advance, with data transfer rates of up to 2Mbps and further improvements likely.

Enhanced Parallel Ports are also *'backward compatible'* with older, non-EPP devices. This means that a computer with a EPP will have the following characteristics:

- Any device that is EPP compatible device will attach to an Enhanced Port and will detect that the port is of the EPP type. Subsequent data transfers will be at the maximum rate allowed by the port. This allows the newer printers and network adapters to operate at their best potential.
- Any device that is not EPP compatible will still attach to an Enhanced Port but the port will operate in standard mode.

If an EPP compatible device is attached to a standard Parallel Port, the device will work in standard mode. For the user, this should be an automatic process as the device software will be able to test the port type and configure itself accordingly.

The EPP was designed for use with hard drives, CD ROMs, LAN cards, etc.

ECP

The Enhanced Capability Port was promoted by Microsoft and Hewlett Packard and is designed for interfacing to the modern range of printers and scanners. While it is capable of operating in other modes, the EPP mode provides added features such as DMA operation and RLE (Run Length Encoding) compression of data. Compression ratios of up to about 64:1 are supported, making it an ideal interface for the transferring of scanned bitmaps.

Windows 95 has built-in support for ECP ports and the its IRQ and DMA can be set up in the 'Device Manager' menu. Naturally, the printer must also be ECP capable.

PARALLEL PORT DEVICES

A whole range of storage and other devices exist for connection to the computer's parallel port. These include 3.5" floppy drives, 5.25" floppy drives, fixed hard discs, removable cartridge drives, optical R/W drives, CD ROM drives and tape streamers (fast-running tape decks using 1/4" cartridges or DAT tapes, for data backup and restore purposes). Peripherals other than storage devices include scanners, video cameras, sound cards and LAN adapters.

The advantages of parallel port peripherals are:

- Ease of connection. There is no need to open machines to fit or configure cards.
- Portability. The peripheral is a free-standing device that will connect to any computer.
- Can be used to extend laptops and notebooks, which lack internal space for expansion.
- Allows a machine with the IDE card limit of two hard discs to attach a third, external, drive.
- Sharing resources. A CD ROM, for example, is not tied to a particular computer; it is neither fitted into a machine nor does it requires an adapter card to be fitted to a machine. This allows the peripheral to easily passed to where it can currently be most usefully employed.
- Sharing Data. Devices such as the ZIP drive allow 100Mb of data to stored on a removable disc that can then be inserted into any other ZIP drive for reading.
- Easy recovery from machine failure. In the event that a machine breaks down, its data will be held on a mass-storage device which can be quickly transferred to another working machine. A portable 1.2Gb hard disc or 2Gb DAT streamer would handle most of an organisation's data comfortably.

To ensure that the computer's only parallel port is not lost to the device, parallel port peripherals normally provide an additional parallel port.

SERIAL PORT

A serial transmission system is cheaper to employ, since it only requires a single channel between the PC and the external device.

In a serial system, data that arrives in parallel format from the bus is converted into a stream of bits that is sent sequentially along the single cable. This conversion task is carried out by a chip called a *UART* (Universal Asynchronous Receiver Transmitter). The PC uses a standard known as RS232C and is implemented as COM1 and, if fitted, COM2, COM3 and COM4.   An updated version known as RS-232D meets CCITT V.24, V2.28 and ISO IS2110 standards.

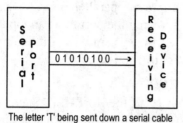

The letter 'T' being sent down a serial cable

Common devices to be found on a serial port are printers, plotters, modems, remotely controlled instruments and machinery.   Although the above example shows data being transmitted <u>out</u> of the port to a device, it should be stressed that the RS232 port is essentially a bi-directional port. This means that data can also be passed <u>in</u> to the port from an external device.

The letter 'T' being received into the serial port

A good example of such a device is a serial mouse.   Other examples are bar code readers, electronic tills and remote monitoring equipment.

In the case of a modem, the port will transfer data both in <u>and</u> out of the PC.

The serial port is often used for instrument control.   The computer sends out commands on the RS232 port to the instrument's serial interface.   The commands may set up the instrument for certain purposes and initiate the resultant readings, which are transmitted back to the computer on the same serial cable. This can be used over short distances for activities such as manufacturing test beds and the digital control of electronic or radio equipment.   When used via modems or dedicated telephone lines, longer distances can be achieved.   This allows for remote control of apparatus and remote data logging.

Like the parallel ports, the serial ports are detected at power up and their addresses stored in memory. The normal address for COM1 is 3F8h and the normal address for COM2 is 2F8h.   As with the parallel ports, the serial port addresses in use on any particular computer can be found by using the MSDOS MSD utility.

Alternatively, the DEBUG utility can be used to interrogate the table with the command:

d0040:0000

The RS232 port and serial communications are covered in detail in the chapter on Data Communications.

UNIVERSAL SERIAL BUS

The Universal Serial Bus (USB) was developed by Intel and promises to be the new general-purpose PC port.   It could eventually replace both serial ports, parallel ports and internal interface cards as the means of connecting slow to medium speed external devices such as keyboards, mice, modems, etc.

Unlike the large 9/25 pin serial connections and the 25/36 pin parallel connections, the USB requires only four wires in a light flex cable.   There is one wire for the common ground, one for data in each direction and a 5v power supply wire.

It has many distinct advantages:

- The bus is relatively, fast with a maximum date transfer rate of 12Mbps.
- USB is Plug and Play compliant.   So, devices can be *'hot swapped'* - i.e. fitted and removed without rebooting or reconfiguring the machine; the configuration problems previously associated with adding and altering equipment is eliminated.   If a new device is fitted while the computer is switched on, it is automatically configured.
- The bus provides its own power supply to any low-power devices that connect to it.   There is no longer any need for each external device to have its own power unit.   This should make peripherals cheaper and eliminates the tangle of power connections at the rear of machines.
- Devices which were once designed to use their own manufacturer's interface cards (eg scanners, some mice) will no longer have this requirement.   This should make the new USB models of the devices cheaper and easier to connect.

USB allows a single port to connect many devices together is in daisy-chain. Up to 127 devices can connect to a single USB port if hubs are used to expand the system. A hub is simple a star-like connector that connects a group of devices to a single connection point.

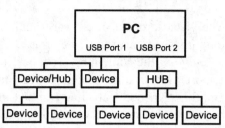

The diagram shows a PC with two USB ports. Port 2 connects directly to a hub and this has three outlets connected to USB devices. Typical USB hubs support four, five or seven port outlets.

Port 1 connects to two devices that are daisy chained to the port. One of these devices also acts as a hub and has two further devices connected to it.

Hyundai 17B+ and 15G+ monitors are available with three USB ports mounted on the base. So, a PC port may connect to a monitor and speakers, headphones and microphones could connect directly to the monitor. Or a keyboard could be designed as a hub, with a mouse, joystick and light pen attaching to a connection at the rear of the keyboard.

Many USB devices are being introduced (eg Canon digital cameras, Logitech mice, Samsung, Philips and Iiyama monitors, Cherry keyboards).

USB is supported by all modern PCI chipsets (ie HX, VX, TX) but is only supported in Windows 95 Release 2; all Windows 3.1 users, most Windows 95 users and all NT users cannot currently access USB facilities.

FIREWIRE

Another high-performance serial bus is IEEE-1394, also known as *'Firewire'*. This was developed from the Apple computer range and is also known as the *'Multimedia Connection'* since it allows camcorders, scanners, disc drives, DVD players, CD ROMs and printers to share a common connecting bus. The common interface means that it is also suitable for the home networking of PCs.

Like the USB system, it supports up to 63 devices. However, Firewire does not require the use of hubs as each device has a common connection to all other devices - including the PC. The standard connecting cables are 6-wire; two for the power and four used to connect to consumer audio and video products (TV sets, VCRs, amplifiers, etc). The four bus wires are configured as two twisted pairs, crossed between ends to provide transmit and receive pairs. Sony uses a four wire variant for its products, using the IEEE-1394.1 standard.

Despite its simplicity, Firewire is an extremely fast interface that can move data at 100Mbps, or 200Mbps. 400Mbps and 1.2Gbps versions are being discussed. Even the slowest speed is capable of simultaneously delivering two full-motion video channels running at the high video rate of 30fps, accompanied by CD quality stereo sound. It multiplexes data such compressed video and digitised audio along with device control commands on the common bus.

DVC (Digital Video Cassette) systems made by Sony already use Firewire on their camcorders. The other major players such as JVC, Hitachi and Philips plan to use Firewire systems on their D-VHS (Digital VHS) recorders. Since DVC requires 3.5Mb per sec (ie 28Mbps), it cannot be handled by USB (12Mbps limit) but is well with Firewire's capabilities. On the other hand, a 90 minute video would require almost 19Gb of hard disc space. This places this aspect of Firewire at the professional end of the video market.

Firewire devices, like USB devices, are hot swappable.

Microsoft intend to support Firewire in their future versions of Windows.

RELATIVE USES

Both Firewire and USB are competing with Ultra SCSI and Fibre Channel for the high-speed bus market. The likely uses of USB and Firewire are complementary rather than competing.

- SB remains a viable option for input devices (mouse/keyboard/joystick), audio (sound/music/ telephone), printers, scanners, storage devices (floppy, tape) and slow speed communications (modems, ISDN)
- Firewire offers a higher performance for top-end devices such as DVD drives, DVC cameras, D-VHS recorders and wide-band networking.

Computer Video

The visual product of the early mainframe computers was only plain text and numbers.   Usually this output was directed to a line printer.   Even when screens became more common, they were mostly used to *'monitor'* the computing process. The introduction of the IBM PC brought the first concession towards a more attractive presentation.   IBM machines introduced its *'IBM character set'* for screen and printer and this provided some line and box graphics.   There was no need for a sophisticated screens and early monitors were crude, low-definition devices.

Two main developments have led to greatly improved monitor design:

- Programs have become increasingly more graphics based (Computer Aided Design, Desk Top Publishing, Windows, multimedia, etc.). These programs required monitors that could display ever more detailed output.
- Users were spending much longer periods in front of the monitor, as the computer developed into more of a tool.   This raised questions of eyestrain, fatigue and other harmful effects, etc., which required to be addressed.

The monitor, and its hardware and software drivers, are becoming increasingly complex devices.   There is a wide choice of specifications, techniques, performances and prices.   There is no overall *'correct'* choice; there is only an appropriate choice for a particular use.   For example, it would be a waste of a company's resources to buy a £2,000 large screen, high performance monitor and video accelerator card for a PC that is used only for occasional word processing.   On the other hand, the same expensive monitor and card might be absolute necessities for detailed work in a design office.   This chapter examines the technology of monitors and computer graphics cards and discusses the technical and operational factors to be considered when choosing - and using - such devices.

MONITOR CONSTRUCTION

MONOCHROME MONITORS

The construction of computer monitors is identical to that of television screens. The monitor is based around a CRT (cathode ray tube) which contains the main elements shown in the diagram, plus control and amplifier circuitry.   The electron gun, or *'cathode'*, produces an electron cloud that is then drawn as an accelerated stream towards the front screen of the CRT which is held at a very high voltage.   When the electrons strike the coating on the inside of the tube they cause a temporary phosphorescence of that area of the tube surface.   This causes a bright spot to appear in the middle of the monitor screen.

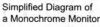
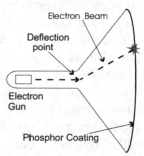

Simplified Diagram of
a Monochrome Monitor

Electron Beam

Deflection
point

Electron
Gun

Phosphor Coating

To produce a picture from this system, the two other requirements are:

- The whole of the screen should be covered by the beam.
- The beam should be modulated, to provide a grey scale.

SCANNING

The CRT monitor is a serial device.   Each individual area of the screen has to be illuminated to different degrees to provide a picture.   It is not practical to have a separate gun for each spot on the screen.   The

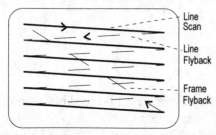

Line
Scan

Line
Flyback

Frame
Flyback

one gun has to handle the whole screen surface. The process of ensuring that the electron beam systematically covers each part of the monitor screen is known as *'scanning'*. The screen scanning process is in the same way that a book page is read - from left to right and from top to bottom, one line at a time. The finished picture is, in effect, composed of a set of parallel lines, called a *'raster'*.   To achieve this, electronic circuitry is introduced to deflect the electron beam in both the horizontal and vertical directions. The movement from left to right, and the accompanying rapid *'line flyback'* from right to left is carried out by the *'line scan'* circuitry.   The slower movement down the screen and the final rapid *'frame flyback'* is carried out by the *'frame scan'* circuitry.   These scans are synchronised by line and frame scan oscillators.

Commencing from the top, left corner of the screen, the beam is moved rightwards at a constant, pre-determined speed.   When it reaches the rightmost edge, the electron stream is switched off, while the deflection circuits 'fly back' the position to the left edge of the screen, ready for the next line of scan. The period when the stream is switched off is known as the *'line blanking'* period.   This process is repeated hundreds of times, until the entire screen is covered. The exact amount of lines depends on the resolution of the screen standard in use - anywhere between 200 lines and 1000 lines or over.   When the last line is traced on the screen, the electron stream is again switched off - the *'frame blanking'* period, while the beam is returned to the top left corner of the screen.

MODULATION

In a TV receiver, the intensity of the beam can be varied continuously across the scan of the line, limited only by the quality of the controlling electronics.   For computer monitors, each line is considered to have a certain amount of elements along its length.   Each element can then be illuminated or not, to produce the picture intelligence.   Each of the picture elements is known as a *'pixel'*.   The number of picture lines and the number of pixels across each line is a measure of the *'resolution'* of the screen picture.   A SVGA screen, for example, has a resolution of 800 x 600 - i.e. is has a matrix of 800 pixels across by 600 pixels down.

If a monitor was to have a modulating input signal that was TTL (transistor-transistor logic) the input voltage would switch between +5 volts and 0 volts.   The electron stream would either be completely on or completely off.   Such a monitor would not be able to provide shades of grey.   If the flow of electrons can be stepped in discrete stages, then a grey scale can be implemented.   The input here would be an analogue signal, which is capable of providing degrees of modulation of the electron beam.   In an ideal world, the modulating signal would vary in infinitely small steps, to display a huge amount of picture detail.   While the monitor can cope with fairly small changes, the memory that would be required to store such variations is currently prohibitive (see later section on memory)

FRAME REFRESH SPEEDS

The screen produced by the above process has only a short life, as the glow from the phosphoresced areas will rapidly die away.   The whole process has to be repeated regularly enough so that the persistence of vision of the human eye perceives the screen as a continuous display, with no detectable flicker. Where the picture has a dark background, any flicker is less noticeable.   Where there is a white background, the constant cycle of lighting a pixel, letting the pixel illumination dull, followed by again fully illuminating the pixel causes the most pronounced flicker.   This can be particularly noticeable with Windows, since most backgrounds are light-coloured.   Initially, 40 frames per second was considered adequate and a refresh rate of 50Hz (cycles per second) was used.   This was discovered to be too slow, as it still produced enough flicker to cause eyestrain and headaches.   40Hz is really the rate at which most people can detect flicker.   Many people are capable of detecting and being bothered by flicker at up to 70Hz. At 72Hz, flicker ceases to be a factor. Consequently, the frame refresh speeds - i.e. the vertical scanning frequency - has gradually increased.   IBM has set the VGA refresh rate at 60Hz or 70z, but VESA has set it at 72Hz. VESA has set 70Hz as the lowest acceptable rate for SVGA graphics adapters, with 72Hz as the acceptable standard. With 1024 x 768, VESA has set the rate at 70Hz, although larger screen sizes often use 76Hz.   NEC now produce a range of 90Hz frame speed monitors and one of the 20" Philips models has the high rate of 160Hz.   These figures are for non-interlaced systems. The pace of improvement has been tempered by the fact that faster frame speeds increase the system bandwidth and thereby cost more to manufacture.

LINE REFRESH SPEEDS

The frame refresh speeds and screen resolutions have a direct bearing on the required speed from the line scan circuitry.   Consider the frame refresh time being kept constant and the resolution being increased. The system has to produce more horizontal lines in the same time, so the line scan time has to be shortened, to get each line drawn faster.   This results in a higher line scan frequency. Similarly, if the resolution remains constant but the frame refresh is speeded up, there will still be more lines drawn in the same time - the line frequency has to be increased.   A VGA monitor has a line frequency of 31.5KHz. This means that 31,500 screen lines have to traced out every second. For a SVGA screen, 48,000 screen lines may be required to be produced each second (see the chart on page 134).

BANDWIDTH

When a monitor is driven at a high resolution with high frame refresh speeds, much data has to be placed on the screen in a very short time. The ability of a system to achieve high throughput is measured by its *'bandwidth'*.   The bandwidth is measured in MegaHertz (millions of cycles per second) and describes how quickly the electronic circuitry can change from the system voltage state to a zero voltage state; this in turn determines how many pixels can be handled per second. A high resolution screen will have more dots along each screen line. This will demand a greater throughput and hence a higher bandwidth. Typical VGA colour monitors will have bandwidths between 30MHz and 100MHz, dependent on price. SVGA monitors can range as high as 200MHz.   Low resolution, slow refresh speeds will require a lower system bandwidth than superior specifications.   The higher the system bandwidth, the more demanding is the monitor circuitry.   This partly explains why a high-performance monitor is more expensive than poorer models.

Simply lowering the frame refresh rate would lower bandwidth and reduce monitor costs. This is an unacceptable solution, since it produces severe flicker problems.   Incompatible cards and monitors may be easily connected, resulting in driving a monitor with a signal that is changing at a pace outwith its bandwidth capabilities.   This would result in the signal not responding fast enough to changes and adjacent unwanted pixels being lit, with the consequent downgrading of clarity.

See page 136 for greater detail.

INTERLACING

To provide high-resolution screens at lower cost, a system of *'interlacing'* is contrived.   Here, the picture is built up in two halves.   Firstly, all the odd lines are built up.   This is immediately followed by filling in all the even lines.   If the frame speed is unchanged, then the whole picture takes twice as long to build up as a non-interlaced model.   This reduces the required bandwidth and hence cost.   The problems of a jerky picture at low refresh speeds are reduced, since each frame refresh manages to update the whole screen, albeit only every other line.   This is an acceptable compromise for many, although non-interlaced monitors are the best performers if they can be afforded. Non-interlaced models are also sometimes referred to as *'sequential'* systems.   They draw every line, both odd and even, in a straight sequence until the whole screen is painted before returning to the top of the screen.

SYNCHRONISATION

The internal circuitry of the monitor contains oscillators to produce the necessary line and field scans. The start of these line and field scans must coincide with that required by the computer's graphics output. The cable between the computer and monitor carries the modulation information.   It also carries line and frame synchronising pulses from the computer.   These pulses are used to keep the oscillators in the monitor running at the correct timing.   Without these synchronising pulses, the screen would soon suffer from *'line tear'* and *'frame roll'* as the slight timing differences between the two units became aggregated.   The sync signals are usually two different TTL lines carrying between 0v and 5v, one each for the line and frame pulses.

ASPECT RATIO

This the ratio of the screen's width to the screen's height.   Monitor CRTs, like conventional TV screens, are built with a ratio of 4:3.   To maintain a uniform screen display, the screen must be driven at the same rate - i.e. there should be 4 pixels across the screen for each three pixels down the screen. If this is achieved, then all the pixels on the screen will be square and graphics drawing is simplified.   This was not the case, however, with earlier screen standards.   For example, the CGA standard produced a screen grid of 640 pixels by 200 pixels.   To fill the screen area, the 200 horizontal lines are spaced further apart than with a higher resolution.   This distorts the horizontal to vertical ratio and results in the pixels not being 'square'. Drawing a box whose dimensions was 20 pixels by 20 pixels would not produce a box, but a rectangle. Similarly, a circle would produce an ellipse.   These problems could be overcome - at the expense of further complexity (i.e. more calculations, more time).   Later standards do not suffer from this problem. The SVGA standard, for example, is 800 x 600, which is exactly a 4:3 ratio.

COLOUR MONITORS

It is commonly held that a colour monitor must always be better than a monochrome model. This is not true. Indeed, in many cases a monochrome monitor will produce sharper results than a colour version. The techniques required to produce colour screens entail a much more accurate alignment than is necessary with monochrome screens. A colour monitor displaying a monochrome screen may not be as clear as the same display on a monochrome monitor. Certainly, a poorly adjusted colour monitor is much more difficult to use than a poorly adjusted monochrome monitor. For this reason, where colour is not an important factor, such as in DTP, many users prefer to use a monochrome monitor.

There are many good reasons why users wish, or need, to use colour monitors:

- Art and graphic packages really require colour to be used to the maximum effect. Professional packages allow for 'colour separations'. The various coloured components of the picture create their own separate printouts on a printer. The masters are taken to a commercial printer, where a separate print run is made for each colour. Each run overlays on the same sheet, to reproduce the original artwork.
- Multimedia and video almost always require colour for maximum realism and impact.
- Computer Aided Design packages make use of colour to represent different elements of the design. A street plan, for example, might show water routes in a different colour from electricity supply routes. Also, when technologists design a printed circuit board, each layer of connecting tracks will be a different colour, with the silk screen layer being a different colour again. These jobs could be accomplished with a monochrome screen, but the viewing would be much more difficult, therefore less productive.
- Some application programs are written to make use of colour to highlight menus, chosen options, etc. A red message on a blue background is perfectly clear on a colour screen. When viewed on a monochrome screen, it is seen as one shade of dark grey on another shade of dark grey. Colour screens make the reading of such menus easier, with less eyestrain
- Sales and business presentations are greatly enhanced by colour.

COLOUR PRINCIPLES

The human eye reacts to light either by processing various light sources that are :
- reflected from the printed page (known as 'subtractive mixing')
- directly targetted at the eye (known as 'additive mixing').

SUBTRACTIVE MIXING

Natural daylight reflecting off a non light-absorbent paper (ie white) allows the full light spectrum to be reflected. These reflected wavelengths are mixed inside the eye and interpreted as white. Adding ink or paint pigment to the paper surface results in the area affected selectively absorbing some of the wavelengths from the white light source. The viewer sees the resultant colour reflection from the mix. Since the introduction of the pigment have taken away some of the wavelengths, the

Primary Colour Mix	Result
Magenta + Yellow	Red
Cyan + Yellow	Green
Cyan + Magenta	Blue
Cyan + Magenta + Yellow	Black

process is termed 'subtractive mixing'. The primary pigments are Cyan, Magenta and Yellow and the result of mixing them in equal quantities is shown in the table. Other colours and hues are obtained by mixing the primary colours with unequal quantities. In practice, it is easier to introduce a black ink (ie one that absorbs all light wavelengths) than to achieve the absolutely equal amounts of Cyan, Magenta and Yellow required for the same effect. Additive mixing uses the 'CMY colour model' and CMYK printers use this principle and add a black ink for more consistent blacks and to achieve faster print speeds..

ADDITIVE MIXING

The colour monitor exploits the fact that the three main colours, as detected by the eye - are red, green and blue. In this case the light is not reflected but is directly transmitted from the CRT screen to the eye. Any other colour of light can be obtained from mixing the three primary colours of light - red, green and blue - in the appropriate ratios. For example, mixing red and green light produces yellow light, while mixing red, green and blue in the same proportions produces white light. Since the monitor CRT uses three different light sources to produce the colours, the process is termed 'additive mixing'. If no light sources are added to the mix, no wavelengths reach the eye and the screen is perceived as being black.

CRT CONSTRUCTION

The monochrome monitor screen was only concerned with *'luminance'* - i.e. how bright a particular pixel on the screen should be.   Screen brightness might vary from being off (i.e. black) through to fully on (i.e. white) and shades of grey (i.e. guns partly on).   The colour monitor is concerned with luminance - but it is also concerned with the <u>colour</u> of each pixel - known as the *'chrominance'* information.   The colour output from the PC is sent out as three separate signals - one each for the red, green and blue components.   Other outputs carry the vertical and horizontal synchronisation signals.   These video outputs are produced by the graphics card of the computer. A specially constructed monitor is required to produce the colour display.

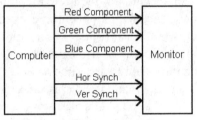

THE SHADOW MASK TUBE

The diagram shows the most commonly used model of colour tube, which is called the *'shadow mask tube'*.   The tube was originally invented by the Radio Corporation of America and first demonstrated as early as 1950.   Although originally produced for colour TV tubes, the same technology is used in most current computer monitors.   More modern, improved, and more expensive alternatives now exist in the *'Trinitron'* tube.

The shadow mask tube is really three tubes in one and has three electron guns, one each for the red, green and blue components of the screen.   Each of these guns produces an electron beam that can be either switched off and on (as in the RGB monitors) or have its intensity varied (as in analogue monitors).

The inside of the tube is coated with many thousands of tiny dots of red, green and blue phosphor. These dots are arranged in triangles comprising of a dot of each colour.   It is this cluster of dots, sometimes referred to as *'triads'*, which provides the luminance and chrominance for a single pixel. When a colour phosphor is hit by an electron beam it emits a beam of coloured light and the mixing of the various beams of colour takes place in the viewer's eyes to produce the final perceived colour for each triad.

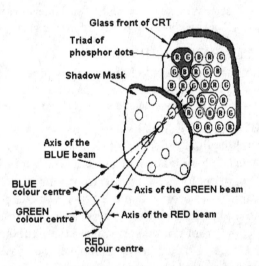

It is the job of each gun to emit, modulate, focus and accelerate its own electron beam towards its own set of phosphor dots.   However, as a single beam scans, it would illuminate dots that were part of another colour set. To prevent this, a metal sheet is placed inside the tube, between the guns and the screen, about 1cm from the screen.   This screen is perforated with tiny holes and these are aligned so that only the 'red' beam will ever be able to illuminate the red phosphors, the 'green' beam will only ever illuminate the green phosphors and the blue phosphors are only ever illuminated by the electron beam from the 'blue' gun.   There is a single hole in the mask for each triangle of dots. The rest of the screen is *'shadowed'* off from the beam by the mask - hence the name 'shadow mask tube', Since the holes only occupy a minority of the area of the mask, the vast majority of the emitted electrons are absorbed by the mask.   As a result, colour tubes need much greater beam currents and a higher final anode voltage than a monochrome tube.

SIGNAL			COLOUR
R	G	B	
0	0	0	Black
0	0	1	Blue
0	1	0	Green
0	1	1	Cyan
1	0	0	Red
1	0	1	Magenta
1	1	0	Yellow
1	1	1	White

COLOURS AVAILABLE WITH RGB

To obtain a pure white screen, all the guns will be driven at the same amplitude. If any of the guns suffers partial or total failure, the picture will have a *'colour cast'*. A total failure of the red gun, for example would result in a cyan cast (the complementary colour of green and blue).   A partial failure of the blue gun would produce a yellowish tinge to the display. Changing characteristics of components might lead to colour casts and these can usually be eliminated by altering variable potentiometers on the printed circuit board. At least one monitor model has external controls to allow the drive of each gun to be altered.

COLOUR PURITY

Colour purity confirms that a pure red (or green or blue) video drive produces a screen that is uniformly red (or green or blue) all over the screen area.   Achieving and maintaining the alignment of each beam with its corresponding set of mask holes and phosphor dots is a tricky business.   This work is carried out by trained staff, who have to open up the monitor case for the adjustments.

The first adjustment is CENTRE PURITY, which ensures that the beams pass through the colour centres. If centre purity is incorrectly adjusted, then a pure red picture would begin by producing red at the left side of the screen.   It would then drift away to other colours.   Another adjustment is EDGE PURITY, which tackles the more common problem of obtaining purity in the corners of the monitor screen.   Here a red picture would produce pure red at the screen centre, with loss of purity at the extremities.   These tests are carried out by using a test screen of solid red, followed by the same tests for the other guns.   In practice, loss of colour purity is not normally sufficiently severe to produce other than 'hot spots' - area where the solid colour suffer a change in tone.

NOTE   This effect can also be caused by shadow mask magnetisation (see next section).   The purity should only be adjusted if de-gaussing proves to be ineffective.

CONVERGENCE

Any picture on a colour monitor is a mixture of three separate pictures. Even a monochrome display on a colour monitor is only a mixture of the red, green and blue pictures, in equal quantities.   It is essential that the three pictures are correctly aligned with each other. This involves ensuring that any one video pixel is achieved by illuminating the phosphors in the same triad. Failures to align are normally at their worst away from the screen centre.   For example a screen filled with a white grid might display properly

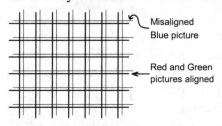
Misaligned
Blue picture

Red and Green
pictures aligned

at the centre while the vertical lines at the edges may be yellow (red + green) with a blue edge (known as *'colour fringing'*). Such misconvergence can vary by 0.5mm to 1.5mm across the screen and is a major cause of eye strain.   Static Deflection is concerned with aligning the undeflected beams (i.e. converging the triad in the centre of the screen).   Dynamic Convergence is concerned with the total area covered by the beam travel.   Note

that a tube may have perfect colour purity and still be badly misconverged.   Convergence tends to alter with age. At least one model has external controls for convergence - all the others have internal variables for use by trained technicians. Misconvergence is not a problem with Trinitron tubes or monochrome tubes, which only have a single gun.

It is not generally the job of the support technician to fix these problems; the technician only has to detect them and report them for repair.

DEGAUSSING

The electron beams are easily deflected by magnetic fields. The shadow mask is metal and therefore able to be magnetised.   It is vital that this does not happen, otherwise the unwanted magnetic fields will distort the beam - causing problems with purity.   In monitors, as in TV sets, a coil surrounds the tube. When the monitor is first switched on, the coil is automatically energised.   A high alternating field is produced by the coil, which is gradually reduced over a period of seconds.   This removes any residual magnetic field that may have been present on the shadow mask.

In adverse conditions, such as using computers on production lines, near heavy machinery, etc., the excessive local magnetic fields may render the automatic degaussing apparatus only partially effective. In these circumstances, the technician can manually degauss the screen using a degaussing coil or wand. These are plugged in to the mains supply and gradually moved in a circular motion over the face of the shadow mask tube for about a minute.   Still maintaining this movement, the coil or wand should be slowly moved away from the face of the screen. At about 6 - 10 feet distance, the degaussing device can be switched off.   Do not switch the device off close to the screen, otherwise the device acts as a gaussing device, instead of a degaussing device!   All monitors provide degaussing at switch-on as standard. An extra refinement is to have a degaussing button that will carry out the function at any time during the running of the system.

TRINITRON CONSTRUCTION

The Trinitron CRT was developed by the Sony Corporation of Japan in 1968. Although the tube's construction follows similar principles to the shadow mask tube, its approach produces a significantly different performance. The screen area (the part seen by the user) of a shadow mask tube resembles part of the surface of a sphere. The screen is curved in both the vertical and horizontal directions. This system provides for easy focusing of the electron beams on to the phosphor inner coating. The screen area of a Trinitron tube looks like part of the rounded surface of a cylinder.

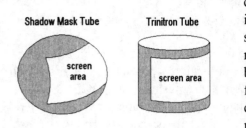

The horizontal direction is still curved but the vertical direction is now flat. The Trinitron is called the FST type (flatter squarer tube) and has the following advantages over the shadow mask variety:

- distortion of displayed lines is minimised
- screen corners are sharper
- suffers less glare from lighting

Another major departure is in the distribution of the tube's phosphor coating. The Trinitron tube moves away from the triad cluster of coloured phosphors. Instead, the phosphors are arranged in vertical strips in alternating colours. These strips stretch continuously from the top to the bottom of the screen.

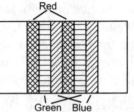

Because the screen is composed of stripes of colour, instead of independent clusters, the quality of the final picture is regarded as being superior - although some have not found it to their tastes. The shadow mask is replaced with an aperture grill that has a vertical slot for each vertical phosphor triad.

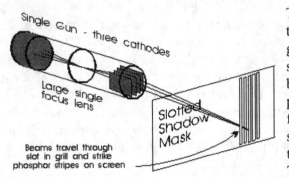

The third important difference is in the construction of the guns. Instead of having three separate colour guns, as in the shadow mask, the Trinitron employs a single gun with three cathodes - it produces three beams. The three beams have a common focus plane, which results in a sharper image and better focusing over the entire screen area. The use of a single focusing lens allows a larger gun dimension than the individual guns of the shadow mask tube. This results in higher beam density. This, together with fewer losses in the mask, results in a much brighter picture. Trinitron quality is measured in 'slot pitch' instead of dot pitch. A 0.26mm slot pitch is about 0.28mm or 0.29mm dot pitch. The aperture grille is held in place by two fine supporting wires which run across the screen. This results in two fine lines appearing on the screen but this generally does not present problems to users. The Trinitron tube is now used in a range of Sony, Taxan, Philips and Eizo monitors.

ENERGY SAVING

The *'green'* machines currently being marketed are ones where positive steps have been taken to protect the environment by reducing the power consumption of the computer, the monitor, or both, during periods of inactivity. A typical 14" monitor, for example, will consume between 65 Watts and 100 Watts of power, while a 17" monitor will consume around 150 Watts. Power-saving efforts centre round:

The Energy Star Programme - this is the voluntary code of practice agreed between the American Environmental Protection Agency and manufacturers. The code stipulates that units will be capable of entering a *'low power'* state of 30W maximum.

The DPMS System - this is the power-saving method recommended by VESA and can be used to meet the Energy Star standard. It is known as the *'Display Power Management Signalling'* system and depends upon the monitor and the video card both being DPMS compatible. Spare lines on the VGA connecting lead are used to carry the control signals from the PC to the monitor. The video card signals to the monitor how to control its energy-consuming components - i.e. the HOR and VER drive circuitry, the very high CRT voltages and the current to the tube's cathode. Differing power savings can be made, dependent upon the time required to bring the monitor back to full operation. The *'Suspend'* operation lowers power consumption to about 10-20% of its normal level and allows for a fairly fast recovery time. The *'Active Off'* operation lowers power consumption to about 5% but has a slower recovery time. An example of a DPMS compatible video card is the GTS Ultra Pro Windows Accelerator and the new Taxan range of monitors.

TCO-92 - this is more stringent standard from Sweden that requires a 30W maximum on standby and 8W maximum on power down.

Meanwhile, Hitachi has produced its own power saving system that is not VESA compatible. It uses a serial port connection between the monitor and the computer. The provided Windows software allows the serial connection to power down the monitor when it is not in use. The software also provides control over the normal monitor settings.

NOTE

Although the main unit consumes less power than the monitor, steps can be taken to save energy by closing down the disc drive power or reducing the disc speed and by running the CPU at a reduced speed. A range of machines, such as the IBM PS/2E, the AST Bravo LP and the Viglen Genie DX2-66EEO are available with the energy-saving techniques implemented either in software or in the BIOS. The facilities range from a single power-down facility to independent power-down times for CPU slow-down, hard disc power-down, monitor power-down and system power-down; intervals can be from one or two minutes up to one or two hours. Major manufacturers such as AMI and Phoenix already produce new BIOS chips. VESA is about to announce a standard for implementing power management via the BIOS - this is known as VBE/PM, the VESA BIOS Extension for Power Management. EIZO monitors already switch themselves off if no incoming signal is detected.

RESOLUTION

The quality of a screen picture, in terms of its detail, can be defined by its *'resolution'*.

Mode	Resolution	Max Colours
CGA	640 X 200	2 colour
CGA	320 X 200	4 colour
EGA	640 X 350	16 colour
VGA	640 x 480	256 colour
SVGA	800 x 600	> 256 colour
8514/A	1024 x 768	256 colour
XGA	1024 x 768	256 colour
EVGA/SVGA	1024 x 768	> 256 colour
Unnamed	1280 x 1024	> 256 colour
Unnamed	1600 x 1200	> 256 colour

The screen resolution is measured by the number of pixels across the screen, by the number of pixels that can be displayed in the vertical direction. The amount of colours for each resolution is merely the most commonly used figures; the colours available for the higher resolutions are really only limited by financial, rather than technical considerations. Monitors, such as the Philips Brilliance range, are available with resolutions up to 1600x1280.

Even these high resolutions are unable to fully meet modern needs. Advertisers used to talk a lot about WYSIWYG (What You See Is What You Get). This meant that the screen would display the image in exact size and detail as would be expected in the final printed output. The higher resolutions of modern printers place an increasing demand on WYSIWYG DTP and graphics systems. Consider that an A4 sheet is approximately 97 square inches - say 80 square inches after taking borders into consideration. A typical laser printer or inkjet printer has an output at 300 dpi (dots per inch), or 90,000 dots per square inch. So, to display a full A4 sheet

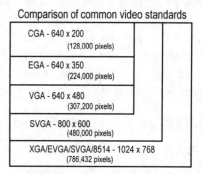

Comparison of common video standards

CGA - 640 x 200 (128,000 pixels)	
EGA - 640 x 350 (224,000 pixels)	
VGA - 640 x 480 (307,200 pixels)	
SVGA - 800 x 600 (480,000 pixels)	
XGA/EVGA/SVGA/8514 - 1024 x 768 (786,432 pixels)	

on screen - at printer resolution - would require 80 x 90,000, or a full 7,200,000 dots. Clearly, even the highest screen resolution is incapable of fully displaying detailed DTP and CAD work. With current printers having 600dpi and 1200dpi capability, the problem is greatly worsened. These limitations are minimised by the *'zoom'* facility offered by many packages; this allows a close up view of a small area of the printed output. While zooming allows the fine detail to be inspected, it is no longer at the correct physical size. Many would argue that this is not a problem since most users could not visually resolve 90,000 individual dots on a one inch square in any case.

DOT PITCH

In a shadow mask tube, the holes in the mask are set at pre-defined intervals across its surface.   The triads of colour phosphors are laid on the inner screen at a matching pitch.   The distance between the centre of one triad to the centre of the next triad is known as the *'dot pitch'*.   The dot pitch, therefore, is a measure of the finest quality possible in the picture from that particular monitor.   The dot pitch is measured in fractions of a millimetre.   The lower the dot pitch value, the more closely spaced can be the individual illuminated spots - hence the better picture detail.   Since the adjacent triad is physically offset, the dot pitch is a diagonal measurement. Some books and magazines also refer to dot pitch as the distance between two triad centres in the same horizontal row or to the nearest centre directly vertical but these would give inaccurate measurements since they don't necessarily measure to the nearest adjacent triad centre. The table shows the dot pitch converted into horizontal *'dots per inch'* which is a more useful measure when deciding the quality of a monitor.

The table shows the maximum number of dots that will appear across different screen sizes.

	14"	15"	17"	20"
Theoretical width of screen	11.2"	12"	13.6"	16""
Number of dots at .26mm dot pitch (80dpi)	896	896	1088	1280
Number of dots at .28mm dot pitch (89dpi)	997	997	1210	1424
Number of dots at .31mm dot pitch (96dpi)	1075	1075	1305	1536

As shown, there is a direct relationship between dot pitch, screen size and the maximum clear resolution.   So, a .28mm dot pitch monitor has around 1210 dots per line on a 17" screen but has only around 997 dots per line on a 14" screen.   The 17" monitor in this case is capable of handling 1024 x 768 mode with ease.   The 14", on the other hand, has many fewer dots on the screen than the number of individual pixels required by the 1024 x 768 picture. The result will be a marked loss of detail and the blurring of small characters. Since these are idealised figures, the 14" monitor is best run at no more 800 x 600.

The exact figures will vary by manufacturer and those in the table are working approximations.   Manufacturers tend to err on the side of over-estimating the active image area of their screens.   An inspection of a range of 17" monitors reveals that the actual screen diagonal size varies from 16.34" down to as little as 15.25".   In the worst case given, the monitor had a dot pitch of .26mm.   So, instead of the 1280 x 1024 resolution claimed, the screen is capable of a horizontal maximum of 1182 dots.

Although the smallest dot pitch is more desirable, they are more costly to manufacture. .24mm and even .22mm dot pitch monitors are available but are expensive. Typical dot pitch sizes for colour SVGA monitors are 0.26mm and 0.28mm; VGA monitors and large-size SVGA monitors normally have a 0.31mm dot pitch. Some manufacturers still claim that a .28mm 14" monitor is a 1024 x 768 model and this is only true if an inferior picture is acceptable, since each individual pixel cannot possibly be separately displayed. For large-screen monitors, the dot pitch can be greater without any loss of detail. Alternatively, the dot pitch can be reduced to .28mm; in this case, more detail can be crammed on the screen (e.g. more columns of a worksheet).

Even where a screen's construction quality allows for the reproduction of high resolution, the higher resolution modes may not be able to be used.   A 14" monitor, for example, would display tiny icons and extra small text if it was driven at high resolutions.   The table shows the most likely resolutions to be used with a particular screen size.

Resolution	Best Monitor Size
640 x 480	14"
800 x 600	15"
1024 x 768	17"
1600 x1200	20"

VIDEO STANDARDS

VESA

The Video Electronics Standards Association was formed out of a group of independent vendors of graphics controllers, who were unprepared to allow IBM to continue to set the standards.   Members include Intel, Orchid, Taxan, Tseng Labs and Video 7. The slowness of IBM in developing beyond VGA and its eventual production of an IBM-bound product in XGA, led VESA to produce their own advanced 800 x 600 standard in 1989; this became known as the Super VGA Standard (see below).   IBM is now a member of VESA, as are over 200 companies internationally.   VESA has gone on to tackle the problems caused by different manufacturers having different standards, by establishing a set of mode numbers which provide a common reference point for all graphics adapters. (See full VESA table later)

COMMON GRAPHICS MODES

Below is a brief description of the most popular graphics modes currently to be found in use. The earlier ranges, such as MDA, Hercules, CGA and EGA, are no longer manufactured but there is still a number of these in use.

MDA

Mono Display Adapter. This was the original screen for the earliest personal computers, as defined by IBM in 1981. It only supported a monochrome text mode of 80 x 25 characters.

HERCULES

This is the earliest high resolution graphics standard. It introduced a graphics mode and could display 720 x 350 pixels, in monochrome only. This mode is supported by much older software.

CGA

Colour Graphics Adapter. This is the original IBM standard for colour monitors. Although introducing colour, the CGA standard had a poorer resolution than the Hercules model. Its maximum resolution was 640 x 200 pixels - and this was in 2-colour mode. In 4-colour mode it could only support a resolution of 320 x 200. In new desk computer systems, it has been replaced by the much improved standards. It had a brief recovery for use in some cheaper portables and notebooks.

EGA

Enhanced Graphics Adapter. Introduced by IBM in 1984 and was a great improvement on the CGA standard. It was able to display 16 colours from a palette of 64, at the much improved resolution of 640 x 350. Like the MDA, Hercules and CGA systems, the EGA is no longer marketed.

VGA

Video Graphics Array. Introduced by IBM in 1987 and remains a popular mode. It introduced the first screen with square pixels, i.e. a 4:3 aspect ratio. It was also the first standard to dispense with TTL levels of screen drive and introduce varying levels of colour intensity. It handles a palette of 256 colours, with a resolution up to 640 x 480. It also supported refresh rates of 60Hz or 70 Hz. The 16-colour version quickly became the industry standard.

MCGA

Multicolour Graphics Adapter. This is basically a cut-down version of the VGA system. To save memory on the video card, it had no 640 x 480 16-colour mode. Since memory is now relatively cheap, MCGA is ignored in favour of VGA.

SVGA

Super VGA. The original VESA specification was for a 16-colour 800x600 screen. This produced over 50% more dots than VGA, for the same screen area. This allowed for example, spreadsheets to display more worksheets columns on the screen, by displaying 132 characters instead of the usual 80 characters. It was also very useful for Windows and its applications, since the user could see more icons on the screen at any one time as well as having improved resolution. This was the most common standard supplied with new models. Later VESA standards allowed for 1024x768 and 1280x1024 resolutions in 16 colour and 256 colour versions. It covers refresh rates of 56Hz, 60Hz or 72 Hz. Modern SVGA cards produce 16,777,216 colours.

8514/A

An IBM top-end product which does not use the memory-mapped method of other graphics cards. It was mainly aimed at the CAD market and has its own separate processor for graphics activities. (See later notes)

EVGA

Enhanced VGA. Introduced by VESA in 1991. A non-interlaced, 70 Hz refresh rate 8514/A standard which is only common in large-size screens.

XGA

Extended Graphics Array. Originally an interlaced standard from IBM which is more versatile than the 8514/A. The 8514/A and the XGA systems failed to replace VGA as IBM hoped. (See later)

NOTES
- There is a certain amount of uncertainty in dealers' specifications. Not all suppliers subscribe to the VESA coding. Often, the term SVGA simply means 'better than VGA'.   A 1024 x 768 card is sometimes called Ultra VGA.   Often, the higher resolution (1280 x 1024 and upwards) models are referred to as *'Workstation'* monitors.
- This confusion also involves VESA members, since they were producing video products before they came together to create common standards.   As a result, a large range of goods produced by VESA members is outwith their own standards. These lower specification products are 'unofficial' VESA standards and products.   This is be a diminishing problem, although many units will remain in use for some time.
- Some monitors are incapable of working down to 800x600 but are still marketed as 'SVGA'.
- A monitor advert which states *'up to 32,767 colours'* may only apply to a low resolution with higher resolutions only supporting 256 colours.
- Clearly, the specification of a monitor should be checked by a buyer, rather than relying on its title in an advertisement.
- Most cards can display a number of colours from a larger possible palette (e.g. 16 colours from 64 or 256 from 32,767).   A piece of software may wish to use more colours than the card is capable of displaying at any one time.   The 'extra' colours are displayed by *'dithering'* using the existing colours, producing a rather coarse hatching effect.   This may be acceptable in some applications but photo-realistic graphics, video clips and multimedia applications would demand a wider displayable colour range.

SCREEN SIZES

Higher resolution monitors allow more information to be simultaneously displayed on the screen - more of a worksheet, more of a database record, an entire A4 page of DTP.

ADVANTAGES
- Less time is spent on scrolling a window on the output.
- More data visible on screen at the same time means fewer errors.

DISADVANTAGES
- Putting more information on the same size of screen means that text, icons and graphics are all smaller than before - and therefore more difficulty to read.   A 14" model of SVGA monitor, for example, is only useful to those with gifted eyesight.
- To maintain the required readability requires a bigger - and therefore more expensive - monitor. The user is forced to move from a 14" model to a 17" or even 20" model.   Unfortunately, there appears to be a geometric ratio between screen size and cost.
- Bigger screens have problems maintaining an even resolution over the entire screen area;   some extreme areas become slightly fuzzy, due to convergence problems. Quality can be maintained over a larger screen area, with 'dynamic beam focusing', but this involves extra construction complexities - at an even greater cost.

The average monitor is a 14" or 15" model with 17" is becoming popular.   20" and 21" models are becoming widespread for DTP and CAD use.   For specialist work, multimedia and other presentations, Mitsubishi and NEC produce a staggering 37" model, at equally staggering prices.

NOTES
- When a manufacturer's specification refers to the screen size, it is describing the measurement between any two diagonal corners.
- This measurement usually does not describe the <u>actual</u> screen area, since it is common for the phosphor coating to only extend over a proportion of the front screen.   In these cases, there will be a permanent, unlit border round the screen area.

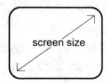
screen size

- The unused area of the screen does not result in any loss of resolution; it just means that the video detail is compressed into a smaller area than the screen dimension suggests.
- Although a small size monitor is capable of displaying a high resolution screen, it is often not a practical situation, since the size of the text can be too small to be readable. This is being countered by the introduction of *'anti-aliasing'*, a technique that adds artificial shading to lines and letters, to give an appearance of added sharpness.

SCREEN DRIVES

RGB

This is the most straight forward of the colour drive methods and is the method used for the older CGA and EGA standards. For CGA, four connections are used to convey the picture information from the computer to the monitor (other connections are used for the signal ground and the horizontal and vertical synchronisation signals). The RGB system operated by switching the red, green and blue guns off and on; from zero volts to around one volt. Any gun, at any time, is either fully switched on or fully switched off. The fourth connection allows any of the eight colours to be displayed in one of two intensities (i.e. - red appears pinkish, etc.). EGA systems provided two wires for each gun - one for on/off and one for intensity. This resulted in 64 possible colours. These drives were described as *'TTL'* types (**T**ransistor to **T**ransistor **L**ogic).

ANALOGUE

For accurate design work a monitor with sharp images in a range of colours is perfectly adequate. However, for art work, a greater degree of diversity of colours is required. After all, a 'real' picture has many shades and hues. With RGB drive, any gun, at any time, was either fully on or fully off. This is unable to meet more sophisticated needs. Ideally, each of the guns should be able to have its intensity varied from fully off to fully on - and every intensity in between. The permutations provided would provide the rich variety we encounter in normal life. It is argued that, for art and graphic work, a greater variety of colours on screen has a greater impact on the viewer than increased screen resolution.

A VGA graphics adapter drives the colour guns at 64 different intensity levels. Since there are three guns, the possible colours produced are 64 to the power 3, which is 262,144 colours. For XGA and SVGA, the guns can be driven at 256 different levels, which results in 16,777,216 different colours.

NOTE   The current construction of some monitors may not allow the display of much more than about 256,000 different colours. The computer system - its memory, its graphics hardware and its software drivers - can now handle over 16 million colours. The drive variations to provide the 16 million colours will still be sent to the monitor but, mainly due to the characteristics of the phosphors, the full range of colours may not be reproduced.

COMPOSITE VIDEO

In this method, the output from the PC is a single signal that combines the three colour components and the synchronisation signals. The monitor has to separate these signals, before applying them to the monitor circuitry. Some PCs (e.g. the Commodore range) have a composite output as well as a RGB output. This allows these models to use some TVs as monitors, which can be useful. However, they suffer from poorer quality; as the extra signal processing circuitry introduces more noise and more signal distortion. For these reasons, this method is only common on home games computers and is not often found as an option for PCs. A 'VGA to TV PAL' card is available that provides a composite video output to connect a PC computer to a domestic TV but results are obviously inferior to a proper monitor.

DISPLAY DATA CHANNEL

VESA has developed a system, known as DDC, whereby the graphics card and monitor can communicate with each other using one of the unused pins on the video connector cable. This is of special significance when used with the Plug and Play facilities of Windows 95. The monitor holds information on its specification and this 128-bit information block is continually transmitted to the graphics card. The data block is called the *'Extended Display Identification'* - EDID. The graphics card can then adjust to the best drive for that monitor. For example, graphics cards will always automatically use the maximum refresh rates supported by the monitor for a particular resolution. It will also automatically use the best screen mode available. These changes take place without any activity on the part of the user although the user is still free to choose the setup if desired.

The current standard has two levels - DDC1 and DDC2. DDC1 describes the basic operation and DDC2 is further split into B and AB categories. The B specification supports a larger range of video modes DDC1 while the AB specification supports a new bus, termed the ACCESS.BUS to control the monitor/graphic card communication. The ACCESS.BUS is a serial system that rivals the USB (see page 120). DDC-compliant monitors include Sony's 20", Goldstar's 21", ViewSonic's 17"and Nokia's 17" models. DDC1-compliant cards include the Diamond Stealth 64 and the Matrox Millenium.

DUAL SYNC / MULTI-SYNC

Some monitors may only operate on a single line frequency. When attached to a computer graphics card, it adjusts its running speed to synchronise to that of the video output. This is a minor automatic adjustment and extends only to very limited frequency boundaries. Producing this single standard model requires less complex circuitry and is cheaper. *'Dual Sync'* monitors sense the frequency of the incoming signal and lock to it if it is one of its two pre-set line frequencies - normally 31.5Khz and 35.5KHz. Many modern monitors are capable of automatically locking to a range of different line and frame scan frequencies within the bandwidth it is designed for. They are said to be 'multi-sync', 'multi-scanning' or 'autosync'. If the upper limit of this scanning range is high enough, an element of future-proofing is introduced, since the monitor will be able to handle any future specification upgrades (new standards will involve higher refresh rates). The fact that a monitor's circuitry can synchronise to a range of different refresh speeds, does not imply that it will perform equally well at all the standards it can cover. A model that can cover CGA will not manage to stretch to cover SVGA. Indeed, models that are designed for SVGA use often perform less well when trying to handle lower standards (most models don't even try to cover CGA or EGA). Generally, analogue signals will not properly drive an RGB monitor and an RGB signal will not properly drive an analogue monitor. Some monitors are advertised as being both analogue and digital. These monitors have added circuitry to make the conversion.

Typical scan frequencies for the range of screen resolutions are given in the table below.

	Line Scan (max)	Frame Scan (typical)
MDA	18.4KHz	50 Hz
HERCULES	18.1KHz	49Hz
CGA	15.7KHz	60Hz
EGA	21.9KHz	60Hz
VGA	31.5KHz	60Hz, 70 Hz, 72 Hz
SVGA	35.5KHz	56Hz
	37.8KHz	60Hz (standard)
	48KHz	72 Hz (VESA)
8514/A	35.5KHz	43Hz interlaced
	48KHz	60Hz, 70 Hz
1280 x 1024	66KHz	60Hz

An autosynched monitor is ready, if the facility is provided, to auto-size the screen image.

AUTO-SIZING

In VGA, 480 lines are used to display a graphics screen, while the VGA text mode uses only 400 lines. An EGA picture only requires 350 lines of a VGA screen. When the program switches mode, the vertical screen size should adjust to ensure that the picture occupies the entire screen area. Consider a screen which is adjusted so that a text mode output fills the screen. If the output is switched to graphic mode - without re-sizing - the graphics screen will be slightly squashed. Conversely, a monitor adjusted to display a graphics will stretch a text output, unless the screen is re-sized.

SCREEN MEMORY

The number of colours that a monitor can produce is theoretically endless. The limitation is in the ability of the computer graphics card to store all the possible colour permutations for each screen pixel. All graphics standards (apart from 8514/A) use a *'memory mapped'* method of handling screen output. An area of computer memory is reserved for holding the individual pixels that comprise the screen picture. This screen memory is <u>additional</u> to the computer's 640k user area; in all but the lowest resolutions, extra memory for storing the screen's composition will be located on the graphics controller card. The data in this memory area is used to regularly update the picture. The computer's CPU has the task of constantly updating the screen memory area. The electronics on the graphics card read this information and use it to control the drive to the monitor. For a simple, monochrome system the storage may only require a single bit per pixel. If the bit is 0, the pixel is left unlit; if the bit is 1 then the pixel is illuminated. In colour systems, extra pixels are required, to store the colour and hue of the pixel.

In text modes, the bit pattern for each displayable character (i.e. the alpha-numeric set, punctuation and the IBM extended character set) is pre-stored and is copied into the screen memory area. It is a much more complex task in graphics mode. To place a straight line on the screen, the CPU must calculate the position of every pixel in that line and write this information to the appropriate screen memory locations. For an arc, there is the added time required to calculate the curve's co-ordinates.

HEALTH & SAFETY

EC directive 90/270/EEC was passed in May 1990. It took effect from 1st January 1993, with all new and modified workstations coming under its terms. All workstations, both existing stations and new sales, are covered by 1st January 1996. The directive ensures that workers using VDUs are:

- given full information on the use of office equipment
- provided with monitors to required standards on ergonomics and emissions.

In the UK, the Health and Safety at Work Act, through the Health and Safety (Display Screen Equipment) Regulations, embodies the EC directive and the British Health and Safety Executive will provide guidelines on the directive. The directive sets out minimum requirements in a range of areas such as VDU, keyboard, desk, chair, lighting, noise, heat and humidity, along with employer obligations to train employees, reduce employee VDU time, protect employees' eyesight and enact worker consultation and participation. The standards of the directive are contained in its annexe and this is largely based on the ISO standard 9241 "Ergonomic requirements for office work with visual display terminals". Of course, the HSE and employers' organisations such as the CBI have differences with the trade unions on the interpretation of individual items of the directive. The aim should be the creation of a safe, functional and productive working environment for the benefit of all.

The legislation ensures that employers will provide VDU operators with a free eyesight test when requested by an operator. If necessary, the employer will also provide *"corrective appliances"* (spectacles). The definition of a VDU operator is one who uses a VDU for between 3 and 5 hours per day. The HSE provide a pamphlet entitled *"Display Screen Equipment Work"* that explains definitions for different types of VDU user.

Legislation also covers the hardware design. As a result of EC action, monitors, like other goods, will carry the *'CE'* mark - an EC safety mark.

RADIATION

The harmful effect of electromagnetic radiation from monitors has been an issue that is controversial and still not satisfactorily resolved. Some reports, mainly from Sweden, Finland and Denmark, suggest that monitor radiation can induce leukaemia and brain cancer. Others, including the Health and Safety Executive, dispute the reports and there are claims that the reports are under-researched and discredited. Still others accept that there is a cancer danger from monitor radiation - but small in comparison to cancer dangers from smoking and diet. Computer monitors produce high magnetic fields. These are essential to the running of the monitor, as high currents are required for the beam deflection circuitry. They are no different from the magnetic fields that are emanated from all 50Hz mains electrical equipment and wiring. It is the effects of sustained exposure that causes concern. After all, a user would not normally sit in front of an electric kettle for 8 hours a day but a computer user could easily spend 8 hours a day less than two feet from a monitor. In this respect, it is similar to the claims of harmful effects of living under high-voltage power lines.

Radiation from monitors occurs mostly from rear although an appreciable amount also occurs from the front. The fields diminish sharply with distance.

For increased safety, the following steps can be taken:

- Use an LCD screen, or other non-CRT display, if this is acceptable.
- Use a monochrome monitor, if possible. These have lower radiation levels.
- Purchase a low radiation monitor (usually tagged as 'LR'). Note that if a monitor has a special screen coating to reduce radiation, this coating also reduces the screen brightness.
- Position the monitor about 30" from the user.
- Ensure that no other workers are seated less than 4' from the rear of the monitor.

The EC Directive 90/270 talks of radiation levels being reduced to *'negligible levels'* and the Swedish MPR-II standard (also called MPR 1990) has become a popular yardstick, because it provides actual radiation levels.   Radiation is categorised as both ELF (Extremely Low Frequency - ie 1Hz to 1KHz) and VLF (Very Low Frequency - ie 1KHz to 400KHz). The chart shows the MPR-II standard.

Frequency Band	Electric Field (in volts per metre)	Magnetic Field (in nano Teslas)
ELF	25	250
VLF	2.5	25

However, the Health and Safety (Display Screen Equipment) Regulations exempt the UK from the requirements of MPR II. The Swedish regulatory body NTUEK, by contrast, works on the assumption of a link between radiation and cancer and has mandatory minimum radiation levels.   Another standard that is sometimes quoted (e.g. from Hitachi) is the TUV standard from Germany.   This standard covers both radiation levels and refresh rates. It is a combination of the MPR standard and ISO 9241 that covers image quality.   The Swedish TCO 1992 standard lays down rules on electromagnetic radiation levels, heat emission, automatic low power switching and electrical safety.

PHYSICAL LAYOUT

The layout of keyboard, monitor and documents in relation to the user's vision and easy physical reach is of great importance.   Prolonged periods of body inactivity, particularly in bad seating, can itself result in backache and neckache.   Add uncomfortable seats and badly laid out desks and the situation is worsened.

Bad desk layouts not only contribute to back problems - they are also a source of eye problems, as users strain to read monitors and documents in adverse conditions.   In a normal day, the human eye experiences a variety of muscle movements.   The eye normally moves rapidly from one object to another, with the vertical, horizontal and focusing changes that are entailed.   In contrast, prolonged viewing of a VDU involves prolonged muscle tension, to maintain concentration on a relatively small flickering viewing area.   VDU users complain of a range of symptoms from redness, watering and ache through to focusing difficulties, loss of clarity and double vision.

A range of measures to improve user conditions includes:

- Size of desk.   An inadequate desk surface usually results in an unmanageable clutter, loss of productivity and user stress.   Consider placing the CPU unit under the desk, or using mini-tower CPU units. Most desks are about 70cm high, which satisfies the average user.
- Seating position. The seat should be comfortable and be of the swivel type, preferably on castors. The seat height and backrest should be adjustable. Certain users may require foot rests to maintain adequate posture.
- Size and type of monitor screen. The screen size should be adequate for the job being carried out. Detailed CAD or DTP work on a small screen is a sure way to cause eyestrain and lost working days.
- Position of monitor. The monitor should be moved to suit the user and not the other way round.   EC regulations require that monitors have positional adjustment (e.g. a tilt and swivel base or adjustable monitor arm).   The VDU user should be able to rotate the display from side to side as well as tilt the screen up and down.   Many users prefer to stand the monitor directly on the desk surface, rather than on top of computer case.   Some desks have glass top so that the VDU can be situated under the glass.   This frees the desk space but may introduce extra reflections from office lighting.   A preferred position would involve the user being stationed about 30" from the monitor and looking down on it from a small angle.   Flickering first affects the edges of a user's vision. If a user sits close to a monitor, the effects of flicker will be more pronounced.
- Position of monitor controls.   These should be front-mounted for ease of access. Thumbwheel controls provide greater precision setting than tiny knobs.
- Protection of monitor controls. Ideally, the controls should be covered by a flap, to prevent accidental changes to settings.
- Regular breaks - necks suffer most when forced to maintain a fixed position for long periods; eyes suffer from maintaining a fixed focal distance.   Those employees on permanent screen operations - data entry workers, database operators, program coders, etc. - should have scheduled breaks in their working day.
- Use of document holders - these can be adjusted for the most comfortable reading position. This avoids the continual refocusing involved when reading documents that are left on the desk.

SCREEN GLARE

The aim is to minimise the amount of office light that reflects from the screen surface of the monitor. Screen glare makes reading the screen data extremely difficult and is very tiring to user eyes.   The aim is to have as little contrast as possible between the screen and its surroundings.   Preventative measures include both lighting and environment changes and choice of monitors.

- Avoid fluorescent lighting completely.   The room lighting should be diffused.   Both the Lighting Industry Federation and the Chartered Institute of Building Service Engineers provide booklets that cover the problems of poor lighting and the lighting required for areas where VDUs are in use.
- Don't place a monitor in front of windows or other bright light sources.   If there is no alternative to having a monitor face a window, use blinds or curtains.
- The room walls and furnishings should have matt surfaces with neutral colouring.
- Use monitors with FST tubes, as they suffer less glare than conventional tubes.

- High quality monochrome VGA grey-scale monitors produce high contrast results and are preferable to a higher resolution colour monitors with fuzzy patches.
- Use monitors whose screens have anti-glare silica coatings. The screen can also be etched to refract the light. A smooth panel can be bonded to the surface of the screen. This lets light out, but minimises glare by breaking up light that strikes the screen. By preventing light entering the tube, the picture contrast is improved - as in Trinitron tubes.
- Use monitors with fast refresh rates as this will minimise the effects of flicker. Some monitor tubes use long-persistence phosphors to minimise flicker, but they also tend to blur movement.
- Fit a non-glare filter in front of monitor screen. These are mostly made from glass, although some are plastic. But beware, the Association Optometrists believe that filters reduce glare - at the expense of making the screen more difficult to read. Keep the screen clean, with an anti-static cleaning compound.
- Use VDU spectacles when working at screens; these are specially tinted and can include prescription lenses.
- Choose screen colours carefully (where the application allows the user to define screen colours). There is some evidence that dark lettering on a light background aids readability and is more protective to the eyes when using typed or printed documentation. There is no need for the user to constantly adapt to differing contrasts. On the other hand, dark backgrounds suffer less from the effects of flicker, although this is now less of a problem with the new higher screen refresh rates.

STRESS

Employees who spend long periods on VDU suffer greater levels of stress than other employees. The source of such stress appears to be the high levels of productivity expected of data-entry workers, poor working environment and the low esteem associated with jobs that have been computerised. This is covered by the EC directive that states

> *"the employer must plan work activities in such a way that daily work on a display screen is periodically interrupted by breaks or changes of activity, reducing the workload at the display screen".*

This is based on the old adage that *'a change is as good as a rest'.* A balanced load of VDU work and other work will improve working conditions and will probably lead to more productivity in the long run.

The Health and Safety Regulations requires that employers carry out risk assessment. This involves assessing the risk to their employees' health and safety, employing competent safety officers, devising appropriate safety measures, and training staff in these safety measures.

ADJUSTMENTS/CONTROLS

Many of the reported problems of users are easy to resolve. Most of the monitor problems come into that category. Often, a monitor is simply badly adjusted, or has gone out of adjustment over time. A few simple tweaks may be all that is required to restore normal working. Most monitors provide the basic control over its operations in the form of adjustable knobs or thumbwheels; a few controls require a screwdriver adjustment.

COMMON CONTROLS
Most quality monitors allow a fair degree of trimming of the monitor performance, as follows:

BRIGHTNESS
This varies the density of the electron beam(s) and hence the amount of screen illumination. In monitors with poor power regulation, an increase in brightness might lead to a shrinking of the picture size. This may appear with manual alterations to the brightness control - or may occur when the screen content switches from a mainly black content to a mainly white content. The monitor power supply cannot cope with the increased current demands and the voltage to the screen scanning circuitry drops. The reduced voltage means that the scan drive is reduced and the picture occupies a smaller proportion of the screen area. At the extremes, this cannot be cured by user adjustment and the monitor has to be sent for repair.

CONTRAST
This control increases the amplitude of the drive to the gun(s) and hence increases the ratio between different levels of screen brightness. Too much contrast drives the light grey details into displaying as white, thereby losing detail. Too little contrast makes all colours tend to grey, producing a wishy-washy screen.

HOR/VER POSITION
These controls adjust the starting points, and hence the stopping points of both the horizontal scan and vertical scan. The effect of these adjustments is to move the picture vertically or horizontally along the screen and this is used to centre the picture.

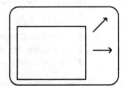

HOR/VER SIZE

The position controls determine the commencing point of the scans. The size controls vary the amplitude of the beam swing in the horizontal and vertical planes and this determines the actual size of the illuminated portion of the screen. Some monitor models can be adjusted so that the scans fill the entire screen area, eliminating the black border. This increases the effective viewing area and aids readability. However, with shadow mask tubes particularly, this may result in the loss of menu options at the corners (this is particularly a Windows problem, where icons like the minimise/maximise icon sit in the extreme top left hand corner of the screen).

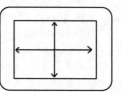

PRE-SET CONTROLS

Monitors come with the following different approaches to their controls:

- Entirely manual - the user has to make adjustments each time the monitor is used for a different mode. This is thankfully now uncommon.
- Auto-sensing . This requires no user intervention, as it works entirely automatically. This is the most common approach.
- User choice from either a set of in-built stored settings or from a set of user-entered settings that were digitally set and stored. If none of these options are taken, the system works in auto-sensing mode.

Where digital controls are used, there are usually 8 or 9 settings, although there can be up to 30 predefined modes & user-defined settings. Now, the monitor circuitry automatically sizes and places images as it switches between resolutions. A block of built-in memory is used to store size and positional information for different analogue and digital sources.

LESS COMMON CONTROLS

VER/HOR CONVERGENCE CONTROLS

Some monitors, such as the Iiyama Vision Master, allow the user to adjust the convergence of the three colour elements of the picture. In most monitors these are internal controls, as best results are obtained with test equipment. A signal which comprises three colour grids, is injected into the monitor, so that the alignment of the colours is achieved more easily. Without a test generator, the adjustment is a more hit-and-miss affair.

PINCUSHION CONTROL

Like the control above, this control is also concerned about the picture's shape, as opposed to its size or position. It is difficult to maintain linearity at the extremes of the picture area and the result is 'pincushion distortion' as shown in an exaggerated form in the diagram. The Compaq V70 monitor, for example, allows the user some control over the screen's beam linearity.

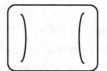

TRAPEZOIDAL DISTORTION

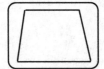

With trapezoidal distortion, the edges of the screen remain straight but the scan length at the top of the screen is progressively lengthened with each successive line scanned. This produces a trapezoidal shape as shown in the diagram. Again, the shape has been exaggerated for clarity. In-built to the Hitachi CM6111ET.

HOR/VER LOCK

This is also called horizontal and vertical phase. Controls are often marked as HSYNC and VSYNC. These controls vary the lock between the incoming sync signals from the computer video circuits and the monitors internal oscillators. The adjustment ensures that the monitor's oscillators maintain synchronisation.

CONTROL OF INDIVIDUAL GUNS BRIGHTNESS

This degree of control allows the user to set the screen colours to match printer colours, where the user has a colour printer. Used in the Mitsubishi Diamond Pro and Philips Brilliance monitors.

> CAUTION
> Internal pre-sets exist for brightness, convergence, etc. Leave these well alone. These adjustments are intended for trained service staff. And, don't forget that there can be as much as 25Kvolts on the final anode of the cathode ray tube!

ALTERNATIVES TO CRTs

LIQUID CRYSTAL DISPLAYS

The Liquid Crystal Display is one of the most popular alternative to cathode ray tube VDUs and is widely used in portable and notebook PCs.   It employs the following principles:

Light is only a very high frequency radiated wave.   In fact, light is *'unpolarised'* - it is composed of waves in angles of every plane. In an LCD display, the source of this light is usually a fluorescent source behind the screen - such models being described as having a *'backlit'* display.   This light is passed through a polarising filter. Only the waves in a single plane will pass through this filter. This single plane is known as the *'plane of polarisation'*. This polarised light is then presented with another polarising filter.   If the second filter has the same plane of polarisation as the first filter, then the light will be able to pass through and be viewed by the user. If the plane of polarisation is opposed to that of the first filter, then no light wave will be able to pass through.

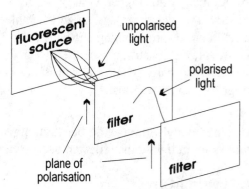

It follows, then, that if the second filter can alter its plane of polarisation, it will control the flow of light waves to the user.   If the diagram was considered as a single pixel and was repeated thousands of times over, as a matrix, then it would constitute a VDU screen.

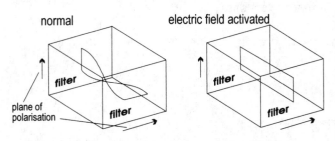

In practice, it is not possible to continually alter the plane of polarisation of the second filters. Instead, a cell is composed of a piece of *'nematic'* liquid crystal between the filters. The planes of polarisation of the two filters differ by 90 degrees.   Now, the light from the fluorescent source still passes through the first filter in a single plane only.   This time, the effect of passing through the liquid crystal is to twist the wave 90 degrees, along the crystal's plane.   When the wave reaches the second filter, it is at the correct angle to pass through since they are both aligned.   So, the normal state is to pass light.   That is why most LCDs have a lit screen as default.   The second diagram shows the effect of applying an electric field to the cell. The molecules of the liquid crystal will line up, its plane will become straight and there will be no 90 degree twist to the light wave as it passes through.   The light's plane is now different from the second filter and no light will pass through the filter.   So, if each pixel area has its electric field switched on or off, pixels will be lit or unlit - i.e. a functioning VDU has been created.   If the two filters are given the same planes of polarisation, then pixels will remain unlit until the electric field is energised.

LCD CONSTRUCTION

In practice, the display is not constructed pixel by pixel.   Instead, the screen is manufactured as a single entity, with a layer of liquid crystal sandwiched between layers of glass.   This, in turn, is sandwiched between polarising sheets.   A grid of wires is used to access any particular area of the screen surface.   A voltage is applied to the appropriate vertical and horizontal co-ordinates, to activate that particular pixel. This is called *'direct multiplexing'* and although relatively easy to manufacture, it is difficult to control drive of the cells.   The main problems are:

- The voltage on the control wires cannot be too high, otherwise there is a likelihood of turning on cells adjacent to the wanted cell.
- The small allowable voltage swings do not provide enough control to achieve satisfactory grey scales and good contrast.
- The scanning arrangements are inadequate.   The data on every pixel in a line can be stored and applied to the vertical wires at the same time.   However, It is only possible to address a single row at any one time.   So, for example, a VGA screen of 480 lines would result in each line only having its pixels set every 1/480th of the time.   The greater the vertical resolution, the less time is available for holding a particular cell in the 'dark' state.   During the rest of the time, the cell is reverting to its 'light' state, with a consequent deterioration of picture contrast.

TFT DISPLAYS

To solve the above problems, a system known as an *'active matrix'* is employed. This uses TFT (thin film transistors) in a matrix, with a single transistor located at the junction of each vertical and horizontal control wire. The voltage at each cell can now be increased, since smaller level signals can be placed on the control wires which will be amplified by the transistor. Since this higher voltage now only occurs right at the cell, there is little chance of activating adjacent cells. The result is a sharper picture. Additionally, the higher voltage swings result in faster cell changes and therefore greater contrast. Finally, the higher voltage range available allows much greater control over grey scales. TFT LCDs also improve on scanning difficulties. The short time available for each cell remains unavoidable. However, the construction of the TFT screen results in a capacitance effect on each cell. This maintains the desired charge while the cell is not being addressed and holds the desired 'dark' state. This also improves screen contrast.

NOTE

In some models, there is no backlighting source. Instead, a mirror is placed behind the display. This allows room light to be reflected back or blocked, dependent on the controlling electric field.

COLOUR LCDs

LCDs are also available in colour versions. These are expensive, since they have even greater production quality control problems than monochrome versions.

They are available in both passive-matrix and active-matrix versions.

ADVANTAGES OF LCDs

- No electron beams - so no linearity problems - no misconvergence, no pincushion distortion, no sizing/positioning
- Low power consumption and low voltages
- Light weight - ideal for portables
- No radiation, unlike CRTs
- Flat displays - hang on wall / easy to locate in work area
- No flicker problems

DISADVANTAGES

- Fixed mode of operation
- Restricted viewing angle
- Poor contrast. Supertwist displays give more contrast but introduce a certain tinge. This is correctable with special film coatings and extra construction complexity. It is called 'triple supertwist'. It is more expensive to manufacture and is used in the best LCD displays.
- Slow speed. When the liquid crystal structure has been pulled into a straight configuration, under the influence of the electric field, it takes a relatively long time to restore to its former state. This explains why LCD screens often 'smear' when scrolling or attempting other fast screen updating.
- Costly to manufacture, due to difficulties of quality control

PASSIVE MATRIX

The cheaper of the versions, this screen is effectively a sandwich of three mono LCD screens, each screen emitting either red, green or blue. To increase efficiency, *'dual scan'* displays are now produced. These split the screen in two vertically and each half is simultaneously scanned and lit. So, a single screen is painted in half the time - i.e. the refresh rate is doubled and flicker is halved.

ACTIVE MATRIX

Each colour triad is comprised of the necessary red, green and blue LCD elements and each is activated by its own switching transistor. In this way, the TFT mechanisms described above take place on light waves of pre-determined colour. Since each element is individually switched, the *'ghousting'* associated with older screens is eliminated. In addition, TFT elements are less sensitive to heat and brighter back lights can be used. Unfortunately, these screen are expensive to produce, since a normal VGA monitor would require almost a million transistors to be assembled on the one screen. A single non-working transistor means that a pixel has lost one of its colour elements and the screen has to be scrapped. About a third of all units produced are unable to meet this very demanding quality control. Models that can handle 24-bit colour and 20" screens are being worked on currently.

GRAPHICS CARDS

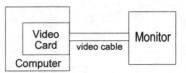

The electronics to drive the monitor is mounted on a separate graphics card that slots into the expansion bus on the computer's motherboard. The output from this card appears on a socket at the rear of the computer case. The diagram shows the two main types of connector used with PCs. The CGA connector and EGA connector are identical and each has two rows of pins while the VGA/SVGA/XGA connector has three rows of pins. The chart shows the use of the pins.

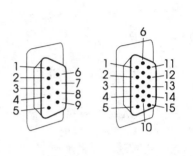

Pin	Mono	CGA	EGA	VGA/SVGA/XGA
1	Ground	Ground	Ground	Red
2	Ground	Ground	Red Intensity	Green
3	Not Used	Red	Red	Blue
4	Not Used	Green	Green	Not Used
5	Not Used	Blue	Blue	Not Used
6	Intensity	Intensity	Green Intensity	Red Return
7	Video	Not Used	Blue Intensity	Green Return
8	Horizontal Synch	Horizontal Synch	Horizontal Synch	Blue Return
9	Vertical Synch	Vertical Synch	Vertical Synch	No Pin (used as key)
10				Ground
11				Not Used
12				Not Used
13				Horizontal Synch
14				Vertical Synch
15				Not Used

There are a number of factors to be considered when purchasing a graphics card. Such a purchase might be as part of an entire system. It is also possible to buy a matching graphics card and monitor, to upgrade the graphics facilities of an existing system. The main considerations are:

A.	RAM size/Resolution/Colour Depth
B.	Bandwidth
C.	RAM type
D.	External bus type
E.	Internal bus size
F.	Refresh rates
G.	Chip Set used
H.	RAMDAC used
I.	Extra facilities (eg video handling), 3D

A. GRAPHICS RAM SIZE

The main memory of the PC was not designed for the current high-resolution screens. The amount of memory put aside to hold the screen information is totally inadequate by today's standards. Out of the 1Mb memory area, a maximum of 128Kb is laid aside for graphics memory. This would directly address a 640 x200 screen of 256 colours. To go beyond this specification, the machine would need to have the additional graphics information stored in <u>extra</u> memory with special software routines to access this extra hardware. Consequently, graphics cards have their own memory chips to store graphics information. The RAM size required is determined by the maximum screen resolution and the maximum colour depth (ie how many colours to be displayed).

The formula to calculate the amount of memory required for a particular screen standard is:
HORIZONTAL RESOLUTION x VERTICAL RESOLUTION x COLOUR BITS / 8
The number of bits for each pixel depends on the number of colours that the pixel has to display. For monochrome, only one bit per pixel is required (pixel is either lit or unlit). For 4 colours, 2 bits per pixel are required, providing 2 to the power of 2 combinations. For 16 colours, 4 bits are required, providing 2 to the power 4 combinations. For 256 colours, 8 bits are required (i.e. 2 to the power 8 combinations). A 16-bit system can provide 65,536 different colours for each pixel (called 'high colour'), while a 24-bit system provides 16.7million colours (often termed 'true colour'). Some cards offer 30-bit depth which produces 1,073,741,824 colours! Other cards use 32-bits to handle true colour at faster rates.
The equation given produces a memory requirement specified in bytes. Dividing the result by 1024 gives a requirement measured in Kilobytes (Kb). There are 1024 bytes to a kilobyte. Dividing by a further 1024 produces a measurement in Mb (MegaBytes).

EXAMPLES

A 16-colour VGA screen would require

640 x 480 x 4 / 8 = 150 Kbytes

A 16-colour SVGA screen would require

800 x 600 x 4/8 = 234Kbytes (i.e. at least a 256k card)

A 256-colour VGA screen would require

640 x 480 x 8 / 8 = 300 Kbytes (i.e. at least a 512k card)

A 256- colour SVGA screen would require

800 x 600 x 8/ 8 = 469 Kbytes (i.e. at least a 512k card)

A 256-colour 1024 x 768 screen would require

1024 x 768 x 8 / 8 = 768 Kb (i.e. a full 1Mb card)

A 24-bit, true colour 1024 x 768 screen with 16.7 million colours would require

1024 x 768 x 24 / 8 = 2.25Mb

Finally, a top of the range system with true colour at 1600 x 1200 would require

1600 x 1200 x 24 / 8 = 5.49Mb

Bits per pixel	Colour Depth
4	16
8	256
16	65,536
24	16.7m

SVGA cards used to be supplied in 256Kb and 512Kb versions; they now come from 1Mb to 4Mb.

NOTES

- A graphics card may be advertised as being, say, a 2Mb memory board. However, the board may not be fully populated. If the board's design allows for future expansion, then extra memory can be fitted to the card to allow it to cope with greater resolutions. Many cards allow up to 4Mb of memory to be fitted while the Chrome 731 card allows up to 40Mb to be fitted.
- Where the fitted RAM size is vastly greater than is currently required for a particular mode, the memory can be divided into *'pages'* - each page containing the data for a full graphics screen. This allows rapid switching between screens, since the second screen can have its pixel pattern built up in memory, while the first screen is being displayed.   This is the basis of on-screen animation.

B. BANDWIDTH

The term *'bandwidth'* is used to describe both memory and graphics needs and there are important differences.   The general description of monitor bandwidth is given on page 124.   With colour monitors, the graphics data is sent in parallel to three separate guns and the amount of colours being used is not relevant to the bandwidth calculation.   The restriction on any one channel's capabilities is measured by the resolution required and the refresh rate.   The formula to calculate the required graphics bandwidth is:

HORIZONTAL RESOLUTION x VERTICAL RESOLUTION x REFRESH RATE / 8

So, a 640 x 480 display with a 70Hz refresh rate requires to cope with

640 X 480 X 70 / 8 =   2.56Mb /sec, ie over 20 million different pixel values per sec

while a 1600 x 1200 display with a 75Hz refresh rate requires to handle

1600 X 1200 x 75 / 8 = 17.17Mb /sec, ie over 135 million different pixel values per sec

Memory bandwidth is much greater than graphics bandwidth for the same screen because it has to store and transfer the colour details for each pixel.

So, a 640 x 480 display, with a refresh rate of 70Hz and 256 colours requires to transfer

640 X 480 X 70 X 8 / 8 =   20.2Mb /sec, ie over 160 million different pixel values per sec

while a 1600 x 1200 display with a 75Hz refresh rate and 16m colours requires to transfer

1600 X 1200 x 75 X 24 / 8 = 137.36Mb /sec, ie over 432 million different pixel values per sec

Where a card is intended for multimedia and video use, the bandwidth capability of both the monitor and the graphics become crucial factors.

C. RAM TYPE

At one stage all graphics cards used standard DRAM (Dynamic RAM) chips as a frame buffer to store the graphics information about that frame.   In this *'Single Port'* system, the CPU has to write <u>to</u> the DRAM using the same data and address buses as that used to get data <u>from</u> the DRAM to the VDU driver circuitry. Since these transfers in and out cannot be simultaneous, a bottleneck existed.   The logic value on a single pin on the DRAM chips controlled whether the memory was in read or write mode.   When toggled to write mode, the CPU updated the screen information.   When in read mode, the chips on the graphics card read the information and processed it to drive the monitor.

The last few years have seen the introduction of cards using VRAM (video RAM) which overcomes the speed limitation imposed by conventional DRAM. With the VRAM *'Dual Port'* system, separate address and data buses are provided for the in an out transfers. Hence, this memory block is capable of being both read and written to simultaneously, with the system preventing attempts to read and write to the exact same memory areas at the same time. Writing will be carried with random access - i.e. only those pixels that need updating need be accessed and altered. Since the stream of data to the monitor is in serial format, the read process will always be a complete sequential read of the frame buffer. This greatly speeds up the screen handling process and the extra cost is justified where fast screen updates are required. VRAM system require their own dedicated controller.

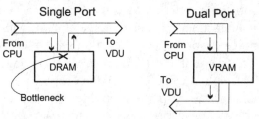

A variation on VRAM is Windows RAM (WRAM).   This is modified dual-ported system and is faster then VRAM and up to 50% faster than DRAM.   It carries out some of the tasks (eg blitting) normally placed on the graphics controller, thereby speeding up processing. It is manufactured by Samsung and can be found in high performance systems such as the Matrox Millenium card. Other options are EDO RAM as found in the VideoLogic GrafixStar card and Multibank DRAM as found in Tseng ET6000-based cards such as the STB Lightspeed 128 and the GrafixStar 600.   See the chapter on Memory for details of these memory chips.

D. EXTERNAL BUS TYPE

A very wide range of graphics cards is available, using every type of data bus system. Since the fastest data buses have the greatest throughput, the graphics card should be matched to the fastest bus.   So, a PCI computer will be able to accommodate a graphics card on either its ISA expansion slot or its PCI expansion slot.   Although an older ISA graphics card will work in the system, a PCI card would show a marked improvement.   Similarly, a VESA card should be used in a VESA local bus machine, although an ISA can be used.   PCI cards and VL cards are not interchangeable.

Older graphics cards are supplied in 8-bit and 16-bit data bus models.   Since the width of the data bus affects the speed of data transfer into the graphics card, users should attempt to purchase a 16-bit model.   Users with 8-bit XT machines have no choice, since their machines only have 8-bit buses. Most standard ISA PCs will make use of the 16-bit model.   The 32-bit models are for use with the *'local bus'* architectures, where greater data transfer rates between the system and the graphics card can be gained. Versions of graphics cards for PCI Pentium boards using a full external 64-bit data bus are developed and the new VESA VL-Bus 2.0 standard aims to retaliate with a specification for a 64-bit wide local bus instead of the usual 32 bit width.

E. INTERNAL BUS SIZE

The bus size in a graphics card's specification refers to its internal architecture, the path between the card's RAM and the card's graphics processor. The most critical element in graphics performance is not data flow into the graphics board; it is how the board organises and manages the frame buffer held in memory inside the graphics board.   Having a 64-bit internal bus greatly speeds up throughput, enhancing the card's performance. It also allows some cards to use cheaper DRAM instead of VRAM. The card's memory is organised into interleaved banks, allowing one bank to be written to while the other is being read. This increases throughput without the expense of VRAM.   However, with increasing resolution, even 64-bit buses can act as a bottleneck and 128-bit versions are now common. The Imagine 128 Series 2 chip from Number Nine has a 128 bit bus with memory interleaved as three banks and a data rate of 500Mbps.   With a maximum memory capacity of 32Mb of DRAM and 8Mb of EDO VRAM, it is optimised for 32-bit operating systems such as Windows 95 and is well equipped for the graphics demands of the future.

F. REFRESH RATES

Greater resolution and greater colour depth (i.e. bits per pixel) both mean that the card has to move more data for a single frame.   This means that cards commonly have lower refresh rates at higher resolutions and at greater colour depths.   For example, even a high performance card like the GrafixStar 700 PCI card has a wide variation in refresh rates. It handles 120Hz at VGA and SVGA, 100Hz at 1024x768, 90Hz at 1280x1024 but is a poor 60Hz at 1600x1200.   An older S3-based ISA card from 1992 fares much worse with respective rates of 70Hz for VGA, 60Hz for SVGA and 1024x768 and an unacceptable 45Hz interlaced format at 1280x1024.

G. CHIP SET USED

To reduce costs, all SVGA graphics cards are based round a limited range of different VLSI chips, sometimes referred to as the *'graphics engine'*. These chips are dedicated to the one task and different manufacturers produce a range of chips with different performances.   Example chips are the Tseng Labs range (from the basic ET4000 to the new ET6000), the S3 range (from the early 86C911 to the 928, 964, Trio64V to the new Virge), the Weitek range (from the 5186 to the new P9100), the ATI range (from the Mach8 to the 3D Rage II), the Cirrus Logic range (from the 5426 to the new GD5480).   All these chips, and the others, provide varying performances.   It is best to compare the working speeds of the chipsets as used on various cards.   This may use 'Wintach' readings, measuring how cards cope with actual applications packages or general card tests may be used, measuring bit manipulation features.

Example chip/card performances are:

Chip	Graphics Card	Memory Type	Refresh rate at 24-bit SVGA	Other features
Matrox MGA-2064W	Millenium card	WRAM	200Hz	220MHz RAMDAC
S3 Virge	Diamond Stealth 3D200	EDO RAM	120Hz	Supports 3D
Tseng ET6000	Hercules Dynamite	SDRAM	90Hz	Hardware acceleration of AVIs and MPEGs
Matrox 1064SG	Mystique card	SGRAM	200Hz	Supports 3D
S3 968	GrafixStar 700	VRAM	120Hz	

METHOD OF SCREEN WRITING

As soon as the PC progressed beyond the CGA standard, the standard machine BIOS (Basic Input/Output System) was inadequate and required extension.   The added graphics functionality is provided by an extra EPROM (Erasable Programmable Read Only Memory) chip on the graphics card.   The efficiency of this BIOS extension affects the screen writing speed.   Some SVGA cards copy the extension software into an area of RAM to speed up screen handling.   This technique is known as *'ROM shadowing'*.   Currently, there are three approaches to screen handling:

- Leave the computer's CPU to do all the screen handling   This is the simplest and cheapest method; it is also the slowest. Watch a screen update in Windows - around 15% of the CPU time is used up in updating the screen cursor alone!   The problems worsen if the system is upgraded. Adding a SVGA card, for example, means the CPU has to handle an even bigger amount of screen data - with no extra computing power to handle it.
- Use a Co-Processor to take on the graphics work. As mentioned above, the 8514/A boards and the VESA XGA boards use a second processor to carry out the graphics tasks.   Typical functions given to a co-processor would be - text display, line drawing, rectangles, ellipses and area colour fills.   Alternative co-processor systems are based around the Texas TI-34000 series.   Expensive and usually found in CAD environments.
- Use a graphics accelerator card, which is also a quick method and generally found in most modern high performance PCs.

When extra cards take over the graphics, the main machine requires to have special software drivers installed, to allow communication to the cards.   For example, Texas uses a memory-resident driver known as TIGA (Texas Instruments Graphics Architecture) to translate Windows drawing commands into the specific commands required by the graphics boards which use their graphics chips (the TI 30410 and the TI 30420).   This is now a *'standard'* in the sense that many boards are now manufactured which are TIGA compatible.

A refinement offered by some cards is *'register-level compatibility'*.   This refers to how closely the card's screen writing corresponds to that of an IBM card, at the lower, register level.   All clones attempt to provide the same functions as the software routines contained in an *'official'* IBM BIOS chip. Often, they succeed in achieving the same end, although the route taken may be different. In an attempt to speed up screen writing, some software entirely ignores the screen handling routines of the BIOS; instead, they write directly to screen memory.   If the graphics card is not constructed in the same fashion as an IBM card, such programs would not work correctly. If the card's register set is compatible with an IBM card, then the card can still run this software.   For example, the Paradise 8514/A Plus card uses a Western Digital register-compatible chipset.

3D CARDS

Games and animations such as walkthroughs and flybys require to show a quick succession of frames with each frame showing the viewer a different viewpoint on the scene.   As the viewpoint is moved, so the shading, shadowing and fine detail will alter.   Each scene comprises a range of objects (buildings, people, etc) and each object is made up from many individual graphics polygons, usually triangles.   Each triangle has its own colour and surface detail (eg grains of sand, bricks, leaves).   The scene will have one or more supposed sources of illumination; this could be the sun, streetlights, etc.   As the viewpoint is moved the light source will illuminate the triangles differently.   To produce a 3D effect, the user is shown perspective (ie distant objects are made smaller than close objects) and defocussing (ie distant object are not as clear as close objects; they are usually dimmed or 'fogged').

The commonly implemented features in 3D cards are:

Facility	Explanation
Z-Buffering	Since x and y describe the horizontal and vertical co-ordinates, 'z' refers to depth. A Z-buffer stores the depth information of objects (eg the dog is behind the tree). This allows *'hidden surface removal'* - ie time is saved by not drawing parts of an object that are obscured by foreground objects.
Flat shading	The polygons are filled with a uniform colour, which is not as effective but is very quick. Flat shading can be implemented to improve frame rates.
Gouraud shading	Obscures the boundaries between polygons by drawing realistic colour gradients ; produces smoother and more natural shapes.
Phong shading	Achieves better results than Gouraud shading but is more demanding of processing power.
Texture mapping	Filling polygons with the same graphics bitmap (eg woodgrain or feathers)
Anti-aliasing	Curved and diagonal edges produce a 'staircase' effect known as *'jaggies'*. If the colours of the boundary's surrounding edges are blended, the effect is minimised.
Perspective correction	If an object is receding into the distance, the bit maps used to texture should also gradually diminish. So, a brick wall bitmap would draw smaller and smaller bricks as the wall shrunk towards the horizon.
Mip mapping	Similar to the above, except that new patterns are rendered for distant polygons.
Bilinear/trilinear filtering	Large areas when rendered can appear like a patchwork quilt, with blocks of slightly differing colouring. Filtering determines a pixel's colour on the colour of the surrounding pixels thereby producing a more uniform transition.
Alpha blending	Controls an object's translucency, thereby providing water or glass effects. It is also used to mask out areas of the screen.
Logarithmic fogging	More distance objects are fogged to grey

The routines to constantly calculate all of these objects and display them on the screen (typically at 20 pictures per second) requires a great deal of computational power.   This is called *'rendering'* and it strains even the most powerful PC.   To overcome this problem, many of these computational routines are embedded in graphics card's chipset and called by special software drivers.   Initially these drivers, known as APIs (Application Programming Interface), were written by graphics card manufacturers for their own range of cards.   The routines for a Matrox card would not work with a VideoLogic card, and so on.   As a consequence, games supplied with one card would not work with another graphics card, as the games were specially written to use the card manufacturer's APIs.   Games bundled with the Diamond Stealth 3D 200, for example, are specially written for the card's VIRGE chipset.

There was a need for standard interfaces and this has been met by Silicon Graphic's OpenGL and Microsoft's Direct 3D.   OpenGL is not designed for the games market.   Windows 95 Release 2 includes DirectX facilities which includes Direct3D.   Card manufacturers only have to write drivers to interface their cards to the Direct 3D API's functions.

MICROSOFT'S DirectX

Microsoft have produced a number of APIs under the title DirectX.   These are:

Direct 3D	Provides a standard interface for 3D object display and rendering
Direct Draw	Reduces CPU time by allowing software direct access to alter video memory
Direct Sound	Reduces CPU time by allowing software direct access to sound hardware. Also provides synchronisation of video and sound data.
Direct Play	Aids running applications over networks or communications lines.
Direct Input	Speeds up mouse and joystick responses.

H. RAMDAC USED

The graphics information is stored in memory in digital format and has to be converted into analogue values in order to drive the gun(s) of the monitor. A chip, known as a RAMDAC (RAM digital/analogue converter) carries out the conversion function.   The frame buffer data for each pixel is read in the order that it will be sent to the monitor for display. This data is passed to the RAMDAC for conversion. With 24-bit colour, the numbers stored in memory exactly relate to the intensity of the red, green and blue elements of each pixel. This makes the digital to analogue conversion simple. However, this is not the method with lower colour depths. It is common that a card can only handle a subset of its full range of colours at any one time. . For example, a card capable of 65,536 different colours may only be using 256 colours in a particular mode. This subset of colours is known as the *'palette'* and is stored in a look-up table in memory.   During normal activities, the screen's pixel colour information is stored as a sequence of logical colour numbers. The colour number for each pixel is read from memory, translated into the values for each gun and these values are given to the RAMDAC to produce the actual colour that will appear on the monitor.   Each Windows application package stores information about the palette it uses. When the application is run, Windows sets the RAMDAC to use that palette. When several applications are open at the same time, each application may have different sets of colour numbers in their required palettes. This can result in unexpected colour changes as the range of colours supported by the card is less than the range of colours requested by the applications.   RAMDAC performance is measured both in resolution (eg 24-bit) and conversion speed (eg 135MHz).

I. OTHER FACILITIES

The preceding list outlines some of the more important features of graphics cards.   There are, however, many more factors that may prove important for a particular user or for a particular activity.   These might include:

- Support for DPMS power saving. The ability of the graphics card to control the power usage of the monitor at times when there is no user activity.
- Virtual Screen or virtual desktop. A user may wish to display a great deal of detail on the screen (e.g. many Windows groups or many Windows applications open at the same time). This would normally require a large screen monitor otherwise the icons would be too small for comfortable viewing. An alternative is to use a normal monitor screen size and only view a part of the full screen at any one time.   Moving the mouse to an edge of the screen scrolls the display in that direction.   Thus a 640x480 screen can act as a window on a larger 1280x1024 display held in screen memory.
- Zoom. The virtual desktop provides a scrolling window on a larger screen.   The zoom facility allows the user to magnify any portion of the screen, usually to allow detailed editing of graphics or DTP.   There is no scrolling in this case.   The Number 9 GXE64 Pro card, for example, magnifies the screen up to 5 times normal size.
- The ability to display input from live video sources such as VCRs and camcorders, as provided in the Media Vision 1024 card.   Again, an extra daughterboard may have to be fitted for this.
- Ease of setup.   There are wide variations in the demands on installers. One card, the Radius XGA-2, has 12 DIP switches and 8 jumpers while another, the Diamond Stealth 64 PCI, is entirely software selectable.
- Drivers to allow the user to switch resolutions without having to reboot the machine to activate the new screen mode.
- Drivers for a wide range of monitors, applications (particularly AutoCAD and 3D Studio) and operating systems such as Windows 95, Windows NT and OS/2.
- RGB output, as provided with the Pegusus VL video card.
- Connectors to extension devices.   This is usually the *'VGA features connector'* which allows connection of other video cards e.g. video capture facilities. Unfortunately, the connection only supports VGA.   In the future this may be replaced by the expected Vesa Media Channel (VMC) currently being developed.   It works with the older ISA, MCA and EISA buses as well as the newer VL-Bus and PCI systems.   It is designed to handle up to fifteen different audio and video sources on a single channel, allowing a great flexibility in connecting together sound cards, video capture cards, MPEG systems, video conferencing systems and anything that the future may throw at it.   Its first appearance is in the Video Logic 928Movie and PCIMovie cards.
- MPEG-2 players, to handle DVD drives.
- Built-in TV tuner.

VIDEO HANDLING

Many graphics cards now support a range of full motion video options. This may include MPEG, Quicktime, Video for Windows and Intel Indeo formats. Video playback is often achieved by fitting an extra daughter board or using additional video handling software. Video for Windows (AVI) is the most common PC video format although MPEG systems are becoming very popular. MPEG requires special hardware to decode the compressed files, although it can use a software method to decode if the computer has a fast CPU. Modern cards should be capable of supporting both of these video standards. See the chapter on multimedia for more details.

Since video playback involves the greatest strain on CPU resources, CPU usage tests can be a valuable indication of a card's performance. Low CPU percentage usage times are the most desirable and large variations can be measured between cards. The Matrox MGA Millenium cards requires almost 25% of the CPU's time to play a 16-bit AVI file, while the Miro 20SD card required less than 6% to play the same file.

CO-PROCESSOR CARDS

8514/A

All PC graphics modes used standard memory mapped techniques until IBM introduced their 8514/A adapter, initially for their PS/2 series of computers. Like other graphics cards, the 8514/A had its own onboard screen memory but this screen memory was not organised by the computer's CPU. The 8514/A adapter board contained its own graphics chip - a graphics co-processor - which relieved the main CPU of this task. Because the chips are processing in parallel, the system speed is significantly improved. The inability of the 8514/A card to handle CGA, EGA and VGA software severely limited IBM's flagship product and all manufacturers (including IBM) have moved on to better things. Ultimately, the 8514/A standard proved to be merely the jumping-off point for other improved standards. An example of this card was the Paradise 8514/A.

XGA

Developed by IBM for their next range of PS/2s. Originally, it was only compatible with the IBM MCA bus. VESA standards for ISA and EISA versions are being developed. The 1024 x 768 mode is interlaced but the VESA standard will be non-interlaced. XGA cards have three modes:
- a normal, memory-mapped VGA mode
- a 132-column text mode
- a mode where the card's graphics co-processor is used.

The card supports 256 colours at SVGA and 1024 x 768 - and 65,536 colours at VGA.

Apart from the above, there is the well-used Texas 340x0 series of graphics co-processors. Example cards are the Hercules Graphics Station 16, the EIZO AA41 (based on the TI 34010 graphics processor), the Number Nine #9GXiTC Ecstasy card, the Chrome 431 and 731 cards and the Rapier 8-24 card (all based on the TI34020 chip).

ACCELERATOR CARDS

Like co-processor boards, the accelerator board is designed to relieve the computer's main CPU of valuable graphics processing time. In a co-processor system, a second processor chip is employed for the graphics tasks. In an accelerator system, the main graphics tasks are implemented in hardware. These main tasks are line and box drawing and 'bitblitting' (bit-to-block transfers - i.e. memory flooding). Since these operations are implemented in hardware, there is no need for a processor to determine what needs to be done - the tasks are pre-defined. The results in the graphics functions being carried out more quickly. Most graphics cards on sale currently use some form of graphics acceleration

NOTE

There can be significance variations in the efficiency of each board's method of handling graphics functions. For example, one particular board may need less information passed to, in order to carry out a particular graphics function, compared to another card configuration. Some cards will carry out a smaller range of graphics functions, the remaining functions being left for the computer's main CPU to process.

CARD PERFORMANCE

There is no doubt that graphics accelerator cards substantially improve a system's performance. However, manufacturers' claims should be put in perspective:

- The claims only consider the graphics functions being tested in isolation.
- When considered as part of the overall activities of an application program, the performance is nowhere near so spectacular.

These figures, although significant, don't begin to approach the raw performance figures. When in the higher 1024 x 768 modes, the cards tended to perform significantly better for certain applications. Word for Windows, for example, showed improvements of between 160% and 490%. Corel Draw, on the other, showed a slightly worse performance compared to SVGA. As expected, the performance of VL-Bus and PCI bus is appreciably better than ISA versions. Not every application can make the maximum use of a graphics card. Improvements tend to be greater at the higher resolution end of their use. Generally, very high resolutions are only usable on larger sized monitor screens, from 15" upwards.

VESA GRAPHICS MODES

VESA has established a set of graphics modes and these are given in the table. This provides a common standard for both the manufacturer of graphics cards and the writers of software. Where a card is described as 'VESA compatible', the manufacturer has ensured that all or a subset of these modes is supported by its card. Similarly, software houses can write software knowing that particular screen resolutions, refresh rates, numbers of colours, etc will be available to run their software. Where graphics cards do not directly support certain modes, software - known as VESA Bios Extensions - can run as TSRs to ensure compatibility.

NOTE: Not all manufacturers stick to this mode numbering scheme.

Mode No (in Hex)	Resolution	Colours	Memory	
0	Text 40 x 25	2	1k	CGA/EGA/VGA
1	Text 40 x 25	16	4k	CGA/EGA/VGA
2	Text 80 x 25	2	2k	CGA/EGA/VGA
3	Text 80 x 25	16	8k	CGA/EGA/VGA
4	320 x200	4	16k	CGA/EGA/VGA
5	320 x 200	2	8k	CGA/EGA/VGA
6	640 x 200	2	16k	CGA/EGA/VGA
7	Text 80 x 25	2	2k	MDA
8	160 x 200	16	16k	IBM
9	320 x 200	16	31k	IBM
A	640 x 200	4	63k	IBM
B	704 x 519	16	178k	
D	320 x 200	16	31k	EGA/VGA
E	640 x 200	16	63k	EGA/VGA
F	640 x 350	2	27k	EGA/VGA
10	640 x 350	16	109k	EGA/VGA
11	640 x 480	2	38k	MCGA/VGA
12	640 x 480	16	150k	VGA
13	320 x 200	256	63k	VGA
25	640 x 480	16	150k	
26	640 x 480	16	150k	
50	640 x 480	16	150k	
53	800 x 560	16	219k	
58	800 x 600	16	234k	
59	720 x 512	16	180k	
6A/102	800 x 600	16	234k	VESA
70	800 x 600	16	234k	
71	800 x 600	16	234k	
73	640 x 480	16	150k	
77	752 x 410	16	151k	
79	800 x 600	16	234k	
100	640 x 400	256	234k	VESA
101	640 x 480	256	300k	VESA
102/6A	800 x 600	16	234k	VESA
103	800 x 600	256	469k	VESA
104	1024 x 768	16	384k	VESA
105	1024 x 768	256	768k	VESA
106	1280 x 1024	16	640k	VESA
107	1280 x 1024	256	1k	VESA
108	Text80 x 60	16	2k	VESA
109	Text 132 x 25	16	2k	VESA
10A	Text 132 x 43	16	3k	VESA
10B	Text 132 x 50	16	3k	VESA
10C	Text 132 x 60	16	4k	VESA
10D	320 X 200	32K	117k	VESA
10E	320 X 200	64K	125k	VESA
10F	320 X 200	16M	188k	VESA
110	640 x 480	32K	563k	VESA
111	640 x 480	64K	600k	VESA
112	640 x 480	16M	900k	VESA
113	800 x 600	32K	879k	VESA
114	800 x 600	64K	938k	VESA
115	800 x 600	16M	1.37M	VESA
116	1024 x 768	32K	1.41M	VESA
117	1024 x 768	64K	1.5M	VESA
118	1024 x 768	16M	2.25M	VESA
119	1280 x 1024	32K	2.34M	VESA
11A	1280 x 1024	64K	2.5M	VESA
11B	1280 x 1024	16M	3.75M	VESA
11C	1600 x 1200	32K	3.43M	VESA
11D	1600 x 1200	64K	3.66M	VESA
11E	1600 x 1200	16M	5.49M	VESA

P.C. Configuration

WHAT IS MS-DOS

MSDOS stands for 'Microsoft Disc Operating System' and is by far the most common systems software used on PCs. It was created for IBM by the giant American Microsoft Corporation and was originally known as PCDOS. The roots of MS-DOS are in the CP/M operating system of the 70's. It first appeared in 1981 and has had 6 major revisions and many minor revisions. Upgrades have seen additions such as handling hard discs, RAM discs, new display standards, mice, memory-resident programs, expanded memory and networks. Version 4, although it broke through the previous restriction on 32Mb disc partitions, never really took off. Versions 5 and 6 have been big successes, due to their extra facilities such as memory management and greater flexibility of some of the commands.

It is still not the ideal operating system and many of the shortcomings were rectified by the user buying add-on utilities such as Norton, Xtree, Magellan, etc. In the last few releases, particularly v6 and 6.2, Microsoft has added many of the facilities that previously were only gained by purchasing add-ons. These additions include virus protection, file defragmenters and disc surface testers.

MS-DOS acts as a buffer between the user and the computer, and makes difficult tasks like the copying and deletion of programs very easy. There are other PC operating systems on the market, such as DRDOS and UNIX, but around 80%-90% of all PC machines in the world use a version of MS-DOS or Windows '95. Version 7, distributed with Windows 95, is a much reduced product since most of the facilities are intended to be embedded in the Windows environment.

THE OPERATING SYSTEM

A computer operating system is required for all personal computers, to provide the user with a range of machine and disc utilities. The operating system provides the control software for all the common input/output facilities e.g. getting a keystroke from the keyboard and displaying characters on the screen at the correct position, reading and writing files, and general housekeeping maintenance.

MS-DOS is not a single program - it is a collection of related programs, as a glance at the DOS directory will show. This collection drives the hardware of the computer and manages its resources. Thus, it provides an automatic buffer between the user and the hardware, as shown.

All operating systems have 2 main objectives.

1. To use the resources of the computer efficiently. Some devices in the computer work more quickly than others. Part of the task of the operating system is to ensure that faster devices are not held up by slower peripheral devices.

2. To conceal the difficulties of dealing directly with the hardware of the computer. The operating system takes care of these tasks. So, those who write or use software do not have to have a detailed knowledge of computer hardware. A single command from the user to the operating system, results in many low level commands on the hardware. For example, if the user wishes to save a file, the system software will automatically handle all the complex tasks of checking whether there is free space on the disc, moving the write head to the free area, writing the file information to disc, updating the disc information area, etc.

As can be seen from the diagram, the user never deals directly with the computer hardware. All user commands are handled by the operating system, which passes the appropriate instructions to the hardware. Many application packages allow the user to carry out file handling activities, such as loading and saving tasks. In these cases, the user chooses options from the application menu and these choices are passed on to DOS to pass on to the hardware.

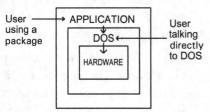

The user talks to the application - the application talks to DOS - and DOS talks to the hardware.

However, for the more complex tasks, the user has to directly interface with the MS-DOS software. Many of the less common, more complex, DOS facilities are not directly available through application packages. These commands have to be directly entered by the user at the keyboard. To obtain the maximum use of the operating system requires an understanding of its composition and its set of commands.

STARTING UP

When a PC is powered up, a procedure known as *'bootstrapping'* occurs. This loads in the MSDOS operating system into the computer and sets up the system configuration. When MSDOS has been loaded into the computer's memory, the operating system's prompt will be displayed to the user. This is normally in the form of the current logged drive, i.e.   C:\>

You cannot run programs or perform housekeeping tasks until the operating system has been loaded.

THE BOOTSTRAPPING PROCESS

The user normally sees the process from interface to kernel to BIOS. The user gives the command at the prompt. This command is processed by the command processor before being passed to the BIOS, via the kernel. The boot procedure follows the reverse order. The diagram shows the process simplified:

The main steps are:

1. The computer initiates a POST (Power On Self Test) procedure that is stored in the system ROM (i.e. the BIOS). The POST conducts a self test of the main board, discs, printer, keyboard, memory, etc. If it finds any fault, it will provide an error message and stop. Error messages can range from *"Hard disc failure"* to *"Time of day clock stopped"*. All checks are carried out with a *'hard reboot'* - i.e. switching the power on. A *'warm reboot'* involves either pressing the computer's reset button on pressing the Alt-Ctrl-Del keys. A warm reboot ignores checks such as memory tests.

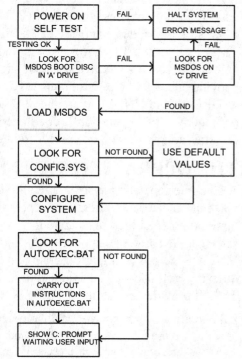

2. The presence of any *'ROM extensions'* are detected. Apart from the BIOS ROM that is present in all computers, some will have other ROM chips installed for extra control purposes. These are fitted on add-on cards such as video cards and disc controller cards. These extra ROMs contain code to control their own card's activities. If the BIOS finds an adapter card, it runs the code in the extra ROM so that the card's control code can be loaded into memory.

3. If the POST is successful, then control is passed to the bootstrap code resident in the BIOS ROM. This small piece of code triggers the loading process. There is enough code to read drive A:, sector 1, track 0 (the floppy disc's boot sector). If there is no disc in A:, it tries to read the same location on C: If no boot sector is found on the discs, an error message is given and the system halts. Where the boot sector is found, the code loaded from the boot sector enables the loading process to continue. The code from the boot sector is used to load the kernel and remaining BIOS. Some systems load both IO.SYS and MSDOS.SYS at this stage. In other systems, IO.SYS is loaded first and it then loads MSDOS.SYS.

4. The system is configured.

IO.SYS, in fact, contains two components- BIOS and SYSINT.

BIOS contains the built-in device drivers that allow standard communications with the computer's keyboard, screen, printer, serial ports, disc drives.

SYSINT carries out a range of functions, as follows:

  a) determines the configuration of available memory and relocates the DOS kernel (MSDOS.SYS) so that it goes down from high memory.

  b) calls code in the kernel to build a table for the devices which the computer will be using.

  c) initialises each of the resident device drivers.

  d) reads CONFIG.SYS and adds any other installable device drivers into the list. These software drivers are all files ending with the .SYS extension (such as RAMDRIVE.SYS, for installing a RAM drive).

  e) sets up buffer space in memory, according to the BUFFERS = command.

Typical configuration details are
- how many files can be open at the same time
- how much memory to allocate to disc buffer space
- any additional device drivers. These are additions to standard MS-DOS, to improve or extend handling of the discs, screen, keyboard, printer.

The CONFIG.SYS file can be omitted altogether, in which case the computer will work on its own set of default values. In this case, the system will still work but some of the desired facilities will probably be lost. If CONFIG.SYS is included, and a system file is mentioned in CONFIG.SYS, the named file must be present in the specified directory.

f) loads command interpreter, or shell. COMMAND.COM is the standard MS-DOS shell. If there is a SHELL = statement in CONFIG.SYS, the specified shell is loaded instead of COMMAND.COM.

5. AUTOEXEC.BAT is executed.

If the configuration process is achieved satisfactorily, the computer will look for an AUTOEXEC.BAT to run. Again, this file is optional but it is present on all systems, since it allows a degree of customisation by the user. This is a normal batch file which is used for purposes such as:
- altering the system prompt
- producing user start-up menus
- loading the driver for a mouse

If the batch file is not present, the user will be presented with the C: prompt. If an auto-execute batch file is included, all the commands must be correct to fully set up the system. If not, an error message will be given.

CONFIG.SYS

The CONFIG.SYS file allows the user to change the system's default configuration settings. Typical contents of a CONFIG.SYS file might be:

It is simply a text file, with each text line containing a description of an alteration to the standard system configuration. This means that the file can be created with any standard text editor such as DOS EDIT or any word-processor used in ASCII mode). It also means that the file can be easily edited to add, delete or modify the commands contained in it.

```
device=c:\WINDOWS\HIMEM.SYS
device=c:\WINDOWS\EMM386.EXE noems
DOS=HIGH,umb
COUNTRY=044,850,C:\DOS\COUNTRY.SYS
DEVICEhigh=C:\DOS\DISPLAY.SYS  CON=(EGA,,1)
devicehigh=c:\dos\ansi.sys
FILES=10
BUFFERS=10
STACKS=9,256
```

NOTE
- None of the changes to CONFIG.SYS take effect until the system is re-booted.
- To work, the file must be in the root directory.
- A configuration file may only contain a few lines. The size of the file will depend on the system and its intended use.

COMMANDS IN CONFIG.SYS

The common commands for enclusion in the configuration file, CONFIG.SYS, are explained next.

BUFFERS

This command is concerned with the transfer of data between the computer and the disc drives. This is a very slow process, compared to transferring data between different parts of the computer memory. Because of the mechanical movements involved in disc activities, it is typically 100 to 1000 times slower than memory transfers!

Often, a file can be split over various parts of a disc's surface. Reading this file involves moving the disc head to the required segment of the program at the required time. It takes a considerable time to move the head to the required track and wait for the wanted segment to rotate under the head. If the program has to re-read the same data, it has to repeat this slow process all over again.

To speed up disc read/write activities, the system can allocate chunks of memory to temporarily store the data that your program most recently read/wrote. These memory blocks are called *'buffers'*. All data flowing between computer and disc passes through these memory buffers. When MS-DOS has to process a disc request, it first looks to see if the required data is already in the buffers. If the required data is found, it is copied into the main computer memory, by-passing the slower disc access.

The use of buffers can have a considerable effect on the overall efficiency of application programs, particularly databases.   Backup & restore, for example, can run in half the usual time, using buffers.

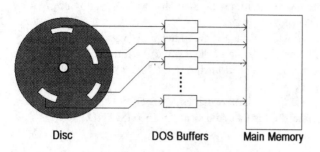

Disc   DOS Buffers   Main Memory

Each buffer needs 528 bytes (512 for holding the data and 16 for information that controls the buffer area).   The allowable range for the number of buffers is between 1 and 99.

The default value (the value given if there is no CONFIG.SYS file) is between 2 and 15, depending on the size of main memory and disc capacity.   In all modern machines (i.e. those with main memory greater than 512k and system disc greater than 360k) the default value is 15.

There is a trade-off in the use of buffers.

1. Initially, extra buffers mean higher performance.   Eventually, however, MS-DOS could spend so much time looking through buffers that it becomes slower than getting the data directly from disc. This point is usually reached when more than 40 buffers are in use. After about 20-30 buffers, there is usually no more noticeable improvement in performance.

2. The buffers have to compete with application programs for the same area of main memory. Since each buffer takes up 528 bytes of main memory, the user has to be careful to leave enough memory to run application programs.

In practice, the buffers should be set to the amount recommended by the software packages in use on the computer.   Otherwise, the default values should be left unchanged - unless actual test runs have been made, to time the effect of different buffer amounts for the particular system in use.   This is useful for older machines but has been overtaken by improved techniques, such as carrying out the caching in extended memory (see SMARTDRV later) or in dedicated chips on a disc cache controller (see chapter on discs).   These can produce much larger cache areas than those available within conventional memory.

FILES

This command is used to set the maximum number of files that can be in use at the one time.   The default value is 8 and this sets up eight places in memory to track information about open files. MS-DOS uses five of these areas for its own use.   Often, eight will be enough but there many applications (such as databases) and environments (such as WINDOWS) where a much higher figure is required. Be guided by the applications to be used - each application specifies its requirements.   The maximum number of files that MSDOS will allow to be open is 255 but versions of MS-DOS prior to version 3.3 only supported a maximum of 20 open files.   Each extra file consumes another 48 bytes of main memory space.   Generally, 30 files should be set for Windows use with another 10 added for each application that is expected to be run concurrently.   So, if only Word is in use 40 files are adequate; if the user has Excel and Word open at the same time, then FILES should be set to 50.
NOTES

- Where a program's memory needs are great, the liberal use of a large number of files and buffers would result in insufficient remaining memory for running the program.
- If a program with a need for a large number of buffers (such as a relational database) has to co-exist on a computer with a program that needs a large number of files (such as word processing) then separate CONFIG.SYS files will have to be created for each application. The appropriate configuration file would be brought in to the root directory and the system would be re-booted.   DOS 6 provides a more convenient facility to choose between different configurations, from a start-up menu at boot time

Such problems will rarely be encountered with DOS 5 or DOS 6, since their memory handling abilities usually result in sufficient main memory being available for even the most demanding programs.   The only real problems are with PCs on networks, since their driver software can be demanding on machine main memory.

COUNTRY

Different countries have different keyboard layouts and screen displays, to match the countries' particular language constructions. Many languages, such as Arabic and Hebrew, require an entirely different character set from the usual 26-character Roman alphabet. Specially tailored versions of DOS are required in such cases. However, a large part of the world uses the Roman alphabet with minor variations. For these a common core system was created, with a single piece of software (COUNTRY.SYS) from which the elements of a particular country could be extracted.

Different countries have different methods of displaying the date, time and the separators between numeric values. For example, countries such as Holland, Sweden and Germany use a comma to separate decimal places and a full stop to separate thousands. So, the British value of 3,000.99 would appear as 3.000,99. The date of 1st October 1993 would be displayed on a British machine as 01-10-1993, on an American machine as 10-01-1993 and as 1993-10-01 in Sweden. The default character set is USA. To establish the UK display, the CONFIG.SYS should contain the command COUNTRY=044, 044 being the international dialling code for the UK. This is set up from the COUNTRY.SYS file in the DOS collection.

Thus, the full command in CONFIG.SYS should be:

> COUNTRY=044,,C:\DOS\COUNTRY.SYS

DEVICE

The bootstrapping process has set up an area in high memory, to hold the details of the default device drivers, as previously mentioned. A device is typically something that can be read from or written to. A device can be hardware with the mouse being a device that is read while a monitor is a device that is written to. A device can also be 'virtual', which means that it can act as a device. An example of this would be a disc file; in this example, the device can both be read and written. The driver is the software that lets the computer communicate with a device. A standard set of device drivers is provided and these are:

CON	A combined keyboard and monitor device. The way that it is used inside a command determines whether it is a read from the keyboard or a write to the monitor.
AUX	A default name for COM1, the first serial port
PRN	A default name for LPT1, the first parallel port
LPTs	The range of parallel port devices
COMs	The range of serial port devices
NUL	This is a dummy device; it does not exist as an actual physical device. It is used for testing or disabling screen output. Examples are given in the chapter on batch files

These drivers are automatically loaded into a list in memory when the computer is first booted up. DOS already has these drivers stored within IO.SYS. This list of devices is created even if the hardware devices do not all physically exist in that machine. Where the user wishes to extend the default list, to provide an enhancement to the system, the extra device driver can be added to this list in memory. Examples of extra drivers would be those for mice, network interface cards, RAM drives, file compressors, plotters, etc. These devices require their own software drivers to interface the computer to the hardware device. When the list of device drivers is compiled in the machine memory, the extra installed drivers appear in the driver list before the standard DOS drivers. This means that an installed driver can be used to replace a standard device driver - since any call to a device will find the installed driver first. For example, ANSI.SYS can be used to replace the standard keyboard driver and the standard screen driver. Any call routed to the keyboard or screen will be intercepted by the ANSI driver to provide extra facilities beyond those provided in the standard drivers. This extra functionality has to be paid for by the loss of machine memory occupied by the extra driver software.

Additions are achieved by the use of the command DEVICE=filename in the CONFIG.SYS file. These files also have the .SYS extension and are loaded and given control. The driver then carries out the configuring of itself and the system for the new facility. There are many such extra devices which are supplied by various manufacturers. If an add-on hardware device is purchased, such as a mouse, the package will usually also contain the necessary software driver.

NOTE

Most drivers are installed as described above but some are installed via AUTOEXEC.BAT instead of CONFIG.SYS. They will not have the .SYS extension but will still be device drivers nevertheless. Examples of such drivers are MOUSE.COM and SMARTDRV.EXE.

DOS DRIVERS

The other device drivers supplied with MS-DOS include:

HIMEM.SYS & EMM386.EXE

These are important memory management drivers and are covered in detail in the later section on memory management.

SMARTDRV.SYS

This driver appeared with DOS version 5 and is used to create a disc cache for the computer, to speed up disc intensive activities.   Like BUFFERS, it sets aside an area of memory to store the most regularly used data read from/written to disc.   With BUFFERS, the temporary storage occupies part of the 640k memory area, lowering that available for application programs.   With SMARTDRIVE, the temporary storage can either occupy extended or expanded memory.   If the SMARTDRIVE disc cache system is implemented, there is little need for large BUFFERS, and these can be reduced to 4 or 5 for use with the computer's floppy drives. The minimum syntax is:

DEVICE=SMARTDRV.SYS

and this would create a default disc cache of 256k.   The allowable parameters are:

DEVICE=drive\path\SMARTDRV.SYS 1024 512 /a

The parameters in the example are:

- drive\path indicates the drive and directory where the SMARTDRV.SYS file can be found.   If no parameter is given, the file is looked for in the hard disc's root directory.
- 1024k (i.e. 1Mb) has been set aside for the disc cache.   Valid sizes range from 128 to 8192, user values being rounded to the nearest 16 if necessary.   If the value given is greater than the memory available, the system sets up the maximum cache that it can.   About 2048k is the highest setting as any extra memory allocated after that produces only a minimal extra improvement; the extra memory is best left for Windows use.
- 512k has been designated as the minimum size to which the cache will shrink.   Some programs (see section on Windows) will seize the cache allocation if the other extended memory is in use. This can reduce the size of the cache to zero and the second parameter specifies the lower limit to which any program can diminish the cache size.
- The /a parameter creates the disc cache in expanded memory. This would also require that an expanded memory manager be first installed.   EMM386.EXE, for example, would appear earlier in the CONFIG.SYS script.   If this parameter is omitted, the disc cache is established in extended memory.   This would require that HIMEM.SYS appears earlier in the CONFIG.SYS script so that it can handle the extended memory activities requested by SMARTDRV.SYS.

NOTE

When determining the maximum size for the disc cache, take into account that application programs probably wish to occupy part of the extended or expanded memory for their own use.

SMARTDRV AND WINDOWS 3.1

With a machine fitted with DOS 5, use the Windows SMARTDRV.EXE product instead of the DOS SMARTDRV.SYS file.   The Windows version is a special version that is much faster due to its improved caching implementation. It also allows Windows to recover some of the cache space for its own use when required.   These maximise the performance of Windows.   With DOS 6 onwards, use the DOS version.

To prevent Windows seizing all the cache space, SMARTDRV can be set up to have a minimum as well as maximum size.   The maximum size determines the most memory space that will be devoted to cache activities.   The minimum size determines the lowest point to which the cache will be reduced.   So a cache configuration given by SMARTDRV 1024 512 would indicate a 1Mb cache which would always have 512k available.

There is a trade off between the amount of extended memory allocated for disc caching and that left for Windows applications.   On the one hand, a windows application requires as much extended memory as it can to store the elements of the program. This avoids the slow process of swapping programs to the hard disc (see the section on virtual memory in the chapter on Windows Configuration). On the other hand, a Windows database will need a large cache area to store as much data as possible.   It follows that the second parameter for SMARTDRV, the one that dictates the minimum disc cache size, should be set at a value corresponding to the applications in use on the machine.

TESTING SMARTDRV

The effectiveness of the SMARTDRV caching can be checked by asking for a report on cache hits and cache misses. A cache hit is an occasion when the data was available in cache memory, while a cache miss involved fetching the data from disc. If the cache hits figure is divided by the total data calls (i.e. cache hits plus cache misses) and multiplied by 100, the resultant figure is a measure of the percentage efficiency of the cache system on that particular machine.

With the example given:

$$\frac{27612}{27612+4062} = 87\%$$

```
Microsoft SMARTDrive Disk Cache version 4.0
Copyright 1991,1992 Microsoft Corp.

Room for 256 elements of 8,192 bytes each
There have been 27,612 cache hits
   and 4,062 cache misses

Cache size: 2,097,152 bytes
Cache size while running Windows: 2,097,152 bytes

         Disk Caching Status
drive  read cache  write cache  buffering
--------------------------------------------
 A:      yes         no          no
 B:      yes         no          no
 C:      yes         yes         no

For help, type "Smartdrv /?".
```

the figure is acceptable. Of course this rating will vary with the amount and type of activity carried out but a figure of 85% upwards would be regarded as an effective caching system while lower figures may require some adjustment in the cache size. The report on cache effectiveness can be invoked by giving the command

SMARTDRV/S

The figure should be calculated over a number of different sessions, so that an average efficiency figure is arrived at. SMARTDRV caches DOS as well as Window operations. If the efficiency of Windows caching alone is to be measured, then tests should be carried out when only Windows has been run since booting up, so that any DOS caching cannot upset the figures. A likely assignment would be:

Memory Size	SMARTDRV Size	
	Normal	Minimum
2Mb	1Mb	256Kb
4Mb	1Mb	512Kb
8Mb	2Mb	1Mb
>8Mb	2Mb	1Mb

The minimum size set for SMARTDRV should not be below 256k if the system is to have any real effect. Each increase in Cache size provides a lesser benefit than the preceding value. A value beyond 2Mb would be wasteful except in circumstances where a CD ROM is being cached. Buffers should be no more than 10 if SMARTDRV is operating; this will save some memory in the conventional memory area.

SMARTDRV and DOS 6 onwards

Microsoft's DOS v 6 provides extra caching facilities from version 4 onwards of SMARTDRV.

DOUBLE BUFFERING

This is provide caching support to older SCSI drives, newer SCSI interface cards already being able to interface to Windows without this special help.

The following line is added to CONFIG.SYS:

DEVICE = C:\DOS\SMARTDRV.EXE / DOUBLE_BUFFERING

in addition to the following line

C:\DOS\SMARTDRV

being added to AUTOEXEC.BAT.

The double buffering scheme requires an extra 2.5k from conventional memory and should only be used where necessary. With these commands in place, the system can be rebooted and the SMARTDRV command given from the DOS prompt. If any of the entries in the 'buffering' column on the right hand of the display show 'yes' then double buffering is required; otherwise double buffering should be removed.

DRIVE CONTROL

Support is provided for *'write caching'* (see chapter on Discs and Drives). Individual drives can have their read caching and write caching facilities set at bootup time. If no drives are specifically mentioned in AUTOEXEC.BAT, drives are given default modes of operation. These can be changed by mentioning the drive and using a + or a - as a switch.

An example assignment might be:

C:\DOS\SMARTDRV C+ D-

The following table shows the variations allowed, using the C: drive as the example.

	Read	Write
C+	ON	ON
C-	OFF	OFF
C	ON	OFF

If no drives are specified, the hard disc(s) is both read and write enabled, while floppies and CD ROMs are read enable and write disabled.

EXTRA SWITCHES

These include

/X	Disables write caching of all drives
/U	Does not load SMARTDRV's CD ROM handling code
/L	Will avoid using the UMB area so that it is free for other programs

Entering SMARTDRV/? displays a list of the switches available for the command.

SMARTDRIVE and Windows 95

SmartDrive is dropped in Windows 95 in favour of its own improved caching system called VCACHE. This caching system does not required user assignment as it dynamically allocates itself to make best use of the available memory at any one time.

ANSI.SYS

This extends the computers control of graphics, by exceeding the normal MS-DOS's 25 screen lines limit, control of colours, etc.   It also allows control of the keyboard.   ANSI.SYS is for DOS use only, not being required for Windows, and is covered in detail later.

RAMDRIVE.SYS

This creates a virtual disc - i.e. RAM disc - in any expanded or extended memory in the computer (see the chapter on memory). The device's exact name and use vary from manufacturer to manufacturer. Often, manufacturers have a similar device driver called RAMDRIVE.SYS. These drivers allow a portion of the computer's memory to be used as though it were a disk drive. It has a drive letter allocated to it and the usual DOS commands (e.g. MD, CD, RD, COPY, DEL) apply to the virtual disc in the same way as they do to an actual physical disc. For example, if the virtual disc is allocated the drive letter 'D', then the command   COPY C:*.* D: is quite permissible.

Since there is no mechanical movement (as in disc access) involved in retrieving information from memory, the virtual disc acts as a very fast drive. Its drawback is that its contents are lost when the power is switched off. Its main uses are:

1. Programs that are so large that it can't all fit into main memory at the one time. Such programs are split into sections - called 'overlays' - and the various sections are loaded into the main memory as and when required. Only parts of the program are in main memory at any one time. If the other overlay sections reside in virtual memory, then they can be called into main memory with great speed. This causes a noticeable improvement in performance with these larger application programs. A batch file could be written to copy the overlay files from the hard disc into the virtual drive prior to running the application and the application could be configured to expect the files to be in that particular drive.

2. The handling of temporary files. Many programs, particularly Windows applications, create many temporary files during their running. These temporary files are then deleted again when the application is exited. When the application crashes, many temporary files are left on the hard disc.   These can range from small files to files of 1Mb or more. The need to continually write to disc can be eliminated if the temporary files are stored in the virtual drive.   This speeds up the running of applications and can be very noticeable when printing from an application.   Windows printing results in the creation of temporary print files and the use of a ram drive will result in control being passed back to the user from a print operation in a much quicker time.   With temporary files, the fact that data is lost from the virtual drive on power down is a distinct advantage; any temporary files left after an application crash are removed automatically and do not clog up the hard disc.   If this technique is used, the ram drive size has to be set at a figure to handle the largest files that are expected to be used, since the application will crash if there is not enough space on the virtual drive to store the temporary file.

The minimum syntax for creating a virtual disc is

DEVICE=RAMDRIVE.SYS

This would allocate a default virtual RAM disc size of 64k.

The allowable parameters are:

DEVICE=drive\path\RAMDRIVE.SYS 1024 512 64 /e

The parameters in the example are:

- 'drive\path' indicates the drive and directory where the RAMDRIVE.SYS file can be found.   If no parameter is given, the file is looked for in the hard disc's root directory.
- 1024k (i.e. 1Mb) of memory has been set aside for the virtual disc.   The allowable range is from 16k to 4096k.   Where no size is given in the command, the default value is 64k.   If the disc demanded is greater than the physical memory present, the ram drive size will be automatically scaled down. Note that Windows is best with at least 4Mb of RAM and allocations for a ram drive and SMARTDRV have to be deducted from the physical size of the machine's memory.
- The virtual disc sector size has been established as 512 bytes.   This is also the default value and is normally left unaltered.   However, the user can choose between 128, 256 and 512 as permissible values.
- The number of files and directories that can be created in the RAM drive's root directory has been set at 64.   This is the default value and the permissible range is 2 to 1024.   In fact, the virtual disc needs four sectors (the boot sector, the FAT, the directory and at least one data sector).   If the size demanded differs from that which can be accommodated, the number is adjusted automatically. Consider the case of a sector size of 512 bytes.   Each directory entry requires 32 bytes, so a 512 sector can contain 16 entries. If the ram drive parameter in the CONFIG.SYS file only requests 7 as a maximum for files and directories, it will be rounded up to 16 entries; if the parameter given is 19, then 16 entries will be allocated.
- The /e parameter creates the RAM drive in the machine's extended memory.   This would require that HIMEM.SYS appears earlier in the CONFIG.SYS script so that it can handle the extended memory activities requested by RAMDRIVE.SYS. If the parameter was specified as /a, the RAM drive would be created in the machine's expanded memory.   This would also require that an expanded memory manager be first installed; EMM386.EXE, for example, would appear earlier in the CONFIG.SYS script. If no parameter is given, the RAM drive is created in conventional memory. Using up conventional memory is to be avoided, as it is likely that all but the smallest of application programs will be unable to fit into the remaining main memory.

If the default sector size and number of entries are acceptable, then these parameters can be omitted. Thus, a 2Mb virtual disc in extended memory would be specified as:

DEVICE=drive\path\RAMDRIVE.SYS 2048 /e

If there is sufficient memory in the machine, more than one virtual disc can be created by the use of more than one 'device=ramdrive.sys' command.

The RAMDRIVE.SYS file is implemented in IBM's PC-DOS as VDISK.SYS and the /a switch to place the driver in expanded memory is replaced with a /x switch.

RAMDRIVE vs SMARTDRV vs BUFFERS

As described, there are a number of ways that the user can speed up access by saving programs and data in memory for quick access.   These cache methods are compared below.

BUFFERS	RAMDRIVE	SMARTDRV
Useful in a machine with no extended or expanded memory. Consumes important conventional memory.	Data is lost if machine is switched off before data is saved to disc. The process is not automatic; the user has to predict what files might be used so that they can be copied into the ram drive. All other files are accessed in the normal, slow, way. A useful place to store temporary files or Windows swap files. Useful in a machine with no extended or expanded memory, as a small ram drive can be set up in conventional memory. The memory allocated to RAMDRIVE cannot be used for other purposes.	The process is entirely automatic. There is no need to predict what data will be used. The system is limitless in the number of files and different sets of data it can handle during the machine's run; it is only limited by the number of files and data sets that can be held in the SMARTDRV memory at any one time. Files are opened and closed to best maintain the fastest flow of data for the user. Changes to files are regularly written away, minimising the loss of data with a power cut.

DISC CACHE and MEMORY CACHE

Disc caching is used to speed up data transfers between the disc drive and memory.   This should not be confused with memory caching which is a way of speeding up data transfers between main memory and the CPU.   Memory caching is dealt with in the chapter on Memory.

DRIVER.SYS

This driver is used to allow an additional external disc drive to be attached to the computer. This is sometimes an unusual combination and the driver can be given parameters to ensure that the system will be able to recognise and control the new drive. Often, PCs have two 5 1/4" floppy drives and users wish to attach an extra 3 1/2" drive or tape drive, with the use of DRIVER.SYS.   When the computer boots up, it checks what peripherals are attached to it and then checks for any installable device drivers in CONFIG.SYS.   The first internal floppy disc drive is assigned the drive letter 'A' and the first internal hard disc is assigned the drive letter 'C'.   A second floppy disc drive is assigned 'B', while any subsequent drives are lettered from 'D' onwards.   Apart from drive letters, the drives are assigned physical drive numbers.   The floppy drives are numbered from 0 upwards, while the hard discs are numbered from 128 upwards.

The syntax for the driver is   DEVICE=drive\path\DRIVER.SYS /d:drivenumber/f:disksize

Permissible values for f are:

0	360k
1	1.2M
2	720k
7	1.44M
9	2.88M

EXAMPLES:

To add an external 720k floppy drive   DEVICE=drive\path\DRIVER.SYS /d:2 /f:2

To add an external 1.4M   DEVICE=drive\path\DRIVER.SYS /d:2 /f:7

Note that the drive number quoted is 2.   This assumes that this is the first external drive to be declared. Such a command would be given even if the machine only had a single existing internal floppy drive (drive 0), since drive 1 would be reserved for any future additional internal floppy drive.   As an alternative to using the 'f:' parameter, the parameter can be replaced with three others.   These are used to describe the physical characteristics of the external drive and are -

/h: the number of heads in the external drive
/s: the number of sectors per track
/t: the number of tracks per side

These can be used to set up a new device that does conform to the normal expected values for disc drives. In such a case, the values will be as given in the documentation supplied with the new device.

EXAMPLES OF PROPRIETARY DRIVERS

The device driver to handle the SoundBlaster Pro sound card is installed by adding the following command to the CONFIG.SYS file:

DEVICE=C:\SBPRO\DRV\SBPCD.SYS

To run the 'Stacker' disc compression system, the following commands would be in the CONFIG.SYS:

DEVICE=C:\STACKER\STACKER.COM C:\STACVOL.DSK
DEVICE=C:\STACKER\SSWAP.COM C:\STACVOL.DSK /SYNC

Note that in the above case, the device drivers also have their own parameters passed in when they are being installed.

Similarly, if the SoundBlaster card is to be connected to a CD ROM, the earlier command would be altered to a command such as:

DEVICE=C:\SBPRO\DRV\SBPCD.SYS /D:MSD001 /P:220

SHELL

The SHELL command is used to specify a different command processor from COMMAND.COM, if this is supplied by a particular software product. The command is:

SHELL=C:\path\filename

This command can also be used where the normal DOS shell, COMMAND.COM, is not to be found in the root directory:

SHELL=C:\path\COMMAND.COM

These commands can include optional parameters:

SHELL=C:\path\COMMAND.COM/P/E:512

The /P ensures that the shell stays permanently, while the E parameter sets up the *'environment'* size in bytes, rounded up to the nearest 16. The environment space is a piece of memory that stores details of PATHs, the PROMPT, DIRCMD details, COMSPEC details, user defined variables and batch file replaceable parameters (see later). The default size of the environment is 256 bytes (160 bytes for DOS 3.2) but it can be increased as above, if programs produce an *'out of environment space'* message. The current contents of the environment area can be viewed by entering the SET command with no parameters. If the /F parameter is added to the command, DOS will provide a *'Fail'* response to a critical error. This avoids the *'Abort, Retry, Fail'* choice when a user attempts to read or write to a floppy drive that does not have a disc inserted. This is usually accompanied by long pauses and several attempts to return to the DOS prompt. With the /F parameter, the user will be given a *'Current Drive not valid'* message and is instantly returned to the DOS prompt.

BREAK

MS-DOS will stop running when either CTRL-C or CTRL-Break is pressed. This check is only made when the computer is taking input from the keyboard or sending output to the screen or printer. Pressing the key combinations have no effect, for example, when reading or writing to disc. Where it is required to extend the abilities of MS-DOS or programs to interrupt the process by pressing either CTRL-C or CTRL-Break, the command BREAK=ON can be added to CONFIG.SYS.

However, this addition forces extra checks for these key presses - and this slightly slows down the computer operations. If this facility is not required, it can be turned off with BREAK=OFF (this being the default condition).

Pressing CTRL-Break during the execution of an application would normally take the user out of the application and return to the DOS prompt. To prevent this happening, most applications trap the pressing of CTRL-Break and take their own appropriate action.

NOTE: Although the BREAK command is often placed in the CONFIG.SYS file, it can also be placed in a batch file, or it can even be entered by the user directly from the keyboard.

LASTDRIVE

This command is used to set the maximum drive letter which MS-DOS will accept. The drive letters vary from A to Z. The default is a last drive of E. Where extra channels are to be added (e.g. extra drives, disc partitions, RAM drives, a network, tape backups) the default can be extended by the command LASTDRIVE=x, where x is the last drive letter in use. Since MS-DOS allocates a data structure for each specified drive, only the drives required should be listed in LASTDRIVE.

SUBST

This command provides a shortcut for users who regularly use a particular directory. It makes a particular sub-directory look a disc drive. Consider the effects of the following command:

SUBST W: C:\APPS\WSTAR\FILES

Here, the command links the drive letter *'W'* to a specified drive directory. After this command, any reference to the W: drive is actually concerned with the FILES sub-directory at the end of the given path. This means that the command COPY *.* C:\APPS\WSTAR\FILES can be shortened to COPY *.* W:

There will be a new logical drive W: and this will have to be taken into account when setting LASTDRIVE, as discussed above. The current list of assignments can be displayed by giving the SUBST command with no parameters. The /D parameter deletes an association between a drive letter and a path. So

SUBST W: /D

will delete the association created in the above example.

Another use for the command is to allow the easy switching of floppy drives where a program insists on fetching data from a particular drive. This can be achieved with

SUBST A: B:

Create or deletion of SUBST assignments should be carried out while within Windows. Also, disc commands such as CHKDSK, FORMAT, DEFRAG and RESTORE should not be used with SUBST drives; such commands should always be used with actual physical drive names.

STACKS

Every computer has a number of memory areas to store signals from *'multiple interrupt devices'* (i.e. LANs and hard discs).   The computer's CPU has only a limited number of internal registers (memory locations built in to the chip at the manufacturing stage).   This can be inadequate for the running of the system.   When a program runs, there is a constant need to:

- Process hardware activities in the most efficient way.
- Pass parameters (data and control information) from one program sub-routine to another.
- Memorise the return memory address of the calling sub-routine that temporarily calls another sub-routine.   This allows control to return to the correct point in the calling program, when the called routine is exited.

An example of stack operations would be a user pressing a key on the keyboard during a file save operation.   The system wishes to process the keyboard activity but it won't stop the disc write activity. So it places the keyboard interrupt on the stack and will process it as soon as the disc write is complete.

The computer can have stacks varying in amount from 8 to 64, the default being nine.   The size of each stack can vary from 0 bytes to 512 bytes, the default being 128 bytes. The default sizes should be left, unless changes are demanded by a particular application. Under certain circumstances, the default values may not be enough and this will result in messages such as *"Internal Stack Failure"* or *"Divide Overflow"*.   In these cases, the stacks can be increased, bearing in mind that extra stacks devour main memory.   Inadequate stack size leads to loss of information or -even worse- loss of program control (known as a *'crash'*).

The command STACKS=10,256 would reserve space for 10 stacks, each capable of holding 256 bytes. The command STACKS=0,0 can be used to eliminate pre-determined memory stacks where each program that will be run provides its own stack arrangements.   When Windows is installed it sets up stacks as 9,256 but this can be reset to 0,0 with no ill effects and memory can be recovered, as long as it does not produce any *'parity error'*, *'Internal Stack Overflow'* or *'Exception Error 12'* messages.

SETVER

Some application programs check the version of DOS that they are running under and this can cause difficulties where the DOS version is newer than an application.   For example, an application written to run under DOS 4.01 will not run under DOS 5, while a program written for DOS 3.3 will not run under DOS 4.01.   Programs that are written to work under a particular DOS version will check to see if that version is in use on the machine.   If it not the recognised DOS version, the program will not load - even if the DOS version on the machine is <u>better</u> than the version being tested for.

DOS 5 onwards provides the solution by maintaining a table of application EXE and COM files, along with the correct version number for the files. If SETVER is installed, then a DOS 4.01 application is told that the machine has 4.01 fitted, while a 3.3 application is told that 3.3 is fitted.   Programs not on the list still work under DOS version 5 onwards.   The utility has to be loaded via a CONFIG.SYS line:

DEVICE=drive\path\SETVER.EXE

This loads a table into memory that already contains a list of programs and their correct version numbers. To view the list, simply type SETVER|MORE.   To add to the list, enter

SETVER drive\path\prog.exe n.nn

where *'prog.exe'* is the file to be added to the list and *'n.nn"* is the DOS version to be tagged to the file. To delete from the list, simply add the parameter /d to the end of the command e.g.-

SETVER drive\path\prog.exe /d

Since SETVER and its table consume memory, it should only be used where problems are being experienced in running certain applications   If a machine contains all the latest software, or the existing software runs happily under the current DOS version, SETVER should be not be included in the CONFIG.SYS file and memory can be saved.

NUMLOCK

The Numlock key controls the use of the numeric keypad section of the keyboard. When presses once, the keypad is interpreted as a set of numbers; pressing the same key again interprets the same key presses as cursor control keys.   If a computer is to always start up with the keypad producing numerics, the line

NUMLOCK = ON

should be added to CONFIG.SYS.   Similarly the command NUMLOCK = OFF will ensure that the computer always starts up with the keypad recognised as a set of cursor controls.

FCBS

In DOS version 1, files were accessed via *'File Control Blocks'* (FCBs). These are memory sections, each 40 bytes, that store file names and other attributes. Very few modern packages use this method, preferring the FILES= command. If an old program is being used, such as dBASE III+, the required FCBS setting will be stated in the program's manual. The syntax is

FCBS = x

where x is the total number of files that can be opened at any one time (from 1 to 255, with 4 as a default). If not required, the value should be set to 1 to recover some memory, as the default value is four. Earlier DOS versions provided a second parameter to protect currently opened files. The default second parameter value is zero and this means that if the maximum files allowed are already opened, a new file can only be opened by DOS automatically closing down the least recently accessed file. The second parameter is the number of files to be protected. Thus

FCBS = 20,5

would handle 20 files with the first five being protected. If the two parameters were given the same value, no new files would be allowed to be opened beyond the given figure.

COMMANDS IN AUTOEXEC.BAT

AUTOEXEC.BAT is a special file that the system looks for, after carrying out the CONFIG.SYS stage of the configuration process. It is an optional file but, if it is present, the instructions contained within it will be executed one after the other.   This file is of the 'batch file' type to be examined shortly. This is a special type of batch file, in that it runs automatically each time the machine is switched on. For this reason, it is used for further refinements to the machine configuration.   The commonly used commands to be found in this file are:

PATH

To run a particular executable program such as an EXE, COM or BAT file, the user normally either;
- moves into the appropriate sub-directory, using CD, and calls up the program by name.
- calls the program using its full description, including the path of sub-directories e.g.
  C:\BUSINESS\FINANCE\123

This is cumbersome and also expects that the user knows the path where the file can be found.   This task can be made much easier by including a PATH command in the autoexec file. This command tells MS-DOS where to look for programs, by giving a list of drives and directories that should be searched. The syntax is the word PATH, followed by the first sub-directory to be searched. Each new sub-directory to be searched can be added to the existing path, being separated from the earlier part of the path by a semi-colon.   Now, as long as the executable file exists in one of the sub-directories contained in the path, it can be called and run from anywhere in the directory structure.

For example, the following PATH command -

PATH C:\MS-DOS;C:\UTILS;C:\FINANCE\123

would instruct MS-DOS to search through the MS-DOS, UTILS and 123 directories, if the wanted file was not found in the current directory. Note that the FINANCE directory is not searched.

If the wanted file is not in the current directory or in any of the directories named in the path list, it cannot be called without the user knowing where it resides in the directory structure.

Since the search is conducted in the order specified by the path, the most frequently accessed directories should appear earliest in the path statement.

The path can be up to 128 characters in length and is stored in the 'environment variables' area, a block of memory taken from the main 640k memory area. Although the PATH command is usually embedded in the AUTOEXEC.BAT file, it can be issued as a direct command from the DOS prompt. Any new paths set up directly from the keyboard will replace any set up by AUTOEXEC.BAT and will remain in force until the machine is rebooted.

To view the currently operating path, the PATH command can be given with no parameters; this will result in the current path being displayed.   To clear the current path setting use the command with a semi-colon as parameter - i.e.

PATH;

APPEND

The PATH command only allows users access to executable files and does not provide access to data files. However, most applications require not only the EXE files, but a number of overlay files, help files, data files, etc. To run such applications, the user requires to access both the executable and non-executable files in an application sub-directory. To achieve this, DOS provides an APPEND command. This command functions in exactly the same way as the PATH command, except that it applies to non-executable files, and has a similar syntax:

APPEND C:\BUSINESS\FINANCE\123;C:\DATAFILES

The above command lets the user access data files in the two sub-directories named in the APPEND command, from any part of the directory structure. Like PATH, the APPEND command can contain up to 128 characters and occupies part of the main memory allocation.

To view the currently operating APPEND path, the APPEND command can be given with no parameters; this will result in the current append path being displayed. To clear the current APPEND path setting use the command with a semi-colon as parameter - i.e. APPEND;

If the command has the /x parameter added, then the APPEND command will also search the APPEND paths for executable files. If the command has the /e parameter added, the path is held as an environment variable called 'APPEND', allowing access to its contents via a batch file.

NOTE Any application called via the APPEND path that needs to create new files will create them in the <u>current</u> directory and not in the application's home directory.

KEYB UK

The KEYB command is used to set up the correct keyboard for a particular country. The default keyboard is an American layout and the diagram shows the different layout of keys on a French keyboard. If the KEYB command is not included in the autoexecute file, it will produce transposed keys (such as the @ symbol, and the double quotes symbol).

To obtain a British keyboard, the command KEYB UK should be given. This assumes that KEYB.COM is in the root directory. If it is not, then the path to it must be given e.g.

KEYB UK,,C:\DOS\KEYBOARD.SYS.

This loads a device driver to interpret the keystrokes from the keyboard as the expected QWERTY layout. Compare this with the French keyboard layout which uses the AZERTY layout. To move from the default USA keyboard to a French interpretation, the AUTOEXEC.BAT script would contain a KEYB FR command. Similarly, GR configures for Germany, IT for Italy and NL for the Netherlands.

PROMPT

The normal on-screen prompt is A>. This can be altered by the PROMPT command followed by the required symbols. The list of symbols and their uses is:

SYMBOL	MEANING
$p	Current drive and path
$g	> symbol
$l	< symbol
$t	Current time
$d	Current date
$v	DOS version number
$n	Current drive
$q	= symbol
$h	Backspace and delete
$_	Carriage return & line feed
$b	The	(pipe) character
$$	Dollar sign
$e	ESC character for ANSI calls

The most common use is PROMPT pg, which displays the current directory in which the user is sitting - e.g. C:\WS5>

If the command is PROMPT $t then the on-screen prompt will be: The current time is 11:17:35.45

If the command is

PROMPT $p time=$thhhhhh $g

the prompt will be altered to something similar to

C:\WS5 time=3:08 >

The details of the current prompt are stored in the environment area.

FASTOPEN

If a user requires to open a file on a hard disc, the system has to locate the exact position on the disc where the file commences, so that the drive mechanism can be moved to that location. This will be true of each file to be accessed. If the files are specified in a PATH or APPEND statement, then the levels of the path have to be searched each time the file is required.   So, even if the same group of files are accessed regularly during an operation, the system has repeat the search process every time it needs the same file.

The FASTOPEN utility employs a portion of memory to store the location of the files that were recently accessed.   Now, if a file is to be accessed, the memory list is checked first. If the file is present in the list, its physical location can be retrieved quickly, thus speeding up disc accesses. Of course, if the file is not in the memory list, the system has to revert to the slower process of interrogating the disc system.

The syntax is   FASTOPEN C:=100

This allocates the C: drive the ability to track 100 files' locations.   The permissible range of files is from 10 through to 999, the default being 48.   Each allocation requires about 48 bytes of memory.   If the /x parameter is used, the list is made up in expanded memory, rather than conventional main memory; there is no option to use extended memory.   If more than one hard disc is in use separate lists can be configured for each drive, thus:

                        FASTOPEN C:=100 D:=150

FASTOPEN is only available for hard discs and will not work with floppy drives. It does not improve performance radically and is not often used.

DIRCMD

As shown in the DOS & Environments chapter, the DIR command has a range of options so that the screen output can be filtered or ordered to the user's needs.   If the user uses a regular format (e.g. always wishes to see files in their descending order of size) then this can be made the default form for DIR. This is achieved with the DIRCMD command as shown:

                        SET DIRCMD=DIR/O-N

This can be embedded in the AUTOEXEC.BAT file so that is set up each time the machine is switched on; the other DIR options can still be used normally at the command line as usual.

SHARE.EXE

This is a dual-purpose command that is used where:
- A PC is part of a computer local area network and file sharing and file locking are required. It is also employed where a PC is used as a multi-programming system.   It is used to provide OLE (Object Linking and Embedding) within Windows applications, thus allowing data sharing between programs.
- The hard disc size, or partition size, exceeds 32Mb and the DOS version is prior to version 5.   Older programs which still employ FCBs require compatibility with partitions greater than 32Mb to prevent loss of data. Provision for partitions greater than 32Mb is provided within the DOS 5 and DOS 6 kernels.

SHARE.EXE is a TSR that can be installed by placing it as a line in the AUTOEXEC.BAT file or via a INSTALL=C:\DOS\SHARE.EXE in the CONFIG.SYS file.   In its first use, the utility prevents two programs opening the same file in write mode at the same time.   File sharing allows a file to be read by two programs at the same time, while file locking ensures that only one program will write to that file at any one time. The command has two optional parameters:

/L   controls the maximum number of files that can be locked at any one time. The default is 20
/F   controls the amount of memory laid aside for storing information on locked files. The default is 2048 bytes.

An example of the command would be:

                C:\DOS\SHARE.EXE /L:100 /F:4096

With older DOS versions, when a PC with a larger disc than 32Mb boots up, DOS will attempt to run SHARE.EXE if no arrangements have been made via CONFIG.SYS or AUTOEXEC.BAT.   In such a case, it will only look for SHARE.EXE in the root directory or in any directory given in a SHELL statement.   If the file is not found, the message *"WARNING! SHARE should be loaded for large media"* is displayed.   In a non-networked DOS 5 machine, the warning can be ignored.

MOUSE

The way that a mouse is installed in a computer varies from system to system. Commonly there is a file called MOUSE.COM which installs a resident program to drive a mouse device. The command MOUSE can be added, if this facility is available and is required. If there is no demand for the mouse, the command should be omitted from the AUTOEXEC file, to avoid wasting memory space. Windows has its own built-in mouse driver and, if all the mouse-driven applications operate under

Windows, there is no need to install a separate mouse driver. Sometimes a mouse driver will be installed as a system file, via the CONFIG.SYS configuration process. Alternatively, the MOUSE.COM file may be called via the AUTOEXEC.BAT file.

MODE

The DOS MODE utility provides control over both printing and screen output. Its main options are:

CONTROLLING THE GRAPHICS CARD

The MODE command can be used to control the graphics card output. A card that is capable of highly detailed colour output may be instructed to alter its output to meet changing needs. Examples might be the needs of a particular package, the use of a monochrome monitor on a colour card or to produce larger screen characters for the visually impaired.

The syntax is MODE display

where the display options are:

40	Use the graphics card with 40 characters per line
80	Use the graphics card with 80 characters per line
bw40	Disable the card's colour and produce 40 characters per line
bw80	Disable the card's colour and produce 80 characters per line
co40	Enable the card's colour and produce 40 characters per line
co80	Enable the card's colour and produce 80 characters per line

In addition, if the ANSI.SYS driver has been installed, the MODE command can be used to control the number of characters in a text line and the number of text lines required to fill the screen.

The syntax is

MODE CON: cols=40 lines=25

where the parameters are:

cols : Either 40 or 80

lines : Either 25,43 or 50, if the display adapter is capable of supporting such definitions.

CONFIGURING PARALLEL PRINTERS

The default settings for a parallel printer are the use of the LPT1 port, with 80 characters per line and 6 lines per inch and no retry parameter. If this is not suitable, then it can be changed with the use of the DOS MODE command.

MODE can be used to configure the printing characteristics of any parallel (Centronics) printer. Parallel devices are designated as PRN, LPT1, LPT2 and LPT3.

The syntax is

MODE LPT1, cols=80, lines=6, retry=b (This can be shortened to MODE LPT1,80,6,b)

The parameters in the example are:

LPT1	:	The printer to be set up. The options are PRN, LPT1, LPT2 and LPT3. PRN and LPT1 can be regarded as interchangeable.
cols	:	The number of columns (characters) per line. The default is 80 but can be changed to 132 for wide-carriage printers.
lines	:	The number of lines in each vertical inch of printed output. The default is 6 but this can be changed to 8.
retry	:	The action to carried out in the event that the computer experiences a time-out from the printer during the printing process, probably from a printer that is busy.
		If this parameter is given, a small portion of code remains in memory to handle the situation according to the following retry options:

	e	Return an 'error' signal when the printer is busy
	b	Return a 'busy' signal when the printer is busy
	p	Continually retry to print until printer accepts computer output
	r	Return a 'ready' signal from a printer that is busy.
	n	Do nothing. This is the default response.

If a parameter is omitted, the command will use the last given value for that parameter.

It may not be necessary to give a MODE command to set up parallel printer settings, since many application packages will carry out the function from within the application configuration.

Microsoft does not recommend that retry values should be given with MODE commands that are used over local area networks. This applies to both serial and parallel printer MODE commands.

SWITCHING PRINTERS

When a user presses PrtScr or re-directs text files to a printer (e.g. TYPE MEMO.DOC > PRN or DIR > PRN), the default is to route the data to the first parallel printer port LPT1.

To route data to a serial port, the user has to give the following DOS command:

MODE LPT1:=COM1:

This will direct any printer output to the serial port until the direction is disabled with the DOS command:

MODE LPT1:

CONFIGURING SERIAL PRINTERS

However, when the above re-direction is given, an extra command must preface it.   It is necessary to inform the system as to the speed of the data and its construction. This is known as the transmission and reception 'protocols'.

Both the computer and printer must be running at the same baud rate (speed of data transfer) and regarding data as having the same number of data bits for each character.   Printers will mostly have DIP switches that allow the user a choice of these settings.   It is vital that the computer is operating at the same settings as the printer, if intelligible results are required.

The configuration is set at the printer end by switches. For the computer, they are established by giving another MODE command. DOS uses the BIOS code to carry out its serial port activities.

A typical MODE command might be:

MODE COM1:96,n,8,1,retry=b

This provides a setup for COM1, with a baud rate of 9600, 8 data bits, no parity, and 1 stop bit. COM port options range from COM1 to COM4.

PROTOCOL OPTIONS

BAUD

Some printers have baud rates ranging from 110bps to 19200bps, which is the full range that DOS is capable of handling. Other printers have smaller ranges of say 1200bps to 19200bps. Only the first two digits of the baud rate are entered, e.g. a baud rate of 4800 is entered as 48.   Valid values are 11, 15, 30, 60, 12, 24, 48, 96 and 19.

PARITY

There are three possible options:

  n : no parity

  e: even parity

  o : odd parity

An extra bit can be included in the data stream, to provide for error-checking at the receiving device.   This bit is inserted between each set of data bits and stop bits. With even parity, the sending device counts the number of binary one bits in the character to be sent.   If the number of these data bits is even, the parity bit is set to zero, otherwise it is set to one.   With odd parity, the parity bit is set to one if there is an even number of binary ones in the character to be sent.   This ensures that the transmitted total bit group (i.e. the data and the parity bit) will always contain an even number of bits for even parity and an odd number of bits for odd parity.   If any of the data bits or parity bits are accidentally altered during transmission, the receiving device can detect the problem.   The parity bit is mostly ignored, since there is no way that a printer can ask for the re-transmission of a faulty character. However, some devices may be set to expect a parity bit, even if it ignores its presence; in that instance, the MODE command must set up the expected odd or even parity.   Mostly, the configuration will demand that no parity be included.

DATA BITS

This can be set to 7 or 8 data bits. 7 bits is sufficient to cover the ASCII values from 0 through to 127.   This covers the entire alpha-numeric range, along with printer control codes such as Backspace and Carriage Return. To print characters from the extended character set, such as box-drawing elements or foreign characters, an 8-bit data stream is required to represent the ASCII codes above 127. Additionally, graphics data requires 8 bits.   If the computer is set up to send 7 data bits, the computer printer data has its most significant bit set to zero. This will obviously cause printer output errors with data that requires 8 bits. Accordingly, printers are commonly set to 8 data bits.

STOP BITS

Offers a choice of 1 or 2 stop bits. Almost always, this will be set for a single stop bit.

RETRY MODE

Some computer programs may simply send data to the printer, without any prior checking of the status of printer port.   If an attempt is made to send to a busy device, then after a time-out period of a few seconds, the user will be given an error message such as *'Not ready error writing device COM1'*.   Other programs check the status of the printer port, before transmitting any data.   If the printer happened to be switched off, then the application would wait for ever and the application would be hung up.   The RETRY parameter is used to prevent this happening. Its options are:

RETRY=NONE   If the printer port tests as busy, a busy code is passed back to the program. If the program continues to attempt to print the data, the user will be given the *'Not ready error writing device COM1'* type message.

RETRY=E   If the printer tests as busy, an error code is passed back to the program, which can then use the code to take abort/retry action. If the program decides to again try printing the data, the memory-resident MODE code will continuously attempt to print the data, unless the user presses the Ctrl-Break keys.

RETRY=B   If the printer port test as busy, a busy code is passed back to the program.

RETRY=R   If the printer port test as busy, the program is told that the printer is actually ready to receive data.   The MODE program then takes over the continual process of trying to send the data to the printer.

RETRY=P   If the printer port tests as busy, the MODE command will continually try to print the data - for ever, if necessary.   This is the mode suggested by the HP DeskJet printer.

Earlier versions did not have the RETRY parameter.

The MODE commands may be included in the AUTOEXEC.BAT file, if it is the permanent printer configuration that is in use.   Bear in mind that part of MODE command will remain in memory, taking up valuable memory space and should only be used where necessary. Default settings are COM1, even parity, 7 data bits and 2 stop bits for a 110 baud rate, with a single stop bit for all other baud rates.   A report on the current usage of a printer can be obtained by entering MODE LPT1/STATUS or MODE COM1/STATUS.

KEYBOARD SETTINGS

The MODE command can also be used to control the keyboard response thus

MODE CON RATE= x DELAY = y

where x is the rate at which any key held press will repeat the keystroke and y is the delay between holding down the key and the keyboard repeat commencing.   The rate can be set between 1 and 32, with 20 being the default.   The delay can be set to 1, 2, 3 or 4 representing quarters of a second, the default being 2 (i.e. half a second).   These settings apply to DOS mode with the response within Windows being set via the Windows Control Panel's Keyboard utility.

SETTING ENVIRONMENT VARIABLES

As explained earlier, the environment area is a section of memory dedicated to holding the details of the PROMPT, the PATH and various other variables.   The environment area is allocated 160 bytes on bootup but this can be increased to as much as 32k using the SHELL command.

The contents of the environment are a series of text statements such as:

COMSPEC=\COMMAND.COM

which tells DOS where to find the transient portion of COMMAND.COM

PATH=C:\;C:\DOS;C:\UTILS

which stores the details of the PATH statement given in the AUTOEXEC.BAT file or a PATH statement subsequently entered directly from the keyboard.

DOS 5 onwards also supports a DIRCMD variable that can be used to change the default display of directory listings.   For example, if a wide directory is preferred, then the AUTOEXEC.BAT file could contain the line SET DIRCMD=/W.   If the AUTOEXEC file contained the line SET DIRCMD=/O:N then all directory listings will be displayed in sorted alphabetical order.   The command will be stored in the environment area.   To view the current environment contents, give the command SET without any parameters.   The prompt and path contents are stored as variables with their variable names.   These variables can be accessed for use within batch files. Thus, a batch file can contain a line saying

echo The current path is %PATH%

Often, applications are required to create temporary files during the running of their programs.   This may be achieved by declaring the sub-directory that will hold these temporary files at the point of installing the application.   Other programs store their temporary files in a directory that is pointed to by the variable TEMP in the environment.   Such a declaration might be:

SET TEMP=C:\TEMP

The application interrogates the contents of the TEMP variable to see where it should write its temporary files. If the machine has been configured to have a virtual disc, then the RAM drive can be made the home for the temporary files. This would greatly speed up program execution, since the reads and writes are to memory and not the hard disc. In this case, the CONFIG.SYS would include:

> SET TEMP=D:\

This technique has another benefit. Applications should create temporary files during the running of the program and then delete these files on leaving the application. In this way, they are never seen by a user. There are times, however, when an application is not exited safely (e.g. the machine is switched before exiting the application or the program hangs and the machine has to be rebooted). In these cases the temporary files are left on the hard disc. The command DIR *.TMP/S will list any unwanted temporary file; do not run this command from within Windows. If the TEMP directory is on hard disc, these files will occupy valuable disc space. If the TEMP directory is a virtual directory in memory then all temporary files will be automatically lost when the machine is switched off, requiring no extra maintenance to keep the hard disc free of unwanted temporary files.

It is also possible to use the SET command to create and initialise variables that can be used by batch files or applications programs.

For example, the SoundBlaster Pro uses the following:

> SET SOUND=C:\SBPRO
> SET BLASTER=A220 I7 D1 T4

DOSKEY

The DOSKEY utility made its first appearance with DOS v5 and it provides four extra facilities:

- Command recall
- Command editing
- Multiple commands on a single line
- Creation of user-defined macros

DOSKEY is a TSR that is about 3k in size. Using DOSKEY also consumes a default 512 bytes of memory to act as a buffer to store command line commands and macros. To alter the buffer size, the command

> DOSKEY /BUFSIZE = n

can be given where n is the required buffer size (256 bytes being the minimum).

COMMAND RECALL

The simplest use of DOSKEY is to include the command, without parameters, in the AUTOEXEC.BAT file. This loads the program as a TSR that stores each command given by the user at the DOS prompt. The number of commands that can be stored depends on the length of the commands and the allocated buffer size. When the buffer becomes full, any new command is stored at the expense of the oldest command. The process can be regarded as a conveyor belt that stores a list of the most recent DOS prompt commands. All of these commands in the buffer are available for re-use. This saves having to repeat the typing of long and complex commands. If they have already been recently entered, they can be recovered from the buffer and run again.

To place the last command in the buffer back into the command line, press the UP arrow key. This is identical to pressing the f3 in other DOS version. However, pressing the UP arrow key again brings the second last command into the command line. Using this, and the DOWN arrow key, all the stored commands can be fetched - one at a time - into the command line. When a desired command is in the command line, the user only has to press the ENTER key to run the command; the command now becomes the last one in the buffer. To jump to the earliest command in the list, the user presses the Pg Up key, while pressing the Pg Dn key fetches the latest command in the list.

Pressing the f7 key display the entire list of commands currently stored in the buffer. The earliest command is preceded by the number 1, the next by the number 2 and so on. Once displayed, the user can press f9, followed by the number of the desired command. This brings the command into the command line from where it can be run. If the user knows the start of the command, the first few letters of the command can be entered at the DOS prompt, followed by pressing the f8 key. This displays the most recent command in the buffer which matches the search text. Pressing f8 will find the next latest command meeting the search text. If there are no commands that match the search text, pressing f8 produces no results and the user is returned to the DOS prompt.

COMMAND EDITING

The DOS editing keys for modifying command line statements were covered earlier, as were the improved editing facilities provided with DOS v5 onwards.

With DOSKEY loaded, any commands fetched from the buffer into the command line at the DOS prompt can be similarly edited before the command is run.   This does not alter the command held in the buffer; instead, the edited version becomes the latest command to be added to the buffer.   DOSKEY offers a few extra editing commands to the normal DOS 5 set.

- CTRL-Left Arrow moves the cursor to the left one word at a time.
- CTRL-Right Arrow moves the cursor to the right one word at a time.
- CTRL-End deletes all the characters from the cursor position to the end of the statement line.
- CTRL-Home deletes all the characters from the cursor to the beginning of the statement line.

MULTIPLE COMMANDS

Before DOSKEY, the user had to use several, independently given commands to carry out complex functions.   The first command would have to be typed in and run before the second command could be entered.   DOSKEY allows the user to type in several commands in the one command line statement (up to a maximum of 128 characters) and have them all carried out when the ENTER key is pressed.
Consider the following set of commands:

        DIR *.BAK/S > BAKLIST
        DIR *.TMP/S > TMPLIST

The commands in the above example produce two text files.   The first command lists all .BAK files which inhabit the disc, while the second creates a list of all existing .TMP files.   The creation of such lists would prove useful in tidying up the disc.   It would be more convenient if the user could combine both command on to the one command line.   After entering the line, the user could then leave the machine unattended and the two files would be created one after the other.
If DOSKEY is installed the user can enter the command as one line thus:

        DIR *.BAK/S > BAKLIST   ¶   DIR *.TMP/S > TMPLIST

The paragraph mark (i.e. the ¶ symbol) is achieved by pressing Ctrl-T.

USER-DEFINED MACROS

A DOSKEY macro is a facility to create 'aliases' - i.e. a list of commands can be called by invoking a single name.   It can be likened to a single line batch file.   The macro name and its associated commands are stored in the buffer area and can be up to 127 characters in length.   Consider the above example of creating lists of backup and temporary files.   If this was to be a regular activity, the user can be saved the trouble of typing in the long command.   The commands can be entered and named thus:

        DOSKEY GETLISTS=DIR *.BAK/S $G BAKLIST $T   DIR *.TMP/S $G TMPLIST

The above command can be entered directly at the keyboard but regularly used utilities can be set up in the AUTOEXEC.BAT file.   When the machine boots up, the AUTOEXEC.BAT commands are carried out and the DOSKEY lines set up the users own defined macros. Note that macros use the dollar symbol and the letter 't' to separate commands, instead of the ¶ symbol used when entering directly from the keyboard.   The redirection of input and output symbols used in normal DOS commands are similarly replaced as shown.

DOS	DOSKEY
<	$L
>	$G
>>	GG
│	$B

In normal batch files, parameters can be passed in and these 'replaceable parameters' are designated from %1 to %9 (see section on batch files for full details).   Macros using DOSKEY can also handle replaceable parameters but they are designated from $1 to $9.   An example macro with replaceable parameters is: DOSKEY GETLISTS=DIR *.$1/S $G FILELIST

DOSKEY can also be used to redefine any existing internal DOS command as in this example
        DOSKEY DIR = DIR/W/P

MIRROR

This command loads a TSR that will create a 'deletion-tracking' file.   The file stores the name and disc location of every file that the user deletes and this file is used to assist the UNDELETE command.   It also creates a copy of the FAT and directory entries, to assist an UNFORMAT command.

VER

Prints out the manufacturer of the DOS and its current version.

CONFIGURING A COMPUTER SYSTEM

Configuring a computer system consists of:

- Setting DIP switches and/or jumpers on hardware such as printers, video cards and the like, as prescribed in the products' manuals. It may also require the selection of specific options from the front panel of printers, monitors, modems, etc.
- Setting up AUTOEXEC.BAT, CONFIG.SYS and any add-on utilities to load the appropriate hardware drivers and balance memory usage to achieve the desired configuration.

MACHINE CONFIGURATION

The actual machine configuration needed may vary from user to user as each may have different memory needs, TSR usage, or requirements for the auto-running of certain batch files, utilities or application programs. Configuration, then, begins with determining the exact needs of the user. Of course, these needs might sometimes conflict. A program with large memory overheads, for example, could not be run in tandem with a large number of TSRs. So, the first job of the support technician is to arrive at a working specification for the machine, in conjunction with the user.

MEMORY MANAGEMENT

The aim of memory management is to utilise the whole memory of the machine in such a way that the maximum amount of user memory is available for application programs and data, consistent with achieving the maximum functionality and speed.

→ Memory usage is explained in detail in the chapter on Memory and should be reviewed before proceeding with memory management.

Until the advent of DOS 5, there was little room for major memory planning. Earlier versions allowed for user setting of FILES and BUFFERS sizes and allowed users to install TSR programs via batch files (mainly AUTOEXEC.BAT) and device drivers via CONFIG.SYS. Careless use of these settings (e.g. installing rarely used device drivers, setting FILES or BUFFERS parameters beyond the actual requirements, setting FILES or BUFFERS below the minimum required by an application, installing many TSRs) could seriously affect machine performance, or even prevent an application running.

These problems could exist while part of the machine memory, areas above 640k, was completely unused. These unused areas - termed *'upper memory blocks'* - were capable of holding device drivers, etc. but DOS was not able to re-allocate into these areas. The gap was filled by add-ons such as *'PC KWIK'*, and 'QEMM' which allowed the allocation of device drivers into unused UMBs.

VIEWING MEMORY STATISTICS

MSDOS provides a utility that displays facts about the machine's memory usage. The MEM command provides information about what is occupying the conventional and upper memory areas of the machine and displays the size and memory location of programs, data, drivers, etc.

It has three different switch options, as below:

/CLASSIFY or /C - lists all the programs that are in conventional memory and upper memory including their size in decimal and hexadecimal. It also provides a summary of the machine's memory usage. An example display may be as shown on the chart on the next page.

/PROGRAM or /P - lists all currently loaded programs, including their name, type (i.e. program, data, environment), size and memory location.

/DEBUG or /D - similar to /P but also includes internal drivers, as shown on the chart on the right.

```
Conventional Memory :

  Name            Size in Decimal        Size in Hex
  ----            --------------         -----------
  MSDOS           26576    (26.0K)         67D0
  HIMEM            1072    ( 1.0K)          430
  EMM386           3232    ( 3.2K)          CA0
  COMMAND          2624    ( 2.6K)          A40
  win386           1584    ( 1.5K)          630
  WIN              1552    ( 1.5K)          610
  COMMAND          2800    ( 2.7K)          AF0
  FREE           615616   (601.2K)        964C0

Total  FREE :    615616   (601.2K)

Upper Memory :

  Name            Size in Decimal        Size in Hex
  ----            --------------         -----------
  SYSTEM         167472   (163.5K)        28E30
  win386          29936    (29.2K)         74F0
  RAMDRIVE         1184    ( 1.2K)          4A0
  ANSI             4192    ( 4.1K)         1060
  DISPLAY          8288    ( 8.1K)         2060
  SMARTDRV        31376    (30.6K)         7A90
  KEYB             6208    ( 6.1K)         1840
  SHARE            6192    ( 6.0K)         1830
  DOSKEY           4128    ( 4.0K)         1020
  UMBFILES         2960    ( 2.9K)          B90

Total  FREE :        0    ( 0.0K)

Total bytes available to programs (Conventional+Upper)
    :   615616 (601.2K)
Largest executable program size
    :   615440 (601.0K)
Largest available upper memory block
    :        0 ( 0.0K)

 15990784 bytes total contiguous extended memory
        0 bytes available contiguous extended memory
  1048576 bytes available XMS memory
        MS-DOS resident in High Memory Area
```

```
Address      Name        Size       Type
-------      --------    ------     ------
000000                   000400     Interrupt Vector
000400                   000100     ROM Communication Area
000500                   000200     DOS Communication Area

000700       IO          000A60     System Data

001160       MSDOS       0013D0     System Data

002530       IO          005380     System Data
             HIMEM       000430     DEVICE=
             EMM386      000CA0     DEVICE=
                         000130     FILES=
                         000100     FCBS=
                         003E60     BUFFERS=
                         0001C0     LASTDRIVE=
0078C0       MSDOS       000040     System Program

007910       COMMAND     000940     Program
008260       win386      000040     Data
0082B0       COMMAND     000100     Environment
0083C0       WIN         0000A0     Environment
008470       WIN         000570     Program
0089F0       win386      0000B0     Environment
008AB0       win386      000540     Program
009000       COMMAND     0000B0     Data
0090C0       COMMAND     000940     Program
009A10       COMMAND     000100     Environment
009B20       MEM         0000A0     Environment
009BD0       MEM         0176F0     Program
0212D0       MSDOS       07ED10     -- Free --
09FFF0       SYSTEM      028E40     System Program

0C8E40       IO          003590     System Data
             RAMDRIVE    0004A0     DEVICE=
             ANSI        001060     DEVICE=
             DISPLAY     002060     DEVICE=
0CC3E0       win386      000090     Data
0CC480       SMARTDRV    007A90     Program
0D3F20       KEYB        001840     Program
0D5770       SHARE       001830     Program
0D6FB0       win386      0000A0     Data
0D7060       DOSKEY      001020     Program
0D8090       UMBFILES    000B90     Program
0D8C30       win386      0073C0     Data


  655360 bytes total conventional memory
  655360 bytes available to MS-DOS
  615440 largest executable program size

15990784 bytes total contiguous extended memory
       0 bytes available contiguous extended memory
 1048576 bytes available XMS memory
         MS-DOS resident in High Memory Area
```

NOTES:

- The /D and /P options show the addresses and sizes in hexadecimal only, with the summary information in decimal.

- If the machine is fitted with extended memory, then this will be included in the display.

- If the machine is fitted with expanded memory, then this will only be included in the display if conforms to LIM 4.0 specification.

- The *'largest executable program size'* displays the largest possible program that the computer's conventional memory can store.

- *'Available XMS memory'* is the amount of extended memory being managed by HIMEM.SYS or other extended memory manager.

MSDOS MEMORY MANAGEMENT

Microsoft overcame many of its earlier memory management limitations commencing with its version 5 of MSDOS.   The current version of MSDOS allows users to maximise the memory available for user programs by placing drivers, etc. into memory above the 640k user area.

Consider the memory map shown in the diagram. This represents a typical machine without any optimisation. The map represents any PC computer later than the XT model, since the XT's 8086 chip was incapable of accessing addresses beyond a 1Mb limit.   The   machine's   AUTO-EXEC.BAT and CONFIG.SYS files will have inserted a range of drivers and utilities into the user memory area, as shown.   Also, the entire DOS kernel sits in the user memory area.

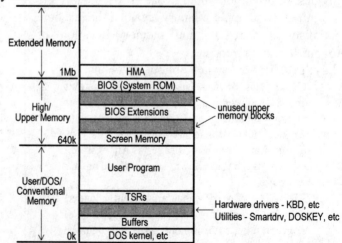

NOTE:

Most books/manuals define the 640k area as conventional memory and the 1Mb area as base memory; others describe base and conventional memory as equivalent terms. All books accept that the 640k can be described as user memory.

Note that while this overcrowding is taking place in the base memory area, it is almost certain that there will be unused areas of memory address in the upper memory area.

Using the DOS MEM/C command would produce a display similar to the display shown.

Note that the total memory available for running application programs is a mere 496Kb, which is inadequate for much modern software.

DOS itself requires about 62K and the rest of the 640k is eaten up with various drivers and utilities.

The solution obviously lies in moving much of the drivers up into the unused areas of upper memory, while still being able to access them for their normal functions. Even better would be to move part of the DOS kernel out of base memory up into extended memory.

```
Conventional Memory :

  Name              Size in Decimal       Size in Hex
  ----              ---------------       -----------
  MSDOS             63424    (61.9K)        F7C0
  HIMEM              3696    ( 3.6K)         E70
  EMM386             3232    ( 3.2K)         CA0
  RAMDRIVE           1184    ( 1.2K)         4A0
  ANSI               4192    ( 4.1K)        1060
  DISPLAY           18048    (17.6K)        4680
  COMMAND            4704    ( 4.6K)        1260
  SMARTDRV          31376    (30.6K)        7A90
  KEYB               6208    ( 6.1K)        1840
  SHARE              6192    ( 6.0K)        1830
  DOSKEY             4128    ( 4.0K)        1020
  FREE                 64    ( 0.1K)          40
  FREE                144    ( 0.1K)          90
  FREE                160    ( 0.2K)          A0
  FREE             508288   (496.4K)       7C180

Total  FREE :      508656   (496.7K)

Total bytes available to programs : 508656  (496.7K)
Largest executable program size :   508288  (496.4K)

15990784 bytes total contiguous extended memory
       0 bytes available contiguous extended memory
 8372224 bytes available XMS memory
    64Kb High Memory Area available
```

USING EXTENDED MEMORY

All PCs, from the 286 series onwards, which are fitted with extended memory can be manipulated with the memory management tools provided in MSDOS version 5 and later. The first 64k of extended memory (i.e. the first 64k beyond the 1Mb conventional memory) is known as the *'HMA'* or *'High Memory Area'*. This should not be confused with the Upper Memory Blocks which reside between 640k and 1Mb. The HMA is largely unused by application programs. It is possible, therefore, to use the HMA to store parts of the DOS kernel, instead of placing it in base memory. To achieve this, the CONFIG.SYS should have the following two lines inserted at an early point in the script:

    device = c:\dos\himem.sys
    dos = high

The first line loads the extended memory manager into base memory; HIMEM.SYS acts as an organiser of both the HMA and the rest of extended memory, preventing the simultaneous use of the same area of memory by different programs. This driver is compulsory where Windows is to be used. Since it manages extended memory and acts as the link between base and extended memory, it follows that this driver must remain in base memory. However, the addition of this extra driver into base memory allows much more memory savings than it devours. The HIMEM line should appear before any other line that seeks to use extended memory.

The second line instructs the HIMEM driver to load the DOS hidden files, MSDOS.SYS and IO.SYS into the high memory area. Since this line appears at an early stage in CONFIG.SYS, it can be assumed that the HMA is unused and so DOS can be safely loaded there.

The MEM/C command would now produce a display similar to that shown. Note that MSDOS now only occupies just under 26k of base memory. If this figure is compared with the previous display on the previous page, it can be seen that exactly 36k of DOS

```
Conventional Memory :

  Name              Size in Decimal       Size in Hex
  ----              ---------------       -----------
  MSDOS             26560    (25.9K)        67C0
  HIMEM              1072    ( 1.0K)         430
  EMM386             3232    ( 3.2K)         CA0
  RAMDRIVE           1184    ( 1.2K)         4A0
  ANSI               4192    ( 4.1K)        1060
  DISPLAY            8288    ( 8.1K)        2060
  COMMAND            2624    ( 2.6K)         A40
  SMARTDRV          31376    (30.6K)        7A90
  KEYB               6208    ( 6.1K)        1840
  SHARE              6192    ( 6.0K)        1830
  DOSKEY             4128    ( 4.0K)        1020
  FREE                 64    ( 0.1K)          40
  FREE                144    ( 0.1K)          90
  FREE                160    ( 0.2K)          A0
  FREE             559600   (546.5K)       889F0

Total  FREE :      559968   (546.8K)

  Total bytes available to programs : 559968  (546.8K)
  Largest executable program size :   559600  (546.5K)
15990784 bytes total contiguous extended memory
       0 bytes available contiguous extended memory
 8372224 bytes available XMS memory
       MS-DOS resident in High Memory Area
```

has been saved from the base memory. Yet, it can be seen that just over 50k of extra memory is now available for user applications, since DOS was loaded into the HMA. The explanation for the difference lies in the added benefits of moving parts of DOS into the High Memory Area. If BUFFERS is set to 48 or less, then these DOS buffers will also be moved up to the High Memory Area. If BUFFERS is set to 44 or less, then even a part of COMMAND.COM is moved up into the High Memory Area. Even with these improvements, a substantial part of base memory is still being used up by device drivers. These can be loaded into the unused Upper Memory Blocks on 386 and 486 machines.

USING UPPER MEMORY BLOCKS

Computers, prior to optimisation, will have a number of unused areas of upper memory that are not currently devoted to servicing added hardware such as local area network interface adapters or add-on ROM extensions.   The fitting of cards results in their control chips being mapped in to an area of the upper memory.   So, for instance, a video card usually is placed at address C000 (i.e. 768k), an XT disc controller may be at C800 and a SCSI card or cache controller may be at DC00.   This leaves areas of upper memory that are not in use at all. If the CONFIG.SYS file is altered, then these unused blocks can be used for loading the device drivers currently occupying base memory.   From 386 machine onwards, the following lines are required to achieve this:

> device = c:\dos\himem.sys
> device = c:\dos\emm386.exe noems
> dos = high,umb

The first line, as before, loads the interface between base and extended memory.   The second line loads the EMM386 driver.   This driver is dual purpose - it allows access to the Upper Memory Blocks and it can also be used to configure extended memory to act as expanded memory for those programs that use expanded memory.   In our example, we wish to use the first facility and disable the second facility. That is the reason for the *noems* parameter, which stands for *'no expanded memory'*.   The 64k that expanded memory would require for its paging area is now available for storing various drivers. Omitting the 'noems' parameter, or using the 'ram' or 'auto' parameters will result in the system using 64k of UMB space as an EMS page frame.

It should be noted that it is unlikely that all these unused areas of upper memory will actually have memory chips fitted.   Yet DOS expects to find all its TSRs and drivers within the 1Mb area.   The EMM386 software solves the problem by storing the drivers, etc. into extended memory and maps (i.e. links) the DOS call to the actual place where the routine is stored.   The third line adds the parameter *umb* to inform the system that a DOS link is established between base memory and the upper memory area.

Now the way is prepared to load devices into any unused UMBs.   In this instance, there will be free memory available in the Upper Memory Area.   On other machines, it would be advisable to run MEM/C to check on whether there are any free UMBbs - and whether any free block is large enough to store the size of the new driver to be loaded.   There are two methods of loading device drivers into upper memory blocks.   This is because device drivers can either be loaded via CONFIG.SYS using 'device= ' commands, or via AUTOEXEC.BAT using COM and EXE files, such as KEYB.COM or SMARTDRV.EXE.

NB - Windows applications do not make use of EMM386, since all their memory management needs are met by HIMEM.SYS.   EMM386 can be used for normal DOS programs, or for DOS programs running under Windows.   The 'noems' parameter prevents the creation of expanded memory under DOS; Windows can still create expanded memory dynamically - i.e. only when it needs it.

DEVICEHIGH

The normal 'device=' type command in CONFIG.SYS can be replaced with the 'devicehigh=' command. Examples are:

> devicehigh=c:\windows\ramdrive.sys 3076 512 200/e
> devicehigh=c:\dos\ansi.sys

LOADHIGH

Instead of simply entering the filename in the AUTOEXEC.BAT script, the command is prefaced with the word 'LOADHIGH'. Examples are:

> loadhigh c:\windows\smartdrv.exe 2048 2048
> loadhigh keyb uk,,c:\dos\keyboard.sys
> loadhigh c:\dos\share.exe

The new, optimised, PC memory map as described in the example now looks similar to:

The MEM/C command would now produce a display similar to that shown.

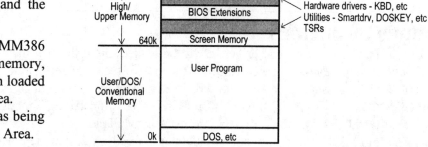

The display now provides statistics on both the base memory and the upper memory usage.

Note that although the EMM386 driver occupies some base memory, all the drivers have now been loaded up into the upper memory area.

As before, DOS is reported as being resident in the High Memory Area.

The base memory now available to user application programs has risen to over 607k.

There is still room in the umbs to load another one or two devices, since the display reports that the largest available upper memory block is just under 29k in size.

NOTE

The order in which drivers appear in the configuration files can alter performance and this is looked at later.

MEMMAKER

DOS 6 introduced an automated system for PC configuration called 'MemMaker'.

When this program is run, it boots the PC and monitors how the various drivers and TSRs listed in CONFIG.SYS and AUTOEXEC.BAT are loaded. It notes the size of each device to be installed. It then compares the available memory blocks with the needs of each TSR and driver. From this it calculates the optimum usage of the UMBs.

It then alters the LOADHIGH and DEVICEHIGH lines so that each item is loaded into the most appropriate slot to provide maximum usage of the UMB areas.

These alterations make use of the new /L switch that is available in DOS 6. This switch forces the TSR

```
Conventional Memory :

   Name              Size in Decimal        Size in Hex
 -------------       --------------------   -------------
   MSDOS               26576     (26.0K)         67D0
   HIMEM                1072     ( 1.0K)          430
   EMM386               3232     ( 3.2K)          CA0
   COMMAND              2624     ( 2.6K)          A40
   FREE                   64     ( 0.1K)           40
   FREE               621600    (607.0K)        97C20

 Total  FREE :        621664    (607.1K)

 Upper Memory :


   Name              Size in Decimal        Size in Hex
 -------------       --------------------   -------------
   SYSTEM             167472    (163.5K)        28E30
   RAMDRIVE             1184     ( 1.2K)          4A0
   ANSI                 4192     ( 4.1K)         1060
   DISPLAY              8288     ( 8.1K)         2060
   SMARTDRV            31376     (30.6K)         7A90
   KEYB                 6208     ( 6.1K)         1840
   SHARE                6192     ( 6.0K)         1830
   DOSKEY               4128     ( 4.0K)         1020
   UMBFILES             2960     ( 2.9K)          B90
   FREE                  144     ( 0.1K)           90
   FREE                  160     ( 0.2K)           A0
   FREE                29632     (28.9K)         73C0

 Total  FREE :         29936     (29.2K)

 Total bytes available to programs (Conventional+Upper)
      :      651600    (636.3K)
 Largest executable program size
      :      621440    (606.9K)
 Largest available upper memory block
      :       29632    (28.9K)

 15990784 bytes total contiguous extended memory
        0 bytes available contiguous extended memory
  8372224 bytes available XMS memory
        MS-DOS resident in High Memory Area
```

or driver into the memory block specified in the address given in the switch, regardless of the order of the lines in the CONFIG.SYS or AUTOEXEC.BAT files.

Finally it reboots so that the changes take effect. If it has inadvertently mapped a device to a memory location in use by an adapter card, this will be detected on the second bootup. The user will be given the choice of undoing the changes or trying again using a less aggressive look at memory.

MemMaker is a handy utility for inexperienced user or for generating a quick memory management setup. However, it does not give perfect results and frequently has to be tweaked to provide the best performance.

When MemMaker is first run, it offers the choice of an Express setup which is fully automatic or a Custom setup which lets the knowledgeable user have more choice over the configuration.

NOTE

The /L switch does not have to be generated by MemMaker and can be directly entered into CONFIG.SYS and AUTOEXEC.BAT by the user who has sufficient knowledge of the machine's memory map and the size of each module to be installed.

```
DEVICEHIGH /L:1,15792 =C:\DOS\DISPLAY.SYS CON=(EGA,,1)
DEVICEHIGH /L:2,12048 =C:\DOS\SETVER.EXE
DEVICEHIGH /L:1,9072 =C:\DOS\ANSI.SYS
```

ORDER OF DEVICES

Where a number of TSRs and drivers are to be loaded, the order that they appear in the CONFIG.SYS can have an important influence over the efficiency of the resultant memory management.   In DOS 5 and in DOS 6 without use of the /L switch, TSRs and drivers are installed in the order that they appear in the CONFIG.SYS and AUTOEXEC.BAT files.   When installing a module, it is placed in the largest available UMB slot, whether or not a more slot is available.   So, for example, a 20k module may be installed into a 32k slot, even though a 20k slot is free.   A 25k module may therefore find that no slot can store it and the module will have to be loaded into conventional memory.   A different order of installation would have placed the 25k module in the 32k slot and the 20k module in the 20k slot, resulting in no wastage of UMB memory and no wastage of conventional memory.   MemMaker, or the use of the /L switch can specify the area to store a module and thereby optimise the use of memory.

Also, if a CD ROM drive is to be cached, then the MSCDEX driver must be loaded before Smartdrive is loaded.

By default, a page frame created by EMM386 will be located in a 64k slot commencing at address 0D00h, often resulting in a spare memory block above and below the page frame area.   Some larger device drivers are unable to fit in any of these spare slots. If the page frame was located at a different starting address, the smaller memory block areas would be able to form a larger contiguous free area. This would allow larger drivers to be installed.   This can be achieved by adding a 'frame= ' parameter to the EMM386 line as in the following example:

DEVICE=C:\DOS\EMM386.EXE FRAME=C800 HIGHSCAN

This command locates the page frame to commence at address C800h, assuming the area is free (check with the MSD Memory utility).   Other possible relocation areas are E000h or E800h.

INCLUDE/EXCLUDE

DOS 6 onwards added the 'include' and 'exclude' commands to its list of memory management tools, to allow for any imperfections in the optimising process.   For example, MemMaker will not include the B000-B7FF (704k to 736k) area in its optimisation, since this is used by SVGA video boards. MemMaker cannot detect the presence of SVGA boards and therefore leaves the area alone. Similarly, EMM386 will not include E000-EFFF (898k to 980k) area in its optimisation, since it is sometimes used for BIOS extensions.

These areas, and others, can be checked to see whether they are occupied by using the 'Memory' option of Microsoft's MSD utility.   This option will display the computer's memory map with information on whether each block of memory is in use or is free.   Using the 'Memory Browser' in the 'Utilities' option will display a list of the ROMs that are installed in the machine, along with the address at which they are located and their size.   From this, it should be possible to appreciate the exact usage of the current machine memory. This examination should also expose any address areas that are being overlooked in the memory management process.

If an unused memory area is to be included in the pool to be used for UMBs, the EMM386 command can be modified with the 'include' option as shown:

DEVICE=C:\DOS\EMM386.EXE I=E000-EFFF I=C800-DBFF NOEMS

In the above example, two unused areas have been included into the UMB pool.   Notice that the addresses are entered in hexadecimal numbering.

It is also possible that an area of addresses could be tested as free when it actually contains a ROM.   In this case, the driver would think it was installed to a UMB area when it actually failed to load (since it impossible to write to a ROM).   An attempt to call the driver would instead run the ROM code and this would result in a crash of Windows or the Windows application. DOS 6 also provides an 'exclude' option to ensure that any such conflicts are avoided.   When the clash of address areas is discovered - and this may be a case of trial and error - the area can be excluded from the memory management process as below:

DEVICE=C:\DOS\EMM386.EXE X=DC00-E000 NOEMS

In this example, the area has been found to contain a ROM for a SCSI card.   Using the X= switch followed by the unwanted area has prevented that area from being added to the UMB pool.

WHO DOES WHAT
Each area of memory is organised and managed by different memory management code as described and these are as shown as a reminder in the following table.

Memory Range	Address Range	Memory Manager
Base	0 - 640k	DOS
Upper	640k - 1024k	EMM386
HMA	1024k - 1088k	HIMEM
Extended (XMS)	1024k upwards	HIMEM
Expanded (EMS)	Page Frame Area	EMM386

ADD-ON MEMORY MANAGERS
The techniques outlined above use utilities that are provided free with Microsoft DOS or Windows. More sophisticated utilities are available from third-party suppliers.   They replace EMM386, etc. and produce better results.   Examples are Quarterdeck's QEMM, Qualitas' 386Max and the shareware program DOSMAX.   Some drivers require more memory during initialisation than they do once installed.   If the early larger requirement is too large for a free UMB, MemMaker will not use that block. This may result in a driver being placed in conventional memory.   The add-on programs provide a 'stealth' facility. This will place part of the code in another memory area during initialisation, knowing that it will be discarded after the driver is installed.   In this way, the driver can be fitted into some UMBs that appear to be smaller than the driver's file size.

MULTI-CONFIGURATION
If a machine is dedicated to the one type of job, then the correct configuration can easily be set up via CONFIG.SYS and AUTOEXEC.BAT.   Where a range of activities has to be carried out then these activities probably have different memory requirements.   One package may require expanded memory while another may wish to use extended memory.   Yet another package may work best with lots of memory configured as a ram drive. This is overcome by having a range of different configurations saved as CONFIG.1, CONFIG.2, etc.   When a particular setup is required, the required file is copied as CONFIG.SYS.   The same procedure applies to the AUTOEXEC files.   When both required files are copied, the machine can be rebooted so that the wanted configuration will take place.

With DOS 6, a much improved system was offered where the different configurations all existed inside the same CONFIG and AUTOEXEC files.   On bootup, the user is offered a menu and only the script lines that correspond with the user's choice are implemented.

EXAMPLE
Consider a user with four distinct needs:
1. A spreadsheet package that requires lots of expanded memory
2. A database package that can make good use of a ram drive
3. Access to Windows
4. Access to a local area network

This requires four different configurations as the machine's available memory would not be sufficient to create expanded memory, extended memory, a ram drive and all the necessary drivers and TSRs.

The listing on the next page shows the script of a 'multi-configuration' system as provided by DOS v6. The heart of the system is the **[menu]** section.   This always commences with the [menu] shown in the first line.   This is then followed by a 'menuitem' line for each option that is required.

The word after the equals sign is the name of the section of configuration code to be run.   This is followed by name of the option as it will appear on the opening screen.   These are separated by a comma.

```
[menu]
menuitem=Lotus, Run the Spreadsheet
menuitem=DataEase, Run the Database
menuitem=Windows, Run Windows
menuitem=LAN, Enter the Network
mencolor=7,1
menudefault=Windows,10

[common]
device=c:\dos\himem.sys
dos=high
files=40
country=44,,c:\dos\country.sys

[Lotus]
device=c:\dos\emm386.exe 4096
device=c:\dos\smartdrv.exe 2048
buffers=40

[DataEase]
device=c:\dos\emm386.exe noems
dos=umb
device=c:\dos\ramdrive.sys 4096 /e

[Windows]
dos=umb
stacks=0,0
buffers=10
device=c:\dos\smartdrv.exe 2048 2048

[LAN]
stacks=9,256
```

In the example, there are four options.   The *'menudefault'* line specifies which option will be taken if the user does not choose within a certain period of time.   This time is measured in seconds and the example will take the Windows option if the user has not decided within ten seconds.

The *'mencolor'* line sets up the screen colours, with the first number being the foreground colour and the second number being the background colour.   The colour numbers are the standard set repeated in the table.

The **[common]** section provides the script lines that are common to all configurations and the lines in this section are implemented no matter which option is chosen.

There then follows each of the four different machine configurations, each with a header that corresponds to the menu section.   So, the menu option for spreadsheets is linked to Lotus in the menu.   The menu then looks for the line **[Lotus]** in the script and runs the code within that section.

In this way, the same CONFIG.SYS file can provide user choices at bootup.   To choose a new configuration, the user reboots the machine and takes a new option.

There is only one drawback with multi-configuration systems. They can't be used with MemMaker.   This is because MemMaker uses the /L switch to place drivers in specific addresses and these will probably differ from application to application.

0	Black
1	Blue
2	Green
3	Cyan
4	Red
5	Violet
6	Yellow or Brown
7	White
8	Black or Grey
9	Bright Blue
10	Bright Green
11	Bright Cyan
12	Bright Red
13	Bright Violet
14	Bright Yellow
15	Bright White

AUTOEXEC.BAT

The same technique can be used with AUTOEXEC.BAT as was used with CONFIG.SYS.

It is possible to run different parts of the file dependent upon the choices taken within CONFIG.SYS.

Passing control to different parts of the script is achieved through the line *'goto %config%'*.   When the user chose an option in CONFIG.SYS - i.e. either Lotus, DataEase, Windows or LAN, that choice was placed in an environment variable called *'config'*. When the CONFIG.SYS file is exited, the variable will still hold the value that was chosen and this can be passed on to the AUTOEXEC.BAT file.   This variable can then be used to decide which section of the script should be enacted.   The environment variable is accessed with the AUTOEXEC.BAT file as %config%. (see later for more details of batch files including the 'goto' command and environment variables).

The example listing shows four distinct sections of code, each corresponding to the choices in CONFIG.SYS.   The first section of code carries out the activities that are common to all choices, such as setting a British keyboard, etc.,

The Lotus and Windows sections simply run the packages.   The DataEase section loads all the data files to be used into the RAM

```
@echo off
prompt $p$g
keyb uk,,c:\dos\keyboard.sys
path c:\dos\windows
goto %config%

:Lotus
cd 123
Lotus
goto end

:DataEase
copy c:\dease\files\*.* c:\ramdisc\*.*
cd dease
dease
goto end

:Windows
win
goto end

:LAN
ipx
netx
login

:end
```

drive for faster processing, before running the application package itself.   The LAN section loads the various network drivers and places the user at the login stage of entering the network.

DEBUGGING THE SCRIPTS

If a machine is not configuring itself in the way that was intended, DOS 6 and DOS 6.2 provide facilities for checking out lines in the CONFIG.SYS and AUTOEXEC.BAT files.   With DOS 6, the machine can be booted and the user can wait until the *"Starting MS-DOS..."* message appears.   Pressing the f5 key at this point will by-pass all the commands in the CONFIG.SYS file.   Pressing f8 at the message allows the user to by-pass individual lines of the CONFIG.SYS file.   In this mode, the user is asked whether the line should be carried out and waits for a Y/N reply; pressing the Esc key at any stage carries out all the remaining commands in the file while pressing f5 ignores all the remaining commands in the file.   With DOS 6.2, these facilities affect both the CONFIG.SYS and AUTOEXEC.BAT files.   Older DOS versions do not have these facilities and require the files to be amended and the machine rebooted.   By a process of removing lines or making lines inactive, the cause of the problem can be located.   A line in AUTOEXEC.BAT can be made inactive by REMming it out.   This means placing the letters REM in front of a command.   It will then be ignored at bootup time.   A line in CONFIG.SYS can only be REMmed out in DOS version 5 onwards; with older DOS versions, the line would have to be temporarily edited out.

ORDER OF COMMAND CALLS

The command processor is called COMMAND.COM and this is loaded into memory when the machine is booted up.   Within that file is a range of utilities.   These are known as *'internal commands'* and are listed below:

> CALL, CHCP, CD, CLS, COPY, CTTY, DATE, DEL, DIR, ECHO, ERASE, EXIT,
> FOR, GOTO, IF, LOADHIGH, MD, PATH, PAUSE, PROMPT, RD, REN, SET,
> SHIFT, TIME, TYPE, VOL

This list of utilities is chosen to contain the most commonly used commands.   To avoid wasting main memory space, not all available MS-DOS commands are included in this file.   The extra commands are available as separate small programs which reside on disc (usually in its own MS-DOS subdirectory).   These commands are only loaded into memory when the program is called.   These are called *'external commands'* and some examples are listed below:

> ASSIGN, BACKUP, CHKDSK, COMP, DEBUG, DISKCOMP, DISKCOPY,
> EDLIN, FDISK, FORMAT, KEYB, LABEL, MORE, PRINT, RESTORE, SHARE,
> XCOPY

The commands that are underlined are no longer included in DOS v6; it introduces some new external commands such as MSD, CHOICE, MOVE and DELTREE.

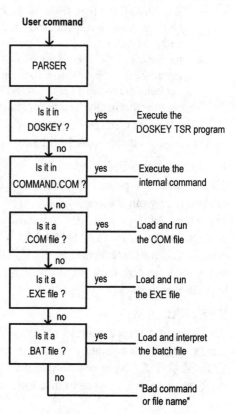

When a command is entered by the user at the keyboard, it is analysed by the COMMAND.COM file. It then carries out the search for the appropriate file to run, in the order shown in the diagram.   The *'Parser'* is a component of COMMAND.COM and its job is to separate the command itself from any of its parameters.   For example, if a command was 'TYPE WORK.DOC', then the program called 'TYPE' would be searched for and given the parameter 'WORK.DOC'.

- First, a match is sought in the memory resident DOSKEY commands.
- If the program is not found, a match is sought in the internal commands within COMMAND.COM
- If the program is still not found, a match is sought for a file with the .COM extension.
- If this file is not found, a match is sought for a file with the .EXE extension.
- If no EXE file is found, a match is sought for a file with the BAT extension.
- Finally, if no match is found, an error message *'Bad command or file name'* is given.

INSTALLING DOS

Modern versions of DOS cannot be loaded or run directly from the manufacturer's floppy discs, since the files are stored in a compressed format.   The files have to be decompressed before use but can be used thereafter from either the hard disc or a set of other floppy discs.   In commercial situations, the files would almost always be held on the machine's hard disc.

Installing DOS on a machine is normally a straightforward process, with little input from the installer.

INSTALLATION PROCEDURE

The DOS disc marked as disc 1 should be placed in the A: drive and the machine should be booted up. This runs the installation program that begins by checking out the computer's hardware configuration.

FIRST SCREEN

It presents a first screen of options with default values as shown.   In the United Kingdom, the Country option should be changed to UK and the Keyboard option should be changed to UK English.

> Date - date currently stored in the machine's internal clock
> Time - time currently stored in the machine's internal clock
> Country - United States
> Keyboard - US English
> Hard Disc or Floppy - Hard Disc installation

SECOND SCREEN

The second screen of options presents the options shown. Normally, the default directory should be left as \DOS. This can create a company standard, as the files will always be found in the same directory on every machine in the organisation.   Similarly, few - if any - organisations would

> Install to - C:\DOS
> Shell on Start-up - Run / Don't Run Shell
> Single DOS partition

wish the DOS shell to be invoked on machine start-up, as this invites experimentation from machine users.   The last option is only available on machines that do not already have a DOS partition and have the free space.   The setup process works with a single partition as its default.   When all the options are selected, the installation program copies the files from the floppies, decompresses them (using the file EXPAND.EXE) and places them in the chosen directory of the hard disc.   The installer swaps the installation discs when requested by the program.   The whole operation takes less than 10 minutes.

UPGRADING DOS

Where an earlier version of DOS exists, an upgrade can be achieved by :
- Deleting all the files from the DOS sub-directory and re-installing as above.   This will refresh the DOS directory's contents and place fresh system files on the disc (i.e. COMMAND.COM, IO.SYS and MSDOS.SYS).
- Replacing the old versions of DOS files on the hard with the newer versions on the floppies and installing the new system files on the hard disc using the command SYS C: from a floppy that contains the modern version of SYS.COM.

The second method may be appropriate when upgrading with earlier versions of DOS which stored the DOS files in uncompressed format but it is a laborious operation with modern compressed files.   The first method produces exactly the same results and is cleaner and quicker.

PROTECTING EXISTING CONFIGURATION

The installation process replaces any current versions of AUTOEXEC.BAT and CONFIG.SYS with default files from the floppy disc.   The current versions would be over-written and this would mean that important settings and drivers would be lost.   So, before carrying out any DOS installation/upgrade, rename these files as AUTOEXEC.OLD and CONFIG.OLD.   When the installation process is completed, the new versions of AUTOEXEC.BAT and CONFIG.SYS can be deleted and the .OLD versions renamed back to AUTOEXEC.BAT and CONFIG.SYS.   In this way, the carefully honed settings are preserved.

SYSTEM DISCS

The support engineer should always carry a floppy system disc, to allow access to a machine where the hard disc fails to operate.   This may happen for a number of reasons, such as the accidental deletion of COMMAND.COM or other system file.   Where a number of DOS versions exist in an organisation on different machines, a system disc for each DOS version would be advisable.

Batch Files

Many day-to-day tasks require the user to enter a series of keyboard commands for their completion. Each day, the user had to repeat the same series of commands to produce the same result.   To ease this burden, MSDOS has the facility to place these commands in a text file. This file is called a *'batch file'*. The file is given the extension *".BAT"*   e.g.:

MOVE.BAT

To execute a batch file, the name of the file is entered, followed by <Enter>, as in other runnable programs.   When the file is found, the MSDOS commands within that file are executed one after another without any further keyboard input.   In addition to the normal DOS commands, MSDOS provides extended commands for use in batch files. So, the entry of a single command, has resulted in a long sequence of MSDOS commands being implemented.

Common uses for batch files are :
* To automate regularly used DOS sequences, as mentioned above.
* To create customised user menus. For example, the batch file clears the screen, displays the program options, waits for the user's choice of key and runs the appropriate program.
* To automatically load and run a program when the computer is first switched on. This special batch file has to be given the name AUTOEXEC.BAT (or, alternatively, the AUTOEXEC.BAT file can call a specially written batch file for the purpose).
* To provide for automated system checks which may or may not trigger activities.   For example, the detection of the date as a Friday may result in all word-processing files being backed up.

In all cases, the user of batch files need have no knowledge of the workings of the PC or knowledge of the DOS structure, DOS commands, etc.   All the intricacies of the system can be hidden to the average user by the writer of the batch file.   The skills of the writer are employed once and the batch file is then used many times over - thus creating a productivity aid.   Since the instructions are embedded in the batch files, it eliminates the many typing mistakes which hold up operations.   If the batch file is written correctly, it should always work correctly.

CREATING BATCH FILES.

Batch files are created using a plain ASCII text editor, such as the DOS EDIT utility or a word-processor used in plain ASCII mode. Each DOS command will occupy a separate line of the program. The completed file is then saved onto disc, with the extension ".BAT"
Again, as in other DOS files, the name given to the file should reflect its contents.
The contents of any batch file can be viewed using the DOS TYPE command as below:

TYPE LOOK.BAT   or   TYPE LOOK.BAT | MORE

EXAMPLE BATCH FILE
Contents of LOOK.BAT

```
echo off
REM This is the first attempt at a batch file !
cls
echo Here is the contents of the DOS Directory ...
cd c:\dos
dir/w
pause
cd \
```

This simple batch file uses a mixture of normal DOS commands and a few commands which only work within batch files.   It is explained line by line next:

* Line 1 switches off the screen display of commands. Normally, each command is *'echoed'* to the screen before being carried out. In other words, the text of the command would be displayed on the screen, prior to it being carried out.   To present the user with a cleaner screen, the ECHO OFF command is used to prevent the commands from being displayed to the screen. The <u>results</u> of carrying out the command are still displayed to the screen - it is only the text of the command itself which is suppressed.   Echoing can be turned on again with ECHO ON.   Mostly, ECHO ON is used to assist debugging a batch file, since the progress of the batch file can be viewed as

each command is echoed to the screen. The final working version then normally has ECHO OFF added as its first line.

- Line 2 allows REMarks to be added to the program, to explain what is happening to the programmer. The lines will not be sent to the screen, if ECHO is set to off.   Since experienced programmers can create batch files of great length and complexity, comments can be used to document each section of the batch file's code.   These comments can prove extremely useful and time-saving when the batch file is viewed at a later date (perhaps with a view to altering it).   REM statements can also be used to preface the batch file with the details of the purpose of the batch file, any instructions for usage, the name of the writer, the date written, etc. The REM can be replaced with a semi-colon and this will produce the same result with a slightly cleaner look. (note that the semi-colon can also be used for other purposes, as seen later).
- Line 3 uses a normal DOS command to clear the screen.
- Line 4 displays a message to the screen. Any text after the command ECHO will be displayed to the screen. This command can be used to temporarily overrule the ECHO OFF command.
- Lines 5 and 6 use normal DOS commands to change the current directory to dease.dir and display the directory contents across the width of the screen.
- Line 7 halts execution of the program, displays the message
    Strike any key when ready ...
  and waits for a key to be pressed before executing the remaining lines of the batch program.
- Line 8 changes the current directory to the root directory.

IMPROVING APPEARANCES

- The ECHO OFF command only takes effect <u>after</u> it has been executed. This means that this 'ECHO OFF' line will still appear on the screen, even if it is the first line in the batch script.   This can be overcome if the first line is changed to @ECHO OFF ; echoing is still switched off but the command does not appear on the screen. This works in DOS from versions 3.3 onwards.

- To produce a more pleasant screen layout, there will be a need to produce blank lines on the monitor screen, usually to space out lines of text.   Entering a blank line in the batch script will not result in a blank line being produced on the screen; the empty script line will simply be ignored.   Also, typing the word ECHO on its own will not work, as this is seen as the same command as ECHO OFF.   A blank line can be produced by using the command followed by a full stop.   Alternatives to the full stop could be one of the following, depending upon the version of DOS being used:
    +   "   / | :   [

For example,

    ECHO+   or   ECHO[
will produce a blank line.   Note that there is no space between the ECHO command and the character chosen from the above list.   The user should experiment to find the version for their own DOS version; the full stop is supported by DOS 5 onwards.

- If you wish to replace the "*Strike any key when ready ...*" message which automatically results from the use of the PAUSE command, the line
    PAUSE > NUL
will prevent the usual message line from being printed on the screen. The system will still pause, waiting for keyboard input . This can be used in conjunction with an echo command, to produce the desired message, as in this example;

```
ECHO Press any key to archive the Corel Draw backups
ECHO or press CTRL-Break to exit
PAUSE > NUL
```

NOTE
    The execution of a batch program can be terminated at any stage, by pressing CTRL-Break.
    The execution can be paused by pressing Ctrl-S and can be restarted by pressing any other key.

OTHER COMMANDS

As shown in the earlier example, the normal MSDOS commands (e.g. MD, CD, etc.) can be used in batch files.   Additional, extended, batch commands such as ECHO and PAUSE are available.
For more sophisticated work, control commands are available.
These include

GOTO
IF
FOR .. IN .. DO

These commands provide for decision-making within the program and the ability to move around different parts of the batch file script, sometimes implementing one section of the script while implementing other section under different conditions. Batch files using these commands are literally computer programs and their construction is considered as *'batch file programming'*.

EXAMPLE BATCH FILE

The following batch file is designed to be run at the end of the day. It will copy all Wordstar files with the extension .BAK to a sub-directory of a floppy disc. The batch file should then delete all backups from the hard disc, to recover disc space.

The batch file program lines should:
- Display a start-up message.   Since the copying may take a little time, it is helpful to produce messages which remind users of the tasks being performed or keep the user informed of the batch file's progress.
- Make a directory on the floppy disc called BACKUPS.WS
- Copy the .BAK files from the WS5\DOCS directory of the hard disc into this new directory.
- Delete all .BAK files from the WS5\DOCS sub-directory.
- Display the message *"ALL BACKUPS COPIED OVER !"*
- Pause.
- Display the files held on the BACKUPS.WS directory.

The resultant batch file script would be:

```
REM WS.BAT
@ECHO OFF
REM   This program is designed to save all WordStar .BAK files
REM    to the BACKUPS.WS of the floppy disc
REM    Written by D. Dick    01/06/97
ECHO Insert a formatted floppy disc in the A: drive and then press any key
ECHO or press CTRL-Break to exit
PAUSE > NUL
MD A:\BACKUPS.WS
COPY C:\WS5\DOCS\*.BAK A:\BACKUPS.WS\*.*
DEL C:\WS5\DOCS\*.BAK
ECHO ALL BACKUPS COPIED OVER!
PAUSE
ECHO Here is the contents of the backups directory on the floppy disc:
DIR A:\BACKUPS.WS
```

NOTES
- The first three REM lines introduce comments about the batch file and are ignored when the batch file is executed.
- The following three lines provide a message to the user and wait for the user to insert a floppy disc. The program does not check to see whether the user actually inserts a disc; it simply carries on processing the batch files commands as soon as a key is pressed.
- The next lines contains a command to create a sub-directory called BACKUPS.WS on the floppy disc.   The first time that the batch file is run, this line will create a new BACKUPS.WS directory.   When the batch file is run on further occasions, the directory will already exist and this line will result in an error message. However, the program will not terminate and will move on to the next batch file instruction.

REPLACEABLE PARAMETERS

Up to now, the functions of a batch file have been pre-determined at the time of writing the batch script. All the information required to enable the batch file to be independently executed are included within the batch script. As a result, the finished batch file will always carry out exactly the same set of tasks each time that it is run.

This means that where a user carries out a number of <u>similar</u> tasks, separate batch files would have to be written for each task. Consider the previous example of the batch file called 'WSBACK.BAT'. This always archives files with the BAK extension. If the user wished to carry out exactly the same tasks with files which had the .DOC extension, then another batch file would have to be written. This new batch file would have the exact same script as the earlier version, except that the letters BAK would replaced by the letters DOC. If files with the extension .TXT were to be similarly archived, then yet another almost identical batch file would have to be created. This method would result in the creation of a whole range of batch files which contained only light differences, to allow users to carry out a variety of tasks.

What is required is a single, general purpose batch file, which is able to accept the required file extension along with the batch file name, e.g.:

WSBACK DOC   or   WSBACK BAK   etc.

Here, WSBACK is the name of batch file and any file extension can be passed in along with the command. The big advantage with this method is that different file extension names can be passed in each time the batch file is called; the batch file is now general purpose.

This should be easily understood by a user, since this technique is already commonly used with the existing range of DOS commands. For example, the command DEL TEST.DOC uses DEL as the actual program command and in this case TEST.DOC is the file name being passed in with the command. Similar techniques are used with the DOS DIR, TYPE, REN, CHKDSK, FORMAT and other commands. The part of the command which can be altered each time the batch file is called by the user is termed the *'replaceable parameter'* portion and can be a filename, a path, or even a DOS command. The actual filename, path or command is supplied by the user at the time of executing the batch file.

NOTE:
Where required, a batch file can have more than one parameter, e.g.:

WSBACK TXT DOC BAK   or   EXAMINE file1 file2

Normally, the parameters will be separated by a space or a comma (although semicolons, colons, etc. can be used).

INSIDE THE BATCH FILE

Since the actual content of the parameter(s) will probably be different every time the batch file is executed, the batch file coding does not know what is going to be passed in. It has to use a general name(s) within its coding. These general names will then take on the values of the parameters which are passed in.

These general names variables inside the batch file are the *'Replaceable Parameters'* and are represented by the percentage character, followed by a digit. These go from %0 to %9. The batch file name is allocated to %0, the first user input parameter is allocated to %1 and so on.

Therefore EXAMINE file1 file2 would result in %0 holding EXAMINE, %1 holding file1 and %2 holding file2.

EXAMPLE
A batch file is to be created to send any given file away to any given sub-directory on an archive floppy 'A' disc.
The batch file will have the following syntax:

STORE filename path

- *STORE* is the name of the batch file.
- *filename* is the file to be archived.
- *path* is the destination directory on the A drive where the file is to be stored.
- A space separates the file name and the directory name.

A complete breakdown of this batch file is as shown.

This program uses two parameters that take the place of the filename and the directory name, being the %1 and %2 parameters.   If the batch file were called as STORE REPORT SALES   then the text *'REPORT'* would replace every occurrence of the %1 parameter, while the text *'SALES'* would replace every occurrence of the %2 parameter.   The batch lines would then be executed as normal.   Such a batch file is much more flexible because different file names and directory names can be used each time the batch file is called.   Now lines 9 and 10 of WSBACK.BAT can be altered to:

```
REM STORE.BAT
echo file backup in progress
echo changing to the A drive
a:
echo creating the new directory
md %2
echo changing to the new directory
cd %2
echo copying files to the new directory
copy C:\%1
echo file %1 copied to A drive
echo returning to the C drive
c:
```

> COPY C:\WS5\DOCS*.%1 A:\BACKUPS.WS*.*
> DEL C:\WS5\DOCS*.%1

to make this batch file able to archive files with any extension given by the user.

BRANCHING & LOOPING

The example batch files given so far have used *'sequential'* coding; each script line is executed in strict order, from the first line to the last line.   This is sufficient for some batch files of limited use.   More often, there is a need to control the order of the lines which are executed, dependent   on the circumstances in which the batch file is run.

Consider the two examples below:

```
XXXXXXX                                          XXXXXXX
XXXXXXX                                          XXXXXXX
XXXXXXX                                          XXXXXXX
Make some kind of test                           XXXXXXX
XXXXXXX )                                         XXXXXXX
XXXXXXX  } If everything's OK then                XXXXXXX
XXXXXXX  } execute these lines                    Make some kind of test
XXXXXXX )                                         if something is wrong, go back up
XXXXXXX )                                         XXXXXXX
XXXXXXX  }                                        XXXXXXX
XXXXXXX  } Otherwise, execute                     XXXXXXX
XXXXXXX  } these lines instead                    XXXXXXX
XXXXXXX )                                         XXXXXXX

      EXAMPLE 'A'                                      EXAMPLE 'B'
```

In Example 'A', the first few lines are always executed.   There then follows two blocks of coding, only one of which is ever executed each time the batch file is run.   If the first block of coding is executed, then the second block is ignored, and vice versa.   An example of this might be a block of coding which displays an error message if something goes wrong.   In Example 'B', all of the lines are executed. However, some lines might be executed many times over before execution continues in a sequential manner.   An example of this is continually checking whether a floppy disc has been inserted before proceeding further.

So, the flow of control may see jumps down to a lower part of the script, or jumps up to previously executed lines.   To allow for these jumps in the script execution, MSDOS allows labels to be added to a batch file.   A label has a name and is preceded by a colon. The first eight characters of a label are significant, so :labelforhere and :labelforthere would be seen as the same label.   At any point in a batch file, the label can be jumped to by the use of the GOTO command.

EXAMPLE

> :LABEL
> DIR A:/W
> PAUSE
> GOTO LABEL

In this very simple example, the directory of the floppy disc would be displayed, followed by the *"Strike a key when ready..."* message.   When a key is pressed, control will be returned to the top of the file and the process will repeat itself again.   This would carry on forever.   The only way to exit from this particular batch file is to press CTRL-BRK.

NOTES

The GOTO line need not use the colon - i.e. the last line could be either

    'GOTO : LABEL' or 'GOTO LABEL'

The colon can also be used to place comments into the program, as an alternative to the REM statement,

e.g.:   REM this is a comment

                    : this is another comment

DECISION MAKING

Batch files only benefit from the GOTO statement when the jumps result from some kind of check.   If the result of the particular check is true, then control can be altered.   MSDOS allows the use of the IF statement within batch files.   It has three uses:

- to compare two strings (called an *"equality conditional test"*).
- to check for the existence of a file on the disc.
- to test *'errorlevel'* values returned from other programs.

EQUALITY TESTS

The command requires the use of two equals symbols (==) to represent equality. Use of the == conditional test allows the creation of batch files which can carry out different parts of the test, dependent on the result of the test.

EXAMPLES:

        IF %1 == BUDGET GOTO :END

If the input parameter is "BUDGET", pass control to the label entitled "END".   Note that the test string is <u>case sensitive</u> - "budget" or "Budget" would not be detected as an input parameter.   If all possibilities need to be tested, then more than one equality check will have to be made (or see using the FOR command later).

        IF %1 == %2 GOTO :SAME

If both input parameters are identical , pass control to the label entitled "SAME".

        IF %1 == DATA.NEW   DEL DATA.OLD

If the input parameter is "DATA.NEW", then use the DOS DEL command to erase the file entitled "DATA.OLD".

IMPROVED WSBACK.BAT

In the earlier version of WSBACK.BAT, the user could nominate files of any extension to be archived. If it was considered necessary to prevent users from archiving .COM and .EXE, for example, then the batch file could be altered to:

```
@ECHO OFF
ECHO Insert a formatted floppy disc in the A: drive and then press any key
ECHO or press CTRL-Break to exit
PAUSE > NUL
MD A:\BACKUPS.WS
IF %1 == COM GOTO ERROR
IF %1 == com GOTO ERROR
IF %1 == EXE GOTO ERROR
IF %1 == exe GOTO ERROR
COPY C:\WS5\DOCS\*.%1 A:\BACKUPS.WS\*.*
DEL C:\WS5\DOCS\*.%1
ECHO ALL BACKUPS COPIED OVER!
PAUSE
ECHO Here is the contents of the backups directory on the floppy disc:
DIR A:\BACKUPS.WS
GOTO END
:ERROR
ECHO EXE and COM files should not be archived ! Please try again....
:END
```

Note that the 'GOTO :END' line is used to jump over the error message line; if that line were not present, then the batch file would always display an error message - even when the program had no errors.

FILE TESTS

The existence of a file on a disc can be tested with the statement

IF EXIST %1 ECHO The file is here !

If the file exists, the test is true and the rest of the line is executed.   If the file does not exist, the rest of the line is ignored and control passes to the next line of the batch file.   A more common use of the command is:

IF NOT EXIST %1 GOTO :END

The NOT is included to reverse the outcome of a test.   So, If the file exists, the test has not proved to be true therefore the rest of the line is ignored and the batch file will continue execution from the next line of the script.   If the file does not exist, the test has proved to be true, the rest of the line is executed and control is passed to the label entitled 'END'.   The code which commences from the label END onwards will probably give an error message to the user and may also terminate the program.

WORKED EXAMPLE   A batch file called MOVE.BAT is required to copy any file from the hard disc's root directory to the hard disc's STORE sub-directory, thereafter deleting that file from the root directory.   This can be easily achieved as follows:

COPY C:\%1 C:\STORE
DEL C:\%1

However, if the program was expected to allow the transfer of the file to <u>any</u> directory specified in the input parameters, the program could be altered to:

COPY C:\%1 C:\%2
DEL C:\%1

A typical call would be:

MOVE letter.doc backups

If the file itself does not exist, then both lines of the batch file will produce an error message upon execution.   The file may not exist, or may exist in a different directory from the one specified in the parameter, or the file name may simply have been misspelled. In such cases, the lines will not execute properly, but no damage will result.   However, there will be a serious problem if the name of the destination directory is mis-typed or does not exist. In this case, the COPY will not be successful, <u>but the file will still be deleted from the root directory.</u>

```
REM MOVE.BAT
@ECHO OFF
CLS
IF NOT EXIST C:\%1 GOTO :ERROR1
COPY C:\%1 C:\%2
DEL C:\%1
GOTO :EXIT
:ERROR1
ECHO The file %1 does not exist ...etc
:EXIT
```

The first problem can be dealt with by testing whether the file exists before carrying out the rest of the program. The program on the right will suffice.   The middle two commands are only executed if the nominated file actually exists.   This batch file could be improved, if an appropriate error message were given to the user, as shown on the left.

```
IF NOT EXIST C:\%1 GOTO :EXIT
COPY C:\%1 C:\%2
DEL C:\%1
:EXIT
```

DIRECTORY TESTS

The worked example pointed out the dangers of working with directories without first checking that they exist on the disc.

The following three commands can be used to make various directory tests.

IF EXIST %1*.* command

This tests whether a <u>directory exists</u> which contains at least one file, in which case the test is true and the command on the rest of the line is executed.   If the test is false, the remainder of the line is ignored and control passes to the next line of the batch script.

IF NOT EXIST %1\NUL command

This tests for a <u>non-existent directory</u>, in which case the test is true and the command on the remainder of the line is executed.   Filenames such as CON, LPT1 and NUL are used to access input/output devices. These are not true file names but some DOS commands see them as present in every directory.   So, if they are not present in the above test, the directory cannot exist.

IF EXIST %1\NUL IF NOT EXIST %1*.* command

This tests for an <u>empty directory</u>, in which case the test is true and the command on the rest of the line is executed.   Note here that one IF statement follows another on the same line.   This is called 'nesting' and allows for more complex tests with a reduced number of script lines.   The second IF statement is only considered if the first IF statement produced a result which was true.   For the overall test to be true, the directory must exist and must contain no files.   If these techniques are used in the example, we can build in error-checking, thus making the program more immune to user typing mistakes or logic errors.   An improved version of the program would look similar to that shown.

If the file or destination directory do not exist, then an appropriate error message is given. If both the file name and directory are correct, then the COPY command will

```
REM MOVE.BAT
@ECHO OFF
CLS
ECHO Running the %0 program ....
IF NOT EXIST C:\%1 GOTO :ERROR1
IF NOT EXIST C:\%2\NUL GOTO :ERROR2
COPY C:\%1 C:\%2
IF NOT EXIST C:\%2\%1 GOTO :ERROR3
DEL C:\%1
GOTO :EXIT
:ERROR1
ECHO The file %1 does not exist ...
GOTO :ERROR3
:ERROR2
ECHO The directory called %2 does not exist !
:ERROR3
ECHO The copy of %1 to %2 was not successful !
:EXIT
```

be executed. The next line checks whether the file exists in the destination directory. This ensures that the DEL line is only executed if the file copy did take place.   Again, an error message can warn the user that the file transfer did not take place.   In fact, the ERROR3 message is used with all three error situations. Note that the replaceable parameters can be used in ECHO statements, to inform the user of what program is running, or what files and directories are being processed.   This is particularly helpful in batch files which produce a lot of activity, to keep the user informed of progress as the file executes.

EMPTY PARAMETERS

Most batch files expect one or more parameters to be entered after the batch file name. For a new user, there is no indication of the expected syntax of the command and often users will enter parameters in the wrong order or will fail to enter a sufficient number of parameters.   The first case can be detected by equality tests, file tests and directory tests.

Consider a batch file with three input parameters.   %0 would be the batch file name and the input parameters would be %1 through to %3.   If a user only entered the batch file name followed by one parameter, then %2 and %3 would both have no contents (they would be 'nul' values).   Testing for a nul value for %3 would then detect that something was wrong and error messages could be given, etc. Testing of the last parameter works for all circumstances where insufficient parameters are given, since the last parameter will always be nul whether one, two or all parameters have been omitted by the user.

Testing for a nul parameter value requires a slight alteration to the earlier equality tests.   It is not possible to use a simple

IF %3 == GOTO :NEXT

since this equality test will compare %3 with the word GOTO.   Additionally, %3 will itself be replaced by a nul value, leaving the left hand side of the equation empty. There must be values on both sides of the equality test.   This is solved by the use of quotation marks eg:

IF "%3" == "" GOTO :NEXT

Now, if %3 has a nul value the test is reduced to

IF "" == "" GOTO :NEXT

The nul value is now detected and control is passed to the coding commencing after the label 'NEXT'. The same effect could be achieved with variations such as

IF %3! == ! GOTO :NEXT

HELP PAGES

Batch files can be written so that they can provide help as to their use, if users enter no parameters, or enter a question mark as the parameter, e.g.:

MOVE ? or MOVE

would produce a statement on the use of the batch file.

An example help page could be :

```
@ECHO OFF
IF %1 == ? GOTO HELP
IF "%1" == "" GOTO HELP
GOTO MAIN
: HELP
CLS
ECHO The MOVE command requires the name
ECHO of the file and the destination
ECHO directory into which it will be placed.
ECHO An example is :      MOVE REPORT C:\SALES
ECHO The file will be deleted from the current directory.
GOTO END
:MAIN
    ...      the main program
    ...      goes here
:END
```

If the user provides a question mark as a parameter, or the user provides no parameter, the help section is displayed and the program skips the main program coding and jumps to the end of the batch file (i.e. returns the user to the DOS prompt. If help is not required, the help lines are skipped over and execution continues after the label 'MAIN'.

Some help pages may require a lot of text and this would result in a great many ECHO commands being executed. The ECHO command is slow to process and a faster alternative would be to enter the help in a text file using the DOS EDIT command.

The batch file could then display this help with a line such as:

TYPE help.txt

FOR..IN..DO

It is possible to make the same command repeat itself - for example, to operate on a set of different files. The DOS FOR command allows the programmer to specify a group of similar parameters which will be substituted into a command, until each member of the group has been processed. This saves considerable typing time. It also makes the program more compact and easier to read.

The general format of the command is

FOR %%variable IN (parameter list) DO command

The %%variable is similar to variables used in algebraic expressions - e.g. $x = y + z$, where x, y and z are used to represent unknown numbers. These algebraic variables can then have any values substituted in them for evaluating the formula. In the same way, the DOS variables can be used to represent any of the individual parameters within the parameter list.

DOS variables are preceded by two percentage symbols, to distinguish them from replaceable parameters. These variables are case sensitive - %%A is not the same as %%a.

In the next example, a simple batch file is used which will allow the deletion of three files from a floppy disc, with a single command, e.g.:

TRASH budget.bak report.doc memo.doc

The batch file would be called TRASH.BAT and would be as below:

```
@ECHO OFF
CLS
FOR %%A IN (%1 %2 %3) DO del a:\%%A
```

The delete command is executed three times - once for each element in the bracketed parameter list. On each occasion, the variable %%A took on the value of the corresponding element in the parameter list. So, firstly %%A will take on the value of %1 (budget.bak in the example) and will delete that file. On the second run through, %%A will take on the value of %2 (report.doc in the example) and delete that file. On the third and last run through, %%A will take on the value of %3 (memo.doc). If the list held five items, then the process would be run through five time with five files deleted.

The parameter list need not contain replaceable parameters. This example places file extensions into the list. The program will now delete all files with .BAK, .TMP and .A extensions.

```
@ECHO OFF
CLS
FOR %%A IN (BAK TMP $A$) DO del a:*.%%A
```

It is even possible to use wildcards in the parameter list. For example, the following line will list all the files in the current directory:

FOR %%A IN (*.*) DO ECHO %%A

EXAMPLES USING FOR .. IN..DO

1.   Obtaining listings of all text files with a single command

The FOR command allows the user to extend the range of facilities offered by DOS. For example, the TYPE command, when entered directly from the keyboard, can only be used with a single file at one time.   Thus TYPE FRED.DOC is permissible but TYPE *.TXT will produce an error message.   This can be got round with the FOR command as below:

```
FOR %%A IN (*.TXT) DO TYPE %%A
FOR %%A IN (*.*) DO TYPE %%A
FOR %%A IN (%1) DO TYPE %%A
```

The first example selects each text file in the current directory in turn and displays its contents on the screen.   The second example will display the contents of all files in the current directory.   The last example displays all the files in the directory given in the parameter %1 - for example, passing in C:*.* as the parameter to the batch file.

2.   Allowing parameters to be non case-sensitive

The example given of WSBACK.BAT was forced to use four equality tests to ensure that the parameters would be identified in both upper and lower case form.   The coding was as below:

```
IF %1 == exe GOTO ERROR
IF %1 == EXE GOTO ERROR
IF %1 == COM GOTO ERROR
IF %1 == com GOTO ERROR
```

The FOR command below has exactly the same effect with only a single line.

```
FOR %%A IN (com  COM exe  EXE) DO IF %%A==%1 GOTO ERROR
```

To extend the tests to exclude BAT files would require another two IF statements; with the FOR command, the words 'bat' and 'BAT' would be added inside the bracketed list.

3.   Comparing two directory's contents

Wildcards can be used in a batch file to compare the contents of the current directory to any other directory. The program can then print out a list of the files that are not on the second directory and a further list of those files that are common to both directories.   The batch file would be called thus:

```
COMPDISC  A:\DATA
```

The coding for such a batch file could be:

```
REM COMPDISC.BAT
@ECHO OFF
CLS
ECHO This directory has the following extra
ECHO files which are not present on %1
ECHO ---------------------------------------------
ECHO.
FOR %%Z IN (*.*) DO IF NOT EXIST %1\%%Z  ECHO ....
%%Z
ECHO.
ECHO The following files appear in both directories
ECHO.
FOR %%Z IN (*.*) DO IF EXIST %1\%%Z ECHO .... %%Z
```

4. Updating date and time stamps on files

There will be occasions when it is desirable to have all the files in a directory updated to the current date and time.   This might be seen, for example, as a desirable way of distinguishing between different versions of programs in development.   It might also be used to show when a group of files were last printed.   The following command can be used to update the date and time stamps on a single file:

```
COPY /B filename+,,
```

Unfortunately, this command will not work with wildcards and so the FOR loop is used to feed each file in the directory to this command one after the other, thus:

```
FOR %%A IN (*.*) DO COPY/B %%A+,,
```

NESTING OF FORs

It is possible to *'nest'* FOR loops; this involves having one FOR loop feed another FOR loop.   This is achieved as below:

```
FOR %%A IN (*.*) DO COMMAND/C FOR %%B IN (TYPE PRINT) %%B %%A
```

If the current directory contained files called PETER, PAUL and MARY, the batch file has the following effect:

```
TYPE PETER
PRINT PETER
TYPE PAUL
PRINT PAUL
TYPE MARY
PRINT MARY
```

SHIFT

An earlier batch file achieved multiple deletions thus:

```
FOR %%A IN (%1 %2 %3) DO del a:\%%A
```

This is inflexible because:

- It always expects a fixed number of parameters (three in the above example)
- Since there are only 10 allowable replaceable parameters (%0 to %9) there is a physical limit to the number of files that can be deleted with the one command.

These limitations can be overcome with the use of the SHIFT command.

This command simply shifts the contents of all 10 replaceable parameters one place down - what was %6 becomes %5, %9 becomes %8. The contents of %0 is lost. There is no backwards shift command, so the old contents of %0 is irrecoverable.

A program to delete any number of files is:

This would be called by the command
SCRUB file1 file2 file3 file4 ... etc

```
REM SCRUB.BAT
:LOOP
IF "%1" == "" GOTO :END
DEL %1
SHIFT
GOTO :LOOP
:END
```

On the first execution, %1 would contain file1 so the equality test on the second line would be false (i.e. - %1 would not contain a nul value). The remainder of that line would be ignored and the program would not be terminated. As a result, the following line would delete file1. The SHIFT command would then place file1 into %0 and file2 into %1, etc.

The GOTO command would take the program back to the top of the coding. Since %1 was still not a nul value, file2 would likewise be deleted. The second execution of the SHIFT command means that the contents of file1 would now be lost, as it was overwritten by file2. %1 now contains file3 and it would be similarly deleted.

The same process would result in the deletion of file4. However, after file4 is deleted, the SHIFT command would move file4 into %0 and %1 would now have a nul value. Control would be passed to the top of the program and this time the equality test would be true, resulting in a GOTO END which would terminate the program.

This type of program is very flexible, since it can successfully run with a large list of file names, limited only by the size of the keyboard buffer. It will also work if the user gives no file name at all. In that case, help page code lines would be useful and could be added.

CALL

Earlier batch files have shown how ordinary .EXE and .COM files can be called from within a batch file, by entering the program's name as a line of the batch file script. When the EXE or COM file is finished, control is passed back to the batch file, to the line below the script line which called it.

It is also possible to call another <u>batch</u> file from within a batch file, by also simply giving the new batch file's name as a script line. However, in such a case, the second batch file is then run <u>instead</u> of the calling batch file; when the second batch file is completed, control does not return to the first batch file and all activity stops - the user is returned to the DOS prompt.

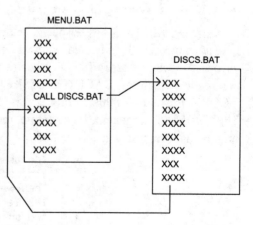

MSDOS provides a CALL command to overcome the above problem. The CALL command allows one batch file to temporarily call another batch file, with the control returning to the first script when the second script is completed. Control would normally pass to the script line below the line containing the CALL command; in the case of the FOR command, control will return in to the loop.

The example shows a line in MENU.BAT temporarily passing control to DISCS.BAT. As can be seen, when DISCS.BAT is finished, control is automatically passed back to MENU.BAT; their is no need for any special code inside DISCS.BAT to ensure that control is returned to MENU.BAT.

Possible uses for the CALL command include:
- Creating a collection of the organisation's commonly-used routines (e.g. giving error messages, file checking, etc.) which can then be called by different batch files when required. This technique resembles the library of 'procedures' or 'modules' found in programming languages.
- Creating a set of linked routines which together comprise a larger program. By writing the large program as a collection of smaller units, each batch file can be tested separately - making large batch systems easier to write and debug.

It is common to construct a collection of batch files, which together comprise a user-friendly front-end for a non-DOS literate user. Such a collection, for example, may have a main menu which offers the user a choice of activities. The user responds by pressing the key which corresponds to the desired activity. Each choice would activate a sub-menu with other choices. The program would then execute another batch file which would carry out the chosen task(s). At the completion of this activity, control would be returned to the main batch file.

PARAMETER PASSING
The CALL command allows the first batch file to send output to the second batch file, eg:
> CALL C:\MENU\DISPLAY %3
This first batch file is calling a second batch file called 'DISPLAY.BAT' which resides in the 'MENU' directory of the hard disc, The first batch file is sending its parameter %3 to this new batch file.

USER INPUT

Batch files were originally created to only have input in the form of replaceable parameters. This is very flexible, because it allows the user to specify different data each time the batch file is run.

However, with MSDOS versions prior to version 6, there is no facility for allowing user input while the program is running. The only user input is the PAUSE command which waits for any key to be pressed. Providing user input greatly broadens the scope of batch files, with new abilities such as:
- allowing the user the choice of activities from within the program. The user could press different keys to run different parts of the batch file (or even selectively call other batch files, utilising the CALL command).
- choosing which floppy drive to work with by hitting the 'A' or 'B' key when prompted by the batch file.
- having the option to create a new destination directory, if an IF EXIST check can't find the directory given by the user as a replaceable parameter.
- having the option to quit a program if an error, or potential error, is encountered (e.g. - "This will erase the existing files. Are you sure Y/N")

Fortunately, MS-DOS has a special variable called ERRORLEVEL which was originally intended to hold a value which indicated whether an application program or DOS command was exited without error. A value of zero usually indicates that the previous program was run without error. Many DOS commands, such as BACKUP, DISKCOMP, DISKCOPY, FORMAT, REPLACE, RESTORE and XCOPY, make use of this facility.

The FORMAT command, for example, returns the following possible ERRORLEVEL values, depending on how the program was terminated:

5	The user answered 'N' to the question 'Proceed with Format ?'
4	There was a fatal error
3	The user pressed Ctrl-C
0	The format was successful

A number of small utilities exist, which interface with MS-DOS batch files. These can be called and will return a value back to the calling batch file, via ERRORLEVEL. The value of ERRORLEVEL can then be tested and used for decision making.   MSDOS v6 provides a file called CHOICE.COM for this purpose and this is covered shortly. For users with earlier DOS versions, user input utilities include many shareware products such as BatMenu, BEN and Bat Utils and the Batch Enhancer utilities of commercial products such as Norton Utilities.

MENU SYSTEMS

The single most common batch file utility allows a single keypress to be returned in ERRORLEVEL, so that it can be used in menus.   If such a utility existed, called 'GETASC' then the outline of a menu program could be as shown.

The check values returned in ERRORLEVEL are the ASCII numbers for the keys 1,2,3 and 4.   Some utilities might convert the ASCII values into actual ERRORLEVEL values of 1,2,3 and 4.   In such cases, values 1 to 4 should replace the values 49 to 52 in the script.

The ERRORLEVEL check values are used in the script file in descending order.   This is important as the ERRORLEVEL command returns a true condition if the ERRORLEVEL is found to be <u>equal to or greater than</u> the test number.   If the order of the equality tests were re-written to be in ascending order, any value of ERRORLEVEL from 49 upwards would make the very first test true, acting upon this line's code and ignoring the following tests.   Thus pressing the 3 key, for example, would invoke the code for option number 1.

This is not fully secure as an unwanted keypress may still trigger the wrong option. Pressing the lower case letter 'n' for instance produces an ASCII value of 110; since this is a higher value than those in the test lines it will trigger the first test.   This can be overcome by introducing a nested IF check thus:

```
REM MENU.BAT
@ECHO OFF
:AGAIN
CLS
ECHO        MENU
ECHO        ====
ECHO.
ECHO  1. FIRST CHOICE
ECHO  2. SECOND CHOICE
ECHO  3. THIRD CHOICE
ECHO  4. EXIT
GETASC
IF ERRORLEVEL 52 GOTO :END
IF ERRORLEVEL 51 GOTO :THREE
IF ERRORLEVEL 50 GOTO :TWO
IF ERRORLEVEL 49 GOTO :ONE
ECHO WRONG NUMBER - TRY AGAIN ...
GOTO :AGAIN
:THREE
REM PROGRAM GOES IN HERE
GOTO :AGAIN
:TWO
REM PROGRAM GOES IN HERE
GOTO :AGAIN
:ONE
REM PROGRAM GOES IN HERE
GOTO :AGAIN
:END
```

IF ERRORLEVEL 49 IF NOT ERRORLEVEL 50 GOTO :ONE

This line insists that the command at the end of the line (in this case the GOTO statement) is executed if <u>both</u> the IF test conditions are met. Since both conditions have to be true, control will only pass to the :ONE sub-routine if the ERRORLEVEL value is exactly 49.

Some utilities allow the user to specify the range of permitted values when the utility is called - e.g. READNUM 1234 or READCHAR ABCDE.   These values are passed in to the utility as the acceptable parameters.   In such cases, the utility prevents the user from proceeding until a keypress from the permitted range is given.   Key presses outside this range may result in an error message or a beep on the speaker.

YES/NO OPTIONS

Some programs require the user to choose form a list of menu options.   On other occasions, the user will only have two choices - e.g. *"Do you wish to format this disc Y/N"* . The batch files only expects a n (or N) or y (or Y) from the keyboard. Since the user might press upper or lower case versions of these letters, both error levels would have to be tested.

```
.....
.....
ECHO DO YOU WISH TO EXIT (Y/N) ?
READNUM
IF ERRORLEVEL 121 IF NOT ERRORLEVEL 122 GOTO :END
IF ERRORLEVEL 89 IF ERRORLEVEL NOT 90 GOTO :END
......
:END
```

The previous examples used a key press utility called 'READNUM'. The equivalent utility in commercial and shareware enhancers may be called 'ASK', 'CHOOSE', 'GETKEY'. Some of these solely return the ASCII value of the key pressed, while others return a value which reflects the position of the key pressed in the permitted list (If the range is A to E, then pressing C might return an ERRORLEVEL of 3). Enhancers can also be easily written using the DOS DEBUG utility, or using Turbo Pascal.

USING CHOICE.COM IN DOS 6

From MSDOS version 6 onwards, the user has access to a new batch utility called CHOICE.COM. This returns an ERRORLEVEL that reflects the position of the key pressed in the list of specified permissible keys. For example,

> CHOICE /C:xyz

uses the /C: to denote that what follows is the permissible list of key presses (x, y and z in the example). When this batch command is reached, the user is presented with the following prompt:

> [x,y,z]?

Pressing the *'x'* key returns the ERRORLEVEL value of 1, pressing *'y'* returns the value of 2, while pressing the *'z'* key returns a value of 3. If the CHOICE utility detects an error condition while it is executing, it returns an ERRORLEVEL value of 255; a value of 0 is returned if the user presses CTRL-C or CTRL-C. The command can be made more user-friendly by adding text, eg:

> CHOICE /C:xyz Enter your option

This will result in the following screen prompt:

> Enter your option [x,y,z]?

Other switches for this command are:

/S	which forces the CHOICE command to only accept case sensitive characters (i.e. - if the permissible list contains a lower case *'c'*, pressing upper case *'C'* will not be accepted). The default is that both upper and lower case version of the characters in the permissible list are accepted).
/N	which displays any text in the command but does not display the characters in the permissible list. Nevertheless, the command still waits for the pressing of a key from that list.
/T:c,nn	which waits for *nn* seconds; if the user has not pressed a key from the permissible list within that time, the command returns the value corresponding to character *c* from the list. The value of *nn* can be up to 99 seconds.

Since the command will only return a value when a key from the permissible list is pressed, the chances of false triggering are greatly reduced. However, the *'IF ERRORLEVEL'* tests will still have to be entered in the batch script in descending order, as shown in the example.

```
REM   MENU.BAT with DOS 6
REM   USING CHOICE.COM
@ECHO OFF
:AGAIN
CLS
ECHO          MENU
ECHO          ====
ECHO.
ECHO  f. FIRST CHOICE
ECHO  s. SECOND CHOICE
ECHO  t. THIRD CHOICE
ECHO  e. EXIT
CHOICE /C:fste Enter your choice
IF ERRORLEVEL 4 GOTO :END
IF ERRORLEVEL 3 GOTO :THREE
IF ERRORLEVEL 2 GOTO :TWO
IF ERRORLEVEL 1 GOTO :ONE
ECHO WRONG NUMBER - TRY AGAIN ...
GOTO :AGAIN
:THREE
REM THE BATCH SCRIPT LINES FOR REM
PROGRAM THREE GOES IN HERE
GOTO :AGAIN
:TWO
REM THE BATCH SCRIPT LINES FOR REM
PROGRAM TWO GOES IN HERE
GOTO :AGAIN
:ONE
REM THE BATCH SCRIPT LINES FOR
REM PROGRAM ONE GOES IN HERE
GOTO :AGAIN
:END
```

PIPES

A number of runnable programs can be linked in the same command, in such a way that the <u>output</u> data of one program will become the <u>input</u> data of the next program. This is known as *'piping'* of data and DOS uses the ¦ symbol to represent piping. A simple example is:

> TYPE filename ¦ MORE

If the file has a large number of lines, the output of the TYPE command is presented to the user a screenful at a time, pausing for a keystroke between screens. Another example is

> DIR ¦ SORT

Here, the output of the DIR command is sorted before being displayed.

The MORE and SORT commands are considered later.

There is no reason why more than one pipe can be employed, to provide even more complex processing of data, for example

command1 | command2 | command3

Here the output of the first command is treated as the input of the second command. When the second command has further processed the data, its output becomes the input of the third and final command.

There is no requirement to insert a space between the commands and the pipe symbol but it is often inserted for reasons of clarity.

FILTERS

MSDOS provides facilities to process a programs results before returning that program's output. This is known as *'filtering'* the program's output (or input). DOS filters provide a useful means of presenting output in a more useful form - either by re-arranging the output or by selecting only a subset of the normal output. Although these activities can be carried out directly from the DOS prompt, they lend themselves admirably to batch file work. The DOS filters are MORE, FIND and SORT.

MORE

This is a simple filter which prevents the output from scrolling off the screen page when there is a large number of lines to be output. It displays a screenful of information at a time and pauses between screens until a key is pressed. The operation of the MORE command is similar to the /P parameter in the DIR command.

Examples:

    TYPE C:\REPORT.MSD | MORE
    DIR/S | MORE

In the first example, the text of the file REPORT.MSD will be displayed until the screen has only a single line left. This line will display the message "--MORE--" and will wait for a key to be pressed before displaying another screenful of the file's text.

In the second example, the contents of the entire disc's file and directory structure will be displayed, with the user being given time to read each screenful of information before moving on.

FIND

This filter ensures that the only output used (or ignored) is that which contains the string of characters given by the user.

The FIND command can be used in two ways:

- To find the occurrences of a particular string of characters in a file.
         e.g. FIND "loadhigh" C:\AUTOEXEC.BAT
  This command will accept more than one input parameter but will not accept wildcards. An example of several parameters might be:
  FIND "MOUSE" C:\AUTOEXEC.BAT C:\CONFIG.SYS
  where this is used to determine whether the mouse driver is in the configuration file or the autoexec file.

- To narrow down the range of output from data supplied by another utility.
         e.g. DIR/S | FIND "<DIR>"
  This will list all directories on the disc, including all sub-directories. It will also show all the "." and ".." directory labels and this can be eliminated by further processing as shown below. DOS versions before v5 achieved a similar result with the following command:
         ATTRIB /S | FIND "<DIR>"

PARAMETERS FOR 'FIND'

If the FIND command is used with the /V parameter, it ensures that only those lines which do NOT contain the sub-string are returned. The above example to show all directories could be modified thus:
         DIR/S | FIND "<DIR>" | FIND /V "."

In this case, the output from the first FIND command still contains the unwanted extra sub-directory labels but the second FIND command filters out any directories which contain a dot. This will work for both "." and ".." directories, since both contain at least the single dot looked for in the match.   This will greatly clean up the final output since all the system sub-directory labels will be removed.

If the FIND command is used with the /C parameter, it returns the number of occurrences of the sub-string found in the named file.

So, entering the command FIND "load" C:\AUTOEXEC.BAT/C would produce the following output, if there were five lines in the references to the search string:

---------- AUTOEXEC.BAT: 5

If the FIND command is used with the /I parameter, it ignores the case of the search string.   If this is omitted, then the search string *"load"* will not find *"LOAD"* as a match, for example.

If the FIND command is used with the /N parameter, it displays a list of the line contents and line numbers where the search string was found.

So, a typical output from running the command FIND "load" C:\AUTOEXEC.BAT /N might be:

```
---------- \AUTOEXEC.BAT
[5]loadhigh C:\WINDOWS\SMARTDRV.EXE 2048 2048
[10]loadhigh KEYB UK,,C:\DOS\KEYBOARD.SYS
[11]rem loadhigh C:\WINDOWS\MOUSE.COM /Y
[12]loadhigh C:\DOS\SHARE.EXE
[13]loadhigh doskey
```

OTHER EXAMPLES

Numbering all lines in a text file

The following command uses two FIND commands with the output of the first FIND being used as the input of the second FIND.   It is used to place line numbers on each line of a text file.   This is very useful for long batch files or assembler listings as an aid to debugging. The command is:

FIND /N/V "###" PROG.ASM | FIND /V "----------" > PROG.TXT

The first FIND is used to produce an output that has every text line numbered.   The search string ('###' in this example) contains a string that will not exist in the input file.   The /V switch ignores lines that contain the search text; since ALL lines fail to match the search text, this ensures that all of the lines are included in the numbered output.   The last FIND is used to remove the opening line which contains a string of minus signs followed by the input file name (see the above example).   The processed data is then fed to a text file for viewing.

Obtaining directory information

If the user gives the command:

DIR\S/AD/B

All the directories and sub-directories on the drive are listed. A sample of such an output would be:

```
D:\NETWORKS\CNE
D:\UTILS
D:\VIRUSES
D:\ZIPS
```

The command can be re-written thus: **DIR\S | FIND "y" | MORE** produces the following sample output:

```
Directory of D:\NETWORKS\CNE
        19 file(s)         160,501 bytes
Directory of D:\UTILS
        12 file(s)         339,307 bytes
Directory of D:\VIRUSES
       130 file(s)       4,959,818 bytes
Directory of D:\ZIPS
        51 file(s)       1,041,879 bytes
    17,827 file(s)     344,733,617 bytes
                       602,865,664 bytes free
```

This produces the following extra information:

    How many files are in each sub-directory
    How much data is stored in each sub-directory
    The total files stored on the disc
    The total data stored on the disc
    The free disc capacity

The FIND command makes use of the fact that the letter *'y'* appears in both the word *'Directory'* and the word *'bytes'* to ignore files names and only extract the lines containing directory and disc information.

Searching for a particular file

The syntax of the FIND command expects to search for a text string in a single file.   However, if a FOR command is attached, the entire contents of a directory can be searched by sending file names one at a time to the FIND command.   In the example shown, the output is sent to a text file for viewing; the text file should be stored in a different directory from the one being searched.

The example shows a directory being searched for the word 'del' ; note that the /I switches ensures that the search is for lower case only.

```
@echo off
del c:\xx
for %%A in (*.*) do find /I "del" %%A >> c:\xx
```

This produces an output similar to:

```
---------- TT.BAT
del tt

---------- CLEANUP.BAT
d:\discutil\delbaks
d:\discutil\deltemp

---------- TEST$$CT.SPD

---------- FF.BAT
del c:\xx
for %%A in (*.*) do find /I "del" %%A >> c:\xx

---------- SD.INI
```

In the example, four of the files contained the word 'del' and the full lines are displayed after the file name in which it was found.

SORT

As the name suggests, this command is used to sort the output in some way. Used without parameters, it will sort the output in ascending order of the first character in each line.   The utility can be tested by giving it some direct text from the DOS prompt.   Enter the following lines, finishing each line by pressing the Enter key:

```
SORT
DAVE
JACK
BILL
f6
```

The three names should be re-displayed in sorted form.   In practice, the input data to the SORT utility would come from an existing text file - or from the output of another utility.

OTHER EXAMPLES

          e.g. DIR/S | SORT

will produce a list of all the directories in ascending alphabetical order.   The output of the DIR command provides the data for the SORT utility.

If used with the /R parameter, the command will sort the data input to it into an output which displays the data in the REVERSE order of each line's first character.   So, the command DIR/S | SORT /R will produce a list of directories in descending alphabetical order.

      TYPE NAMES | SORT > SORTED.LST   *or*   SORT < NAMES > SORTED.LST

The above commands both take a file called *NAMES* and produce another file called *SORTED.LST* which contains the names sorted into ascending alphabetical order.

If used with the /+n parameter, where n is the number of characters along the line, the command will sort the lines of data input into an output sorted into an order which is based on the data contents found in the column number given in the parameter.

From DOS 5 onwards, users can list only the files in a directory by giving the command:

      DIR /A-D/OS

Earlier DOS versions can achieve the same result with the SORT utility thus:

    DIR /A-D | FIND /V "<DIR>" | SORT / +16

In a DIR's output, the 16th column is the start of the information on the files' sizes. So, sorting on this column will display files in ascending order of size. The FIND command is used to eliminate directory entries from the output.

REDIRECTION

The default operation of a PC is that the input comes from the keyboard and the output goes to the screen. It is taken for granted, for example, that the DIR command will send its output to the screen. However, the default situation is easily changed, both from commands given at the DOS prompt or from commands embedded in batch files. This allows, for example, the output of a DIR or other command to be sent to the printer instead of the screen, so that a permanent copy can be made. If preferred, the output can be sent to a file on a disc, so that the output can be read later - or used by some other command. Similarly, data input need not come always come from a keyboard. MSDOS can connect programs with data files, so that the program's normal input is replaced by the data in a given data file. This provides scope for creating a range of batch files tailored to the particular needs of a user, with different utilities being linked together through their common use of a data file.

REDIRECTION OUT

The DIR command normally sends its output directly to the screen. However, this output can be redirected to the printer thus:

    DIR > PRN   or   DIR > LPT1

If required, the DIR output can be sent to a disc file thus:

    DIR > filename

In this case, the filename can be on any drive/path; the command automatically creates a file of the given name in the given path.

    COPY *.* A: > NUL

Normally, the effects of a command are echoed to the screen, even if the actual command is not seen, due to the use of the ECHO OFF command. So, in the above example, all the names of the files being copied to the A: drive would be displayed on the screen. Placing '>NUL' at the end of the command redirected the screen output to the NUL file. No actual file is created but the screen no longer displays the COPY command operations.

NOTE

The > symbol will send the output to a newly created file. So DIR A: > DISC.CAT will create a file which contains a list of the file contents of the floppy disc. If a file of that name already exists, its contents will be over-written by the new data. Where the output is required to be added to the end of an existing file, two of the > characters should be used. Thus, DIR A: >> DISC.CAT will concatenate the floppy's file contents on to an existing file called DISC.CAT; if DISC.CAT does not exist, the command will create a new file of that name. This command can be used to catalogue a collection of floppy discs. Each disc's list of files is added to the DISC.CAT file and the final text file contains a list of the entire floppy contents. Such a command could best be incorporated in a batch utility that prompted the user to change discs, checked whether the disc had been changed etc.

REDIRECTION IN

Consider an example where a file called LIST contains a list of names and addresses, as below:

    ANDERSON   COLIN   9 MARCH BANKS   GLASGOW
    JACKSON   MARK   22 THE CRESCENT   BIRMINGHAM
    SMITH   ANGELA   17 TWEED RD   MANCHESTER
    DOCHERTY   JENNIFER   5 ELMONT HSE   GLASGOW
    STEWART   ALISTAIR   8 MOUNT SQ   LONDON
    BOYLE   MARY   15 GEORGE ST   BIRMINGHAM
    GREEN   ERIC   14 PORTER LODGE   LEEDS
    JOHNSON   ARTHUR   3 BRENT TOWERS   LONDON

Such a file could be used as an input source for the filter commands, as in the following examples:

SORT < LIST   or <LIST SORT
> will take the LIST file and present it to the screen in ascending order of surnames.

SORT/R < LIST
> will display a descending list, based on surnames.

SORT/+12 <LIST
> will display a list which ascends on the forenames.

<LIST FIND "MARY"
> will display any lines which contain the word 'MARY'. Note that this command is case sensitive; it will not find 'mary' or 'Mary'.

<LIST FIND/V "GLASGOW"
> will display all the lines which do NOT contain the word *'GLASGOW'* in them.

<LIST FIND/C "LONDON"
> will display the number of occurrences of lines which contained the word *'LONDON'*.

IN/OUT

MSDOS allows both input and output redirection to be used in a command. In this way, an input list can be used to produced an output file which is a sorted version, or a chosen sub-set of the list.

EXAMPLES:
> SORT < LIST >LISTSORT

will take the file LIST, sort it in ascending order of the first character and save the sorted version as LISTSORT.

> <LIST FIND "BIRMINGHAM" > BRUMLIST

will produce a file which contains only Birmingham addresses.

> DIR C:*.BAK/S > BACKUPS.LST

This command will list all files with the .BAK extension. The /S parameter ensures that the entire directory structure is covered. The output is then redirected to a file for later viewing/printing.

VARIABLES IN BATCH FILES

DOS allows variables to be set up inside the memory's *'environment'* area which can be used as temporary stores of data. The environment area already stores its own variables such as the *'path'* and the *'prompt'* data. These can be added to by the user, either directly at the keyboard or within batch files. The values of these new variables are set up by the SET command e.g. SET NAME=ARTHUR, or SET NAME=%1 where the value is being sent in as a parameter to a batch file. There should be no space at either end of the = symbol.

The value can be cleared by using the SET command with no value
> e.g. SET NAME=

If the SET command is entered by itself, the contents of the environment area (i.e. the *'environment strings'*) will be displayed, with the output being similar to below:

```
COMSPEC=C:\DOS\COMMAND.COM
WBLIB=D:\WB;
TEMP=d:\
NU=d:\norton\NU
PROMPT=$P$G
PATH=C:\DOS;C:\;C:\WINDOWS;C:\WINDOWS\SYSTEM;D:\UTILS;D:\NU
```

When used in a program for test purposes, the variable is enclosed in percentage symbols,
> e.g. IF %NAME%==%2

The variable can also be displayed with the ECHO command
> e.g. ECHO %NAME%

NOTE
> If running a batch file produces an *"out of environment space"* message, alter the CONFIG.SYS file to provide more memory for environment variables (see the chapter on on PC Configuration).

Computer Memory

MEMORY USAGE

The memory inside a computer stores a variety of information.

- A computer loads a program into its main memory, from where it can be run. A computer program is a list of instructions for the CPU, each instruction being stored as a numeric code.
- Computer programs exist to manipulate data. The data may be loaded from disc or CD, entered from the keyboard, downloaded via a modem - and a range of other input devices. The data may be in the form of database records, wages data, etc. Whatever its format, the data will always be held in the form of numeric codes.
- The computer requires to store some of its own system programs (such as the components of the MSDOS operating system) and its own system information (such as the nationality of the keyboard in use, screen display information, etc.).

All of the above must share the same pool of memory held inside the computer. In addition, the machine stores much of the code it requires to handle its hardware in programs that are permanently blown on to chips. If the computer is to avoid getting into utter confusion, it must allocate these activities to separate areas, each with its own distinct boundaries within the machine's addressable memory. The description of these functions and the memory areas they occupy is described as a *'memory map'*.

MEMORY ACCESS

The machine has to be able to separate one program instruction from the next. This is achieved by storing the machine instructions in different memory locations. This means having each consecutive instruction stored in its next consecutive memory address. It is important to differentiate between an address and its contents. The address is a unique location in memory. The contents of this address may be part of an application program or system program, or may be data.

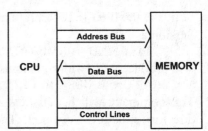

The CPU will fetch an instruction from the memory by placing the instruction's memory address on the Address Bus and a Read signal on one of the Control Lines. The memory chip places the address's contents on to the Data Bus and this is picked up by the CPU. The CPU then carries out the instruction. If the instruction involves writing a piece of data to memory, the appropriate location is placed on the Address Bus, the value to be written is placed on the Data Bus and a Write signal is placed on one of the Control Lines. Once the instruction is completed, the CPU can fetch the next instruction, often stored in the next consecutive program memory address. The simplified diagram uses a single bus for both data and program instructions. This is very common and is called the *'Von Neuman'* architecture.

THE PC MEMORY MAP

The early IBM PC, the XT, appeared in 1981 with an 8088 processor and only 16k of main memory (with a recommended figure of 64k). These chips had a 20-bit address bus and could only address 1Mb of memory. This now seems a ludicrous limitation, in the days of 10Mb application. In 1978, though, when the 8086 was brought out, memory chips were extremely expensive and personal computers would have been lucky to have 100 kilobytes of memory. 1Mb was something to look forward to for large mainframe computers. The ability of the 8086/8088 chips to address a full megabyte of memory was regarded as a luxury that was unlikely ever to be used. This may have been a

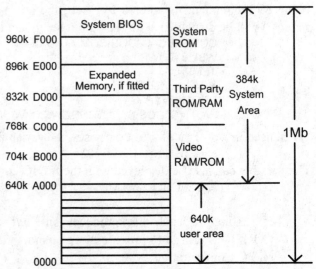

reasonable assumption at the time but holds up poorly in the light of the drop in memory prices, the development of more powerful processors and the creation of huge software applications.   Overcoming these design shortcomings is dealt with elsewhere.

The diagram that displays the allocation of memory to different parts of the computer system is known as a *'memory map'* and is explained below in terms of a basic configuration, without any memory management.

The entire machine memory is divided, for historical reasons, into segments of 64k.   The segments are not shown to scale on the diagram, to aid clarity.   The map shows both decimal numbering and its hexadecimal notation equivalents, since this is commonly shown on computer system manuals.

USER AREA

Also known as *'Low-DOS'*, the lower 10 segments make up the 640k user area, where DOS and the user applications reside.   The bulk of this area is provided for application programs, but some is devoted to system programs and variables.

SYSTEM AREA

The remaining six segments, a total of 384k, are variously called the *'system area'*, the *'upper memory area'* or *'high DOS'* area.   This is occupied by the ROM BIOS, various device drivers such as video adapters and disc controllers, and video memory.   These are not all shown on the memory map, since individual configurations can vary greatly.   The map, as an example, shows the location of expanded memory.   In fact, the great majority of PCs do not have these expanded memory expansion cards fitted. The exact map locations for scanners, modems, data acquisition equipment, etc. would vary, since their actual addresses might well have to be altered to prevent clashes of addresses. This would be achieved by setting the values of DIP switches mounted on the cards.

The diagram also shows that two 64k sections of memory are set aside for the computer's video needs. The exact amount of video memory that is used depends on the screen standard in use (refer to the Chapter on Video for more details on video modes).   The early MDA mode was mapped to address B000.   When CGA was introduced, it was mapped to B800. This allowed both MDA and CGA to co-exist in independent memory areas.   It was expected that CGA would be used for colour graphic applications, while MDA would still be used for text-based applications, due to its superior text quality.

Hercules screens, on the other hand, were mapped to B000, with MDA text compatibility.   The higher resolution modes also are mapped to B000 as their default, although the actual memory required will depend on the screen resolution and the number of colours on screen. For example, a 16-colour EGA can just fit into main memory, commencing at A000.   It is possible to steal up to C400 in some EGA modes and C800 in some VGA modes. Most VGA and higher modes cannot fit into main memory, even

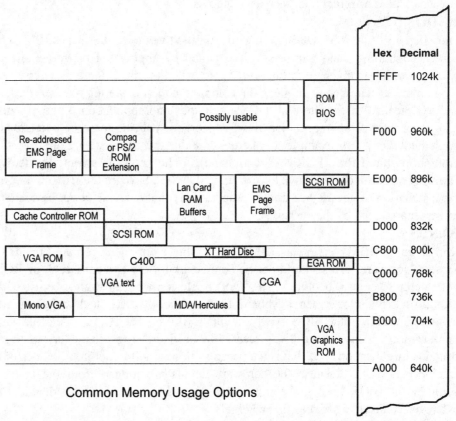

Common Memory Usage Options

commencing at A000 and have to use extra memory on graphics boards.

Much of the upper memory space is unused, since the designers over-estimated the amount of space that would be required by future add-ons and extra system ROMs; the idea that programs would be available as plug-in ROMs never developed. This space can be used for other purposes, as described in the section on memory management.   The diagram shows the most common memory areas and their uses.

NOTES

- Any memory block is exclusive to one use.   For example, if the address range D000h to E000h is being used for expanded memory, any LAN card or disc controller card would require to be set for operation in another - unused - part of the memory map.
- The ROM BIOS is always located from F000h to FFFFh.   This is because the PC always looks for an instruction at FFFFh when the machine is switched on.   This instruction starts the bootup process.
- Not all memory usage may be accurately reported by the MSD Memory utility and this can cause memory conflicts which may hang the machine.

DOS AND THE MEMORY MAP

MSDOS is fundamentally a program loader and file handler and comprises of three elements:

- A command processor
- A system kernel
- A hardware-specific BIOS

The separation of the system into parts allows the maximum flexibility when it comes to developing the system and producing improved versions.   The first two software components are written to be independent of the physical requirements of the hardware. They are concerned with the functions and interface to the user.   The last component has the responsibility of controlling the actual hardware components of the computer system.   Since only the BIOS is hardware-dependent, the user interface and system kernel do not have to be revised to accommodate new hardware devices that might be developed.

The DOS distribution disc contains three files:

COMMAND.COM

This provides the standard DOS user interface and prompt, and interprets user commands.   DOS has a standard character-oriented user interface but, because it is a separate module, it can be supplemented or replaced with a different one, such as Windows.

MSDOS.SYS

The Microsoft title is MSDOS.SYS, while the IBM version is known as IBMDOS.SYS. This is the DOS kernel, containing many services.   It is called by application programs and provides an applications interface which is invisible to the user.   It is called by the ubiquitous interrupt 21h call, much loved by programmers. The kernel contains the compiled code for the internal services, such as file management and I/O, needed to execute both DOS commands and application program calls.   Note that this is the high level control of information flow, concerned with the logic of operations and not their hardware implementation. For example, the kernel contains the file system code (e.g. the sequence of steps and prompts required for a FORMAT command).   The kernel is essentially hardware-independent. So, a hardware vendor does not have to rewrite MSDOS.SYS to get it to run on a new machine. Furthermore, the installation of new device drivers requires only that a device driver be written and linked into a list of drivers maintained by the kernel.

IO.SYS

Known in its IBM version as IBMIO.SYS, this component contains the BIOS (Basic Input Output System) software. This should not be confused with the System BIOS, or ROM BIOS, which is burnt onto a chip to control bootup.   The IO.SYS file contains hardware-specific code, including a collection of built-in drivers for screen, keyboard, hard and floppy disc, clock and serial and parallel ports.   Some, or sometimes all, of the BIOS may be stored in ROM.   The BIOS code deals with devices on a low level. For example, it moves the disc's read/write head or writes characters to the video display.   It also contains initialisation code that is temporarily brought in to interpret the lines of the CONFIG.SYS file at machine start-up.   Because the hardware details are hidden from the rest of the operating system, additions at BIOS level make it possible to add support for new devices without having to make extensive changes to services in the kernel.

NB - All these components have to present for the machine to function. IO.SYS and MSDOS.SYS are normally hidden files. If any one of three is deleted accidentally, then the machine would fail to operate.

USER ALLOCATION

The user allocation is shown in the unscaled memory map. The bottom 256 bytes are always reserved for the machine's interrupt vector table. This is a set of pointers which contain the addresses of particular sets of code to be run, if particular interrupts are triggered. These pointers are held in RAM, so that an expert programmer can alter them to change program functions. For example, a programmer can prevent the PrtScr key from carrying out a screen dump, instead pointing to code which plays a tune! This area should not be touched by the inexperienced. The DOS kernel is the heart of the operating system and has to be permanently present in main memory. The actual amount of space that it occupies depends on the DOS version and whether memory management techniques have been applied. DOS can leave as little as 537k for user use (DOS v4.01) and as much as 617k (DOS 5 with memory management).

Notice that COMMAND.COM is loaded as two separate portions. The lower section is known as the *'resident'* portion and it handles program termination (i.e. pressing Ctrl-Break) or user program errors resulting in program termination. This section provides all the standard DOS error messages. The upper section is known as the *'transient'* portion and provides the user's interface to DOS. It provides the DOS prompt, provides for EXE and COM files to be run and also contains the batch processor (to interpret and execute batch file commands). This portion also processes the *'internal'* DOS commands (DIR, COPY, etc.).

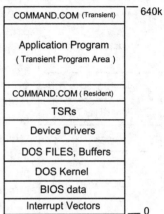

The memory needs of the DOS buffers, device drivers and TSRs have to be added to the overheads of DOS itself. They occupy a significant proportion of the so-called 'user area'. The user allocation of 640k can quickly diminish to 500k, or even less.

When the demands on the system are extreme, there can easily be conflicting demands for machine configuration. The setup for one application might slow down another's operations. In some cases, it may prevent another application from loading. At worst, it may allow a program to load, then prevent the work from being saved back to disc. Such difficulties are usually overcome by the re-allocation of programs within the machine memory - a technique called *'memory management'*.

DEVICE DRIVERS

A device driver is simply a piece of software that is used to provide the correct interface to a particular piece of computer equipment. The equipment might be some external device, such as a printer, plotter or mouse; it might be an internal device, such as a graphics card. It might also be a different way of treating conventional equipment such as a RAM disc or screen writing. DOS, after all, has its own default software for driving the screen, printer, etc.

Consider how data is handled by a printer and a plotter. The output to a printer is transmitted one character at a time, as a series of ASCII characters. The received ASCII value is used by the printer to select the appropriate sequence of dots, in dot matrix, laser or inkjet printers, or appropriate rotation on a daisy wheel printer. Regardless of the printer type, there is a standard output from the computer's printer port. Plotters, on the other hand, work in an entirely different way. The final print is a result of a series of lines drawn by pen activities. These activities consist of pen up, pen down and pen horizontal movements. Such movements are not the standard output from a printer port. The plotter device driver is the software that translates the data into the corresponding sequence of pen movements. Similar conversion software is required for mice and graphics cards. The software is particular to the piece of equipment in use and therefore the driver would be supplied along with the equipment.

DOS supplies a few of its own device drivers. These are optionally installed by the user and are therefore taking up memory space if the user has a requirement for them. The most used of these is the ANSI.SYS driver, which provides extra facilities for screen handling and keyboard operations. One of the main uses of the ANSI.SYS driver is to intercept output intended for normal video BIOS routines, such as writing a character to the screen. The ANSI driver can provide software to change screen foreground and background colours, alter the cursor position, etc. DOS also provides drivers to create ram discs and handle various other devices. If the extra facilities are not required, the drivers are not installed and memory is not used up.

DOS TSRs

Often, an application cannot provide all the functions that a user might wish. For example, a user may be running a word-processor and wish to enter the client's address, next Wednesday's date or a net price after adding mark-up and VAT. Despite sitting in front of a very expensive database and calculator (i.e. the computer), the user still has to resort to the filofax, calendar or pocket calculator. That is where TSR programs aid productivity. They allow more than one program to be in computer memory at one time. Without leaving the word-processor, the user can temporarily call up an on-screen calculator or other utility, use it, and return to the word-processing program.

DOS supports the use of TSRs ('*Terminate and Stay Resident*' programs), also known as '*memory-resident*' programs. These differ from DOS programs in the way that they use memory and the way that they are called. A DOS program is invoked by executing the appropriate COM or EXE file. This results

Application Program
Productivity Suite TSR
Print Utility TSR
Calendar TSR
DOS Area

in the program taking the amount of memory it requires. When the program is exited, the memory is released. A TSR program is also installed by executing a COM or EXE file. This loads the program into the lowest available memory above the device drivers. In some cases, the program is immediately run and is eventually exited by the user. In other cases, it loads itself into memory and immediately returns to the DOS prompt. To the unwary, it may appear that nothing happened. In either case, when the program terminates, it does not release the memory space it occupied. Instead, the program remains in memory and can be called up to be run. A normal DOS program, or even another TSR program, can now also be loaded into memory and loads commencing from the upper address of the first TSR. As the diagram shows, TSRs can be stacked up in memory. Some may be single utility programs, while others may contain a suite of facilities.

All TSR programs sit inactive in their memory areas, while the main program runs.

At any time, TSRs can be called by the user pressing 'hot key' combinations; perhaps holding down the ALT key and a particular letter key, or pressing both Shift keys simultaneously. Even while the main application is running, DOS is checking in the background for keyboard operations. As soon as it detects the TSRs hot key combination, control is passed to the TSR program, with the main application being temporarily suspended. Most often the TSR program 'pops up', i.e. the screen of the application is seen as a background with a window displaying the TSR program. The main application is still sitting in main memory and is frozen at the point of TSR invocation. When the TSR is exited by the user, the main application re-occupies the whole screen and carries on from where it was suspended. The TSR program remains in its own memory area awaiting a future invocation.

DISADVANTAGES

If one or more TSR programs are installed, they may not leave enough space in the memory to allow a large application to be loaded. Space is recovered from some TSRs by executing it a second time with an 'uninstall' parameter; this reclaims the TSR's memory space for other use. In most cases, however, the only way to reclaim the memory space is to reboot the machine. This initialises the system with a new low marker, indicating the starting point for the loading of applications.

Often, TSRs are included in the AUTOEXEC batch file, so that they are automatically installed in memory at switch on. This is a convenient way to configure a machine to have regularly-used TSRs in place. Of course, in these cases, rebooting the machine will not reclaim the space, since the AUTOEXEC file will always install the TSR. The line invoking the TSR will have to be removed from the batch program script and only installed by the user at the DOS prompt, when required.

TSRs that are always used should be included in the AUTOEXEC.BAT file, while others should be manually invoked. TSRs are available for a wide range of uses, such as spell checkers, thesauruses, calculators, keyboard enhancers, communications programs and small databases and text editors. The most famous of these is the Sidekick program, which has a wide range of facilities and is flexible in its installation options. For example, if memory space is tight, a limited version can be installed which omits the notepad, calendar and dialler. Other files can be run to install other variations. It should be noted that a few TSRs load in at the top of available memory.

The most common TSRs are SHARE.EXE, KEYB.COM and a range of different virus checkers.

NOTE
> Although more than one program is in memory, it is not a *'multi-tasking'*. Multi-tasking systems run several programs 'simultaneously'. Usually the CPU time is, in fact, shared between each process, each having a *'time slice'* in a rota. The time slots allocated to each program are small, so the CPU quickly moves from application to application. To the user, each program seems to be running continuously. With TSRs, several programs reside in memory, but only one program ever runs at a time. If a TSR is invoked, the CPU time is devoted entirely to that process. When the TSR is exited, the CPU time is devoted solely to the application program.

DOS OVERLAYS

Even at best, the user area of base memory is around 620k. Computers based on the 8086 are unable to add any extra memory, either extended or expanded. Machines based on 286's onwards can address more memory, but may not actually have any extra memory fitted. How then, does a machine manage to run today's large application programs? If an application is 1Mb, 2Mb or 3Mb in size, and some are much larger still, it cannot possibly fit into the user memory area. The solution rests in only loading and running a <u>part</u> of the program at any one time. Accordingly, the program is divided up by the programmer into sections of code that are able to fit into memory; these are called *'overlays'*. dBASE IV, for example, is organised as a core program and a set of overlays. These overlays are not independent programs; they are not EXE files that can be executed by entering their name at the DOS prompt. They will usually be identified by the file extension .OVL or similar. Since the overlays cannot be run independently, the application always maintains a core program in memory. This keeps track of all data and decides what overlays should be brought in at any particular time.

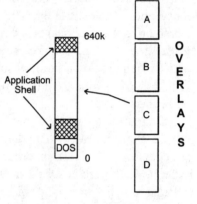

For example, a word processor such as Wordstar would not keep its thesaurus or spell-checker in memory at all times, since they are not frequently required. If the user requests a spell-check, then the core program would fetch the spell-checking overlay from disc and place it in the main memory. When spell-checking is finished, another overlay can be fetched from disc and its contents can overwrite the spell-checking overlay. This is not the ideal way to run an application, since time is taken in swapping overlays from disc. Alternative methods of handling large programs exist, either accessing the memory more efficiently or providing additional memory.

PAGING

Overlays suffer from two main problems:
- They require the <u>programmer</u> to split the program into manageable chunks.
- They can be inefficient. An 200k overlay may be loaded just to access one of its 2k long routines

Paging solves the first problem by having its own *'paging unit'* inside the Pentium's memory management unit. This divides the program into chunks and handles the loading and unloading of these chunks to and from memory. These chunks, known as *'pages'* are normally only 4k in length and this minimises the wasted time involved in handling excessive chunks of program.

Paging also provides a *'virtual memory'* system, where the program can be larger than the physical size of the computer's memory. A 386, 486 or Pentium has a maximum physical address range of 4Gb. Thus, a total of one million 4k pages are supported. Since computers have only around 8k to 64k of memory installed, any extra pages required for a program can be stored to disc. When a particular page is required, it can be fetched from disc and used to replace another page which is already in memory, using a number of possible *'page replacement policies'*. The continual swapping of pages between memory and disc allows the computer to run a much larger program than would otherwise be supported.

MEMORY ORGANISATION

As discussed earlier, the computer's memory, both RAM and ROM, is regarded as a contiguous list of locations. Each location is identified by its unique memory address. In fact, the memory is organised as a matrix of storage cells, as in the diagram. For simplicity, the diagram only shows 16 rows and 16 columns, providing 256 addressable locations or cells. Any cell in the matrix can be accessed by specifying its row and column co-ordinates. The memory chip circuitry has to translate any memory address into the corresponding co-ordinates.

In the example, the CPU requests access to address 227 (i.e. 11100011 in binary. This binary pattern is placed on the address bus.   The four least significant bits (0011) are used by the column decoder to

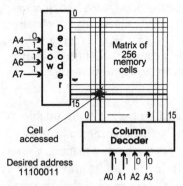

Cell accessed

Desired address
11100011

determine the column co-ordinate, known as the Column Address Select (CAS) line.   In the example the CAS value is 3.   The four most significant bits (1110) are used by the row decoder to determine the row co-ordinate, known as the Row Address Select (RAS) line - in this case 14.   The row and column address lines then access only the single unique cell which corresponds to the address supplied.   Note that the convention is to number address bus lines and data bus lines commencing with line 0.   So, a 16-bit address bus would number its lines from A0 to A15 and an 8-bit data bus would number from D0 to D7.   As can be seen, any cell in the matrix can be individually accessed. Hence the description as a random access device. Also, accessing each cell will incur the same circuit switching time overhead.   This is the chip's access time.

To simplify the diagram, only the address lines are shown.   There will also be data lines to transfer data in and out of the cells to the CPU. A data transfer will either be a read operation (the cell's contents are copied on to the data bus) or a write operation (the contents of the data bus are copies into the cells).   To instruct the chip on which operation is required, it is fed read/write information on its control lines.   If the CPU requires data from memory, it issues a read instruction along with the address to be read.   To write data to memory, the CPU places the data on the data bus and issues a write instruction along with the address location.

The diagram shows only a matrix of 256 bits.   A practical chip would involve the same architecture, only on a larger scale.   The diagram describes a 256 x 1 bit chip, since only one bit at a time can ever be accessed.   To read or write a byte, eight of these chips would require to be accessed in parallel. Example commercial DRAMs are 256k x 1 devices, 64k x 4 devices (four 64k devices parallel configured in the same chip) or 1M x 8 devices (a full byte-wide set of 1Mb matrix capacity)

NOTE   - The cells accessed may contain a program instruction or program data.   The circuitry can't distinguish between instructions and data and the programmer has to ensure that the correct addresses are being accessed.

UMA

Unified Memory Architecture is a memory organisation standard set by VESA.   Motherboards supporting UMA allow the CPU and video system to share the same pool of main memory.   There is no need for video cards to be fitted with 2Mb, 4Mb or more of their own separate memory.   This should make these cards significantly cheaper.   Additionally, chunks of the memory on the current standard video cards will be unused when the card is used in low resolution or low colour depths.   This may be occurring while there is a real shortage of main memory for user applications and data.   With UMA boards, lowering the resolution or colour depth reduces the amount needed by video and the remainder is released for use by programs.   Unfortunately, such systems are slower by up to 10% due to the extra processing required to manage the memory and because of the loss of memory from the normal pool available for Windows, applications, etc. UMA provides cheaper but slower computer systems.

ROM SHADOWING

The code inside the system BIOS ROM comprises of a set of utilities.   The internal POST code checks out the computer hardware on bootup.   Thereafter, a set of utilities can be called upon by DOS or by applications. Examples are program code to read a character from the keyboard or write a character to the screen.   Similarly, the ROM chip built in to a video card has code to handle the card's screen handling activities.   The routines contained in the ROM chips are accessed on a very regular basis but the time required to access code from a ROM is several times longer than accessing data from RAM.   If the BIOS code and video code were held and accessed in RAM then their operations would be greatly speeded up and the machine performance would be significantly improved.

Facilities exist to copy the system BIOS and the video ROM code from the ROM chips into normal RAM - a process known as 'ROM Shadowing'.   Shadowing is normally enabled or disabled via the BIOS setup. The BIOS setup normally allows for either only enabling the System BIOS or only enabling the video BIOS code, or enabling both.   The chosen ROM code is copied into unused areas in the system area (ie 640k to 1Mb).

CPU CACHE MEMORY

Standard memory speeds have not progressed at same rate as processor speeds. As a result, the CPU can process data faster than the data can be fetched from memory or placed in memory. The Pentium mother board operates at no more than 66MHz while CPUs can run at up to 266MHz. Consider that a 133MHz CPU cycles every 7ns while the access time for main memory is usually 70ns. This means that the CPU has to stand idle while the required location in memory is accessed for data to be transferred. This waiting is enforced by *'wait states'* which prolong the CPU's access cycle time. While this matches the performance of the CPU to that of the computer memory, it slows down the effective CPU operating speed. This bottleneck could be overcome if the much faster Static RAM was used as main memory. However, the cost of using SRAM for 640k, or 1Mb or 16Mb of machine memory is entirely prohibitive at the present time. It would also be extremely wasteful to have expensive RAM sitting doing little, while most of the computer activity centres round only a small portion of the memory at any one time.

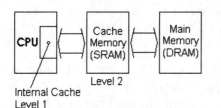

A favoured solution is to use a small block of fast RAM between the CPU and the main memory. This is known as *'cache memory'*. Any data held in the cache memory can be transferred to the CPU at greater speeds, due to its faster access time. This means that the CPU can access memory without the need for wait states. The result of using cache memory is to dispense with wasted CPU time and to increase computer efficiency. Since the block of fast SRAM is likely to be substantially smaller than the computer's main memory, the cache memory can only hold a portion of the data that is resident in main memory. The aim is ensure to ensure that only the data most likely to be required is stored in cache memory.

This relies on two established facts, collectively known as the *'principle of locality'*.

- The running of applications programs involves jumping and looping through different parts of the long list of program instructions. Despite this, most program activities are sequential - an instruction follows from a previous program instruction, with occasional jumps to other program areas. When arrived at the new program area, the machine then progresses sequentially through the new area. Often, the same few instructions are repeated over and over again as part of some iterative process.
- The data for programs is often grouped together in sequential fashion. For example, a payroll program will process employee 75 after employee 74, and so on. Also, data recently read is likely to be the data to be written. The same payroll program, for example, will read an employee's wage record, calculate new figures and write the new results over the old record data.

If the data is often accessed sequentially, then a group of data is transferred from main memory into cache memory. This one-off transfer will take place at the slowest speed - i.e. that of the main memory, wait states and all. Any subsequent requests for data will be transferred to the CPU at the higher cache memory speed. Concentrating the programs main data into the fast memory ensures that the performance is optimised. When another area of data is requested - one not already stored in cache - the data is transferred from main memory into cache memory, along with the contiguous data in main memory. The fetch of the first piece of data, in this case, is actually slower than normal, since an entire block of data was transferred at a wait-state speed. However, since subsequent fetches from that memory block will be faster, the <u>overall</u> effect is to speed up processing.

Therein lie the limitations of cache memory:

- If the cache contains data transferred due to a previous CPU request, there is no guarantee that the next CPU request will be for data from the same block. In that circumstance, there will be no *'cache hit'*, i.e. the requested data is not to be found in cache memory. The requested data, as part of a new block of data, will be transferred from main memory to cache. This means that the time taken to transfer the previous block was largely wasted and the efficiency of the computer has been reduced.
- The benefits of caching vary with the type of application in use. A program that uses a lot of data transfers benefits from a large cache memory. On the other hand, a program that is processor intensive (any number-crunching application) requires less data transfers and does not benefit to the same extent.

Despite the limitations listed, the net effect of using cache memory is to improve the computer's processing times. Intel state that their cache tests show a hit rate of around 88%. In other words, only about 12% of the data accesses results in wait states, with most of the accesses involving no wait states. This produces a much improved throughput and a rate of around 90% is the optimum value.

CACHE ORGANISATION

Just as any cache memory is better than no cache memory, the way that the cache memory is organised and read/written has a bearing on its performance.   The material so far has outlined how data is fetched from main memory to cache, to CPU.   Of course, any data that is <u>written</u> to cache memory also has to be reflected in changes to main memory.   A number of different methods of reading and writing exist and they affect the performance of the cache.   These methods do not commonly appear on advertising material but may appear in manufacturers' brochure specifications or magazine reviews.   As expected, the faster the method, the more costly the product.   Users have no control over the method of reading and writing cache, other than at the purchasing stage.

READ METHODS

LOOK THROUGH - The CPU requests data from the cache. If it is not in the cache, the CPU requests the data from the main memory.   This would involve a second read request which would slow the process.

LOOK ASIDE - The CPU interrogates the cache memory and the main memory at the same time.   If the data is in the cache memory, it is transferred at the faster rate; otherwise, it is fetched more slowly via main memory.

WRITE METHODS

WRITE THROUGH - The CPU updates the cache and the data in the cache is used to update the contents of main memory.   An improvement on this method is to store all writes to main memory in a queue within the cache and copy from the queue to main memory.   This requires an area of cache memory to be set aside to store the data queue but it has the advantage of allowing the cache to write data to the main memory at a quiet time on the data bus - and without tying up the CPU.

WRITE BACK - This is similar to the improved 'write through' method, except that the main memory is only updated if there is a difference in the contents of the cache and the corresponding section of main memory

CACHE ARCHITECTURE

The data transfers are carried out by dedicated 'cache controllers'.   When the CPU requests access to the data at a particular address, the address is used by the cache controller, to see whether that address appears in the cache memory.   If the address is in the cache memory - a 'hit' - then the address contents can be used by the CPU without recourse to the main memory.   If the address is not found in cache memory - a 'cache miss' - the cache controller has the job of accessing the main memory and of updating the cache memory.   The hit rate of the cache is determined by:

- The cache size. A large cache stores more address information and increases the likelihood of the required data being in cache. This can be improved by adding increased memory to the cache and is a good way to improve a machine fitted with slow main memory chips of, say, 100ns access time.
- The bus size between main memory and cache. A wide bus transfers data between main memory and cache memory at a faster rate, for those occasions when a cache miss is encountered.
- The way the cache is organised. The common methods are 'direct mapped' and 'associative cache'. These control the link between main and cache memory and cannot be altered.

With large caches, a lot of time can be spent searching the cache. If the wanted data is not present, then the extra time has been wasted.   However, if multi-tasking is required, then a large cache size will speed up processing.   Off-the-shelf computers are supplied with a variety of cache options.   Some have no cache memory fitted; most have 64k, 128k or 256k of cache; others have as much as 512k or even 1Mb.

PRIMARY/SECONDARY CACHE

Note that the Intel 486 and Pentium chips already have a small area of cache memory built in to CPU chip. This is known as 'Primary Caching' or 'Level 1 Caching'.   This is often considered inadequate and can be supplemented with the addition of extra 'Secondary' or 'Level2' caching. The 486 has 8k of primary cache while the Pentium has 8k for instructions and another 8k for data.   The Pentium Pro, like the Pentium, has two 8k caches but it also includes its secondary cache of 256k within the CPU itself rather being an external add-on.   This allows internal cache operations to take place simultaneously with external DRAM operations.   The Pentium II reverts to an external cache.

BURST MODE

When the CPU accesses a location from main memory, the desired address is sent out and the data from that location is placed into the cache. With burst mode systems, the memory chip's own circuitry calculates the next address locations (usually the next three consecutive addresses) and thus minimises the work of the CPU.   This speeds up throughput and makes it faster than ordinary EDO memory.

Similarly, cache memory can operate in burst mode, speeding up data movements between the second level and first level cache. A typical Pentium 66MHz motherboard system requires 6 clock cycles for each DRAM memory request, while each SRAM request require only 3 clock cycles. Chips that are optimised for *'pipeline burst mode'* achieve subsequent memory requests in only a single clock cycle.

DRAM	6+6+6+6 =	24
SRAM	3+3+3+3 =	12
Pipeline Burst RAM	3+1+1+1 =	6

MEMORY CATEGORIES

A summary of the main memory definitions is given below; these will be explained in greater detail later.

Type	Where used
DRAM (Dynamic Random Access Memory	Once was the only type used for main memory. It is used for the User Area, System Area and both Extended and Expanded Memory.
EDO	Extended Data Out A new, faster alternative to DRAM chips. 50ns, 60ns or 70ns access time.
BEDO	Burst Mode EDO memory. Sends a group of data bytes to the CPU without involving the CPU in much of the process. Faster than ordinary EDO memory.
SDRAM	Synchronous DRAM. Keeps the CPU and memory timed in step, thereby minimising the control signals between them and greatly increasing data transfer rates compared to both DRAM and EDO.
SGRAM	An even faster version of SDRAM which can operate in burst mode for both write and read operations (SDRAM can only read in burst mode).
SRAM (Static RAM)	Fast access memory normally used for caching the CPU (see below)
VRAM (Video RAM)	Latest dual-port memory technology used in newer video cards to speed up screen updates.
WRAM	Windows RAM. Developed by Samsung for video cards. It is dual-ported like VRAM but supports a block write mode for faster data rates.
Multibank DRAM (MDRAM)	20ns access time. A cheaper alternative to SRAM for cacheing and a faster alternative to DRAM for video cards.
Rambus (RDRAM)	2ns access time. Synchronised to the bus clock and provides data on both edges of the signal
Cache RAM (Level 1)	Memory built in to a CPU and sitting between the CPU and external memory to speed up data access. Access times are from 5ns to 10ns.
Cache RAM (Level 2)	Memory on the motherboard between the CPU and main memory to speed up data access.
CMOS RAM	Small block of additional memory is used to store information about the computer (e.g. type of drives in use, amount of memory in the machine, etc.)
Environment	Part of main memory that is set aside for storing information about the current prompt, search paths and user-defined variables.
User Area	Also known as Base Memory and Conventional Memory. All DOS programs and parts of Windows applications run in this area. Extends from address 0 to 640k.
UMA (Upper Memory Area)	Also known as the System Area and the High DOS area. Extends from 640k to 1Mb and is used by the ROM BIOS chip and the ROM chips that are fitted on expansion cards. The parts not used by ROMs are available to provide the window into Expanded Memory, with unused areas being called Upper Memory Blocks (see below)
UMBs (Upper Memory Blocks)	Unused areas of the UMA. Can be used to store device drivers and TSRs if the machine has been memory managed.
EMS (Expanded Memory)	The original way to create extra memory beyond the 1Mb limit. A block of memory (often chips on a separate card) can have a part of its contents viewed at any one time through a *'window'* in the UMA. Mostly used by games.
HMA (High Memory Area)	The first 64k block of memory above the 1Mb boundary. Used to store part of DOS when the system is memory managed.
XMS(Extended Memory)	The area of memory above 1Mb. Used by Windows and by a wide range of utilities such as disc caches, ram drives, print spooling, etc.
ROM BIOS	The ROM chip fitted in every PC. When the machine is switched on, it tests the system and loads DOS.
BIOS Extensions	The ROM chips that are fitted to add-on cards to control their operations (e.g. video cards or disc controller cards)

MEMORY TYPES

A range of memory products exists, with differing characteristics. However, there are two basic types:
- Those whose contents can only be read, during the running of a program. Some memory's contents may be permanent, while other memory chips may be removed from the computer and re-programmed. Examples of this type are ROM, PROM, EPROM and EEPROM.
- Those whose contents can be read and also written to. Examples are DRAM, SRAM and EDO.

Apart from the above characteristics, memory can be graded in terms of capacity and speed of access. Take, for example, a memory chip that is coded as:

> 41256-60

The first two digits indicate the product range, the rest of the numbers before the hyphen indicating the chip capacity (measured in thousands of bits).   The numbers after the hyphen indicate the chip access time, where 60 means 60 nano-seconds, 70 means 70ns.   Note, however, that 10 means 100ns and 20 means 200ns, rather than the 10ns and 20ns that might be expected. The example is a 256k, 60ns chip.

ROM

These are *'Read Only Memory'* chips and they are *'non-volatile'*; their contents will not be lost if the power is removed. These chips are used in a wide range of electronic control circuits, from industrial machine tools to domestic washing machines. They are also the ideal choice for computer control. A computer's control programs require to be non-volatile.   The computer's basic functions are controlled by system software and there is a potential Catch-22 situation, in that

> *"the computer needs a program to be loaded, so that the computer can load a program'*

By placing part of the operating system software into a ROM chip, the system BIOS, the basic machine control programs are available to be run as soon as the computer is switched on.   The programs in the ROM provide the machine's basic input and output functions, to allow application programs to be loaded and run.   Unfortunately, if the system is to be updated, the BIOS chip has to be replaced with a new chip that contains the new program routines.   This requires opening the computer case and is a job for experienced support staff or technicians.

ROM chips are *'mask programmed'* devices; the layers of the integrated circuit are manufactured using specifically designed masks. These produce chips that are only capable of performing the required pre-determined programs.   Due to the cost of manufacturing ROMs, they are only used in large quantity runs.   This, in turn, means that they are only made when the manufacturer is certain that the programs they contain are debugged.   These chips are also fitted in video, network and disc controller cards.

PROM

This stands for *'Programmable Read Only Memory'*.   With ROM, the internal program is dedicated at the production stage; the program itself determined the physical construction of the ROM chip.   A cheaper method for small and medium scale use is a ROM-type chip that is able to be programmed, after the construction stage.   Such chips are mass produced by a chip manufacturer, who has no idea of the use to which they will be put. Once the chip is purchased by a computer manufacturer, the company's programs can be embedded in it.   This is achieved by *'blowing'* fusible links inside the chip, to form the binary codes representing the program's machine code instructions.   Every intact link represents a binary 1, with a blown link representing a binary 0.   Like the ROM, the PROM chip is also non-volatile.

EPROM

The initials stand for *'Erasable Programmable Read Only Memory'* and it was introduced as a development tool.   The problem with ROM and a programmed PROM was that, once produced, they were unalterable. This is perfectly fine for a computer manufacturer - once the program contents are fully debugged. The EPROM is used to test the program. Like PROM, its links are blown to the needs of the test program.   The EPROM can then be used on the test computer. If the program is satisfactory, it can be used to create mass ROM or PROM versions.   If the program needs alteration, the EPROM is subjected to ultra-violet light for a few minutes. This 'heals' the ruptured links, allowing the chip to be blown to the next test program. The blowing and wiping clean process can be repeated many times over, before the chip fabric starts to degenerate. An EPROM chip is easily identified as it has a glass window on top of the chip to allow entry of the ultra-violet light. Due to its expensive construction,

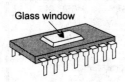
Glass window

it is only a viable alternative to ROM and EPROM for small scale use. Example EPROM chips would be the 2764-20 (64k - i.e. 8k x 8 bits) and the 27512-20 (512k - i.e. 64k x 8 bits). The equipment required to program and erase EPROMs can be cheap enough for individual or hobbyist use. For continual development use, the EPROM is often replaced with a *'ROM emulator'*. This is a piece of equipment that plugs into the ROM socket and acts like an EPROM. It contains RAM to avoid the program-erase cycles. Since it is self-powered, it appears to the main computer as a piece of ROM.

EEPROM

A variation on the EPROM is the **EEPROM** - the *'Electrically Erasable and Programmable Read Only Memory'*. Like EPROM, it has holds its contents when the power is removed. However, its contents can be overwritten without resorting to prior cleaning with ultra-violet light. It is currently significantly more expensive than other memory devices but is a likely candidate for future use in computers.

MAIN MEMORY

The variations on ROM memory outlined earlier are primarily concerned with the computer's basic control functions, with application programs being loaded from disc into main memory. This is not always the case. Many palmtop computers use ROM to store application programs, to overcome the storage problems associated with such small machines. Due to their tiny physical dimensions, there is no space for a hard disc to store application software. So, the machine stores a word processor, spreadsheet, personal organiser, etc. in ROM.

In most computers, however, the application software is loaded into, and run from, main memory. In addition, there is a need for an area to store program data and video data. These memory areas use RAM which stands for *'Random Access Memory'*. Unlike ROM technology, RAM chips are volatile which means that the data stored in the chips only remains there as long as the chips are powered. When the machine is switched off, the chips lose their contents. That is why users are always reminded to save all their data before switching off their machines. In fact, to ensure complete data integrity, the application should be exited, i.e. getting back to the DOS prompt, before switching off. This ensures that any data held in the computer's memory buffers are flushed away to disc. A database, for example, will not save each record as it is entered; it will save a number of records into a buffer area and then save the groups of records. Although they appear to the user as having been saved, they are still vulnerable to loss, if the power is switched off. The term *'random access'* is used to distinguish it from serial access devices. With serial access devices, such as tapes, the data is read in with one item following the other. The last item takes longer to fetch than the first item. Random access means that any cell address in the entire memory area can be accessed with a uniform time overhead.

NOTE   Confusingly, ROM chips are also random access devices. The difference between ROM and
        RAM variants is not in their access methods, but in their volatility (or lack of it) and speed.

RAM TYPES

Computers use two types of RAM. These are termed Dynamic Ram and Static RAM and they have differing constructions and characteristics. These characteristics include, speed, complexity and cost. The speed of the chip is termed its *'Access time'* and is measured in nano-seconds (i.e. 10 to the power minus 9). Both types use arrays of transistor switches to store the binary data. The main difference lies in how the transistors are switched and it is this which affects the chips' characteristics.

NOTE   Both types use different circuitry and are therefore <u>not</u> interchangeable. Static RAM
        cannot be plugged into sockets intended for Dynamic RAM and vice versa.

DRAM

Dynamic Ram, or DRAM, is commonly used for the computer's main memory. An incoming data signal with logic level 'on' (i.e. logic 1) to a cell is used to charge a capacitor, which holds the transistor in its switched state. The charge in this capacitor quickly leaks away and the transistor would lose its information. To prevent this, the capacitor has to be constantly *'refreshed'*. On a regular basis, the contents of the capacitor have be read. If it contains a value, the capacitor is fully re-charged to maintain its *'on'* state.

When an incoming logic level wishes to store an *'off'* state (i.e. logic level 0), the capacitor is discharged. With a main memory of 640k, and 8 cells to every byte, this involves reading and writing to 6,720,000 different cells. If the machine has an 8Mb memory, then over 64 million cells have to be refreshed regularly.   For this reason, DRAM - despite technological improvements - is a relatively slow memory system.   120ns or 150ns would be considered as slow access times for modern DRAM, while 70ns or 80ns would be average and 60ns would be considered fast.   Example DRAM chips would be the:

      4164-12   with 64k x1 bit organisation and a speed of 120nS
      44256-70 with 256k x 1 bit organisation and 70nS access time
      41256-60 with 256k x1 bit organisation and 60nS access time

A 256Mb DRAM has been announced by IBM, with a claimed halving of access times.   NEC are working on a 1Gb DRAM.

SRAM

Static RAM, or SRAM, does not use the capacitive method. Each cell represents a single bit and the value is held by a more complex set of transistors that are configured as a bistable (commonly called a *'flip-flop'*).   The output of this flip-flop can be 'set' or 'reset', to store either a binary 0 or a binary 1.   In this chip, the cell's state will maintain itself, until it is either altered by a new value, or has its power removed.   There is no need to constantly refresh the cells' contents.   The result is that the static RAM chip is significantly faster than dynamic RAM.   An access time of 20ns to 45ns would be considered slow, while 15ns would be average and 10ns would be considered fast.

Static RAMs have one major drawback.   They require a more complex structure, with a greater component count for each cell.   As a result, the fastest static RAM is larger and much more expensive than dynamic RAM.   For this reason, it is not used for the main memory chips of the computer.   They are, instead, used for fast cache memory (see later section).   All SRAM chips are of the SIL type (single in-line) and are of the SIMM (single in-line memory module) or SIP (single in-line package) variety.

Example SRAM chips are:

      1Mb x 9 -80   with 1Mb x 9 bit organisation and 80nS access time.
      4Mb x 9 -70   with 4Mb x 9 bit organisation and 70nS access time.

Special very fast SRAM is used for cache memory (see later).

SPEEDING UP ACCESS

There are a number of ways that have been developed to improve on the access times produced by the basic method described earlier.   These include:

FAST PAGE MODE ACCESS

The normal basic access method splits the incoming address value into a Row Address and a Column Address. Where access to the memory is random (i.e. an incoming address is completely different from the previous address accessed) the process already described has to be undertaken.   However, there are many times when the access is sequential (i.e. the data to be fetched consists of a block of contiguous addresses).   Examples of sequential access would be fetching graphics data or a block of text.   With sequential access there is no need to recalculate the Row Address for each cell and a block of data can be accessed by changing the Column Address values alone.   The data fetched is known as a *'page'* and is accessed at a faster rate than conventional methods.

INTERLEAVING

This also speeds up sequential accesses and is achieved by splitting the memory up into two or four separate banks.   All digital circuits move between high and low states and, after being switched, need a specific time to recover before being switched again.   This slows down memory access rates.   With interleaved systems, sequential data is stored over the various memory banks.   This means that one bank can be accessed while the previous bank is in recovery time.   This reduces waiting time and increases sequential data access rates.   It also allows banks to perform read/write operations at the same time.

SYNCHRONOUS OPERATION

Normal DRAM works asynchronously - the CPU and the memory chips have to use an elaborate set of signals to control data operations.   The time to generate these signals and the time for the signals to be recognised impose time delays upon the data transaction.   Synchronous operation ties the CPU and the memory in step with the same clock.   This eliminates the need for much of the handshaking signals and the generation by the CPU of a wanted address location results in the transfer of a copy the location's contents without the need of any further CPU to memory communication.   Commonly used with Pentium cache RAM (486s used asynchronous cache), it is now appearing for use with main memory.

FAST ACCESS MEMORY TYPES

A range of memory chips take advantage of the above techniques, and others, to improve memory performance. These memory types currently are:

EDO RAM This stands for *'Extended Data Out'* memory and is used both for main memory and in video cards as a replacement for VRAM (see below). It is an extended version of page-mode working. With normal page-access memory, the data is removed from the chip's output buffer when the Column Address line is de-activated. With EDO, the data stays available while the chip is getting set up for the next access. Access delays are reduced in this way and a complete memory transaction can take place in a single clock cycle instead of the normal two clock cycles. This will not double the chip's overall speed, since it only improves sequential access times. Overall, typical speed improvements of 5% to 10% are expected. Can't be used in 386s, 486s or older Pentiums. Available as 72-pin SIMMs or 168-pin DIMM versions (at 3.3v or 5v).

BEDO Burst Mode EDO memory is essentially EDO with the addition of burst mode operation plus some tweaks to the memory access cycle.

VRAM This is a variation on DRAM chips, where normal data write operations and constant sequential reads occur at the same time. This is specially useful for video memory and is explained in the chapter on Computer Video.

SDRAM Synchronous DRAM uses synchronous working as outlined earlier. For even faster working, it also uses both interleaving and burst mode techniques. This ensures speeds up to 100MHz, in burst mode, compared to EDO's 50MHz maximum speed and BEDO's 66MHz maximum. Because of its reliance on its clock speed, SDRAM performance is measured in MHz. Current chips are roughly equivalent to 10-12ns access times.

WRAM Windows RAM was developed by Samsung specially for use in video cards. It is dual-ported like VRAM but supports a block write mode for faster data rates.

MDRAM Multibank RAM is applies the interleaving technique for main memory to second level cache memory to provide a cheaper and faster alternative to SRAM. The chip splits its memory capacity into small blocks of 256k and allows operations to two different banks in a single clock cycle.

SGRAM The *'Synchronous Graphics Ram'* is an even faster version of SDRAM that can operate in burst mode for both write and read operations (SDRAM can only read in burst mode). This increased writing speed is very important in graphics applications. 10ns, 12ns and 15ns access times.

RDRAM Dispenses with the page mode type of interface in favour of a very fast serial interface operating at 500Mbps. This *'Rambus'* interface is a fast local bus between CPUs, graphics controllers and block-oriented memory. Currently adopted for some Nintendo machines and destined to find its way into the PC market.

CHIP TYPES

RAM and ROM chips are available in a variety of different physical constructions as follows.

DIP

Dual in-line packages; sometimes also known as DILs. These are the traditional outline for industry logic chips and other integrated circuits and were used on early PCs. They are rectangular blocks with connecting pins down two opposite sides. The pins can be soldered directly on to the computer motherboard, or plugged into board-mounted receptacles, called *'I.C. sockets'*. The diagram shows an example; the actual amount of pins will probably be much more, depending on the amount of address lines and data lines required.

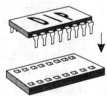

SIPs

The SIP (Single In-line Pin package) is only found in older models. It is very similar in its construction to the SIMM board, except that its connections are to a row of pins instead of a row of printed circuit pads. These pins are then plugged into a special socket on the motherboard or soldered into place.

SIMMs

The *'Single In-line Memory Module'* is the standard for most current machines and consists of a set of memory chips mounted on a small printed circuit board. There may be eight or nine chips on the board,

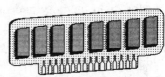

dependent on whether parity checking is in use. The board has an edge connector similar, although smaller, to that used on add-on cards. The memory board plugs into a special set of slots on the motherboard. Since the board is clipped into place, it provides a more secure connection than earlier DIP chips. The constant heating and cooling of memory chips made them regularly expand and contract until they sometimes popped out of their holders - an effect known as *'chip creep'*. This is avoided with SIMMs making their use more reliable. SIMMs are available in two basic types - 30-pin and 72-pin; this refers to the numbers of pads on the edge connector.

30-PIN

These are used with 286's and most 386SX's, 386DX's and 486's. They have an 8-bit data width, with an extra ninth bit if parity is used. So, a chip advertised as *'1 x 8 '* indicates that it is of 1Mb capacity - ie 1 million bits times 8. A *'1 x 9'* is a 1Mb chip including parity checking. 30-pin SIMMs have to be used in sets of 4 to connect to a 32-bit data bus. They are supplied with 3 chips or 9 chips on the board. Newer *'composite'* SIMMs have improved chips that are capable of replacing three conventional memory chips. Thus, a 3-chip board and a 9-chip board both provide 4Mb of memory but with different chips on the board. These boards, despite having the same capacity, are not usually interchangeable.

72-PIN

These are used with some 386DX's, some newer 486's and Pentiums. They are supplied with 8 or 9 chips on the board. They have a 32-bit data width and will have four extra bits if parity is being used. The extra pins to the board carry the address lines and control lines from the motherboard. It can be thought of as four separate 8-bit chips used to construct a 32-bit wide data path. So, a chip advertised as *'1 x 32 '*

30-pin	72-pin	Parity	Access Time
x8	x32	No	70ns
x9	x36	Yes	70ns
-	EDO	No	60ns

indicates that it is of 4Mb capacity - ie 1 million bits times 32, divided by 8. Similarly, a *'1 x 36'* is a 4Mb chip including parity checking. An *'8 x 32'* is a 32Mb SIMM while a *'8 x36'* is a 32MB SIMM with parity. 72 pin SIMMs are available in 1Mb, 2Mb, 4Mb, 8Mb, 16Mb, 32Mb and 64Mb varieties.

SIMM BANKS

Motherboards provide slots for inserting SIMMs and these groups of slots are known as *'SIMM banks'*. It is important that the motherboard manual be consulted, as different configurations are possible.

386/486

The average 386/486 motherboard has eight 30-pin SIMM slots and the slots can be configured to take either 256k, 1Mb or 4Mb modules. Most motherboards split the eight slots into two banks of four slots. The four slots in the bank must be populated and the four SIMM boards fitted must be of the same type. It is not possible, for example, to have two 4Mb modules and two 1Mb modules in the bank. There would have to be four 4Mb modules or four 1Mb modules. This is because a 32-bit data bus width needs to connect to 32 bits of RAM. Since each 30-pin SIMM provides 8 bits, four boards allow the full 32 bits of data to be accessed at the same time. If data was accessed a byte at a time, it would require four separate memory accesses to build up a 32-bit data word, resulting in much slower transfer rates. Some other models, including Pentium motherboards, have only two banks of 2 slots.

Some boards also demand that the configuration of the second bank be identical to that used in the first bank. So, if the first bank contained four 2Mb modules, the second bank would also have to contain four 2Mb modules. Some motherboards provide jumpers so that the second bank can have a different configuration from the first bank. This allows the first bank to have, for example, four 2Mb modules while the second bank has four 1Mb modules - giving a total of 12Mb. If this flexibility is not allowed on the motherboard, then upgrading memory can be expensive as SIMM boards may have to be discarded to allow higher capacity boards to replace them. It also important that each SIMM board use chips with the same access times. If SIMMs have different access speeds, the computer will either operate at the speed of the slowest board or the system may crash if the BIOS has not been configured for the slowest speed.

Since the 486 has a 32-bit data width, it can be fitted with a single 72-pin SIMM.

Pentiums

The Pentium CPU has a 64-bit data bus and therefore requires that two SIMMs be fitted at a time. The two SIMMs must be of the same capacity - ie using two 16Mb SIMMs provides 32Mb of main memory. Although all Pentiums support 72-pin SIMMs, there are variations in the type of memory supported by particular motherboards. Try to avoid mixing parity and non-parity SIMMs. Fitting parity SIMMs to non-parity motherboards will probably crash the system; fitting non-parity SIMMs to a parity system will probably disable the parity checking of existing parity SIMMs. Try to avoid mixing memory speeds as adding a slower SIMM usually brings the whole bank down to its access speeds. It is usually possible to mix pairs of SIMMs- eg one pair of 16Mb and a pair of 4Mb. VX and HX chipsets allow each bank to have different memory types (eg FPM in one bank and EDO in another bank) and runs each bank at its best speed. FX chipsets allow the mixing of EDO and FPM in the same bank, with all SIMMs being treated as FPM. Note that some very early Pentiums used 30-pin SIMMs.

FPM and EDO SIMMs are identical in appearance. To find out what is currently installed on a computer either check the motherboard manual, use a SIMM tester (this may involve visiting a repair shop) or watch the messages on booting up the computer. Many BIOS chips will produce a message such as "BANK 0 : EDO" if EDO installed.

DIMMs

Starting to appear in the more expensive machines is the *'Dual In-line Memory Module'*. It is a 168-pin module that has electrical contacts on both side of the board. It has a greater reliability than SIMMs and is available as a non-parity board. It has a 64-bit data width which directly matches the Pentium's 64-bit data bus width, allowing a single DIMM to be fitted. Newer motherboards will only support only DIMMs, requiring less memory banks and providing a more compact layout. DIMM boards are available with either FPM, EDO or SDRAM fitted. Using DIMMs does not in itself lead to any speed improvement as it is only a connection type. It is the use of SDRAM on DIMMs with interleaving that makes these particular DIMMs faster. DIMMs are available in both 3.3v and 5v versions. Most motherboards are fussy over the use of DIMMs with SIMMs and the manual should be consulted; some or all of the SIMMs may have to be removed to allow the DIMM to function.

DATA INTEGRITY

The movement of data in and out of memory is carried out by the 'memory controller'. This circuitry can be configured to check the integrity of the data being held in memory. Lower-end models tend to have no integrity checking, mid-range systems tended to have parity checking, while top-end systems such as networks servers have ECC. With the production of ever more reliable memory chips, parity has tended to be dropped, leaving ECC provided on systems requiring the ultimate in reliability (known as 'mission critical' systems). The integrity checking, if any, is determined before purchasing a machine.

PARITY

Many machines have built-in parity bit writing and parity checking. This technique attempts to ensure that the data stored in any particular memory location is identical to the original data written and has not been accidentally altered by:

- electrical disturbances (such as transients - i.e. spikes - on the power)
- faulty RAM chips

Faulty memory chips will be detected during the POST (Power On Self Test) when the ROM BIOS tests out the system when it is switched on or given a hard reset. Other memory problems, such as power surges, can occur <u>during</u> the user's session and these can cause the alteration of some memory contents. It is these problems that parity checking is designed to detect.

From a user point of view, memory is seen as being a byte in width. The eight bits of the byte are used to store the program data. In fact, parity memory s attach a ninth bit to each data byte. This is the 'parity bit'. When data is written to memory, a count is made of all the binary 'one' bits in the data byte. If the total is odd, then the parity bit is set to one, otherwise it is set to zero. This is an automatic process. When the data comes to be read, the same calculation on the byte's contents are made prior to sending it to the CPU. If the calculated parity contents are different from the value in the parity bit, then an error is known to have occurred and an error message will be given to the user.

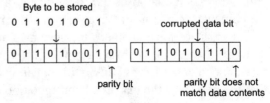

If the expected value and the stored value are identical, it is likely that the data is unchanged (this is not guaranteed, since a number of bits in the byte could have been altered and still produce the same parity value as the original data).

In the example given the value 01101001 is being stored in a memory location. It has an even number of binary 1's, so the parity bit is set to 0. If the data is corrupted as shown in the second diagram, there would be five binary 1's which should result in a 1 in the parity bit. Since the parity bit contains a 0, the error is detected.

A single bit parity is not foolproof, since the corruption of two bits in a byte might render a correct parity check even though the byte is corrupted. As a result, it is not supported by Triton-chip Pentium motherboards; parity SIMMS can be fitted but the parity bit will be ignored.

Note that if the data was altered due to a permanent fault on the chip, the faulty address would be detected by the computer when it makes its self-test on being powered up.

PRACTICAL EXAMPLES

As a consequence of using parity checking, memory boards are often populated with chips in groups of nine. For example nine 1M x 1 chips would use eight of the chips to produce 1Mb of storage (1m x 8 bits) while the other million bits would be used to store the parity for each byte. An alternative board has three chips - two 1M x 4 chips to produce 1Mb of storage (i.e. 1m x 8 bits) and a 1m x 1 chip for the parity bits. With modern 72-pin memory modules, data is organised on 32-bit width and each byte of the 32-bit word would have its own parity bit.

A non-parity system can be fitted with parity RAM; the parity bits are simply not used. However, a parity system has to be fitted with parity Ram or it will not work.

FAKE PARITY

A simple check was used to check whether a SIMM was parity or non-parity; A two or eight chip SIMM was non parity while three or nine chip SIMMs were parity types.

However, a number of SIMMs have appeared for parity motherboards that use *'fake parity'* or *'logic parity'*. This reduces the price of the SIMM by not providing the extra memory to store the parity bits. Writes to the SIMM discard the parity calculations since it cannot store them. During memory reads, the SIMM generates the correct parity bit expected by the motherboard. The motherboard is fooled into thinking that parity checking has been carried out and no memory errors have been found.

ECC

Parity circuits are designed to detect memory errors; they are unable to correct them. The Error Correction Code (ECC), also described as 'Error Checking and Control', system is able to detect and correct single bit errors. A five-bit error checking code is used to provide reliable detection of corruption. Since there is great detail in the checking code, the information can be used to restore the data byte to its original value. Any corrections are made without the user even knowing that a problem had occurred; it will not produce error messages. ECC systems will also detect multiple bit errors. Unlike parity systems, ECC will detect multiple bit errors where two bits appear to self cancel (ie one bit changes from 0 to 1, while another bit changes from 1 to 0).

PRACTICAL EXAMPLES

ECC systems can use specially designed RAM chips (ie x39 or x40 - those with 39 or 40 bus width). A common alternative is to use two SIMMs that are x36 (ie 36 width bus). This provides a total bus with of 72 bits. Of these, 64 bits are used for data storage and 8 bits are used for ECC information. However, x36 chips are also commonly used for parity systems. In this case, the way the integrity locations are used depends upon whether the memory controller works on a parity or an ECC system.

CMOS

This stands for *'Complimentary Metal Oxide Semiconductor'* and is a low power consumption memory chip. In PCs it comprises of a small block of additional memory that is used to store information about the computer (e.g. type of drives in use, amount of memory in the machine, etc.).

It is not part of the computer's memory map and is associated with the computer's real-time clock chip. The real-time clock is always supplied with power as it has its own rechargeable battery. This means that the contents of the CMOS will remain even when the power is switched off. The CMOS ensures that the details of the machine's configuration are always available when the machine is first booted up. The contents of the CMOS memory can be altered via the BIOS setup procedure offered during bootup. Depending upon the BIOS type, pressing the Delete key or the f1 key during bootup will take the user into the BIOS setup routine.

BREAKING THE 1Mb BARRIER

As mentioned previously, the early PCs could only address 1Mb of main memory due to their 20-bit address bus. Apart from memory addressability, IBM made a design decision that has affected PC development ever since. It decided that the <u>top</u> of the map should be given over to system use. There was no problem with the XT range. Their processors could address 1Mb and their boards allowed for the fitting of up to 1Mb of ROM/RAM. The restrictions became clear when the processor range was upgraded. The 80286 chip had a 24-bit address bus, capable of accessing 16 million different memory locations; the 80386/80486 chips have 32-bit address buses, capable of accessing 4Gb of memory. Memory chips are now comparatively cheap and extra memory can easily be fitted to the motherboard.

This extra memory could have been accessed with relative ease - if only IBM had decided that the system area would be located at the <u>bottom</u> of the memory map. As it stands, there cannot be a contiguous block of memory, since the 384k system block breaks up the user memory area. This causes difficulties for programmers and hardware manufacturers alike.

IBM must privately regret the impediment they have inflicted on their own product range. There is no technical difficulty in producing a PC product with a different memory map. The system area could be placed at the bottom of the memory map, allowing limitless future expansion above it. The problem is not one of technology, it is one of compatibility. No existing software or add-ons would work with this new machine and this has been the deciding factor in maintaining the present architecture - warts and all. All subsequent PC hardware and software developments struggle to get the best from this bad situation.

The attempts to increase memory addressability, while still living with the current architecture, have revolved around the development of Extended Memory and Expanded Memory.

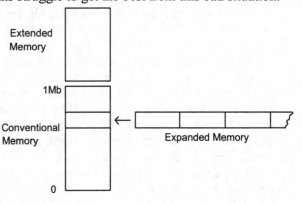

- With XMS, the extra memory is added to the memory map above the 1Mb line.
- With EMS, the memory consists of banks of memory that can slot into the existing DOS memory area.

The 1Mb area is commonly known as *'conventional memory'*.

EXTENDED MEMORY

Extended memory is memory that is mapped to the addresses above 1Mb. It is mostly known as *'XMS'*, for Microsoft's e<u>X</u>tended <u>M</u>emory <u>S</u>pecification. XMS cannot be used with 8088 or 8086 machines, since they are only capable of addressing 1Mb. For machines from the 80286 on, there is the alternative of the Extended Memory system. These computers make use of extended memory for purposes such as:

<u>Making better use of conventional memory</u>

DOS 5 onwards and utilities such as PC KWIK, Above Disk, QEMM, etc. use extended memory to hold parts of the DOS kernel and the many device drivers that previously occupied normal user memory. This solves the many problems that arise when machines have to connect to networks, use a number of TSRs, etc. These ancillary programs consume considerable amounts of main memory, resulting in users having insufficient remaining memory to run application programs. The memory management utilities are able to re-locate many device drivers, TSRs and even part of the DOS kernel into extended memory, thus allowing the maximum usable space in the conventional memory area. This technique is not restricted to extended memory. Memory managers can also make use of unused UMBs (upper memory blocks) in the upper memory area. This is also beneficial, but there may well not be as much memory to play around with - particularly if the upper memory area is heavily populated with ROMs and adapters, or if there is a lot of drivers, etc. requiring to be moved up.

<u>Providing extra facilities</u>

DOS and commercial packages provide utilities to use the extended memory for new uses, such as print spooler, hard disc cache and RAM disc

<u>RAM DRIVE</u>

 An area of memory, whose size is set by the user, is allocated to act as a temporary disc drive. Files can be saved to the RAM drive and loaded back from, in exactly the same way as a hard disc. The usual DOS copy and directory commands work with the RAM drive. It provides a very useful fast drive - much faster than fetching from disc. The only storage limit is the amount of memory that is set aside for the system.

HARD DISC CACHE - SMARTDRV.SYS

An area of the extended (or expanded) memory can be set aside to store information from the machine's hard disc.   This area is termed the *'disc cache'*.   It works like memory cache, except that it is even more efficient. Like memory cache, a block of memory is inserted between the CPU and the storage medium.   Memory cache is a small block of fast memory interfacing the CPU to slower memory.   Disc cache, on the other hand, is a much larger block of memory (between 256k and 2Mb) which is inserted between the CPU and a very much slower disc drive.   The ability to often fetch information directly from this memory copy rather than from disc can greatly enhance applications that have extensive disc read activities.

PRINT SPOOLER

A printer's mechanism works at a very slow rate, in comparison to the speed that print data can be sent to it by a computer.   Most printers now have a small in-built block of memory, called the *'print buffer'*.   This buffer holds data from the computer, stores it and passes it to the print head control circuitry as and when required. This is fine for small documents, as the entire data can be transferred to the printer leaving the computer free for other operations.   For large documents, the printer buffer is too small and the computer will be tied up while the printing proceeds.   To prevent this, an area of computer memory can be set aside to hold printer document data.   The computer can then be used for other processing, while data is sent to the printer in the background

DEVELOPING MORE POWERFUL APPLICATIONS

The addition of extra memory does not in itself result in its use by DOS applications, since they still work within the 1Mb memory range.   From the 80286 onwards, the CPU was capable of addressing larger memory ranges. To ensure backwards compatibility, the chips have two operating modes:
- REAL MODE - which simulates normal 1Mb DOS running.   It acts like a 'real' 8086 and allows the running of 'older' programs.   In this mode, the chip is only using 20 of its 32 address lines.
- PROTECTED MODE - which supports the wider addressing capability, amongst other advantages such as multi-tasking.

Accessing extended memory requires running the CPU in protected mode. Programs used *'DOS extenders'* to allow MSDOS programs access to XMS. DOS extenders are an interface between a program running in protected mode and the machine's operating system. They automatically switch between real and protected mode.   Programs that take advantage of extended memory include Lotus 123 v3.1, AutoCad and DataEase 4. DataEase 4, for example, uses the XMS memory to store and sort records, which is much faster than sorting to and from disc. Many DOS extender applications use the base memory (i.e. 640k) for the program and the extended memory area for the data.

Windows uses the now standard Microsoft multi-tasking DOS extender, called DPMI (DOS Protected Mode Interface), to allow applications to be executed entirely within extended memory. This eliminates time delays introduced with program overlay swapping and EMS page swapping, since the entire program can be fitted into extended memory - and run from there.   This DOS extender is built-in to Windows and is automatically used by all appropriate programs which it runs in protected mode. DPMI can also be used on 286 machines. The extended memory is accessed via an XMS driver, such as HIMEM.SYS.

EXPANDED MEMORY

In 1985, Lotus, Intel and Microsoft co-operated in a system to use extra memory, known as EMS - the Expanded Memory Specification. It is also referred to as LIM memory, after the developers, **L**otus/**I**ntel/**M**icrosoft.   It is used by programs such as Lotus 123 v2.1, dBASE IV, AutoCAD and Supercalc. The expanded memory manager software is called EMM.SYS and the industry standard is version 4, issued in 1987. It can handle up to 32Mb of expanded memory.   Note that the previous version, 3.2, can only store data in the expanded memory. The EMS system carries out its processing in the normal DOS space (within the 1Mb range) and can therefore also be used by the humble XT machines. On the other hand, it is slower, more awkward to use and more expensive than extended memory. This is due to the way the expanded memory is organised and accessed.

BANK SWITCHING

EMS reserves up to four 16k areas of memory in an unused section of the upper memory area, above 640k   These new areas are called *'page frames'* and they act as 'windows' on the main EMS memory. The area used starts at address 832k, which is D000 expressed in hex notation. The EMS memory is also divided into up to 2000 different 16k areas, dependent on the memory size. These areas are called *'pages'*. The application is loaded into EMS memory but, at any one time, a portion of this memory (and its contents, either program or data) is electrically switched into a page frame address area. This allows it to be accessed by any normal DOS program that recognises the EMS system.   The EMS expansion card is fitted with memory just of the same type as found in main memory.   These memory chips differ from main memory chips in that they do not connect to the machine's address bus.   EMS memory chips have to connect to their own address bus on the expansion card. This is wider than the machine's address bus, as it adds extra bits to identify each page number.   Therefore, it follows that a single CPU address would match many different EMS locations.

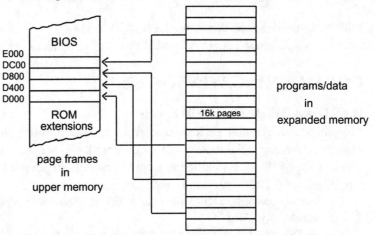

The program that is using EMS has to give the page number as well as the required address. After all, address 1100 in page 3 is a different location from address 1100 in page 9.   The page number is used by the card to ensure that the appropriate page of data is switched in to the page frame in conventional memory.   Placing the page frames in the user area is precluded, as there is no way to disable any main memory and two memory chips cannot be simultaneously read. It would also completely confuse existing DOS programs. Different card manufacturers will have different physical board designs, but they will all conform to the Expanded Memory Specification.   Each card will be supplied with its own expanded memory manager. This communicates with the EMS device driver, sometimes called a *'LIM driver'*. This is usually called EMM.SYS for a 286 machine, EMM386.EXE for a 386 machine, or similar. When a software house develops a product to use EMS, they will not be aware of the specific boards on which it will be used. This will not matter, as the boards, in following the same specification, will respond to the same EMS memory call interrupt (67H).   When the interrupt is issued, control is passed to the EMS driver. This driver is written to specifically match the design of the board and it converts the standard arguments sent by application into the control sequences required by the particular board.

PAGING

If a machine is already fitted with extended memory, the system can be configured so that the CPU sees the XMS as EMS memory.   Since there is no specialised EMS circuitry, the bank switching principle cannot be utilised.   Instead, a slower system of paging is employed. When the application wishes to address a particular memory address which lies outside the 1Mb memory, the EMS manager copies the appropriate page (i.e. the one with the requested address) into one of the 16k windows in upper memory. It is now available for accessing and the EMS manager will make the translation from the requested address to the address where it will actually be found in one of the page frames.   Eventually, all the page frames will be occupied.   When another address is requested which requires another page to be loaded, there will be no vacant page frame to load it into. In this case, one of the current page frames will be written back to EMS memory (since its contents may have been modified) and another page can be loaded by overwriting this frame.   In this mode, it acts like an I/O device.   In this case, however, the data is being moved in and out of a large pool of EMS memory, rather than disc or external ports.

The software driver (called EMM386.EXE in DOS 5) acts as an EMS emulator and is hence sometimes called a *'Limulator'*. It will switch into protected mode to copy the data from extended memory into the page frame, then revert to real mode to run in DOS mode.   Other EMS emulators are part of DRDOS and QEMM.   Using extended memory in this way provides EMS activities without the expense of the EMS board.   On the other hand it is much slower since page transfers take milliseconds, compared to microseconds for bank switching. Overall, the EMS system involves complex and time-consuming page swapping or bank switching techniques and is slower than accessing conventional memory, although still faster than disc accesses. For 8088/8086 machines, it is the only available method for running larger applications from memory. For these machines, it allows access to such luxuries as giant spreadsheet worksheets. All machines wishing to use the EMS system will require:

- to be fitted with a memory board to hold the EMS chips and control circuitry, or have extended memory to configure as expanded memory.
- the application to have the necessary software to automatically detect and control the board's circuitry.

The use of EMS in new applications has died away, in favour of XMS systems.

Configuring Windows

Microsoft has replaced Windows 3.1 with Windows 95. Windows 3.1 requires the presence of DOS for its operation, although latest NT and Windows '95 versions are designed to replace MSDOS.

CONFIGURING WINDOWS 3.1

HARDWARE REQUIREMENTS

To gain the maximum performance from a Windows-driven system, certain hardware and software requirments have to be met. Windows will not operate on a 8086 machine. Real Mode, which allowed use of Windows - albeit at a crawl - on XTs expired with Windows 3.0.

For Windows 3.1, the minimum requirements are:
- A 286 upwards, with 1Mb total RAM for Standard Mode and at least 6Mb of hard disc space (preferably 9Mb)
- A 386 upwards, with 2Mb extended memory for Enhanced Mode and at least 8Mb of hard disc space (preferably 10Mb)
- An EGA monitor upwards
- DOS ver 3.1 onwards
- A Mouse (not strictly essential, but highly recommended)

The lower figures for hard disc space assume no extras such as network drivers, printer drivers, etc.

Standard Mode

Standard Mode runs around 20% faster than Enhanced Mode. A machine will be automatically in Standard Mode if it is a 286 or is 386/486 with less than 2Mb of memory. This mode allows the machine to run as many Windows applications as machine memory will allow. However, DOS applications must be full screen (i.e. not in a Window) and run in the foreground; there is task switching of non-Windows applications instead of multi-tasking. When it is anticipated that the user will only ever run a single application on the machine, then that program can be speeded up by using Standard Mode - even if the computer is capable of running in Enhanced Mode. So, machines which support Enhanced Mode can be put into Standard Mode by calling Windows with the /S parameter - i.e. WIN/S

Enhanced Mode

The 386 onwards can create virtual 8086 partitions and DOS applications can run in these partitions. This means that DOS applications can be multi-tasked and run from a window as well as full screen. So, cut and paste operations (via the clipboard) are possible:
- between DOS applications
- between DOS applications and Window applications

Enhanced Mode also supports *'virtual memory'* - a technique that treats hard disc space as memory. A machine will be automatically in Enhanced mode if it is a 386 onwards, with at least 2Mb extended memory. If the machine has only 1Mb total RAM (i.e. 640k + 384k) then it can still be run in Enhanced mode although its performance will be slower than in Standard mode. In such a case, or if a 386 machine has been previously using Windows in Standard mode using the /S switch, Windows can also be used in Enhanced mode by calling it with the /3 switch - i.e. WIN/3

MULTI-TASKING

All Windows users will be engaged in multi-tasking activities at some time or another, even if they don't consciously choose to do so - or even know that they are doing so. There are obvious benefits in running more than one program at a time. A user could, for example, have Windows open on several packages at the same time and copy data from one application to another with copy or cut and paste activities. This may involve copying text, figures or graphics from databases or spreadsheets into word processing or DTP applications. A user may also choose to have a database carry out a detailed search and report activity, while he/she carries on typing a document in a word processing package. The typing operation is a *'foreground'* activity, while the database activity is carried out in the *'background'*, i.e. there is no apparent signs that it is going on. When the database is next returned to by opening its window again, the report will be compiled and ready to use.

Many users may shy away from running several complex applications simultaneously. However, this does not mean that their machines are not multi-tasking. A document that is being printed out while the user types the next document, the handling of drop-down or pull down menus, the handling of dialogue boxes - these are operations that are carried on while the main application appears as a continuous operation to the user. Multi-tasking is a main feature of Windows.

INSTALLATION

The purpose of this section is to briefly describe the installation of Windows on to a standalone computer and to outline the main options that are available for configuring the machine resources for maximum Windows performance.

INSTALLATION TASKS

The purpose of the SETUP program is to:
- Check that the computer hardware is compatible with Windows
- See which mode, Standard or Enhanced, the computer is capable of supporting
- Copy and decompress the Windows files into a sub-directory of the hard disc.
- Set up the machine's SYSTEM.INI and WIN.INI files. These are the Windows initialisation files - text files which hold the details of the machine's Windows configuration. These are read on Windows startup and used to configure the machine.
- Automatically find any Windows applications and create the corresponding program icons
- Automatically find any <u>known</u> non-Windows applications and create program information files (PIFs) and program icons. Other DOS applications can be added subsequently (see later)
- Modify the machine's AUTOEXEC.BAT and CONFIG.SYS files.
  The AUTOEXEC.BAT file has a path to the Windows directory added and a variable TEMP is set in the batch script to point to a TEMP directory that is created in the Windows directory. If supported by the machine, SMARTDRV.EXE will also be added as a script command.
  The CONFIG.SYS file experiences a number of modifications as below:
  - HIMEM.SYS is added as a device driver
  - Updates RAMDRIVE.SYS to the Windows version, if it is currently installed.
  - Updates EMM386.EXE to the Windows version, if it is currently installed.
  - Updates the EGA.SYS driver if an EGA monitor is in use.
  - Updates the mouse driver
  - Deletes any device drivers which would prevent or inhibit the normal operation of Windows. Therefore, it is advisable to make a backup copy of the original CONFIG.SYS, so that any major changes will be known.

INSTALLATION STEPS

The initial steps in the installation are:
1. Place the first Windows installation disc in drive 'A'
2. Enter A: [ENTER]
3. Enter SETUP [ENTER]
4. Read the Information screen
5. Choose either Express Setup or Custom Setup

EXPRESS SETUP

This choice allows the program to make the installation decisions; the hardware is checked and the program configures Windows as it decides best suits the machine. This includes choosing between Standard and Enhanced mode; if the machine is short of disc space, the installation program will suggest a curtailed installation, omitting some or all of the optional components (such as screen savers). User input is restricted to inserting installation discs as instructed by the program - and answering a few simple questions:
- User name and company name
- Brand of printer to be used
- Which output port the printer is connected to (e.g. LPT1, COM1)
- Whether the user wishes to run the Windows Tutorial

The AUTOEXEC.BAT and CONFIG.SYS files are automatically updated and the Windows files are stored in \WINDOWS sub directory of the hard disc.

CUSTOM SETUP

The Express Setup is useful for inexperienced users but the Custom Setup allows greater flexibility of installation. Custom Setup allows control over the configuration by allowing the user input to the questions mentioned above, plus the following additional questions:

- The directory name where the Windows files are to be stored
- The type of computer to be used
- The type of monitor, mouse and keyboard to be used
- The language that Windows will display
- The type of local area network in use, if any
- Whether to change the AUTOEXEC.BAT and CONFIG.SYS files
- Which Windows components are to be installed and which are to be omitted
- Any changes to virtual memory settings (see later)

The support engineer should have all the required facts at hand before running Custom Setup.

NOTE   A machine that has been installed using the Express Setup can always be altered later using the Windows 'SETUP' option from within Windows.

UPGRADING FROM EARLIER WINDOWS VERSION

It is possible to install a version of Windows without first removing an earlier version.   In such a case, the installation process will replace system files, device drivers and Windows utilities where a new version exists.   All the other old files and Windows applications are untouched.   This means that all the hardware settings regarding monitor, keyboard, mouse, network, etc. are preserved.   Similarly, all Program Manager groups are preserved.

POTENTIAL SETUP PROBLEMS

The main difficulties in installing Windows are caused by:

- Windows not able to correctly identify the hardware in use.   If the installation is invoked by the command SETUP/i, the hardware check is ignored and the Custom Setup is used to allow the technician to specify the hardware in use.
- Active TSRs which are incompatible with Windows.   The most well known ones are reported during Setup and the SETUP.TXT file on Windows Disc 1 outlines the steps to be taken with particular programs. Problem files include commercial products such as various Norton, PC-Kwik and PC Tools utilities as well as Microsoft's own JOIN, KEYB, MIRROR and FASTOPEN utilities.

Any DOS screen savers should also be removed or disabled before running Windows Setup.

The Windows User's Guide gives information on configuration options and the Windows 'Getting Started' booklet contains a useful troubleshooting section.   In addition, the following text files are installed along with Windows:

> SETUP.TXT, README.WRI, PRINTERS.WRI,
> NETWORKS.WRI, SYSINI.WRI and WININI.WRI.

These files can be read for the latest information on using Windows with new hardware devices not previously mentioned.   It pays to read these documents, as it can often save a great deal of otherwise wasted effort.   Ideally, the documents should be printed out and bound into a reference document.   The files can then be deleted from the Windows directory thus freeing up around 250Kb of hard disc space.

ALTERING INSTALLED OPTIONS

If, during Custom Setup, a reduced set of Windows components was installed, the extra components can easily be added at a later date, using the 'Add/Remove Windows Components' option within the 'Options' choice of Windows Setup (to be found in the Main group). The boxes denoting the desired extra components should be clicked as active (i.e. a cross will appear in the box) and the 'OK' button clicked.

Similarly, if free hard disc space becomes a problem or the README files, etc. become superfluous, then these components can be removed by making their boxes inactive (the cross is removed from the appropriate boxes) and the 'OK' button is clicked.

	Windows Setup	
The following optional groups of files (components) are installed on your system.		OK
To remove a component, clear its checkbox.		Cancel
To install a component, check its checkbox.		
To remove or install specific files within a component, choose Files... for that component.		Help

Component	Bytes Used	Add/Remove Individual Files...
■ Readme Files	15,694	Files...
■ Accessories	1,283,601	Files...
□ Games	0	Files...
■ Screen Savers	59,216	Files...
□ Wallpapers, Misc.	0	Files...

Disk Space Currently Used by Components:	1,358,511	Bytes
Additional Space Needed by Current Selection:	0	Bytes
Total Available Disk Space:	78,364,672	Bytes

SETUP OPTIONS

The main configuration options requested in the Custom Setup routine are also achieved via the *'Setup'* utility in the *'Main'* group. The choices are:

COMPUTER

In most cases, the default option of 'MS-DOS System' will be the appropriate choice. However, there is the option to choose specific machine models; these are listed in the Windows documentation, or the list can be viewed at Setup time. These machines include all the Hewlett-Packard range, some Toshiba portables, along with assorted NEC, AST and Zenith models. If in doubt, consult the documentation, as incorrectly choosing the standard default option could cause problems later. Not available via the Setup option in the Main Group.

DISPLAY

Normally, the display as estimated by the installation program will be correct but there are occasions when this can be improved through an alternative choice. For example, standard VGA mode is only 640x480 resolution in 16 colours, while many modern video boards are capable of the SVGA mode of 800x600. In these cases, the display option can be altered to choose the generic 800x600 SVGA driver supplied with Windows.

Additionally, some portables will provide a better picture if driven in *'Mono VGA'* mode (i.e. simply black and white) rather than standard VGA mode which provides 16 shades of grey.

Finally, many modern monitors are driven by cards capable of 1024x768 resolution or even 1280x1024. Often, these systems are optimised to work with Windows and have their own software screen drivers. If the standard Windows drivers (which cover a range of video cards such as 8514/a, Trident, Video7 and XGA types) are inadequate for the card, then the video card's own driver can be added to the list of available screen drivers. This is achieved by choosing the *'Other'* option from the menu of Window drivers. The program then prompts for the drive and path where the manufacturer's driver is stored. When the driver is chosen from this disc, its files are copied into the Windows sub-directories.

Changing between display modes can be achieved at any time by double-clicking the Windows Setup icon within the Main Windows group. A window displays the current display, keyboard, mouse and network settings, as shown. If the *'Options'* choice is taken, the title changes to *'Change Windows Settings'* and any of these settings can be altered. If the *'Display'* choice is taken, a drop-down menu of available drivers is displayed and can be chosen or added to as previously described.

KEYBOARD

Most keyboards are covered by the *'Enhanced 101 or 102 key US and Non US keyboards'* category, but the option can be changed from within the Windows Setup utility, opening the drop down *'Keyboard'* options menu within *'Change System Settings'*.

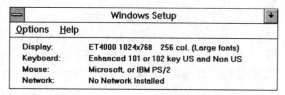

KEYBOARD LAYOUT

The *'Keyboard'* option chooses the physical size of the keyboard (e.g. an 83 key or a 102 key layout) and its electronic configuration - it says nothing about what each key actually represents. Different countries place different characters and symbols on the keycaps (see section on keyboards). To ensure that key presses correspond to the language of the country in which it used, the keyboard layout has to be notified to Windows. In the United Kingdom, that would mean choosing an English (International) setting as opposed to the English (American) setting, which places certain symbols on the keyboard in a different layout from British users. This option can also be changed after setup by using the *'International'* option within the *'Control Panel'* icon of the Main menu (see later).

KEYBOARD CUSTOMISATION

If the *'Keyboard'* option is chosen from the *'Control Panel'*, the response of the keyboard can be altered via the controls shown. The *'Delay Before First Repeat'* determines how long a key will be depressed before it begins to auto-repeat the character. The setting is achieved by dragging the marker block to a faster or slower setting along the speed bar. The *'Repeat Rate'* determines the speed at which the key will auto-repeat the character. This setting is also achieved by dragging the marker block to a faster or slower setting along the speed bar. Below the speed bar there is a test box that allows the

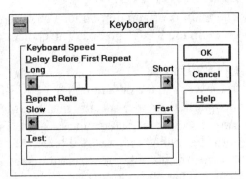

settings to be tested, before exiting the window by clicking on the *'OK'* button..

MOUSE SELECTION

Most varieties of mouse are Microsoft compatible but a range of drivers for other brands is supplied - including Logitech, Genius Olivetti and Hewlett-Packard. If the mouse in used is not specifically mentioned in the list, it should either be selected as a Microsoft option, or should come with its own specific driver on disc.

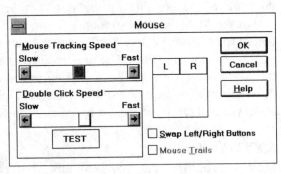

Any new mouse driver can be added to the list via the Windows Setup utility. If non-Windows applications are to be run in a Window using the mouse, then the mouse driver will have to loaded prior to entering Windows. This can be achieved by adding DEVICE=C:\WINDOWS\MOUSE.SYS in the CONFIG.SYS file or calling MOUSE.COM from the AUTOEXEC.BAT file. Both files are resident in the WINDOWS sub-directory. Special configuration for the Genius mouse, Logitech mouse and others is covered in the README.WRI file.

MOUSE CUSTOMISATION

If the *'Mouse'* icon is chosen from the 'Control Panel' menu, a mouse customisation window is opened.

The *'Mouse Tracking Speed'* determines the speed of the mouse pointer across the monitor screen and the setting is achieved by dragging the marker block to a faster or slower setting along the speed bar.

The *'Double Click Speed'* is also determined by dragging the marker block to the desired setting. Below the speed bar there is a test box that will change colour if the box is double clicked within the time span set.

If the user of a machine is left-handed, the mouse will be manipulated by the fingers of that user's left hand. The role of the mouse buttons can be reversed, so that the left button carries out the functions of the right button and vice versa, to make for more natural use of the mouse. To enable this function, activate the box marked *'Swap Left/Right Buttons'*.

A mouse used with an LCD screen can be made more visible if the movement of the pointer leaves a trail behind it, the trail rapidly fading away. If the machine's video hardware does not support this function, the *'Mouse Trails'* box will not be activated as a valid choice for customisation. If the box is activated, the machine can have mouse trails enabled or disabled by clicking the box to contain a cross or be empty respectively.

NETWORK

Network options vary from having no network attached (the most likely option) to a wide range of commercially available local area network systems - including many Novell, 3 Com, Banyan and Lan Manager versions. Again, new products can be added to the list via the Windows Setup utility. Configuring and using Windows over a network is a complex process and some organisations have placed copies of Windows on every machine, rather than attempt to run Windows over a network.

Certainly, the documentation given in the Windows books, the NETWORKS.WRI file and other works should be carefully read before attempting to use Windows over a network. This will not be a problem for Workgroups for Windows which was designed to integrate Windows and networking.

Change System Settings

Display:	ET4000 1024x768 256 col. (Large fonts)
Keyboard:	Enhanced 101 or 102 key US and Non US keyboards
Mouse:	Microsoft, or IBM PS/2
Network:	Novell NetWare (shell versions 3.21 and above)
	No Network Installed
	Novell NetWare (shell versions 3.21 and above)
	Novell NetWare (shell versions 3.26 and above)
	Novell NetWare (shell versions below 3.01)

LANGUAGE

A range of working languages is offered during Custom Setup and this can also be altered using the *'International'* option within the *'Control Panel'* icon of the Main menu. This option controls the way

International

Country:	United Kingdom	OK
Language:	English (International)	Cancel
Keyboard Layout:	British	Help
Measurement:	Metric	
List Separator:	.	

Date Format
10/06/95   Change...
10 June 1995

Currency Format
£1.22
-£1.22   Change...

Time Format
08:36:43   Change...

Number Format
1,234.22   Change...

applications will sort data, taking into account any special or accented characters in a language.

The *'Country'* option is used to determine the Windows date and time formats (i.e. DD/MM/YY or MM/DD/YY), along with numeric and currency formats (i.e. £ symbols or $ symbols, using commas as numerical separators instead of full stops, etc.). This option is not offered during Setup.

The *'Measurements'* option determines whether to use metric or English units of measurement. This option is also not offered during Setup.

PRINTERS

Installing printers under Windows involves three stages:
- Choosing the required printer type(s)
- Choosing which printer port will service which printer
- Choosing any printer settings

PRINTER SELECTION

Printer options can be set up using the *'Printers'* option from the *'Control Panel'* icon or the *'Print Manager'* icon, both in the Main group. This displays any printer drivers that are already installed (this will be zero for a new installation). Since hundreds of possible drivers exist, only the ones actually required by the user reside on the machine's hard disc; the others are either resident on the Windows installation discs or are supplied with a particular model of printer. New drivers can be installed by clicking the *'Add >>'* button. This displays a large list of all printer drivers that are currently held on the Windows installation discs. When the desired printer is highlighted and the *'Install'* button clicked, the user is prompted to insert the particular disc that contains the specified printer driver.

Printers

Default Printer
IBM 4039 LaserPrinter PS on LPT1:

Installed Printers:
HP LaserJet 4L on LPT1:
HP LaserJet on LPT1:
HP LaserJet Series II on LPT1:
IBM 4039 LaserPrinter PS on LPT1:
IBM 4039-12R Print Accelerator on LPT1:

Set As Default Printer

☒ Use Print Manager

List of Printers:
Agfa Compugraphic 400PS
Agfa Compugraphic Genics
Apple LaserWriter
Apple LaserWriter II NT
Apple LaserWriter II NTX
Apple LaserWriter Plus
Apricot Laser

Close
Connect...
Setup...
Remove
Add >>
Help
Install...

The driver is then copied on to the machine's hard disc (in the WINDOWS\SYSTEM sub-directory) and added to the list of installed printers. If the required driver is supplied with a particular printer, then it is installed by choosing the *'Install Unlisted or Updated Printer'* option from the list of printers. If there is no available driver for a particular printer, consult the printer manual as the machine might be compatible with or emulate a listed printer. Alternatively, Microsoft, the printer manufacturer or a public domain library may supply the wanted driver.

DEFAULT PRINTER

The default printer is the one that will be used when a job is printed out without first specifically mentioning which printer should be used. It follows that the default printer should be the one mostly commonly used. If there is only one installed printer then it is automatically the default printer.

PORT SELECTION

Once installed, printers are designated a particular output port for their operations, from the usual choices of LPT1, LPT2, LPT3, COM1, COM2, COM3 and COM4. The actual port chosen may be a parallel port or a serial port, dependent upon the printer to be connected. Assigning a port to a printer is achieved by highlighting the desired printer and selecting the *'Connect'* option from the *'Printers'* panel of *'Control Panel'*. A panel offers a range of port choices, with the possible options shown as being present. Not all the ports displayed in the list may be physically connected (not many machines, for example, have four serial ports) and a port which does exist may already be in use for another device, such as a mouse. Any port which is not available is displayed as not being present. The required port is highlighted and the *'OK'* button clicked.

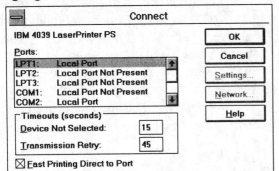

The *'Device Not Selected'* figure is alterable and determines the number of seconds that will elapse before Windows reports that the printer is unavailable. The *'Transmission Retry'* figure is also alterable and determines the number of seconds that will elapse if a printer is currently busy before a message is given that the printer will not accept the print job.

The *'Fast Printing Direct to Port'* option can be enabled/disabled by clicking on the box; an 'X' in the box denotes that fast printing is enabled. If fast printing is enabled, Windows writes directly to the printer, by-passing MSDOS; when disabled, DOS print interrupts are used and this slows printing down somewhat. If an application requires the use of DOS print interrupts, then the *'Fast Printing Direct to Port'* option should be disabled.

CONFIGURING SERIAL PORTS

If a serial port is chosen for a printer then the configuration of that port is achieved by clicking on the *'Settings'* button which appears in the *'Connect'* display. This allows the baud rate (i.e. speed of transmission) and the composition of the data (i.e. size of data packet and whether the printer expects parity bits and stop bits) to be set up, along with the transmission protocols (i.e. whether the usual Xon/Xoff method of flow control is in operation or whether the printer carries out its own hardware control of data flow). The correct settings for these parameters can be found by consulting the manual for the serial printer to be connected.

PRINTER SETTINGS

This reveals a configuration panel as shown. This allows printer characteristics such as printer resolution, paper size (A4, fanfold), paper feed type (tractor, manual, auto sheet feeder) and print orientation (portrait, landscape) to be established. The actual choices offered depend upon the printer being configured. For example, an Epson dot-matrix printer will not offer the option to choose printer cartridges because it does not support them. Similarly, a sub-menu of the printer menu may offer options to download fonts to a laser or ink-jet printer. Options will also allow the print intensity and the graphics dithering method to be established. Where a printer has plug-in font cartridges, a list of supported cartridges will appear as a menu option and the user can click on the ones actually in use. Information on problems with specific printers is given in the PRINTERS.WRI file which is installed along with Windows.

Another setting lets the user decide the priority to be given to printing(the background job) over normal Windows applications processing (the foreground job)

The selection can be made via the *'Background Printing'* option of the Print Manager's *'Options'* menu.

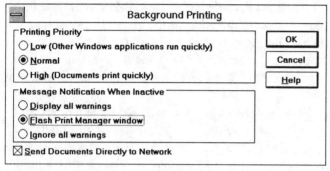

If printing is given a Low priority, the print tasks are only carried out while the application package is not occupying processor time. This slows down the printing process but speeds up applications.

If printing is given a High priority, the printing will be much faster but the application may slow down almost to a stop.

The Normal priority is a compromise on printing and application processor time.

VIRTUAL MEMORY

Computers with 80386 chip upwards support *'virtual memory'* techniques. This allows Windows to use free space on the hard disc as if it was extra computer memory. In this way, the computer is fooled into thinking it has more memory at its disposal than actually exists. When Windows runs out of extended memory, its hardware routines swap part of the memory contents to a disc file. Indeed, Windows doesn't even know whether any particular part of its information is being stored in memory or on disc, as the operations of virtual memory are invisible to it. The overall result is that the machine is able to run more programs at any one time than would otherwise be possible. This avoids the dreaded *'out of memory'* messages that can occur when a machine with little extended memory attempts to open a second window. Temporarily storing information from memory on to hard disc frees that amount of memory for another program. The larger the disc area used, the more programs can be accommodated. The area of disc space that is used to store the information is occupied by a *'swap file'*. The virtual address space is handled in 4k pages. When a required page is not currently held in actual memory, the contents for that page have to be fetched from disc.

There are two types of swap file:

- TEMPORARY SWAPFILE

  These files are only present when Windows is being run and they are deleted again when Windows is exited. The temporary swap file is called WIN386.SWP. Using temporary swap files is the slower of the two methods, since it has to make use of the normal DOS calls and normal ROM BIOS routines for its disc operations. Since these only work in Real mode, file activity has to be achieved by temporarily switching from Protected mode to Real mode; after the file activity, Protected mode is restored again. Although slower, this method has the advantage of maximising the amount of free disc space for applications.

- PERMANENT SWAPFILE

  A permanent swap file will remain on the hard disc as hidden files, even when they are not currently storing any information. To achieve this, a permanent and contiguous area of free disc space is dedicated for use as a swap file. The main swap file is called 386SPART.PAR and is hidden in the drive's root directory; it is accompanied by a read-only file called SPART.PAR that resides in the WINDOWS directory. The hidden file in the root directory is the larger file and requires a large contiguous area of disc space. This ensures that reading from the disc is not slowed down by constant references to the disc's FAT table (see section on disc structure). Since the 386SPART.PAR is always located at a known point on the hard disc, a contiguous read from the disc surface can be obtained with reduced movement of the read head. The net result is that this is a faster method than temporary swap files. If a user has a small RAM size, 4Mb or less, and runs a number of large programs, the time saving can have a significant effect on overall machine performance. Unfortunately, it also means that a sizeable section of hard disc has to be permanently devoted to the swap file - even when the machine is only running in normal DOS mode.

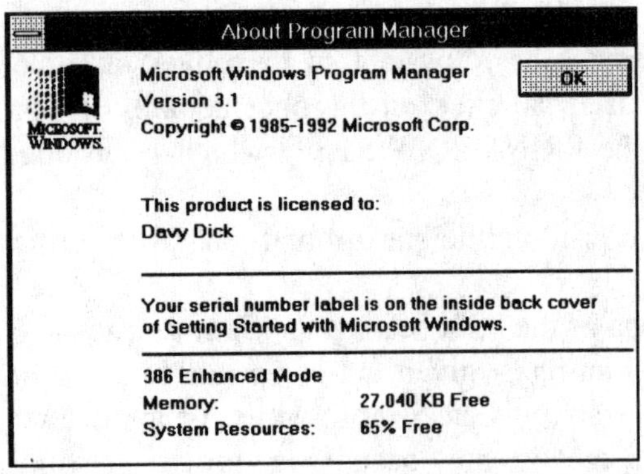
About Program Manager
Microsoft Windows Program Manager
Version 3.1
Copyright © 1985-1992 Microsoft Corp.
OK
This product is licensed to:
Davy Dick
Your serial number label is on the inside back cover of Getting Started with Microsoft Windows.
386 Enhanced Mode
Memory: 27,040 KB Free
System Resources: 65% Free

If the *'About Program Manager'* box is clicked within *'Program Manager'*, a window opens to provide the user with information about the current operating mode for Windows. It displays the mode as either Standard or Enhanced. It then displays the amount of memory available for Windows processing. The picture shows that around 27Mb of memory is available on that particular machine. In fact, the machine has 16Mb of RAM fitted, of which 3Mb has been devoted to a RAM drive. The figure displayed is a combination of the actual physical memory available and the virtual memory provided by a permanent swap file. As can be seen, the total is well beyond the actual physical memory resources of the machine and, therefore, plenty of opportunities exist to extend Window's processing memory, if this is desired.

The '*System Resources'* figure reports on the usage of the 64k block of memory used by Windows for its housekeeping. This area is known as the FSR (*'Free Systems Resources')* and stores information on windows, icons, fonts, dialog boxes, etc. If its usage exceeds 75% (i.e. only 25% free), the system faces becoming unstable. When there is only 15% free, the system will be unable to open another window, regardless of how much other memory is available.

OMITTING A SWAP FILE

It should be noted that, since disc access is much slower than memory access, using virtual memory slows down program execution. For machines with lots of memory, 16Mb or more, swap files can be dispensed with altogether and all operations can be run within the existing actual extended memory. This results in a faster operation than disc-based swap file activity. Also, if a user only runs one or two applications at any one time (a common situation), there is no real benefit in having a swap file.

SETTING SWAP FILES

If the *'Virtual Memory'* button is clicked in the *'386 Enhanced'* window from the *'Control Panel'* icon in the Main Menu, the virtual memory settings are displayed and can be altered. These settings are:

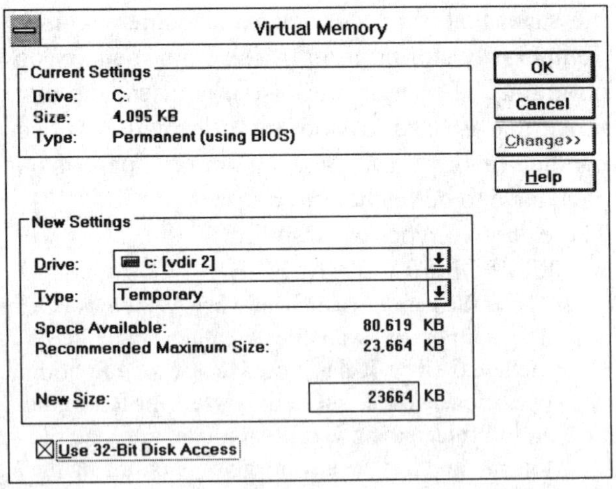
Virtual Memory
Current Settings
Drive: C:
Size: 4,095 KB
Type: Permanent (using BIOS)
OK
Cancel
Change>>
Help
New Settings
Drive: c: [vdir 2]
Type: Temporary
Space Available: 80,619 KB
Recommended Maximum Size: 23,664 KB
New Size: 23664 KB
Use 32-Bit Disk Access

DISC DRIVE

This allows the drive for a swap file to be chosen. If the disc is partitioned, choose the partition with the most free space. If a disc compressor such as Stacker or Superstore is being used with a disc, a permanent swap file should be allocated to the uncompressed portion of the disc. This solves the problem of Windows wanting to talk directly to the disc controller, while the compression device driver software requires all disc activity to be directed through it.

SWAP FILE TYPE

The user can choose the type of swap file from *'Permanent'*, *'Temporary'* and *'None'*.

If the *'None'* option is chosen, then Windows will operate within the restrictions of the machine's physical memory size. If the *'Temporary'* option is chosen, the optimum use of disc space is calculated and presented as a recommended choice. This would be around half of the available disc space, or four times the size of the actual RAM, whichever is the smaller value. This choice can be altered by typing a value into the *'New Size'* box.

If the *'Permanent'* option is chosen, the recommended size takes into account how much contiguous free space exists on the disc. It is therefore advisable that the disc be defragmented before taking this option, using Norton's Speedisk or other similar defragmentation software.

In any case, when the *'OK'* button is clicked to decide the chosen method, the user is invited to reboot Windows to allow the settings to take effect.

32-BIT ACCESS

The normal disc access process is slow, consisting of applications calling a DOS interrupt (int 21h), the DOS interrupt calling a BIOS interrupt (int13h) and the BIOS controlling the disc controller.   With 32-bit access enabled, Windows detects whether the machine's disc controller is capable of 32-bit access mode.   If so, it will communicate with the controller card directly, using 32-bit instructions.

This feature is implemented while still in Protected mode and produces an improved virtual memory performance, due to faster disc access times.   Suitable controllers are Seagate ST506 or Western Digital 1003 compatibles; this covers most modern systems apart from SCSI and ESDI types.   Direct 32-bit access also allows more DOS applications to run than there is physical memory, something that cannot be done otherwise.   Without 32-bit disc access techniques of paging, DOS applications are not able to be written to virtual memory, even if a permanent swap file is present.   This option is only enabled if the hard disc controller can support this feature.   The default is to have 32-bit access toggled off, as it can cause disc error problems when used with battery-powered portable machines.

WINDOWS FONTS

Fonts are collections of alphabetic, numeric, punctuation and symbol characters as will be seen on the computer monitor or printed to paper. Fonts have three characteristics:

TYPE FACE -   the actual *shape* of the characters, such as Arial (a sans serif face i.e. plain outline with no feet or twirls), Times Roman (a serifed face used in many publications) and Gothic.

TYPE SIZE -   the actual *height* of the characters as measured in points, there being 72 points to an inch. A 36-point headline, then, will be half an inch high.

TYPE STYLE -   such as bold, italics or underlined.

In addition, Windows handles screen and printer fonts in two ways:

BITMAP

A bitmap font holds an actual picture of each character, composed of a collection of pixels.   This means that each point size must either have a different bitmap or an existing bitmap has to be scaled up or down. In addition, each type style has to be independently stored. So, there is a bitmap for the normal version, the bold version, the italicised version and the underlined version - not to mention the bold underlined, etc.   Bitmap fonts occupy lots of disc space, particularly for the larger point sizes. They are faster than True Type since the image can be dumped to the printer without any translation.

TRUE TYPE

True Type fonts do not store an exact bitmap picture of every type face, size and style.   Instead, it stores a description of a type face.   This description is stored as geometric mathematical formulae that outline the shape of the various parts of the character in normal, bold, italic and bold italic modes. When an application chooses to use a particular font, the font description is fetched and scaled to the required type size.   Windows then generates a bitmap of the font for use with the screen or printer. This process is known as *'rasterising'*. A slight manipulation of the factors in the formulae allows the faces to be scaled to any size. This has two distinct advantages:

- The computer need only store the set of four descriptions for each type face, compared to a set for every font size with bitmaps.
- The mathematical formulae of true type fonts maintain smooth curves even with large type sizes, whereas bitmaps tend to become very 'blocky' and ugly at larger sizes.

FONTS AND PRINTING

The fonts to be selected for use on a particular machine will depend on the type of printer it is connected to. The common methods for printing text are:

- Using the font resident in the printer.   Installing a printer's software may have resulted in fonts being added to the Windows system.   If these fonts are used, Windows is compatible with the printer and, after a minimum of setup, the data is sent to the printer as a set of ASCII codes.   This is a fast method, since there is no special translation required.   However, the printer software may not have installed a matching set of screen fonts and Windows will have to use the closest match. Hence, the user will have lost WYSIWYG (What You See Is What You Get).
- Sending the bitmap straight to the printer.   This may be from a bitmap font or may be the bitmap that was created by rasterising a True Type font.   A normal A4 page would need around 1Mb to store all the page's information.   However, it is common for printers to only have an internal

memory buffer of 512k or less.   That is why a highly complex sheet is often ejected after only printing the top half of the page.   The solution lies in adding more buffer memory to the printer or in using some method of compressing the data.

- Describing the fonts to be used to the printer.   Once the printer has stored the definition of each font, the computer can send plain ASCII with the consequent saving in time.   There are various methods dependent on the printer in use.   These include PCL5 (Hewlett Packard's Printer Control Language 5) and Postscript. In each case the printer driver converts each font before sending it to the printer.   Printers that support PDL (Microsoft's Page Description Language) have some True Type fonts already embedded in the printer. Since the fonts don't have to be download, printing is greatly speeded up. They are also able to download True Type fonts at a faster rate than PCL5 or Postscript downloads.

SETTING UP FONTS

The management of fonts is carried out from the *'Fonts'* option in the *'Control Panel'*.

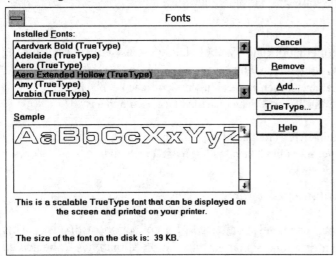

This displays a list of the fonts that are already installed in Windows and a font can be highlighted to see a sample of that font, as shown.   These are the fonts that will be available within Windows applications such Word, Draw, etc.

Clicking the *'True Type'* button produces a small menu which allows Windows to use Truc Typc fonts which print exactly as seen on the screen; these are scaleable fonts and each font is comprised of two files with a .FOT and a .TTF extension.   This mini-menu also offers that only True Type fonts be used (i.e. raster fonts and other vector fonts are ignored in Windows applications).

A font can be removed from the installed list by highlighting the font and clicking on the *'Remove'* button.   The font is not removed from the hard disc; it simply no longer appears as a Windows font option.   However, if the *'Remove Font from Disc'* box is enabled the font is deleted from the hard disc.

A font can be added to the installed list by clicking on the *'Add'* button.   The drive and path of the disc which contains the new font are entered.   This will result in a list of the available new fonts being displayed in the boxed titled *'List of Fonts'*.   If all the fonts are to be installed, the *'Select All'* button is clicked, otherwise the desired font is highlighted. Clicking the *'OK'* button adds the font(s) to the installed list.   Remember that too many installed fonts will impede the operation of Windows.

Add Fonts		
List of Fonts:		OK
BahamasHeavy (TrueType)		Cancel
BahamasLight (TrueType)		
barcod39 (TrueType)		Select All
Bard (TrueType)		
Bedrock (TrueType)		Help
Beehive (TrueType)		
BLADES bold (TrueType)		

Directories:
c:\windows\system

🗁 c:\
📂 windows
📂 system

Drives:
💾 c: vdir 2

☒ Copy Fonts to Windows Directory

SETTING THE DATE AND TIME

The computer's real-time clock can be set within Windows. It has exactly the same effect as using the DATE and TIME commands under DOS.

The facility can be called up via the *'Date/Time'* option in *'Control Panel'*.

Date & Time	
Date	OK
10/06/95	Cancel
Time	Help
09:51:54	

ALTERING THE DESKTOP

The Windows environment can be customised for the individual user's taste. This includes the type of background 'wallpaper' or pattern and the type of screen saver. Access to these changes is via the *'Desktop'* option in the *'Control Panel'* choice within the Main group.

The Windows default desktop colour is grey and this can be altered to a pattern chosen from the given list. If preferred the *'Edit Pattern'* button can be clicked and the user can create his/her own design. An alternative to a pattern would be to have a picture as a background, known as *'wallpaper'*. This can be chosen from the given list or the user can activate the Wallpaper *'File'* box and type in the drive, path and filename of any existing graphics file with a .BMP extension.

Windows requires more system resources to display a graphics wallpaper file than it requires to display a pattern or a solid colour. This means that a complex BMP file can consume sufficient resources to prevent Windows functioning efficiently. If available, an .RLE graphics file can be used as this will use up much less resources.

Finally, the Screen Saver option is designed to replace the normal screen contents after a user-defined delay. This is aimed at preventing degradation of the phosphor coating on the CRT if the machine is left on with a static screen image. The screen saver is normally some kind of moving display to prevent localised phosphor burns. A minor industry has sprung up to provide a huge variety of amusing and novelty screen savers.

CREATING PROGRAM GROUPS

Windows will create a number of default Program Groups, such as 'Main' and 'Accessories'. When applications are installed, they mostly create their own groups. Each group is a window in which icons of a similar nature are placed. So, the Accessories Group will have icons for Windows Write, the Calendar, Calculator, etc. Users may wish to have a collection of their own regularly used utilities placed in a single group. The steps for creating a new Program Group are:

- Choose *'New'* from the File Menu of Program Manager.
- Choose *'Group'* when asked to select a new Group or a new Item.
- Enter the name of the Group in the *'Description'* dialog box. The name entered here is one used as the title below the group icon.
- Click on the *'OK'* button.

An existing group can be deleted by highlighting the icon and pressing the 'Delete' key.

CREATING PROGRAM ITEMS

Each item in a group window is a utility, a program or a document file. Double clicking on an icon or application icon will run that particular program. Double clicking on a document opens the application that created the document (e.g. Word or Excel) then opens the document within that application.

An item can be added to a group by following these steps:

- Highlight the group into which the item is to be added.
- Choose *'New'* from the File Menu of Program Manager.
- Choose *'Item'* when asked to select a new Group or a new Item.
- Enter the name of the item in the *'Description'* dialog box. The name entered here is one used as the title below the icon in the group window.
- Enter the program filename, including drive and path (e.g. C:\UTILS\CORETEST.EXE) in the *'Command Line'* dialog box. If the location of the wanted file is not known, the directory structure can be inspected using the *'Browse'* option.
- The *'Working Directory'* is the name of the current directory while the program is running. The name of the directory can be entered so that any other existing components of the program (and any other files the application creates) can be accessed.
- The *'Change Icon'* button allows a choice of icons if the default icon is not wanted.

CREATING CUSTOM OBJECTS

Many users may constantly work with the same few files - e.g. a spreadsheet for the company budget, a database of customers, a standard word processing letter template, etc. After loading Windows, the user would have to load the appropriate package and then load the required file. Creating custom Program Groups would improve the situation as outlined above. Even better would be a Program Group that contained icons of the actual <u>files</u> that the user would wish to use. Double-clicking on an icon would both load the application and the desired file in the one operation. This can be achieved as below:
- Create a new Program Group, as outlined above.
- Open File Manager and size and position it so that the File Manager and the Program Group are both visible.
- Use the File Manager to find each file that is regularly used.
- Drag each file into the Program Group.

WINDOWS AND DOS

As time goes by, more and more applications work under Windows but there is still a wide variety of DOS programs in use. It is important that DOS utilities and applications are still able to be run under Windows.

A DOS program can be run by using the *'Run'* option in the *'File'* menu of Program Manager, or by double clicking on an icon for a DOS package.

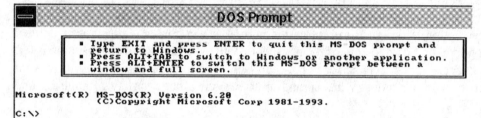

If fuller access to the DOS directory system is required, the user can shell out to DOS via the *'Dos Prompt'* icon as shown. This opens a window in which the user can carry out all the normal DOS activities (e.g. DIR, FORMAT, COPY, etc.) or run a DOS package. When first opened, the DOS window will not occupy the whole screen. For a larger viewing area, the window can be maximised by pressing the Alt and Enter keys. Pressing the same key combination a second time toggles the window down to the initial partial Screen size.

When the DOS session is over, it is important that the user returns to the initiating Windows code. Opening Windows from the DOS prompt at this stage will attempt to open another occurrence of Windows and places a great strain on resources. If this is carried out several times, the system will run out of resources and will probably crash.

BALANCING DOS AND WINDOWS

It is not possible to balance Windows resources between different Windows applications - all are treated equally. However, it is possible to dictate how time resources are divided between DOS tasks and Windows tasks. This is achieved through the *'Scheduling'* selections in the *'386 Enhanced'* option with the Control Panel Group.

If the *'Foreground'* and *'Background'* values are equal, then DOS and Windows run at the same speeds whether they are in the foreground or the background. A large foreground value means that a DOS application in the background will run very slowly; if the *'Exclusive in Foreground'* button is made active, completely stops a DOS application running in the background.

The *'Minimum Timeslice'* value sets the time each Windows application gets before control is passed to the next Windows application. Small settings mean smoother transitions between applications - but they run more slowly. A larger timeslice sacrifices smooth transitions for faster speeds.

WINDOWS CONFIGURATION FILES

Every time Windows is entered, it looks up the contents of two files - SYSTEM.INI and WIN.INI, which are both stored in the WINDOWS directory.   The information held in these files is used to set up Windows to match both the existing computer hardware and the declared needs of the user.

SYSTEM.INI

The SYSTEM.INI file stores configuration information on how Windows interacts with the machine's hardware.   It can be regarded as the Windows equivalent of CONFIG.SYS.   The file is created automatically during the Windows installation process, with some of the information being supplied by the user during the Setup procedure.   Many of the settings can be altered by the various options offered within Control Panel.   The panel displays only a sample of the settings that are stored within the SYSTEM.INI file; many of the settings are omitted for ease of reading.

As can be seen, there are a number of different sections, each section heading being enclosed by square brackets.   The lines below each heading contain specific information on particular aspect of the configuration.

The **[boot]** section contains details of all the drivers and Windows modules. The first line informs Windows that the Program Manager shell should be used upon entry.   If Norton Desktop were to be used instead, the line would be changed to SHELL=NDW.EXE. The network assignment line has no filename attached to it. A blank indicates the default situation, in this case indicating that no network is attached. The language dll (dynamic link library) is set to English, possibly via the Control Panel.

The **[keyboard]** section shown indicates that a UK keyboard is in use and that the keyboard is of the 101/102 keys types.

The **[boot.description]** section contains a list which describes the present settings for all those settings that can be altered during Setup.

The **[386Enh]** section contains the settings used for running in 386 Enhanced Mode. These include the disc drive where the swap file is located, the size of that swap file and whether 32-bit access is enabled.

```
EXTRACT FROM A TYPICAL SYSTEM.INI FILE

[boot]
shell=progman.exe
mouse.drv=mouse.drv
network.drv=
language.dll=langeng.dll
sound.drv=mmsound.drv
comm.drv=comm.drv
system.drv=system.drv
keyboard.drv=keyboard.drv

[keyboard]
keyboard.dll=kbduk.dll
type=4

[boot.description]
display.drv=S3 V1.4 1024x768 16/256 colors (Large fonts)
mouse.drv=Microsoft, or IBM PS/2
network.drv=No Network Installed
language.dll=English (International)
system.drv=MS-DOS System
codepage=437
woafont.fon=English (437)
keyboard.typ=Enhanced 101 or 102 key US and Non US keyboards

[386Enh]
32BitDiskAccess=on
MinTimeslice=20
WinTimeslice=100,50
PermSwapDOSDrive=C
PermSwapSizeK=17892

[standard]

[NonWindowsApp]

[mci]

[drivers]
```

The **[standard]** section contains similar information for use in Standard Mode.

The **[NonWindowsApp]** section contains information about the use of DOS applications when used within Windows.   Typical information may be the number of text lines on the screen or the disc to be used for swapping DOS applications when in Standard Mode.

The **[mci]** section contains a list of the drivers being used to play files via the mci (Media Control Interface), such as CD players, wave players and synthesisers.

The **[drivers]** section is used where an installable device driver requires a parameter.   The [drivers] section links an alias to the command and parameters. This alias is then used in the [boot] declaration.

Since any changes to SYSTEM.INI alter the Windows views of the hardware, the user will have to exit to DOS and re-enter Windows for any changes to take effect.

Further details are contained in the SYSINI.WRI file which is installed with Windows.

WIN.INI

This file is often described as being concerned with the *'look'* and *'feel'* of the Windows environment. While this is largely true, the file also contains some hardware configuration information, such as the keyboard and mouse response times.   This is generally a much larger file than SYSTEM.INI, since it records information on many of the Windows applications.   The file can easily be hundreds of lines long, when all the applications and their configurations are recorded.   Again, therefore, the example shown displays only a small fraction of the assignments which appear under each heading.   In addition, not every heading is described.   Some of the more significant sections are:

EXTRACT FROM A TYPICAL WIN.INI FILE

```
windows]
spooler=yes
run=
Beep=yes
DoubleClickSpeed=724
KeyboardDelay=2
KeyboardSpeed=31
ScreenSaveActive=1
ScreenSaveTimeOut=120
load=
MouseSpeed=1

[Desktop]
wallpaper=marble.bmp

[Extensions]
pcx=pbrush.exe ^.pcx
wri=write.exe ^.wri
hlp=winhelp.exe ^.hlp
doc=C:\WINWORD\winword.exe ^.doc
ico=icondraw.exe ^.ico

[intl]
sLanguage=eng
sCountry=United Kingdom
iCountry=44
iTime=1
iCurrDigits=2
iMeasure=1
sCurrency=£
sShortDate=dd/MM/yy

[ports]
LPT1:=
LPT2:=
COM1:=9600,n,8,1,x
COM2:=9600,n,8,1,x

[Sounds]
SystemStart=tada.wav, Windows Start
SystemExit=chimes.wav, Windows Exit

[colors]
Background=192 192 192
Window=255 255 255
WindowText=0 0 0
ActiveBorder=192 192 192
Scrollbar=128 128 128

[fonts]
Arial (TrueType)=ARIAL.FOT
Arial Bold (TrueType)=ARIALBD.FOT

[PrinterPorts]
HP DeskJet Plus=HPDSKJET,LPT1:,15,45
```

The **[windows]** section contains some of the *'look and feel'* settings, with items such as the rate at which the cursor blinks, the width of the borders round windows, whether the machine will emit a beep if an error is encountered, keyboard repeat times and mouse response times.   This section, via the spooler= line, dictates whether the Windows Print Manager is enabled.   Any file(s) named in the load= assignment will be loaded and run minimised when Windows is entered.   Any file named in the run= assignment will be loaded and run in the main window when Windows is entered.   This can be a data file such as C:\LETTERS\REPORT.DOC.   There is no need to specify the application as Windows will associate the file extension with the appropriate application package.   It will automatically load the package and then load the specified file.

The **[Desktop]** section contains most the details of the appearance of the Windows desktop, with items such as the spacing between icons, what wallpaper should appear in the background and whether the wallpaper is centred or tiled.

The **[Extensions]** section links particular file extensions with their associated application programs.   For example, the Paintbrush program uses .PCX files.   This means that when a file is selected from File Manager, it first loads the required application then loads the selected file into the application, saving time.

The **[intl]** section dictates the format in which dates, times and number formats will appear.   The i before an assignment indicates that the parameter is an integer (i.e. a whole number with no decimal part) and an s prefix indicates that the parameter is a text string.   The example shows that the country is UK, the language is English and that the currency is a pound symbol.   The iCurrDigits indicates that there should be two decimal places after the decimal point in any currency display.   The iMeasure indicates 1 for English and 0 for metric measurements.

The **[ports]** section indicates the machine's parallel and serial ports and dictates the speed and protocols for serial ports.

The **[sounds]** section links particular sound files to events - e.g. what tune or sound clip will be played when Windows is opened or closed, or replacing the default beep sound.

The **[colors]** section dictates the colours to be used to paint the various parts of the Windows components, e.g. menu backgrounds and foreground, choice button backgrounds and foregrounds.   Each component is named and is followed by the RGB (red, green and blue) proportions to be used to determine the colour.   These numbers range from 0 to 255.

The **[fonts]** section contains a list of all the fonts which are to be loaded when Windows is entered. The list consists of the font name as it will appear in Windows dialogue boxes, then an equals sign followed by the filename of that particular font. Note that adding a font to the WIN.INI file does not make the font available to Windows - it must be installed via the *'Fonts'* option of the *'Control Panel'*.

The **[printerPorts]** section determines which printer driver is attached to which printer port.

Further details are contained in the WIN.INI file which is installed with Windows.

Most of the settings in WIN.INI are changed via the options in *'Control Panel'*. However, there will be occasions when it would be useful to directly edit INI files. For example, changing the fonts that are used to display text beneath icons can only be achieved by the direct editing of the WIN.INI file. If an INI file becomes corrupted it can prevent Windows from running. In such a case it may be easier to edit the system files than entirely re-install Windows.

OTHER INI FILES

The details of many Windows applications will be stored in their own separate INI files. Typical INI files might be MOUSE.INI, LOTUS.INI, MSACCESS.INI or EXCEL4.INI. These files will contain the particular colour settings and other configuration details for these applications.

MODIFYING INI FILES

All INI files are stored in plain ASCII format. This means that they can be readily altered using any ASCII editor, such as the DOS EDIT utility. Windows provides a utility known as SYSEDIT, which resides in the Windows\System sub-directory. This utility can be added to the Main or Accessories group, if it is anticipated that it will be required from time to time. Otherwise the file SYSEDIT.EXE can be invoked via File\Run. When run,

SYSEDIT displays the CONFIG.SYS, AUTOEXEC.BAT, WIN.INI and SYSEDIT files in four separate windows. The user can move between each window to read the file contents and alter any lines as required. Always make a backup of the files before any editing is attempted, in case there are any unexpected results. The editing process may involve tweaking some of the parameters that the Desktop cannot reach or it could involve using some of the undocumented features of Windows assignments. Another good reason for invoking SYSEDIT is to tidy up INI files. When applications are added to Windows, the system files may be updated to reflect the new configurations. However, removing applications icons does not alter the lines of system files. Even deleting the application completely from the hard disc will not alter the lines of INI files. When an application is removed from a machine, the INI lines of that application have to be removed by hand.

CONTROLLING USERS

In a work environment, it may be desirable that users are prevented from customising their own machines or from experimenting with various utilities. The Windows Control Panel provides many of the customising options and these facilities can be removed from the user's access by editing the CONTROL.INI file to include a [Don't Load] section.

The following example shows how the Network, Sound and Colour options can be disabled:

```
[Don't Load]
Network=true
Sound=true
Color=true
```

It may also be desirable to prevent users from using the *'Run'* option, thus preventing them from installing or running unauthorised software. The PROGMAN.INI file can be amended as shown:

```
[Restrictions]
NoRun=1
EditLevel=4
```

The *'NoRun'* line prevents the *'Run'* option from being available to users and they can only launch applications that have their own icons in a Program Group. This can go a long way to control games and viruses on office PCs. To be fully effective, File Manager has to be removed from these machines as WINFILE.INI cannot be edited to prevent the launching of applications. The *'EditLevel='* line prevents users from creating, deleting or renaming Program Groups as well as preventing the creation, deletion, moving and copying of program items. If the line *'NoFileMenu=1'* is added, it will remove the entire File Menu from Program Manager and users will be unable to create or delete items or groups or change program properties.

A less strict approach allows users to alter groups and items during a session, while ensuring that Windows always restarts with the default arrangements. In that way, users cannot permanently alter the Windows environment. This can be achieved by omitting the *'EditLevel'* line, or setting the level to zero, and adding the line *'NoSaveSettings=1'*. The *'NoSaveSetting='* line disables the *'Save Settings on Exit'* option in Program Manager's Options Menu and overrides and *'SaveSettings='* line in the [Settings] section of PROGMAN.INI.

Another options for the [Restrictions] section prevents the user from exiting Windows and entering DOS. This is achieved by adding the line

```
NoClose=1
```

and by deleting the DOS Prompt icon from the Main Group. If a user requires access to a DOS package, a PIF file can be created for the application and the user can access the package via the icon rather than via the DOS prompt.

TIDYING WINDOWS

Windows and Windows applications require hundreds of files for their operations. In addition, each application will modify the Windows configuration files as well as often adding their own INI files, DLL files and driver files. Many of these additions are necessary to allow wanted applications to run but many others are the result of trying out programs (particularly those that are given away with magazines). All unwanted components are occupying disc space as well as tying up valuable Windows resources. Windows INI files can become huge, filled with unused and unwanted lines and Windows 3.1 does not provide an uninstall utility. Fortunately, there is a trend among better software providers to provide their own facility to de-install their own package.

UNINSTALLING COMPONENTS

If, during Custom Setup, the full set of Windows components was installed, the unwanted components can easily be removed at a later date, using the *'Add/Remove Windows Components'* option within the *'Options'* choice of Windows Setup (to be found in the Main group). The boxes denoting the unwanted components should be clicked as active (i.e. a cross will appear in the box) and the *'OK'* button clicked. This will delete all the files in the named group (e.g. Accessories or Games). If certain files are to be deleted from a group while the rest remain, the *'SelectFiles'* button should be clicked; this will list the files in that group, allowing only nominated files to be deleted.

DELETING FILES

The *'Remove Windows Components'* process makes particular programs inactive (e.g. removing the program items or program group) but this does not remove the files from the hard disc. There is a wide range of files that can be removed without losing much Windows functionality:

- Unused Windows utility files (e.g. Calendar).
- Windows text files (e.g. WININI.TXT) and WRI files (e.g. PRINTERS.WRI).
- Unused application files.
- Temporary files left behind after a system crash (i.e. all .TMP files).

UNINSTALL UTILITIES

A range of Windows utilities has appeared to help the user to control the Windows environment. These include Uninstaller, Clean Sweep and WinDelete. These programs include facilities to detect unreferenced drivers and unused fonts and provide facilities to delete a program and all its linked components.

CONFIGURING WINDOWS 95

Like Windows 3.1, Windows 95 is a multitasking system although '95 performs these tasks much more efficiently.   Applications in 3.1 load in all the DLLs (software components) that it may need during the running of the application; with several applications running, there is soon a shortage of memory. Applications in Windows 95 only load in DLL components when they are required; this results in less memory overheads and so more applications can effectively multitask.   Windows 95 also supports multithreading which allows different parts of the same application to run at the same time.   A user, for example, can carry on using a word processor while it carries of a spell check or a file search.

HARDWARE REQUIREMENTS
For Windows 95, the minimum requirements were previously described.   The package comes in both CD-ROM and floppy disc versions; it is also available as an upgrade for existing DOS or Windows users and as a full installation version for new machines.

INSTALLATION STEPS
The steps in the upgrade from Windows 3.1 to '95 are:
1. Insert the installation disc in drive 'A'
2. Call up the Windows Program Manager.
3. Choose the *'File'* option within Program Manager.
4. Choose the *'Run'* sub-menu option.
5. Type A:\SETUP or use the 'Browse' option to locate the SETUP file.   The setup program will load in the files necessary to run 'Windows 95 Setup Wizard' which will then control the rest of the setup process. If floppy discs are being used, the user will be asked to change discs from time to time.
6. The Setup Wizard begins by interrogating the computer system.
7. The Option is given to
    a) install Windows 95 in the existing Windows directory on top of the 3.1 system
    b) install to another directory to create a *'Dual-Boot System'*.   This allows the user to choose during the boot up sequence to run Windows 95 or the existing DOS/Windows operating system software.   Pressing f4 during the bootup sequence runs the old software.   Since all the old settings are maintained, the user has to reinstall all the Windows applications in Windows 95.
8. The option is given to save the DOS and Windows 3.1 system files so that Windows 95 can be uninstalled later and control returned to the previous setup.
9. The Setup program checks the hardware components, enters the results in the Registry (see later) and then offers a selection of Setup Options:
    a) *'Typical'*   Best for most purposes.
    b) *'Portable'*   Also installs software for laptop systems to facilitate file transfers.
    c) *'Compact'*   Installs the minimum set of files; for computers with small hard discs.
    d) *'Custom'*   Allows the expert user to fully customise the system during installation.
10. The *'Typical'* setup option then request the following:
    ● User name and company name
    ● Confirmation of some hardware items (eg confirming that a CD-ROM drive or video capture card is in use).
11. The option is given to create a startup disc.   This copies all the files required to run the computer in the event that the hard disc develops a problem and creating the disc is highly recommended.
12. After creating the startup disc, the Setup Wizard copies the files from the installation floppies or CD on to the computer's hard drive.
13. Restarting Windows boots the computer into Windows 95.   The hard disc's boot sector (see chapter on disc drives) has been modified to run Windows 95.
14. Once rebooted, the Wizard performs some final activities such as setting up program icons in the *'Start'* menu.

INSTALLATION FROM DOS
The steps in installing Windows 95 on a machine that does not already use Windows 3.1 are:
1. Insert the installation disc in drive 'A'
2. At the DOS prompt type A:\ setup
3. The setup program runs ScanDisk to check the integrity of the machine's hard disc.
4. The remainder of the installation is as described above.

CUSTOM SETUP

The *'Typical'* Setup is useful for most purposes but the Custom Setup allows greater flexibility of installation. Custom Setup allows control over the configuration of a range of hardware and software components. The support engineer should have all the required facts at hand before running Custom Setup. If there is any doubt, the 'Typical' setup should be used. A machine that has been installed using the Typical Setup can always be altered later

UN-INSTALLING WINDOWS 95

If the old Windows and DOS configuration was saved during the installation process, Windows 95 can be easily removed. The steps are those described below for removing programs, with Windows 95 being chosen as the component for deletion.

OSR2

Windows Operating System Release 2 (OSR2) is currently only supplied with new systems and is not available as an upgrade. The main improvements over standard Windows 95 are:
- It handles hard drives that are larger than 2Gb without resorting to partitioning.
- It uses disc space more efficiently, producing less waste.
- It provides better support for playing CD-I movies.
- It provides added network and Internet features including DirectX
- It supports MMX chips.
- It brings together all the bug fixes, patches and 'service packs' that have been issued over the years.

On the down side, it uses a different disc format (known as FAT32) from Windows 95 (FAT16). This means that many existing low-level utilities will not work with OSR2. Microsoft's own Scandisk and Disk Defragmenter still work with OSR2 as do Norton Utilities 2.0.

INSTALLING/DELETING SOFTWARE

During the Setup process, applications may have been added to the *'Programs'* sub-menu of the *'Start'* menu. Additional 3.1 applications can be added in the conventional way by running the application's Setup program via the *'Run'* option on the *'Start'* menu. Windows 95 intercepts some of the normal installation activities and converts them into its own format. For example, additions to Program Manager are converted into Windows95 start menu shortcuts and INI entries are entered in the Registry. Windows 95 applications can be added as above or can be added via the following steps:

1. Open the *'Start'* menu.
2. Choose the *'Settings'* option.
3. Choose the *'Control Panel'* option.
4. Choose the *'Add/Remove Programs'* option.
5. Choose the *'Install'* option from the *'Install/Uninstall'* option.

The Install Wizard then carries out the required installation activities. Since Windows 95 applications are designed to provide uninstall facilities, they can removed simply by highlighting the application name on the pick list and choosing the *'Remove'* option.

Windows 3.1 application can also be installed using the Wizard but since they have built-in uninstall facilities, they cannot be automatically removed at a later date..

ADDING/DELETING WINDOWS COMPONENTS

Since the Typical Setup installed a minimum set of Windows components, extra components can be added at a later date, using the *'Windows Setup'* option within the *'Add/Remove Programs'* Window. A list is displayed with the installed components having their boxes checked. The boxes next to the desired extra components should be clicked as active (i.e. a tick will appear in the box) and the *'Apply'* button clicked. Similarly, components can be removed by making their boxes inactive (the tick is removed from the appropriate boxes) and the *'Apply'* button is clicked.

ALTERING THE SETUP

The main configuration options as determined by the Windows 95 Setup routine can be altered to suit personal choice or changing hardware and software demands.   This can range from adding and deleting programs as already described, through to altering the configuration of hardware such as keyboard, monitor, modem, printers, mouse and sound cards. It can also the system settings such as date and time, fonts to be used, user passwords, etc.   These alterations are made via the *'Control Panel'* which is accessed as an option from the *'Settings'* option on the *'Start'* menu.   The diagram gives an example of the alterations that may be available and some of the most common alterations are described below.

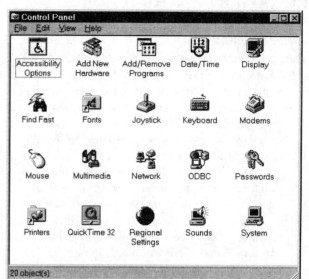

DISPLAY

Choosing the *'Display'* option in the *'Control Panel'* offers four choices for altering display properties. The *'Settings'* menu, as shown in the diagram, alters the main display characteristics. These are:

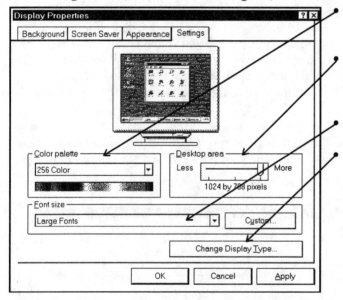

- Selecting the number of colours to be used (this depends on the maximum number of colours offered by the video card).
- Setting the screen resolution by clicking on the slider and moving it to the required setting (the maximum resolution depends on that supported by the screen and be the video card).
- Selecting large or small fonts for use with text to be displayed on the desktop.
- Selecting the video card and monitor to be used. Choosing this option results in options to change both the video card type and the monitor type. In each case, a list of manufacturers' types are displayed and the desired choice can be highlighted and the *'OK'* button clicked. Where the desired type is not in the list (probably because it has been introduced since Windows 95 was written) the *'Have Disk'* option can be clicked.   This allows the appropriate software to be loaded from the disc supplied by the manufacturer of the video card or monitor.

The *'Appearance'* option allows the screen display to set to the user's preferences. This includes the colours for Window text, message boxes, etc. Alternatively, a number of default colours schemes can be chosen from.

The *'Screen Saver'* option lists a selection of possible screen savers and these can be previewed before one is selected.   A 'Wait' text box sets the time delay before activating the screen saver.

The *'Background'* option allows the setting of:

- a background pattern
- a background wallpaper
- a background wallpaper made up from any other graphic on the hard disc, selected via the *'Browse'* option.

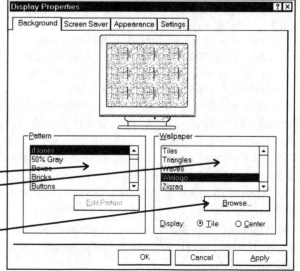

KEYBOARD CUSTOMISATION

If the *'Keyboard'* option is chosen from the *'Control Panel'*, the response of the keyboard can be altered via the options shown.

The *'Language'* sub-menu, as shown, provides for:

- Determining the keyboard layout. Different countries place different characters and symbols on the keycaps.   To ensure that key presses correspond to the language of the country in which it used, the keyboard layout has to be configured in Windows. In the United Kingdom, that would mean choosing an English (British) setting as opposed to the English (American) setting, which places certain symbols on the keyboard in a different layout from British users.

- Determining the keyboard variations within certain counties.   This does not apply to Britain and the standard *'British'* option would be chosen.

- Setting up hot-key switching between languages, where the same machine is used in a multi-lingual environment.   The *'Add'* option allows extra keyboard options to be added to the choice list.

The *'Speed'* sub-menu provides for:

- Setting the *'Repeat Delay'*.   A slider control determines how long a key will be depressed before it begins to auto-repeat thc charactcr; thc value is set by dragging the slider to a faster or slower setting along a speed bar.

- Setting the *'Repeat Rate'*.   This determines the speed at which the key will auto-repeat the character.   This setting is also achieved by dragging the slider to a faster or slower setting along a bar.   Below the speed bar there is a test box to test the settings, before exiting the window by clicking on the *'OK'* button.

- Setting the *'Cursor Blink Rate'* .   This determines how quickly the cursor will flash control and is also set by dragging a slider control.

The *'General'* sub-menu provides for matching the software to the physical keyboard in use. Most keyboards are covered by the *'Standard 101 or 102 key or Microsoft Natural Keyboard'* category, but the option can be changed by clicking the *'Change'* option and selecting the keyboard type currently in use.

MOUSE CUSTOMISATION

If the *'Mouse'* option is chosen from the *'Control Panel'*, the response of the mouse can be altered via the options shown.

The *'Motion'* sub-menu provides for:

- dragging a slider control to set the speed at which the pointer moves across the screen.

- dragging a slider control to set the length of trails from the moving pointer. A mouse used with an LCD screen or large screen monitor can be made more visible if the movement of the pointer leaves a trail behind it, the trail rapidly fading away. The machine can have mouse trails enabled or disabled by clicking the box to contain a check or be empty respectively.

The *'Buttons'* sub-menu sets up the mouse for left or right-handed use. If the user of a machine is left-handed, the mouse will be manipulated by the fingers of that user's left hand. The role of the mouse buttons can be reversed, so that the left button carries out the functions of the right button and vice versa, to make for more natural use of the mouse.   The *'Double Click Speed'* is determined by dragging the slider control to the desired setting. Below the speed bar there is a test box.

The *'Pointers'* sub-menu offers choices on the shape of mouse cursor or pointer during operations such as *'Busy'* or *'Select'*.

The *'General'* sub-menu provides for the selection of the mouse type currently in use. Most varieties of mouse are Microsoft compatible but a range of other common mouse drivers can be chosen from a pick list.

PRINTERS

Printer options can be set up using the *'Printers'* option from the *'Settings'*
option in the *'Start'* menu. This produces the screen shown on the right.
Clicking the *'Add Printer'* icon runs the Add Printer Wizard which steps the
user through the installation options.

Clicking on a particular printer icon produces a status window for that printer.
Clicking the *'Properties'* option in the *'Printer'* menu produces the screen
shown on the right. The *'General'* sub-menu allows a test page to printed to
check that the printer is functioning properly.

The *'Details'* sub-menu offers the following:

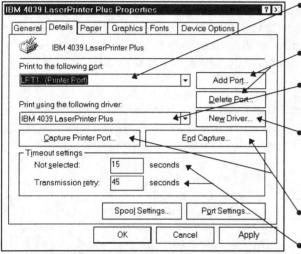

- Set the printer port to be used for the printer connection. The pick list displays the possible ports to choose from (eg LPT1, LPT2, COM1, COM2).
- This list can be altered by adding extra ports or deleting existing ports.
- Set the printer driver to be used with the printer. The pick list displays any drivers that are already installed.
- New drivers can be installed by clicking the *'New Driver'* button. This displays a pick list of all available Windows printer drivers. If the required driver is not in the list but is supplied with a printer, then it is installed by choosing the *'Have Disk'* option.
- Direct printing to a remote printer on the network or to the local printer attached to the computer.
- Set the amounts of time that will expire before a *'Not Selected'* message is displayed or before attempting to re-send a document to the printer.

- The *'Spool Settings'* button opens a sub-menu to configure print spooling arrangements. Windows 95 speeds up operations by creating a temporary file for a file that is to be printed. The temporary file provides the source for the printer allowing printing in the *'background'* - the user can carry on with other processing. There are options to commence printing as soon as the first page of a document is spooled or after the entire document is spooled. The first option is faster but the second option provides smoother background printing. The sub-menu also provides selection of two data formats for the spool file. EMF is the normal choice with RAW being used for Postscript printers. A final option allows printers that have bi-directional ports to be configured.
- The *'Port Settings'* button opens a sub-menu that allows for the spooling of MS-DOS print jobs.

The *'Paper'* sub-menu offers:

- Setting the paper size to be used in the printer.
- Setting printing to portrait or landscape mode.
- Setting the way paper will be handled (eg hand-fed single sheets or automatically from paper trays).
- Setting the number of copies that are to be printed.
- Determining whether to print in duplex mode (ie on both sides of the paper); only available if the printer is a duplex machine.

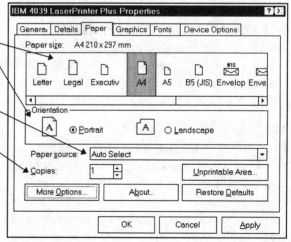

The *'Graphics'* sub-menu sets the printing resolution
in dots-per-inch (if the printer supports high resolutions, the graphics will be clearer), the method
dithering to print colour graphics as greyscales and
the intensity of shading to be used.

The *'Fonts'* sub-menu allows printers that have add-on fonts cartridges to be recognised. It also allows
True Type fonts to be downloaded as Bitmap soft fonts or to be printed as graphics; the latter option is
useful where a document uses many typefaces.

The *'Device Options'* sub-menu allows printers that have been given extra memory extensions to have
that extra memory recognised by Windows 95. It also allows control over the memory usage so that
large files do not result in running out of memory.

DEFAULT PRINTER

The default printer is the one that will be used when a job is printed out without first specifically mentioning which printer should be used. It follows that the default printer should be the one mostly commonly used. If there is only one installed printer then it is automatically the default printer. This is set using the 'Set as Default' option within the 'Printers' sub-menu of the 'Settings' option in the 'Start' menu.

CONFIGURING SERIAL PORTS

If a printer's serial port is to be used then the configuration of that port is achieved by clicking on the 'System' icon which appears in 'Control Panel'. Clicking on the 'Device Manager' option reveals a list of the machine's resources. This allows the baud rate (i.e. speed of transmission) and the composition of the data (i.e. size of data packet and whether the printer expects parity bits and stop bits) to be set up, along with the transmission protocols (i.e. whether the usual Xon/Xoff method of flow control is in operation or whether the printer carries out its own hardware control of data flow). The correct settings for these parameters can be found by consulting the manual for the serial printer to be connected.

COUNTRY SPECIFIC SETTINGS

Windows can support a range of different languages and these may have different date time formats (i.e. DD/MM/YY or MM/DD/YY), along with numeric and currency formats (i.e. £ symbols or $ symbols, using commas as numerical separators instead of full stops, etc.). These options can be accessed via the 'Regional Settings' icon in 'Control Panel'.

- The 'Regional Settings' sub-menu offers a range of countries and the desired country can be chosen from a pick list. This option controls the way applications will handle and present data, taking into account any special or accented characters in a language.
- The 'Number' sub-menu determines the way numbers will be presented in Windows applications such as Excel. The results of any changes is shown in sample windows.
- The 'Currency' sub-menu alters the symbols that will be used for currency and also the symbols to be used for decimal and thousands separators.
- The 'Time' and 'Date' sub-menus determine the way that the date is displayed within Windows (eg in the UK dates are shown as day-month-year while the US uses month-day-year).

SETTING THE DATE AND TIME

The computer's real-time clock can be set within Windows. It has exactly the same effect as using the DATE and TIME commands under DOS. The date and time settings within 'Regional Settings' only control the way they are displayed; they do not alter the computer's internal clock. This facility is called up via the 'Date/Time' option in 'Control Panel'.

MANAGING MEMORY

The concept and principles of virtual memory were explained earlier in the chapter.

Windows 95 automatically grabs all available physical memory in the computer, intending to use it for a range of utilities such as disc cache, fonts, etc. This memory is held by Windows 95 even when it is not in use. So, even a newly switched on machine will show that all the available memory is allocated.

As the program runs, Windows dynamically shares the memory between the system's resources and the user's applications. This does not always work out very efficiently and can leave a user's application being swapped to the 'virtual memory' on the disc drive, while the memory set aside for disc caching is not being fully utilised.

Windows automatically detects the amount of memory available for cache and sizes the cache to that value. However, as the program tasks are regularly being switched in an out of memory, the constant resizing of the cache leads to extra disc activity (called 'thrashing') as everything is moved around in the memory to fit the new size.

The wasted time and wear can be minimised by setting the maximum and minimum values of the disc cache. The following lines can be added to the SYSTEM.INI file:

```
[vcache]
MinFileCache =1024
MaxFileCache=8192
```

The maximum value depends upon the actual amount of physical memory present. About half the actual memory is a reasonable figure for the setting. These settings speed up normal processing as more of the application is in memory and disc trashing is greatly reduced. Where users are carrying out heavy database, video or imaging work, the settings may be increased to reflect the greater reliance on sustained data throughput.

VIRTUAL MEMORY

Windows 95 also detects how much disc space is available for virtual memory and automatically resizes the virtual memory amount when required. Windows 95 is normally left to organise its own management but user configuration can be achieved via the *'System'* icon in *'Control Panel'*. Clicking the *'Performance'* option followed by the *'Virtual Memory'* option reveals dialogue boxes to set the drive to be used along with minimum and maximum sizes. Setting a high value minimises the number of times that the memory area will have to be resized.

Where there is more than one disc drive in the computer, the drive with the fastest access times and the highest data rate should be used for the swap file. This will improve overall performance.

WINDOWS FONTS

The general description of fonts was given on page 227 and the main differences between font handling in Windows 3.1 and Windows 95 are:

- With Windows 3.1, a family of fonts had both a FOT and a TTF file; Windows 95 only require a TTF file for each font.
- With Windows 3.1, fonts were listed and loaded via INI files. In Windows 95, font control is vested in the Registry, although a WIN.INI file remains to maintain backward compatibility with 3.1 applications.
- With Windows 3.1, every font was loaded in during the startup process.
  Windows 95 has immediate access to the fonts through the Registry and does not require to pre-load all the fonts.

SETTING UP FONTS

The management of fonts is carried out from the *'Fonts'* option in the *'Control Panel'*.

This displays a list of the fonts that are already installed in Windows; these are the fonts that will be available within Windows applications such Word, Excel, etc.

The *'File'* sub-menu allows:

- The addition of new fonts via the *'Install New Font'* option on the *'File'* menu. This opens an *'Add Fonts'* window where the location of the new font can be given and the name of the font highlighted before clicking the *'OK'* button. The location can be a floppy disc and a box can be checked to copy the font(s) from the original location into the Windows fonts directory.
- The deletion of existing fonts from the system. Highlight the font from the pick list and choose the *'Delete'* option from the *'File'* menu.

CUSTOMISING THE START MENU

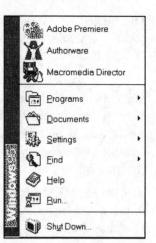

When the computer boots into Windows 95, it displays a *'Start'* button on the bottom taskbar. Clicking this button displays a menu similar to that on the right. The bottom seven entries on the menu are the standard choices. Where an entry has an arrowhead, clicking the entry produces another menu. The top three entries have been added later so that commonly used applications can be quickly accessed without hunting through sub-menus. This is achieved by:

- Choosing the *'Settings'* option from the *'Start'* menu.
- Choosing the *'Taskbar'* option from the *'Settings'* menu.
- Choosing the *'Start Menu Programs'* option from the *'Taskbar'* menu'.
- Choosing the *'Add'* option from the *'Start Menu Programs'* menu.
- Typing in the full name of the application file (ie drive, path and filename) or using the *'Browse'* utility to search for the file on the disc.
- A screen such as that below displays the user's disc structure and the wanted folder should be highlighted before clicking the *'Next'* button. If required, a new folder can be created at this stage.

If the *'Start Menu'* is chosen as the destination option, the application will appear on the Start Menu on bootup.

If the *'Programs'* option is chosen, the application will appear in the Programs menu.

If a sub-folder is chosen (eg *'Internet'* in the example shown) then the application can be run by opening that particular folder.

- When a folder has been selected, the application name, as it will appear in the menu can then be entered.

An existing application can be deleted using the *'Remove'* option in the Taskbar properties menu.

USING DOS FROM WIN95

Users have the option of using DOS from inside Windows 95, where DOS activities appear within a window area. This can be invoked by clicking the *'Start'* Button, choosing *'Programs'* from the pick list displayed and selecting the *'MS-DOS Prompt'* option. DOS commands and DOS application programs can be run from within this window, although this is not the best method if regular DOS work has to be carried out. Where a user requires to access DOS on a semi-regular basis, it can be accessed without any Windows overheads via the system boot options.

STARTUP OPTIONS

During the machine's bootup sequence, it will display a *'Starting Windows 95'* message. If the f8 key is hit at this point, a menu is displayed as shown. Choosing the sixth option takes the user directly to the DOS 7 prompt without loading Windows. Option 7 is similar except that it does not attempt to use the AUTOEXEC.BAT and CONFIG.SYS files. The first option is used to run Windows 95 as normal. The second option creates a text file that lists all the files and drivers that were loaded during the bootup process. The text

```
Microsoft Windows 95 Startup Menu
==============================
   1. Normal
   2. Logged (BOOTLOG.TXT)
   3. Safe mode
   4. Safe mode with network support
   5. Step-by-step confirmation
   6. Command prompt only
   7. Safe mode command prompt only
Enter a choice :
```

file reports on whether the loading of each piece of software was successful. Option 5 is useful for debugging a configuration as each step of the configuration process waits for the user to confirm whether to attempt the next configuration command. This gives the user time to see the effects of each command and watch for error messages.

The third and fourth options ignore all but the essential drivers and provides a minimum setup (ie no CD-ROM, no printers, only VGA resolution), allowing the user to eliminate the effects of rogue hardware or software elements that prevent the system from booting up correctly.

BOOTING INTO DOS

The startup menu method of obtaining access to DOS is cumbersome, as the user has to wait for long periods while the system boots. Similarly, when the DOS application is finished, typing *'EXIT'* returns the user to Windows before the shutdown option is available.

For regular users of DOS, there are a couple of methods of speeding up DOS access. They both involve amending the MSDOS.SYS file which is located in the root directory of the boot drive. Since the file is a hidden file, it will have to be unhidden by highlighting the file name within Explorer, clicking the right mouse to reveal a drop-down menu, choosing the 'Properties' option and unchecking the *'hidden'* and *'read-only'* boxes. The MSDOS.SYS file is a plain ASCII text file and can be edited with any plain text editor such as WordPad or DOS EDIT. The section in the file called [options] can be amended so that the Startup menu is always displayed upon bootup, without the user having to press f8 at exactly the right time. This is achieved by adding the line *'BootMenu=1'* in the [options] section. Adding the line *'BootGUI=0'* in the [options] section ensures that the user is always taken directly into DOS upon bootup. To get into Windows, the user has to type WIN.

DEVICE MANAGER

The Device Manager is the most important tool for viewing and altering the configuration of the computer's hardware. The Device Manager is accessed via the *'System'* icon in the *'Control Panel'*, which is an option in the *'Settings'* menu off the Start menu.

It offers two views:

- Listing all hardware in order of their type (eg all hard drives are grouped together regardless of whether they are EIDE or SCSI)
- Listing all hardware in order of their type of connection (eg all SCSI devices such as disc drives and CD ROMs are grouped together, while all the serial devices are listed together).

In the example, an exclamation mark is present against the SCSI controllers. This indicates that a conflict has been detected between the resources allocated to the device and resources required for its proper operation.

Double clicking on a device produces a screen that reports on the configuration and state of that device.

The example shows a report on a sound card and the address space, IRQ and DMA channel used is clearly displayed. The bottom box also reports that the configuration of the device is not conflicting with the usage of other hardware devices in the computer. Unchecking the *'Use automatic settings'* box allows the values to be altered. The setting to be altered can be double clicked and a new value can be entered.

The 'Driver' option displays details of the current software driver being used to handle the device. Again, this can be altered if a newer driver is issued.

Similar reports are available for all devices on the system, including disc drives, the mouse, keyboard, monitor, modems, serial and parallel ports and network cards.

THE WINDOWS 95 REGISTRY

The hard disc of Windows 3.1 users soon contained a large collection of files that held all the Windows components and applications together. This was made up of the Windows INI files and usually separate INI files for each application. Added to this was the clutter of duplicated DLL files as different applications installed exactly the same DLL (eg Visual Basic DLLs) in various directories across the disc. Maintaining the system caused problems. Users found, for example, that deleting components for one application often removed a DLL that was shared with another application, thus preventing the second application from running.   With Windows 95, the collection of INI files and duplicate DLLs is replaced with a single database of all system and application information. This is the SYSTEM.DAT file and it includes both hardware and software information, although support for separate INI files is present for backward compatibility.

Additionally, users can have their own personalised desktop, held in a USER.DAT file.   The *'Passwords'* icon in *'Control Panel'* allows the machine to be set up with different desktop options for different users.   Users are then free to set up their own preferences and these are associated with that user's password.

Windows provides a program for editing the Registry, called *'REGEDIT'*; it is stored in the Windows directory.   The left window of the Editor displays the Registry information under six sub-groups.   The right window has two columns, displaying the name of each configuration detail and the data stored. The utility also has a 'Find' facility which can be used to locate a particular device in the Registry.

WARNING

Altering the Registry should only be tackled by experienced users as incorrect changes can prevent Windows 95 from booting up.

REGISTRY BACKUPS

If the Registry is corrupted or damaged, some or all of the machine's configuration can be lost.   There are many utilities which create backups of the Registry to allow for the Registry of a clean copy in the event of problems.   Microsoft provide two such programs on the installation CD, inside the *'Misc'* sub-directory of the *'Other'* directory.   These are called *'CFGBACK'* and *'ERU'* and both contain instructions for use.

Discs & Drives

DISC BASICS

The computer's disc systems are designed for the long-term storage of programs and user data.   When the power is removed from a machine, the contents are lost from memory, so the discs (sometimes called *'backing store'*) are used for their preservation.   The disc systems used to store data range from large hard disc packs used in large mainframe computers, to tiny 1.5" and smaller hard discs in portable notebook computers.   In addition, almost all PCs allow data to be stored on removable discs called *'floppies'*. This allows data to be moved around by carrying discs from machine to machine, or sending a disc through the mail.   Hard discs, on the other hand, are permanently built-in to the machine and are not normally accessible by the user.   Some new systems employ removable hard discs, to exploit the high capacity of hard discs while still retaining the mobility of floppy discs but these are still relatively uncommon.

Despite the wide differences in size and storage capacity, all magnetic discs work on the same basic principles.   Even the newer optical discs, while using substantially different technology, adopt the same general approach.   Disc drives are *'direct access"* devices, which means that the reading and writing of data can occur at any part of the disc.   Tape storage, on the other hand, is a serial device - the system has to search from one end of the tape until the wanted data is found.

TRACKS

Data is written to a disc magnetically in a similar way to recording on audio tape or video tape.   In this case, however, the media used is not a long continuous cassette of tape but the same type of surface material in the shape of a disc. The disc is rotated to allow access to all parts of its surface.   So, data will be written in circles round this disc. Regardless of the type of disc, the data is organised on the disc in concentric circles known as *'tracks'*. The tracks number from the outside of the disc to the inside, with the outermost track being called track 0.   The number of tracks on a disc varies from 40 or 80 on floppy discs to about 1000 on some hard discs.   The *`density'* of a disc is the number of tracks that the disc can handle eg for 3.5" discs, Double Density means that it can support 80 tracks per side.

The density of a disc is often quoted in TPI - tracks per inch.   A 3.5" floppy is a 96tpi disc which indicates that each track is 1/96th of an inch wide.   So, an 80 track disc would use up slightly less than one inch of the available disc diameter.   A 48tpi disc is usually used for 40 track discs.

WRITING/READING DATA

A disc is coated on both sides with a magnetisable material, to allow it to store a magnetic pattern that will represent the computer's data. Iron-oxide coatings were universally used in older drives, with improved cobalt-oxide coatings appearing in newer models.   The coating is magnetised under the influence of a coil of wire called the read/write head (the same coil that writes data is also used to read back data when required).   The disc is mounted on a vertical shaft that spins it at 300 rpm in the case of floppy drives and from 3600 rpm to 10,000rpm for hard disc drives. The read/write head can be moved to any track on the disc by an electric actuator and it floats just above the surface of the disc.   This movement is organised by electronic circuitry known as the *'disc controller'*.

So, by moving the head to the desired track and waiting until the desired portion of the track rotates under the head, any part of the disc can be accessed for reading or writing.   Writing involves energising the coil to create a magnetic field which, in turn, creates an altering magnetic pattern on the disc surface. At a later date, when the magnetised area of the disc is passed under the head, the magnetic fields on the disc induce a current in the read coil. These pulses of current are cleaned up and used to convert back to the binary data that was originally recorded.

The dimensions of the read/write head areas are dependent on the number of tracks that will be used on that disc.   If a 5.25" floppy disc drive only has to cope with 40 tracks, its head will be twice as wide as another 5.25" drive which has to cope with 80 tracks on the same disc radius.   On a large capacity hard disc with many hundreds of tracks, the head dimensions are even more finely engineered.   The heads commence their numbering from head 0.

SECTORS

A single track can hold from 4.5k to over 18k of data, dependent on the floppy disc type.   To make the most economical use of tracks, they are divided into compartments known as *'sectors'*. Sectors number from 1 upwards and each sector normally holds 512 bytes, i.e. 1/2k, of data.   So, a 9-sector track on a floppy stores 4.5k of data, while a 36-sector track on a hard disc stores 18k of data. The number of sides and the maximum number of tracks is determined by the hardware of the disc drive and is outwith the control of the user.   However, the size and number of sectors are set under software control (hence the description *'soft-sectored'*)

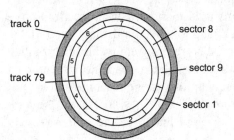

In fact, at the end of each sector there are two bytes that are additional to the 512 of the sector.   These are not used to contain user applications and data but are used to ensure the integrity of the data in the sector.   These are known as *'Cyclic Redundancy Check'* bytes.   When the data is written to the sector, a formula is applied to the data to produce a check number to be placed in the extra two bytes.   When the data is to be read back again later, the data from the sector is stored in a buffer before being passed on for processing. The same formula is applied to the data in the buffer and it should produce the same answer as that stored in the two check bytes. If the computed CRC figure accords with the stored CRC figure, the data in the buffer is fit to be passed on. If there has been any corruption of the data in the sector, or even any corruption of the check bytes, then the formula will produce answers that do not match. When the machine's built-in test routines in the BIOS find this error, it sends an error code to the application program that is using the disc reading code.   For example, if DOS is using the BIOS code to read a sector, a corrupted sector will produce the familiar *"Sector read error, Abort, Retry, Fail?"* message. The CRC bytes occupy disc space but do not appear in the figures for usable disc space (e.g. a 1.4Mb disc is the user's figure after taking into account CRC bytes).

CLUSTERS

In practice, sectors are often grouped in a unit called a *'cluster'*. The cluster is the smallest area of disc that can be used to store an independent item of data. So, if a particular disc used 4 sectors to a cluster, a batch file of only a few hundred bytes would still consume 2k of disc space.   If a program or a piece of data requires more than one cluster's worth of space, it can be stored in subsequent unused clusters.

FORMATTING

All discs, whether floppy or hard, have to be formatted, a process sometimes also called *'initialisation'*. This involves laying down data on the disc that is outwith the data seen by users.   This data is solely used to distinguish between one track and another and between one sector and another.   The read/write head is moved to the desired track and sector before reading or writing data in that sector.   So, every block of data can then be uniquely addressed by the read/write head used, the track used and the sector used to store it. Before any read or write operation is started, the system wants to ensure that it has really arrived at the correct track and sector.   Any mechanical or electronic glitch may result in the head being positioned over the wrong sector.   This would result in either reading the wrong data or overwriting data. To overcome this, the data sections laid down on a disc are preceded by a Sector ID which contains the track number, the sector number and the sector size.   If the information in the sector ID matches the desired location, the read or write operation will go ahead normally.   In the event of an incorrect head movement, the sector ID will not match the wanted location and the head is returned to track zero for another attempt.

The process of preparing a hard disc with sector IDs is known as *'low level formatting'*.   A complimentary *'high level formatting'* process consists of preparing the disc for use by DOS.   A low level format is carried out by the disc controller card and results in a disc that has its sectors identified and organised according to the required interleave (see later).   A high level format uses some of these sectors to set up the structures needed to store details of the fields and their whereabouts. This includes the boot sector area, the File Allocation Tables and the root directory, all of which are dealt with later. For hard discs, a low level format is carried out by invoking a special utility and a high level format is carried out by giving the DOS FORMAT command.   With floppy discs, the FORMAT command carries out both low and high level formatting.

FLOPPY vs HARD DISCS

Floppy discs comprise a single disc with two sides, while a hard disc will comprise several discs, with more sides and therefore greater storage capacity. This, coupled to the more precise engineering of hard disc, means that hard disc capacities far outpace those of floppies. The largest commonly used floppy disc stores 1.44Mb of data while the smallest hard discs currently available store 500Mb of data, with larger models storing up to 10Gb of data. Fetching data from a hard disc is much faster than from a floppy disc. This is due factors such as:

- The increased speed of rotation of a hard disc (this is 30 times or more faster than a floppy disc)
- A hard disc is spinning continuously while the computer is switched on, while a floppy drive motor is only energised when data is to be read or written. This means that a hard disc is always ready at the correct speed of rotation while a floppy drive has to get up to the correct operating speed before any disc activity can take place.
- The data is packed more tightly on a hard disc, so more data is read off from the reading of a single track compared to a floppy disc's track.

As programs become more sophisticated, they become ever larger, with some packages needing as much 90Mb of disc space. The extra capacity and vastly better speed make hard discs the obvious choice for storing application programs. Where large data files are in use, such as databases and graphical/DTP activities, there is also a speed advantage to storing the data on a hard disc. Floppies have the advantage of being cheap and portable and are a popular choice for storing backup copies of data. Some software is supplied on a set of floppy discs, with larger applications being supplied on CD-ROMs (see later).

FLOPPY DISCS

Floppy discs for PCs come in two sizes - the older 5.25" and the current 3.5" size. This refers to the diameter of the discs inside the protective casing. Both discs are made from mylar plastic coated with ferric oxide. The floppy drive is normally known as the A: drive; if a second floppy is fitted in a machine, it will be known as the B: drive. The hard disc is called the C: drive. A machine can have one or two 3.5" drives or one or two 5.25" drives or often one of each type. Most machines have a single hard disc, although others can be added as Drive D, Drive E, etc. Some hard disc systems only allow two hard discs per machine, while other allow four hard discs. A modern floppy disc drive has two heads (one for each surface). The earliest floppy discs were single-sided (i.e. only one read/write head on one side of the disc) but these are almost all gone from use, leaving all floppy drives as double-sided models. The table shows the characteristics of the floppy disc types commonly in use.

	Tracks/ side	Sectors/ track	Capacity	Sector Length (outer track)	Sector Length (inner track)	Bits/inch
5.25" Double Density	40	9	360k	1.66"	1.1"	6000
5.25" Quad Density	80	15	1.2M	1"	0.66"	9869
3.5" Double Density	80	9	720k	1"	0.73"	8717
3.5" High Density	80	18	1.4M	0.55"	0.37"	17000

5.25" DISCS

The disc sits in a vinyl wallet, or 'jacket', to protect the magnetised surface from exposure to dust or grease. The disc spins at 300 rpm inside the jacket, so the jacket lining is coated with a soft, non-woven material that is very lightly lubricated to minimise friction. The write-protect notch allows or prevents writing to the disc. A tab can be placed over the notch to disable any writing to the disc. In this way, important data can be written to the disc and then protected against accidental erasure or modification. When the tab is removed, the disc is again able to be written to. The wallet has a slot in both sides, to expose the surface so that the read/write heads can reach the magnetised coating on the disc. The read/write head is brought close to the disc surface by the action of closing the disc drive lever after the disc is inserted. When not in use, the disc should be kept inside its cardboard sleeve, to protect the exposed area. This disc also has an 'Index Hole'. This is a hole that is cut both in the jacket and in the disc itself. As the disc rotates inside the jacket, a point will be reached when both holes will align. At this point, a light from one side of the disc is able to pass through the hole and be detected by a light sensor on the other side of the disc. The timings of these pulses of light tell the computer exactly how much rotation has taken place. This information, when combined with the head movement, can place the read/write head on any sector on any track with great accuracy.

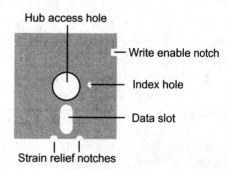

Hub access hole
Write enable notch
Index hole
Data slot
Strain relief notches

In the centre of the disc, there is a *'Hub Access Hole'*; this is the hole in the disc that allows the mechanism's drive hub to hold the disc while it is being rotated. The 360k discs usually have a Hub Ring added round the hub hole to increase the strength at this point, since this is where the disc is being held by the rotating mechanism; these are not present on 1.2Mb discs.

Another feature of 5.25" discs is the set of *'Strain Relief Notches'* on the disc wallet. These are notches cut in the jacket close to the head access slot, to reduce creasing when the jacket is stretched.

The lower density product - i.e. Double Density - uses 40 tracks and 9 sectors per track. This means that there are 360 sectors on each side, giving a total of 720 sectors on the entire disc. Since each sector is 512 bytes, the disc can store 360k of data. The higher density version - described as Quad Density - increases the number of tracks to 80 and the number of sectors in each track to 15, giving a storage capacity of 80 x 15 x 2 sides x 512 bytes = 1.2Mb. A double density disc has a coercivity of 300 Oersteds while a quad density disc has a coercivity of 600 Oersteds (see later).

When data is written to a disc, the level is taken as being 100%. When that same data is read from the disc, its level is lower than the original figure. This reduction is known as the *'clipping level'*. A known-brand disc normally returns a clipping level of around 50%, while bulk discs are around 40%. Disc drives, however, are able to adequately cope with clipping levels down to about 20%.

PROBLEMS WITH 5.25" DISCS

Trying to format a 360k to Quad Density usually results in a substantial proportion of the disc being seen as bad sectors. This is due to the coercivity of the disc surface being too low, allowing the magnetised areas to have an undue influence on each other, resulting in the inability to accurately store data. This means that even those sectors that are initially reported as being usable can often cause problems with time, as one magnetic area starts to influence a neighbouring area. Since the outer tracks are less densely packed than the inner tracks, they are the least affected by these problems. While it is possible to format a Quad Density disc to 360k, there are possible problems inherent in using the higher write head current with the lower coercivity surface. In any case, there would be few occasions when a user would wish to use a high capacity disc in low capacity mode.

Always use discs at their intended capacity, to prevent unwanted side-effects. For instance, a disc that a user has written to in both 360k and 1.2M drives will have data laid down in both wide and narrow formats, since the 1.2M drive has a narrower write head. This can lead to occasions when a narrow track of data (i.e. the one written to in a 1.2M drive) is sitting inside a wider track of data (i.e. one written earlier on a 360k drive). When the data is read on a 1.2Mb drive the narrow head only reads the narrow track and all is fine. However, when the same disc is read in a 360k drive, the wider head picks up the pattern on the wider track as well as the pattern on the wanted track. The results can be unpredictable.

3.5" DISCS

The inner disc of this type of floppy is constructed similarly to the larger floppy, except that it has smaller dimensions and a higher quality coating. It can store more data than the 5.25" despite its smaller proportions. The 3.5" is more robust since it is housed inside a rigid plastic case. The read/write slot is protected by a metal or Teflon slider that covers the slot when the disc is outside the drive. When the disc is placed in the drive, the drive mechanics push the slider back so that the read/write head can gain access to the magnetic surface. 3.5" discs have a write-protect hole that can be covered or uncovered by sliding a plastic cover over it. When the hole is covered, the disc can be written to. This is the opposite of the 5.25" disc that can only be written to when its write-protect notch is <u>uncovered</u>.

Double Density discs have 80 tracks with 9 sectors per track. This gives a capacity of 80 x 9 x 2 sides x 512 bytes = 720k. High Density discs have 80 tracks and 18 sectors in every track. They have double the capacity of double density discs - giving a capacity of 1.44Mb. Some dealers offer *'2Mb discs'*. These are just high density discs, being quoted with their unformatted capacities; when the formatting data is placed on the disc, the disc is left with a usable capacity of 1.44Mb. The coercivity of a 720k disc is 600 Oersteds and a 1.4Mb disc's coercivity is 700 Oersteds.

A high density disc has a permanent extra hole punched in its body; this hole is not designed to be covered and uncovered like the write protect hole. The hole's presence or absence indicates whether the disc is a double density or high density version. The drive decides to use high or low head currents by checking for the presence or absence of this hole.

PROBLEMS WITH 3.5" DISCS

Like the case of 5.25" discs, the 3.5" disc increases its storage capacity by increasing the number of sectors in a track - in this case from 9 sectors to 18 sectors per track.   A 720k disc writes 8,718 bits of data for every inch of track, while a 1.4Mb disc requires to write 17,434 bits per inch.   Unlike the 5.25" disc, both the DD and HD versions of the 3.5" disc have 80 tracks.   This means that the read/write head dimensions in a 720k drive are identical to those of a 1.4Mb drive, eliminating the problem of tracks embedded within tracks.

Again, the reduced sector length results in storage integrity problems that are solved by doubling the coercivity of high density discs.   This requires a particularly thin coating, under one micron, of fine grain oxide, compared to the 720k disc coating of just under two microns.   So, 1.4Mb drives can write and read 720k discs without difficulty.   While 720k drives cannot read 1.4Mb formatted discs, they can reliably read double density discs that have been formatted to 720k in a 1.4Mb drive.

Users should still not attempt to format 720k discs to beyond their rated capacity.   Although 3.5" discs will report less sectors errors when formatting, the surface is still less reliable than would be expected. The high density notch is designed so that 1.4Mb drives would detect the presence of an HD disc. However, some machines are not equipped to make this detection.   It should be noted, that the difference between DD and HD discs is not the hole's presence or absence, but the coercivity of the disc surface.

PROTECTING FLOPPY DISCS

The disc media is easily affected by the environment and users should be encouraged to practise good housekeeping. As the diagram shows, the gap between the head and the oxide coating is tiny compared to commonly found elements in the real world.   A smoke particle is around 250 microns, a fingerprint is around 300 microns, a dust particle is around 400 microns, while a human hair is a gigantic 0.03 ins.

If a particle of smoke or dust was to be trapped between the head and the disc surface, the oxide coating would be torn from the disc and the surface would almost certainly be permanently damaged.   The data contained in that sector, cluster, or even entire track would be lost forever. In extreme cases, the head itself could also be damaged.

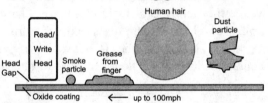

This problem is greatly minimised with hard discs, as the mechanism is contained within a sealed unit. But, with floppy discs, the danger is much greater.   That explains why users are recommended not to smoke in the presence of computers. Of course, smoking does not automatically mean that damage will occur.   Luckily, smoke and dust particles often bounce off the surface and are not trapped in the head gap.   However, there is an added danger with 5.25" discs.   The disc surface is open to outside corruption through the head access slot.   If a user holds a 5.25" disc such that a fingerprint or palm print is placed on the disc surface, a layer of grease is deposited on the oxide coating.   If this happens, a smoke or dust particle can become embedded in the grease. Now, the particle won't bounce off and is more likely to be dragged into the head gap.

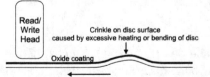

Other problems can be caused by leaving the disc exposed to excessive heat.   This may warp the disc surface as shown in the diagram.   If a 5.25" disc is forced into a drive, or bent in any other way, the disc will be similarly warped or crinkled.   This raised portion will hit the read/write head as it rotates and part of the disc surface will be scraped off, with resultant damage to the disc and the loss of data.

Apart from protecting the discs themselves, there is a need to take care of the disc drive mechanisms. From time to time, computers have to be transported from one place to another.   The sudden jolts to the machine could cause the read/write heads to bounce around and crash against each other.   A cardboard or plastic insert can be placed in the drive and the drive door closed.   This layer of card prevents the heads from bouncing around and allows the drive to be moved around in safety.   With hard discs, this is not possible as they are housed in sealed cases.   Hard disc heads must be moved to a part of the disc surface where no data is stored. Here, they can safely rest on the disc surface without scraping the oxide coating.   This is called *'parking'* and is covered later.

DO'S & DONT'S OF DISC HANDLING
- Avoid keeping computers in dusty surroundings; enforce smoking bans in computer areas.
- Avoid placing or storing discs in excessive temperatures.
- Don't touch the exposed surface of a 5.25" disc; keep unused discs in their protective envelopes.
- Avoid magnetic fields - don't place discs on top of printers, loudspeakers, telephones, etc.
- Floppy discs should never be folded or bent in any way.
- Always insert floppy discs carefully into drives.

DETECTING DISC CHANGING
A floppy disc drive needs to detect that a disc has been removed from a drive and a new disc has been inserted. This may take the form of a microswitch inside the drive that is depressed when the disc is inserted. The switch changes state when a disc is removed changes state again when a new disc, or even the same disc, is inserted. The status of this *'media change line'*, line 34, is used by various applications and utility programs. If a drive is not fitted with this mechanism, or the mechanism becomes faulty, the machine will not know that a disc has been changed. This can lead to unexpected results. For example, a user gives a DIR command on a disc, swaps the disc and gives another DIR command. Instead of displaying the new disc's contents, the files of the original disc are displayed once again. Since the system does not know that the disc has been changed, it is displaying the old directory contents directly from the copy of the FAT and directory stored memory rather than reading the new directory information. Worse still, any new writes would be based on the memory version of the disc's FAT instead of the actual disc FAT - with data being written to the wrong part of the disc.

HARD DISCS
Hard disc systems are composed of:
- A sealed drive unit
- Disc controller electronics, either on a controller card or built in to the drive.
- Connecting cables between the drive and the computer motherboard.

While the floppy is a single plastic disc, hard disc units are comprised of two or more discs in the one sealed unit. The extra discs boost the drive's storage capacity and each of these discs is known as a *'platter'*. The term applies to both sides of that particular disc. So, if a drive had three platters, it would contain 6 sides. Like floppies, areas of the hard disc's coating are magnetised and demagnetised to store

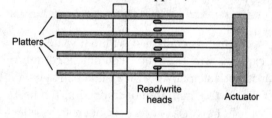

the data. The disc is aluminium and coated with ferric oxide or cobalt oxide. In some newer models, the disc is made of glass.

The original XT was composed of two platters and had a capacity of 10Mb. Modern drives can have many platters, depending on the capacity of the drive. A 210 Mb hard disc may have six platters (i.e. twelve sides) while Fujitsu's 8.8Gb model has ten platters.

The older models of hard disc drives were 5.25" and newer models are 3.5" in diameter. There is no relationship between the size of the disc and its capacity. The 3.5" models are generally faster and quieter than the 5.25" version. A full-height drive is about 3.25" high, while a half-height drive is about 1.63" high. Nearly all 3.5" drives are half-height models.

CYLINDERS
Many specifications and publications refer to the term *'cylinders"* when describing a disc's construction. Mostly, the term is used freely as the equivalent of *'tracks'*. With hard discs there are a number of different platters and the heads are mechanically linked and are therefore placed over a <u>set</u> of tracks at any one time. The collection of tracks covered is known as the drive's *'cylinder'*. In a hard disc, each platter will have an identical set of cylinder numbers and these number from zero upwards. So, cylinder 2 would be the third track on side 0, the third track on side 1, the third track on side 2 and so on. Since a floppy disc has only two sides, the term is never used. The inner tracks are smaller than the outer tracks, so the data is stored more densely in the sectors of these tracks. The density of the innermost track determines the drive's maximum capacity.

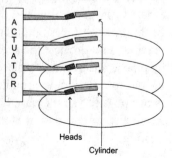

When a disc is constructed, it is provided with one or more extra inner tracks. These are used to provide a landing zone for the read/write heads. When older machines are given a *'park'* command, or newer machines are powered down, the read/write heads are moved to sit in the landing zone so that they will not be able to scratch the surface of any sectors used for storing data. A drive rated as 771 tracks might only format the disc to 770 tracks, using track 771 as the landing zone. Some systems also use spare inner tracks to make up bad tracks. This can result in different utilities displaying different results; some are counting the tracks for data while others are counting the total tracks.

With IDE and SCSI systems, the electronics can be used to hide the *real* surface structure from the machine. As far as the machine is concerned, the drive has say 953 tracks, with each track containing 36 sectors. This will, indeed, be the *'logical'* view given to the machine by the drive. In fact, the drive may well have a completely different physical layout. Since the disc's outer tracks cover a much greater surface than the inner tracks, the outer tracks can be used to store up to three times more sectors per track than the inner tracks. This is known as *'zone bit recording'* and provides greater storage with improved reliability. The exact internal layout need not be known by the machine or by the user, since the electronics on the drive make the drive appear to have the normal regular track and sector layout.

HEADS

Each side requires its own read/write head and these number from zero upwards. All the heads are mounted on the same actuator arm, so that they all move in unison as a single unit. When one head is on the sixth track in from the edge, then all the other heads will be on the sixth track of their disc sides. This is used to achieve economy of head motion. All the sectors in the same cylinder number (of all platters) will be used, before moving the head inward to the next cylinder number.

The maximum read without moving the head to another track is calculated by multiplying the number of sides by the number of sectors in the track; this is then multiplied by the sector size, usually 512 bytes.

> So, for the XT machine, 4 x17x0.5 = 34k could be read .
> For a 201Mb hard disc, 12x36x0.5 = 216k could be read.

Each platter has a read/write head for each side. Where a drive is reported to have an odd number of heads, it is due to the extra head and side being used for storing positional information instead of data. The smaller the dimensions and tolerances, the more likely that the drive could go out of alignment. To prevent this and the effects of temperature changes (see later), one disc side is given over to *'servo tracks'* that ensures that the head assembly maintains its tracking. As long as the head on the servo track's side is kept in alignment, then the other heads must maintain alignment, since they are mechanically linked.

ELEVATOR SEEKING

Modern hard disc electronics use a technique known as *'elevator seeking'*. The requests for disc reads are stored in a queue so that reads located in the same disc area are read while the head is at that location. The reads are not in the same sequence as originally requested and the electronics sorts out the data to compensate. This technique reduces the amount of head movement thereby speeding up disc access.

CALCULATING DISC CAPACITIES

Like floppy discs, the capacity of a hard disc is found by multiplying the total number of sides by the number of tracks by the number of sectors per track by the number of bytes per sector.

For example, the hard disc issued with the IBM XT machine had 2 platters, 17 sectors and 305 tracks. Since each sector was 512 bytes, it had a capacity of 4 x 17 x 305 x 512 = 10Mbytes. The IBM AT machine had the same specification, except that it had 615 cylinders. So, its capacity was 4 x 17 x 615 x 512 = 20Mbytes. However, there are a number of other factors that have to be taken into account when attempting to calculate the usable surface of a hard disc.

A WORKED EXAMPLE

Consider the case of a disc that is advertised as a *"210Mb"* disc. This is based on the following formula

```
       sides   tracks   sectors
        12  x  953  x  36    = 411696 sectors at 512 bytes = 210,788,352 bytes.
```

However, this is not a 210Mb disc. The final figure has to be divided by 1024 to arrive at the total expressed in Kb (since there are 1024 bytes in a kilobyte).

Dividing the result by a further 1024 produces an actual disc size of 201.02Mb. This a full 9Mb less than the manufacturer's advertised size.

However, this is not the end of the story.   The disc space that is actually available to the user to store programs and data is smaller still.   The hard disc is consuming the following overheads:

	Sectors	Bytes
Partition	36	18432
DBR	1	512
FATs	402	205824
Directory	32	16384
totals	471	241152

The Partition, DBR, FAT and Directory are covered later.   The final user area is comprised of 411225 sectors of 512 bytes.   This provides a user area of 210,547,200 or 200.8Mb.   The so-called 210Mb hard disc, in fact, provides a user area of 201Mb.

To compound matters, some manufacturers and suppliers used to quote the <u>unformatted</u> size of a hard disc.   The sector numbering which is written during formatting consumes a considerable amount of the disc surface and the *'formatted capacity'* is a more accurate reflection of the true usable size of the disc.   The total capacity of a disc is generally around a quarter more than the final formatted disc capacity.

COMPARISON OF SECTOR CODING

The BIOS always identifies a particular sector by a three-dimensional co-ordinate - the cylinder number/side number/sector number.   On the other hand, DOS (e.g. DEBUG) and many add-on utilities refer to sectors by their ascending sequential number - in the above example going from 1 to 127,738.

The conversion of DOS logical sector numbering and the actual physical layout of sectors/tracks/heads is carried out by the machine's BIOS.

INCREASING DISC CAPACITY

The capacity of disc surfaces is continually rising as improving technology allows the packing of ever more data on to each square inch of disc surface.   This increased packing density, also known *as 'areal density'* relies upon:

- improved surface coatings
- improved head technology

DISC COATING

To achieve higher data density, the number of tracks is increased and the length of a sector is shortened.   This means that the area free to be magnetised to store a single bit is diminished in both directions, both in length and in breadth.   If no steps were taken, the magnetised effects on the disc surface would influence each other and upset the data storage.   To prevent this, the disc has a surface coating that is difficult to magnetise.   This reduces the interference between the adjacent magnetised areas.

The degree of resistance to magnetisation is known as *'coercivity'* and is measured in units called *'Oersteds'*.   It measures the amount of magnetic force that will be required to change magnetic particles from sitting in a North-South orientation to a South-North orientation. A low coercivity disc will have its magnetic particles in the disc coating more readily affected than those of a high coercivity coating.   A 3.5" floppy disc has a coercivity of 700 Oersteds, while modern drives have ratings of around 2,000 Oersteds.   Research is continuing to produce surfaces with higher ratings, allowing more data to be stored on the disc surface.

DISK HEADS

The write head uses a magnetic field to alter the flux pattern of the disc coating.   The magnetic field from the head spreads out like an umbrella, increasing in width as it approaches the disc surface.   The first diagram shows how a head with a large gap requires a large surface to store a single piece of data.

In the second diagram, the head is flying much lower, the gap is smaller and the area covered by the magnetic pattern is much reduced.   Reduced

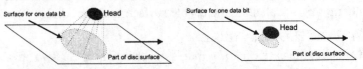

head gaps result in greater areal density.   The original flying height of read/write heads was over 12 microns and now range from 2 to 6 microns.   The current tiny high capacity drives are achieved by having the heads fly at less than one micron above the disc surface.   With the head being closer to the surface, the head's magnetising effect is also increased.

This technique is currently maximised through *'Proximity Recording'* where the head flies at only 0.8 microns from the disc surface.

Another technique is to make the head of narrower width so that the tracks are closer together and more tracks can be placed on the disc surface. This allows for increased capacities (ie more data on the same disc size) or smaller diameter discs (ie the same data on a smaller size). Increased packing density also means that manufacturers can make discs cheaper by having less platters and heads.

MAGNETORESISTIVE HEADS

As the area allowed for each bit is reduced, the signal picked up by the normal inductive read head is weaker, reducing the reliability of the data read. Techniques to improve the signal pickup include:

Technique	Effect	Limitations
Move head closer to disc surface	Increased flux at head increases signal	Head gaps already very small
Place more turns on head coil	More sensitive head increases signal	Increases losses at fast speeds
Move data past head faster	Greater rate change of flux increases signal	Head speeds already very fast

One of the improvements in head technology is the Magnetoresistive (MR) head. MR heads have the following features:
- Separate read and write heads.
- The write head remains an inductive head but with much less windings on the coil. The extra windings were required for adequate data reads but resulted in writing too wide a track. Less windings means the head produces a narrower magnetic pattern and more tracks can be placed on the surface and more bits can be placed on each track.
- The reduced inductance of the write head also means that it can write at faster speeds.
- The read head is made from an alloy whose resistance changes in the presence of a magnetic flux. It is velocity independent - ie it is the presence of the flux and not the rate of change of flux that produces the read signal; increasing or decreasing the disc speed has no effect on the signal.
- The read head is tiny and can detect a much reduced data area. Areal density can therefore be increased.
- The read track is smaller than the write track so even slight head mis-alignment will not produce noise (the read head remains within the written track and does not read data from adjacent tracks).

PRML

Traditional drives translate the incoming signal from the head into digital data using *'peak detection'* - reading a peak value as a binary 1 and lower values as a binary zero. This is an increasingly difficult task for the electronics when the incoming analogue stream is very fast and contains noise. PRML (Partial Response Maximum Likelihood) converts the incoming signal into a digital waveform and runs it through a series of filters. A group of bits is compared at a time which produces more reliable data translation. The increased reliability allows for a more efficient coding method when writing data; the RLL coding system requires less redundant data. This results in greater capacity from the same disc area.

MAXIMUM DISC HANDLING

Available disc drives sizes grew at a rate that overtook the computer's handling capacity. Early DOS versions, prior to v3.31, had sixteen bits embedded in the disc boot sector to store the total number of sectors allowed per logical drive. Since the maximum different binary combinations from a 16-bit address is 65,536 and each sector is 0.5k, the maximum disc partition size on early PCs was 32Mb.

This restriction was lifted from v3.31 onwards, when a four byte area was put aside in the boot sector area. This is a 32-bit number and can theoretically store a partition size up to 2 Terabytes. However, the standard BIOS for PC compatibles has a design that limits it to handling a maximum of 1024 tracks on any one hard disc, 63 sectors per track and a maximum of 255 read/write heads, while the IDE interface can handle a maximum of 65,536 tracks, 255 sectors per track and 16 heads. A disc system can only work at its lowest common denominator; there is no point in the BIOS supporting 255 heads, for example, if the IDE electronics can only handle a maximum of 16 heads.

This means that a normal IDE disc system can only operate with a maximum disc size of 16 heads covering 1024 tracks with each track holding a maximum of 63 sectors. With the normal sector size of 512 bytes, the maximum disc size supported is:

	BIOS	IDE	Actual best
Sectors/track	63	255	63
Number of heads	255	16	16
Number of cylinders	1024	65536	1024
Maximum capacity	7.84Gb	127.5Gb	504Mb

16 x 1024 x 63 x 512 = 504Mb

This restriction can be overcome by bypassing the drive mechanism program code in the BIOS. The normal calls to the BIOS disc routines are intercepted and sent to a conversion routine which translates between the normal physical CHS (cylinder/head/sector) values and logical CHS values which can have a greater range than those contained in the BIOS. Ultimately, the logical values, when multiplied together, cannot exceed the product of the BIOS values.

EIDE drives address the problem by using LBA (logical block addressing) on the disc controller card along with an LBA-aware BIOS chip. Every sector on the drive is numbered in sequence from zero upwards. The modified BIOS takes the CHS information that is passed to it (via the DOS Int 13h call used for disc reads/writes) and translates it into a 28 bit address specifying the disc sector. Since the largest disc size supported by the BIOS is 7.8Gb (63 x 255 x 1024) any system using the LBA BIOS routines have this as a maximum figure.

Nevertheless, the maximum partition size remained at 2Gb for some time. This limit was imposed by the design of DOS, Windows 3.1 and the first release of Windows 95. The second release of Windows 95, OSR2, is capable of handling the full 7.8Gb as a single partition. Windows NT has its own filing system (NTFS). This does not use the BIOS for its disc handling and can therefore handle beyond the 8Gb limit. The SCSI interface, due to its disregard for physical disc geometry, has no limitations on the number of heads it can support; SCSI drives have always used a form of LBA working.

For older machines whose BIOS code does not support large discs, a software patch is installed which extends Int 13h working.

HEAD ACTUATORS

The set of read/write heads in a hard disc assembly is moved in unison, under the influence of a single actuator mechanism. The head mechanisms come in two varieties:

STEPPER MOTORS

Stepper motors rotate by a small pre-determined amount when the motor coil is energised. Each step moves the read/write heads in or out exactly one track. This is the cheap system but is slow and is no longer used. Stepper motor systems are also more prone to temperature changes than voice coil types. The physical dimensions of the disc expand and contract with temperature changes. Since the stepper motor always moves the heads by the same amount with each step, they might not position the head exactly between the track boundaries. That explains why users are recommended to switch on their computers for some time before using them, if they have been lying in a cold office overnight. If the heads and tracks are not in exact alignment, then data reads might be inaccurate, as the read head may be reading partly from a neighbouring track. Even worse problems may result if the user tries to save data under these conditions; the data may be written partly on the wanted track and partly overwrite data on a neighbouring track. Stepper systems also require a *'park'* utility to move the head away from the active disc surface when the machine is being transported. When the power is removed from a stepper motor drive, the read/write heads settle on the disc surface at the last track stepped to. This system is no longer used.

VOICE COILS

A voice coil actuator is the more modern method and is given its name from the coil that moves the cone of a hi-fi loudspeaker coil. Like the loudspeaker coil, the head coil is within the influence of a permanent magnet. When the current through the coil is increased, the coil moves. Since the coil is connected to the head and actuator arm, the arm moves and therefore the heads are moved. This movement is against the action of a spring. When the current is removed, the spring pulls the heads to an area of the disc surface that does not store data; this is achieved without the user having to run a *'park'* utility - in effect, these discs *'auto-park'*. Voice coil systems are faster and more reliable.

The disc in a voice coil drive will shrink and expand with temperature changes, just like any other hard disc. The voice coil mechanism, however, is designed to overcome this particular problem. Instead of moving the heads by an exact amount, regardless of the prevailing disc temperature, the heads are moved to exactly the correct part of the track. In effect, the heads may move by a slightly different amount for differing temperatures. The heads find out the exact stopping positions for each track by sensing positional information laid down on a special track laid aside for the purpose. As the disc expands, the positional information will also move outwards and the heads will come to rest at the new altered position. This extra track is called the *'servo track'*.

DISC RELIABILITY

Manufacturers usually quote their discs' reliability figures in terms of *'Mean Time Between Failure'* or *'MTBF'*.   With older drives MTBFs were of between 20,000 hours and 50,000 hours - i.e. between about 800 days and 2,000 days of continuous use.   Modern drives are quoted as having MTBFs of between 300,000 and 500,000 hours.   Allowing for manufacturer's optimism this still results in drives that would never become faulty during their useful lives. In this context, 'useful life' would be the functional, rather than mechanical or electrical, life of the drive.   Drive technology is moving ahead at a rate that encourages organisations to upgrade their drive systems prior to them becoming faulty beyond repair.

PROTECTING HARD DISCS

Hard discs require most of the safety precautions already mentioned concerning floppy discs to be observed. The need to keep the disc unit away from strong magnetic fields, avoiding smoke and dust, etc. apply as much to hard discs as floppy discs.   On the one hand, the hard disc is in a sealed unit and therefore has a better chance of surviving a hostile climate.   On the other hand, the repercussions of disc failure are much more serious.   If a floppy disc is damaged, it can be thrown in the waste bin at little financial loss.   If a hard disc is damaged, it is a very costly item to replace.   In addition, a damaged floppy disc should have its backup copy immediately to hand and so productivity is not affected.   With a hard disc failure, a new disc has to be ordered up, fitted and have all the backup files restored before the machine is ready for use.

Apart from the above environmental problems, hard discs are particularly vulnerable to knocks and jolts. Unlike the floppy drive, the user is unable to mechanically stabilise the head assembly. If the case of the machine should be jolted while the machine is switched on, the head may make contact with the surface of the disc and scrape off some of the coating from the tracks. If this happens, the data in these sectors will be lost and considerable permanent damage can be caused to the disc surface.   This is termed a *'head crash'* and it takes out sectors from the system.   If the head crash happens when the head is positioned over the system areas (see notes on the Master Boot Record and DOS Boot Record) then the disc can be rendered unusable, since the system files cannot be relocated to any other sector - they must be found in specified tracks and sectors of the disc.

To minimise possible damage, modern drives have auto-park mechanics; that means that the read/write head is positioned out of the way of the data tracks when it is not involved in read or write operations. With older drives, software utilities are run to place the head out the way of data tracks before switching off the machine.   If an older machine is switched off without previously parking the heads, then as the motor slows down, the heads drop down from their cushion of air and land on the disc surface.   When the machine is later switched on again, the head is dragged across the disc until such time as the motor speed is sufficient to lift the head off the disc.

DISC SPEED

The speed of a disc drive is based on
- The time to get to the required data (known as the *'access time'*)
- The time taken to read that data from the disc (known as the *'data transfer rate'*)

ACCESS TIME

The time taken to reach the required data is based on two factors:
1. The time that the head takes to get to the wanted track (seek time) measured in milliseconds.   Each track-to-track jump time may be different, since some head movements will wish to move across a larger amount of the disc than other movements.   Due to the way that files are written, most track-to-track movements are not very distant.   So, the average access time is calculated on the basis of 1/3rd of the tracks, instead of the expected half of the tracks.   A poor seek time would 25ms and a fast seek time would be 8ms.   Drives with seek times lower than around 25ms are using voice coil actuators rather than stepper motor actuators.
2. The time taken to get to the wanted sector (latency period).   This is the time spent waiting for the wanted sector to rotate to the position directly under the read/write head. On average, this is half a disc revolution.   At 3600 rpm, this would be 8.33ms, at 4,500 rpm this would be 6.67ms and at 10,000 rpm it would be 3ms.

The original PC's 10Mb hard disc had an access time of 80ms and the AT was quoted at 40ms.   Modern drives range from about 16ms to under 8ms.

DATA TRANSFER RATE

The rate at which a small amount of data (e.g. a single sector) is transferred is determined by the above factors and is a physical restriction that cannot be adjusted by the user.   When a number of sectors require to be read, the most common case, the way that the disc is low-level formatted plays a large part in achieving the maximum data transfer rate.   Low level formatting separates each sector with *'sector IDs'* that determine the sector boundaries.   The maximum data transfer rate is reached when the head reads from a contiguous set of sectors, without having to move the head to another track.   In such a case, the rate would be determined by the sector size, the number of sectors per track and the speed at which the data passes under the read head.

With a floppy drive, the disc rotates at 300 rpm and so the 18 sectors on a 1.44 Mb floppy would be read in 0.2 secs.   The transfer rate would be:

0.5k x 18 / 0.2 = 45k bytes/second or 360Kbits/sec

Now, even a slow hard disc spins much faster, at 3600 rpm, giving a track reading time of only 0.01666 secs.   So, for a hard disc with 36 sectors the data transfer rate would be:

0.5k x 36 / 0.01666 = 1.08Mb/second or 8.6Mbits/sec

With models rotating at 4,500 rpm the track reading time is 13.33 and the data transfer rate would be:

0.5k x 36 / 0.01333 = 1.38Mb/second or 10MBits/sec

So, reading a 1Mb file from a large hard disc can take a second, around twenty times faster than reading from a floppy disc.   Of course, the access time for both drives has to be included and this slightly reduces the dramatic gap in performance between the two drive types.   Most controllers also have to decode various timing pulses before sending the data to the computer.   Dependent on the type of card used, this produces various levels of delay and affects the overall data transfer rate.   The above figures are maximums, in that they assume that all the data will be read in one contiguous read, with no additional track-to-track movements.

Another major factor in determining data transfer rate is the efficiency of the electronics in the disc controller card.   A very fast disc requires that the controller be able to transfer the data to the motherboard at the same rate.   This is covered later.

INTERLEAVE

The <u>floppy</u> controller circuitry can easily cope with the amount of data being transferred. The slow speed of the disc rotation means that data is read off slowly and is easily processed by even the slowest electronic circuits.   With much faster hard disc speeds, there is a potential problem for hard disc controllers.   The sectors of a floppy disc are contiguous on the disc surface as shown in the diagram; this is 1:1 interleave factor.

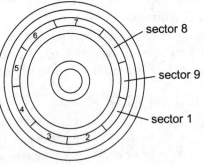

If sectors are contiguous on a hard disc, the controller circuitry may not be able to keep up with the tasks of processing each sector. The controller has to verify that sector's data integrity and pass on the data to the BIOS, before reading the next sector.

If the sectors are contiguous on the disc, the controller may find that the following sector has already passed under its head when it wishes to read the data.   This would involve waiting until that sector rotated back under the read head again.   The result would be a slow data transfer rate.

To overcome this, the sectors of a disc can be arranged so that sector 2 will not be placed on the disc directly after sector 1, sector 3 will not follow directly after sector 2 and so on, as shown below.   In the diagram, a disc with 17 sectors per track and 1:3 sector interleave is shown. The controller attached to this drive requires time to process the data from the sector 1 before moving on to read sector 2.   Therefore, sector 2 is not contiguous to sector 1 and is placed further along the track.   The distance between sector 1 and sector 2 represents the time required for the controller circuitry to cope with the processing.   A 1:3 interleave means that the next required sector is always spaced 3 sectors away from the current sector.   For a slower controller card, the spacing between sector numbers would be increased.   A 1:6 interleave would mean that sector 2 would be spaced 6 sectors away from sector 1.   It was common to have older machines supplied with an incorrect interleave factor.   In such cases, a simple interleave adjustment would increase disc performance by as much as 50%.

In many cases, the machines as supplied by manufacturers had a higher interleave setting than was necessary. The disc controller could often cope with a lower interleave setting than the one configured on the disc. It is certainly worth checking the interleave ratio on existing machines and adjusting them where this can be done. If a disc is checked with a diagnostic utility such as Spinrite, the range of results for different interleave ratios is displayed and the user is informed of the optimum setting for that particular controller.

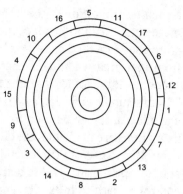

Reducing the interleave ratio can have a dramatic effect on data transfer rates. For a 26 sectors/track disc, for example, a 1:1 interleave is four times faster than a 1:4 interleave.

Note that any trouble with interleaving is a problem with the controller not the hard disc itself. If a controller has inefficient circuitry, replacing it with a more modern card will improve disc performance. The effects of the change of card will be seen when the disc surface has its interleave altered to match the improved capabilities of the controller.

NB : Modern machines are supplied with a controller that is capable of handling 1:1 interleave arrangements. Virtually all IDE, EIDE, ESDI and SCSI drive controller are pre-set to 1:1 as standard and should not be altered by the user.

CHANGING THE INTERLEAVE RATIO

Disc utilities are available to alter a hard disc's interleave ratio, including Spinrite, Norton Utilities Calibrate and Disc Technician. These test the controller for the lowest ratio that can be safely used. This is dependent on the controller card, any caching and the size and speed of the bus. It works by reading the data in the present interleave sequence and timing that read. It then reads these sectors in different sequences, again carrying out timing of each sequence. The table of interleave timings found is then displayed. The user can then choose to have the disc altered to work with the optimum interleave ratio and the program will then automatically carry out the alteration. The utilities carry out the process in a 'non-destructive' fashion, which means that the original data can be left on the disc.

ENCODING METHODS

Magnetising and demagnetising the disc surface as the head passes along a sector allows the magnetised and demagnetised areas to be written in accordance with the binary 1s and 0s of the data to be written. When the head comes back to read that sector, the magnetised pules, and their patterns, can be translated back into a stream of 1s and 0s in the same pattern as the original written data.

However, it is not quite that simple. If a long series of 0s were to be written to a sector, this would cause problems when the data was later read. A long time span without pulses leaves the electronic circuits unsure of the exact number of 0s in that stream. This may be aggravated by slight speed differences in disc motors. This synchronisation problem would cause probable data reading errors. As a consequence, the pattern written to the sector has to contain synchronisation information along with the actual data. Earlier solutions lay in recording extra synchronisation pulses on the sector along with the actual data, in the ratio of one synchronisation bit to one data bit. Although this scheme - known as 'Frequency Modulation' - worked, it was extremely wasteful of disc space. This technique was employed in the 100k BBC floppy disc drives.

MFM

The MFM - Modified Frequency Modulation - system is the original PC technique and is used for floppies and many older hard discs. This uses a more compact encoding method that produces a reliable disc drive but consumes a rather large amount of the information in each sector for synchronisation purposes.

RLL

The RLL - Run Length Limited - technique has been popular since 1986 when it was patented and introduced by IBM. Improved hard disc tolerances has meant less surface undulations, allowing the read/write heads to fly closer to the disc surface - as low as 8 microns. New cobalt coatings have higher coercivity. The combination of lower-flying heads and more coercive materials has meant that more data can be packed on to the same disc area. RLL uses a more complex encoding algorithm which means that a smaller proportion of the information written to a sector is synchronisation information - thus allowing more actual data to be placed a disc of the same physical capacity. These factors result in storing 50% more user data on the disc. Also, since more data can be stored in a specific area of disc surface, reading from that area when RLL-encoded will bring in more data than when reading that same area if MFM encoded. Put another way, the data transfer rate of an RLL drive is greater than that of an MFM drive. Manufacturers don't actually manufacture RLL and MFM drives. Whether a drive can be used for RLL encoding or has to be used for MFM encoding is a result of the quality of that disc's surface. Almost all new drives are made to RLL quality. If an RLL quality disc is quoted as 30Mb, this assumes that an RLL controller is used in conjunction with it. If it is controlled by an MFM controller card, it will only be able to operate to 21Mb capacity. It is no fault of the drive; it is a measure of the efficiency of the controller card. In this example, the MFM card would be formatting the disc to 17 sectors per track instead of the 26 sectors per track of which the disc surface is capable. Also, MFM quality drives should not be used with RLL controllers as pushing 26 sectors on to tracks with densities designed for 17 tracks will cause disc read errors, either immediately or with increasing frequency at a later stage.

INTERFACES

The *'controller'* is the electronic circuitry used to control the operations of the drive mechanism and the head read/write activities. In some machines, this circuitry is built on to the machine's motherboard but it is mostly implemented by a separate card that plugs into an expansion slot on the motherboard.

In early systems, manufacturers produced their own interface arrangements and this meant that users had to always use the manufacturer's specific card and drive components. Nowadays, one group of manufacturers, such as Western Digital, produces controllers while other manufacturers, like Seagate and Maxtor, produce the hard drives. As a result, a number of standard interfaces have been arrived at, to allow the devices to communicate. While the interface card is mainly for controlling the hard disc, most cards also have on-board electronics to control floppy discs.

The mechanics of drives mostly work in the same way but there are differences in the way that the drive communicates with the motherboard. The most common interfaces are described below.

ST506

The oldest interface is the ST506. It was produced by Alan Shugart of Seagate Technology and appeared at the time of the introduction of the IBM PC. It was originally used with 5Mb drives and has a maximum disc capacity of 140Mb. The stream of data bytes, timing pulses and separators read from the disc is translated into data which is placed on the computer's data bus via the card's connection to the expansion slot. This transfer of data between controller card and expansion slot is shown in the diagram as the flow of *'actual data'*. The data from disc to controller card, i.e.

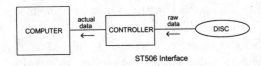

ST506 Interface

the *'raw data'*, is in serial (therefore slower) format. ST506 drives are produced in MFM and RLL types with disc to controller transfer rates of 600kb/sec and 900kb/sec, assuming both drives are operated at 1:1 interleave. When 1:1 interleaves are used, there is no further improvement can be made between the drive and the card, since all other factors (i.e. speed of rotation, encoding method, sectors/track) are either standard or maximised. An improved version of the ST506 is the ST412, which meets the IEEE 412 specification and uses voice coils for controlling head movements instead of stepper motors, to speed up disc access times. The ST412 also carries out elevator seeking. Most ST506/412 systems use MFM coding with equal amounts of recorded data being stored on each track. As shown in the diagram, the ST506/412 drive connects to the motherboard via cables to the disc controller card. A 34-wire cable is used to control the drive's choice of head and move the heads to the various tracks, etc. The wires are also used to dictate whether reading or writing is to take place.

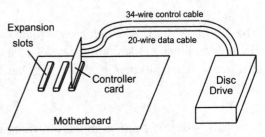

Another cable, of 20 wires, is used to carry the data between the controller card and the drive.

The data is in serial format, despite the number of wires in use; the other wires are reserved or earthed.

ESDI

The Enhanced Small Device Interface was produced by a consortium of manufacturers who required better performance than the ST506/ST412 standard. ESDI is also a serial method but the interpretation of the timing pulses is carried out on the drive itself rather than in the controller card. This process is unaffected by any noise on the drive/controller interface and, as a result, the ESDI interface produces a higher data transfer rate.

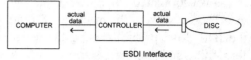

ESDI Interface

Other improvements include improved disc motor speed tolerance, an improved disc surface (i.e. a higher surface coercivity) and a reduced space between the head and the disc surface (down to 10 microns or less), allowing more sectors per track. In addition, ESDI drives can report their size and layout to the controller, eliminating the need for the user to know and set up the exact disc configuration (numbers of heads, cylinders, sectors, etc.).

Although a device-level system, the ESDI drive possesses a degree of high level communication with the machine. For example, an ST506 controller attempting to format a hard disc would require to given a very long series of commands to move the heads and energise the write heads in the appropriate sequence. With the ESDI system, a single command is passed to the circuitry on the controller and it will carry out the process without any further intervention from the computer. The cables are identical to ST506 cables; it's just that the data they carry is different. So, the physical layout of an ESDI is identical to the diagram already given for the ST506/412 system.

The data from disc to controller is, nevertheless, in the slower, serial format. Most ESDI systems produce over 1Mb/sec transfer rates with 1.25Mb/sec being typical. Both drives and controller are available in different speed formats, so not every drive can be expected to work with every controller. Often produced in high capacity versions and used in higher performance systems, particularly on single-user systems. The ESDI system was most commonly found on the IBM PS/2 range of computers. The ESDI standard is now obsolete, with support moving to SCSI systems at the higher end of the market and to IDE systems at the lower end.

IDE

The system, introduced by Compaq in 1987, stands for Integrated Drive Electronics, sometimes described as Intelligent Drive Electronics, or even Imbedded Drive Electronics. This system is really an ST506/ST412 setup that puts the entire controller circuitry on to the drive itself, to eliminate any losses between drive and controller. With this improved reliability, IDE drives have increased numbers of sectors per track, allowing even greater data density on the drive. Most have 34 or more sectors per track and a 36 sector per track drive is not uncommon. They use 1:1 interleave and, also taking into account that the data from the disc is now in faster parallel format, produce fast performances. Theoretical data transfer rates of up to 5Mb/sec are possible although around 4Mb/sec is more typical.

The fact that the IDE system is designed to appear to the machine as an ST506 system means that the original AT BIOS chip can always accommodate an IDE; there is no need to change the BIOS chip to get it to communicate with the drive system.

IDE drives connect to the computer in one of three ways:

1. Using a *'pass-through'* board that plugs into a spare expansion slot. There are no electronic processing components on this board and it is used solely as a means of making connection to the motherboard (hence the term *'passing through'*). The board contains only bus buffering chips and some address decoding chips and it has a 40-wire ribbon cable that connects to the IDE drive. 16 of these wires are used as a parallel bus for faster data transfer.

2. Using a special IDE connector on the motherboard, to avoid using up any expansion slots. The electronics for the drive is already mounted on the computer's motherboard in these instances. The drive is simply plugged into the motherboard connector. In these cases, separate circuitry is provided to handle the floppy drives.

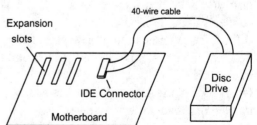

3. Using the old *'hardcard'* method. Here the drive and controller circuitry are situated on the same expansion card that fits into a spare expansion slot on the motherboard. Low profile drive mechanisms are required, to allow neighbouring expansion slots to be used. These are no longer produced.

IDE is the popular choice of drive with new machines due to its general reliability and its relative cheapness (due to the reduced circuit complexity as a result of the data interpretation work being done on the drive). However, it does have the one drawback. If problems are encountered, the drive cannot be low-level formatted. IDE drives are low-level formatted at the factory and only give the appearance of an ST506 system to the machine. So, if the problems cannot be resolved at a higher level, the design of the IDE drive prohibits using the usual software to carry out low level operations such as low-level formatting and interleave setting.

IDE systems use logical addressing which leaves the job of translating logical sector numbers into actual head, track and sector information to the electronics on the drive. This is an advantage since it simplifies operations, with the drive taking over some housekeeping. For instance, if the drive detects that a track is deteriorating, it can transfer the data to a spare track and mark the original track as bad - all without the knowledge of the main machine. As far as DOS is concerned, the data is still in the original track - the task of translating what DOS thinks is the wanted sector into the actual new location is the job of the drive circuitry. That is why the normal utilities which work an absolute sector level have problems with IDE drives. However, file utilities such as defragmenters operate at a higher level and can therefore still work with IDE drives.

IDE drive controllers are unable to co-exist on the same machine with ST506 controllers or ESDI controllers. If a machine is to be given a second drive as an IDE drive, the original drive must also be an IDE type. IDE systems only support two drives. Most IDE drives are compact 3.5" models. IDE hardware is almost only targeted at the AT market onwards, although a few XT cards can be found.

EIDE

The rapid development of the other parts of the computer system has left the disc subsystem as the bottleneck for many activities. Although IDE is the most common interface for current machines, it has a number of disadvantages:

- Its peak data transfer rate, at 4.1MB/sec, is now inadequate. The low transfer rate is not a limitation with ordinary 16-bit ISA busses, since they are only capable of working up to a maximum rate of around 3Mb/sec. The PCI and VL busses can handle much faster rates, but the IDE controller card is designed to fit into the ISA expansion slots of these machines. Such machines are therefore incapable of handling even the IDE's peak rate and an improved disc interface would be wasted on ISA based computers. A disc interface capable of plugging into the PCI or VL expansion bus could utilise the faster potential on these buses - hence the development of EIDE.
- It is only designed to interface hard discs. Other devices are not easily connected to the interface, although some CD ROMs now provide IDE connections.
- It can only handle two drives per controller. Many machines do not support more than a single controller, limiting the computer to a maximum of 1Gb spread over two drives. At best, a computer will support two controllers, allowing 2Gb of disc.

1995 saw the more widespread use of an improved interface known as EIDE or E-IDE (Enhanced IDE). This interface can handle four drives with a maximum drive capacity of 8.4Gb. The devices will mostly be disc drives but the interface will also easily handle CD ROMs and tape drives. It is also cheaper than the other alternative fast interface - the SCSI interface.

The EIDE interface offers significant improvement in speed over the standard IDE interface, with a range of possible rates as laid in ANSI specifications.

ATA, AT Attachment, is the general standard and ATA-1 describes normal IDE working.

ATAPI, ATA Packet Interface, describes the ability of the interface to work with other devices beyond disc drives. If a scanner or CR ROM is described as having an ATAPI standard, it means that it connects to the IDE controller.

ATA-2 is the foundation of a range of EIDE interfaces.

Some of the transfer modes use PIO, Programmed Input/Output, which means that the computer's CPU is in control.

Other modes use DMA, Direct Memory Access, where the controller card relieves the CPU of much of its memory read/write activities.

An EIDE disc drive remains compatible with the normal IDE system. Such a drive can be connected to an IDE controller and will work happily, although its transfer rate will slow down to that of the normal IDE performance. It is this compatibility that gives the Enhanced IDE its name.

There is a wide range of performances available when choosing disc systems, as shown in the table.

Some modes, such as the PIO Modes and the SCSI modes, are standards.

Others were developed by disc manufacturers to improve performance, although these are being adopted by other manufacturers. Fast ATA and Fast ATA-2 were initiated by Seagate, whereas Ultra ATA was initiated by Quantum.

Comparison of different drives and interfaces

	Max Burst Rate
Normal IDE	4Mb/sec
Normal SCSI-1	5Mb/sec
Fast SCSI	10Mb/sec
PIO Mode 3	11.1Mb/sec
DMA Mode 1	11.1Mb/sec
Fast ATA	11.1Mb/sec
Fast ATA-2	16.6Mb/sec
DMA Mode 2	16.6Mb/sec
PIO Mode 5	20Mb/sec
Fast Wide SCSI	20Mb/sec
Ultra ATA	33Mb/sec
Ultra Wide SCSI	40Mb/sec

DRIVES AND THE BIOS

The early XT machines expected the user to set switches on the controller card to inform the system of the drive number in use with the card. The XT controller card had its own BIOS chip and it stored a table of the most popular types of drive.   Each number in the table corresponded to a set of disc parameters.   This was satisfactory at the time, since only a limited range of disc types and sizes were available.   From the AT onwards, the motherboard BIOS made provision for disc handling and it originally contained a disc table of types 0 to 14.

The machine's BIOS uses an area of CMOS (Complimentary Metal-Oxide Silicone - a type of low-power RAM) which is permanently powered by the machine's internal automatically recharged batteries. This is the same battery that keeps the internal clock operating.   The CMOS stores the details of the number of disc drives in use, their type and size. The hard disc details include the number of cylinders, number of sectors per cylinder, number of heads and write pre-compensation tracks. The user runs a setup program and chooses the appropriate description; the type number is used to set up the parameters in the CMOS memory.

Below are extracts from an AMI BIOS :

Drive Number	No of Cylinders	No of Heads	Start of WPC	Landing Zone	Sectors/ track	Disc Capacity
1	306	4	128	305	17	10M
2	615	4	300	615	17	20M
3	615	6	300	615	17	30M
4	940	8	512	940	17	62M
5	940	6	512	940	17	46M
6	615	4	65535	615	17	20M
7	462	8	256	511	17	30M
8	733	5	65535	733	17	30M
9	900	15	65535	901	17	112M
...	...	...	...	...	...	...
42	981	5	981	981	17	41M
43	755	16	65535	755	17	100M
44	887	13	65535	887	34	191M
45	968	10	65535	968	34	161M
46	751	8	0	751	17	50M

Since the original table originated with the XT, the list is not exactly exhaustive or up-to-date.   The original table grew to some 47 entries, some of which still describe small disc sizes that will rarely be found in use any longer.   To further complicate matters, some manufacturers' tables list their own versions of what characteristics match what table number; fortunately, most lower entries remain identical.

Entries 0 to 14 are identical to the entries in the original AT set.   However, a number of entries thereafter have been altered to allow the inclusion of higher-capacity drives than previously specified. This, of course, means that the modified numbers in the table only correspond to that manufacturer's BIOS and will not be available in other BIOS tables. Indeed, the table may well not be the same in future issues of the same manufacturer's BIOS.   Unfortunately, since disc technology is racing ahead, there are increasingly many disc types that are not covered by the existing tables held inside most BIOS chips, regardless of manufacturer.   A way had to be found to future proof the BIOS, otherwise the chip would have to be updated whenever new drive types became available.

ENTRY 47

Fortunately, modern BIOS systems (e.g. IBM, AMI, some Phoenix, etc.) have deliberately left the details for table entry 47 left undefined. This allows a custom configuration to be entered by the user as entry 47. In this way, a BIOS will not age too quickly.

If option 47 is chosen as the drive type, the user is then prompted to enter the following information:

Entry	Meaning
Cylinders	The number of cylinders
Heads	The total number of read/write heads
Write Precompensation - WPC	The starting cylinder for write precompensation to take effect
Landing Zone - LZ	The cylinder to be used as the landing zone for parking the read/write heads
Sectors per track - ST	The number of sectors per track
Size in Mbs	The capacity of the disc expressed in Megabytes

The entries listed are the ones to be commonly displayed by a utility. In fact, there are two other entries held in the table. These are:

- Size in millions of bytes - this holds the disc's capacity in millions of bytes, as opposed to Megabytes.
- Control Byte - the individual bits in this byte are used hold information such as whether the disc has more than eight heads, is a servo drive, etc.

Since the values in the table do not cover new drives, the values that are placed in the CMOS can be any set of values which result in the same, or less, sectors than the actual drive used.   As long as the formula

$$\text{total tracks x number of sectors per track x number of heads}$$

produces a value that is equal or less the sectors value given in the drive specification, the IDE electronics can handle the logical to physical translations. If the total value of sectors exceeds the actual physical sectors, incorrect clusters will be overwritten and data will be lost.

SCSI

The SCSI interface standard is the Small Computer Systems Interface (pronounced 'scuzzy').   This is an old interface, adopted as an ANSI standard in 1986, which has made a serious impact on the general storage market.   The SCSI drive has the controller circuitry built-in and, like the EIDE, it uses logical addressing methods. The drive is connected via a 50-wire or 68-wire cable to an adapter card that connects to one of the computer's expansion slots   Since the controller circuitry is on the drive, the card is described as a 'host adapter' rather than a controller card. Its only real job is to allow SCSI devices to connect to the computer bus.   Since it is a simple device, it is able to connect up to seven or sixteen different devices.   The connecting cable can have a number of connectors attached to, to connect to a number of internally fitted SCSI devices.   External devices, such as DAT drives and external CD ROMs, can connect to the bus via a D-shell connector on the SCSI adapter card.

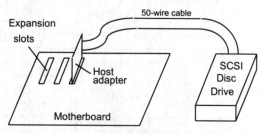

When several devices are connected, the system is described as being 'daisy chained'.   The total length of the chain must not exceed 19 feet (reducing to 9 feet for Wide SCSI and only 5 feet for SCSI-3), to minimise transmission errors.   Each end of the chain must also be fitted with terminating resistors. These terminate the cable and prevent signals being reflected back down the cable as noise.   The terminators may comprise of resistors built in to the device and activated by DIP switches, or they may be separate terminating plugs or 'blocks'.   Each external device has two connectors - one for connecting to the existing chain and one for either extending the chain or terminating the chain.

The intelligence built in to the host adapter is designed to relieve the machine's CPU from the tasks of organising the control of the various devices attached to it.   The machine CPU can transfer these responsibilities to the circuitry of the host adapter card so that it can carry out other activities.

The IDE drive receives instructions that are both disc-specific and low-level. The SCSI controller, on the other hand, communicates at a higher level and is data-specific, leaving the physical considerations entirely to the device's on-board circuitry. The generalised nature of this interface means that it is able to connect more than just disc drives to the motherboard.   A range of devices, such as CD ROMs, tape drives, scanners, etc., can be connected to the SCSI interface with ease.   Each device must be given a different ID number.   With SCSI-1 and SCSI-2, these range from 0 to 7 and the host adapter usually defaults to ID 7. Wide SCSI-2 and SCSI-3 support up to 16 devices. The ID number is set in each device with the DIP switches or jumpers on the cards. Adaptec, a major SCSI adapter manufacturer, pioneered the ASPI (Advanced SCSI Programming Interface). This is a single driver that lets DOS communicate with the adapter card and another driver for each device on the chain.

Since each device on the chain may be able to communicate at a different data rate, the adapter card has to alter its data rate to match each device it is working to any particular time. The card can work at the faster rates for faster devices and will slow down to the rates of the slower devices. To achieve this, the card has to set its standard for communicating with each device.

SCSI VERSIONS

A range of different SCSI standards have evolved with the following data transfer rates from the device to the adapter card. These use different data bus widths and different electronic controls.

Bus widths are either 8-bit or 16-bit. This is the bus between the controller and the drive; the controller may well have a 32-bit interface via the PCI connector.

Fast SCSI doubles the transfer rate by using more stringent electronic parameters which allow timings to be altered and overheads reduced. Ultra SCSI's electronics run at double the normal clock frequency and this produces transfer rates that are double that of Fast SCSI.

Type	Data Rate	Data Path	Comments
SCSI-1/ SCSI-2	5Mb/sec	8-bit	50-pin connector. Asynchronous
SCSI-2 Fast	10Mb/sec	8-bit	50-pin connector . Synchronous
SCSI-2 Fast Wide	20Mb/sec	16-bit	68-pin connector
SCSI-3 Ultra	20Mb/sec	8-bit	50-pin connector. Also called Fast 20.
SCSI-3 Ultra-Wide	40Mb/sec	16-bit	68-pin connector
Ultra-2	40Mb/sec	8-bit	Also called Fast 40.
Ultra-2 Wide	80Mb/sec	16-bit	
	80Mb/sec	serial	Being worked on

Since the data transfer rate between the adapter and an ISA based computer works out at around 2Mb/sec, a SCSI adapter that connects to PCI or VL bus produces far better results.

SCSI systems do not use the machine's BIOS, having placed a device driver in the CONFIG.SYS file to install the necessary control software. This means that a SCSI drive can cohabit with an ST506 or an IDE system in the same machine without any conflicts. In addition, since devices of different transfer rates can work with the same adapter, upgrading to a faster SCSI hard disc will involve no changes to the SCSI adapter. Many CD ROMS, scanners and Postscript printers now have SCSI-2 interfaces.

NOTES
- The best EIDE performances compete with the middle/top SCSI performance but SCSI systems also have an edge on performance in multitasking environments. The CPU can send an instruction to a SCSI device and carry on with other tasks until the device responds. With EIDE, the CPU has to wait until the device responds before carrying out other tasks thereby slowing down throughput, particularly in situations of multiple I/O requests.
- The performance of the interfaces has outstripped the speed of most current drives which run at about a 10Mb/s sustained data transfer rate. Even the most modern and fastest drives (such as the 10,000 rpm Seagate Cheetah) can only provide a sustained transfer rate of up to 30Mb/sec.
- An ultra-wide controller card, such as the Adaptec 2940UW, has both 68-pin connectors (for ultra-wide devices) and 50-pin connectors (for SCSI-2 devices).

WRITE PRECOMPENSATION

IDE and SCSI systems use the disc surface to the maximum advantage. They write more data on the more spacious outer tracks and less data on the more compressed inner tracks. To the outside world, however, they present a logical view that represents the disc as having an identical number of sectors in every track. For other systems, this facility is lacking and this can cause problems of reading and writing data evenly over the disc surface. The sectors that are on the inner tracks on a disc (the higher numbered tracks) are smaller in size than the tracks on the outer surface of the disc. Yet, the track has to hold the same amount of data, for say 36 sectors, whether it is on the inner or outer edges of the disc. It follows, then, that the data is more compressed on the inner tracks than on the outer tracks. The computer data is written on to the disc surface as a stream of magnetised sections, with each section having its own north and south poles like any other magnet.

Magnetised section are separated from the each other by a small unmagnetised area. Problems arise when the inner tracks locate these *'magnets'* closer together, with smaller spaces between them. Their proximity results in the magnetised areas affecting each other, with similar poles repelling and opposite poles attracting. The slight alteration of the magnetic pattern may be sufficient to prevent the data being read back correctly. To correct this, the writing process can treat the inner tracks differently from the outer tracks, by taking into account the likely distortions when placing the data on the surface. The writing process is compensating in advance for the problem, so that the final written information will be where it ought. It is this *'compensating in advance'* that gives the process the name *'precompensation'*. When the data is later read, the inner and outer tracks are read and processed in the same way. Since precompensation is concerned with writing data to the correct place on the disc surface, it only affects the writing process and is not used for reading data.

The parameters for each drive include a write precompensation number. This is the number of the first track at which to apply precompensation when writing data. If a 953 cylinder disc has a precompensation value of 150, then write precompensation starts at track 150 onwards. If the value for the same drive is 953, then no precompensation is applied to that particular disc (this might also be stored as -1).

The reduced physical size of disc area for the storage of each data bit can cause another problem. The electric current used to produce the data writing to the outer tracks could result in each data write occupying too large a disc surface area in the inner tracks. The separating non-magnetised areas disappear and the data elements begin to overlap into each other. To prevent this, the current supplied to the write head is reduced on the inner tracks, creating a smaller write area on the disc surface.

CACHE AND CACHE CONTROLLERS

The speed of a computer's throughput is not solely determined by the raw speed of the CPU. Many applications are disc based and large database applications are specially disc-intensive in their operations. So a large proportion of the time is spent in disc activities rather than processing activities. Windows also makes heavy use of disc operations, particularly if machine memory is small and swap files are in operation. In any case, Windows uses many DLL (Dynamic Link Library) files which function like overlay files with the added benefit that the DLL file can be used by various applications. However, this technique also increases the number of disc accesses required to run applications.

There has been continual progress in CPU development from the days of the 8088 processor. Disc development, although making rapid progress of late, has remained the main bottleneck in the system as it is still largely limited by the mechanical nature of its operations.

Cache controller cards have been developed as a highly successful method of improving disc access times. They work on the same principle as memory cache systems explained previously. Memory cache acted as a high-speed buffer between the fast CPU and slower memory. With disc caching, memory chips are used as a high-speed buffer between the fast CPU and very much slower disc devices.

In fact, DOS buffers is an elementary form of caching. Each buffer stores 512 bytes of data - the same size as a disc sector. With buffers set at 20, 10k of memory is set aside for disc caching. With today's giant applications, this is totally inadequate and most modern disc drives use *'track buffering'* instead of sector buffering. This means that an entire track (or more likely several entire tracks) is read at a time into a memory buffer that is located on the drive's own electronics circuit board. The memory chips for these buffers are soldered directly on to the disc drive's own printed circuit board and cannot be added to. The normal buffer size is between 32k and 512k.

Full disc caching can be implemented in two ways:

1. Using memory chips located on the disc controller card and not part of the PC's normal memory map; they constitute extra memory that is dedicated to interfacing slow disc access with fast CPU access. The controller card is used to replace the normal IDE, ESDI or SCSI controller and is plugged into the normal expansion bus on the machine's motherboard.

   Many of these cards also provide for the control of floppy drives. The memory chips used are normal SIMM boards. With the decreasing price of memory chips, this method has fallen out of favour.

2. Using a chunk of the computer's memory, usually extended memory, under the control of DOS or Windows SMARTDRV utility, or Windows 95 VCACHE utility.

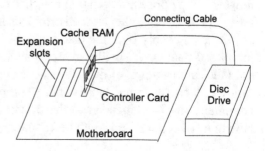

Both caching systems work in the same way. The CPU demands data at a much faster rate than the disc mechanism can fetch it. The cache memory on the controller card - or in smartdrive memory - stores copies of the data that was previously read or written. It also reads ahead - it reads in data from sectors beyond that requested. If the machine wishes to read a file, there is a fair chance that the data is already stored in the cache memory. If so, then it can be transferred at a much faster rate than would be the case with reading directly from disc. If the data is found in cache, then it is described as a *'hit'*; if it has to be fetched from disc, then it is a *'miss'*. To improve the *'hit rate'*, the controller predicts the next data to be read (see notes on the principle of locality) and pre-loads this data into cache memory. This is particularly effective with database records and other data that is organised on a sequential basis.

Caching algorithms can deliver around 90% of data requests from the high-speed cache, avoiding interrogating the hard disc. On the other hand, when there is a cache *'miss'*, the system actually operates more slowly than a non-cached system. There is wasted time, while the cache is fruitlessly searched, before the data is fetched from the disc. Of course, if a very large quantity of data is to be handled, a small controller cache, or a small smartdrive cache, will have only a limited effect on efficiency. The larger the cache memory size, the more likely that the data will be found without recourse to disc access. If the user is working with huge database records, or large graphics files or DTP files, then each read required could be larger than the actual cache size and large disc reads would be required on every occasion. This will slow down throughput and give a poor hit rate. (NOTE : This effect should be borne in mind when measuring cache efficiency with SMARTDRV/S; it is possible that the same machine might be perfectly efficient at handling other processing chores).

When fresh data is to be read in, there will be occasions when the cache is already full of older data. The controller has to decide what data should be overwritten by the new data. This is either based on algorithms called the *'Least Frequently Used'* or the *'Least Recently Used'* methods. As the names imply, either the least popular (the data least requested) or the oldest data is chosen to be overwritten. The LRU (Least Recently Used) algorithm is most commonly used as it is the fastest. This is method that Windows itself uses when deciding which DLLs should be sent to the swap file when its memory resources become tight.

Implementing cache in hardware offers the benefit of greater throughput, since little processor time need be dedicated to cache activity; the controller's built-in CPU decides when data should be read from or written to disc. The controller card may contain a 68000 or an 80186/80188 processor. Controller cards also offer the possibility of elevator seeking techniques, as explained previously, to minimise read/write head movement. The top of the range controller cards also offer *'disc mirroring'*, where the data is written to two different hard discs. If one disc should break down, the data is instantly available from the second disc. There is no down time while the system is replaced and the data is restored.

It is common for modern drives to have 32k, 64k, 128k, 256k or 512k of cache memory built-in to the drive. These are usually referred to as *'track buffers'* Cache controller cards increase this to 2.5Mb up to about 16Mb. It is also argued that the reduced need for disc accesses results in less disc wear, thus prolonging the disc's life. The expected effective access times for cache controller systems are around 0.3ms, which is about 40 times better than a hard disc used without caching.

WRITE CACHING

Some caching only operates for disc reads. If required, the benefits of caching can be applied to disc writes. With write-behind caching, data to be written disc is not written immediately, but is held in the cache memory until the machine's CPU is free. In this way, the machine's throughput is not slowed down by forcing the CPU to deviate from other work to carry out the disc writes. Giving the command SMARTDRV/S produces a display that informs whether its write caching is in operation. With a controller card, the writing to disc can be undertaken by the circuitry on the card, fully relieving the CPU. While write-behind caching improves machine performance, it also leaves data vulnerable. While these systems have a time limit (say four seconds) of holding write data in the cache, this still leaves scope for problems. If for example, there is a power failure, then data that is being held temporarily in the controller memory will be lost. Similarly, any batch files that reboot the machine (such as a batch file to choose from different CONFIG files) might reboot while data was still in the cache. In these circumstances, the data should be flushed to disc prior to rebooting - or the write-behind facility itself should be disabled. Disc controllers can have the system set between either write-through or write-behind. This is also possible with SMARTDRV.

Many publications state that SMARTDRV is a read-ahead only cache and does not have write-behind facilities. This is not so. If the command SMARTDRV/C is added to the batch file prior to rebooting, any data in its cache will be flushed to disc. If it is vital that there be no opportunity for losing data, then write behind caching can be disabled by the SMARTDRV command followed by the drive letter and the minus symbol e.g. SMARTDRV C: - and restored again by the command SMARTDRV C: +
To have read-only cache on a permanent basis, the Windows SMARTDRV.EXE file in the AUTOEXEC.BAT file (or the SMARTDRV.SYS file in the CONFIG.SYS file, if not using Windows) should only have the SMARTDRV command and the drive letter. If a system does not provide write behind caching, it is said to use the *write through* method; in fact, it is simply a normal read-ahead system. Many users prefer to disable write-behind caching since Windows applications are still prone to crashing and this could result in loss of data, corruption of data or even the disc's filing system.

WINDOWS 95 CACHING

Windows 3.1 and DOS use SMARTDRV as the cache controlling software. Windows 95 replaces this replaced with VCACHE. SMARTDRV has minimum and maximum values set during configuration. VCACHE is more intelligent and is able to use the available memory to best advantage. The amount of memory used depends on the demand on the systems resources and the application packages. Depending upon the amount of RAM available at any time, it allocates the amount it needs for cache at that time. If the system demands change, then VCACHE automatically reallocates the amount allocated to caching. Another benefit of VCACHE is that it caches CD-ROMs. If a Windows 95 user also wishes to run DOS programs, then SMARTDRV can still be placed in the AUTOEXEC.BAT file for use with DOS.

DOS DISC ORGANISATION

Like a floppy, when a hard disc is formatted, it creates four areas of the disc, plus an additional area for the Master Boot Record (not required for floppies). The actual order on a disc is as follows:
- Master Boot record
- Boot Record
- FAT
- Directory
- Data Area

Each of these areas occupies differing amounts of disc space, dependent upon the disc's overall capacity. Each is described below, with the order changed to ease the explanation.

DATA AREA

This is by far the largest area of the disc and it contains all the data files and directories (a sub-directory acting in a similar fashion to a data file).
The formatting process sub-divides the data area into many equal sized portions known as *'sectors'*. A sector is the smallest area of the disc that can be independently identified. DOS supports sector sizes of 128, 256, 512 or 1024 bytes but has standardised on a sector size of 512 bytes. Sector size is under software control, hence the description of *'soft-sectored'* discs. Older systems actually punched holes in the disc to define sector boundaries and were described as *'hard sectored'*. These holes were punched in the inner track of the disc and a photoelectric cell detected a light beam as it shone through each passing hole. The number of light pulses detected, when compared to an index hole, determined which sector was being read. This meant that the size and shape of the disc could not be changed but it had the advantage of using all of the surface of each track. Soft sectored systems are more flexible but require to use some of the track area for the synchronising information previously supplied by the punched holes. The ability to control the layout of data on a disc is exploited in some early copy protection schemes. To prevent unlawful copying of discs, manufacturers resorted to non-standard formats such as including a sector that was larger than the rest, or having eight sectors on a particular track instead of nine. Since DOS did not know of their changed layout, the disc could not be read by normal COPY, XCOPY or DISKCOPY commands and the disc could not be duplicated. The disc could still be run, as the program coding would know of the non-standard sections and treat them accordingly.
Note that some utilities report on sectors as 'sector 17551' while others may refer to cylinder 2, head 3, sector 4'. This is because DOS does not wish to know the exact location of a sector in terms of heads and tracks; it prefers to number sectors in continuous ascending order - sector 0,1,2,3,4....15001, 15002, 15003 and so on.

Disc layouts in PCs can be viewed as having two formats:
1. The physical format that is used by the ROM BIOS.   This sees the actual layout in terms of the number of heads, the number tracks, the number of sectors per track and the sector size.   These are termed the *'absolute sectors'* and an absolute sector is identified by its cylinder/head/sector.
2. The logical format as used by DEBUG and various other disc utilities.   This sees the sectors as continually incrementing from sector one, commencing on the first head and the first track and moving inwards.   These are termed the disc's *'relative sectors'* and comprise of single numbers.   These absolute sectors can be mapped into the actual physical DOS absolute sectors.

Cylinder 0/head 0/ sector 1 contains the hard disc's master partition information and is therefore not included in the DOS sector numbering scheme. Cylinder 0, head 1, sector 1 is the equivalent of DOS sector 0.   This sector contains the DOS Boot Record and is normally also ignored in the numbering scheme.   The remaining sectors on the disc are then included in the DOS numbering.

EXAMPLE
In a typical 36-sector disc with 4 heads, side 0 track 5, sector 3 would be an absolute sector.
To have got to that position, four full tracks of 36 sectors must have been scanned by all four heads.
So, 4x36x4 = 556 sectors. The head, having returned to head 0 is moved to sector 3.
This means that the relative sector is 556 + 3 = 559.
Therefore, the absolute sector given by side 0, track 5, sector 3 maps to relative sector number 559.
Note that this will only be the case with discs with four sides. If the disc had six sides, the relative sector would be (6x36x4)+3 = 867.

CLUSTERS
With hard discs, like floppies, space for data is allocated on the basis of *`clusters'*.   A cluster is the smallest group of sectors that can be utilised as a single unit.   A cluster is the smallest disc space that will be allocated to a file, no matter how small the file may be.   There can only be one file in any one cluster, although one large file can span many clusters.   A cluster is composed of one or more sectors.

The cluster size varies with the disc and its formatting.   The actual number of sectors in a cluster depends on the type of disc.   A table of typical examples is given below:

Typical Disc Size	Max Disc Size	Sectors/cluster	Cluster Size
360k 5.25" floppy disc		2	1024
1.2Mb 5.25" floppy disc		2	1024
720k 3.5" floppy disc		2	1024
1.44Mb 3.5" floppy disc		1	512
32Mb hard disc	< 64M	2	1024
100Mb hard disc	< 128M	4	2048
210Mb hard disc	< 256M	8	4096
500Mb hard disc	< 512M	16	8192
850Mb hard disc	< 1Gb	32	16,384
1.3Gb hard disc	< 2Gb	64	32,768
Any disc with OSR2	< 8Gb	8	4096
Any disc with OSR2	< 16Gb	16	8192
Any disc with NT	Any size	1	512

There is a compromise between maximising read speeds and getting the maximum use out of disc space. Large cluster sizes lead to faster access times and faster transfer times but it does waste disc space for smaller files.   However, since many larger applications use large files both for programs and data, it makes sense to use larger cluster sizes in the larger capacity discs.   Floppy discs always have very slow access times due to their design.   Since speed is not the major factor for floppies, they can concentrate on storage efficiency. The 1.44Mb disc, for example, only has a single sector as a cluster.

The clustering of sectors only occurs in the disc's data area - the directories and FATs are organised on an individual sector basis.

The larger the cluster size, the greater potential loss of disc space due to lost capacity in underused clusters.   For example, a small batch file of 30 bytes consumes 512 bytes on a 3.5" HD disc - and as much as 32k on a large hard disc.   Since a file is never likely to use exact multiples of the cluster size, it follows that there is quite a bit of wasted space on a disc. The DIR command only shows the amount of data stored in a file and does not give the actual amount of disc surface allocated to store the file.

Consider the diagram on the next page, which is for a hard disc with 32k clusters. The first two columns display the file names and extensions. The third column shows the file sizes as displayed when a normal

	Displayed size	Actual size
AUTOEXEC BAT	482	32768
BACK TXT	962	32768
BACKCHK DAT	28	32768
COMMAND COM	47845	65536
CONFIG SYS	224	32768
FILELIST DOC	4880	32768
GETCHAR COM	32	32768
HISCORES 3D	275	32768
MENU BAT	572	32768
PCXLIST	57	32768
POWERPNT INI	414	32768
VGA_BIOS EXE	77133	98304
WORD BAT	25	32768
	-------	-------
Totals	132,929	524,288
	-------	-------

DOS DIR command is issued.   According to the DOS report, the 13 files appear to consume 132,929 bytes of hard disc space and they appear to have an average file size of 10.2k.

In fact, they consume 524,288 bytes - a difference of over 291,000 bytes and the average file size is actually 40.3k .

The best case is the COMMAND.COM file, which produces very little waste. The file has been allocated 47,845 bytes and actually consumed 65,536 bytes, with 17,691 bytes being wasted.   The worst case is the WORD.BAT file which only uses 25 bytes of the 32,768 byte cluster.

It follows that the user should avoid the creation of lots of little batch files for trivial jobs that could be carried out from the command line with little extra effort.

As an alternative, thought could be given to producing DOSKEY macros, since they can be embedded in the AUTOEXEC.BAT file and consume no other disc space.

MASTER BOOT RECORD

The Master Boot Record comprises a single sector - sector 1 (i.e. side 0/track 0/sector 1).

The sector contains partition table and other information.   A partition is a portion of the hard disc that appears, and can be treated as, a separate disc drive; not only do partitions act like separate hard discs, they are allocated disc drives letters, 'D', etc.

A partition is a set of contiguous tracks and a partition has to start on the first sector of a track and end on the last sector of a track.

A disc can have more than one partition.

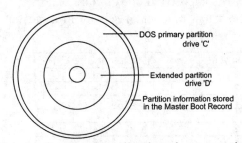

DOS primary partition drive 'C'

Extended partition drive 'D'

Partition information stored in the Master Boot Record

This could be through necessity if older DOS versions are in use, since pre-DOS 4 versions could not handle a hard disc that was larger than 32Mb and Windows 95 Release 1 cant' handle about 2Gb. .   In the case of larger discs, the actual large disc surface would be configured to logically appear as several separate hard discs - disc drive 'C' would be supplemented by drive 'D', drive 'E' or even drive 'F'.

Modern versions of MSDOS can handle larger partitions, but the disc is sometimes partitioned for operational convenience (e.g. placing all applications in one partition and data in another partition).

On other occasions, the hard disc is partitioned so that completely different operating systems can reside in different partitions of the disc. Examples of this are:

- DOS on one partition and UNIX on another partition.
- DOS on one partition and Novell NetWare on another

FDISK is the utility that creates disc partitions. After partitioning, each partition can be formatted to the layout for the particular operating system. The partition table stores the location and length of each of the disc partitions.   There must always be a partition table, even if the disc contains only a single partition.   The number of partitions on a disc and the size of partitions can be later altered with FDISK but, since this process destroys the data in partitions, a full backup would be undertaken before altering disc partitions.

Each DOS partition will contain:

- A DOS boot record, as explained below.
- A FAT for the files in that partition (plus a backup FAT)
- A directory structure for the files in that partition.
- The data area for that partition.

If a disc has more than one partition, then the above will be repeated for each partition, although there will still only be one Master Boot Record with the disc's partition table.   Where there is more than a single partition, the partition table stores a marker for the active partition.   When the machine is booted up, the MBR contains a startup program that passes control to the boot program in the active partition.

Where a disc has more than one partition, the DBR will be repeated at the start of each partition.

The diagram illustrates the layout of a disc that is partitioned into three logical drives.

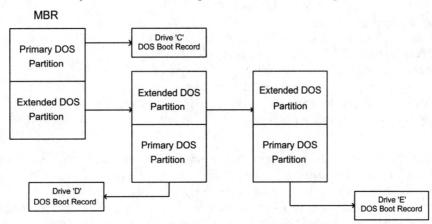

The format of the Master Boot Record can be viewed with any disc editor such as Norton's Utilities:

```
Side 0, Cylinder 0, Sector 1 ═══════════════════ Partition Table format ═

                        Partition Table Editor

             Starting location    Ending location     Relative    Number of
System  Boot Side Cylinder Sector Side Cylinder Sector Sectors      Sectors

DOS-16  Yes   1      0       1     5    320     11         17        32719
DM      No    0     642      1     5    818     17      65484        18054
EXTEND  No    0     321      1     5    641     17      32742        32742
?       No    0      0       0     0     0       0          0            0




                    Press Enter to continue
Help    2Hex    3Text    4Dir    5FAT    6Partn  7       8Choose 9Undo   10QuitN
```

If a disc was partitioned into several logical drives, then the master boot record would be displayed in a similar fashion to the one shown on the diagram, the exact locations being dependent on the size of the hard disc and the proportions in which the space was divided.

DOS BOOT RECORD

The first sector of any DOS partition area is the DOS Boot Record, or *'DBR'*. This sector contains disc information and the code that is used along with IO.SYS and MSDOS.SYS to both cold boot or warm boot the machine. It contains a short machine-code program to load the operating system from disc to memory - if the disc is system formatted (i.e. contains COMMAND.COM, IO.SYS and MSDOS.SYS). The boot record is always created, even if the area is not formatted as a system disc. The boot record also stores details of its own formatting - e.g. bytes/sector, sectors/track, etc. For a floppy, there is no master boot record, so the DOS boot record will be in sector 1 of track 0, side 0. If this sector were viewed with Norton Utilities, the first few lines of the screen dump would look like this for a 720k disc:

```
Side 0, Cylinder 0, Sector 1
EB3C9049 424D2020 352E3000 02020100 027000A0 05F90300 ó<ÉIBM 5.0. etc
09000200 00000000
```

There is a three-byte offset followed by:
- Eight bytes containing the system ID
     (in this case the hex characters 49 42 4D 20 20 35 2E 30 representing the text 'IBM 5.0')
- Two bytes containing the number of bytes per sector
     (in this case 00 02; since Intel stores numbers in reverse order, this is 0200, which is 512).
- One byte containing the number of sectors per cluster (in this case 02)
- Two bytes containing the number of reserved sectors at the beginning
     (this is 01 00, or 1, for current-sized floppy discs)
- One byte containing the number of copies of the FAT (in this case 02)
- Two bytes containing the maximum number of root directory entries supported
     (in this case 70 00 , or 0070h which is 112).

- Two bytes containing the total number of sectors on the disc
  (in this case A0 05, or 05A0h, which is 1440).
- One byte containing the format ID
  (in this case F9 for 720k or 1.2M . A 360k floppy is ID FD,
  a 1.44Mb disc is ID F0 while hard discs are ID type F8).
- Two bytes containing the number of sectors per FAT (in this case 03 00, or 3).
- Two bytes containing the number of sectors in each track (in this case 09 00, or 9).
- Two bytes containing the number of read/write heads (in this case 02 00, or 2).
- Two bytes containing the number of special reserved sectors (in this case 00 00, or zero).

NOTE

The numbers are displayed in hexadecimal, or 'hex', format. This numeric system uses the base of 16 rather than the decimal base 10. So, numbers in any column start at 0 and rise to a value of 15. Since numbers above 9 cannot be shown as a single character, they are replaced by letters of the alphabet. The number 10 is represented by the letter A, the number 11 by the letter B and so on up to 15 being represented by the letter F. The right-most column in a hexadecimal number is to the base 1, while the next column is to the base 16, the next to the base 256 and so on, incrementing by a factor of 16 in each column. To distinguish hexadecimal numbers from decimal numbers, the suffix 'h' is usually added to a hexadecimal number. So 11h and 11 are different, since 11h is 17. In the example display above, the total number of sectors on the disc was displayed as 05A0. Starting from the right-most column the number can be calculated thus: 0 lots of 1 + ten lots of 16 + 5 lots of 256 = 0 + 160 + 1280 = 1440.

The comparative figures shown by Norton for a 1.4Mb disc are:

```
Side 0, Cylinder 0, Sector 1
EB3C904D 53444F53 352E3000 02010100 02E00040 0BF00900 ó<ÉMSDOS5.0.  etc
12000200 00000000
```

These are similar results to the 720k disc, with the exception of:
- the number of root directory entries allowed which is 00E0 or 15x16 = 240.
- the total sectors on the disc which is 0B40 or 11x256 + 4x16 = 2816+64 = 2880.

The comparative figures shown by Norton for a 210Mb hard disc are:

```
Side 1, Cylinder 0, Sector 1
EB3C904D 53444F53 352E3000 02080100 02000200 00F8C900 ó<ÉMSDOS5.0.  etc
24000C00 24000000
```

The main points to note are:
- There are 8 sectors per cluster.
- There are 0200h = 512 entries allowed in the root directory.
- There are 00C9h = 201 sectors storing the data for each FAT.
- There are 0024h = 36 sectors in every track.
- There are 00C0h = 12 read/write heads on the drive.

FILE ORGANISATION

DOS handles file saves and file reads using a combination of the disc DIRECTORY and the disc FILE ALLOCATION TABLE (known as the 'FAT'). The disc Directory stores the list of the files on the disc along with file information such as creation date, etc. (the columns that are viewed when a DIR command is given). The FAT is a table with an entry for each DOS cluster and is used to map the storage of files. DOS uses buffers to cache copies of the FAT and directory.

DIRECTORY

The File Directory is a table of all the files on the disc. A hard disc can accommodate 512 directories in the root directory. The DBR stores the number of directory entries that are allowed for a particular disc. Each directory entry is 32 bytes in length and stores information such as the file name, extension, size, attributes and time and date of creation, as shown in the table.

The **filename** is allocated 8 bytes and the characters must be in

Purpose	Number of bytes
File Name	8
File Extension	3
File Attributes	1
Unused	10
Date Created/Last Updated	2
Time Created/Last Updated	2
First Cluster	2
File Size	4

upper case.   The filename must contain at least one character and if the name is less than eight characters, then the entry is padded with space characters (i.e. ASCII character 32).   If the first letter in the entry is a dot (2Eh) then the entry is for a sub-directory.   If the second byte is also a dot, then the entry contains information on the parent directory of the current directory - the cluster number held in the entry points to the parent directory that calls it.

The **extension** is three bytes long and can consist of no characters at all.   Again, any unused bytes are padded with spaces.

The **attributes** byte consists of eight individual bits, each containing separate information about the file. Each bit has the following meaning, if the bit is set to 1:

Bit 0 : the file is read-only (it cannot be modified or deleted).
Bit 1 : the file if hidden (it cannot be seen by DIR commands).
Bit 2 : the file is a system file (same as hidden).
Bit 3 : the entry is a volume label (it is the disc's volume label and must be in the root directory.   The name and extension data can be combined, allowing a volume label of up to 11 characters.
Bit 4 : the entry is a sub-directory (it points to the sub-directory chain in the FAT - see later. The entry has no data in the file size field).
Bit 5 : the file will be used in an archiving program, such as BACKUP
Bits 6 and 7 are unused

So if a file has an attributes value of 23h or 35, it means that bits 0,1 and 5 are set - so the file is a hidden, read-only file with the archive flag set.

The **time** data is stored in two bytes that record the time that the file was created or was last changed. The system uses a 24-hour clock. The value is valid to the nearest 2 seconds and is calculated thus:

$$\text{Time value} = \text{hours} \times 2048 + \text{mins} \times 32 + \text{secs}/2$$

So, a time of 22:31:12 would result in a value of $22 \times 2048 + 31 \times 32 + 12/2$.

This results in a value of 46,054 which is B3E6h and would be read in a utility as E6 B3.

The **date** is also stored in two bytes and stores the date that the file was created or was last altered.   The value is calculated thus:

$$\text{Date value} = (\text{current year} - 1980) \times 512 + \text{current month} \times 32 + \text{current day}$$

So, the 15th October, 1993 would be stored thus:

$(1993 - 1980) \times 512 + 10 \times 32 + 15 = 6991 = 1B4Fh$ or 4F 1B on a sector editor

The **first cluster** data points to the beginning of the file's allocation chain, as explained later.

The **file size** data is four bytes long and contains the size of the file.

All entries in a newly formatted disc have the first byte in the name set to 00. When a DEL, COPY, DIR, etc. command is given, DOS stops looking for files when it reaches a 00 first byte - knowing that there are no further files on the disc.

A directory entry for a file also includes the first cluster number on the disc that stores the file - this points to starting point in the FAT so that the rest of the file can be traced should the file require more than a single cluster.

A Norton display of a typical root directory is shown below:

```
┌ Sector 403-404 ═══════════════════════════════ Directory format ═
│ Sector 403 in root directory                      Offset 0, hex 0
│                                                    Attributes
│Filename Ext      Size      Date      Time    Cluster   Arc R/O Sys Hid Dir Vol
│        ══
│▓▓▓▓▓▓  SYS      33430   11/11/91    5:00        3         R/O Sys Hid
│MSDOS   SYS      37394   11/11/91    5:00       12         R/O Sys Hid
│MS-DOS_5                  4/01/93   16:32                 Arc                  Vol
│123                      20/10/92   20:11       34                         Dir
│AA                       30/10/92   22:36       39                         Dir
│ACCESS                   15/01/93   16:14       40                         Dir
│ADA                       3/12/92    3:59       41                         Dir
│BANNER                   19/01/93   19:33    10840                         Dir
│CWORKS                   25/01/93   14:37      223                         Dir
│DCDJPG                   16/01/93   14:33       56                         Dir
│DEASE                    20/10/92   21:04       57                         Dir
│DGD                      13/01/93   19:51       60                         Dir
│DISCUTIL                 20/10/92   22:53       61                         Dir
│DOS                       8/10/92   15:49       22                         Dir
│EXCEL                    20/10/92   19:48       74                         Dir
│GRAPHICS                 20/10/92   21:25       88                         Dir
│        ══
│            Filenames beginning with 'σ' indicate erased entries
│                      Press Enter to continue
│1Help  2Hex  3Text  4Dir  5    6Partn  7     8Choose 9Undo  10Quit
```

UNDELETION

When a file is erased, the first byte of the filename is set to E5h - all the other Directory information is left undisturbed.   This ensures that the file will be ignored in any DOS activities such as DIR and COPY, as files commencing with the E5h character are by-passed.   The contents of the file are not deleted since this would involve needless extra time-consuming disc activity.   If a new file to be written needs the space occupied by a deleted file, it can overwrite it at any time. Since the 'deleted' file's data is left intact, it can be easily recovered. Assuming that there has been no further file saves which have overwritten the deleted file's directory or FAT areas, a deleted file can be recovered. An `unerase' utility, such as the MSDOS UNERASE command or disc tool utilities for users with pre-DOS 5 versions, can be used to search for filenames that begin with the E5h character; the rest of the filename is then presented to the user, who can type in the file's commencing letter.   This letter is written back to the directory entry so that it replaces the E5h value.   The file will again be recognised by DOS commands is recovered.

FILE ALLOCATION TABLE

Commonly called the `FAT', the table immediately follows the boot record. The disc space required to store the FAT depends on the size of the disc (e.g. a 1.2Mb floppy needs 14 sectors to store its FAT, a 20Mb AT disc needs 82 sectors and a 201Mb disc requires 402 sectors).
Examples of the different disc sector layouts are:

Disc Type	Boot	FAT	Directory	Data	Total
360k	1	4	7	708	720
720k	1	6	7	1426	1440
1.2M	1	14	14	2371	2400
1.4M	1	18	14	2847	2880
32M	1	126	132	63597	63856
201M	1	402	32	411225	411660

The partition table is not included in the hard disc calculations.   Since floppy discs and small hard discs (up to 16Mb) only support a maximum of 4096 clusters, the FAT size is set at 12 bits, since 12 raised to the power of 2 is 4096.   With larger discs, 16-bit FATs are used, to allow up to 65,636 entries.   16-bit FATs are only supported in DOS from version 3.3 onwards.   12-bit entries are an inheritance from the days when hard discs were small and all disc space was precious.   The table contained in the FAT stores an entry for every cluster on the disc.   The value held in the FAT indicates whether that cluster is:
- Already in use (i.e. is storing user data)
- Free for use (i.e. can be used for storing a new file, or part of a new file)
- Marked as Unusable (i.e. there is a faulty sector in that cluster).

The possible values in the FAT are:

Purpose	Contents
In Use (part of a chain)	Another cluster number
In Use (end of a chain - EOF)	FFF8-FFFF
Free/Available	0000
Reserved	FFF0-FFF6
Bad Cluster (marked by FORMAT)	FFF7

With floppy discs, the value for unusable will be FF0-FF7, while EOF values will be in the range FF8-FFF.   Like the directory area, the FAT values are set to 00 when the disc is first formatted.   The first entry in the FAT is always the disc ID - F9 for a 720k or 1.2M floppy, FD for a 360k floppy, F0 for a 1.44Mb floppy and F8 for a hard disc).

READING A FILE

If a file is short, under 4k, it will only occupy a single cluster.   In such a case, the cluster number stored in the directory entry points to the sole cluster of the program.   However, most files are longer than 4k and would therefore occupy several, or many, clusters.   The collection of clusters for that file is known as a 'chain' or 'allocation chain'. The start of the chain is the commencing cluster stored in the directory entry.   In the example this is cluster 77. If entry 77 is examined in the FAT table it will indicate whether any further clusters are required to be read for that file.   For a small file of a single cluster, entry 77 would store the end of file marker - a value between FFF8 and FFFF. No further clusters are read.
For larger files, as in the example, entry 77 stores the location of the next cluster that comprises the file's chain (cluster 78).

Cluster 78, in turn stores the location of the third cluster in the file's chain. Notice that this is cluster 80, since cluster 79 was not written to due to it being a bad cluster. Cluster 80 then points to the fourth cluster of the chain. In fact, this is the <u>last</u> cluster of the chain, as indicated by end of file marker stored there. The system continues to read data until the end of the chain is reached, or the data read equals the size of the file as stored in the directory.

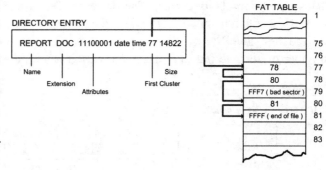

CREATING A FILE

When a <u>new</u> file is written to disc, its details are placed in the Directory, in the first unused entry. This may be a previously unused entry, or it may be overwriting an erased entry. The first FAT entry that is marked as free is used to store the first cluster of the file and two bytes of the directory entry are used to store this initial cluster location. If the file is small enough to fit in the single cluster, the FAT entry is set to FFFF, to indicate end-of-file. For larger files, the next free cluster is found, further user data is stored there and the contents of the initial cluster number in the FAT table are updated to point to this second cluster. This will continue until the entire file is stored - at which point the FAT entry for the last cluster to store that file's data is given the end-of-file value FFFF. When the disc is formatted (or re-tested later with a utility), faulty sectors are isolated by placing the value FFF7 in the corresponding FAT entry. DOS will not attempt to write to these clusters, when allocating new files.

NOTES
- Since the FAT is a central part of the entire disc operation, a second copy is also stored on the disc. Both copies are updated for each file write. The primary FAT is the working version used for DOS reads; the secondary copy is used as a backup in the event of FAT corruption problems. When writing to a file, both FAT copies are updated; when reading files, only the main FAT is used.
- The CHKDSK command does not make good any difference in the two FATs, although add-ons, such as Norton Utilities can detect and repair any FAT damage.
- CHKDSK only reports on the FAT entries which are already marking clusters as bad; it does not detect any newly faulty clusters. Only a special utility program, of which there are many in the commercial and shareware market, will test and mark any faulty clusters that are not currently marked in the FAT as bad. With DOS 6.2, SCANDISK will carry out this task.
- To save storage space, 12-bit FATs only occupy the FAT space that they actually require. For floppy discs, early small hard discs under 16Mb and small partitions - in fact, any situation where there are less than 4096 clusters - the 12-bit code is used and occupies 1½ bytes. So, FAT entries are bunched into pairs with a pair occupying three bytes of the FAT. This improves storage at the expense of a more complex algorithm to extract the chain values from the FAT. This means that a user cannot directly examine a floppy disc's file chain by directly reading the values in the FAT. Fortunately, many utilities allow the FAT to be viewed directly with the conversion being carried out by the utility. With modern hard discs, the task is more direct, since the FAT entries are 16-bit. This means that each entry in the chain occupies a distinctive pair of bytes in the FAT and tracing of the chain is therefore simplified.

HANDLING SUB-DIRECTORIES

The above example was a simple case where all files resided in the root directory of the hard disc. In fact, most files will reside within sub-directories of the disc, to various layers of depth. This means that the sub-directories and their files must fit within the structure outlined above. This is achieved by making a sub-directory an entry within the main root directory, similar to making an entry for a normal file. It will have a directory entry similar to a file directory entry. In this case, however, the *'Directory'* attribute is set to indicate that it is not a file. In this instance, the *'First Cluster'* stored in the directory entry points to a cluster similar to the layout in the diagram. The cluster holds information on the files in its directory in the same way they are stored in the root directory. The cluster stores all the normal date, time and size information.

It also stores the starting clusters of these files which can then have their chains traced in the usual manner, as previously described. The first two entries in the directory cluster are the single dot and double dot that appear whenever a DIR command is issued in a sub-directory.

These are compulsory entries. The dot entry refers to the sub-directory itself and the double dot entry points to the parent sub-directory (i.e. the directory that called it).

At the first level down from the root, all sub-directories will have a double dot entry with a cluster number of zero, to indicate that it was called from the root directory. If the cluster number is not zero,

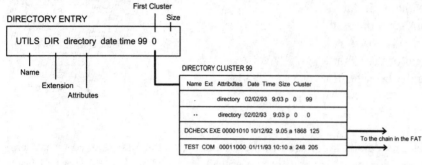

then that sub-directory is more than one level down from the root directory and it stores the cluster number of the sub-directory which is its parent.

A large hard disc with a 4096 byte cluster can hold a maximum of 128 entries, since each directory entry is 32 bytes long. The 128 entries may be a mixture of files and other sub-directories, as required. When using smaller discs, or when requiring to store more than 128 files, a second or further directory clusters would be required to store all the additional entries. Where more than a single cluster is devoted to a sub directory, the FAT table is used to point to the next cluster in the sub-directory chain. With a single-cluster sub-directory, the FAT entry will store the end of file marker.

NOTE

Since the files and directories in the root directory are created in purely chronological order, many hundreds of files will already be present in the root directory prior to some important directories being created. These directory entries appear well down the list of root directory entries. Should the sub-directory wish to be accessed, the whole directory must be sequentially searched until the sub-directory entry is found. This can slow down file accesses and it would improve matters if directories could appear further up the directory table. Fortunately, Norton has a utility called DS.EXE which can re-write the directory so that sub-directories appear at the top of the table, prior to single files. The directories and files can be sorted into alphabet order or, if desired, the order of individual directories can be decided to allow the most-frequently accessed directories to appear at the top of the directory table.

FRAGMENTATION

Often, a file can be stored as one contiguous block of disc space. However, files can end up occupying several non-contiguous areas of the disc, when:

- An existing file is added to. Unless it is the last file in the FAT table (very unlikely), the extra data will have to be placed in the first free clusters.
- A new file is allocated the space of a smaller erased file. Again, the extra data is forced to overflow into a non-contiguous area of the hard disc.

The resultant diffusion of files across the disc can be viewed using the `disc map' facilities of DOS 6 'DEFRAG' or Norton Utilities or PC Tools. The continual movement of the head from one area of the disc to another can substantially slow down data retrieval, up to around 25% extra wasted time.

Fragmentation can be overcome by backing up and restoring the disc, although this is a bit drastic. A better option is to use utilities such as the DOS 6 DEFRAG command, Norton's `Speed Disc' or PC Tools' `Compress'. These can re-order the allocations to achieve contiguous space for files. The result of defragmenting is to have each file occupying consecutive disc clusters.

Defragmentation utilities cannot run under multi-tasking environments, including Windows, since disc accesses might be required to maintain multi-tasking disc swaps. Windows, for example, may wish to use virtual memory to effect multi-tasking and it would be impossible to carry out defragmentation while another program was writing to disc. Even Windows versions of defragmenters only work if no other applications are running. And, it is always best to carry out a disc defragmentation before attempting to establish permanent swap files in Windows, since these files require a contiguous disc area.

USING DEFRAG

The command can be used with or without switches. When switches are used, these are given at the command line prompt. When used without switches, the user is taken into a more user-friendly front end that provides the same services. The first screen requires the user to choose what disc to work on.

When the drive is selected, a map appears on the screen displaying the used spaces and free spaces on that disc. The user is also given a short report and recommendation similar to that shown. The user can then choose between the *'Optimise'* and *'Configure'* options.

> 98% of drive C: is not fragmented
> Recommended optimisation method:
> Unfragment files only

The Optimise option defragments the disc according to its own recommendation.

The Configure options provide for:

Full Optimisation - All directories are brought to the front, all files are made contiguous and are shuffled to the front of the disc, after the directories. This is the most thorough option but is also the slowest.

Unfragment Files Only - This is the faster option since it only ensures that all files are left contiguous. There is no shuffling of files to the front so gaps will be left between files. This speeds up the access of the existing files on the disc but future files are liable to fragmented due to the gaps left between files.

File Sort - The Directory area stores filenames in random order of chronology - i.e. a new file is added to end of the current Directory entries. Defrag allows for files to be stored in ascending or descending order of file name, file extension, date & time or file size.

If entered at the DOS prompt, the drive letter must be entered and the following possible switches:

/F	Carry out a Full Optimisation	/U	Unfragment Files Only
/SN	Sort files in ascending order of filename	/SN-	Sort files in descending order of filename
/SE	Sort files in ascending order of file extension	/SE-	Sort files in descending order of file extension
/SD	Sort files in ascending order of file date & time	/SD-	Sort files in descending order of file date & time
/SS	Sort files in ascending order of file size	/SS-	Sort files in descending order of file size

EXAMPLE:

DEFRAG C: /F /SS-

will carry out a full defragmentation of the C: drive with files sorted in descending order of file sizes.

FAT PROBLEMS

The FAT and directory are the parts of the disc that are continually read and written. Every time a file is created or modified, the directory and FAT entries are updated. Since these areas are the most used on the disc, they are most at risk of corruption through hardware, software or power problems.

USING CHKDSK

The MSDOS CHKDSK command can be a useful utility as long as the user knows what it can and cannot do. It is not a particularly user-friendly repair utility, although it can be a useful diagnostic aid. When run, CHKDSK compares the size of each file as given the directory entry; it then checks whether there are the correct number of clusters in the file's chain to accommodate the file. In making these checks, a number of problems are detected along the way. These problems are rarely hardware faults - they are usually software glitches that have made rogue writes to the FAT, or users switching off the power before a program has completed its disc housekeeping, or users pressing Alt-Ctrl-Del to escape from a problem they don't understand. Although CHKDSK can be used to effect some disc repairs, it is better to use a more intelligent utility such as Norton's Disk Doctor since it provides a better chance of cleaning up the disc structure without loss of data. Of course, on seriously corrupted discs, even Disk Doctor will report that it cannot successfully recover a disc.

ALLOCATION ERRORS

The file's size is held in the directory entry. From this can be calculated the number of clusters that it ought to require to be stored. If a file's size indicates that it requires 4 clusters and CHKDSK detects a chain of 3 clusters or 5 clusters it will produce an *'allocation'* error message.

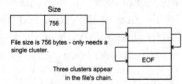

INVALID CLUSTER

Every chain in the FAT table ought to terminate in an end of file marker. If CHKDSK discovers that a chain terminates in a value of zero or a bad file marker, it will produce a *'file has invalid cluster'*

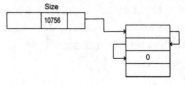

message. CHKDSK will tidy up the situation by truncating the file.

If the situation remains undetected, then the cluster will be used in a future file allocation. So two file chains will point to the same cluster (see the later section on cross-linked clusters).

LOST CLUSTERS

If the user aborts an application in the middle of a disc write operation, the application should complete the file activity before closing down. If the application is poorly written, or if there is a power glitch or

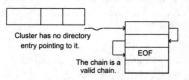

Cluster has no directory entry pointing to it.

The chain is a valid chain.

EOF

the user has simply turned off the machine prematurely, the file activity may be halted before completion. Since the last act of a file write activity is the updating of the file's directory entry, the chain can end up written to disc without being pointed to by a directory entry. Other causes of 'lost clusters' messages are applications which only partially delete their temporary files and programs which write directly to the directory and FAT areas. Every time a file is deleted, DOS should mark all the clusters in the chain as being free, thereby putting them back into the general pool for future file allocations. Anything which prevents these clusters being marked as free results in them being ignored in the allocation of future files - even although they are not being used to any good purpose.

Running CHKDSK, dependent on the DOS version, produces one of the following messages:

Errors found, F parameter not specified	Errors found, F parameter not specified.
Corrections will not be written to disk	Corrections will not be written to disk.
1 lost allocation units found in 1 chains.	4 lost clusters found in 3 chains.
1024 bytes disk space would be freed	Convert lost chains to files (Y/N)?

In fact both messages merely report on the problems found; selecting the 'Y' option makes no difference whatsoever as the problem is not cleared up. It will produce a report similar to the following:

210546688 bytes total disk space
856064 bytes in 199 directories
16384 bytes would be in 3 recovered files

This option merely reports on the likely effects of cleaning up the disc. To effect a repair, the CHKDSK command should have the /F parameter added at the end. This provides an option to "Convert lost chains to files?". If the user answers 'N' then the clusters in the chain are marked as free in the FAT table, to return them for further use. If the user answers 'Y' then the program attaches a directory entry to the chain. Since the original file name is not known, DOS gives it the name FILE0000.CHK, with any subsequent recovered files being titled FILE0001.CHK, FILE0002.CHK, etc. The recovered files can be examined to see if the contents are usable. Often, the recovered file is a valueless temporary file or the file may be in machine code and therefore unreadable without a disassembler utility. However, text files may be examined and the file may be brought back into use and renamed if desired.

CROSS-LINKED CLUSTERS

If the chains of two different files point to the same cluster, a 'cross-linked clusters' message results. This is usually the result of clashes of software or disc hardware problems. DOS does not have a utility to repair this situation. However, utilities, such as Norton's Disc Doctor, can carry out an

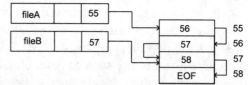

intelligent repair. If there is no utility to hand, the only other method is to save the affected files with new names, delete the original affected files and then rename the files back to their original names. This is not usually fully successful and a file may end up with too much data or data loss. An examination of the recovered files contents is possible if they happen to be text files; it takes a lot more skill to unscramble files containing machine code instructions. If at all possible, EXE, COM and overlay files which have been cross-linked should be replaced with the original files from the installation discs.

DIRECTORY CORRUPTION

If the directory area becomes corrupted, the chains that comprise the files are still intact in the FAT area, but the directory entries no longer point to the start of the chains as they once did. If the user edits the directory with a disc editor such that the first cluster field contains 00, then the CHKDSK/F command will recover the file into a new file called FILE000.CHK and can then be renamed. In this way, the file is recovered without the need to carry out any intensive search of FAT chains. Of course, if many files are corrupted, the above process would produce lots of files which would have to be interrogated, identified and renamed. This might be an essential - if boring - task where a data file has no backup copy.

In the case of application files, it is much quicker to simply re-install the application.

SCANDISK

DOS 6.2 introduced the *'ScanDisk'* utility which is a preferred alternative to CHKDSK. Like CHKDSK, it can carry out tests and repairs on the disc's FAT, directory structure and files. It can also check the disc for faulty clusters, whether or not the cluster currently is being used to store a file. It can check the DOS boot sector and works with hard discs, floppy discs, PCMCIA memory cards and even RAM drives. It is not capable of testing remote drives such as those over a network or over DOS Interlink. It must not be used when other programs are running. It can be called with no parameters and this checks the current drive, or it can be used with a named drive (e.g. *'SCANDISK D:'*), multiple drives (e.g. *'SCANDISK C: D:'*) or can check out all local drives on the computer (e.g. *'SCANDISK/ALL'*).

DOS RECOVER COMMAND

Finally, a word of warning about using the RECOVER command. It has a helpful-sounding name but it can have lethal consequences. The DOS manual states that it *"Recovers readable information from a bad or defective disk"*. To achieve this, it checks out every cluster in a file or a disc. If a cluster in a chain is found to be defective, the other parts of the chain are saved under a new name and the defective cluster is marked as bad in the FAT. This is not as useful as it may seem, since if a single sector in the cluster is bad, the contents of the entire cluster are ignored in the recovery process. Other disc editors could be used to recover the data from the functioning sectors and thereby recover more information than with the DOS command. The real problem with RECOVER is its ability to check an entire disc. If the command RECOVER C: is given, it moves all files into the root directory, deleting all sub-directories. If that wasn't bad enough, it then renames every single file in the hard disc as FILE0001.REC, FILE0002.REC, etc. - including the system files! And, since the root can only hold 512 entries, all other files are lost! It would be a good idea, therefore, to remove the RECOVER program from every DOS directory on every machine in an organisation, to prevent the unwary from using the program. DOS gives the following warning when the command is used for an entire drive:

> The entire drive will be reconstructed,
> directory structures will be destroyed.
> Are you sure (Y/N)?

The reader of Microsoft's manual on the other hand will be told that:

> *"When you recover an entire disk, each recovered file is placed in the root directory in a FILEnnnn.REC file"*.

This is a misleading statement to say the least, since it could lead to operators using the program in the belief that only corrupted files would be affected by the changes.

WINDOWS 95

Windows 95 reorganises the old file structure to provide the following benefits:

- Supports partitions greater than 2Gb (Release 2 only)
- Minimises disc wastage by using small cluster sizes (Release 2 only)
- Supports long filenames

FAT32

With Release 2 (OSR2) the filing system has become known as FAT32, as distinct from the 16-bit FAT16 that hard discs use with DOS, Windows 3.1 and Windows 95 Release 1.

The chart on page 270 shows the makeup of a 32-byte directory entry. Two bytes were allocated to point to the starting cluster of a chain. 16 bits can only store up to 65,536 different numbers making that the maximum number of clusters for a disc of even the biggest size. This means that an 8Gb disc would have to use clusters of 128k (ie 8Gb/65536) and a future 32Gb disc would require a cluster size of 512k. This means that a small batch file of 100 bytes would occupy a 0.5M of disc space! FAT32 future proofs the computer by using two of the ten 'reserved' bytes in the Directory to provide a four byte address for clusters. A 32-bit location can store four thousand million different numbers; this allows the maximum size of a disc to be 4G x 512 bytes - ie 2 Terabytes. It also means that the size of a cluster could be reduced to a single sector.

Max Disc Size	Sectors/cluster	Cluster Size
< 8G	8	4096
< 16G	16	8192
< 32Gb	32	16384
> 32Gb	64	32768

To minimise the size of the disc's two FAT areas, a compromise minimum cluster size of 4k is used. This cluster size also allows VCACHE to speed up disc accesses by keeping a copy of the FAT in memory as best it can.

LONG FILENAMES

A benefit of Windows 95, in both Release 1 and Release 2, is the ability to have file names that are up 255 characters in length, accept spaces and full stops, allows upper and lower case - and still remain backwards compatible with DOS and Windows 3.1.

When upgrading to Windows 95, there is no need to re-format the discs as the long filenames can be integrated into the existing Directory and FAT structures. The older files will continue to use the storage methods described earlier, while files under Windows 95 will use extensions to the existing system to provide both 8.3 and long file name versions of files that it stores.

The 32 byte Directory entry described on page 270 remains in use under Windows 95. This only provides for 11 characters for the file name. This cannot be increased without making the file structure incompatible with DOS and Windows 3.1. The solution lies in the attribute byte,

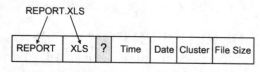

REPORT.XLS

| REPORT | XLS | ? | Time | Date | Cluster | File Size |

shown shaded in the diagram. The purpose of each bit in the byte is explained on page 271. There is no occasion when the first four bits are all set at the same time (ie the directory entry cannot be both a volume label and a system file).

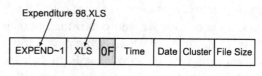

Expenditure 98.XLS

| EXPEND~1 | XLS | 0F | Time | Date | Cluster | File Size |

Microsoft takes advantage for long filenames by setting the first four bits (ie the byte stores the value 15 or 0Fh). DOS and older Windows applications do not test for this and therefore only see the traditional 8.3 file format. Windows 95 applications and utilities check for the attribute byte being set to 0Fh and detect that a long file name is present. It then uses a chain of LFN (long filename) directory entries, each entry storing another part of the name; this works as an altered version of sub-directories as explained page 273/4.

Since DOS and older Windows applications require the traditional file naming, the long name is truncated to 6 letters, a tilde sign and a number as shown in the example. Extension names are unaffected, as are filenames that are 8

Long File Name	Truncated File Name
REPORT.DOC	REPORT.DOC
Minutes of October	MINUTE~1
Minutes of November	MINUTE~2

characters or less. Where a file's first six characters are identical to another file, the number at the end of the file name is incremented.

Many of the existing utilities are designed to run at a low level and do not understand the mechanisms being used by Windows 95. As a consequence, they cannot be used and Windows 95 version of disc utilities have to be purchased. Microsoft's Disk Defragmenter and ScanDisk utilities, as supplied with Windows 95, understand the new structure and are safe to use.

INITIALISING A DISC

Most disc drives arrive pre-formatted. Indeed, many have DOS and/or Windows pre-installed. If this is not so, then the disc will have to be initialised for use. In addition, there are occasions when the best solution to surface problems seems to be clean the disc back to scratch. This involves:
- low level formatting
- partitioning
- high level formatting

Any files on the hard disc are destroyed by the formatting/partitioning process and must be backed up before the process is started. However, if Partition Magic or the FIPS freeware programs are used, then non-destructive partitioning can be carried out. Partition sizes can be re-allocated without loss of existing disc contents. Also, a floppy disc (of the type which is suitable for the machine's A drive) must be formatted as a system disc and the FDISK and FORMAT files must be placed on this disc.

LOW LEVEL FORMATTING

The routines for low level formatting are usually tucked away and are accessed in one of three ways:
- Via a hard disc drive utility supplied with the machine.
- Via a BIOS routine called from the setup menu offered during bootup.
- Via a BIOS routine called via DEBUG.

In each case, it is important that the user either knows which type to pick from the pre-defined hard disc table, or already has a list of the required parameters such as number of tracks, sectors, write precompensation details, etc.   The exact list of pre-set drive configurations offered depends on the BIOS in use.   Earlier BIOS versions obviously were introduced before new larger drives became available.

To use the DEBUG utility, the following steps should be taken:

1. Run DEBUG and at the prompt, a minus sign, enter D C800:00.   This should display the BIOS copyright message for the common Western Digital controllers.   If the copyright message is not displayed, enter D CC00:00, which is the other common BIOS address for disc calls.
2. If none of the above produce a copyright message, consult the disc controller manual.
3. When the correct location is found, enter G=C800:5 or G=CC00:5 or the address given in the disc controller manual.   This will usually display a menu allowing the declaration of the disc's parameters and low level formatting of the disc.

This information is stored in a block of CMOS memory, a small area of RAM that is permanently powered up by the machine's internal rechargeable batteries.

The above instructions are for MFM and RLL systems. Remember that IDE drives cannot be low-level formatted as they come pre-formatted from the factory and can't be re-formatted.

PARTITIONING

Creating DOS partitions is achieved using the DOS FDISK command.   In DOS versions prior to 4.01, each partition had to be 32Mb or less.   From version 4.01 onwards, there has been no such restriction and an entire disc up to 2Gb could be created as a single partition.   For non-DOS partitions, the utilities for partitioning would be supplied by the particular manufacturer.

FDISK provides for two different kinds of hard disc DOS partition:

1. The DOS primary partition - this contains the DOS system files and is the 'C' drive.
2. The DOS extended partition - this partition area can be further divided into other logical drives, 'D', 'E', etc.   If it remains as a single drive partition then it is logical drive 'D'.   Remember, each logical drive is only a proportion of the actual surface area of a single hard disc.   From a DOS point of view, it is a completely separate drive, with its own boot record, FATs and directory.   As such, it functions as an independent disc drive and can be treated as such when it comes to formatting and ordinary disc read, write and copy activities.

Only one partition can be active at any one time and the primary partition must be the active partition if DOS is to be available at bootup.

If Partition Magic or the FIPS freeware programs are used, then non-destructive partitioning can be carried out. Partition sizes can be re-allocated without loss of existing disc contents.

Running FDISK produces a menu as shown on the right.

Option 4 can be run to display current partition information, if the disc has previously been initialised. This can be carried out without any loss of data. However, if the utility is used to change partition sizes, then the data on the disc will certainly be destroyed and a backup of all disc contents should be backed up prior to any partition changes.

```
            MS-DOS Version 5.00
           Fixed Disk Setup Program
      (c) Copyright Microsoft Corp. 1983-1991


                FDISK Options


    Current fixed disc drive: 1


    Choose one of the following:

    1. Create DOS partition or Logical DOS Drive
    2. Set active partition
    3. Delete partition or Logical DOS Drive
    4. Display partition information

    Enter choice: [  ]
```

A report on a typical hard disc is:

```
Display Partition Information

Current fixed disk drive: 1

Partition Status  Type   Volume Label  Mbytes  System  Usage%
C: 1      A       PRI DOS  MS-DOS_5     201     FAT16   100%
```

The 'A' in the second column indicates that it is the active partition.

Where the same disc is partitioned into two, the display might show the following:

```
Display Partition Information

Current fixed disk drive: 1

Partition Status  Type   Volume Label  Mbytes  System  Usage
C: 1      A       PRI DOS  MS-DOS_5     51      FAT16   25%
   2              EXT DOS               150             75%
```

In this case, since there is more than one partition, the user will be offered the opportunity to view the information on the logical drives in the extended partition.

A typical display would be as shown in the diagram:

Note that if a partition was smaller than 16Mb, it would only need a 12-bit FAT to store its chain and the second last column would then read FAT12.

```
Display Logical DOS Drive Information

Drv  Volume Label  Mbytes   System  Usage
D:   GRAPHICS      50       FAT16   33%
E:   APPS          100      FAT16   67%

Total Extended DOS Partition size is 150
Mbytes
```

The steps involved in partitioning a drive are:
- Delete any previous partitions on the disc, using option 3.
- Create a primary partition, using option 1. This offers options to create a DOS Partition or a Logical DOS Drive. When 'Create Primary DOS Partition' is chosen, the option is then given to have the primary partition as the sole partition on the disc. If a single partitioned disc is required, opt to have the primary partition as the maximum possible size. This will be drive C and will be the active partition.
- If a second partition is required, then call option 1 for a second time, followed by choosing the 'Create Extended DOS Partition' option. The remaining disc space is offered as the size for the extended partition. Since only one extended partition can be attached to each drive, the size entered should be the total amount of remaining disc space.
- If a second partition is created and sized, a new menu appears to offer the creation of Logical Drives in the extended partition. If a single logical drive is required, simply press the return key; this results in the entire partition being described as drive D and being allocated all of the disc space given to the extended partition. Otherwise, the amount of extended partition space required for the D drive should be typed in (either in Megabytes or as a percentage of the available partition space, followed by the percentage symbol), followed by the return key. This will call the logical drive D and allocate it the nominated amount of extended partition space. Other drive allocations can be similarly made, until the extended partition space is used up.
- If more than one partition is created, option 2 must be invoked, to make the primary DOS partition the active partition. If this is not done, the machine will not be able to boot up from the hard disc.

Where a machine has more than one hard disc, using FDISK will result in an extra option in the opening menu. This is option 5 which offers 'Choose Current Fixed Disk Drive'. This allows either disc to be accessed for FDISK operations. The second disc can be either a single partition or can also be partitioned with multiple logical disc drives. Any logical drives on the second disc will commence after the last drive letter used in the first drive. In any case, the machine will always boot to the C drive.

HIGH LEVEL FORMATTING

When FDISK is exited, the machine displays a message saying 'System will now restart' and the system disc should be inserted in the A drive. This returns the system to the prompt. If the machine is switched off at this stage, a later reboot will only result in an 'Invalid media' message. In this case, the machine should be re-booted from a system floppy disc that contains the DOS FORMAT program.

The disc is still unable to be used and each partition has now to be individually formatted. Use the DOS command FORMAT C:/S to format the primary partition with the DOS system files. Any logical drives can be formatted with the unadorned command e.g. FORMAT D:, FORMAT E:, etc. The high level format generates the boot sector, produces a FAT and directory and checks for defective sectors.Note that using the FORMAT command with a floppy disc carries out both a low-level and a high-level format.

PROTECTING FILES

Computers are excellent tools but are susceptible to temperature, power cuts or fluctuations and magnetic fields. This can lead to a sudden breakdown of a machine and the collapse of the program it is running. Worse still, it can lead to the loss or corruption of important data. In most organisations, the data held in the machine is more important than the machine itself. If a hard disc crashes, it is a simple matter of purchasing and fitting another disc. However, if scores of Megabytes, or even Gigabytes, of data are lost, then countless amounts of man-hours are required to replace this data. In many cases the data can be reconstituted from paperwork (e.g. customer forms, order forms, etc.). In other cases, the data has no paperwork equivalent (e.g. telephone orders or data that was automatically gathered from remote stations) and this can be lost forever.

Despite all efforts to achieve reliability, these losses remain a distinct possibility. The only defence is to ensure that important data is copied away at regular intervals, thus creating backup copies. In the event of machine failure and data loss, the user can reconstitute the data using the backup version. The user then only has to add the changes that have occurred to the data since the date and time of the backup.

FREQUENCY OF BACKUPS
The frequency of backups is a matter for the individual organisation; there is no one answer. The question can be answered by asking *"how much extra effort would be required to reconstitute lost data if backups were carried out weekly instead of daily?"* or *"is there any data that can afford to be lost at all?"* If data changes slowly on a particular machine, there may be less need to carry out frequent backups. Where the data on a machine is regularly changing, then degree of change should be reflected in the frequency of backing up. Although this holds true for most circumstances, there will be occasions when frequent backups are important for even slowly moving data. In circumstances where the data being added contains vital information, then it may be that a more frequent backup is required to ensure that this information is not lost.

BACKUP STRATEGY
Most organisations conduct their backup activities in an organised way to minimise duplicated effort. When the disc is backed up for the first time, a full backup is carried out requiring many floppy discs to store the hard disc's data. Where cost effective, tape streamer backup drives can be used, some with removable tape cartridges. In general, there is little need to back up application programs since they are readily available from the installation discs that came with the application's purchase. The only exception may be where an application is heavily customised at installation time and backing up would save these settings.

When the time came for the second backup, a great deal of time can be saved if only new files and those files that have been altered are backed up to disc; there is no point in wasting time and discs to back up data which has not been changed since the last backup. When the third backup is carried out, again a smaller number of discs are used for the backup. The discs are grouped and labelled for an incremental restore, if need be. Eventually, the older sets of discs would be brought back into use to store fresh backup data. Every so often, say monthly, a complete backup would be instigated to freshen the set of backup discs.

DOS provides two commands to handle backups
1. The BACKUP command creates the backup copies. This can be a copy of the contents of a single directory, with or without its lower subdirectories. This means that the user start from the root directory and backup the entire disc, if required. As a refinement, the user can decide to only back up selected files, rather than all files in a directory.
2. The RESTORE command recreates the copy on the original disc, if required.

Normally, the BACKUP command will be used regularly, say daily, while the RESTORE command will only be used in an emergency.

USING BACKUP
The basic syntax of the command is as below:
BACKUP C:\TEST.DIR*.* A:
This command will make a backup copy of all the files in the TEST.DIR directory of the hard disc on to the 'A' floppy drive. It is important to note that this command will delete all the previous contents of the destination disc.

The BACKUP command does not work like the COPY or XCOPY commands, which copy the files in their original format. With these commands, the individual files can still be accessed on their own. The BACKUP command copies the files over to the destination disc in a coded form and they cannot be accessed until they have been re-processed with the RESTORE command. The main data files are compacted into a single file, along with a control file that is used to track the files in the backup file. An example of a backup disc is shown. If a backup requires several floppy discs to hold the data, the program will prompt for the disc to be changed. In that case, DOS numbers each disc label as BACKUP 001, BACKUP 002, etc. and the files on the disc are numbered as BACKUP.001 with CONTROL.001 onwards.

```
Volume in drive A is BACKUP  001
Volume Serial Number is 3038-1A01
Directory of A:\

BACKUP  001   166484 14/06/97  18:57
CONTROL 001      889 14/06/97  18:57
     2 file(s)   167373 bytes
             562176 bytes free
```

Like most DOS commands, the BACKUP command allows a number of different parameters to provide added flexibility.

These are:

/s	Also backup the files in any sub-directories.
/m	Back up only those files that have changed since the last backup.

/m Back up only those files that have changed since the last backup.
This also turns of the 'archive' attribute on the original file, so that it will not be backed up in a future /m backup (unless it has been modified in the meantime, thus turning back on the 'archive' attribute).

/a Append the backup files to those already on the floppy disc. The destination disc is not deleted and the new backup data is merely added to the disc.

/l Create a log file (BACKUP.LOG) of all the files backed up. This is a text file that lists all the files that were backed up, along with date and time information. This is a recommended option, to make it easier to trace backup activities.

/d:dd-mm-yy Only back up files created or modified on, or after, the given date.

/t:hh:mm:ss Only back up files created or modified on, or after, the given time.
If this parameter is used, the /d parameter must also be used.

These options can be entered in upper or lower case and can be used in any sequence or combination.
A typical BACKUP.LOG file might be as shown on the right.
The date and time of the backup are stored, followed by each file in the backup file. The list shows the sub-directory from which the file came. The backup disc used to store the files is also stored; in this case, all the files are in the first backup disc and this is shown by the '001' in the first column.

```
14/06/1997  18:57:13
001  \WINDOWS\256COLOR.BMP
001  \WINDOWS\ARCADE.BMP
001  \WINDOWS\ARCHES.BMP
001  \WINDOWS\ARGYLE.BMP
001  \WINDOWS\CARS.BMP
001  \WINDOWS\CASTLE.BMP
001  \WINDOWS\CHITZ.BMP
001  \WINDOWS\EGYPT.BMP
001  \WINDOWS\FLOCK.BMP
001  \WINDOWS\HONEY.BMP
```

BACKUPS AND BATCH FILES

When a BACKUP command exits, it returns a value in errorlevel that indicates the level of success of the process.
The possible errorlevel values are:

0	Backup was successful
1	No files were found to back up
2	Some files not backed due to file sharing problems
3	The user stopped the process (pressing CTRL+C)
4	The backup stopped due to an error

These errorlevel values can be used within a backup batch file, to report on the success, or otherwise, of the batch file's progress.

RESTORING FILES

This command is used to restore backed up files to their original destination. As with BACKUP, if the files are stored over several discs, the RESTORE program will prompt for the next disc to be inserted, as appropriate. An example would be:

RESTORE A: C:\TEST.DIR

The destination directory must be specified as the same one from which the backup was made. If the files do not exist on the hard disc, then they will be created. If they do exist, they will be over-written.
A range of parameters can be also be used with RESTORE.

/s Also restores the files in any sub-directories.

/m Only restores files that have been modified since the last backup. This saves time over-writing files which are unchanged since the backup.

/n Only restores files that no longer exist on the original drive.

/p Prompts for confirmation before restoring files that are read only or have changed since the last backup.

/b:dd-mm-yy Only restores files modified on, or before, the given date.

/a:dd-mm-yy Only restores files modified on, or after, the given date

/e:hh:mm:ss Only restores files modified on, or before, the given time.
If this parameter is used, the /d parameter must also be used.

/l:hh:mm:ss Only restores files modified on, or after, the given time.

EXAMPLES:

RESTORE A: C:*.* /S

restores all files, including any in any sub-directories from the A drive on to the hard disc root directory.

RESTORE A: C:\WINFILES*.DOC /m

restores all the files with the .DOC extension that have been modified since the last backup, back in to the WINFILES directory.

BACKUP FOR WINDOWS

This is a more powerful and more user-friendly product than the earlier DOS BACKUP command. Its menu is shown in the diagram and offers three levels of backup, chosen from the *'Backup Type'* window.

<u>Full</u> - Backs up all files on the disc. A thorough option that would only be required on an infrequent basis.

<u>Incremental</u> - Backs up those files that have been modified since the last backup. The archive bit is reset for each file that is backed up. This means that a full restoration requires the files from the initial full backup and the files from every subsequent incremental backup. This requires the storage of the set of all backups and is recommended where different files on a disc tend to be used and altered.

<u>Decremental</u> - This also results in the backing up of all files that have been modified since the previous

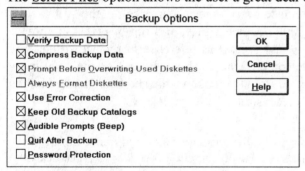

full backup. The difference with this method is that backups after the initial full backup do <u>not</u> result in archive bits being reset. This will backup all files that have been altered since the full backup, even if these files were backed up in a previous decremental backup. Thus, the new decremental backup supersedes all previous decremental backup files. This method only requires the storage of the full backup and the last decremental backup and is recommended where the same files are regularly being modified - e.g. budget files, price lists.

The <u>Select Files</u> option allows the user a great deal of flexibility over which files or directories should be included in the backup, with the use of *'Include'* and *'Exclude'* options on individual files.

The <u>Options</u> menu provides the facilities shown in the diagram. The files and options chosen for the backup can be saved as a *'Setup File'* for later use using the *'Save Setup As'* option.

This means that a set of such files - e.g. *'DOCSBACK'* , *'PICSBACK'*, etc. - can be called from the *'Setup File'* window.

COMPRESSION UTILITIES

With the ever-increasing size of application packages, particularly with Windows based products, there is an inescapable rule of computing which says *"no matter how big your hard disc is, it's not big enough"*. The 1Gb disc that was meant to solve all storage problems rapidly fills up and the previous 500Mb system looks decidedly small. The room full of 40Mb machines is relegated to running older applications with the hope of a future upgrade. To relieve storage problems, software houses have proposed an alternative approach. Instead of making the discs bigger, the files could be made smaller! This does not involve the writing of new, smaller files. It takes the existing files and stores them in a more compact form. File compression can work at one of two levels:

- On an individual file, or group of files, basis, such as PKZIP or LHA
- On an entire disc basis, such as with Stacker or SuperStor

The files cannot be used without first being restored to their original form. They are only <u>stored</u> in a compressed format; they have to be used in their original format. Some utilities require the user to actively carry out the decompression before using the file. Other utilities make the process invisible to the user who can be completely unaware that compression and decompression are taking place.

FILE COMPRESSION

ARC and ZOO were early compression utilities and can these can still be found in use. PKZIP is currently the most-commonly used file compressor program. These are all shareware programs. Other shareware utilities include LHA (which uses .LZH files), SLIM, PAK and ARJ. Some utilities are optimised for specific files. For example, the ALCHEMY program can be used to compress graphics files by huge amounts. The difference is that it uses a *'lossy'* algorithm; it sacrifices some tiny details for increased space savings. This is acceptable for graphics or sound files, whereas other data files and program files require to be stored with absolute accuracy. Absolutely accurate reproduction requires *'loss-free'* algorithms. Most files, whether programs or data files, contain a large amount of repetitious and redundant information. If the storage of this information is re-organised, vast savings can be made. It is possible, on <u>average</u>, to reduce files by up to 50% or more, dependent on the file's format. Some graphics file formats, for example, are already stored in a compressed form and these will produce poorer results than plain ASCII files. The table shows some typical compression results:

File used	Original size	Compressed Size	Program used	Percentage saved
CONTROL.HLP (in Windows)	121672	87028	PKZIP	29%
MONEY.BAS (in DOS)	46225	11081	PKZIP	77%
MARBLE.BMP (in Windows)	27646	8355	PKZIP	71%
NEWMACRO.DOC (in Word)	110383	43007	PKZIP	62%
NETWORK.BMP (digitised image)	921656	57992	Alchemy	96%

These results are achieved by attacking the file's areas of repetitious data. Consider, for example, a graphics file that has large areas of blue background. Instead of storing every blue pixel separately, the area could be stored as *'5000 pixels of blue'*. This is called *'Run Length Encoding'*, or RLE. When decompressed again, the coded information restores 5000 separate elements of pixel data.

If a file is compressed with a particular utility, it has to be uncompressed by the same utility, since different utilities use different algorithms to achieve compression / decompression. There are only three or four compression algorithms and utilities use variations on these. The PKZIP and ARC utilities use the LZW (Lempel-Ziv-Welch) algorithm, while ALCHEMY uses a form of Huffman coding to produce JPEG files. The LZW method requires that a table be created, which places different strings from the file in different elements of the table. So, element 400, for example, would represent a particular string in the file being compressed. The code 400 can now replace every other occurrence of the string in the entire file. The string could be an English word within document files, or a run of pixels in graphics files. As the file is compressed, the table is filled up and is used as reference to replace strings with shorter codes in the compressed version. When de-compressing, each occurrence of the code in the compressed file results in the actual string being retrieved from the lookup table and being restored in the decompressed version. In this way, the original file is reconstructed with no losses.

FACILITIES
- To assist in the management of large groups of compressed files, there have appeared front ends such as SHEZ for DOS and D'Compress for Windows. These essentially provide a friendlier user interface to the basic compression utilities (PKZIP and ARJ respectively).
- To simplify the storage and manipulation of compressed files, most utilities can compile a set of files into one single compressed file.
- To automate file decompression, some utilities will create a self-expanding file. The file, or files, are compressed into a single file which then has the decompression utility embedded into the file. This creates a single .EXE file which, when called, runs the decompression code and reconstructs the individual files. It should be noted, however, that the sub-directory will still hold the .EXE file in addition to the decompressed file. This can occupy substantial extra disc space if not deleted.

TYPICAL USES
Universally used by Bulletin Boards, since download times are reduced; if a file is half its original size, it will only take have the time to transmit over the telephone network. The latest standard for modem data compression - V42bis - uses BTLZ , a British Telecomm variety of the Lempel-Ziv algorithm. The compression of a group of files into a single file also simplifies downloading. Often used in application packages' distribution discs, with the ARC format. DOS itself uses compressed files on its installation discs, as do many modern application packages. This reduces the number of discs that have to be distributed with the package. It also reduces the number of discs that the installer has to swap to effect an installation. If an application is run infrequently, it can be stored in its sub-directory in compressed form. When it requires to be used, the files can be decompressed. One batch file could be written to compile the application files into a single compressed file for storage while another batch file could unpack the file for use.

DISC COMPRESSION

Rather than tackling compression at a file level, modern techniques address the disc as a whole. They concern themselves with *'disc compression'* rather than *'file compression'*. These utilities are often known as *'disc doublers'*, since they can make the hard disc store twice as much data as before. To achieve this, the files on the disc are compressed and decompressed *'on the fly'*; this means that files are compressed before being saved to disc and decompressed when read from disc. This happens in real time, hence the expression *'on the fly'*. With file compressors, the individual files remained as normal DOS files and could be copied in their compressed state. With disc compressor, this is not possible due to the way that the files are stored.

The disc is effectively sectioned into two. The smaller section is the normal DOS section on which the machine will boot up; it contains the DOS system files and the CONFIG.SYS and AUTOEXEC.BAT files. A huge hidden file within the DOS partition is used as the store for the compressed files. This much larger section is organised on the basis of individual sectors of 512 bytes. So, data is stored on sector basis, rather than on a cluster basis. This makes for more effective use of the disc surface, since a cluster can be up to 8k or over in size. Small files, or parts of files, can be stored much more economically on

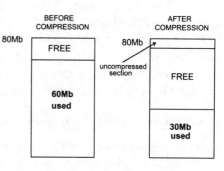

a surface based on 512 byte chunks, rather than in 8k chunks. There is no need to format or partition the disc to achieve this; the task of creating these sections is carried out by the utility's installation program. The installation creates, in effect, an extra drive within a drive complete with its own FAT.

A device driver is loaded in via CONFIG.SYS (either into conventional memory or upper memory) and this can be regarded as sitting between DOS and the disc controller. Almost all applications make disc requests by calling up the BIOS disc routines via an interrupt 13h call. With disc compressors, these calls are trapped by the extra layer and the data is compressed before being written, or decompressed after being read. Buffers are used to hold the data while it is being processed.

As far as DOS is concerned, it is dealing with a perfectly ordinary disc drive; the driver presents the compressed section as an extra logical disc drive, e.g. drive 'D'. To keep the process invisible to the user, Stacker then swaps round the 'C' drive and the 'D' drive. This means that when the machine is booted up, the system is configured from the normal DOS partition (i.e. the

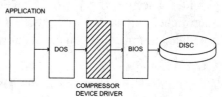

actual 'C' drive) and then the compressed section is presented to the user as the logical 'C' drive. The normal section can still be accessed as the 'D' drive. Since the utility is hardware-independent, it can be used with a range of storage devices. It will work with floppy discs or Bernoulli drives, optical drives and even RAM drives. The drive types used can be MFM, RLL, ESDI, IDE or SCSI.

If an existing disc is to be compressed, the installation will also involve an initial compression of all files already on the disc.

PERFORMANCE

Apart from the space savings to be made from the use disc compressors, there may be some benefits to be gained in overall machine throughput.

Using a disc compressor produces two contradictory time factors:
- Compressors speed up disc access times. Since the files to be read/written are smaller, they take less time to read/write.
- The compression/decompression of the files consumes valuable CPU time, thus slowing down the machine.

With older machines, this overall effect may be to slow down operations. With fast machines, the CPU can quickly encode/decode the data and the overall result is an improvement in machine performance.

LIMITATIONS
- If an old machine is fitted with a 50Mb or 80Mb hard disc, the cost of installing a disc compressor is not really economic. Doubling a machine's capacity from 50Mb to 100Mb does not provide a lot of extra storage capacity, except in percentage terms.
- The compressor device drivers consume memory

- Can't be used with Windows 386 Enhanced mode with a permanent swap file, since Windows by-passes DOS routines and carries out disc access directly.   In such cases, a temporary swap file should be used or the permanent swap file should be created in the normal DOS section of the disc.
- Software that writes directly to disc, by-passing normal DOS calls, can cause a lot of damage to files that are stored in compressed format.   This includes some disc utilities and virus-checking programs.   Careful reading of the disc compressor manuals is required, to prevent the use of these programs.
- De-installing a compressed section can be a problem.   This can be eased if the disc happens to have enough free to store all the files when they are in their decompressed state. Since the whole point in disc compressor is to maximise disc usage, this is not a likely situation.   So, removing a compressed section will involve making a complete backup of all the compressed files, de-installing the compressed area, then restoring as many files on to the disc as it will hold.

Examples of these products are Stacker, SuperStor and XtraDrive.   Initially brought out as DOS add-ons, Stacker was temporarily bundled with MSDOS and SuperStor is bundled with DRDOS.   This makes sense, since these major disc utilities are now lined up with major disc operating systems.   Of course, the use of these utilities is optional.

LARGE CAPACITY DISCS

There is a phenomenal growth in mass-storage devices such as CD ROM and floptical discs.   These are now widely available in the commercial and home market and the forecast is for continuing future growth. The read-only versions are used to hold application packages, databases, educational encyclo-paedias, clip art collections and PC support information.   Increasingly, programs are being freely distributed in a demonstration format so that users can test the package's abilities. The entire program is already on the CD and a user can call the distributor to purchase the package by credit card. The user is then given a password code to allow them to access the entire package. All the above programs or data are written permanently at the manufacturing stage and cannot be altered by the user.   There are also two types of device that can be user modified. The WORM drive (write-once read many) is used for archiving company audit material; the data is written to disc and cannot be altered thereafter. This provides a secure, if expensive, method of mass storing information than was previously committed to microfiche.   The new generation of rewriteable CD ROMs and MO discs (large capacity floppy discs) use magneto-optical systems that allow the data on the discs to be modified.

CD ROM

The simplified diagram shows the basic layout of a side view of a section of a CD ROM disc.   The plastic disc has an embossed surface comprising of areas of normal thickness ('lands' or 'hills') and sunken areas ('pits'). The discs are stamped out from a master disc. After the high initial costs of

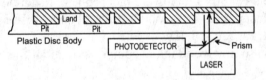

creating the master disc, individual CDs can be stamped out very cheaply as can be seen by the number of computer magazines that include free CDs of shareware and program demonstrations.   The changes of height along the track represent the data on the disc, although the coding method is more complex than the simple storage of the data's 1's and 0's.   The top surface of the disc is coated with a layer of reflective aluminium (the shaded area of the diagram) and this is covered with a protective plastic layer; the total disc thickness is 1.2mm.

The disc is read from its underside by firing a laser beam at the revolving surface.   The beam reflects from the aluminium coating and is diverted to a photo sensor by a prism. The normal depth areas - the 'lands' - reflect back most of the laser beam while the 'pitted' areas scatter the beam as shown in the diagram.   So, the photo sensor will detect different reflected strengths from the two different surface areas.   The laser beam passes through focusing lenses so that the beam is a tiny spot at the point of contact with the disc surface.

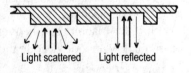

The spot is only 1 micron in size - one millionth of a metre. This means that much more data can be packed on to the disc surface compared to standard magnetising methods. This explains the ability to pack up to 650Mb of data on to a single disc. Since the head does not require to be close to the disc surface, it does not suffer the risk of head crashes associated with normal floppy and hard discs.

The laser, prism, lenses and photodetector are all enclosed in a single unit that is moved from track to track. It is the equivalent of the ordinary read/write head of a hard disc. The disc contains only a single track, organised as single spiral similar to a long-playing record, except that the disc is read from the centre outwards. Reaching a wanted sector requires the head to be moved to the approximate location on the spiral track. The head then follows the track until it reaches a sector header; this header information is then used to locate the wanted sector.

Although CDs use a number of error detection and correction techniques, they should still be handled with care. Grease from a fingerprint diffuses the laser beam while surface scratches deflects the beam.

DISC ORGANISATION

The disc is 120mm in diameter with a 15mm hole is punched in the centre. A 6mm area of the surface, next to the hole, is used by the drive mechanism to clamp the disc while rotating. The next 4mm area is used to store information regarding the disc's contents; this is known as the VTOC (volume table of contents). The data area width is 33mm and comprises a single track spiralling outwards about 20,000 times and totalling around 3mile in length. The outer area of 3mm is used for handling the disc.

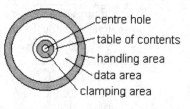

centre hole
table of contents
handling area
data area
clamping area

A single-speed drive reads 75 of these sectors per second, giving a transfer rate of 150kb/s. A double-speed drive reads 150 sectors/sec while a 10x drive reads 750 sectors/sec, giving transfer rates of 300kb/s and 1,500kb/s respectively. The original single speed model spins at 300rpm and other models are multiples of this - ie a quad speed rotates at 1,200 rpm and a 6x rotates at 1,800rpm. Most CDs have a 2,352 bytes sector size of which 2k or over is used for data and the remaining bytes for error-detection information.

Hard discs specify a particular disc area in terms of track and sector. CD ROMs, showing their origins as audio discs, specify areas in terms of minutes, seconds, and sectors within each second.

Thus, a 74 minute CD has a capacity of 74 x 60(secs) x 75(sectors) x 2k = 650Mb of user data area.

There are two methods of organising data on the spiral:

CLV - Constant Linear Velocity. This was the most common method and is that used with audio CDs. All disc sectors are of identical length. The outer spirals on the surface are longer than inner spirals and can store more sectors per spiral than those closer to the centre. Therefore the disc spins slower when reading outer tracks compared to inner tracks. A 4x drive may spin at over 2,100 rpm on inner tracks and only 800rpm on outer tracks. This system achieves the same amount of data read per second, no matter where on the disc the data is stored. A good quality motor is required to handle the constantly changing rotational speed.

CAV - Constant Angular Velocity - This is currently used in hard and floppy drives and being increasingly adopted by CD drive manufacturers. The disc motor rotates at a constant speed making it easy to manufacture. The outer spirals store less sectors per inch than inner spirals; it stores the same amount of information for every single revolution. Its access time is faster than a CLV model since it does not suffer delays while the motor speed changes between inner and outer spirals. Pioneer, for example, claim that their 10x has a 65ms access time in CAV mode compared to around 150ms for CLV models. Many CD drives are a CLV/CAV hybrid, using CLV (ie changing speeds) on the outer tracks and CAV (ie constant speeds) on the inner tracks.

RECORDABLE CD

For large quantity production of CDs, a master copy is laser cut into a glass master copy and this is used to stamp out the lands and pits on the reflective layers of each blank CD. The master copy costs around £500 to produce but subsequent stamped CDs

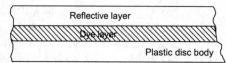

Reflective layer
Dye layer
Plastic disc body

are relatively cheap (which is why they are given away with computer magazines and audio magazines). For small quantities this is an expensive option and CD-R (CD-Recordable) systems utilise a CD writer that uses discs of a different construction from the standard pressed discs. Recordable CD blanks have a layer of dye that can be spot heated by a laser beam to fuse the dye with the plastic substrate and create pits. The blank discs are supplied with a 'pre-groove' moulded on its surface. The groove provides tracking information for the drive's head servo and provides a cheap way to ensure quality tracking.

The individual blank disc is more expensive than a pressed disc but there is no expensive master to create. CD-R discs can be read on any normal CD drive. CD Writers are also capable of reading normal CDs. The dramatic fall in the price of CD writers has led to their widespread use as a backup device.

CD ROM PERFORMANCE

The performance of CD-ROM is determined by the following factors:

- The access time of the drive. These times vary from 110ms to 250ms for newer models and 350ms to 900ms for older models. Compared to hard disc speeds, these are very slow times. That is because there is one single continuous spiral track. The read head cannot first go to the exact track and wait for the wanted sector to come round. It has to make an approximation to the correct distance in then wait for the first sector header to tell the system where the head is positioned. It then makes a second seek to get to the correct position. This slows down the sector access times.
- The data transfer rate of the drive. The most common rates are:

Data Rate	Description	Data Rate	Description
150kbs	single-speed	900kbs	6x
300kbs	double-speed or 2x	1200kbs	8x
450kbs	triple-speed or 3x	1500kbs	10x
600kbs	quad speed or 4x	2400kbs	16x

These figures do not give a complete picture since a quad speed drive will not provide double the throughput of a double speed, and so on. This is for a number of reasons:

- The higher transfer rates only applies to long sequential reads. If the head has to make a number of random access seeks, the faster transfers are offset by the substantial individual access times. The result is an average figure somewhat less than the performance suggested by the 2x, 3x, 4x, 6x, 8x and 10x ratings.
- With CLV models, there is an additional time delay while the motor changes speed when moving between inner and outer tracks.
- For the same reasons above, the sustained data rate shows up better with bigger files.
- AVI video files are often created to be run at double speed and drives with faster rates have to work at the slower rate to be compatible with the data being presented.
- The detection and elimination of read errors. Errors can occur due to slight imperfections in the boundaries of cells or due to data reads caused by fingerprints or scratches obscuring the data read. For small data losses, the error detection system also has an error correction system that alters the read data to the original information. This is an improvement on normal discs and provides a more secure storage medium.
- The size of the drive's buffers. The current drives cache sizes vary from 16k to 1024k, mostly available in 128k or 256k. The cache size can have a significant influence over the smooth performance of multimedia presentations. SmartDrive can be used to gain a reasonably useful improvement in CD ROM performance and products such as PC Kwik and Norton's SpeedCache Plus can achieve significant improvements. Utilities such as CD-Speed copy the CD's most commonly used files to the hard disc to speed up their access.

PRACTICAL NOTES

- CD drives are available as internal and external models. External models connect via the computer's parallel port or via proprietary cards with external connections that plug into the CD ROM unit. An alternative is to wire the external unit via the external connection of a SCSI card.
- With some models, the disc is placed in a plastic caddy for extra protection from scratching or dust. This case is then placed into the CD drive for use. A slider on the underneath of the caddy is then moved aside, in the same manner as that of a 3.5" disc, to reveal the recorded surface. Other models simply require the disc to be placed in a tray like audio CD players or placed in a top loader.
- Four different interfaces can be used to connect the CD to the computer. Some older models use a connection from a SoundBlaster Card or other sound card; these have the required circuitry to control the CD ROM. Other systems connect to a special proprietary interface card; these are sometimes a cut-down version of a SCSI card. Most modern systems connect to the IDE or the faster EIDE (known as 'ATAPI'- Attach Packet Interface) interface. Faster still is the SCSI interface. This is also a cheap option if a SCSI card is already in use for the hard disc.
- The hardware requires two drivers - the hardware-specific driver software supplied with the particular CD and MSCDEX.EXE, the Microsoft CD-ROM Extensions for DOS. The first driver is installed via CONFIG.SYS and the Microsoft Extensions software is installed via AUTOEXEC.BAT. The MSCDEX utility is a TSR that reads the standard ISO 9660 CD discs (i.e. it makes CD files look like normal DOS files); it also provides audio support. The Windows 95 equivalent is the 32-bit CDFS driver.
- Front panel features include the volume control, headphone socket, activity light and disc eject button.
- Dust protection is improved through double door mechanisms, unit seals and automatic lens cleaning systems.

CD STANDARDS

Many of the standards are named after the colour of cover used to report on the new standard. So, the standard for audio on CD became known as the Red Book standard because it had a red cover.

ISO 9660

Often known as *'High Sierra'*, since it was first discussed in the High Sierra Hotel in Nevada in 1985. By 1987, a superset of High Sierra, known as ISO 9600, was agreed as the common standard for computer CD ROMs. All drives conform to this standard for handling files and directories, with different drivers to allow the standard to work with PCs, Macintosh computer and Unix systems. The PCs version is implemented with the MSCDEX or CDFS driver software.

Standard	Purpose
Red Book	Audio CDs
Yellow Book	Computer data (eg application installation CDs)
Green Book	CD-Interactive applications, games and, entertainment
White Book	Video CDs
Blue Book	Music CDs with text
Orange Book	Recordable CDs
Photo CD	Kodak's multi-session picture storage

RED BOOK

Established in 1980, it is also known as CD-DA (Digital Audio). The *'Red Book'* standard was the first of the series and defined the specification for the audio CD currently in use. It specified that the audio would be stored in digital format, compressed and subject to error detection and correction. Each sector stores 1/75th of a second of digitised audio and occupies 2,352 bytes. Data is stored for stereo 16-bit audio with a sampling rate of 44.1KHz with a theoretical maximum of 74 minutes of audio per disc. It can handle 99 audio tracks and its TOC stores the starting point of each track (measured in minutes, seconds and sectors).

YELLOW BOOK

The *'Yellow Book'* standard of 1985 defined the computer data CD specification now commonly known simply as CD-ROM.. This standard is really a storage medium with improved error correction and has three modes:

Mode 1 uses a maximum disc capacity of 666Mb to store computer data. It uses the same 2,352 byte sector size as Red Book but uses 2k of each sector for data with the remaining bytes being used for synchronisation and error correction codes.

Mode 2 was the original attempt at CD-I and provided for compression of audio and graphic information. It offered a 765Mb maximum capacity since it dropped the error correction bytes, allowing each sector to store 2,336 bytes of data. Since the disc was spinning at the same speed, its data transfer rate was also greater - 170kb/s instead of the normal 150kb/s. Mode 2, however, was unable to access computer data and audio/visual data at the same time, since they were stored on different tracks of the disc (only one mode is allowed per track). This limited its usefulness and Mode 2 was never developed.

Mode 3 was termed Mixed Mode as it allowed computer data tracks and audio tracks to be placed on the same disc. Usually, the first track contains the computer data with the remaining tracks containing audio data. The audio tracks could be played through a domestic audio CD player in which case the player would be stepped over the data track. A CD ROM drive would recognise the computer data tracks and would be able to play the audio through its audio output. However, it could not do both at the same time.

Some references to Mixed Mode refer to a drive that can handle both Mode 1 and Mode 2.

CD XA

It is possible for audio and graphic information to be stored in different CD tracks. When each of these data items is used separately, there is no problem but multimedia demands that both audio and graphic information be presented in a synchronised manner and this is not easily achieved. The Extended Architecture (XA) specification allows both audio and graphic data to be stored in the same track in an interleaved fashion, thus allowing greatly improved synchronisation. This extends the Yellow Book Mode 2 by having a Form 1 for computer data (2k of data/sector with error detection) and a Form 2 for audio and video data (2,324 bytes of data/sector with no error detection). Since Form 1 and Form 2 work under the same XA Mode, they can both be placed on the same track. XA also saved space for the storage audio by using a method called ADPCM (Adaptive Delta Pulse Code Modulation). This stores the difference between sound samples rather than the values themselves and results in smaller values being produced and saved.

GREEN BOOK

This is also an extension of the Mode 2 of the Yellow Book, designed for playing CD-I interactive applications. It stores files compressed to the MPEG format and interleaves the picture and sound elements. All CD-I tracks are in Mode 2 XA format. Unlike White Book, it does not provide the standard ISO9660 access and requires a special CD-I player, a PC upgrade such as ReelMagic, or a special device driver, since a normal CD ROM drive cannot handle the format. Dedicated CD-I players are available with their own CPU and video memory and these connect to a monitor or TV.

CD-BRIDGE

As the name implies, this standard allows a drive to handle CDs that were both XA and CD-I compatible. This special bridge CD disc is really a CD-I disc with extra XA information added to it. The Photo CD discs explained below are an example of a bridge disc. The disc has more than one disc label and this allows the same disc to be played in a CD-I player or an XA CD drive.

WHITE BOOK

Used for Video CD - i.e. the storing of full-motion MPEG-1 video. The output cannot be taken directly to any ordinary video card. It has to feed a decompression card to restore MPEG files to their original size. MPEG 1 compression results in a CD with up to 74 minutes of VHS-quality video and stereo sound track. Videos that are longer than 74 minutes have to be split up over two discs. MPEG-1 handling now appears on many video cards, usually with software decompression. Video CD uses XA's Mode2/Form2 working and requires a Mode 2/Form 2 compatible player.

BLUE BOOK

Also known as CD Plus or CD Extra, this is designed to provide multiple sessions on a disc. The first session contains audio tracks and the second session contains computer data. The main TOC (table of contents) contains information on audio tracks and points to a further TOC storing data tracks. If the disc is used in a normal hi-fi CD audio player, it will not attempt to play the data tracks as it will not recognise the second TOC. A blue book drive will recognise and use both TOCs. The most likely use for Blue Book systems appears to be in the music industry where a CD can be played both in a standard audio CD player or in a computer CD drive. In the latter, the music can then be augmented by photographs and text about the performers. This, along with White Book covers most manufacturers approaches to multimedia CDs.

ORANGE BOOK

Also known as CD-R (CD-Recordable) this describes the writing of CD discs. The three parts to the standard are:
  I. The use of Magneto Optical drives which allow data to be written to disc, then erased or overwritten.
  II. The use of the *'Write Once'* format, where the data is written in a single session or multiple sessions but cannot be altered after it is written.
  III. The Rewritable format (CD-RW) which allows the disc to be re-written up to 1,000 times. Requires a Multi-Read CD drive or a DVD drive to read discs written by a CD-RW writer.
CD Writers can produce disc in CD-ROM, CD-DA, Mixed Mode, XA and CD-I format and a quad-speed drive will record an entire disc in about 15mins.

KODAK PHOTO CD

CDs are capable of storing large graphics files and the Kodak Photo CD system allows photographs taken with an ordinary camera to be placed on CD discs. When the film is taken to the developer, the images can be reproduced in both standard photographic print format and in CD format. Such photographs can be viewed in the same way as any other graphics file stored on a CD. A standard CD can store 100 photographs and the full 100 may be built up over a period of time with additional photographs being added at later dates. This is not a problem as Kodak can add any new photographs to the CD. However, a normal CD is not capable of reading any added data since each new additional group has its own unique storage key and this cannot be accessed by the old technology. If this extra facility is required, a *'Multi-session'* model must be purchased as this is capable of reading any subsequent additions. Almost all models currently on the market are now multi-session. CD-I players or CD drives that support XA Mode 2/Form 1 are capable of reading these files.

FUTURE TECHNOLOGY

A range of techniques is being developed to improve both the capacity and speed of CD ROMs. The main areas are:
  - Creating multiple levels of disc. IBM are developing a sandwich of ten CD-R discs. By changing the beam's point of focus, different discs in the sandwich are used.
  - Using higher frequency lasers. Blue violet lasers have a higher frequency (ie shorter wavelength) than red lasers and so smaller pits can be cut - more data per spiral. Up to 10Gb per disc.

DVD

The capacity limitations of current CDs have led to attempts to put a full-length movie on to a single CD. The initial steps towards a *'Digital Video Disk'* centred round:
  - The MMCD (Multimedia CD) or High Density CD developed by Sony and Philips. It aimed to produce a single-sided disc with 7.4Gb capacity.
  - The SD (Super Density) format from Toshiba. It aimed to produce a double-sided disc with 9Gb capacity.

The *'Digital Versatile Disk'* represents a merger of the above Sony, Philips and Toshiba systems. It is mainly viewed as a mechanism for distributing films and the first DVD discs are of this type. It also provides an ideal medium for a wide variety of applications ranging from training material to encyclopaedias.

Book	Specification
A	DVD-ROM
B	DVD-Video
C	DVD-Audio
D	DVD-WO (Write Once)
E	DVD-E (Erasable)

The disc remains at the conventional CD diameter of 120mm but can be double sided and can have two separate layers that are capable of storing data. The DVD specifications are known as *'books'* and are as shown in the table. Since it is aimed at the production of quality video discs, it supports both MPEG-1 and MPEG-2 video standards (ie 352x 240 at 30 fields per second up to 720x480 at 60 fields per second).   DVD discs interleave the video and audio streams.

The likely final products are shown in the table. A 4.7Gb disc stores the equivalent of around 133 minutes of video and three audio streams.   DVD5 drives are currently available (eg the Hitachi GD-2000 and the Toshiba SD-M1002).   The Hitachi has a peak data transfer rate of 2.76Mb/sec using CAV techniques.

Product	Capacity	No of layers	No of sides	Mode
DVD5	4.7Gb	1	1	Playback
DVD9	8.5Gb	2	1	Playback
DVD10	9.4Gb	1	2	Playback
DVD18	17Gb	2	2	Playback
DVD-R	7.6Gb	2	2	Record-once
DVD-RAM	5.2Gb	2	2	Record-many

Single layer discs, both single and double sided, are manufactured in a very similar way to current CD-ROMs.   The second layer comprises a resin layer with partially transmissive qualities.   The reflections from both layers vary only slightly in intensity requiring a particularly sensitive detection system.

How a DVD stores 4.7Gb on a single side

A CD's basic capacity is 765Mb; this is reduced to around 650Mb for the user's use after the overheads for error correction are deducted.   DVD uses a combination of more precise engineering, higher laser frequency, and improved modulation and error correction techniques, to dramatically improve the capacity of a single disc side.

	Standard CD layout	DVD layout	Improvement Factor	New Capacity
Smaller pit length	0.972 microns	0.4 microns	2.4300	1.82 Gb
Narrower track pitch	1.6 microns	0.74 microns	2.1622	3.93 Gb
More surface used for storing data	86 sq cms	87.6 sq cms	1.0186	4.00 Gb
Better error correction	25% of data area	13% of data area	1.1062	4.42 Gb
More efficient channel bit modulation	08:14	08:16	1.0625	4.70 Gb

Advantages of DVD Drives

- Supports high quality MPEG-2 video
- Supports a range of screen aspect ratios, from 1.33 (TV and monitor standard) to 2.25 (wide screen).
- Supports three 'theatre quality' sound formats - Dolby AC-3 surround sound, MPEG-1 audio and MPEG-2 audio.
- Choice of up to eight language tracks
- Choice of up to 32 tracks for subtitles and menus.
- DVD drives can read CD-ROM and CD-R discs.

Disadvantages

- Requires a MPEG-2 decoder and a sound card that can handle the disc's audio formats. These cards will be available separately as upgrade kits or will be available bundled with DVD drives.   Software implementations may be marketed (eg CompCore's SoftDVD) although their performance is likely to be poorer since they use CPU resources rather than dedicated hardware.
- Each DVD has a 'country lock' - a code specific to a region of the world. DVD discs will only run in players which have the same zone code. This prevents US discs being played on European DVD drives.
- As yet, recordable DVDs are not available.
- Normal CD drives cannot read DVD discs.

MAGNETO-OPTICAL DRIVES

There is a growing demand to be able to both read and write to mass storage discs.   Products on offer vary from 128Mb 3.5" discs to 1,000Mb 5.25" discs. The most common format is the 600Mb and 650Mb 5.25" disc.

Uses for such devices include:

- large-scale data backup, particularly network servers
- storage of large company databases
- storage of groups of large graphics files associated with DTP, CAD and multimedia
- DIP systems (Document Image Processing - the scanning and storage of all incoming documents and correspondence).

Magneto-optical (MO) drives use metal granule coatings on the disc surface. Unlike normal hard discs where the surface area is evenly coated, the MO disc has a raised bump for every data bit on the entire disc.   Each data bit occupies an area of just 1 micron in diameter. This surface is then covered by a plastic or glass-based protective coat. The 5.25" types are double-sided discs with two independent sides glued together.   The 3.5" type is single sided. The completed discs of both types are enclosed in cartridges similar to the construction used for 3.5" floppies, although larger and about 11mm in thickness. Each disc side has tracks with discrete physical cells capable of storing data.

Each data cell is written to in at least two stages - erase the old data and write the new data. This is often accompanied by a third stage to verify the write operation.   Mostly, this is achieved during separate revolutions of the disc.   This means that writing to a disc is substantially slower than reading from a disc, although research is being conducted into single-pass systems.

The coating used has a very high coercivity which means that it is normally very difficult to change its magnetic polarity.   But the coating is also susceptible to heat. To alter the contents of a cell, a laser beam is directed at it, on a high-power setting.   This raises the temperature of the cell to just under 200° C.   This greatly reduces the coercivity for a brief period and during this period a magnet is used to set the cell to the desired polarity.   When the cell cools again, the magnetic polarity is effectively locked into the disc.   Only the cells that need to have their contents altered require to be subjected to this process.

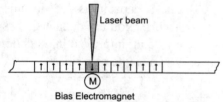

To read the disc, the same laser beam reverts back to a low-power setting and is reflected of the disc. The magnet is not used in the read process. This reading method does not use the <u>amount</u> of reflection as used in the CD ROM.   Instead, it analyses the <u>polarity</u> of the reflected beam, since the beam will be slightly polarised according to whether it is reflected from a '0' or a '1' cell - a phenomenon known as '*The Kerr Effect*'.

The most commonly used discs employ CAV (Constant Angular Velocity) which places data on the tracks using a fixed speed motor. This results in data on the outer track being less densely packed than data on the inner tracks.   It is a simple but wasteful system.

Other systems use ZCAV (Zoned Constant Angular Velocity) which keeps the motor speed constant within any one track but has a faster speed on outer tracks than inner tracks.   This is more complex but packs 50% more data on to the disc surface, taking storage to almost 1Gb.

5.25" DISCS

These appear in four capacities.

- 512 bytes/sector discs. These produce 600Mb systems, with 300Mb per side.
- 1024 bytes/sector systems produce 650Mb versions, with 325Mb per side.
- 1.3Gb systems
- 2.6Gb systems

The drives offer only slow access times of between 19ms to 90ms; they act like slow hard discs.   The Pinnacle PM0-650 and Optical Sunset 1300 drives have the fastest current seek times of 19ms which is still slower than modern hard discs.   Rotational speeds vary from 1,800rpm to 3,600rpm and data transfer rates vary from 522kbs to 4,096kbs.

Hewlett Packard produce jukeboxes of the larger discs so that storage of between 40Gb and 618Gb is available.

3.25" DISCS

These appear in two capacities.

- 128Mb, using CAV
- 230Mb, using ZCAV

They have rotational speeds of 3,000 rpm to 3,600 rpm and these result in transfer rates of 610kbs to 2,100Kbs. Access times are between 30ms and 55ms.

The hardware is expensive to buy initially but the discs are relatively cheap so it is an economic proposition for large storage needs. The more data that is stored the cheaper it becomes in terms of pence per Mb. Some rewriteable optical systems can be configured to also act as a WORM drive, where data security is important.

Magneto-optical discs, like standard CD discs, are robust discs and have life expectancies of 10 years and over. Manufacturers claim that the discs have write/rewrite cycles of between 10 million and 1,000 million. All these drive systems use SCSI interfaces.

NOTE

An MO drive uses a motorised ejection of the disc under software control. Although there is an eject button, this is not operational when the power is switched off. The drive should not be moved when a disc is in the drive. The head is held in a locked position when there is no disc in the drive, but the head is free to move when a disc is inserted. Moving the drive without the head being locked might cause damage.

PHASE-CHANGE DISCS

Some systems, such as the Plasmon PD2000 and the Matsushita PD, do not require magnetism to alter the state of the disc surface. These are called *'phase change'* systems and use a disc whose coating can adopt one of two conditions - amorphous or crystalline. The drive mechanism's laser beam can produce two levels of heat at the disc surface. Heating the coating to just below melting point produces a crystalline structure during the rapid cooling down period. Heating to just above melting point destroys the crystalline structure producing the amorphous state at that point on the surface. Unlike conventional MO systems, phase change drives can write the surface in a single pass and this reduces the time for write operations.

During read operations, the different surface structures reflect different amount of light from the scanning laser beam and these differences are detected and interpreted in the same way as normal CD drive systems.

FLOPTICAL DISCS

These are based on ordinary floppy disc technology with the disc surface being magnetised to the store the data. The disc is also stored in a normal 3.5" plastic case. The difference lies in the addition of special optical servo tracks to the disc surface to ensure very accurate alignment. These extra tracks appear between magnetic tracks and are used to ensure that the read/write head positions itself exactly in the middle of the desired track. An infra-red LED light source reflects off the servo tracks and is picked up by a photodetector. The information indicates the exact position of the read/write head. This increased accuracy allows more tracks to be place on a 3.5" disc size and this results in higher capacity discs. Since the tracks are very narrow, a special narrow head is used to read and write the data.

With drives that are backward compatible - i.e. can also read standard 720k and 1.4M floppies - the drive mechanism also has a second wider head to read these wider tracks.

Compaq produce a 120Mb floptical drive.

LARGE CAPACITY CARTRIDGES

Large capacity discs using conventional magnetised surfaces are available, although they have to be packaged in special cartridges. This means that discs for cartridge drives and standard floppy drives are not interchangeable. The Iomega 'Zip' drive has a capacity of 100Mb capacity, while their 'Jaz' model has a capacity of 1Gb and has a head for each side of the disc. The Zip drive has a seek time of 29ms and the Jaz seek time is 12ms. The Zip has an inferior performances compared to IDE or SCSI hard discs, while the Jaz is almost comparable. Another cartridge systems is the SyQuest EZFlyer at 230Mb, single-sided, 13.5ms seek time.

Interface types used are either the SCSI, IDE or proprietary card, with the parallel port being used for external models.

Computer Viruses

VIRUSES IN PERSPECTIVE

Computer viruses of various types have gained a great deal of publicity and have diverted a great deal of resources to overcoming their effects. Nevertheless, viruses represent only a small part of an organisation's overall problems of security, integrity and reliability. While a definite area of concern, there are still much more important threats to an organisation. A company might fit virus protection software to all machines, to prevent the corruption of data. At the same time, little or no thought might be given to the physical security of the data; e.g. is it held in a machine in a secure room; is the computer password-protected, etc.

To date, apart from a number of well-publicised cases, virus problems are not yet general; many organisations carry out their daily work without any reported virus infection whatsoever. Nevertheless, computer viruses pose a mounting threat to data and have to be taken seriously. They can range from harmless messages to damage and/or loss of data. They are not the glamorous product of a *'hacker'*, as viewed by wide-eyed schoolboys. They are, in fact, a nuisance which causes much extra work and anxiety to computer departments. As time progresses and systems become ever more complex and more interlinked (via local area networks and Workgroups for Windows), organisations come to rely more and more on the quality of their data as stored on computers. This, in turn, is likely to lead to viruses becoming a greater threat than at the present time and all PC support groups should attempt to keep up with the latest trends in viruses.

VIRUS DEFINITIONS

It is generally accepted that the first PC computer virus was *'Brain'* which appeared in January 1986 as a floppy disc virus. This changed the disc label and used up three extra disc sectors. This was fairly harmless but variations have been developed to infect hard discs, hide themselves from detection and destroy the disc's FAT. This is a good example of the evolution of viruses. Although there are now thousands of listed viruses, many are variants on others and only about 50 viruses are commonly to be found. The general *'virus'* categories are:

- VIRUS - a program that attaches other runnable copies of itself to the machine code of other programs and may, or may not, carry out other activities (often described as the *'payload'*).
- WORM - similar to a virus but is aimed at attacking the resources of the computer system, rather than its files. It continually creates copies of itself, thereby clogging up a system. They are commonly found spreading on network systems.
- TROJAN HORSE - disguises itself as something else, such as a game, a utility or a graphics demonstration. When run, the program will carry out some irritating or harmful activity. A Trojan Horse does not normally replicate itself and so, when an infected file is deleted, it is gone from the system.
- TIME BOMB - a Trojan Horse that watches the clock. It will be activated on a certain date or a certain time of day.
- MACROS - a piece of code embedded inside Word document templates or Excel spreadsheets. Opening the document initiates the virus code.

Where the activity is initiated by a certain event, the program is also described as a *'Logic Bomb'*. Examples of triggering events are the number of times a program has been executed or the number of times the machine has been rebooted. Some may trigger in combination - i.e. when a certain file is run at a certain date or time. So, the elements of a logic bomb can be found in viruses and in Trojan horses. Virus variants means that there is an ever-increasing number of viruses to be detected.

NOTE:

This section outlines virus problems and solutions. Since virus numbers increase at an alarming rate, every publication or anti-virus program is out of date as soon as it is produced. The examples, then, are not meant to represent the current state-of-the-art viruses; they are used to illustrate typical strains and their effects. The user is advised to maintain current lists of viruses and maintain the anti-virus software in as current an edition as possible.

The material does not dwell on the exact mechanisms that a virus uses. This is intentional; it is not the purpose of this material to point the way for potential virus writers.

The modification or loss of data through a virus is an offence under Section 3 of the Computer Misuse Act of 1990, which states:

> *3.(1) A person is guilty of an offence if -*
>
> *a) he does any act which causes an unauthorised modification of the contents of any computer: and*
>
> *b) at the time when he does the act he has the requisite intent and the requisite knowledge.*

Since almost all viruses are imported from overseas, prosecutions under this Act will mostly apply to home grown virus writers.

Writing or owning a virus is not an offence but the infection of someone else's computer certainly constitutes an offence under the Act.

FILE INFECTION METHODS

Viruses only infect executable code since they need to be able to gain access to computer processing time. Any machine code is therefore vulnerable to virus attack including:

- COM, EXE, BIN, DRV, SYS and overlay files
- DLL, ICO, PIF, FON, PRG, PGM, CMD, APP and VxD files
- Disc boot sector or partition record
- Macros which invoke application or system code when they are invoked

When an infected file is executed, the virus code becomes memory resident and is free to carry out its designed disruption. The virus has to ensure that its code is always run before any code of the file to which it is attached, since that is the only time that it can guarantee that it will capture processing time.

Files are infected by one of the following methods:

APPENDING: The most common method, it involves attaching the virus code to the end of the file. Every COM file has an initial jump instruction which passes control to the program's main code. The virus simply alters the jump address to the start of the virus code; the virus code is run and control is finally directed to the actual program code. Similarly, with EXE files, the code entry point is altered to the start of the virus code before passing control to the actual program. The virus code will contain a section to replicate itself, plus other possible code sections for activities such as delivering any payload, any triggering routines and any stealth mechanisms. Since the program has extra code added to it, its overall size is increased - a good indication of a virused file. The *'Cascade'* and *'Jerusalem'* viruses are of this type.

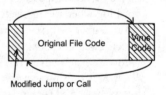

Modified Jump or Call

PRE-PENDING :   Similar to the above, except that the virus code resides at the beginning of the affected program.   Only affects COM files and the overall file length is increased by the infection.

OVER-WRITING :   The virus code replaces the actual code at the beginning of the file, normally a COM file. In this way, the overall file size is unaffected.   When the program is run, the virus code is executed instead of the expected code.   Since the original code is lost, the program's intended function is lost and the file is irrecoverable.   Rarely used, since it is so easily spotted.   However, some programs will have an unused area at the end of its final sector and the virus code could position itself in this area without affecting the original program code, or altering the original file's size. The *'Number of the Beast'* virus uses this technique.

COMPANION :   As previously explained, if two files have the same name, the one with the COM extension will take precedence over the one with the EXE extension.   This facility has been used by applications, with the COM file being used to set up any specialist configuration before loading the EXE file of the same name.   The virus writer takes advantage of this order to introduce a companion virus file.   The virus is created as a COM file with the same name as a normal program EXE file, with the COM file's attributes set to hide the file from normal view.   When the user attempts to run the EXE file, the COM file is run first and the virus activity is executed.   Again, this is not a popular virus as it is easily detected. *'Aids II'* and *'Twin'* are of this type.

CLUSTER :   Here, the file is left uninfected.   However, the Directory entry for the file is altered, so that the starting cluster points to the virus code instead of the wanted file.   The virus runs its own code then runs the file wanted by the user. Many entries may be affected, each pointing to the same virus.

AIMS OF VIRUSES

REPLICATION

The number one aim, sometimes the only aim, of a virus is to replicate itself on to other executable files. This is carried out quietly, to avoid bringing itself to the attention of the user - there are only a few viruses that produce a message during the replication stage. Some viruses are restricted to this activity; they spend their lives on the machine with the aim to simply infect other programs. They can be termed *'passive viruses'* from the point of view that, while being a nuisance, they do not threaten the integrity of existing data. Of course, while many will be actual passive types, some may be more lethal - its just that the correct conditions have not been there for it to activate. It makes sense, then, to treat all viruses with seriousness.

SURVIVAL

Once attached to a computers files or resources, the virus may attempt to escape detection and elimination. This is covered more fully later.

NUISANCE

These are sometimes termed *'irritant viruses'*. They display messages, change round keyboard responses, slow down the system, play a tune or affect the screen display in some way. They may also result in RAM being occupied while a genuine program is trying to run. *'Cascade'* is a nuisance virus that becomes memory-resident when an infected COM file is executed. The virus then infects other COM files and causes the letters of a piece of text to crumble to the bottom of the screen. *'Cascade'* began life as a Trojan horse which did not infect other files - another example of the evolution of viruses. *'Joshi'* is a boot sector virus that activates on the 5th January, requesting the user to enter *"Happy birthday Joshi"*; failure to enter the text hangs the machine.

DAMAGE

These are viruses that result in damage to files or discs. Examples are deleting files, scrambling file contents, creating cross-linked files, increasing files sizes to the extent that the program will not load into memory, or formatting the hard disc. Even irritant viruses can result in problems. Consider the result of losing all screen display when in the middle of a complex set of data entry. Irritant screen messages can also result in a program crashing when the message is written during the execution of the application code.

An example of drive damage is when a virus tells the read/write head of a floppy to move to an inner track which does not exist, the head can become jammed in the inner section of the floppy drive. Damage to hardware is, however, rare.

'Disk Killer' is an example of a boot sector virus that becomes memory resident and encrypts data in files. It overwrites valid sector data with its own code and the data in these sectors is therefore permanently lost. *'Dark Avenger'* infects COM, EXE and overlay files. When one of these infected files is executed, the virus becomes memory resident. It then infects other files and occasionally overwrites the data in a sector with a message. *'Tequila'* is a virus that infects EXE files, increasing their size by 2468 bytes; this is hidden from the user since a DIR command does not display this extra size. This upsets the CHKDSK check of the FAT, producing CHKDSK error messages. The number of entries in the FAT chain may be greater than the size of the file as reported by the virus. If the user runs CHKDSK/F as a consequence, the files are scrambled, as sectors will be released from the chain in the belief that they are surplus to the file. *'Jerusalem'* is a virus that affects COM and EXE files, adding 1813 extra bytes to the infected file; for that reason, the virus is also known as *'1813'*. COM file sizes are increased once only but EXE files can be repeatedly infected, increasing the file size by 1813 bytes every time. When the date is Friday, 13th, any infected files are deleted; it also produces a black rectangle on the screen. It also slows the machine's performance considerably.

NOTE :

If a file is <u>infected</u> by a virus it contains the virus code. If it an executable file, the virus can be run from that file; if it is a data file, the virus is present but is never run. Additionally, every file is capable of being <u>affected</u> by a virus - i.e. the file is corrupted or lengthened in some way.

VIRUS ACTIVITY

The activities of a virus can be viewed as different stages. Not all stages need be coded in a virus, although some activities are common to all viruses. The main stages of activity are:

Activation - caused when infected code is invoked

Trigger - caused by the occurrence by a particular date, time or event. This stage is not included as part of the code in most viruses.

Infection check - tests to see if a targeted file is already infected. The virus can do this by examining the DOS directory structure to find a suitable target, or it might lurk in memory waiting for an executable program to be run.

The Vienna group of viruses, for example, (648, Austrian, Charlie, etc.) set the file's time stamp to 62 seconds when they infect a file.   This time stamp is used when the virus looks to see if a file has already been infected. Times such as 60 or 62 cannot be seen in a DIR command and could only be detected with a disc editor utility.

Infection - If not already infected, the targeted file has the virus code attached to it.   This stage would be omitted for simple Trojan Horse and Time Bomb viruses.

Activity - A particular action such as displaying a screen message, playing a tune, deleting a file, etc.

Evasion - Another stage which may be present is the virus evading detection by deleting itself from the location where it carried out its particular activity.

The simplest case is that shown for the Trojan Horse. It is activated when the infected file is invoked and it performs its particular task.
The second diagram shows the stages of a Time Bomb; as can be seen, it is similar to the Trojan Horse, with the addition of a triggering mechanism - it will not always run the virus tasks when the infected file is invoked; it will await the pre-determined circumstances.
The third diagram shows the infection stages of a virus. The virus makes an attempt at infecting its target file. The diagram shows that it will carry out a particular activity; this is not always the case as certain viruses exist with the sole purpose of breeding.

BOOT SECTOR PROBLEMS

As explained in the chapter on discs, the Boot Sector is the first sector of any floppy disc, or the first sector in a hard disc partition.   The boot sector is a mere 512 bytes long and contains a small program which is loaded into memory by the BIOS when the POST check is completed. This program loads in the DOS components from the disc. This piece of code is the first code which is able to be modified after bootup, since any previously executed code was of the permanent type burnt into ROM.   The virus works by relocating the boot sector code into another sector and placing itself in the vacated position. When the boot sector code is to be executed, the DOS 13h interrupt (for disc read/write operations) is intercepted and the virus code is run before control is passed on to the genuine boot sector code. With a hard disc, this means that both the partition table and the DOS partition are affected. The virus code is loaded into memory when the machine is booted up; in fact, the virus code is loaded before other system and program files. The virus may well place the boot sector code and any virus code beyond that which will fit in the boot sector into another disc sector. It then marks that sector as bad so that it will not be over-written.   The most common example of this type is *'Stoned'*.   Its varieties include producing messages, affecting the partition table and hanging RLL disc controllers.

SOLUTIONS

With a hard disc or bootable floppy disc, if the DOS command SYS C: or SYS A: is given, the boot sector virus can be over-written by a fresh boot sector code. This should be done after the machine is re-booted on a virus-free boot floppy. With non-bootable floppy discs, the files should be copied from the disc (with COPY or XCOPY, never DISKCOPY), the disc should be formatted and the files should be copied back to the disc. With DOS 5 onwards, use the /U parameter to the FORMAT command, so that the boot sector is re-written.

PARTITION SECTOR PROBLEMS

Some viruses, such as *'Michel-Angelo'* infect the Master Boot Record, or partition table. This is the first sector on a hard disc and contains information about the disc (number of sectors in each partition, etc.) and a short piece of executable code to read the DOS boot sector. Every time the machine is booted up, the short program is executed.   The MBR virus infects the partition table code so that the virus code is run every time the machine is booted up.   When the partition sector is infected, the brute force recovery method is to back up all the disc's files, carry out a low level format and re-partition the disc.

SOLUTIONS

If DOS 5 onwards is available, a quick solution is to boot the machine from a clean boot disc and give the command FDISK /MBR. This eliminates the virus code from the master boot record on the hard disc but will not repair a damaged partition table.   It is useful method to anticipate this problem and create backup copies of the partition table. This can be carried out with the DOS 5 command MIRROR/PARTN. This creates a file called PARTNSAV.FIL on a floppy disc.   In the event of partition table corruption, the drive would not be recognised - but the machine can be booted from the floppy and the command UNFORMAT/PARTN can be given. This will restore the partition table to the hard disc. Of course, this only cleans up the partition table; a check will still have to be made of the actual executable files on the hard disc, otherwise an infected file might re-infect the partition table.

FILE VIRUSES

File viruses can have the following characteristics:

- **TSR**   Many viruses operate as Terminate and Stay Resident programs.   When an infected file is executed, the virus code in the file is run first. This code places the virus in memory from where it executes.   The virus code then monitor the system, intercepting calls to run executable files (usually through the normal DOS 21h interrupt).   It is then able to infect the file that is being loaded. To further complicate matters, many TSR viruses, such as *'Brain'* and *'Yale'*, are able to survive a warm boot, i.e. pressing Ctrl-Alt-Del, since the TSR can detect and intercept the key combination.   For this reason, the machine should be cold booted - i.e. switched off for a few seconds and then switched back on again.

- **NON-TSR**   In these cases, the virus code is run once, before passing control on to the actual file's code. It does not install itself in memory. It only executes the virus code each time that the infected file is run.

- **STEALTH**   Stealth viruses are TSR viruses which intercept any calls to read a file's directory information, via the DOS 21h interrupt.   Since most files which are infected have grown in size, reading the file size from the directory would reveal the infection.   So, the stealth virus code detects the directory request, subtracts the virus code length from the actual directory reading and presents the user with the truncated file size. From the user's point of view, the file size has not been altered and it appears unlikely that the file has been infected. The same technique is used to hide any alteration of the disc's boot record or partition table. Such viruses will not be found by anti-virus checksumming systems which simply look for a file's size increasing. This is an old technique which appeared in *'Brain'*, the first recorded virus.   The fact that it is still commonly in use is a comment on its effectiveness.   *'Frodo'* and *'666'* use this technique. However, using CHKDSK will result in the loss of these files!   Additionally, viruses may ensure that when they infect a file, the normal file write update in the directory does not take place. This means that the date and time modified data is left unaltered, so that a change will not betray their presence. Fortunately, stealth viruses cannot hide their presence in memory and anti-virus software can detect memory-resident viruses.

Rarely viruses infect both boot sectors and files - known as *'multipartite viruses'*.   Examples of multipartite viruses are *'Tequila'* and *'Spanish Telecom-2'* (also known as *'Telefonica'*).

MICROSOFT MACRO VIRUSES

Until recently, all viruses were contained inside the actual machine code of a program or routine.   When Microsoft brought out Word 6 it also introduced WordBasic which is used to create *'macros'*.   Excel uses Visual Basic for Applications to create spreadsheet macros.   Macros are simply small, usually single-purpose, helpful routines that can be invoked by clicking an icon or when the Word or Excel document is opened.   When an infected document is opened the macro programming language runs the virus code. To date, the Excel virus does no more than replicate itself.   There are various types of Word macro virus as listed in the table.

DMV	Replicates itself
Concept	Replicates itself
Nuclear	Adds the message "STOP ALL NUCLEAR TESTING IN THE PACIFIC!" to all printouts
Colors	Changes the screen colours
FormatC	Attempts to format the C: drive
Hot	Deletes the contents of a document then saves the empty version.

SOLUTION

Microsoft provide a file called mvtool.exe which is the Macro Virus Protection Tool.   This utility will detects documents that use macros and will report if it finds the *'Concept'* virus which is the most common.   Office 97 automatically detects viruses when a infected document is opened.

VIRUS DETECTION/PREVENTION

Viruses can either be found by inspection of machines or by reported faults.   Viruses often become noticeable when several machines exhibit the same characteristics; a problem on one machine could be a hardware or software fault but a number of machines with the same effect probably indicates a virus. Obvious virus problems are those where the effects are easily seen - e.g. unwanted screen messages, music, etc.   Other problems may only be noticed after a while - e.g. file sizes being increased, data being corrupted or lost, cross-linked files, a file's DOS date and time being altered, unusual error messages, a shrinking of the available main memory, programs taking longer to load than previously, the hard disc light coming on at unusual moments, etc.   Virus protection software works in one of two ways, either through scanning existing files on a disc or memory, or by logging file characteristics and monitoring for any changes. The first method looks for the <u>existence</u> of viruses in a file or memory; the other method looks for the <u>effects</u> of a virus on a file.   Either method can be used and for added security both methods should be used.   Of course, a detection system is spotting a virus <u>after</u> it has affected the computer system; a prevention system is designed to spot a virus <u>before</u> it has a chance to affected the system.

SCANNING TECHNIQUES

Anti-virus software has to detect the presence of a virus by looking for the characteristics which viruses portray.   This can mean one of two things:

- A virus will have a distinctive piece of code within it (e.g. writing a message to the screen) which can be detected by the anti-virus software.
- Viruses have to open files, write to files, alter file sizes, write to the boot sector, write to the partition table, etc.   Any unusual attempts to carry out these activities can be detected as a possible piece of virus code.

Broadly speaking, the presence of infected files can be detected by looking for the source of the infection or by spotting the tell-tale signs of effects of the infection.   This can be achieved in two ways:

- the user loads and runs detection software.
- the detection software can be pre-loaded as a TSR which tests every executable file for viruses before allowing them to be run. This slows down program loading and uses up precious memory but is able to detect viruses before they can spread or cause damage.

These methods are complimentary to each other and both are encouraged.

SIGNATURE SCANNING

This type of detector scans memory, the boot sector, the partition table and the executable files. It is searching for the occurrence of the string of instruction sequences which are mostly unique to particular viruses.   This pattern is usually called its 'signature' and is usually about 16 to 24 bytes in length. Although the virus code can be mostly randomly encrypted each time it infects a file, it still needs a section of unencrypted code to carry out the translations.   This code section is its signature. This means that the software is virus-specific; if a new virus appears, a new version of the scanning software is required.   The more up-to-date the version of scanning software, the more known signatures will be searched for, thereby increasing the chances of detecting viruses. When a known signature is detected, the file or sector is reported to the user as being infected.

To prevent detection, some viruses randomly generate what appears as a completely new encrypted code each time it replicates itself.   These are known as *'polymorphic'* viruses and the encryption code is often given the glamorous title of *'Mutation Engine'*. In these varieties, even the previously unencrypted code is altered.   This is achieved in a number of ways - e.g. adding redundant instructions, changing the order of certain instructions, storing values in different registers or using alternative instructions that carry out the same end result as another set of instructions.   This produces many possible permutations. When these viruses appear, a huge range of potential signatures would require to be searched for, making their detection almost impossible.   An example is the *'Pogue'* virus which plays music and corrupts hard disc data. In response, anti-virus software introduced the *'wildcard'* into their virus checking algorithms. This knows where some of the redundant instructions are situated and ignores their specific contents in the signature search.   Unfortunately, the added complexity leads to slower operations.   Due to the ever increasing complexity of viruses, searching for signatures is regarded as an activity with diminishing returns.   Examples of signature scanners are FindVirus and VirusGuard from Dr. Solomon's Anti-Virus Toolkit and VSafe with DOS 6.

GENERIC SCANNING

A scanning variation is to ignore signatures which can have many variations. Instead, the scanning software looks for machine code instructions which would result in executable files being written to. These are known as *'generic scanners'* or *'monitors'*, since they look for points that are common to a range of viruses, rather than any specific virus.   To that extent, they are more future-proofed. However, some applications require to re-write their EXE files to reflect a user's configuration and this might be reported as a virus. In development environments, such as software houses and colleges, EXE files are regularly created and modified and this could also lead to many spurious reports of file corruption.   Even DOS commands such as FORMAT.COM and SYS.COM might be reported as viruses.   This makes a generic scanner an imprecise weapon but it is useful nevertheless.

Some memory-resident versions of generic scanners overcome this problem by detecting the attempt to write to disc and provides the user with an option to continue with the operation or to abort.   This can be used to prevent unauthorised disc formatting, programs going memory-resident and writing to the disc boot sector.   For example, if a memory-resident scanner intercepts a call to write to disc, its program can test whether the boot sector or FAT is being written to and prevent or present the user with control over that activity.   This is successful unless the virus code writes directly to the hard disc controller via the BIOS, by-passing the DOS calls.   This has to be combated by detecting calls to INT 13, INT 26 and INT 40, which are direct BIOS disc calls.   Checks should include spotting attempts to change file attributes from read-only to read-write, renaming COM and EXE files, writing to executable files and writing to the boot sector.

FILE FINGERPRINTING (Checksumming)

The other detection method concerns itself with the original characteristics of a file and the effects of an infection.   Every new .COM and .EXE file added to a disc can have a CRC check code (sometimes called a *'validation code'*) calculated and logged. Adding together the values of all the bytes in a file would produce a large number which could act as a simple checksum; using a mathematical formula to the bytes produces a figure which is more unique to that file. These checksums can be attached to the files concerned or they can be held in a separate database.   The anti-virus software can then later check these codes for any sign that any file has been altered.   This is a more efficient means of detecting virus attacks.   Of course, by definition, the viruses are only detected <u>after</u> they have infected the system; this method does not detect the infection process itself.   The checking of the existing set of files on the disc can be an automatic process, initiated by a command in AUTOEXEC.BAT.   Each file can have its checksum calculated and compared to its previous value.   Any difference in values will result in an error report. This can be a time-consuming business, with large hard discs but is very efficient.   However, the calculation of checksums for new files has to be carried out regularly and added to the checksum list, if the system is to maintained at an efficient level.

Viruses mostly work by changing the first 'jump' or 'call' instruction in a file; the pointer is altered to point to the added virus code rather than the normal program code.   So, in many cases, testing the checksum of the first few dozen bytes will detect whether the file is infected.   To counteract this, some viruses leave the first pointer untouched and alter the next pointer which is embedded deeper in the file's code. This evades a simple checksum system and requires a checksum on the entire file to be carried out; this takes longer and occupies more storage space. Examples of checksumming are ChkVirus from Dr. Solomon and Anti-Virus in DOS6.

ANTI-VIRUS PRODUCTS

An ever-increasing range of anti-virus products are becoming available. Most are software products but a couple of hardware alternatives are around in the shape of cards that fit into the normal expansion bus. These are particularly useful in dealing with boot sector viruses, both on the hard disc and on floppies. Many software programs are normal commercial products and a few are shareware varieties. Considering the practical problems, then, a preferred anti-virus product should include the following facilities:

- The ability to run the utilities automatically, e.g. through CONFIG.SYS or AUTOEXEC.BAT.   If a utility has to be actively executed by a user, it will often be ignored. The experience of creating backups has shown this.   The virus checking should be able to run without user-activation, if required.
- The ability to run its utilities as TSRs, preferably in extended or expanded memory.   This should be able to scan all files that are executed, modified, copied or unarchived (i.e. restored from compressed form).
- The anti-virus software should be able to test itself for signs of viruses.
- The ability to check memory, disc partition tables, boot sectors, normal files and compressed files.
- The ability to choose between making all tests or making specified checks. A virus can infect an overlay file and although these are commonly given the extensions .OVR or .OVL, they can really be given any extension from a particular application. So, there is no way that a scanner can tell whether a file is a data file or an overlay file containing infected executable code. To be absolutely certain that a machine is virus-free, every file on the disc would have to be checked, not just the .COM and .EXE files.   While this is slower, it is a more secure option.
- The ability to detect as large a range of viruses as possible.

- Few false detections. For example, the virus search strings embedded in one scanner's code should not be detected as a virus by another scanner. This can be avoided by a scanner which encrypts its search strings, which is common in modern anti-virus software. An uninfected machine should produce no false alarms.
- A virus-specific scanner.
- A generic scanner.
- A checksumming program (creating and checking check sums) for both hard discs and floppy discs.
- The ability to test all of a file or only selected parts. Most viruses can be detected by checksumming the first or last section of a file. This is a less secure method but operates much more quickly than a full checksumming routine.
- The ability to handle 'stealth' viruses.
- The ability for users to add known signatures to their check list, including wildcards.
- The ability to prevent viruses writing to the boot sector or partition table.
- The ability to repair infected files.
- The ability to immunise files - fool the virus into believing that the files are already infected.
- A boot sector and partition table restoration facility.
- The ability to create a *'rescue'* disc to store the partition table, boot sector, FAT and CMOS settings.
- A reasonable execution time, although this must always remain subordinate to having the fullest tests carried out. The longer the list of possible signatures, the greater will be the scanning time required; TSR virus monitors require processing time. These are facts of life that have to be lived with.
- A reference book, or dictionary, of all known viruses.
- The availability of regular updates.
- Help line and/or bulletin board service available.

Anti-Virus

Example utilities include Dr. Solomon's Anti-Virus Toolkit, Central Point Antivirus (as used in MSDOS v6), Norton Anti-virus, Vaccine from Sophos, and McAfee's Viruscan.

USING MICROSOFT ANTI-VIRUS

With MSDOS v6 anti-virus utilities are supplied with the operating system. The scanning utility is invoked by calling the MSAV DOS-version program or clicking on the anti-virus icon in the Windows 3.1 version.

The opening screen provides the following facilities:

```
┌─────────────────────────────────────────────────────┐  ▼
│ ═                                                     │
├─────────────────────────────────────────────────────┤
│  Scan   Options   Help                                │
│ ┌──────────────────────┐   ┌──────────────────────── │
│ │ Drives:              │    Status:                   │
│ │  ┌──┐                │    Selected:                 │
│ │  │═ │ A:             │         1   Drives           │
│ │  ┌──┐                │       172   Directories      │
│ │  │═ │ B:             │      3884   Files            │
│ │  ┌──┐                │                              │
│ │  │═ │ C: [MS_DOS_6]  │    Last Virus Found:   None  │
│ │  ┌──┐                │    Last Action:        None  │
│ │  │═ │ D:             │    Date:          24/01/94   │
│ │  ┌──┐                │                              │
│ │  │─ │ E: [MINERVA3]  │                              │
│ └──────────────────────┘                             │
│              ┌──────────────┐  ┌──────────────────┐   │
│              │   Detect     │  │  Detect and Clean│   │
│              └──────────────┘  └──────────────────┘   │
└───────────────────────────────────────────────────────┘
```

- The choice of which drive to check (although the user can set up the Windows version so that it will automatically scan a specified drive when the program is run). Whatever option is chosen, the utility will always check the computer memory for any memory-resident viruses before checking the specified disc.
- The option to simply detect viruses or to both detect and eliminate viruses.
- An elaborate *'Help'* system that guides the user through commonly used terms and step-by-step instructions oj using the program.
- A *'Scan'* pull-down menu that offers a comprehensive description of all viruses it can detect, along with some other facilities. An example of a virus description, in this case for the Tequila virus, is as shown.

```
┌──────────────────────────────────────────────────────────┐
│ ═                                            ┌──────────┐  │
│                                              │   OK     │  │
│  Tequila virus:                              └──────────┘  │
│                                              ┌──────────┐  │
│  This file virus is 2468 bytes long. It infects .COM      │
│  and .EXE files.                             │  Print   │  │
│                                              └──────────┘  │
│  It remains resident in memory, uses stealth techniques,  │
│  uses self encryption, and uses self modifying code.      │
│                                                            │
│  Side effects include corrupted data files, damaged file  │
│  linkage, corrupted program and overlay files, and        │
│  changes to system run time operation.                    │
└──────────────────────────────────────────────────────────┘
```

- An *'Options'* dialogue box as shown:
  The main options are:

```
┌──────────────────────────────────────────────────────────┐
│ ▭                                                          │
│                                            ┌────────────┐  │
│                                            │     OK     │  │
│  ☒ Verify Integrity          ☒ Prompt While Detect        │
│                                                            │
│  ☐ Create New Checksums      ☒ Anti-Stealth               │
│                                                            │
│  ☐ Create Checksums on Floppies   ☒ Check All Files       │
│                                                            │
│  ☐ Disable Alarm Sound       ☐ Wipe Deleted Files         │
│                                                            │
│  ☐ Create Backup                                          │
└──────────────────────────────────────────────────────────┘
```

'Verify Integrity' - This enables the checking of executable files, to see if their size has been altered compared to its previous checksum size stored in the CHKLST.MS file.

'Create New Checksums' - This creates the *'fingerprint'* for each file and stores the file details in CHKLST.MS.   A separate CHKLST.MS file is created for each directory.   This should only be carried out when the user is certain that the files on the disc are free from viruses, as the checklist files will be used to detect future virused files.   A separate option exists to 'Create Checksums on Floppies'.

'Anti-Stealth' -   This enables the generic scanning option (see page 247) to detect as yet unknown viruses - those using Stealth techniques to avoid detection.

'Wipe Deleted Files' - This changes the user option when a viruses file is detected. The user normally is asked if the infected file should be deleted; with this option enable, the user is asked whether the file should be wiped (i.e. every cluster of the infected file is overwritten)

When the 'Scan' of the disc is completed, a report will be displayed similar to that shown:

	Scanned	Infected	Cleaned
Hard Disks	1	0	0
Floppy Disks	0	0	0
Total Disks	1	0	0
COM Files	856	0	0
EXE Files	1500	0	0
Other Files	13268	0	0
Total Files	15624	0	0
Scan Time	00:25:14		

VSAFE

Microsoft also provide VSAFE which is a memory-resident program (TSR) requiring 44k of memory. It employs the signature scanning technique to detect virus problems as they occur.

VIRUSES AND WINDOWS 95

Windows 95 does not come with anti-virus software unlike Window 3.1.   Due to the changes to the operating system for Windows 95, long file names, 32-bit file access, etc, software houses produce virus checkers that are specifically designed for Windows 95.   Earlier versions used TSRs to detect unauthorised disc access. With Windows 95, the TSR equivalent is the virtual device driver (VxD) and a virus checking VxD will intercept disc access to 32-bit disc drivers.   Few Windows 95 specific viruses have been found but running 16-bit applications (ie all programs that are specifically designed for Windows 95) still allows viruses into the system.   If the computer is run in DOS mode, the old TSR utilities are still required while DOS programs run in DOS session within Windows 95 are still protected by the VxD.

VIRUS ELIMINATION

When a virus is detected, swift action should be taken, since delays will result in further potential data loss or corruption.

The action required should include:
- Immediately isolate the machine. Disconnect from any local area network or a peer-to-peer system. No further activity should be carried out on the machine until the infection is cleared.
- Inform management and users.
- Collect any discs that were used in the machine.
- Test all machines that used discs taken from the infected machine.
- Check all machines in the organisation. If an infected game has passed round, employees will be reluctant to admit they used the disc. So, a check should be carried out nevertheless.
- Trace and eliminate the original source of the infection. This is not always an easy task but overcoming the effects of a virus without eliminating the source of the infection only means that the whole process may start over again.
- If the virus is a new strain, report it to the various anti-virus software houses and the police Computer Crime Unit on 0171-725-2306.

The practical steps to eliminating viruses from a hard disc are:
- Boot up the infected machine from a write-protected, virus-checked floppy. This should be a boot disc containing FORMAT, FDISK, UNFORMAT, DEBUG, and copies of the partition table, boot sector, FAT and the CMOS settings. (NB - if the recovery disc contains a CONFIG.SYS or AUTOEXEC.BAT file, ensure that the script lines only refer to files on the floppy disc, since system files on the hard disc may be infected). From DOS 5 onwards, use the /U switch with the FORMAT command; this ensures that the boot sector of the disc is re-written in the case of suspected infected discs.
- Run the virus checking software from a write-protected, virus-checked floppy.
- Identify the infected areas (e.g. memory, boot record, particular files, etc.)
- Use the anti-virus software to disinfect the affected areas, where this is possible and there is no alternative (i.e. there is no backup of the file). This re-writes the files date and time stamps and rewrites the first few bytes of the program code (where the jump to the virus code normally resides). This data is taken from a list in the anti-virus program. This is not entirely successful.
- For added security, delete all infected files and re-install them or restore them from backup discs. Re-installing from the original discs is preferable, since restoring from backups might restore virus if it found its way on to the backup disc.
- Re-run the virus checking software on the entire machine.
- Run the virus checking software on all floppy discs that have been used in the machine.

VIRUS PREVENTION

If a computer system anti-virus strategy is adequately planned and implemented, the risk of virus infection is minimised. The adage *'Prevention is Better than Cure'* emphatically applies to viruses. A rigorous approach to virus prevention can save countless hours repairing the effects of a virus attack. The hours spent in implementing prevention measures will repay themselves many times over in preventing lost production caused by virus attacks. Nevertheless, viruses will still be a threat and it is far better to have a recovery strategy in place before any attack, than running round in a panic when the attack has already occurred.

There are a wide range of activities that can be carried out to provide as virus-free an environment as possible. Remember, a completely virus-free environment is still not a reality, since anti-virus software follows virus development. The degree of enforcement of the activities depends upon the importance of the system in use. Viruses finding themselves on to a home user's machine is less of a problem than viruses finding their way on to a network. Large organisations, with heavy reliance on their computing effort will want to make use of as many safeguards as possible. For these bodies, the data is far more precious than the hardware and the extra time and effort involved is worthwhile. The organisation has to consider the amount of financial loss that would result from a loss of data. The losses could include:
- Repairing or replacing any damaged equipment.
- Lost output while the machines are down.
- Paying for incoming expert help (very expensive).
- Restoring available computer data (from backups).
- Re-entering available data, held on paper.
- Re-collecting data not held on paper (e.g. telephone orders which were directly keyed into computers) and re-entering this data.

The strategy for virus prevention and elimination should be adopted as the organisation's policy at as high a management level as possible. This prevents friction at a later date, when machines are declared out of bounds and individual managers are losing precious processing time.

Virus prevention measures can tackle the problem both at the machine end and at the introduction of software into the system. Both activities are complimentary. A virus-prevention strategy should therefore address both the existing machines and any new software that might be introduced to them. The anti-virus strategy should include

- Naming staff responsible for maintaining current anti-virus software.
- Naming staff responsible for eliminating any virus outbreak.
- Securing outside consultants for anti-virus and data recovery work.
- Compiling detailed procedures for dealing with suspected files, discs, computers or networks.
- Staff training on virus issues.

PROTECTING THE MACHINE

- Ensure that access to machines is restricted to only those who require it. This prevents unauthorised access and narrows down the source of any future virus problems. On a standalone machine, special password protection programs can be installed. On local area networks, the system passwords can be rigorously used. Machines should not then be left unattended and switched on, otherwise these passwords are by-passed.
- Where economically practicable, install anti-virus software on each machine. This is usually a cost-effective measure, as the alternative is to have the PC support technician running round all the machines with the single licensed copy. The extra costs of purchasing multiple copies is soon recovered. The purchase of a site licence can make their installation cheaper still.
- Document the existing machine configuration. This should involve noting the size, checksums and date and time of creation/modification of system files and device drivers. This information is vital in future checking for any corruption of the machine. Even better, create a 'rescue' disc. This is a boot disc that is tested as virus-free and contains a copy of the partition table, boot record and machine CMOS settings. This is normally provided as an option with anti-virus software.
- Ensure that the files and sub-directories of the disc are protected as far as possible. For a standalone machine, this involves setting most file attributes to read-only. Many viruses reset the file's attribute while infecting it, but it is successful in preventing infection from some viruses such as 'South African'.
- On a local area network, sub-directory rights should be set to the minimum access rights possible. For example, if a server directory contains only program files, then access to the entire directory should be on a read-only basis. This is not always possible, as some applications need to write their configuration information. Individual files within read/write sub-directories should be set to read-only, where possible. Individual users on the network should be given no more rights than they actually require.
- Ensure that regular backups are carried out, so that the effects of a virus attack can be quickly overcome. Removing the virus may only be part of the recovery process. Deleted and corrupted files have to be replaced and carrying out a restore can be an effective method of replacing these files. Backup copies should not consist solely of a single backup; copies of previous backups should also be kept, since a virus may not have been detected and the newest backup may itself be infected. From time to time, test that the restore procedures actually work; there is little point in rigorously backing up data if the restore mechanism is flawed (e.g. the tape player may not actually be recording the backup data).
- Enforce strict bans on users bringing games, or even their own utilities. The most common means of spreading viruses is through the mobility of floppy discs. Many organisations, where data integrity is crucial, have policies of dismissal where unofficial use of floppy discs is spotted. No discs should be brought into, or taken out of, the computer environment. Where this is impossible, such as with users of portable computers, every disc taken from the laptop or notebook must be virus checked before being placed in a main machine. Note that this restriction should also be enforced with visiting computer service engineers; any diagnostic discs must be virus checked before being used on a machine. Similarly, demonstration discs brought in by salespeople are a likely carrier of infection from company to company. These discs should be rigorously checked before being run.
- Ensure that only data is kept on users' floppy discs; this minimises viruses spreading since there are no executable code for the virus to attach to. If users are trained to write-protect floppy discs when they only contain readable data, then virus spread via disc boot sectors is also minimised.
- Undertake a training campaign amongst staff, so that the problems from viruses are fully understood; this may well prove a more effective weapon than the big stick and training videos are available.
- Use more than one anti-virus product, since no single piece of software detects all the available viruses.
- Keep the most up-to-date possible versions of anti-virus software, to minimise the prospects of data loss or corruption. The producers of anti-virus software supply monthly or quarterly updates.
- Buy a selection of books on computer security, virus protection and disaster recovery. Evolve the best strategy for the organisation, taking into account the amount of data, its importance, cost, etc.

INSTALLING/USING NEW SOFTWARE

Included in the organisation's policy statement on virus prevention should be a section on the introduction of new software into the organisation.   This may involve the centralisation of software purchasing and installation so that the policy can be fully implemented.   The policy should include:

- Buy only from reputable dealers; avoid the bargains which may be imitations.
- Don't be tempted to use pirate copies. It is illegal and it carries a high risk of infection.
- Do not use bulletin board software, postal shareware and public domain discs or 'free' discs supplied by magazines or dealers until they have been fully tested.
- Write protect original discs, whether operating system disc, application discs or even small utility discs, as soon as they are removed from their delivery wrapping.
- Make a copy of the master discs and write protect the working set of discs.
- Thoroughly test new software before introducing it to the working situation.   This should be carried out in a 'clean' environment; ideally, this should be a standalone computer with no other hardware present except the operating system.   Prior to testing the software, the hard disc contents can be completely erased and fresh system software and anti-virus software installed.   Even the NVR (non-volatile RAM) area should be erased and re-written.   This ensures that there is no unknown influences on the test. Equally, it ensures that any virused software is unable to affect any other working software.
- Test the software with as many anti-virus packages as possible.   Each package tackles the checks in slightly different ways and has different strengths and weaknesses.   The range of viruses found by each package is different.   So, if several packages are used, the chances of detecting a virus are improved.
- If the tests do not expose any viruses, the software should be documented before being brought into use. This will involve noting, for each file, the file size, file checksum and creation date and time.   This can be used to check if files are later affected and altered by viruses.
- Store the master set of discs in a secure place.

COMMON VIRUSES

Below is a table outlining the characteristics of some of the most common viruses. The chart concentrates on the damage caused by the virus; nuisance effects such as playing tunes, etc. are not listed.

	Stoned	Jerusalem	Cascade	Dark Avenger	Nomenclatura	Vacsina	Joshi	Yankee Doodle	AIDS	Michelangelo	Ping-Pong	Pogue	Tequila	Telefonlca
Infects Boot Sector	X						X		X	X	X			X
Infects Partition Table	X						X			X			X	X
Infects EXE files		X		X	X	X		X					X	
Infects COM files		X	X	X	X	X		X				X		X
Infects overlay files				X	X	X								
Infects COMMAND.COM				X	X									
Stays memory resident	X	X	X	X	X	X	X	X		X	X	X	X	X
Uses STEALTH methods								X					X	X
Uses self-encryption			X									X	X	X
Corrupts file linkage	X			X				X		X			X	X
Affects run-times	X	X	X	X	X	X		X	X	X			X	X
Corrupts program files		X	X	X	X	X	X	X	X				X	X
Corrupts overlay files		X	X	X	X	X	X	X	X				X	X
Corrupts data files						X		X						X
Reformats part of disc										X				X
Overwrites part of disc										X				X
Changes to boot sector	X						X			X				X
Changes partition table														X
Affects peripherals (eg printers, monitor, etc)	X	X	X				X				X		X	X
Renew Boot Sector	X			X			X			X	X			X
Clean Partition Table	X						X			X			X	X
Delete and replace virused files		**							X					
Virused Files may be able to be disinfected		X	X	X	X	X		X				X	X	X

** With Jerusalem, if infected files have not increased in size, the file must have been overwritten. In these cases, the files can not be disinfected and must be replaced.

PC Support

The term *'PC Support'* has different meanings in different organisations, dependent upon that organisation's specific needs.   However, the functions of PC support staff might include:

HARDWARE

- Advising on new purchases.   Support technicians can provide invaluable information about the reliability of certain brand names and the quality of their after-service.   Most technicians also have a very good appreciation of any inadequacies in the organisation's computing system and are among the staff most likely to be up to date on what equipment is necessary and available.
- Installing and testing new computers; connecting computers to local area networks.
- Installing hardware upgrades, such as adding extra memory modules, modems, fax cards or network interface cards (with any corresponding driver software).
- Carrying out system preventative maintenance such as the periodic examination, cleaning and testing of equipment and running regular diagnostics checks.
- Carrying out first-line repairs such as replacing faulty boards or cables, The extent of the fault-finding and repair activities may vary widely with the organisation and with the capabilities and experience of their support technicians.   Some sections may contain staff who are trained service technicians with the ability to repair equipment.   Other staff need have no skills with a soldering iron; their role is to find the faulty component and have it replaced or sent for repair.   Other organisations have maintenance contracts and PC support is confined to minor hardware and software problems.

SOFTWARE

- Installing new software.   This will involve the installation and testing of the software prior to its use by the organisation.   It may also require the creation of a training programme for the staff who will be using the software.
- Upgrading existing software - both system software and application software.   This may involve upgrading DOS 5 to DOS 6 or replacing an application package with the latest version number or the Windows version or network version of the product.
- Re-installing individual files that have been corrupted or inadvertently deleted.
- Removing viruses from computers and restoring working applications and data.

OPERATIONAL

- Carrying out any necessary I.T. staff training.   This could be on the use of hardware (e.g. a modem), a new application package, or on carrying out new office procedures using existing equipment.
- Maintaining data security.   This may involve the regular backing up of important company data, either on individual standalone machines or on the network server.   It may also involve the recovering of data and files from damaged discs.
- Advising and checking on Data Protection Act guidelines.
- Advising and checking on Safety at Work regulations.
- Running a user help desk for users in the organisation
- Maintaining records of machine configurations, what applications are on each machine, the specific data held on each machine, the detailed fault history of each piece of equipment, etc.

SOURCES OF USER SUPPORT

A variety of user support mechanisms are used by organisations and these are:

Manufacturers

Where the goods are supplied directly by a manufacturer, they have the responsibility of ensuring that the product carries out its function correctly.   This may take the form of repairing hardware or configuring software.   The level of warranty support depends upon the terms of the contract, ranging from same-day, through to next-day, to two-working-days and so on.   The fast response time is the most expensive but is required where products are used for essential operations (eg medical, financial, real-time, etc).   Where a manufacturer is remote from an organisation, a local service company is often used to provide a speedier response time.   The service staff probably cover a wide range of products and will not necessarily be expert in the product to be serviced.   This can be significant, as clear-up time is as important as the response time. After all, the user wants the visit to be effective as well as quick.

In addition to direct maintenance, many hardware and software manufacturers run support lines, bulletin boards and internet Web sites.   These are dedicated to answering specific user problems, publishing FAQs (answer to frequently-asked questions) and providing patches, upgrades and updated software drivers.   Examples of this are Adaptec (manufacturers of hard disc controllers) and Microsoft (software producers).

Dealers

Where good are supplied via a dealer, the dealer has the legal responsibility for the warranty, since the contract was with the dealer. Most dealers also offer extended warranties where, for an extra charge, the maintenance of the products are covered for a longer period. Dealers can also be contracted to provide improved response times since, in general, they are located closer to their customers. Many dealers will also provide user training as part of the sales package or for an additional charge.

Third-Party Support

Third party support is independent of the manufacturer and supplier of the products and the services cover a wide range of support levels. These range from supplying a diagnostics software package (where the user requires the knowledge and skills to use it) through to full-scale outsourcing (where all the organisation's problems are covered by an external company). In the first case, a one-off payment is made; with outsourcing, a negotiated annual fee covers the cost of the service. Although third-party charges can be expensive, they are often regarded as an efficient option compared to maintaining an in-house facility with permanent staff, accommodation, training costs, etc.

Other third-party services, which are covered later, are:

- Commercial held desks
- Support on CDs
- Training
- Consultancy

In-house Support

For smaller organisation with few computing resources, the cost of a permanent support staff is not justified. For larger organisations, in-house support groups provide the ability to call upon instant services. Additionally, the support staff have intimate knowledge of the organisation's needs and priorities and have local knowledge of the equipment and software in use. The scope of the services can also be much wider as staff can be trained in specialist areas.

Support Methods

External hardware support methods - on-site, back-to-base and swap-out, are covered in the chapter on System Selection. Software support methods are covered later in this chapter.

SYSTEM MAINTENANCE

Preventative maintenance is preferable to waiting for equipment to fail and then repairing it. It is normally easier to carry out and is also cheaper in the long run. Repairs are often seen as money well spent, as it puts the organisation back into working order, while regular maintenance is often viewed as a tiresome and unproductive task. Any such attitudes - whether among management or support staff - need to be changed, as a defined maintenance programme will both reduce system failures and save money. There is a school of thought which advocates a policy of *'if it aint broke don't fix it'* and it is certainly true that the over frequent pulling and prodding of equipment can cause problems. As often in life, a balanced approach to maintenance is the correct one. Elements of the computing system should get as much attention as they actually need in practice. This will mean there will be different cycles of maintenance for different pieces of equipment. This chapter suggests that three levels of maintenance provide an adequate cover.

REGULAR MAINTENANCE

The definition of *'regular'* depends on the organisation's structure and policy. For example, a widely dispersed organisation with far-distant local branches would pose problems for a weekly routine. Generally, a regular routine means a fortnightly or monthly cycle, depending on how hash the computing environment.

The elements of regular maintenance would be:

- Check all external cables for any mechanical damage e.g. fraying, crushing, stretching, etc.). Also check that all cables are properly seated in their respective sockets and that none are only partly plugged in. These checks should be of video cables (between unit and monitor), printer cables (between Centronics or RS232 port on computer and the socket on the printer and the power cables (between the units and the mains supply) and any other cables such as mouse, modem or keyboard cables. Any partially connected cables will result in incorrect operation. In the case of power cables, poor connections might result in arcing (i.e. the mains supply jumping the gap between the plug and socket) at the connections and even result in fires in extreme cases.
- Clean the computer's outside case. This does not directly affect the performance of the machine. It simply keeps the computer looking smart and encourages best practice from its users. In a clean environment, this will be a quick operation. If the cleaning removes a lot of dirt, then it indicates a dirtier environment and this may mean that these machines will require a more frequent internal clean (see later). After all, if the outside is getting dirty quickly, this must also apply to the inner machine.

The rules for cleaning a computer case are:

- o   Always use a proprietary case cleaning fluid; this is usually of the foam type.   Never use normal domestic cleaning fluids as these are often abrasive.
- o   Always use a clean cloth of lint-free material, to avoid introducing lint fragments into the case via the ventilation slots.
- o   Never spray or apply the cleaner directly to the case as this may penetrate the case via the ventilation slots. Always apply the cleaning fluid to the cloth, then apply the cloth to the case.

- Clean the monitor.   The monitor screen has a high voltage on its inside coating and this attracts dust very quickly, making the monitor the item most likely to need cleaned first in any system.   Again, use a proprietary cleaning solution.   The type purchased should be an anti-static cleaner; this type will avoid aggravating the always present static problems inherent to monitors of the cathode ray tube type.

- Clean the laser printer.   The internal paper passages can be cleaned by running through special cleaning papers that are available in laser cleaning kits.   The kits also include swab sticks for cleaning the corona wires.   In some cases, the printer's ozone filter may also need to be replaced.

- Clean the keyboard.   This is the hardware component which is subjected to most abuse.   It is pounded by greasy fingers, its users drop biscuit crumbs and cigarette ash over it and even occasionally spill coffee or Coke over it.   Not to mention dead skin cells and airborne dust. Like the monitor, it is almost certain to be in need of regular cleaning.   If left untouched, it will produce symptoms such as missing or repeated letters.

The PC keyboard is a capacitive device.   The electronics in the keyboard detect a keystroke by sensing a change in the capacitive potential of a wire matrix mounted behind the keys.   The matrix is laid out on a circuit board that contains small "plates". The electronic circuits connect to these plates and monitor the capacitive levels.   When a plastic keycap is pressed, it pushes a conductive plate closer to the plates on its parts of the board and thus changes the capacitive potential of the wire matrix. The keyboard electronics then detect this change and send the corresponding scan code to the computer bus.   Anything which obstructs the mechanical movement or alters the capacitance of the matrix will affect the keyboard's performance.

The steps to clean a keyboard depend upon the severity of the problem and could be one of the following:

ROUTINE CLEANING

- o   Hold the keyboard upside down and gently shake it to dislodge loose crumbs, etc.
- o   Vacuum between the keys, ideally using a 'mini-vac' designed for the purpose. This produces a sucking action but cleaning is usually most effective with a blowing action this helps to dislodge particles.   If available, use canned air which is available from electronic or office suppliers.   A cheaper alternative is the use of a keyboard 'sweeper' brush.
- o   Clean the keys with swabs dipped in cleaning solution.

PROBLEM KEYBOARD

In extreme cases, such as the spilling of sticky drinks over the keyboard, the keyboard may have to be dismantled for cleaning.   In most cases, this will still only involve the removal of the keycaps and the cleaning of the external case beneath the caps.   The steps are:

- o   Remove the keycaps. These can be gently prised off, always using an upwards motion.   Some keycaps have small springs under the caps and care must be taken to ensure that none of these are lost.   Do not remove the space key cap unless necessary, as they can be very difficult to refit.
- o   Remove any sticky material from the keycaps and clean them in warm soapy water. Rinse the keys well to remove all traces of soap and ensure that they are properly dry before fitting again later.
- o   Use a low-pressure hose, hair dryer or canned air to blow an airstream down the key tubes, to loosen any internal particles.   Do NOT put your mouth to the tube and blow your own air down the tube as this will introduce moisture into the matrix and possibly upset the capacitance between the plates.
- o   Carefully clean the board area under the keys, especially round the plunger mechanisms; making sure that all debris and sticky substances are removed and that the each keys plunger moves freely.

If the liquid has entered the internal matrix, the matrix will have to be dismantled for cleaning; this is a tricky task.   The keyboard has to be carefully dismantled and even more carefully re-assembled after the cleaning operation.   All the components have to correctly locate and the springs have to correctly adjusted.   It is a delicate and time-consuming operation. In the commercial environment, it is usually more cost-effective to completely replace a badly-contaminated keyboard compared to the man-hours involved in a major strip-down.

- Clean the mouse.   The normal opto-mechanical mouse uses a ball to rub against and rotate a couple of rollers which are housed inside the mouse casing. The mouse ball is designed to be pushed along a flat surface such as a desktop or a specially made mouse mat with the correct surface resistance.   As the mouse moves the ball picks up any dirt or dust on the mat and introduces it into the mouse casing. Eventually, the ball and the roll both become coated and the result is that the mouse movement becomes jerky and erratic.   The ball can be removed by rotating the ring which holds it in place; this is on the underside of the mouse casing. When the ball is removed, the rollers can be seen and these should be cleaned with a swab dipped in cleaning fluid.

Make sure that all the perimeter of both rollers are cleaned. The mouse ball should be washed in warm soapy water and properly rinsed and dried before re-insertion into the mouse.

- Check that the user is carrying out backup procedures. Exhortations and office memos to staff urging regular backups are common. It is unclear how well such a policy is implemented. The service check-up is a good time to check whether backup discs are in use.
- Have a word with the users about the machines; this will pick up any training needs of the staff or may identify a problem not detected by the checks (e.g. intermittent problems).

LESS REGULAR

Again, the definition of this time scale is loose but could be quarterly or six-monthly, dependent on the amount of use and the amount of changes that are predicted for the machines. The tests are aimed at picking up any deterioration of the disc surface or disc fragmentation due to prolonged file activities. The tests are also aimed at ensuring that the machine configuration - both the DOS and the Windows configuration, if appropriate - is optimised for the current use of each machine.

The elements of such a programme would be:

- Check the integrity of the surface of the machine's hard disc; this can be done with the DOS CHKDSK or SCANDISK commands or a utility such as Norton's Disc Doctor utility. If any problems are detected, they should be repaired by a utility and the nature of the problems should be recorded; Norton provides for the creation of a text file report on the surface test and this can be printed out and filed. Where surface problems are detected, a more regular visit should be paid to the machine to ensure that the disc is not rapidly deteriorating. If a later visit shows even greater surface problems, it indicates disc deterioration and a replacement should be considered before any precious data is lost. Of course, a problem with the disc surface may be a one off (e.g. jolting of the disc due to moving the machine from office to office or due to the effects of the office Xmas party) and will not repeat itself at a later test. In these cases, the sector corruption was not due to long-term deterioration of the surface but due to physical damage. If future checks show no further sector losses, the test routine can revert to the normal cycle.
- Check the fragmentation of the disc with the DOS 6 DEFRAG command or the Norton SpeedDisc utility. Again, if a particularly badly fragmented disc is encountered, this fact should be noted since the machine might be visited more often.
- Tidy the disc. Over a period of time, the hard disc will accumulate unwanted files. These might be files that were created and forgotten, data files left over from an abandoned project, or program files from an unused application. In addition, many programs including Windows create temporary files which are meant to be automatically deleted after their use; such files have extensions such as .A or .TMP. If the program should be unexpectedly halted, then the files are not deleted and still occupy disc space. Some of these temporary files can be quite large - 1Mb or more. Temporary files can be identified with a DOS command such as DIR *.TMP/S or a utility such as Wincheckit and deleted. Other unwanted files should be identified, usually in consultation with the user, and then deleted. In some cases, entire sub-directory structures may be deleted. This may result from unwanted applications or directories created for purposes that no longer exist. The technician has to tidy the machine's directory structure and alter the machine's PATH to reflect these changes.
- There are many ways to delete files and directories, depending on the DOS version and utilities available. These include the following, assuming that a directory called 'example' and its contents are to be removed:

In DOS versions up to v5:   In DOS v6:
     CD example and DEL *.*   DELTREE example
     RD example

In DOS v5:   In DOS Shells, Windows File Manager, etc:
     DEL example   Highlight choice(s) and click on icon or
     RD example   menu option that invokes file deletion

Be very cautious when using the DOS 6 DELTREE command as it is very powerful; it not only deletes the files in the nominated directory and removes that directory - it also deletes all files and sub-directories under the directory specified as the parameter. The command does ask the user whether to continue but it is still too easy to delete huge chunks of the hard disc structure in a careless moment.

- Check that the machine's CONFIG.SYS and AUTOEXEC.BAT settings are correct for the current use of machine. If a machine's main use has altered, the existing configuration may no longer be the optimum setting. The number of buffers may need altering or the allocation of the extended memory may require altering. This should be checked and re-set if necessary.
- Check SMARTDRV for optimum operation. As above, if the machine's use was changed - say to more disc-intensive activities - the existing allocation of memory to SMARTDRV may no longer be sufficient to run the system at optimum efficiency. The operation of SMARTDRV should be checked and altered if necessary.

- Check that the Windows configuration is correct for optimum performance with the current applications. The WIN.INI and SYSTEM.INI can be examined if you understand how they are composed; if not, check the configuration through Windows Control Panel, etc.
- Check that all Windows program groups and items are correctly set up, to reflect the applications currently in use. Programs may have been deleted or moved to other sub-directories and the given paths may no longer point to the programs' actual locations.
- Check that the computer's physical operating environment has not altered. Check for:
  - Exposure to excesses of temperature or of rapid temperature change.
  - Exposure to dampness, dust or vibration.
  - Exposure to strong magnetic fields such as lifts, machinery, office equipment. Strong fields can corrupt disc, taint the monitor purity and produce unpredictable printing.
  - Exposure to strong radio signals such as the office paging system or local taxi transmitter.

ANNUAL MAINTENANCE
These activities address the longer term problems that arise with PCs and are:
- Clean inside the computer unit's case. Over a period of time, dust settles on the components on the boards. This acts as a thermal insulator and reduces the ability of the component to dissipate its heat into the air. The result is overheating of components and an increase in their failure rate. Cleaning the board, therefore, increases the working life of the machine. The cover should be removed from the unit and the boards should be brushed down with a soft-bristled brush. Even better, use one of the small vacuums to ensure that the dust is completely removed and does not simply settle down on another part of the board.

  NB Before cleaning inside a machine, always make a backup of the hard disc contents as a precaution.

- Check the seating of internal cards and internal cables. Each time the computer is switched on it warms the components and they expand; when the computer is switched off again, the components contract. Different components expand and contract at different rates and this tends to make I.C. chips gradually lift out of their socket holders. Similarly, boards tend to lift out of their expansion slot sockets.
  Re-seat chips by applying a firm but even pressure over the whole surface of the chip; this ensures that none of the chip's pins are accidentally bent. You may have to support the underside of the board while applying the pressure, to prevent undue strain on the board. Don't forget to use a wrist earthing strap to prevent any damage to the chips from body static discharge. Similarly, when re-seating a card, ensure that the edge connector is properly lined up with the expansion socket. Avoid excessive force and the use of a rocking motion on the card - from edge to edge - will probably help the insertion process. Don't forget to tighten the card's securing screw once the card is inserted.
- Clean the edge connectors on expansion cards and cables. The accumulation of dirt on contacts increases their electrical resistance and can result in data transfer errors; the binary signal is reduced to a level where the next processing stage is unsure whether the signal represents a binary 1 or a binary 0. Edge connectors can be cleaned with a lint-free cloth or swab dipped in cleaning solution. Cable connectors can be cleaned by unplugging and re-plugging the connector a number of times; this releases any trapped dirt and the abrasive effect cleans the joint between the connecting areas.
  Don't forget to note the orientation of the cable, to ensure that the plug is re-inserted correctly in its socket. Some cables will have special markings and these should be noted before removing the connector. Ribbon cables, for example, usually identify pin 1 with a red stripe on the edge of the ribbon. Often the printed circuit board or the socket will also be marked with a 1 against pin 1 and this greatly reduces the possibility of errors. Other connectors only plug in one way round and this solves the problem. Of course, don't remove all the cables at the one time, in case you have trouble remembering what cable is attached to which connector.
- Clean the machine's floppy disc's read/write heads. Like an audio cassette player or video player, the disc drive's performance will degenerate if the head is coated in dirt or magnetic oxide; the coating increases the gap between the head and the magnetised surface and causes read and write errors to occur. The drive's head can be cleaned using a special cleaning disc that is readily available. Always use the 'wet' cleaner type rather than an abrasive type; this uses a disc which is impregnated with cleaning fluid and has minimal abrasive
   effect. The special disc is placed in the drive and spun like any normal disc; the cleaning disc can then be removed and should be discarded since it will probably now be holding the dirt particles. It is not a wise move to re-use the same disc; this may save money but introducing a disc with dirt particles is equivalent to using an abrasive type cleaner. Hard discs are enclosed in air-tight casings and are therefore not prone to the same degree of the ingress of dirt.
- De-gauss the monitor if necessary. If the screen displays a *'moiré'* pattern then the internal metal screen has become magnetised and requires to be de-magnetised with a de-gaussing coil (see the section on video). This is usually only a problem with older monitors, since newer models have automatic de-gaussing circuitry.

A MAINTENANCE STRATEGY

The tasks and their timings in the preceding pages are intended to be an indication of the likely elements of a company strategy on system maintenance. The final policy has to take into account any existing maintenance agreements with third parties, the conditions of any equipment guarantees, the current age and condition of the equipment, the severity of the working environment and the abilities of the staff in the support section. While the exact final policy is a matter for each organisation there is one matter which is clear - each organisation must have a clearly defined maintenance strategy, so that the reporting and recording procedures, job descriptions, training needs, backup procedures, equipment stock levels, purchases and maintenance budgeting can all be easily understood and implemented.

PROBLEM DIAGNOSIS

A large part of the PC support technician's life is spent handling *'non-routine conditions'* with hardware and software. This term describes any situation where the system does not perform as expected. This can vary from the keyboard *'hanging up'* to smoke belching from the system unit! From a user point of view, most problems are perceived as hardware faults whether the hardware or the software is at fault. For example, a user report that *'the printer won't work properly'* could be traced to a lost software printer driver or user inexperience with the application package.

The technician has to make a few of basic decisions:

- Is the fault really in the hardware ?
- Am I competent to deal with the hardware/software fault ?
- Is the faulty apparatus worth repairing ?

Only those with specialist knowledge should attempt electronic repairs or adjustments. However, many problems can be tracked down and eliminated with a little thought and a systematic approach. When the fault is found, it will not always be repaired. A look at the previous fault history of the machine might reveal a series of similar problems and there are occasions when a complete replacement is cheaper than continual repair. Examples of this include old computer motherboards that are regularly producing new faults and hard discs that are deteriorating. In these cases, regular motherboard repairs and hard disc low-level formatting and file restoring is not an economic proposition. Such decisions are based on a review of the machine's previous fault record, hence the importance of record-keeping.

But the support technician's task is not solely about fault diagnosis and elimination. The technician has to work to a company code which probably includes the following principles:

- providing a prompt response to user requests
- using a systematic method to diagnose faults
- estimating down time of systems
- keeping records on hardware and software
- ensuring safe practices
- ensuring legal practices

PROVIDING A PROMPT RESPONSE

The response to user complaints has to be as prompt as possible for the following reasons:

- To safeguard the health and safety of the workforce or public
- To reduce user frustration.
- To reduce machine down-time and maintain user productivity .
- To minimise the possibility of further damage to equipment or data.

The fault report form should include a section for the date and time of receiving the complaint; it should also contain an entry for the time of the first attendance and an entry for the time the fault was cleared. This is important to maintain a record of the efficiency of the support section. For office sites that are remote from the head office, an early response might be an initial phone call to identify the symptoms and suggest any simple remedies, with problem faults being attended to by as early a visit as is practical.

SUPPORT LEVEL

The level of response and problem resolution for any user depends upon the importance of that user's work and the table shows typical examples:

User category	Type of work	Response Time
Occasional	Any non-essential or irregular user	Next-day or later
Regular	Typist, programmer, graphics designer	Same-day
Essential	Process control, medical, financial	Measured in hours or even minutes

USING A SYSTEMATIC METHOD

The process of detecting the fault should not be intuitive, using inspiration or guesswork. Neither should it be a haphazard elimination process, trying out a series of random tests and equipment replacements until the problem is solved. For all but the simplest of faults (i.e. broken cables or other visible effects), a systematic approach should be adopted. This may take the form of a flow chart, a check list or even a computer expert system. In all these cases, the previous experience of technicians has shaped the best method of diagnosing problems. That experience is then available to others through their following the flow of questions and tests in the diagnostic system. If the system is followed, the technician should be provided with an answer which accurately diagnoses the problem.

ESTIMATING DOWN TIME

Once a fault is diagnosed, the user will require an estimate of the likely down-time of the machine. All users will be eager to know how long the machine will be out of action and managers may wish to move employees to other jobs where a substantial delay is expected. In extreme cases, such as waiting for replacement parts, another machine may have to be allocated and the backup discs from the faulty machine used to restore files to the replacement machine, in order to maintain office productivity. An organisation's maintenance strategy will often contain response time and problem resolution time targets.

FACTORS IN ESTIMATING DOWN TIME
- Does the company have a maintenance contract ?
- If so, is it a 24-hour response contract ?   Bear in mind that the response time is the time elapsing before a <u>visit</u> and not necessarily the time elapsing before a <u>repair</u>.   It is not uncommon for on-site technicians to take the machine back to their workshop for repair. The initial visit may be on site but the repair may still be carried out remotely. This only happens when the fault is complex and therefore it may well involve waiting for parts, thus further delaying the machine's return to active service. Try to press the visiting engineer for a realistic estimate of the time the machine will be gone.
- Is the problem affecting occasional, regular or essential users?
- If not maintained externally, is it a hardware or a software problem?
    IF HARDWARE:
    - o Is the equipment under guarantee ?
    - o If guaranteed, is it a return to base guarantee ?   The time taken to pack and deliver the faulty item can add to the delay in getting it back into service.
    - o If guarantee is a site visit, what is the response time ?   Similar factors to those for maintenance contracts apply here (i.e. repair not be within time of first visit).
    - o If not maintained externally, are there established sources of supply of replacement components ; are the most commonly used replacement components (disc controller cards, cables, etc.) kept in stock ?

    Most hardware faults, apart from cables, mice, keyboards, etc., produce longer down times, caused by site visit delays or waiting for parts, etc.
    IF SOFTWARE:
    - o Is it a machine configuration problem (e.g. memory management, incorrect CONFIG or AUTOEXEC settings, poor Windows configuration, missing DOS files, damaged Registry, etc.) ?   For the experienced support technician, these difficulties are generally easily cured and the down time is therefore not significant.
    - o Is it an application problem ?   This could include simple user errors in using the package or tricky interrupt problems between different programs.   The latter may take some time to resolve; the former may take even longer, since user training may be required.

KEEPING RECORDS

Every support group has a responsibility to maintain a current database on the organisation's hardware and software, down to individual machine level.   This should include case histories of all problems encountered on each machine.   This is important to track recurring or developing problems and thus prevent future difficulties.   The data kept by a support group or help desk (see later) should be collected as part of a hardware and software 'audit'.   Items in an audit should include:
- The manufacturer, model, serial number of each computer in use.
- Details of hard disc type (i.e. RLL, IDE, EDSI or SCSI) and capacity.

- Details of floppy drive quantity, type and capacity (e.g. two 3.5" 1.4Mb drives).
- Details of machine bus (i.e. whether ISA, MCA, EISA or PCI).
- The manufacturer, model, serial number of each piece of ancillary equipment in use (e.g. printers, modems, plotters).
- The location of each item of equipment within the building.
- Any restrictions on access to the equipment (is computer in security room requiring special permission for access).
- Purchase date of equipment and details of guarantee and any maintenance agreements.
- Copies of the CMOS settings of each machine. Ideally these should be disc copies for easy restoration (using a CMOS saving/restoration utility). As a minimum, there should be manually recorded details, particularly of the hard disc drive number).
- Copies of each machine's CONFIG.SYS and AUTOEXEC.BAT. Where machines have Windows, then copies of WIN.INI, SYSTEM.INI and the INI files of applications should also be stored.
- Details of the cards fitted to each machine, including their purpose (e.g. scanner or fax card), manufacturer, model and serial numbers.
- Copies of the DIP switch positions and jumper settings on each motherboard.
- Copies of the DIP switch positions, jumper settings, address allocation and IRQ requirements for each card.
- Copies of all installation guides, hardware manuals and technical notes.
- Master copies of all the installation discs.
- Details of all the software used on the machine.
- Copies of all software master discs.
- Where practical, the original packing and anti-static storage bags, for the easier packing and return of faulty equipment.
- Details of the service history of each item of equipment.

It can be a time-consuming operation to collect data and document the entire existing system in an organisation. Because of this, the process may be best undertaken as part of a rolling programme. Each new purchase may automatically be documented at installation time, while each existing item may only be recorded at the time of a repair or as part of a major equipment service. On the other hand, this system will pay dividends in the long run. The software audit ensures that future purchase requirements are more accurately identified. The hardware audit also aids future purchasing decisions and also prevents a whole range of potential difficulties - e.g. highlighting potential address clashes or IRQ clashes between existing and proposed new cards on a motherboard. The storing of copies of configuration information (CMOS settings, CONFIG.SYS, WIN.INI, Registry, etc.) can greatly speed up the restoration of a machine which has had its configuration inadvertently altered or deleted.

ENSURING SAFE PRACTICES
There are two separate issues involved:
- Safe practices as applied to users
- Safe practices as applied to support staff

SAFE USER PRACTICES
The organisation should be raising user awareness on issues of safe working practice. Since many user deficiencies in this area will be spotted by support staff, much of the direct input on good practice will come from technicians. The serious issues of staff's physical safety and well-being are covered later in this chapter. This leaves the instilling of good practice on equipment and data handling.
Good practice issues include:
- Cold Starts. Never use a computer that has been standing for a long time in a cold environment without first waiting until it has reached a normal room temperature. Writing to cold hard discs, which have been slightly reduced in dimension as a consequence, could result in data loss.
- Moisture. Similarly, a machine which been exposed to a moist atmosphere should be given time to normally dry out before being put into use. Placing voltages on damp circuitry is risking component breakdown as well as data loss.
- Viruses. All staff should appreciate the problems that can be caused by bringing in and using pirate software and be fully aware of any penalty that the company may impose on employees found bringing in or using virused software.
- Disc Handling. All staff should understand and implement rudimentary rules on handling floppy discs to prevent data loss (see section on discs and drives).

- Maintaining the machine's environment. No smoking, eating or drinking at the computer.
- Backups.   All staff should fully understand the benefits of carrying out regular backup procedures and have an agreed procedure which they implement.
- Reporting Any Problems.   The first person to detect any problem with a machine will be the user. Users should be encouraged to report all problems, even those where there is uncertainty as to whether a fault actually exists.   A quick call to the support room or the help desk will soon clear up whether the user is misusing the equipment or whether a problem is developing on the equipment.

SAFE TECHNICIAN PRACTICES

The technician's good practice list is identical to those of the users with the addition of others particular to his/her job. These should include:

- Use proper tools. Using the same screwdriver for all jobs risks personal safety and can damage equipment. Use the proper tool for the job and always carry around a tool set composed of:
  - o Box spanner. This is a preferred method of removing the screws that secure the computer's cover, power supply, expansion cards, etc. Using a screwdriver, particularly one of inadequate size, can chew up the head's slot, resulting in the whole screw having to be drilled out to remove it. Additionally, screwdrivers are prone to slip from the head's slot. This can have dire consequences such as scoring the computer's outer case, technicians stabbing themselves with the screwdriver or the screwdriver plunging though another component. With the box spanner, the screw head is held much more tightly and the chances of damaging the screw or other items is negligible.
  - o Small and medium sized screwdrivers.   If a DIP switch requires to have its settings altered, a small screwdriver is ideal. For larger jobs, discard the small screwdriver and use the one up to the size of the task. Using too small a screwdriver can damage both the screw head being worked on as well as damaging the screwdriver itself.
  - o Neon screwdriver. This is useful to confirm that there is no mains leakage to the computer casing or to the mains earth. The neon screwdriver is held in the hand and the tip of the screwdriver is placed on the area to be tested; the technician's thumb is placed over the cap at the end of the handle. If the neon bulb glows, then there is an unwanted mains voltage at the spot touched.
  - o Phillips head screwdriver. This is often used as an alternative to box spanners where the screw head is of the X-slot Phillips type. This is probably a slightly less safe method than a box spanner but has a lot more grip than a standard slot screwdriver. Where the screw has a rounded Phillips head, this screwdriver has to used.
  - o IC extraction/insertion tools.   The pins of ICs (integrated circuit) chips are very fragile and are very easily bent or broken. Always attempt to use the specially designed tools for extracting and inserting chips.   These are designed to remove chips in a straight upwards motion to avoid pins being bent; prising the chip's end with a screwdriver removes the chip by bending it in its connector and risks damage to the pins.   If a pin becomes bent, an attempt to straighten it with a pair of fine pliers often results in the pins snapping off. An IC insertion tool is designed to ensure that a chip's pins are all lined up correctly with the chips holder. It also ensures that an even pressure is applied to the chip when it is being inserted into its holder.
  - o A pair of fine pliers. These are useful in changing jumper settings and recovering screws that may fall into the computer case.
- Familiarise yourself with Safety laws, as covered later in the chapter.
- Read the equipment's safety notes, <u>before</u> starting a particular job.
- Avoid Static.   The electro-static charge on the body can rise to several thousand volts and can wreak havoc on any chip that is touched, either directly or by touching part of the card or motherboard.   This can be prevented by the wearing of a static earthing band; this attaches to the technician's wrist and has a wire which earths the body to mains earth.   The wire must contain a resistor of at least 1MegOhm to limit the current if live mains happens to be touched by the wearer. Some also advocate leaving the computer's mains cable plugged in but switched off at the mains.   Since the mains switch does not actually switch the earth connection, the earth is always connected through to the chassis of the computer. This allows the user to touch the chassis and dissipate any static charges prior to handling cards or components.
- Always handle cards by their edges.
- Always leave cards in their anti-static packing until required.
- Never work on a live computer, particularly one that is faulty. A mains supply fault could result in lethal voltages present inside the computer case. With monitors, this is even more important, since around 25,000 volts is present inside the casing.

- Never add or remove a card while a board is live board. In both cases there will be a point when part of the card's edge connector is making contact with the socket on the motherboard, while other parts of the card's connector are unconnected. This could easily result in chips on the card being blown and having to be replaced.
- Never force cards into expansion slots or force connectors together. If there is a particular difficulty, check that the card is free to be slotted in - i.e. there is no debris in the expansion slot and its blanking plate and retaining screw have been removed. With cables, check that they are being aligned properly; most cables terminate in plugs which have keys to ensure that they are only entered in the correct way round.

ENSURING LEGAL PRACTICES
Apart from the Health and Safety regulations that technicians will wish to enforce, there are a number of other areas that could lead the organisation into legal difficulty. These are:
- The use of unauthorised software, eg *'pirate'* copies of games or utilities.
- Licensing agreements (e.g. no more than 20 simultaneous users of a package on a network).
- Copyright.
- Data Protection Act.

These issues are covered elsewhere in detail.

RUNNING A HELP DESK
Running an organisation's internal help desk tends to require a broader coverage than commercial help desks which are mostly devoted to a particular product. The help from commercial desks concentrates on support of a particular item of hardware or software, although some general help lines are available.

AIM OF A HELP DESK
The aim of the help desk is two-fold:
- To cure the immediate user problems, maintaining productivity and protecting data/equipment.
- To improve the long-term quality of IT in the organisation, through measures such as problem prevention, user training and informed future purchasing.

The task of a help desk is to solve user problems quickly and courteously. The technicians on the desk cannot possibly know the solution to all problems. Their job is to know where to find the solutions to all problems. Apart from the most obvious problems (e.g. printer out of paper), the degree of spontaneous help from a support technician will be in direct proportion to the knowledge and experience of that technician. The remainder of the help must come from an organised system of initial remote diagnosis. The technician has to work from the information supplied by the user to identify solutions.

SCOPE OF A HELP DESK
Some organisations restrict the help desk's activities to that of clearing I.T. problems. Other organisations expect a wider role from the desk, so that it becomes the clearing house for all company gadgets such as or photocopiers, fax machines, telephones, lifts, coffee machines, shredders, etc. These pages restrict themselves to the computer role of a help desk.

RECORD KEEPING
A fault report form should be completed for each call. It includes the date and time of call, the caller's name and telephone number and a number of the details that would already appear in the report form issued to users for their use prior to calling the help desk. So, by the time the user calls the help desk, he/she will have already formulated a version of the fault. The form has additional information for the use of the desk technician. This would include:
- Whether cleared by phone; if so, the call duration would be logged.
- Whether passed on to supplier. This would be the result of a diagnosis of a non-trivial fault on a machine that is under guarantee. If passed on, the time would be recorded and a reference number obtained from the supplier.
- Whether passed to maintenance third party, if an agreement exists and the fault is non-trivial. If passed on, the time would be recorded and a reference number obtained from the supplier.
- Whether the site requires a visit. This report might be passed on to another technician - if so, record the name of the technician and the time of passing on the form. Also record any equipment or software that might be required to cure the problem. This may be DOS boot discs, utility discs, spare cables, or whatever is required.

OUTLINE FAULT RECORDING FORM

Help Desk Technician's Name		Date of call	
		Time commenced	
Reported by		Time completed	
Tele No.		Location	
Machine No		Inventory Reference	
Make & Model		Processor	
RAM size		Monitor	
Windows version		Hard disc size	
DOS version		Network type	

Problem Description

Diagnosis

Cleared by phone			
Passed to	Supplier	Time	Ref No.
	Third Party	Time	Ref No.
Requires visit	Visiting Technician		Time

Equipment Required

Comments   (e.g. case history)

IDENTIFYING PROBLEMS

The technician has to determine whether the complaint is of a hardware or software variety. This will often have to be obtained through effective questioning techniques, since the user will often blame the hardware for many software or user errors.   There will usually be more hardware than software faults and always more operator errors than either computer faults.   The questions asked allow the technician to determine the likely cause of the problem.   Many problems are of a minor nature. Probably around a third of calls could be saved by training users in the basics of DOS and their applications. Possibly another third are *'printer out of paper'* or *'printer off line'* type of problems - i.e. problems that can be diagnosed and made good without a technician's visit to the actual machine.   Of course, it is difficult to judge whether a user knows the answers to the questions being asked, since user understanding will vary enormously. If the organisation is sufficiently compact, it pays to get to know the users because this provides a basis on which to judge how much to trust their information.   In large organisations, it may pay to have complaints routed through a section contact (the most computer-literate person in the section) so that the help desk becomes familiar with the contact and his/her capabilities.

AIDS TO DIAGNOSIS

- Use an inventory of the organisation's computing system; know what software and hardware is on the reported machine - just by asking for the machine's identification code. Apart from diagnosis, this can be an aid to maintaining the office's normal operations. For example, if a machine has to be withdrawn to await spare parts, it can't be replaced by any other machine - account must be taken of any particular cards that may be inside the problem machine. Replacing the machine might otherwise lose the office its modem link or its fax connection.
- Explain to the user how to use Microsoft's MSD utility (only available with Windows 3.1 or DOS v6). Ask for reports on the suspected areas, explaining to the user how to produce and display the desired report. For example, it is possible to detect that a printer is off line or out of paper using this utility, without visiting the computer's site.
- Use a remote access system to the user's computer. This is extremely useful in a largely dispersed organisation with computer sites remote from the help desk. Remote control software allows the help desk to link one of its computers to the computer at the remote site via modems. With this software, the help desk monitor will also display whatever the remote user is seeing. Even more important, the desk keyboard will act as if it were an additional keyboard on the remote computer. This way, the help desk technician can take full control of the remote system to examine many of its hardware aspects and all of its software aspects. Examples of this remote control software are Microcom's Carbon Copy Plus, Telesystems' PCAnywhere and Central Point Software's Commute.
- Consult the machine's previous case history. Use this information to detect a possible recurring fault or a developing problem. This also allows the desk to discover the most common faults, both within company and on any particular machine.

HELP DESK RESOURCES

As stated earlier, the help desk has to be the source of all knowledge and experience. The resources have to be built up to make this possible and the desk should not rely on the expertise stored in the head of an experienced technician. Fortunately, a number of different resources are available to build up the desk's reference abilities. These include:

- All hardware and software audit records as previously outlined.
- All software and hardware manuals and technical guides.
- Previous case histories of all equipment.
- Statistical records previously compiled from the above.
- Notes from attendance at training courses.
- Use of suppliers' and dealers' support lines.
- Use of consultants for major difficulties.
- Specially commissioned diagnostic packages as described below.
- Proprietary logging packages as described below.
- Journals and memos from User Groups. These can include Windows, Lotus, Novell and Independent PC Users. Membership provides reports on others' problems and allows questions to be raised.
- Copies of computer magazines and periodicals.
- Copies of training videos.

CALL LOGGING PACKAGES

This software is created for use on help desks and provides the following facilities:

- Call logging; each call is recorded and saved.
- Call prioritising; the order of the queue of callers can be altered to match the estimated severity of the fault and the seniority of the person complaining.
- Call tracking; used where a fault is not cleared in the one call.

An example is HelpDesk for Windows by Utopia.

SUPPORT ON CD-ROM/DISC

Support On Site is a CD ROM from Computer Library, a subsidiary of the mighty Ziff-Davis publishing empire. This comes as an annual subscription service with the following facilities:

- Updated CD sent every month
- Text retrieval based on a word or a phrase
- Dozens of software products supported - including dBase, WordPerfect, Wordstar and most of the Lotus and Microsoft range. A LAN Support version is available.
- Product manuals
- Product technical notes
- Drivers, patches and bug fixes

Other products include:
- Diskbase for Windows with a database of 4,600 different disc drive specifications and 750 disc controller specifications
- Windows Help file creators, such as HDK and SOS Help Info Author, to create pages of user help files in the standard Windows format.
- Laplink 6 for Windows provides remote control facilities such as file transfer, chat mode and the ability of the helpdesk to control the remote PC.
- CheckIt Analyst collects machine data, analyses it and reports on a range of installation and troubleshooting options.

CUSTOMISED SUPPORT PACKAGES

These are packages that are built to order and can cover specific software or hardware, or both.   These packages are expensive but they address the specific needs of a support desk that may not be covered in general-release products such as the Support On Site CD ROM.   These are based on expert systems and lead the desk technician through the likely symptoms for different faults.   If the organisation has staff with programming skills, then packages such as these can also be developed in-house.

ASSISTING USERS TO ACCESS SUPPORT

There are times when the aim will be to help user to help themselves. This usually depends on the size of organisation.   If there is an internal support group, then the management will probably wish that all problems would be directed to the group. In a small company, where there is only a small training / PC support force, they may wish to show users how to get their own help.   The most common methods are:

PEER SUPPORT

This merely entails finding someone who already has the skills in a section, to provide the basic help that is mostly required.   Of course, this may involve a process of training of key individuals in departments.

USING ON-LINE SUPPORT

There are now a number of bulletin boards which can provide answers to problems.   Some, like the Microsoft On-Line board, are run by the software house concerned while others, like the Compuserve and CIX boards, are general service boards.   All that is required is a modem connection for the PC to the telephone network. The user can then dial up, log in and either read existing help pages or leave a specific question on the board.   Some areas of bulletin boards are free while others are chargeable; in all cases there will be telephone call charges and possibly extra connect charges.

The recent growth of Internet subscribers means that many companies and individuals have access to this international network.   Many Special Interest Groups exist on the Internet and these cover all kinds of hardware and software areas.   Problems that are placed in this arena will receive replies from the best minds throughout the globe.   There are very few queries that go unanswered on the Internet.

Another definition of on-line help is the mass of help information that is now provided within many application packages.   Some outstanding examples of this can be seen in Windows applications that even include built-in tutorials.   This is not *'on-line'* in the sense of being connected to a telephone line; however, it does provide a high degree of assistance that is always available to the user.   The time spent showing users how to access this information can save a great deal of support time in the longer run.

USING A HELP DESK

Help desks, unlike bulletin boards, are able to provide immediate support for a problem.   Dialling the help desk number and giving your customer number provides the verbal link between yourself and, hopefully, the expert in the subject area.   Help desks can either be internal (i.e. run by the company itself) or external (i.e. a commercial operation).

EXTERNAL HELP DESKS

These are normally run by software suppliers (e.g. IBM, WordPerfect), user groups or software maintenance firms.   Some are free for the first year; most have annual charges; at least one provides a credit service, where advanced payment covers a specified number of calls to the hot-line.

INTERNAL HELP DESK

This is run by the company's own PC support team and is dedicated to the company's particular hardware and software needs.   In some cases, the support staff can take control of the user's computer in order to analyse and fix the problem; the support technician can see the users screen and can alter the flow and data on the user's machine from the remote help desk console.   This is particularly useful where a company has sites that are scattered from the main office.

FAULT REPORTS

In the case of both external and internal help desks, the user has to make some preparations prior to making the call. These are:
- To save any embarrassment, check the problem against manuals. With Windows, check out the hypertext Help menus
- Make the call when the computer is switched on and the program is running.
- Complete a report form such as the example given.

The example report may prove not to contain enough information for the support technician and extra information may be required. Often, this information can be got from running the Microsoft Diagnostics program that comes with DOS 6 onwards and with Windows 3.1 onwards. This is called MSD.EXE and is explained later. The help desk technician can elicit further information by getting the user to run specific tests. For example, the 'L' test will show whether the printer is on line and whether there is paper in the printer.

PRINTING A DIAGNOSTICS REPORT

If the user is at a remote site and the problem is complex, one of the options in the Alt-F menu is to print out a full report on the system. This covers all the areas shown in the main menu plus others such as copies of CONFIG.SYS, AUTOEXEC.BAT and any Windows INI files. This report can be printed out by the user and posted on or faxed to the help desk for analysis.

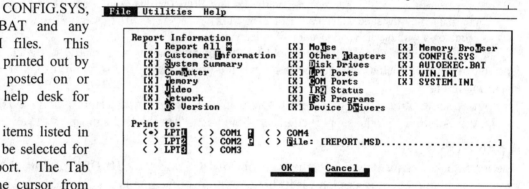

One or more items listed in the menu can be selected for a reduced report. The Tab key moves the cursor from item to item. Pressing the spacebar checks the box to select it for inclusion in the printed report.

If the printer is busy, the report can be saved to a file for later review or printing.

OUTLINE SUPPORT REQUEST FORM

		Date of call	Time of call
Make		Model	
Location		On network?	
List of add-ons			
Software including version number			
Outline of Problem State as succinctly and clearly as possible; when does problem arise - what stage in program/process			
Any error messages			

SYSTEM DIAGNOSTICS

A huge range of utility programs exist to aid the user or technician in maintaining the system in peak performance.   Hundreds of commercial products exist with varying strengths and weaknesses.   Some, like QEMM and PCKWIK are concerned with maximising the machine's performance.   Others, like Sleuth and Checkit, are concerned with analysing and testing the system hardware.   Some, like PC Tools and Norton Utilities have elements of both testing and optimising.   Of course, the programs have a large degree of overlap in terms of their functions.

When the technician wishes to test out a system, one or more utility packages are probably available to him/her.   Since, the commercial products will vary from company to company, only the general utilities can usefully be covered in this section.

Some problems are easily diagnosed; a disconnected cable or a missing system file are quickly spotted and corrected.   Other problems are more difficult to diagnose. These include:

- o not having enough memory to run a program
- o not knowing the efficiency of components - e.g. the disc caching efficiency, the performance of the disc drive (date transfer rate, fragmentation, corruption of disc surface, etc)
- o experiencing conflicts between different programs
- o experiencing conflicts between the addresses and IRQs (hardware interrupts) of different cards (e.g. a newly-installed sound card refuses to work)
- o problems with the size and location of video memory
- o being unable to adequately test the printer ports, communications ports, mouse, keyboard, etc

The list of such problems can become large and the use of diagnostic software can save many hours of experimentation.

Of course, some utilities are supplied by Microsoft and these are therefore readily available on every machine.   Additionally, the support engineer should carry discs with diagnostic software.

Up to DOS 6

The main disk diagnostic tool in earlier versions of DOS was the CHKDSK command.   It is a useful program to highlight errors - as long as its limitations are borne in mind.   CHKDSK compares the details in a file's Directory entry against the details for the file's FAT entry (see section on Discs and Drives). This ensures that no two files are using the same disc space, as held in the FAT.   It also ensures that the size as recorded in the Directory entry is consistent with the actual amount of clusters devoted to it in the FAT (for example, a file with a size of 15k recorded in the directory entry should occupy 4 clusters (in a 4k cluster disc) or 16 clusters (in a single-sector cluster disc; any allocation which is larger or smaller than this is an error).   If a problem is found, CHKDSK responds with a suitable error message such as *'Allocation Error'* or *'Cross-Linked Clusters'*.

So, if CHKDSK finds a problem, then there is certainly something wrong with the disc.   However, the converse is not true - the fact that CHKDSK may produce no error message cannot be taken as indicating that the disc is in good condition.   That is because CHKDSK only concerns itself with files; it does not look at the condition of the rest of the disc surface.   So, a damaged sector would not be found until a file had been saved to it.   CHKDSK does not attempt to write and read back test data to all sectors of the disc; another utility would be required for that type of test.

With DOS 6

DOS 6 also contains the CHKDSK utility - but adds a few very useful extra utilities such as:

MSD

The Microsoft Diagnostics utility is comprised of two files, MSD.EXE and MSD.INI and is a MS-DOS-based program that is also supplied with Windows 3.1.   It is designed to display diagnostic reports on a wide range of hardware and software items from a user-friendly front end.   The command's syntax is:

msd [/f <filename> or /p <filename> or /s <filename>]

Without any parameters, the user is asked to wait while the system is analysed; then the diagnostics menu is displayed, providing various reports from a top menu bar and 13 other choice buttons.   An option from the menu bar is selected by holding down the ALT key and pressing the first letter of the desired menu (e.g. - the Utilities menu is selected by Alt F).   A button option is selected by pressing the same key as the highlighted letter in the button text (e.g. - the Disc Drives report is selected by pressing D). Alternatively, the user can point and click on the menu or button option with a mouse.

MSD Button Options

The buttons produce displays on the following:

Computer: Displays information on the computer manufacturer, processor type, bus type; ROM BIOS manufacturer, version, and date; keyboard type; DMA controller configuration; presence of maths coprocessor

Memory: Displays a map of the computer's upper memory area - the area between 640K and 1Mb

Video: Displays information on the video card manufacturer, model and type; video BIOS version and date; current video mode

Network: Displays information on the network configuration, if the machine is linked to a LAN

Operating System: Displays information on the operating system version, location of MS-DOS in memory, the drive the system was booted from, the current environment settings, the path from which MSD was run

Mouse: Displays information on the MS-DOS mouse driver version, mouse type, mouse interrupt request line (IRQ) number,

Other Ports: Dynamically displays the game card status for up to two game devices or joysticks

Disk Drives: Displays information on the size/number of bytes free on local and remote drives

LPT Ports: Displays information on the port addresses of all installed parallel ports and dynamically displays the status of each port

COM Ports: Displays information on the port addresses and current communications parameters of all installed serial ports and dynamically displays the status of each port

IRQ Status: Displays information on the configuration of the hardware IRQs

TSR Programs: Displays information on the name, location in memory, and size of each program loaded in memory at the time MSD was run

Device Drivers: Displays the names of all device drivers installed at the time MSD was run

Choosing a button displays a window of information on that particular topic. Where there is more than one screenful of information, the information can be scrolled through, using the up and down arrow keys or the PAGE UP and PAGE DOWN keys. Alternatively, a mouse can be used to activate the scroll bars on the right side of the window. Pressing the Enter key or clicking the OK button will close the window and return the user to the main menu.

MSD Menu Options

File Sub-Menu

Find File:	Search for a named file and allow viewing of the file's contents
Print Report:	Send a copy of the report to a printer or file
Exit:	Exit MSD
AUTOEXEC.BAT:	Display the contents of the AUTOEXEC.BAT file
CONFIG.SYS:	Display the contents of the CONFIG.SYS file
SYSTEM.INI:	Display the contents of your Microsoft Windows SYSTEM.INI file
WIN.INI:	Display the contents of your Microsoft Windows WIN.INI file

The options from the *'Print Report'* menu are as shown and individual sections of the machine can be reported on by placing the cursor on the appropriate box and pressing the spacebar to select that area for inclusion in the report.

```
 File  Utilities  Help
──────────────────────────────────────────────────────────
 Report Information
   [ ] Report All         [X] Mouse          [X] Memory Browser
   [X] Customer Information [X] Other Adapters [X] CONFIG.SYS
   [X] System Summary      [X] Disk Drives    [X] AUTOEXEC.BAT
   [X] Computer            [X] LPT Ports      [X] WIN.INI
   [X] Memory              [X] COM Ports      [X] SYSTEM.INI
   [X] Video               [X] IRQ Status
   [X] Network             [X] TSR Programs
   [X] OS Version          [X] Device Drivers

 Print to:
   (•) LPT1   ( ) COM1   ( ) COM4
   ( ) LPT2   ( ) COM2   ( ) File: [REPORT.MSD.................]
   ( ) LPT3   ( ) COM3

                OK     Cancel
```

Utility Sub-Menu

Memory Block Display	Display the machine's memory allocation. This gives the starting address of each block and its size in bytes.
Memory Browser	Search selected ROM and RAM areas for strings such as "copyright" and "version" to determine ROM manufacturer and type.
Insert Command	Allow for quick insertion of a command in the appropriate file; the list of commands you can choose from is stored in the [commands] section of the MSD.INI file.
Test Printer	Prints a page to test that the connection between the computer and printer is functioning.

SAVING THE REPORTS

MSD provides a variety of switches to send the reports to a disc file for later printing. The printed report can be stored for future reference or can be sent to Microsoft or a maintenance company to solve complex problems. The report can also be used as the reference when calling a help desk.

The file switches are:

/f <filename>	Saves a complete MSD report to the named file. This option requests information such as name, company, address, telephone number, and comments and is intended for posting to Microsoft or handing to an external maintenance technician.
/p <filename>	Saves a complete MSD report to the named file without requesting any information. These can be stored as an original configuration on each machine.
/s <filename>	Saves a summary MSD report to the named file and can be used to locate problems and, for this purpose, can be compared to an earlier report on the machine in working condition.

Choosing Exit from the File menu or pressing the F3 function key to exits MSD.

SMARTMON

This utility first appeared in DOS version 6 and is a real-time monitor of the efficiency of the machine's Smartdrv settings.   Giving the command SMARTDRV/S from the DOS prompt provides the raw figures on the number of cache hits (data obtained from memory) and cache misses (data obtained from the disc) and the user can calculate the cache efficiency as a percentage using the formula:

$$\frac{\text{number of cache hits x 100}}{\text{total data requests (i.e. total of cache hits + cache misses)}}.$$

A satisfactory figure would be upwards of 85%, with a lower figure indicating a possible need to increase the cache size.

> NB   The cache efficiency figure should be calculated over the range of different activities actually in use on the machine, over a period of time, in order to get an accurate picture.   For example, calculating the cache efficiency after running a disc defragmentation utility will produce ratings as low as 2% or 3%; this is because the utility is constantly using direct disc access and bypasses caching.   The tests therefore are best carried out over a day's actual use rather than simply switching on the machine and taking a reading.

While the calculations can be recorded and calculated manually, SmartMon supplies a method of automatically providing the necessary figures, plus some other useful facilities.

SmartMon's main features are:

- It provides a continual on-screen icon as shown to report the cache efficiency on an ongoing real-time basis; this icon appears when the main SmartDrive Monitor menu is minimised. When the cache system is in use, the percentage figure in the icon is the instantaneous hit rate for the sampling period. If the cache is idle, the average hit rate is displayed.

- Its main screen provides information on the memory size allocated to caching.   The allocations can be viewed but cannot be altered via this screen; alterations have to be set up via the normal CONFIG.SYS declarations.

- Its main screen displays a histogram of the instantaneous cache hit rate; this Cache Hit Rate chart can be set for a given number of time intervals, and a given sampling frequency.

The number of time intervals defaults to 30 and the frequency to 500 ms.

These settings can be altered through the Options dialogue box.

The instantaneous cache hit rate is calculated by the following formula:

$$\text{Efficiency} = \frac{(\text{Current number of hits - Previous number of hits}) * 100}{\text{Current total of data requests - Previous total of data requests}}$$

When the cache is idle, the Current total of data requests is the same as the Previous total of data requests and therefore the histogram will not be updated.

- It displays the Average Cache Hit Rate in the information bar at the bottom of the SmartMon window. This number shows the cumulative hit rate since the time SmartMon was started, or the last cache reset.
- It allows the user to select any drive and view and alter their cache modes. This is via the *'Drive Controls'* section of the screen and the possible cache settings are:
  - o Cache Read Only
  - o Cache Read and Write
  - o No Caching

The mode for the selected drive is chosen by clicking the appropriate button.

- It provides an *'Options'* dialogue box to configure its own SmartMon parameters, and these are saved in the [smartmon] section of the WIN.INI file.

The Options include:

o Altering the Cache Hit Rate. The Hit Rate display can be set to a sampling frequency between 50 and 10000 milliseconds, 500 being the default. The number of histogram display intervals can be set to between 3 and 100, 30 being the default.

o Creating a Log File. This is very useful for checking the cache performance over a variety of conditions. The average cache efficiency may be reasonable and hide particularly poor performances with certain applications such as databases. If the figures can be logged to a text file as they are collected, the file can be later read and inspected for the lowest sets of readings. For logging cache activities to file, you type in the desired name in the 'File Name' box (including drive and path information) and enter the desired automatic stop time. If the named log file already exists, SmartMon will append the new figures to the end of that file; otherwise, a new file will be created. The log file thus created contains three columns of information. The first column displays the timer tick count since the beginning of the current Windows session. The second column displays the total number of cache accesses since the time SmartDrive was loaded. The third displays the number of cache hits since the time SmartDrive was loaded.

The Automatic Stop time can be set to terminate the file logging after a pre-set number of minutes. The minimum is one minute, the maximum is eight hours, the default being two hours.

```
Cache Hit Rate
  Sampling Frequency (in msec)      500
  Histogram Display Intervals        30
Log File
  File Name   smartmon.log
  ☒ Automatic Stop (in minutes)     120
Drive Control
  ☐ Save Setting in DOS Batch File
  File Name   C:\AUTOEXEC.BAT

  [ OK ]    [ Cancel ]    [ Help ]
```

ticks,	total,	hits
12332584,	532434,	495911
12345602,	533142,	496538
12345766,	533143,	496539
12348513,	533145,	496540
12350710,	533163,	496555
12351259,	533164,	496556
12366638,	533191,	496580
12367187,	533192,	496581

DEFRAG

Also bundled with DOS 6 is a disc defragmentation utility. This is called DEFRAG and is identical to the Speedisk utility from the Norton collection. This produces a report on the degree of fragmentation of files on the disc surface (see the chapter on Discs and Drives). The Windows 95 version is called Disk Defragmenter.

OTHER DIAGNOSTIC UTILITIES

CORETEST

A number of very useful public domain (i.e. free) and shareware (i.e. pay a fee which is normally a great deal less than commercial rates) utilities are available. Some are single purpose utilities to test the machine's memory or the hard drive; others are more general purpose programs.

Typical of these is the CoreTest program issued by the *'Core'* disc manufacturing company. It checks

```
                   DRIVE  EVALUATION  COMPARISON

                       Data Transfer  Average Seek   Track-Track   Performance
            Make       Rate KB/sec    Time   ms      Seek   ms     Index
--------------------------+-------------+---------------+-------------+----------
    Hard Disk 0               1734.8          0.7            0.1        92.459
    CORE HC650                1408.0         17              5          11.5
    Compaq 386/25              852.0         23              5           7.5
    CORE Optima 80             471.0         13              3           7.1
    IBM PS/2-80 70mb,ESDI      800.0         36             15           6.3
    IBM PS/2-70 115mb,ST506    663.0         25             12           6.2
    IBM PC/AT 20mb             160.0         35              6           2.5
    IBM PC/XT 10mb              85.0         79             31           1.2
```

the disc's data transfer rate and the head track-to- track seek time, displaying the results and converting them into a performance index that compares the performance with that of the original hard disc on the XT computer.   In the example shown on the previous page, the higher performance is due to disc caching being in operation (this was detected and reported by CoreTest on a previous screen).   This is a handy little utility to use as a first test on a machine that is reported as being a slow performer.   Before delving into the machine's configuration or the application's setup, simply slip in the floppy disc containing the utility, run CORETEST and look at the results.   A machine may have been supplied with the wrong interleave or the wrong controller card.   If possible, check the performance against others of the same manufacture and model.   Only if the results are similar, should the longer process of machine and software analysis be opened up.

WINCHECKIT

At the other end of the scale of complexity is the WinCheckit program used for a wide variety of system tests.   The diagram shows the range of hardware and configuration options that can be tested. Finding faults without such utilities is possible but is much slower.   It also

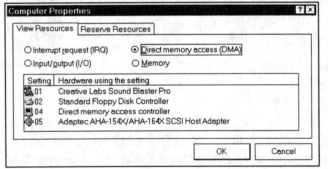

provides a *'Clean Up'* facility to detect duplicate files and a *'Tune Up'* facility that provides advice on improving the system's performance.

Other very informative packages are First Aid from Cybermania and WinProbe from Quarterdeck.

WINDOWS 95

A number of new diagnostic features are available with Windows 95.   Choosing the *'System'* icon within *'Control Panel'* offers four menu choices.

The *'General'* option reports on the CPU type and operating system in use.

The *'Device Manager'* option displays a list of the hardware resources.   Choosing *'Computer'* from the list and clicking the *'Properties'* button produces the screen shown.   The example shows the DMA assignments in the computer and clicking other buttons will reveal how the IRQs, I/O addresses and memory is allocated.

All hardware devices used by the computer are displayed within Device Manager.   Highlighting an individual device, such as the mouse or monitor, and clicking the *'Properties'* button produces information on that device.   If the device is correctly configured and is functioning correctly, a

   'This device is working properly'
message will be displayed; otherwise a
   'This device is not present, not working properly,
   or does not have all the drivers installed'
message is displayed.

The *'Performance'* option allows the optimising of Graphics (ie hardware acceleration features), File System (ie CD ROM speed and cache settings, disc drive read-ahead optimisation) and Virtual Memory (ie automatic or user-determined settings).   Each of these reports on the current settings and allows them to be adjusted by the user.

The example shown has also detected that the computer disc system is not running at maximum efficiency due to some of the drives having only 16-bit drivers.

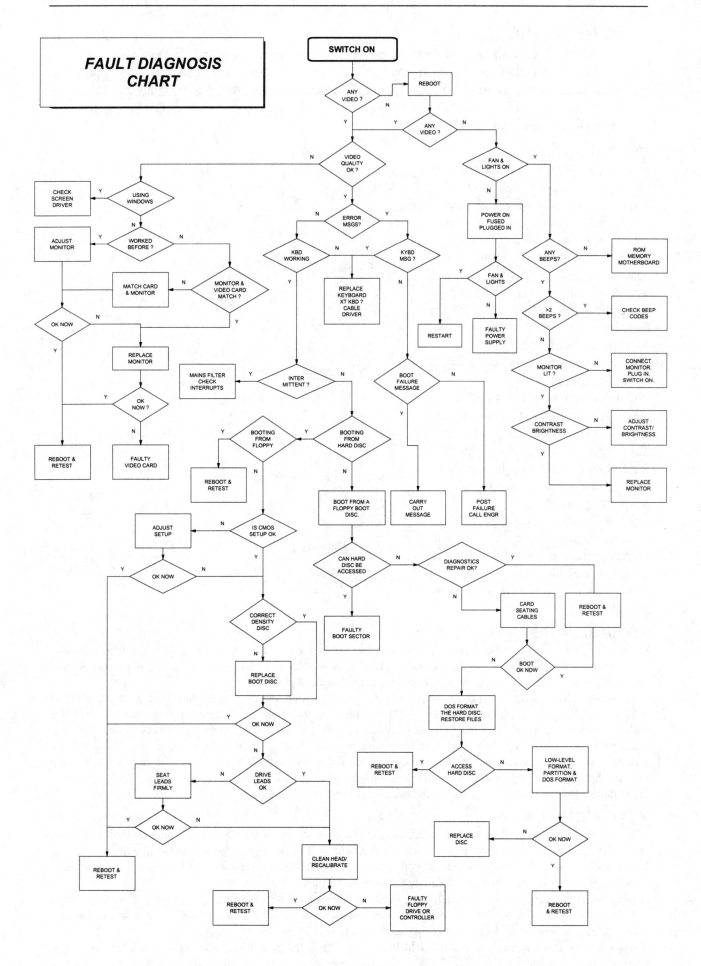

FAULT FINDING

The chart on the previous page gives a small example of a systematic approach to fault diagnosis. It is <u>not</u> a complete fault-finding chart. It does not, for instance, have a section on printer faults, or communications faults, network faults, etc. It cannot hope to cover all the possible faults that can occur. It is intended to act as the basis of a systematic approach to locating system faults. The following pages discuss sections of the chart in more detail.

INITIAL CHECKS

Many of the faults reported by users are of the simplest nature, such as equipment not plugged into the mains supply, not switched on or not even connected to each other.

Other faults are beyond the normal responsibilities of the support technician and are either a job for the company repair staff or a job for the external service company or maintenance contractor.

This section of the chart covers both these types of problems.

When the machine is first switched on, the computer motherboard and the monitor should both be powered up. This should result in some form of screen output; this might be the results of the computer self-test and the normal C: prompt.

If no video output is apparent, it would be wise to give the machine another hard boot, before carrying out the rest of the checks, since the machine will sometimes work perfectly happily thereafter.

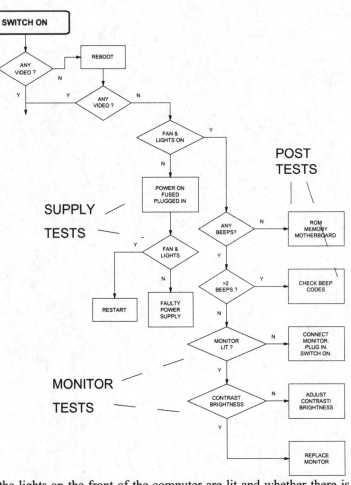

NO LIGHTS/FAN

If there is still no video output, check whether the lights on the front of the computer are lit and whether there is any noise from the computer's disc drive or fan. If there are no lights or motor noises, check that the computer is switched on, attached to a mains supply and that the mains socket is switched on.

If necessary, make good any shortcomings and check whether the computer now shows signs of life. If the computer appears active, restart the system and test again. If the computer remains lifeless, there is a problem with the machine's supply. This might be as simple as a blown fuse or a broken wire inside in the mains cable (so try another as a temporary replacement), a blown fuse internal to the machine (so check it out, if there is no company maintenance engineer, you know what you are doing and you obey all safety precautions) or it might indicate that the computer's internal power unit has failed (so call out the engineer). Its also worth trying plugging the unit into another mains socket, just in case the wall socket itself is faulty.

FAN/ LIGHTS OK

When the computer is first switched on, it automatically performs tests on the CPU, ROM, memory, motherboard, etc. The machine will not carry on if it finds any fault and will warn the user by producing a series of warning bleeps and/or displaying an error message on the screen. If the machine does not produce any beeps, it could mean either power unit failure, ROM failure or motherboard failure.

If there is a single beep, the POST check has passed the computer system as operable. Note that the POST test is not nearly as thorough as the checks used by diagnostic software. So, a POST failure definitely means a problem, while a POST pass does not necessarily mean that the machine is 100% OK.

If there is more than one beep, or a continuous beep, then a fault has been found; the number and duration of the beeps denote a particular fault. The ERRCODES.TXT file lists the error beep warning codes and also gives a comprehensive list of the DOS error codes. DOS error codes are numeric and are organised in a set of linked errors in each series. For example, the error codes from 100 to 199 (called the 1xx series) indicates system board errors, while the 6xx series covers floppy disc errors. The errors range from older system problems (e.g. the 5xx series reports on CGA errors) to modern system errors (e.g. the 215xxxx series reports on SCSI CD-ROM errors).

MONITOR CHECKS

If the computer unit appears to be functional (i.e. the lights are on, the fan is working and the single beep indicates that the unit has passed the POST test), there remains a possible problem with the monitor, its hardware and software drivers or its connections.

First, check that the mains indicator on the monitor is lit. If the indicator is unlit, then in similar fashion to the computer, check that the monitor is switched on, attached to a mains supply and that the main socket is switched on. Remember, in some cases, the monitor receives its mains supply from a cable attached to a rear socket on the computer, while other monitors have their own independent mains connections. In addition, check that the computer and monitor units are connected together - i.e. the video cable from the monitor is plugged into the video output socket of the computer. If necessary, make good any shortcomings and check whether the monitor now shows signs of life.

If the monitor remains lifeless, there is a problem with the unit's supply. This might be as simple as a blown fuse or a break in the mains cable (so try another as a temporary replacement), a blown fuse internal to the monitor (so check it out, if there is no maintenance engineer) or it might indicate that the monitor's internal power unit has failed (so call out the engineer).

If the monitor is lit but does not display any screen output, it may simply be that the monitor is in need of adjustment. Ensure that the brightness and contrast controls are at the correct settings; if in doubt, a mid-point setting should provide a viewable screen from which to make the necessary adjustments.

If screen adjustments provide a screen display, then the fault flow chart can be traced again from the beginning if necessary. If the monitor fails to respond to adjustments, then the unit ought to be replaced by a known working model. If the monitor still shows no video, then the computer's video card must be faulty; if the monitor now displays an output, then the original monitor is faulty and should be repaired.

ERROR MESSAGES

The computer may pass the POST check successfully (indicated by the single beep), the screen may display acceptable video but still produce one of a number of possible error messages, in text form. The most common messages are:

'KEYBOARD FAILURE'

If the screen displays a keyboard failure message, the following may require to be checked:
- Is the keyboard plugged into the computer?
- Is keyboard of the correct type (e.g. an XT keyboard is accidentally plugged into an AT machine, or perhaps a multi-purpose keyboard has its switch set to the XT position instead of the AT position)?
- Are any of the keys jammed in the down position?
- Is the correct keyboard driver being used?

A more precise approach is possible if a keyboard error code is displayed. These are in the 3xx series and cover stuck keys, keyboard cable faults and even displays whether a lockable keyboard has been left locked. If in doubt, the keyboard can be temporarily replaced by a known working model.

'BOOT FAILURE'

If the machine is unable to load DOS it may produce one of the following messages:

Disk Boot Failure
> This indicates corruption of the boot sector and action should be taken as per the flowchart choice 'not booting from the hard disc'.

Non-System disk or disk error
> This often occurs when a user manages to delete the system hidden files IO.SYS and MSDOS.SYS. If these are simply copied from another PC onto a floppy and placed in the machine's root directory, they will not be recognised by the boot system. The hidden files must the first two files in the directory.

No Boot Device
> The device itself is not being detected. This may be due to disc controller failure or simply badly seated cards or loose connections.

Even if there is no boot failure message displayed, the problem may still lie in the boot device and the same steps should be taken as per those for the 'Disk Boot Failure' message.

Most boot failure problems are complex and may well involve a call to the engineer.

INTERMITTENT PROBLEMS

There will be occasions when there are no error messages displayed and the unit, keyboard, monitor, etc. all seem to be functioning satisfactorily.   The problem seems to be an intermittent one, with the machine hanging up when it is required to be used or crashing in the middle of a program.   These problems can be caused by either hardware or software problems.

If the fault develops when there is no software loaded, then the source is easier to determine; the fault must be a hardware one.   While the source of the difficulty may be known, however, tracing the cause of the problem may be more difficult, since the fault cannot be reproduced to order.

Intermittent hardware problems may be

- Overheating faults.   As manufacturers race to bring ever faster performance machines on to the market, the CPU and other chips are forced to run at alarming clock rates and chip temperatures increase beyond the point of stability.   So much so, that some CPU chips have fans built on to their heat sinks, to dissipate the enormous amounts of heat that they generate.

- Design faults. Using memory chips which are not always able to keep up with the speed of the CPU.   Try clicking the machine off the turbo mode and see if the intermittent fault disappears.

- Intermittent connections.   These may be dry joints in soldered connections to the motherboard, power supply, disc drive, etc.   These may be either component or wiring connections.   The application of heat (by a hair dryer or similar) to an area of the board will expand any metal and hopefully expose the intermittent connection.   Conversely, if the problem is already present, the application of a freeze spray (available from electronic component suppliers) to selected areas will cool the area and hopefully restore normal operations, thereby showing up the problem connection.

- Software problems are more difficult to detect, as the fault may only occur under specific circumstances.   For example, it may require a particular clash of interrupts such as when using a particular function of an application over a local area network.   There are so many possible permutations that this may take exhaustive tests to expose. A lot of time can be saved if users are encouraged to note down exactly what they were doing at the time of the fault.

Lastly, the problem may be due to spikes or fluctuations in the mains supply affecting the data on the buses and causing the machine to crash. This may require the fitting of an uninterruptable power supply (UPS) to the computer.   This will be particularly important for local area network servers and other important machines in the company.

VIDEO PROBLEMS

If a monitor produces a display that is of poor quality, it may be due to a number of problems, either in the monitor itself, in the computer's video card, or in the interface and compatibility between the two.

SCREEN DRIVERS

These are the pieces of software that are used to ensure the correct interface between the monitor, the video card and even particular application programs.   For instance, Windows provides a set of drivers to match itself to most screen standards and most graphics cards.   Check that the correct driver is in use; a 1024x768 SVGA driver will not display properly on a normal VGA monitor, for example.

MONITOR ADJUSTMENTS

If the computer systems worked previously and there has been no alteration to the driver, the monitor may have gone out of adjustment.   Monitor adjustments are covered in the section on Video but might include adjusting the brightness, contrast, hue, horizontal or vertical position, the horizontal or vertical size, convergence, pincushion or horizontal or vertical locks.   Do not attempt internal adjustments unless you know what you are doing and observe all safety precautions.   Remember, a monitor has high voltages on some of its components - ranging up to around 30,000 volts!

If adjustments do not cure the problem, try temporarily replacing the suspect monitor with a known working model. If the computer now displays properly, the original monitor was obviously faulty.

If the replacement monitor will not work either, the computer's video card is faulty. As a double check, attach the monitor that you removed from the affected machine on to another working computer; the monitor should work happily on the new machine.

If the system has never worked together as a combined unit before, then the problem may be one of compatibility of the units. Check that the video card and the monitor type are a proper match. A CGA card will not properly drive a VGA monitor, for example. Also, check for the correct settings on the video card DIP switches (refer to the card's manual).

If the text characters on the screen flicker or alter then this is probably bad memory chips on the video card; try another video card.

NOT BOOTING FROM FLOPPY

Although most computers always boot up from the hard disc, there will be occasions when the machine will require to be booted up from a system floppy disc. These might include running diagnostics software or booting from a known virus-free disc before carrying out virus checks on the machine. Also, if the machine fails to boot up from the hard disc, the machine will have to be booted from a system floppy disc, to access the hard disc and diagnose its problem.

If the floppy drive is inoperable, it will be unable to carry out any of the above- mentioned tasks.

The computer's CMOS stores information about the machine's configuration and if this is altered, or the internal rechargeable battery is low, the information may no longer be correct. The setting can be checked by the machine's SETUP program; this is invoked by pressing the Delete key during the POST check for the AMI BIOS and Ctrl-Alt-Esc for the Phoenix and Award BIOS. Check that the A: drive is listed as being present and alter the setup if necessary. If the setup is altered, reboot the machine and see if the problem is now solved. If the internal clock is not keeping the correct time or date, then the internal battery is probably in need of replacement.

If the machine will still not boot from the floppy disc, check the disc itself. The disc may be a 1.4Mb high-density type, while the floppy drive may only be a 720k model. Or the disc may be corrupted; test the disc by using it to boot another computer; if it fails to boot a machine of suitable drive capacity, the disc should be replaced by a new boot disc.

If the disc is OK, it is time to look at the floppy drive itself. Check that the drive connections are seated firmly and reseat if necessary. Clean the floppy drive head using a proprietary head cleaner.

Finally, check the drive calibration using a diagnostics disc; the drive head or motor speed may require to be re-calibrated.

If all of the above fail, the fault must lie in the drive itself or in the drive controller card. Substitution of the card or drive should indicate which component is to blame.

NOT BOOTING FROM HARD DISC

If the computer fails to boot from the hard disc, it may display an error code from the 17xx series for ST506 systems, the 104xxx series for ESDI systems or the 210xxx series for SCSI systems. If so, the error code indicates the area that requires attention.

If there is no error code, boot the computer from a floppy system that is known to be working correctly.

Now try to access the hard disc by typing C: If the hard disc can now be accessed, it would indicate a faulty boot sector on the hard disc. If the hard disc still cannot be accessed, try running a disc diagnostics program (such as Norton Disc Doctor or SCANDISK) on the hard disc in an attempt to effect a repair. If the disc repair software reports a repair, then reboot the machine and retest.

If the repair software is ineffective, check the physical installation of the hard disc; is the disc controller card properly seated in the bus slot; are the power and data cables properly and securely connected to the unit. If necessary, make good any suspect connection and reboot and retest.

If the machine still fails to boot, carry out a high level DOS format on the hard disc and reboot. If the disc now boots correctly, restore all the backup files and use the machine as before.

If the machine will still not boot, carry out a full low-level format, followed by partitioning with FDISK and a high-level DOS format. This is the ultimate activity on the hard disc and the machine should be rebooted and tested. If the machine now operates and the hard disc can be accessed, the backup files can be restored and the computer can be used as before.

If the computer still refuses to boot, then there is a hardware problem with the hard disc and a new drive cable can be substituted as the easiest possible test. This is an uncommon problem and it is more likely that a new disc drive should be fitted.

HEALTH AND SAFETY

There are many hazards to employees in the workplace; these are not confined to the 'dangerous' jobs such as mining, construction or heavy engineering. Every day, employees suffer accidents at work or slowly impair their health by their work practices. The Health and Safety at Work Act came into force in 1975 and acts as the basis for safety law in the UK. It provides a legal framework outlining the responsibilities of both employers and employees, overseen by the Health and Safety Executive. Any employer with more than five employees is obliged under the Act (Section 2(3)) to maintain a written policy on health and safety, open to view by all employees. The Act is a complex 117 page document and only the main points are covered in this section. Other related measures, standards and recommendations are:

- ❍ The Office, Shops and Railway Premises Act of 1983.
- ❍ BS6266 - Fire Protection for Electronic Data Processing Installations.
- ❍ The Illuminating Engineering Society's (IES) recommendations on lighting standards, titled 'Code of Practice for Interior Lighting'.
- ❍ The Fire Precautions Act 1971.
- ❍ The IEEE Wiring Regulations.
- ❍ The Health and Safety (First Aid) Regulations 1981.
- ❍ The Sex Discrimination Act 1986.
- ❍ The Race Relations Act.
- ❍ HSE pamphlet 23 - "Hours of employment of women and young persons".
- ❍ HSE pamphlet 36 - "Working with VDUs".
- ❍ BS7179 and ISO9241 standards on monitor image quality.
- ❍ The EEC Directive 90/270 on VDU radiation levels.

Before acting upon any information in this section, the appropriate material should be fully read over. As far as the computing environment is concerned, healthy surroundings are in the interests of all. A smoky, dusty, damp or cold working environment is against the interests of the people who have to work there and is also damaging to the machine and their data. In addition, the loss of skilled staff through ill-health is not in the interests of anyone; employees lose out physically and the company loses out in loss of output. Implementing the legislation should not be viewed as a penalty but as an investment to retain and expand productivity with a more contented staff. PC Support health and safety issues can be roughly divided into two:

- • Those that are general to all offices - e.g. heating, lighting, working space, fire hazards, working ergonomics, etc.
- • Those more peculiar to computer environments - keyboard injuries, damage from monitors, harmful ozone from laser printers, etc.

NB : It is not the job of the PC support technician to sort out the health and safety problems that he/she encounters. The law ensures that proper machinery is in place with office safety representatives and probably safety committees. However, it would be the responsibility of the technician, both legally and morally, to ensure that any situations which break the law - unintentionally or otherwise - are reported to management or safety representatives.

Some of the more common problems to be encountered are:

GENERAL

- • Are work areas kept clean and tidy? Are waste bins emptied at least once a day?
- • Are work areas overcrowded? Is there the legal minimum of 11 cubic metres of space being provided per employee (with any roof area above 3m in height being excluded from the calculation)?   Are these area allocations compromised by excessive furniture, storage boxes, equipment, etc.?
- • Is the working environment satisfactory? Is it properly lit to prevent eye strain, headaches or accidents?
- • Is the workplace properly ventilated to prevent headaches and sinus problems?   (see HSE Guidance Note EH22 on Ventilation of Buildings).
- • Are there excesses of temperature (i.e. not less than 60°F after the first hour and not exceeding 72°F)?
- • Is the working environment excessively noisy? The 1972 Department of Employment 'Code of Practice for Reducing the Exposure of Employed Persons to Noise' stipulates 90db(A) as the maximum steady exposure to noise for an eight hour day or 40 hour week. For an office environment, a maximum figure of 60db(A) should be aimed for; conversations should be able to be conducted at a normal level.
- • Is the furniture laid out to provide the best ergonomic conditions and reduce backache, neckache, etc.?

- Is welfare accommodation satisfactory? Are there sufficient suitable sanitary conveniences, washing facilities (see Section 9 of the Office, Shops and Railway Premises Act) and places for keeping clothes (see the HSE booklet 10 - "Cloakroom Accommodation and Working Facilities 1980)?
- Are there adequate canteen facilities? See the Department of Employment's Health and Safety at Work booklet 2.
- Are the floors, passageways and stairs safe? Are floor coverings well maintained? Are areas of movement free from obstruction and slippery substances?
- Are all electrical installations in safe condition? Are appliances checked regularly?
- Are the fire precautions adequate? Are all the fire exits in working order and free from obstructions? Are all flammable materials safely stored? Are fire alarms regularly tested? Does the building have a fire certificate? (required where a building houses more than 20 employees or where ten employees work above or below ground floor level)
- Are there adequate first-aid facilities? Are employees trained in first-aid techniques?
- Is there job design to minimise occupational stress? Has attention been paid to job rotation, job enrichment, staff training, removing job isolation, adjusting supervision levels, improving internal communication, providing adequate rest breaks and workplace creches, having clearly defined standards for employee/client communications?

COMPUTER-RELATED

All of the earlier questions on general office environments also apply to computer environments and can have a detrimental effect on staff and output. In addition, there are other hazards which are encountered by computer users compared to other office staff.

VDU HAZARDS
This issue is fully dealt with in the chapter on computer video.

RSI
The general points on ergonomics are also covered in the chapter on computer video. However, a serious problem affects workers who are employed on prolonged keyboard work, particularly fast data entry work. This can cause discomfort, pain or even crippling disability. These symptoms are caused by the swelling and toughening of the muscles at the base of the wrist. The muscles eventually become so thick that they press on the nerves which pass through the wrist. The hand and wrist can become weakened to the point of irreversible damage. This is known as *'repetitive strain injury'* and it is important that the symptoms are spotted at an early stage. If diagnosed early enough, the damage can be arrested by means such as job rotation with non-repetitive tasks, reducing the work rate, introducing more work breaks or moving the employee to another job. Surgery has also proved successful with RSI cases when detected before it has reached an irreversible stage.

REPORTING PROBLEMS
It is best if a working relationship is established in advance with the organisation's safety representatives and the company employee charged with responsibility for health and safety matters. If the lines of communication are clearly understood in advance, it will reduce any tensions arising from any deficiencies which are reported. Since the PC support staff are among the few employees who move around the entire building, they are the most likely to get soundings of employee complaints and problems. Ideally, a report form should be devised and accepted as the standard method of notifying any potential or actual health and safety problem.

GETTING THE FULL FACTS
For a more full account of safety regulations, contact:

> The Health and Safety Executive
> Baynards House
> 1 Chepstow Place
> London W2 4TE
> Tel 0181-243-6000

who can supply the *"Essentials of Health and Safety at Work"* and a range of other such material. Many titles are free and they supply a twice-yearly list entitled *"Publications in Series"* which can be purchased at HSE centres or at book shops who stock HMSO titles. Many of the free pamphlets can be obtained directly from the regional offices of the HSE (see phone book).

Upgrading A Computer

Upgrading a computer consists of altering or adding to its component parts, so that the overall system is improved.   This improvement may be one of speed, or it may be one of added functionality.   In some cases, this upgrade can be achieved by external add-ons, or it may result from additions or alterations inside the computer case itself.   An example of an external improvement would be the fitting of an external modem or mouse, while an internal upgrade would be adding extra memory or a sound card. The upgrade process would usually consist of the following stages:

- SELECTION
- FITTING
- SAFETY/HANDLING
- TESTING
- COMPATIBILITY
- DOCUMENTING

SELECTION ISSUES

The technician has to know the best component to fit for a particular situation.   An example would be knowing the required specification for a video output card.   There would be no point in buying an PCI card if the machine only had an ISA expansion slot, for example.   It is also important to check that the new card will be able to be installed without any interrupt clashes, DMA clashes or I/O address clashes (see later). This would probably involve checking that the add-on card allowed for a range of different settings to be chosen. Incorrect selection could lead to poor performance or the failure of the system to operate.   For example, one particular video capture card will not work in a machine that is fitted with 16Mb of RAM.   These issues should be investigated and settled <u>before</u> the purchase of the item.

COMPATIBILITY ISSUES

The technician has to ensure that the equipment intended for adding to the computer is fully compatible with the existing system.   This may involve physical, electronic and software considerations.   A technical specification may indicate that a card is satisfactory for a particular purpose but other factors may come into play.   For example, the new device may be a full-length card but the computer may only have a half-length expansion slot left unused.   The following guidelines should prove useful:

- Check that the computer will work in the planned operating environment (eg is the temperature too high or too low, is the humidity too great, is the computer to be located close to sources of electrical interference such as machinery, does the site suffer from mains noise requiring the fitting of a mains filter, etc).   Check the computer's specification for the temperature and humidity tolerances.
- Always read the instructions before carrying out any activity; don't hurry into the upgrade.
- Before installing any equipment, carry out a dry run to ensure that there is adequate space to house the equipment and that all the necessary leads will stretch to connect to the new equipment.   This may include control/data cables from the disc controller card, connector cable from a SCSI card, audio lead to a sound card, etc.   It would certainly include making sure that there was a spare power lead on the power supply's cable loom and that the connection would reach to the new equipment.   If there is no spare connection, a 'Y' connector can be bought.   This involves removing a lead from an existing piece of equipment and inserting it into the Y connector.   This connector has two outputs - one to go to the original piece of equipment and one for the new apparatus to be installed.
- Check that the card's IRQs, DMA channels and I/O address locations do not clash with any existing card in the machine; if necessary, consult the manuals of the other cards.   If there is any clash, set the jumpers on the new card to avoid any collision.
- Always test the new equipment - both its hardware and any software; do not assume that it must be working.   Remember that some problems may be immediately obvious while others, such as intermittent clashes of interrupts, may only lead to system crashes on a sporadic basis.

SAFETY/HANDLING PROCEDURES

There are a number of general safety, handling and organisational procedures that should be observed when tackling any upgrade.   These are designed to both protect the technician and safeguard the equipment.   They should become second nature to the support technician and are as follows:

- Always use the correct tools for the job.
- Do not work inside the machine with the power connected.
- Always wear an earthing strap when handling boards and equipment.   Use a proper earthing strap with a built-in 1Mohm resistor; do not make up a simple connection between wrist and earth as this can be fatal if a live connection is accidentally touched.

- If any internal connectors are temporarily removed, record which socket they were removed from and note the orientation of the plug in that socket.
- Do not remove the add-on card from its anti-static protection until it is actually required.
- Avoid excessive handling of the card; hold the card by an edge that has little or no etched tracks.
- When installing the card, ensure that the edge connector is properly lined up with the expansion socket.
- Avoid excessive force in installing the card; gently rocking the card from edge to edge with a firm pressure is sufficient.   If the card is hard to fit, check that there is no other problem such as an obstruction or a misalignment of the card with the slot.
- Avoid excessive force in plugging in connectors to the card.   If the plug is hard to fit, check that there is no other problem such as an obstruction or a reversal of the plug.
- Ensure that the card is securely screwed to the computer chassis.   The screw used to secure the blanking plate will be used for this purpose.

PRACTICAL IRQ CONSIDERATIONS

Each IRQ number corresponds to a physical hardware line - e.g. an activity from a mouse connection or a modem connection.   Each IRQ line is allocated to an interrupt number that links to the corresponding routine for handling that device.   So, for example, a mouse might be attached to the COM1 port which is IRQ1.   Any mouse movement will trigger the IRQ1 interrupt and this will call the mouse handling routine.   When the user installed the mouse driver, the routine was placed in memory and the address of the routine was placed in the interrupt vector table.

SHARING IRQs

It follows that only one routine can be linked to a single IRQ number at any one time.   It is possible to have to two add-on cards set up with the same IRQ number, as long as they are not used simultaneously. If two devices have the same IRQ setting and both attempt to invoke a call at the same time unpredictable results can be expected, since only one device handler is in memory.   Devices, such as a scanner and a modem are unlikely to ever be required at the same time.   In this case the two cards can both have IRQ settings at the same IRQ number.   As long as only device is ever used during any computing session, the driver for the desired device can be installed and the device will be able to be used with no difficulty.   Of course, this would require different drivers to be set up for a session that used the other device on the same IRQ.   This would result in using different CONFIG.SYS files for different sessions, so that the driver software would be installed for the device to be used during that session.   If the DOS version supports multi-configurations, this nuisance can be minimised.   It is possible to have both drivers installed as TSRs and re-write the vector values when changing from one device to another but this is more of a programmer's challenge than one for support technicians.   If possible therefore, every card should use a different IRQ setting.   This is possible in a computer with few add-ons but conflicts become more likely as more and more adapter cards are added to a system.

CHOOSING AN IRQ

When a new device is to be added to the system, its IRQ requirement must not clash with any existing IRQ requirements of existing cards in the system.   All add-on cards will allow some amount of alteration of their IRQ settings, through the adjustment of jumpers or switches.   The documentation that accompanies the card will give details of the default IRQ setting and the other settings that it can adopt. Sometimes, there are only a few alternatives while other cards offer a range of 8 alternative IRQ settings to allow the greatest opportunity for fitting the card without interrupt clashes.   The first stage would be to check the usage of the IRQs within the existing system. Utilities such as Sleuth or Checkit or the Properties option within Windows 95 Device Manager can be used for this purpose.

```
    IRQ   Address      Description        Detected      Handled By
    ---   ---------    ---------------    ----------    ----------------
     0    0566:00D2    Timer Click        Yes           MOUSE
     1    CF01:1923    Keyboard           Yes            Block Device
     2    F000:EA97    Second 8259A       Yes           BIOS
     3    F000:EA97    COM2: COM4:        COM2:         BIOS
     4    0566:02CD    COM1: COM3:        COM1:         Logitech Serial MOUSE
     5    F000:EA97    LPT2:              No            BIOS
     6    F000:EF57    Floppy Disk        Yes           BIOS
     7    0070:06F4    LPT1:              Yes           System Area
     8    F000:EA42    Real-Time Clock    Yes           BIOS
     9    F000:EECF    Redirected IRQ2    Yes           BIOS
    10    F000:EA97    (Reserved)                       BIOS
    11    C94C:091F    (Reserved)                       SCSIMGR$
    12    F000:EA97    (Reserved)                       BIOS
    13    F000:EED8    Math Coprocessor   Yes           BIOS
    14    F000:E845    Fixed Disk         Yes           BIOS
    15    F000:9272    (Reserved)                       BIOS
```

Sleuth is particularly helpful as it can produce a list of all IRQs with the word *'Available'* appearing against all unused IRQ numbers. The table shows the result of the IRQ display option of Microsoft's own MSD utility. The display will vary with differing machine hardware configurations but most IRQ assignments will be similar.

NOTES:

- IRQ numbers 0, 1, 4, 5, 6, 7, 8, 9 and 14 will be used in almost all machines.
- IRQ numbers 0, 1, 2, 8 and 13 are not wired to the expansions slots.
- **IRQ2** When an IRQ between 8 and 15 is activated, it is using its own PIC, known as the slave PIC. This PIC does not have its own connection directly to the MI line of the CPU. It has to notify the CPU through the master PIC - the one that services IRQ0 to IRQ7. It does this through the master PIC's IRQ2 line and the Master PIC activates the CPU's MI pin. This process is known as *'cascading'* which is implemented in hardware - the actual interrupt 0A is not used. This often means that IRQ2 can be used for another device, being mapped to the IRQ9 line of the slave PIC; any card configured as IRQ2 is really using IRQ9.
- **IRQ3** This is allocated for a second serial port, COM2. In the example display, a second port is installed on the machine so the IRQ is in use. Where a second port is not fitted, the line can be used by another device. If a second printer port is fitted but not in use, it may be possible to disable the second port's IRQ line, releasing IRQ3 for another device.
- **IRQ5** This is allocated for a second parallel port, LPT2. Since a second port is rarely fitted, the IRQ can be used by another device. If the second port is fitted but not in use, it may be possible to disable the second port's IRQ line, releasing IRQ5 for another device.
- **IRQ7** This is allocated for the first parallel port, LPT1. The printer port only needs an IRQ line if it is carrying out bi-directional data transfers. Disabling the IRQ7 line of the printer port allows all the normal printing operations to be carried out, along with the usual out-of-paper and off-line detection. In this way, IRQ7 can be released for another device.
- IRQ10, 11, 12 and 15 are likely to be available for use, despite being displayed as *'Reserved'*. In the example, IRQ11 is being used for the SCSI controller card.

DMA

Some devices require data to be transferred between themselves and the CPU at the fastest possible speed. These are usually devices handling bulk data such as network cards, scanners, sound boards and hard discs. Slower devices such as floppy drives and serial/parallel ports do not have as demanding a speed transfer requirement. The slow devices use the CPU to organise the transfer of data between memory and the devices. All the data has to pass through the CPU and this ties up a lot of processing time, slowing down the computer's throughput.

To handle the faster devices, the PC uses a special technique known as *'Direct Memory Access'*. This extra chip handles the transfers to and from memory, leaving the CPU to get on with other tasks. This results in a more efficient system and increased throughput.

The XT has four DMA channels, three of which appear on the expansion bus. The AT onwards has eight DMA slots, with DMA4 being used to

```
= Check√It 3.0 ================================================
    ┌────────────────────────────────────────────────────────────┐
    │  SysInfo    Tests    Benchmarks    Tools    Setup    Exit   │
    ┌─ Interrupt Usage ──────────────────────────────────────────┐
    │ INTERRUPT ASSIGNMENTS:              ┌─ DEVICES WITH NO IRQ ─┐│
    │ IRQ 0   System Timer,win386         │ COM1                  ││
    │ IRQ 1   Keyboard                    │                       ││
    │ IRQ 2   [Cascade]                   │                       ││
    │ IRQ 3   COM2                        │                       ││
    │ IRQ 4   MOUSE                       │                       ││
    │ IRQ 5   Available                   └───────────────────────┘│
    │ IRQ 6   Floppy Disk                                          │
    │ IRQ 7   LPT1                          STANDARD DMA ASSIGNMENTS:│
    │ IRQ 8   Clock/Calendar                DMA 0                  │
    │ IRQ 9   VGA, (Active)                 DMA 1                  │
    │ IRQ 10  Available                     DMA 2  Floppy Disk     │
    │ IRQ 11  Available                     DMA 3                  │
    │ IRQ 12  Available                     DMA 4  [Cascade]       │
    │ IRQ 13  80486 FPU                     DMA 5                  │
    │ IRQ 14  Hard Disk                     DMA 6                  │
    │ IRQ 15  Available                     DMA 7                  │
    │                                                             │
    │          F2 - Copy to Activity Log ▌ ESC - Cancel           │
    └─────────────────────────────────────────────────────────────┘
```

cascade to the CPU. DMA Channels 0 through to 3 are used for 8-bit transfers, while Channels 5 to 7 are available for 16-bit transfers only. The current DMA usage is not available through MSD but can be obtained via Sleuth, Checkit or the Windows 95 Settings/Control Panel/System/Device Manager/Computer option. The above diagram shows the Checkit display for both IRQ and DMA usage. Some installation routines, such as that for sound cards, will carry out their own check of DMA usage and report any possible clashes. Unlike IRQs, no two devices can share the same DMA channel. Older cards did not tend to support DMA.

I/O ADDRESS CLASHES

The section on buses explained how the data in memory could be accessed for reading and writing. This entailed placing the address of the wanted location on to the Address Bus and enabling the Read or Write lines as required. A Write enable would result in the data on the Data Bus being written into the memory location specified in the Address Bus. A Read enable would result in the data held in the specified address being placed on the Data Bus. In this way, data could be moved round the internal system.

I/O Address	Port Use
0000 - 000F	DMA Controller
0020 - 002F	Interrupt Controller (Master)
0040 - 004F	Timer
0060 - 006F	Keyboard Controller
0070 - 007F	CMOS Real Time Clock, NMI mask
0080 - 008F	DMA Page Registers
00A0 - 00AF	Interrupt Controller (Slave)
00C0 - 00DF	DMA Controller 2
00F0 - 00FF	Math Coprocessor
01F0 - 01FF	Hard Disc Controller
0278 - 027F	LPT2
0278 - 027F	LPT1
02B0 - 02DF	Alternate EGA
02E1 -	GPIB Adapter (0)
02E2 - 02E3	Data Acquisition
02F8 - 02FF	COM2
0300 - 031F	Prototype Card
0360 - 036F	PC Network
0380 - 038C	SDLC Communications
0390 - 0393	Cluster (Adapter 0)
03A0 - 03A9	BSC Communications (primary)
03B0 - 03BF	Mono Display
03C0 - 03CF	EGA Adapter (primary)
03D0 - 03DF	CGA Adapter
03F0 - 03F7	Floppy Disk Controller
03F8 - 03FF	COM1

The same technique is used for all the add-on cards such as disc controllers, video cards, sound cards, network interface cards, serial ports, etc. These cards attach to the system via the connections on the expansion slots. Each card will have a unique address, or range of addresses, for its own use. The card will ignore any other addresses on the Address Bus and will only respond when an address from its own range appears on the Address Bus. This means that no new card can use the same I/O port address as that already being used by an existing device.

The problem only exists between hardware devices, since the system can differentiate between memory and hardware addresses. The CPU has a number of control lines that tell the system whether memory or a device is to be read/written. These control signals are:

MEMR	Read from memory
MEMW	Write to memory
IOR	Read from I/O device
IOW	Write to I/O device

The chart shows the lower range of I/O addresses and this will vary slightly dependent upon the machine configuration in use. As can be seen, many of the addresses have their functions allocated, leaving a small range of addresses into which must be fitted additional cards. The range 200h to 20Fh is often used for the fitting of a games port while the 300h to 31Fh range is the common area used for the addition of extra cards (eg a Novell network card). Again, utilities such as MSD, Sleuth and Windows 95 Device Manager can show some of the current I/O port address usage on the machine.

THE FIRST STEPS

The first steps in carrying out any internal upgrade will be the same and these are:

1. Switch off the machine. Ensure that the mains plug is removed from the mains socket. Remove all other cables that connect to the machine.
2. Fit an earthing strap to wrist and earth or computer chassis. This minimises the risk of body static blowing any chips on the card or motherboard.
3. Remove the cover of the computer main unit. There are normally 4 or 5 screws along the rear which secure the cover to the main chassis. In some models, the screws may be along the side of the casing. In a very few cases, it is simply a matter of pressing in two side buttons and hinging up the cover. Check the manual, as the some of the rear screws might be used for other purposes such as securing the fan casing or the power supply.

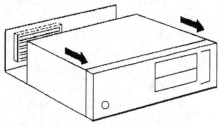

4. The screws should be placed in a safe place. If there is much disassembly work involved, the various screws should be placed in labelled envelopes.
5. Where the add-on interfaces to the outside world (e.g. an internal modem connects to a telephone line, whereas an extra hard disc is entirely internal to the case) remove the blanking plate that blocks off the slot in the external casing. Do not remove more blanking plates than are required, as these are used to prevent dust and debris from entering the case.

FITTING A CPU UPGRADE

The CPU is the 'heart' of the computer and fitting a faster CPU increases the performance of the computer. However, it is not simply a matter of fitting a new CPU in place of the slower model. Older chips ran on 5volts while modern CPUs run on 3.3volts. Fitting a 3.3v chip into a 5volt socket will destroy the CPU and therefore upgrade chips place an extra small board between the CPU and the motherboard. This contains a voltage regulator which allows the newer chip to be compatible with older motherboards.

Overdrive Range	
From	To
486 / 25MHz	486DX-75
486 / 33MHz	486DX-100
486 / 25MHz	Pentium 63MHz
486 / 33MHz	Pentium 83MHz
Pentium 60MHz	Pentium 120MHz
Pentium 75MHz	Pentium 125MHz
Pentium 66MHz	Pentium 133MHz
Pentium 90MHz	Pentium 150MHz MMX
Pentium 100MHz	Pentium 166MHz
Pentium 100MHz	Pentium 100MHz MMX

Most motherboards fit the CPU in a ZIF (zero insertion force) socket which uses a lever to grip and release the CPU pins, preventing possible bent pins caused by forcing the chip into the holder. A few other motherboards were manufactured with an additional socket for future upgrading.

Fitting an upgrade CPU is very easy if the following rules are followed:
- Ensure that the upgrade is pin-compatible (see the ZIF socket table)
- Ensure that the upgrade is voltage compatible (see motherboard manual)
- Ensure that the chip is inserted with the correct orientation (ie pin1 to pin 1)

100MHz DX4 chips plug into the DX upgrade socket on the motherboard.

Almost all 486 motherboard have a P24T socket (consult the manual), and are capable of taking an Intel *'Pentium Overdrive'* upgrade chip.   The 486-to-Pentium version of the chip is designed to match 486 motherboards which only have 32-bit data buses compared to the Pentium's 64-bit data bus.

Socket Number	Number of Pins	Motherboard	Description
1	169	486	Accepts 486 Overdrives only
2	238	486	Accepts 486 and Pentium Overdrives
3	237	486	A 3.3v version of the above
6	235	486	Accepts 486 DX4 CPUs
4	273	Pentium	Accepts 120MHz and 133MHz Overdrives
5	320	Pentium	Accepts 150MHz Overdrives
7	321	Pentium	The current Pentium standard socket

The steps for fitting an upgrade are:
- Carry out the first four steps outlined on page 335.
- Locate the existing CPU, open the ZIF lever and remove the CPU with the tool supplied with the Overdrive CPU.
- Align pin 1 of the overdrive CPU to the motherboard socket pin 1 and press home.
- Close the ZIF lever.
- Reassemble the PC.

Although the process is simple, consideration should be given to the expected extra performance compared to the extra cost. Consider the following points:
- In many cases, adding more RAM has a greater impact on the computer's performance than upgrading the CPU.
- Although the CPU is working at a faster pace after the upgrade, the rest of the system has not necessarily speeded up.   The 486/33MHz upgrade, for example, achieves its extra CPU performance by internally multiplying the computer's 33MHz clock rate up to 83MHz.   The motherboard is, nevertheless, running as a 33MHz board.   A normal 60MHz Pentium, on the other hand, will have both its CPU and its board running at 60MHz.   A normal 90MHz Pentium system will run its board at 60MHz and multiply its CPU by a factor of 1.5 to achieve 90MHz clock speeds.   This is not a consideration when upgrading an existing Pentium system.
- Although the raw speed has been increased, many of the benefits of Pentium systems are still not available (eg improved chipsets, improved caching, USB ports, power management).

Since Overdrive chips are relatively expensive, a replacement CPU + motherboard might be a more cost effective alternative to CPU upgrading.

MOTHERBOARD UPGRADE

The most dramatic improvement in performance from an upgrade is replacing the motherboard/CPU combination. This need not be over expensive, since all or most of the original components (case, discs, memory, video card, etc) can all be re-used on the new board.

SELECTION

A large range of options are available and the main considerations are:

CPU	Pentium 60MHz and 90MHz CPUs are being dumped cheaply while the newer 233MHz and 266MHz models are still commanding premium prices.
Chipset	The facilities of the supporting chipsets are explained in the chapter on Architecture
Board dimensions	Most boards conform to the 'AT' standard but a number of manufacturers have their own non-standard layout. Will the new board fit in the old case?
Board type	The newest ATX boards have different cooling arrangements and require that the case also be upgraded to an ATX type.
Memory type	New motherboards are 72-pin SIMMs and some are now DIMM sockets only. Does upgrading the board require upgrading memory at the same time? Should 30-pin to 72-pin adaptors be purchased so that old memory SIMMs can be used in the new board?
Manual	Never buy a motherboard that is not supplied with a manual - it may become essential.

REMOVING OLD BOARD

The steps for removing the old motherboard are:
- Carry out a backup of the disc's contents as a precaution.
- Carry out the activities listed on page 335
- Note the way that the motherboard is mounted; where are the mounting holes?; are plastic stand-offs or mounting posts being used?
- Remove the add-on cards from the motherboard's expansion slots (eg video card, sound card, disc controller).
- Unplug the cables from the motherboard, noting their function (eg cables to floppy drives, CD-ROMs, power supply, internal speaker, turbo button, reset button, disc lights, keyboard lock).   Note the orientation of cables that are temporarily removed from add-on cards (most cables have a red stripe on one side).
- Unscrew the motherboard and remove it.

FITTING NEW BOARD

The steps for fitting the replacement board are:
- Set any jumpers on the motherboard.   Check the manual for details.   Likely settings would be the clock speed, the CPU multiplication factor and disabling on-board sound circuitry where a sound card was to be fitted.
- Fit the memory SIMMs or DIMMs.
- Fit the CPU if it has not been supplied pre-installed.   This involves opening the lever on the ZIF socket, carefully inserting the CPU with the correct orientation and closing the ZIF lever.
- Hold the board over the case chassis and check that all the mounting holes on the motherboard line up with stand-offs on the chassis.   In some cases, fresh holes may require to be drilled in the case to fir mounting posts.   Never drill or file the motherboard as this may damage the tracks on the board.
- Fit the motherboard, ensuring that it is clear of the metal casing at all points.
- Fit the add-on cards to the motherboard. If the board layout is different from the old board, the cards may not fit in their original order. If a cable is now found to be too short, the cards will need to be fitted on the board in the best order for all the connecting cables to reach.
- Re-connect the cables to the motherboard.   Again, if the motherboard layout is different, cables may have to be re-routed or even extended.
- AT power cables from the power supply are usually wired to two separate plugs, each with six connections. The black leads of each plug should be located together at the middle of the socket and the orange cable should be lined up with pin 1 of the connector. Take care over this - double-check the particular system's connections - as incorrect wiring could damage the motherboard.
- Switch on the computer and run the BIOS setup to configure any alterations to the setup.

UPGRADING VIDEO

Most computers are capable of having their video capabilities improved.   The additional hardware involved can be fairly expensive and would normally only be undertaken if there was a good operational reason.   The adoption of Windows or DTP software might be reasons for such a move.   Indeed, a piece of software may specify that its minimum hardware requirements include, for example, a VGA screen.
An upgrade is in three stages:

- Obtaining the correct components
- Fitting the graphics card
- Installing the software drivers   .

CHOOSING THE CORRECT COMPONENTS

Before contacting dealers, it is important to know exactly what is required. Detailed descriptions of components are in the previous pages, but the specification has to consider:

RESOLUTION

If upgrading a machine from CGA or EGA, should the top screen resolution of the new graphics card be 640 x 480, 800 x 600, 1024 x 768 or higher.   The current upgrade may require, say, VGA resolution.   However, new software tends to demand ever higher screen resolutions.   In that situation, consideration should be given to increasing the resolution to be 800 x 600, or greater.   Increasing the specification allows the system to cope with possible future demands.   Buying for the future may save money in the long term, although it will probably cost more in the short term.   A financial compromise might be to purchase graphics boards that are socketed to allow the expansion of the video memory, by plugging in extra memory chips later.

FEATURES

Requirements for handling 3-D or multimedia files would demand a card that was optimised for these purposes.

SCREEN SIZE & TYPE

If the software demands a high resolution, it will also require a larger size monitor screen, which can make a substantial difference to the upgrade price.   Consideration should also be given to the local operating environment and whether FST tubes or anti-glare screens should be purchased.

COLOUR

There is a golden rule about graphics colours; more colour equals more memory and more memory equals higher price.   In addition, more colours may mean added circuit complexity, such as high performance RAMDACs.   This will also increase the price.

SPEED

The upgrade may be to allow the running of an application, such as a spreadsheet, in high resolution mode.   Here, the speed of the   CPU or the maths co-processor will be more significant than the speed of the screen update.   Here, a cheaper board might be sufficient.   In other situations, such as DTP or graphics animation, the speed of the graphics updates demands that the best performance possible is considered.   A graphics accelerator card or a graphics co-processor card will be essential.   Factors such as the use of VRAM or a PCI bus card should also be considered.

COMPATIBILITY

An upgrade will almost certainly entail the purchase of both a new graphics card and a new monitor.   If the current monitor is a CGA or EGA type, it will have to be upgraded to allow it to meet the new higher specification. It is vital that the all the components are compatible with each other.
The following questions should be addressed.

- Does the graphics card match the machine? Does the graphics card have an ISA, an EISA, an MCA, a PCI or a VESA Local Bus connection? Is this the same type as that used on the machine's expansion slot?   To get the maximum performance, should consideration be given to changing the computer motherboard to one with a PCI Bus system or a faster processor?
- Does the graphics card match the monitor?   Is the monitor of sufficient resolution for the new task - and for any future task? Should extra be paid to ensure future compatibility? Does the monitor support non-interlaced mode? Does the graphics card support non-interlaced mode?

The above paragraphs are only a summary of some of the points to be looked at by the support staff, since they are often consulted about future purchases.   The previous chapters covering video standards, card descriptions, computer bus types, etc. should be consulted for greater detail.   Remember, often purchases are a compromise between users' demands, performance specifications and budgetary constraints.

FITTING THE CARD

The first five steps are the basic ones already outlined in page 335.   These steps should be followed by these next stages:

6. Remove any existing graphics board.   It is unlikely that the graphics circuitry will be mounted directly on to the motherboard.   The only exception would be for a new card that worked in conjunction with the existing video card.   In this case, the two cards would be linked by way of the old card's feature socket.

7. Locate a free expansion slot. Most models have the output sockets from the card exit at the rear of the machine, although in some models, such as the Amstrad, the card sockets extend from the side of the machine.

8. Remove the rear blanking plate currently blocking this slot. One screw holds this plate.

9. Set up any DIP switches or jumper connectors if required. This is not normally required, especially moving from VGA upwards. Be advised by the documentation that comes with the graphics card. This outlines the card's requirements and this can be compared to any existing card's requirements.

10. Insert the new card carefully into expansion slot. The card's output socket should protrude from the empty slot.

11. Secure the card using the same screw removed with the blanking plate.

12. Replace the machine cover.

13. Plug the monitor cable into the graphics card socket.

14. Re-assemble the case and cabling and switch on.

INSTALLING THE DRIVERS

These are specially written software programs, designed to drive the new graphics hardware to the best performance.   These, and the accompanying installation instructions, will be supplied along with the graphics board.

MONITOR CONNECTIONS

The computer's graphics display circuitry may be mounted directly on the PCB of the motherboard. Alternatively, it may comprise of a card plugged into the expansion bus.   In both cases, the display output is taken to the rear of the computer, where it is wired to an output socket.   A cable, or cables, then connect this output to the monitor.

CGA/EGA

Both have 9-pin D-type sockets at the rear of the PC.   The pin layout and numbering is as shown in the diagram and is the view as seen by a user.

VGA/SVGA/XGA

The analogue connectors use a 15-pin D type socket.   In this way, RGB and analogue cards cannot be mistakenly matched with the wrong type of monitors - a VGA monitor lead will simply not plug into a CGA card, for example.   The pin layout and connections are shown.

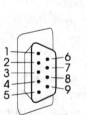
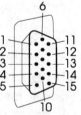

With some high-performance, large-size screens, the red, green and blue signal connections are taken to the monitor on separate co-axial cables with BNC (bayonet) connectors. This minimises interference that may be caused by the colour signal on one lead being induced onto another colour lead.

Pin	CGA	EGA
1	ground	ground
2	ground	Secondary Red
3	Red	Red
4	Green	Green
5	Blue	Blue
6	Intensity	Secondary Green
7	unused	Secondary Blue
8	Hor sync	Hor sync
9	Ver sync	Ver sync

Pin	VGA/SVGA
1	Red
2	Green
3	Blue
4	unused
5	ground
6	Red return
7	Green return
8	Blue return
9	unused
10	Sync return
11	unused
12	unused
13	Hor sync
14	Ver sync
15	unused

NOTE - The monitor also needs a mains supply to power its internal circuitry. This is sometimes supplied by a direct cable to a 13-amp plug; sometimes a mains cable connects the monitor to a socket on the rear of the computer - this reduces the number of leads floating around.

ADDING MEMORY

There are a number of very good reasons why a machine should have its memory size increased.

TO HANDLE MODERN APPLICATIONS

Early PCs were supplied with the basic 640k of RAM and most applications did not even use the full memory. With the development of ever larger operating systems and user applications, 8Mb has emerged as an absolute minimum requirement.   If large files, multimedia, real time video capture and editing and so on are to be accommodated, main memory should be much greater as shown in the chart below.

Category	Examples of Use	Min Recommended RAM
Light User	Word-processing, e-mail	8Mb
Medium User	Database applications	16Mb
Heavy User	Large databases, multi-tasking	32Mb
Power User	Multimedia authoring, DTP, photo-editing, CAD	64Mb
Design User	3D-CAD, CAM solid modelling	128Mb

TO CREATE A VIRTUAL DISC

Adding extra memory provides the capability of configuring it as RAM drive.

TO ACHIEVE GREATER SPEED

Extra memory speeds up Windows applications. The Windows Enhanced Mode uses a scheme called *'virtual memory'* that utilises the hard disc's unused contiguous space as if it were an area of memory.   Since the access time of a disc may be 10ms compared to 70ns for actual memory, Windows will run much faster if it can directly use extended memory.   Some DOS packages can also utilise this extra memory. DataEase, for example, will sort its records in any extended memory rather than use slow disc operations.

TO HANDLE MORE DATA

Lotus 1-2-3, for example, can use expanded memory to store and work with larger worksheets

TO ALLOW MULTI-TASKING

Extended memory can be used to run several programs simultaneously.

TO PROVIDE A DISC CACHE

Smartdrv and VCACHE use a section of extended memory as a disc cache to speed up disc access times.

TO CREATE A PRINT SPOOLER

TO GAIN ACCESS TO SOFTWARE WHICH USES EXPANDED MEMORY

TO ALLOW MEMORY MANAGEMENT

More efficient use can be made of the user memory area, using DOS 5 or DOS 6, DRDOS or QEMM; this allows programs to run where they would otherwise be prevented by lack of memory.

WHERE TO ADD

There are two methods used by different systems to install extra memory:
- On the computer's motherboard. This is now relatively rare.
- On the manufacturer's own memory expansion boards, the additonal cards being described as *'memory modules'*.

WHAT TO ADD

Motherboards may arrive fully populated or partly populated. If a new motherboard is bought, it may have no memory fitted whatsoever.   The first step is to determine the kind of memory is to be fitted.

The most common formats are explained in the chapter on memory and the most likely types to be used in an upgrade are SIMMs, as it is uneconomic to upgrade a computer that requires any older memory type.   The different sizes and possible combinations available should be carefully examined before the chips are purchased.   For example, a Pentium must upgrade memory at least two at a time, since chips are 32-bit and the Pentium has a 64-bit bus.

FITTING SIMM BOARDS

Find the SIMM banks on the motherboard and note the orientation of the current SIMM boards. These boards have holes to engage with pegs on the slots.   Before handling the SIMM discharged your body static or preferably wear an earthing wristband.   Place the SIMM into the socket at an angle of about 30 degrees and engage the SIMM's pegs into the matching holes in the motherboards slot. When the board is gently pushed home and rotated vertically, it will click into place in the bank's retaining side clips. Take care when inserting SIMMs since the pegs break quite easily.

Alter any DIP switch settings or jumper settings as necessary, to configure the motherboard to recognise the new memory.   This is mostly only required by older motherboards, as newer boards automatically detect the amount of memory fitted.

UPGRADING AN IDE HARD DISC

Many older machines are still perfectly functional but are burdened with very small hard discs of 100Mb or 200Mb. While adequate in the past, these discs are incapable of supporting the much larger DOS and Windows programs that are now being produced. These notes cover the two possibilities - replacing the old disc with a higher capacity model, and adding an additional hard disc to the system.

SELECTING

SIZE - This issue is covered in the chapter on system selection. 1Gb has become the minimum requirement for commercial use.

TYPE - Ensure that the model is an IDE type; the existing setup can be identified by the cables that connect the drive to the controller card. The possibilities are:

IDE	A single, 40-pin strip
SCSI	A single, 50-pin (SCSI-2) or 68-pin (UW) strip
RLL, MFM or ESDI	A 34-pin control strip and a 20-pin data strip

If the controller card is an old MFM or RLL type, then the upgrade will include purchasing a new IDE disc controller card to replace the old card, as an IDE drive can not be run from an old RLL or MFM disc controller card.

SPEED - The speed tends to vary with the disc's size and a 12ms access time is typical of a 500Mb disc, dropping to about 10ms for a 1GbMb model.

FITTING

The steps for renewing an old hard disc are:

- Ensure that the new disc's parameters are known; this is likely to be printed on a label on the disc. If this is not provided, contact the supplier for the information on number of tracks, number of sectors per track, etc. Do not proceed with the remaining steps until these facts are known as the BIOS will have to be set up to these parameters.
- Ensure that the new disc is configured as a *'master'* disc. The drives can be set as *'master'* or *'slave'*. The *'master'* setting is for a first disc drive and is the one that the system will boot from; the *'slave'* is the second drive. The jumper settings on the drive configure it and the actual settings vary from manufacturer to manufacturer. Consult the installation notes that come with the drive.
- Make a complete backup of all the existing files on the old hard disc.
- Carry out the initial steps outlined on page 335.
- Remove the power cable and ribbon cable from the old hard disc.
- Unscrew and remove the old hard disc from its drive bay. Place the old drive to one side and retain the screws.
- Fit the new drive into the unused bay and secure with the same screws.
- Fit the power cable and ribbon cable to the new disc drive.
- Refit the computer case and mains cable.
- Reboot the machine and run the setup program for that machine (see computer's manual)
- Alter the BIOS settings, so that the size and parameters of the new hard drive are saved to the machine's CMOS.
- Partition and high-level format the disc, using FDISK and FORMAT utilities from a floppy boot disc (see chapter on hard drives).

FITTING A SECOND IDE HARD DISC

The following steps outline the addition of an extra IDE drive to a machine with an existing IDE drive.

- Carry out the initial steps outlined on page 335.
- Ensure that the existing setup is an IDE system (the ribbon cable between the controller card and the drive should be a single 40-pin strip).
- Ensure that the machine has:
  - A spare drive bay
  - A spare power connector (if not, use a 'Y' power adapter)
  - A spare connector on the ribbon cable.
- Ensure that the machine's BIOS allows the new configuration to be setup. The CMOS has to store the information on the new drive and this has to come from the BIOS settings. Each BIOS chip contains a pre-defined set of drive numbers and each number corresponds to a set of drive parameters. Where there is no match in the pre-defined set, the BIOS provides a type 47; this is a drive number that is user-defined and parameters not in the given sets can be nominated. The parameters are entered by the user via the

keyboard and the data is stored in the CMOS. This means that there will be no problem if both discs are of the same size with the same parameters, as the parameters for the new drive are already stored in the CMOS. There will also be no problems if the new drive's parameters exist in one of the existing sets in the BIOS table. In that case, the CMOS is informed that the 'C' drive is of one particular drive number, while the 'D' drive is of another particular number. However, there may be a problem if the new drive is not in the BIOS table and the existing drive has used entry 47 to a different user-defined set. The only solution is to fit a BIOS ROM that has two user-defined drive numbers - type 46 and type 47. This allows the two drives to be independently configured to different specifications and still be recognised by the system.

- Configure one of the drives as the *'master'*. This is the drive that the machine will boot the system from. IDE hard discs are supplied configured as masters but it may be required to be informed that a slave drive is connected (by setting a *'Slave Present'* jumper).
- Configure the other drive as the *'slave'* (see drive's installation notes).
- Fit the new drive into the unused bay and secure with the screws provided with the installation kit.
- Fit the power cable and ribbon cable to the new disc drive. The drives can be connected to the ribbon cable's in any order; there is no requirement for the master disc to be on the first connector.
- Refit the computer case and mains cable.
- Reboot the machine and run the setup program for that machine (see computer's manual)
- Alter the BIOS settings, so that the new hard drive size and parameters are saved to the machine's CMOS.
- Partition and high-level format the disc, using FDISK and FORMAT utilities from a floppy boot disc or from the existing drive, if it is the master drive (see chapter on hard drives).

UPGRADING TO AN EIDE HARD DISC

A general description of EIDE drives is given in the chapter on Discs and Drives. The general instructions for handling and fitting IDE disc also apply to EIDE drives but there are some important differences. Older BIOS chips will support EIDE drives and this leaves three options:

- Change the BIOS chip to one that support EIDE - not usually a practical proposition
- Use special software drivers that match the new EIDE drive to the existing BIOS. EIDE drives will provide their own drivers on floppy discs that come with the hard disc. This works well but does not allow for a second EIDE channel for connecting further EIDE devices such as CD-ROMs.
- Replace the existing IDE controller card with an EIDE interface card. The EIDE cards have their own BIOS chips built in and these supplement the existing computer's BIOS.

If the EIDE drive is simply replacing an existing IDE drive, it is a straightforward one-for-one physical replacement, followed by the installation of the additional driver software. If the IDE controller card is also being replaced, then the old card's cables to the drive and floppy disc should be removed. The power cable should be disconnected and the drive unscrewed and removed. The new drive should be screwed in place and all the cables connected to it. Like the IDE installation previously described, the CMOS setup has to be altered to store the new drive's geometry (ie the values for cylinders, heads, etc should be placed in the Type 47 entry. Finally, partition and high-level format the disc.

UPGRADING TO A SCSI HARD DISC

A general description of SCSI drives is given in the chapter on Discs and Drives. After the SCSI type has been decided and the drive purchased, fitting is the easiest of all the drives. SCSI works well alongside existing hard disc systems inside the computer as it does not use the computer's BIOS chip, relying instead upon additional software that talks to the additional SCSI controller card that needs to be fitted. The additional driver software comes with the new drive. If, however, the drive is being used to replace an IDE system, then a SCSI interface card that has a BIOS ROM has to be fitted so that the disc will act as a bootup drive.

Fitting the SCSI involves the following steps:

- Fit the controller card in a spare expansion slot.
- Set the ID value of the SCSI drive (usually setting jumpers - see the manual)
- Screw the disc drive into a spare bay
- Connect the controller cable to the drive.
- Connect a power cable to the drive.
- Install the software driver.
- Configure the SCSI software or the SCSI BIOS.
- Partition and high level format the disc.

FITTING A 3.5" FLOPPY DISC DRIVE

There are a variety of reasons for fitting a 3.5" floppy drive to a computer. These are:
- Replacing a 5.25" drive with a 3.5" drive
- Adding a 3.5" drive to a computer with an existing 5.25" drive.
- Adding a floppy to a new motherboard or new controller.
- Adding a second 3.5" floppy drive.

The first steps in the fitting are the basic ones already outlined in page 335. Each of the fitting options is carried out with slight differences and the remaining steps to be followed are detailed separately.

REPLACING A 5.25" DRIVE WITH A 3.5" DRIVE
- Check that the system supports an HD floppy drive. Old XT machines, based on the 8086 or 8088 CPUs, only support double-density drives. From the 286 chip onwards, high-density formats were supported.
- Check that the machine's BIOS will support HD drives. Run the BIOS Setup to see whether it offers a 1.44Mb option.
- Remove the power and data ribbon cables from the old floppy drive.
- Unscrew and remove the old drive from its bay. Place the drive to one side and retain the screws.
- Fit the new floppy drive into the unused bay and secure with the same screws. Since all mounting bays are 5.25" wide, this requires the floppy to be fitted to a mounting kit which adapts the 3.5" case to a 5.25" bay. If the adaptor kit does not come with the drive it will have to be purchased separately.
- Fit the power cable to the new disc drive.   The power plug for a 5.25" is larger than that used for a 3.5" and a power adaptor will have to be fitted between the drive and the power plug. If this is not supplied with the drive, it will have to be purchased separately.
- Fit the data ribbon cable to the new disc drive.   The data connector for a 5.25" drive is different to that used for a 3.5" model. This may require the cable to be replaced with one that fits a 3.5" drive. Some computers are fitted with universal adaptors like that shown in the diagram. It has connections for either 5.25" or 3.5" drives.   If fitting the cable for the first time ensure that the red stripe is lined up with Pin 1 on the controller socket.   Note that the drive select and motor controls for drive B: are reversed compared to drive A.   Floppy drives are supplied preset to be Drive 1 and if the cable has the twist then an extra drive can be fitted without altering jumpers.   If the existing cable is not twisted, then the 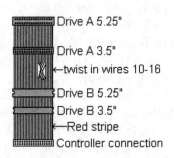 second drive to be fitted will have to be set as Drive 2 using jumpers.   If a flat cable is in use and the new drive does not have drive selection jumpers, then a twisted cable will have to be fitted in place of the flat cable.

NB: The cable is wired so that the drive at the end connector is regarded as drive A.

- Refit the computer case and mains cable.
- Reboot the machine and run the setup program for that machine (see computer's manual)
- Alter the BIOS settings, so that the machine's CMOS stores the size of the new drive (ie 720k or 1.44Mb instead of 360k or 1.2Mb)

ADDING A 3.5" DRIVE TO A COMPUTER WITH AN EXISTING 5.25" DRIVE.

The steps are similar to those above except that the old drive is not removed.   The extra drive is fitted into an unused bay and an additional power lead has to be connected to the drive, via the 3.5" power adaptor.   If the computer does not have a spare power connector, a 'Y' connector (see page 332) should be fitted.   If the data cable only has 5.25" connectors, it cab be replaced with a universal type as shown above.   Alternatively, an adaptor plug can be purchased which fits between the data connector on the cable and the drive's connector.   The machine's BIOS settings will need to be altered to add a second drive of 1.4Mb capacity, while retaining the original drive in the configuration.   Lastly, make sure that the LASTDRIVE setting in CONFIG.SYS allows for the addition of the additional drive.

ADDING A FLOPPY TO A NEW MOTHERBOARD OR NEW CONTROLLER.

This is straightforward since the connections of the new controller card and drive will be compatible. Similarly, the power connectors of a new system will support 3.5" drives.   After fitting, set the machine's BIOS to recognise the drive.

ADDING A SECOND 3.5" FLOPPY DRIVE.

This is also a simple matter of fitting the drive, attaching the data and extra power leads and altering the BIOS to recognise the extra drive. Ensure that the LASTRDIVE setting allows for the added drive.

FITTING A UPS

An uninterruptable power supply (UPS) runs the computer on its own batteries in the event of a power failure.   They are available in a wide range of capacities.   Some last for only a few minutes while more expensive models maintain the system for substantially longer periods.   The smaller capacity models are adequate for many standalone PCs while the higher capacity models are common on network servers. The aim of a UPS is not to maintain normal working for any prolonged period as the cost of the batteries would be prohibitive.   The UPS aims to allow the machine to close down naturally without loss or corruption of files.

The installation steps are:
- Load the UPS software.
- Carry out the initial steps outlined on page 335.
- Set the card's I/O port address. With some cards this may happen at a later stage as some setup software autodetects and informs the user what address to select.
- Plug the card into a spare expansion socket and screw into place.
- Unplug the power cable coming from the power supply to connect to the motherboard.
- Connect this cable to the UPS card.
- Connect an additional supplied power cable from the UPS card to the motherboard.
- Connect the external UPS supply into the mains supply.
- Amend the machine's configuration files according to the manual, to load the monitoring TSR routine. This may be automatically carried on running the setup program.

The battery pack is kept charged by a regulated mains supply.   The diagram shows that the normal computer power supply is still used but is routed through the UPS card.   There are two major types of UPS, these being:

OFF-LINE MODELS

The Off-line UPS lets the computer power supply provide the power for the system under normal conditions. If the mains power fails completely or drops below a tolerable level (a *'brownout'*), the UPS card senses the loss and takes control. The backup battery is then used to feed the inverter and the inverter converts the battery's low voltage into the

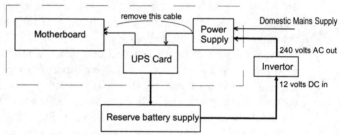

normal mains supply voltage.   This provides enough mains power to alert the user and save files.   This changeover period lasts a couple of milliseconds and most computers can handle this small loss.   In the diagram, the heavy lines indicate the activities that are activated upon mains power loss.

ON-LINE MODELS

The On-line UPS is similar to the above diagram. In this case, however, the domestic mains supply is not connected to the PC.   The PC is permanently supplied by the inverter. The role of the domestic mains is to keep the batteries topped up.   This is a more costly option but it has these extra advantages:
- Since the computer is not directly connected to the domestic mains, it cannot be affected by mains fluctuations, voltage spikes and other line noise.
- There is no switchover delay as the supply is constantly being fed.   This means that there is no possibility of the machine going down during a changeover period.   This is a more secure option for servers and machines where there should be no margin of error.

SELECTING A UPS

Each UPS has a power rating which is measured in VA (Volt Amperes).   This is equivalent to one Watt of power.

To determine the VA rating for a particular station:
- Decide which devices require to be protected; this would include the computer and the monitor, but probably not the printer.
- Add together the power requirements of each of the protected devices.
- Since a UPS is usually around 80% efficient, multiply the total by 1.4 to provide the true working rating.
- This gives the <u>minimum</u> rating required.   For a longer protection time, increase the VA rating. Typical UPS ratings are from 500VA to 2000VA.

FITTING A SOUND CARD

The variety of sound cards (eg whether wavetables or MIDI facilities are required) is covered in the chapter on multimedia.

The first steps in the fitting are the basic ones already outlined in page 335.

The additional steps are:

- Alter the card's base address, DMA and/or IRQ setting if these clashes with an address, DMA or IRQ already in use on the computer. Utilities such as Sleuth, Checkit or Windows 95 Device Manager/Properties will list addresses already in use.
- Insert the card into a spare expansion slot and secure with a screw.
- If the computer has a CD ROM drive fitted, its audio output can be connected to sound card, so that normal music CDs can be played through the card and its speakers. The connecting cable can normally only be fitted in one way.
- Insert the card's software installation disc into the floppy drive and run the INSTALL program. This will install all the software files onto the hard disc and will set up the matching Windows applications.
- Test the card's ability to play
    - music CDs
    - digitised sounds
    - synthesised sounds

FITTING A SCANNER

Scanners versions are available for a variety of purposes, common examples being:

- converting simple line drawings into graphics files
- converting photographic images into high-resolution, multi-coloured graphics files
- using OCR (optical character recognition) software to convert scanned printed pages into text files.

Most hobbyists use hand-held scanners where the scanner is rolled over the image to be scanned. Commercial users tend to use either flatbed scanners (where the image is placed on a sheet of glass similar to a photo-copier) or sheet-fed scanners (where a pile of sheets can be automatically fed through the scanner). Flatbeds are useful for quality photographic work while sheet-fed systems are useful for document management systems where scanning piles of correspondence is productive. Models are also available in a variety of resolutions and colour depths. Early models were monochrome whereas current scanners range from 300dpi, 256-grey-scale models through to 2400dpi, 16.8m colour models.

NB: when choosing a model, consideration has to be given to the capabilities of the rest of the computer. Consider scanning a graphics image that is 3 inches square. If this is scanned by a 300dpi, 256-colour scanner, its storage capacity can be calculated as -

900 dots horizontally x 900 dots vertically	= 810,000 dots
256 colours, so each dot requires 8 bits; image needs 810,000 x 8	= 6,480,000 bits
divide by 8 to get the answer in bytes; 6,4800,000 /8	= 810,000 bytes
divide by 1024 to get the answer in kilobytes; 810,000 / 1024	= 791k

However, for a full A4 sheet at 2400dpi with 16.8 million colours (ie 24-bit), the calculation is

11.65" x 2400dpi x 8.3" x 2400dpi x 24 / 8 /1024 /1024 = 1592Mb

This single file requires huge storage space and provides huge memory problems in trying to load and manipulate the image in paint and photo-retouch packages. Careful thought has to be given to the use of scanners before choosing the specification.

The fitting mostly requires the installation of an interface card, unless a parallel port model is purchased - or a SCSI model is purchased to connect to an existing external SCSI interface. The first steps in the fitting are the basic ones already outlined in page 335. The additional steps are:

- Alter the card's base address, and/or IRQ setting if these clashes with an address, or IRQ already in use on the computer. Utilities such as Sleuth, Checkit or Windows 95 Device Manager/Properties will list addresses already in use.
- Insert the card into a spare expansion slot and secure with a screw.
- Insert the card's software installation disc into the floppy drive and run the INSTALL program. This will install all the drivers and any software files such as OCR programs onto the hard disc.

For SCSI models, there is no extra card and the scanner's cable is plugged into the external SCSI connector at the rear of the computer. The scanner's SCSI ID will need to be set up with jumpers. Ensure that the scanner is properly terminated.

With parallel port models, the scanner's cable is plugged into the computer's parallel port.

FITTING A CD-ROM

Many applications, such as Corel Draw and Windows 95, are now available on CD-ROM as well as floppy disc format.   CD-ROMs also are used to supply shareware, clip art, databases, dictionaries, encyclopaedias, games and a wide range of multi-media files (sound, animations, graphics).   The range of CD-ROMs is growing rapidly.

SELECTING

The choice depends on the performance and facilities required. The following decisions are required:

STANDARD

The standards of CD ROMs are explained in the chapter on Discs and Drives and the correct specification (eg Green Book, White Book, Blue Book) has to chosen for the use required.

SPEED

Like a hard disc, the speed of a CD-ROM can be measured in terms of its access time and its data transfer rate. The performances of different models vary greatly, with a seek time of 250ms being the best option, 300ms being acceptable and 350ms or greater being for budget use only.   Similarly, different units have varying data transfer rates, from single speed to ten times standard speed.

PHYSICAL TYPE

CD-ROMs are available in both internal or external models.   If the machine has a spare front 5.25" drive bay (as in, for example, a tower or mini-tower model) then the user has the option of having an internal unit fitted. Otherwise, the external model can be fitted. With both models there is a further choice, as the CD-ROM can be connected to the motherboard in several ways.   See the chapter on Discs and Drives for interface details.   The correct model and interface have to be purchased.

OPTIONS

Some CDs support Kodak Photo-CD to store processed photographs on CD discs.   In addition, some models further support *'multi-session'* working, which allows users to have new photographs added to the disc and be viewable; a non multi-session model will not be able to access any files added to the original set.   Most CD ROMs will play normal audio CDs.   Models come with either top-loading or caddy-holding methods of holding the disc in the drive.

FITTING

Carry out the first five steps described on page 335.   The steps thereafter depend on the type of CD-ROM unit bought.

INTERNAL

- Choose the machine's drive bay and expansion slot that allow the connecting cables to reach both components without undue strain.
- Remove the front blanking plate; this is usually a plastic plate that can be popped out.
- Install the CD-ROM into the guides and firmly press into place.
- When the front of the ROM unit is flush with the front of the computer casing, secure the unit to the casing with the screws provided.
- Connect one of the spare power connectors on the power loom to the CD-ROM.   This has a unique shape and can only be connected one way round.
- Fit the controller card, or sound card, into the chosen expansion slot on the motherboard.
- Connect the ribbon cable between the CD-ROM and the card.   This carries the data and control wires and the connectors only connect one way.
- If the computer has an audio card, connect the audio cable between the CD-ROM and this card.   This cable carries the audio from the CD-ROM to the card and is keyed to only connect one way.

EXTERNAL

- Remove the blanking plate from a spare expansion slot.
- Fit the host adapter card into the expansion slot and screw the card to the computer casing.
- Refit the case cover and screw into place.
- Plug the CD-ROM cable into the host adapter's external socket.

INSTALLING SOFTWARE

The following steps apply to both internal and external CD-ROMs.

- Replace the computer cover and re-insert the machine's power cable.
- Install the device driver to CONFIG.SYS.
- Update the AUTOEXEC.BAT file.
- The above steps may be carried out with the install disc supplied with the CD ROM.

- The CD ROM would normally be designated as the 'D' drive. If the machine is fitted with other devices (a RAM drive, extra hard discs, tape backups, etc.) the CD ROM will be designated the next free unused drive letter. If this takes the drive beyond the default set of A-E, the AUTOEXEC.BAT file will have to have a line inserted to include the new drive letter (LASTDRIVE=F).

TESTING

- Insert a CD in the CD's tray; or insert the disc into the caddy and place the caddy in the CD drive.
- Re-boot the machine so that the configuration settings take effect.
- Issuing a 'DIR' command to the new CD-ROM drive (e.g. DIR D:) should produce a directory listing of the inserted CD-ROM.

FITTING A NETWORK INTERFACE CARD

This section covers the fitting of a network interface card to a normal computer, so that the machine can be added to an existing Novell Ethernet local area network that uses ThinNet coaxial cable (the most common method of using a LAN).

SELECTING HARDWARE

The important selection factors are:

Network Type	Ensure that the card is a bus, i.e. Ethernet, card. There are a number of other systems available, notably the IBM token ring network; the cards are not interchangeable.
Bus Width	Normal ISA machines can support an 8-bit (NE1000 range) or a 16-bit card (NE2000 range). The 16-bit card is more expensive but can pass data between computer and card at a higher rate. 32-bit cards are also available and these versions require to be fitted to an MCA, EISA or PCI bus.
Card type	The cards are available in three types - DMA, shared memory and I/O mapped. A mixture of these cards is allowed on the same network.

FITTING

- Carry out the five steps outlined on page 335.
- Check the card's IRQ and address space allocations to ensure that they do not conflict with the allocations for any existing card. Alter the network card's jumpers if necessary.
- Insert the card into a spare expansion slot and secure with a screw.
- Refit the computer cover.
- Fit a BNC *'T-piece'* connector to the interface card's BNC outlet socket.
- Interrupt the present cabling so that card is added into the bus; this will require an extra length of cable with BNC plugs.

NB   Unless the wall connection is a make-before-break type (eg Safertaps) then breaking the bus connection will bring down the network. The wiring of the cable to the network card should only be carried out when there is no activity on the network.

INSTALLING SOFTWARE

The computer only requires two small files to be added to convert it into a network node. These are:

IPX.COM

This file is used to establish the link between the computer and the card. It is hardware-specific - i.e. the code has to be specific to the actual make and model of card in use. Novell supplies a utility to generate the appropriate shell.

NET3.COM, NET4.COM, NETX.COM

The DOS *'director'* - decides which commands are sent to the machines internal command processor and which are sent to the server via the interface card. NET3 is used with DOS 3, NET4 with DOS 4 and NETX with later DOS versions.

TESTING - LOGGING IN

- Enter the command IPX followed by Enter.
- Enter the command NETX (or its variation) and press Enter. This should establish the server's hard disc as the local computer's F: drive.
- Enter F: followed by Enter. This should make the server's hard disc the current drive, present the F: prompt on the local computer's screen and the user should be in the LOGIN sub-directory. At this stage the user is not logged into the system and cannot move from that directory.
- Enter the 'LOGIN' command followed by the server name (if there is more than one server on the network), the user login name and password when prompted. This should let the user into the network server with the security provisions already set up by the network supervisor.

FITTING A SERIAL PORT

There are a variety of reasons for fitting a new serial drive to a computer. These are:

- Upgrading a slower model with one a faster model (see the chapter on Data Communications).
- Replacing a faulty serial card.
- Fitting a serial card to a new motherboard.
- Adding a second serial card to the computer.

Most cards are provided with two serial outputs and one parallel output. The first steps in the fitting are the basic ones already outlined in page 335. Each of the fitting options is carried out with slight differences and the remaining steps to be followed are detailed separately.

UPGRADING/REPLACING A CARD

- Unscrew and remove the old card from its slot. Place the card to one side and retain the screws.
- Since this is a replacement card, the IRQ and I/O addresses already allocated to the old card should work with the new card. Check that these have not been changed from the standard addresses as shown in the chart. Utilities such as Sleuth, or Windows 95 Device Manager/Properties will list addresses already in use If the addresses have been altered for any reason, the new card should be set those addresses (usually by setting jumpers - consult the card's instructions).

Port	I/O Address	IRQ Address
COM1	03F8	IRQ4
COM2	02F8	IRQ3
COM3	03E8	IRQ4
COM4	02E8	IRQ3
LPT1	0378	IRQ7
LPT2	0278	IRQ5

- Insert the new card into the empty expansion slot and secure with a screw.

FITTING A FIRST CARD

The fitting instructions are identical to those above except that consideration has to be given to the addresses for the other components being fitted to the motherboard. A computer may wish to work with a number of serial devices (eg mouse, modem, scanner, serial printer) and these should not share the same addresses. If the mouse, for example, is to be set to COM1 with IRQ4 then a modem or scanner card would have its jumpers set for other I/O and IRQ addresses from the list above.

ADDING A SECOND CARD

A second serial card would only be required if the computer was to interface to more than the two serial devices supported by a normal card. The problem with a second serial card is that of avoiding address clashes. The chart above shows that while COM1 and COM3 have different I/O addresses, they have the same IRQ setting. This may not be a problem where devices are never used simultaneously (ie a scanner on COM2 is never used at the same time as a modem on COM4). Where devices require to be used simultaneously, (eg a mouse and a modem) they cannot share the same IRQ as the computer would not know which device to service. Since most computers do not require two parallel devices, one of the COM ports could use its IRQ address if it is not already in use. So, for example, COM2 could be 02F8/IRQ3 while COM4 could be 02E8/IRQ5.

CONNECTING A MOUSE

The mouse can be connected to the computer in a number of ways, as long as the appropriate driver is used. The alternative connection methods are:

- Using the computer's serial port, either COM1 or COM2, as the connection device. This is simple to install and use and is an almost universal option (a few manufacturers, such as Amstrad and Commodore, have their own dedicated mouse and interface connectors). The only potential problem is that the existing serial port might be required for another present or future purpose, such as servicing a printer or modem. Since serial ports come in 9-pin and 25-pin varieties, an adapter might be required to match the mouse to the particular computer.
- Using a dedicated mouse interface on the motherboard. This has a socket into which the mouse cable is plugged. Mostly, this is of the PS/2 6-pin outline, with the exception of Amstrad and Commodore. Converters are available to match a mouse to a PS/2 type port.
- Using an add-on card that plugs into a spare expansion slot. This may be the only option, if the existing serial port is occupied. Unfortunately, a valuable expansion slot is used up this way. Since a special card has to be bought, the bus mouse is also more expensive. With an add-on card, check that it does not use IRQs (hardware interrupts) currently in use by other devices in the machine; check with the manual or use MSD. Adjust the mouse card's jumpers if necessary; check the card's installation notes for guidance.

- Using a cordless connection between mouse and computer. A number of these devices use infra-red light or radio waves as the transmission medium, rather than a length of cable. The infra-red models need to have the beam of the mouse pointing at the receiver, while the radio model only need be in the general local vicinity to be picked up by the radio receiver. Radio-linked mice, such as the Logitech MouseMan Cordless, allow for one of 8 channels to be selected. This is insufficient for a large office and machines sharing the same radio frequency can expect interesting interference problems! These are not commonly used.

MOUSE DRIVERS

The translation of the incoming data stream into screen activity is carried out by a special piece of software called a *'device driver'* that has to be installed before the mouse is used (See the chapter on PC Configuration). The mouse driver might be a file called MOUSE.COM that can be included in the AUTOEXEC.BAT file or it might be automatically installed by the application package. Windows, for example, has its own mouse device driver, MOUSE.DRV. Installation is normally automatic, with the user perhaps being asked whether the mouse is to be used with the COM1 or COM2 port. When a mouse is purchased, it will include a disc containing the device driver and probably some drawing utilities. The most significant mouse standards are the Microsoft and the Mouse Systems standards. Virtually all mice conform to the Microsoft standard and many also conform to the Mouse Systems standard. If the mouse is not Microsoft-compatible (e.g. models such the Logitech Series 9), then the driver supplied with the mouse must be used. Using the wrong driver may produce erratic results. Windows allows the sensitivity of the mouse and other details to be set by the user (see the chapter on Windows configuration).

FITTING A ZIP DRIVE

One model of the Iomega ZIP drive is supplied as an external model with a parallel port connection and is fitted very easily:
- Unplug the printer cable from the LPT1 connector at the back of the computer.
- Plug the ZIP cable into the LPT1 connector.
- Plug the other end of the cable into the ZIP drive's rear socket marked 'ZIP'.
- Plug the printer cable into the ZIP drive's rear socket marked with a printer symbol.
- Plug the drive's power supply into the mains and the supply's output into the drive's power socket.
- Run the install program supplied on a floppy disc by Iomega. This can be run through DOS or through Windows.
- Install the utilities supplied on the 'ZIP Tools' cartridge supplied by Iomega.

The above instructions provide a permanent host for the ZIP drive. However, the drive can be carried to another computer. Running the 'guest' program on the floppy allows the new computer to use the cartridge without having to install the driver or tools.

WINDOWS 95

The *'Control Panel'* has an *'Add New Hardware'* option which invokes an installation wizard to select and configure new hardware, prompting for installation discs if required.

Clicking the *'System'* icon in Control Panel displays a *'System Properties'* menu from which the *'Device Manager'* option displays a list of existing hardware. Clicking on a hardware item displays the menu shown. The *'Resources'* option displays the current I/O and IRQ settings. If the *'Use automatic settings'* box is unchecked, the values can be altered. In the example shown, Windows 95 reports that no conflict has been detected between this device and others.

The *'Port Settings'* option allows the baud rate, parity and flow control to be altered. The *'Driver'* option displays the software drivers that handle the device.

The *'General'* option displays information such as the detected manufacturer of the device.

System Selection

Choosing the correct computer system is a difficult decisions to be made by home and professional users alike. This is due to the thousands of different products and their ever-changing specifications. Any book, by the time it is published, is out of date in terms of hardware/software specifications and prices. However, the approaches to evaluating, choosing and purchasing hardware/software remain unchanged.

If cost is not a problem, then there are few other problems. The user can simply purchase the most powerful computer incorporating the latest technology, a large screen, high resolution, colour monitor and a high definition colour laser printer. Suitable extras might be a colour flat-bed scanner, video and sound cards and a high-speed modem. This setup covers virtually all possible uses and mainly exists as an ideal. For most individuals, and certainly most companies, there are severe financial constraints and expensive equipment is only purchased if it is absolutely essential. Therefore, the selection of computer systems becomes a vital process, as purchasing mistakes might prove costly.

The considerations are not solely technical - there is little point in buying a machine with every conceivable bell and whistle, if it is always breaking down and the technical support from the manufacturer is poor. Questions of warranty and after-sales service can be as important as the technical specifications. When choosing equipment, there is no 'correct' answer - there is only a correct choice for a particular set of circumstances. For example, a 20" colour monitor is entirely unnecessary for use with a computer used for normal text-based programs such as fleet control, many databases, network servers, etc. On the other hand, for some graphic-based programs - such as CAD (computer aided design), professional DTP, map drawing, etc. - a large-size monitor might be an essential purchase. The needs of different parts of an organisation are different; the accountant may require a wide-carriage dot-matrix printer, while the typing pool requires a high-quality laser printer. This means that the final decisions must be based on knowing what equipment is available and on understanding what is suitable for each situation. The main stages of the selection process can be defined as:

- DEFINITION OF NEEDS
- EVALUATION OF PRODUCTS
- PURCHASING POLICY
- POST-DELIVERY ACTIVITY

Companies may well divide these into further sub-activities. For example, the evaluation process may involve both the technical staff (to evaluate the technical specification) and financial controllers (to evaluate purchasing, running and maintenance costs).

DEFINITION OF NEEDS

The definition process can be treated as two separate, although linked, stages:

- define the purpose of the purchase
- define the equipment to meet that purpose

In many cases, the demand may be for a multi-purpose machine; the users may require to have word-processing, spreadsheet and database facilities on each machine in the office. In other cases, a single machine may be required to only run a single package, such as computer aided design software. The important starting point is that <u>software needs determine the hardware requirements</u>

If the general-purpose computer is based on running Windows products, there will be greater demands on the machine; the machine will need more extended memory than would be required on a computer only running DOS-based applications. If a database is to be regularly, then a fast hard disc will make the machine more productive. In the CAD case, extensive screen activities are involved in continually re-drawing the intricate designs and specially fast video cards would improve that machine's performance. The two examples will probably also have different requirements for add-ons; the first case may only require a simple dot-matrix printer, while the second case may require an expensive plotter.

RATIONALISATION

The exact number of machines and the exact software requirements have to be determined as the first priority. This may be a matter of negotiation, since users may well wish to have more software on their machines than they will normally use. Since most packages cost hundreds of pounds, over purchasing of software is extremely wasteful. If a number of machines are in the same room, then perhaps only one computer should be fitted with the software that users rarely use and this machine can be shared by users when required.

LOCAL AREA NETWORKS

If many users require access to the same packages, and especially if they require access to the same sets of data, consideration should be given to placing these machines on a local area network. This involves cabling the machines together so that they are all able to share the one version of each package and the one version of the communal data. The licence for multiple users on a network is generally appreciably cheaper than buying multiple copies to place on each individual machine.

CREATING A LIST

A list of equipment requirements should be provisionally agreed as the basis for the preparation of the detailed list of hardware and their specifications. In the light of the evaluation stage results, there may be some amendment to this list, due to financial or other constraints. Indeed, the hardware definition stage might also force a review of needs, due to technical considerations.

HARDWARE DEFINITION

The next part of this chapter concerns itself with the relative merits of different computer components as an aid to decision making. For more details on a particular topic, the appropriate chapter can be read. To make an informed decision, the full range of facts must be available for comparison. These facts will include product specifications, independent reviews and reports from user groups. Hardware decisions are required on the items listed and guidance is given as to their respective merits for specific purposes.

CASE TYPES

A first consideration is the environment for using the system. The options are:

TOWER   This type has a large, vertical case with plenty of space inside for the inclusion of  extra equipment.   The case should have extra drive bays, so that CD ROMs, extra hard discs, etc. can be easily fitted. The main board used in these models should have plenty of unused expansion slots, so that extra equipment cards can be plugged in. This is the first choice for a system that carries out a lot of the office's extra activities.   Examples of this would be using the machine as the server in a local area network or using the machine as the office's main resource for fax cards, modems, scanners, tape backup, etc. The unit normally sits on the floor and the monitor sits on the desktop. Now supplied in AT and ATX forms.

 MINI-TOWER   This type has a vertical construction as above but is not so tall. It can store less than a tower but is more expandable than the average desktop machine. It is a good compromise for size and expandability. It usually sits on the desk top with the monitor close by.

DESK TOP   This is the most common of all case types and is a horizontal box of varying dimensions, on to which most users place the monitor.

LOW-PROFILE   This is a smaller *'slim line'* version of the above, specially miniaturised to occupy less desk space; they are often also of the *'small footprint'* variety, i.e. they have smaller breadth and depth dimensions than ordinary desktop machines and therefore take up less of the desk area. They are neat machines and pleasing to the eye but they have a major drawback with their expandability. Since the case is of a low profile, there is not enough height in the machine to plug any expansion cards straight into the board's expansion slots.   A special *'plane'* board has to be fitted vertically into one of the expansion slots. The expansion cards then plug horizontally into one of the expansion slots on the plane board. This normally results in fewer slots being available in low-profile models and, in some cases, the power supply has to be unscrewed to allow the extra cards to be fitted.   Unless future expansion of the machines is ruled out, this would not be the first choice for office machines.

PORTABLE   These machines are about the size of a portable typewriter and are  designed for use with internal batteries, the car's 12 volt lighter socket or a mains adapter. This means that they are very portable and are in regular use by those who require computing facilities away from the office. They have small screens built in to the case lid and these are inferior to standard monitors, particularly for prolonged use.

NOTEBOOK   A notebook is an even smaller version of the portable and is around the size of an A4 sheet of paper.   Unlike the portable, they are small enough to carry in a briefcase along with other material and are now more popular than portables.

CPU OPTIONS

The type and speed of the computer's CPU have a great bearing on the system's ability to handle tasks. The difference between different chips and chip speeds becomes more noticeable with the increasing complexity of software. For example, Windows runs substantially better with a Pentium-based machine than with a 486 machine. Programs designed to take full advantage of the Pentium Pro code will only give this extra performance to those who purchase Pentium Pro machines.

NB The available choices for machine CPU types are covered in the chapter on Computer Architecture and should be considered again at this stage.

OTHER CPU FACTORS :

Processor Upgrade Options : Some computers allow the CPU to be removed and replaced by a more up-to-date version. This may involve buying a computer whose motherboard supports such an upgrade option. Often, the upgrade is as not effective as a newly purchased system, since the other components in a new machine (ie disc speed, bus type, video cards) will have improved greatly since the older models was phased out. However, upgrading does provide a degree of *'future proofing'* - i.e. it allows the machine to partially keep up with new technology without the expense of being completely replaced.

Chipsets : The CPU is supported by a *'chipset'* on the motherboard. The set of supporting chips are designed to handle memory and peripheral interfacing. The older chipsets are cheap but support only basic facilities such as EDO memory while the more expensive later chipsets support BEDO, SDRAM, USB, etc. See the chapter on Computer Architecture for more details.

Portables : These machines are mainly battery powered and therefore require low-power version of CPUs. The older portables only lasted around 3 hours on one charge of the internal batteries but the newer chips are even more low-powered to allow the machine to run for up to a full day on a single charge.

MOTHERBOARD OPTIONS

FACILITIES

For those concerned with future-proofing their machine, consideration should be given to purchasing computers that support DIMM sockets and the new Universal Serial Bus.

EXPANSION SLOTS

Each computer has a main board which has a number of extra slots into which additional hardware boards can be fitted. These are known as *'expansion slots'* and the more that are provided, the more expandable the machine becomes. Typical cards to plug into these slots are modems, hard disc controllers, video capture cards, sound cards and cards for the control of electronic apparatus. These slots are provided for different card types and a typical computer will offer a number of PCI slots and a number of ISA slots. If the machine is likely to have a range of add-ons fitted, the number of expansions slots provided on a motherboard is important. In addition, the points made about low profile cases might further restrict the actual number of cards that can be fitted - even in a machine with several free slots.

EXTERNAL PORTS

The machine should be supplied with at least one parallel port, for the printer, and two serial ports, one for the mouse and one for add-ons such as a modem. Some computers have a dedicated, built-in mouse port in the form of a PS/2 socket. Some motherboards provide enhanced serial ports for faster data transmission when using modems. Similarly, some motherboards also provide EPP (Enhanced Parallel Port) bid-directional parallel ports so that parallel port devices such as scanners and external hard discs will provide a faster performance.

MEMORY OPTIONS

SIZE

Machines are provided with a wide variety of memory amounts installed. The amount of memory required for a particular machine can be stated at the time of placing the order, or extra memory can be fitted at a later date as an upgrade (see the chapter on upgrades). Many DOS-based programs are designed to run in the normal 640k user memory supplied as standard on all machines. If this software is the only software to be used on the machine, then a basic memory configuration can be bought - i.e. one without any extra expanded or extended memory. Some DOS software can make use of any expanded memory or extended memory fitted in a machine; if the machine does not have this memory, the program still runs but at a less efficient rate. So, if a computer is destined for prolonged use on such software, it should be fitted with the necessary extra memory. The memory requirements of a particular application will appear on its specification; this is printed in the application's manual and is usually printed on the box packaging. If the computer uses Windows and Windows-based applications, the machine will need lots of extended memory. The minimum memory expected by many Windows applications is 4Mb and can be as much as 32Mb. Windows can run on less memory but is too slow for commercial efficiency. Conversely, the more extended memory that is fitted, the more efficiently Windows applications will run.

TYPE Both expanded memory (EMS) and extended memory (XMS) are used to allow computers to break out of the 640k user restriction imposed by the IBM original architecture. EMS was available as an expansion slot add-on card but has disappeared from new machines. Most new software, and all Windows software, is designed to use extended memory. DOS allows extended memory to be configured to act as expanded memory, for those occasions when older software is required to be run.

SPEED The memory chips fitted on current machines normally have an access time of 70ns, with poorer systems having an 80ns access time. Older systems used 100ns memory but this is no longer supplied with new models. The most efficient modern systems have memory access times of 60ns. Of course, these times have to be viewed in conjunction with the CPU speed, as previously mentioned. The presence of wait states on main memory reflects on the quality of motherboard and the CPU in use. A memory system should require no wait states for the greatest machine throughput.

FORMAT Most modern motherboards use 72-pin SIMMs as a means of holding memory chips. This system also allows easy upgrading of memory, should the need arise. The user simply purchases extra memory modules and inserts them in unused slots.

CACHE MEMORY This is a small block of ultra-fast memory that is inserted between the CPU and main memory to greatly speeds up data transfers, particularly with databases. It is available in 64k, 128k and 256k and 512k cache sizes. 64k and 128k sizes are suitable for DOS packages and 256k or 512k is best for Windows applications and Pentium machines.

MONITOR OPTIONS

SIZE Normal supplied size is 14" and this is adequate for general purposes. The supplying of 15" monitors is also common and provides an improved viewing area for the user. For graphics applications such as CAD, artwork, multimedia and DTP, a larger size screen may be necessary. These are normally 17" and 20" models.

RESOLUTION Most machines are now supplied with SVGA (800 x 600 pixels) monitors and new software is written to this standard. Of course, older software was developed before SVGA was common and such software cannot take advantage of the improved resolution. On the other hand, specialist graphics software is capable of working at very high resolutions (1024 x 768, 1280 x 1024 or higher) and an SVGA monitor will enable the user to take advantage of the improved detail.

DOT PITCH A dot pitch of 0.28 is more general for SVGA work. If affordable, a 0.25mm pitch is preferred for high resolution work.

REFRESH RATE The higher a monitor's screen refresh rate, the less will be the flicker and the less will be the risk of eyestrain for users spending prolonged periods at the machine. A refresh rate of 70Hz or 72Hz is satisfactory.

VIDEO CARDS If a machine is to be used for Windows applications or extensive graphics work, a high performance video card or Windows accelerator card should be bought. However, a card that is optimised for Windows often slows down DOS applications. If only occasional Windows work is envisaged, a normal video card is preferable. For normal work, an ordinary card with around 1Mb of on-board memory should be sufficient; for software working to higher resolutions, a card with at least 2Mb of on board memory should be purchased.

OTHER FACTORS If a machine is to be used for prolonged periods, or placed in an environment with bright light or shiny surfaces, an anti-glare screen should be fitted to the front of the monitor. If a machine is in regular use, or is positioned next to other staff, a low-radiation model should be purchased. If a portable or notebook computer is in regular use, a separate monitor should be purchased, so that the user can connect the machine when appropriate (e.g. a salesperson may use the notebook with its small screen to collect orders during the day and then connect to the large external monitor for calculating and summarising information back at the hotel or head office). An FST monitor (flatter, squarer tube) provides a screen that maintains its clarity for a longer period than the conventional tube. It has no convergence problems and it is an ideal monitor for intricate design work.

HARD DISC OPTIONS

SIZE The purchase should be based on the fact that most computers use up more disc space than first predicted. Calculation of the disc's size should not be a simple sum of all the expected hardware, since each application will generate its own sets of data. A machine used in a typing pool, for instance, may well result in the production and storage of scores of letters every day. A hard disc size of 200Mb may be sufficient to store a number of DOS-based applications but it may not be large enough to store the resultant data files. If Windows applications are to be used, then a much larger hard disc size will be required - a

500Mb or even 1Gb may not be enough to store all required applications and data.   A single Windows application can require upwards of 40Mb of hard disc space just to store its program files.

TYPE   The current choices of drive type are the IDE, EIDE and SCSI systems.   The IDE drive is the one that is supplied as standard with computers and is a fast system at a reasonable cost.   EIDE is faster than IDE and is quickly becoming the standard drive offered on new machines. SCSI drives are even faster but are significantly more expensive. As a consequence, they are normally only available as an optional extra.   SCSI drives are a likely choice for multimedia and video editing activities.

SPEED   The speed of a disc is measured in average access time and can range from 9ms to 18 ms.   If a disc is rated in excess of 18ms, it is probably old stock.   For applications that are *'disc-bound'*, i.e. use a lot of disc access such as databases,   a fast access time can have a significant effect on the machine's overall performance.

BIOS   The BIOS chip is a key component in the system and well-known manufacturers like AMI, Award and Phoenix are safe choices.   These manufacturers ensure that the code in the BIOS chip is compatible with new hardware developments.   Key questions are the ability to handle the speed of the system, compatibility with the CPU and its support chips (normally known as the *'chipset'*), the ability to configure the BIOS (usually with a hotkey combination during bootup), the ability to handle large hard discs and provision for password protection of the system.   Another important consideration is the set up of multiple hard discs on the system.

The hard disc in a system is recognised from data held in the machine's CMOS.   This data can be taken from pre-stored data in the BIOS chip (if the set which matches the drive happens to be stored), or can be from a user-defined set of data.   Some BIOS chips only allow one user-defined set of data (type 47) while others allow more than one set (e.g. types 46 and 47).   If a disc drive is set up according to a user-defined set, then any second disc drive that is added must be of the same type as the first drive - if there is only support for a single user-defined type.   Where the BIOS supports more than one user-defined type, drives of different types can be fitted.

FLOPPY DISC OPTIONS

QUANTITY :   Most machines will provide a single 3.5" disc drive as standard.   If a machine has to be compatible with older machines using 5.25" drives, then the new computer should have a second floppy drive fitted.   If there are no compatibility questions, a machine may be ordered with two 3.5" drives where there is likely to be a regular need to make copies of discs.   Using one drive for the source disc (the one to be copied) and another drive for the destination disc (the disc to be copied on to) makes copying a simple process with no need to constantly swap disc in and out of the same drive.

CAPACITY : In most cases, the disc drive is a HD (high density) model - i.e. it can read and write to both HD 1.44Mb and DD 720k floppy discs.   Since DD floppy drives cannot read the high density discs, they are less flexible.   Purchasers should check that they are being provided with high-density drives.

MISCELLANEOUS OPTIONS

POWER SUPPLY :   A power supply has to be able to handle the current needs of the equipment fitted in the computer case - i.e. the motherboard, hard disc, floppy discs and any cards plugged into the expansion slots such as disc controllers and video cards.   The supply also has to cope with any future add-ons that are plugged into the expansion sockets such as modems, etc.   Additionally, the supply has a wiring loom that provides a few spare power connections.   These are left floating around in the case and can be used to power up add-ons which do not connect directly to the expansion bus. An example of this would be a CD ROM.   A computer power supply of 200W would be needed if the machine is expected to host extra equipment.   For a tower machine used as a network server or power workstation, a 230W or 250W would be more appropriate.   Another consideration with power supplies is their safety, since they handle mains voltages.   The supply should have a safety kitemark or other seal of approval.

KEYBOARD   :   An otherwise good machine can be spoiled by a cheap and nasty keyboard of an unknown brand. The machine should be purchased with a known brand name such as Keytronics or Cherry.

MOUSE   :   A poor mouse, with a sticky and jerky operation, hinders Windows operations and a quality mouse should be purchased with the machine.   More and more DOS-based programs are making use of a mouse and a smooth model will improve productivity as well as tempers.

PRINTER :   Quality, and cost, is on a rising scale in the following order - dot-matrix printers at 9-pin, 24-pin and 48-pin, ink jets and lasers at 300dpi, 600dpi and 1200dpi.

EXTRAS :   These may include scanners, modems, sound cards, video capture cards, etc.

TECHNICAL CHECK LIST

Purpose for Machine	
Case	Tower / Mini-Tower / DeskTop / AT or ATX form Low Profile / Portable / Notebook
CPU	Type : Pentium / Pentium MMX / Pentium Pro / Pentium II Speed : 90MHz / 100MHz / 120MHz / 150MHz / 200MHz / 233MHz / 266MHz Upgradeable : Yes / No
Chipset	FX / HX / VX / TX LX
Memory	Size : 8Mb / 16Mb / 32Mb / 64Mb / 128Mb Speed : 60ns / 70ns Cache Size : None / 256k / 512k Fitting : SIMM / DIMM Type : DRAM / EDO / SDRAM
Hard Disc	Size : Interface Type : IDE / EIDE / ESDI / SCSI-2 / SCSI-UW Access Time : 9ms / 10ms / 12ms / 13ms BIOS supports LBA Yes / No
Floppy Disc	Quantity : One / Two Capacity : 1.44M / 2.88M / ZIP drive / JAZ drive
Monitor	Size : 14" / 15" / 17" / 20" / 21" Resolution : 800x600 / 1024x768 / 1280x1024 / 1600x1200 Dot Pitch : 0.31mm / 0.28mm / 0.25mm / .22mm Refresh Rate : 70Hz / 72Hz / Higher Radiation : Standard / Low radiation FST : Yes / No Anti-glare screen : Yes / No Energy saving : Yes / No
Video Card	Windows accelerator Yes / No 3D accelerator Yes / No Card matches monitor : Yes / No
Ports	Serial : 1 / 2 Fast Speed Yes/No Parallel : 1 / 2 Enhanced Yes/No PS/2 Mouse: Yes / No
Power Supply	Capacity : 200W / 230W / 250W Safety marked : Yes / No
Mouse	Required : Yes / No Type : BUS / PS/2 / Mouse Card
Printer	Dot-Matrix : 9-pin / 24-pin / 48-pin InkJet : Laser : 300dpi / 600 dpi / 1200dpi Colour : Yes / No LAN compatible : Yes / No
Extras	
Warranty	1 year / 3 years / 5years Back to base / On site / Collect and Deliver / Replacement
Make	
Model / Price	Model : Price : £

EVALUATION

For a large contract, or a likely repeat contract, a thorough evaluation process would be carried out. This is aimed at pinpointing problems in advance and thereby preventing future difficulties. The evaluation process should include:

- EQUIPMENT TESTING (reliability, compatibility)
- EQUIPMENT COSTING (purchase costs, installation costs, training costs, running costs, maintenance costs)

EQUIPMENT TESTING

RELIABILITY

The single biggest factor in commercial computing equipment is reliability. This is even more important than the raw speed of a system. If a system breaks down, data may be lost or be temporarily inaccessible. This could have severe consequences for the organisation and must be taken into account during the purchasing of new equipment. Check whether the manufacturer / supplier is running a quality control system to BS 5750 accreditation, or to the ISO 9002 quality assurance standard. In addition, any reputable dealer will be willing to demonstrate equipment. Where a large order is involved, the dealer should be willing to loan equipment so that a thorough test can be carried out. As a minimum, the dealer should offer a 30-day money-back guarantee if the equipment is not suitable. This time should be used to check the machine performance under all possible conditions - running databases, number crunching, graphics, etc.

Many items of equipment are tested by manufacturers who produce figures on the likely running time before there are any problems. This is the MTBF, Mean Time Between Failures, and is measured in thousands of hours. Equipment with a high MTBF rate is likely to run with fewer faults than equipment with a lower rating.

COMPATIBILITY

Another important factor in a purchase is its compatibility with current and new hardware and software. Typical questions are:

- Is the current equipment PC compatible? If a company is currently equipped with Apple Macintoshes, purchasing PC equipment will pose problems of using each other's files. This may not be a problem if the Macs are only used for graphics work while the PCs are restricted to clerical or commercial work.
- Is the speed of the new machine's CPU too fast for the existing old software in the company? If there is a heavy investment in existing software, this may be a problem. Many computers provide a *'turbo'* button to reduce the computer's clock speed and allow older software to be run.
- Is it a UK version? Sometimes bargain hardware and software are non-UK versions being dumped.
- Does new software read old data? Ensure that working data import/export facilities exist.
- Does new software run on intended old machine? Consult the software's minimum requirements. This is particularly true for Windows software.
- Remember that an MCA bus needs MCA cards, a PCI card needs a PCI bus, etc..
- Is the machine's CPU an Intel-compatible? A CPU chip should act exactly like an Intel chip, since software assumes that a 100% Intel is in use.

EQUIPMENT COSTING

The cost of computer hardware and software is not the price paid for their purchase; there are a great many extra factors to be considered. These include:

PURCHASE COST

Many dealers reduce the advertised price of their products by omitting components from the package. Typical *'extras'* may be such essential components as monitors and hard discs. So, check the exact items included in any quoted price. Items to confirm include monitor, DOS, Windows, mouse and any bundled software. Ensure that there are no hidden extras.

INSTALLATION COSTS

For a simple, single computer purchase, there may be no extra cost; the machine may be set up by the dealer as part of the delivery, or it may be installed by company support staff.

For larger or more complex purchases, there are other considerations:

- The time required for installing and testing multiple stations and their software

- The time and material involved in installing a local area network of machines
- The amount of software customisation required. This may be programs specially written by a software house or application packages customised to companies needs. In both cases, time is required to fully test out the software.
- Duplication of effort when running the old manual system and the computerised system concurrently. This may be required until the robustness of the new system is proven.
- Any extra costs, such as improved seating or desks, or alterations to the office lighting.

RUNNING COSTS

The organisation has to budget for the future replacement of faulty or obsolete equipment. This involves estimating the useful life span of the new purchases and the likely costs for replacements at the end of that period.   In addition, an estimate has to be made of likely annual consumables such as discs and toner or ribbons for printers.

MAINTENANCE COSTS

The costs do not end when the systems are bought and installed.   Provision has to be made to keep the systems running as smoothly as possible, with as little loss of processing time as possible from breakdowns.   The main considerations are:

WARRANTIES

Most warranties last a year, with a few dealers offering two or three year warranties.   The first year usually covers all parts and labour and the type of cover thereafter has to be checked. Some, for example, only provide parts cover in the second and third years.   Also, the conditions of the warranty vary and the most common arrangements are:

BACK-TO-BASE

This is a cheap option for the supplier and the user. The repair is carried out at the supplier's premises reducing labour costs and delivering a cheaper maintenance contract.   However, these policies have negative features:
- loss of use of the machine for days
- risk of damage in transit
- costs in preparing the crate for transporting to the supplier

This option is suitable for computers that are not in regular use or handle low priority work.

ON-SITE

An on-site policy is an expensive option since it includes the payment of engineer's travelling time. It is a useful option for users as it involves little disruption and the symptoms and operations are more easily explained to the engineer.   The guaranteed response time - i.e. the time delay before a visit - should be confirmed.   Of course, a fast response time, does not guarantee a fast repair and the item remains unusable during that period.   This option is suitable for medium to high priority items.

REPLACEMENT POLICIES

For a price, a replacement, or 'swap out' policy can be obtained. The defective item is replaced with a working equivalent while the repair is being carried out (either on-site or at the supplier's premises) . This allows the organisation to continue with the minimum disruption.   Faster response time to effect the replacement are more expensive than slower responses.   This is the best solution for essential items such as printers, peripherals, network servers, etc.   In the case of defective computers, replacing the machine usually results in the data on the defective machine being temporarily unavailable - unless the data is transferable to the new machine, or the computer is a network node using centralised data.

MAINTENANCE CONTRACTS

When the normal guarantee period expires, some suppliers provide an extension to their cover and this cost should be confirmed.   If there is no policy of extending maintenance cover, terms have to be sought from a separate maintenance company.   In both cases, the terms of the service (i.e. on-site, back-to-base or temporary replacement) have to be considered.

OTHER SUPPORT

Some manufacturers provide lifetime telephone support for their machines and the availability and quality of this should be checked (e.g. the times the service is available and whether software, peripherals and network problems are included).   Others provide customer support for the first year and charge thereafter. This may be on an annual charge basis or on a per-call basis.

Finally, if a local area network is established, a network supervisor has to be trained and given time to administer the system.

TRAINING COSTS

A factor often overlooked in the costing process is the adequate training of the staff expected to use the new hardware and software. The cost of training soon repays itself in increased productivity. The degree of training required for personnel has to be determined (e.g. some staff to a basic level and others to an advanced level) and costed.

PURCHASING POLICY

The company should have a set of rules on general purchasing and they will mostly apply to computing purchases. These rules may include:
- Dealing directly with the computer manufacturer; this cuts out the middle man and lowers prices - a system known as *'Direct Sales'*.
- Choosing a company with a known track record.
- Placing orders that are conditional on specified delivery times, pricing, an agreed returns or refunds policy.
- Keeping a copy of all material - adverts, order forms, invoices, receipts, correspondence and records of telephone conversations.

No goods should be charged for until they are despatched.

If personally buying, use a credit card, as buyers are covered by the credit card company's insurance scheme if the supplier ceases trading before the goods are dispatched.

POST DELIVERY

When the system arrives, the contents of all the boxes should be checked and tested.

CHECKING

The organisation should have a system for checking and documenting the receipt of all incoming goods. Failure to deliver in time is a breach of the supplier's contract and it may be that the lateness renders the equipment useless. In such a case, the box may be returned to the supplier. If the goods are in time, equipment testing can proceed. At its simplest this may be only a checklist to compare and sign if correct. The first check will be to see that the goods have arrived within the required time. . Each item is given an initial visual examination to check for obvious damage and to ensure that the item is of the type ordered - e.g. correct model, size, capacity, etc. If the item is present, correct and apparently undamaged, the checklist will be ticked against that item.

TESTING

Computer equipment should not be placed in a storage cupboard; it should be tested upon arrival. The extent of testing will depend upon the apparatus. The minimum checked should be on basic functionality - i.e. does the printer actually print, do all the keys on the keyboard work, does the monitor display a satisfactory screen. Further checks can be conducted where required - e.g. do all the printer emulations work, does the monitor handle all the required resolutions, etc. All testing must be carried out within the manufacturer's instructions.

If the system is in any way incomplete or non-functional, the supplier should be contacted immediately. Speed and accuracy in reporting any discrepancy or damage is important. Suppliers must deliver the goods as advertised and purchasers are protected by consumer law. In many cases, the initial contact with the supplier will be carried out by the technician, so that the technical details can be clearly explained. The technician should also inform the administration of his/her own organisation since any legal and financial consequences will be pursued by them.

CONSUMER LAW

The main points of the Sale of Goods Act are:
- Goods must be accurately described
- Goods must be of merchantable quality
- Goods must be fit for the purpose for which they have been sold

The main consumer laws are the Consumer Protection Act, the Fair Trading Act, the Sale of Goods Act, the Trades Description Act and the Supply of Goods and Services Act. For example, if goods are bought unseen, the Mail Order Code of Practice recommends that the user is able to return the goods within 30 days if they are not suitable. In this case, some dealers charge a fee when goods are returned, called a *'re-stocking fee'*, and the consumer may have to pay the transit charges.

Data Communications

There has been a great expansion in demand for communication between computers to allow a variety of data sharing and mailing facilities. Within an organisation this is met by creating multi-user systems that connect PCs via a local area network or a Unix system. The demand for communications within an organisation has been matched by the demand for individuals and organisations to communicate. This communication may remain within a town or may stretch between cities or across the globe. A wide variety of services have been developed to handle the following facilities:

> Speech, file transfer, FAX (including high volume, high-speed Group 4 FAX), voice mail, LAN connection, information and database services, telemarketing (e.g. home/catalogue shopping), image transfer, videoconferencing, e-mail, electronic newspapers, remote surveillance/ security/ monitoring/ diagnostics, telemetry (reading meters from a distance),   EPOS/data transfer, home banking, teleworking, teleconferencing, remote training, remote learning, distributed processing and video on demand services.

BASICS

Within a computer, most data is moved round in parallel format on the various internal buses. Between the computer and the average printer, the connection is also parallel. Parallel systems allow the maximum amount of data to be transferred at any given time. However, this is not practical over long distances as it would require many separate wires for each connection, making the link extremely expensive.   Consequently, most long-distance connections are made using serial transmissions. The actual link may consist of telephone wires, coaxial cable or even fibre optic links. Nevertheless, the data is being carried one bit at a time.   The data travelling along the computer bus in parallel format has to converted into a stream of bits to be sent out of the computer.   This can be carried out in two ways:

- Data is sent to a converter chip mounted on the computer's motherboard. The chip is called a *UART* (Universal Asynchronous Receiver Transmitter) and it sends the serial data out of the computer's serial port.
- Data is sent to a converter chip that is mounted on a modem card fitted in an expansion slot inside the computer. The serial data is directly used by the rest of the modem card's electronics.

The conversions work in both directions, so that data can be transferred both in <u>and</u> out of the PC.

INTERFACES

An interface is the point of connection between two pieces of electronic equipment. To communicate properly, the devices must both conform to the same specification. The specification will include the following requirements, with the examples in brackets being for the RS232 interface:

MECHANICAL	Covers the physical elements such as the connection type (eg 25-pin, pin layout) and cabling type (eg a 15m maximum between devices).
ELECTRICAL	Covers the signal voltage levels passing between devices (eg -5volts to -15volts representing a logic 1) and the way that the data is passed (eg serially, synchronously, asynchronously).
FUNCTIONAL	Covers the purpose of each signal (eg carrying data, sending requests, detecting the condition of connected devices).
PROCEDURAL	Covers the control and timing of signals between devices (eg handshaking procedures).

Practical international standards exist for both analogue and digital transmissions and these issues are covered in the following pages.

TERMINOLOGY

The following terms are commonly used in describing communication equipment:

DTE   Data Terminal Equipment. A device that can send/receive data. Usually the microcomputer or printer.

DCE   Data Communications Equipment (mostly now called Data Circuit Terminating Equipment).
A device that facilitates serial data communications. From a user point of view, this is usually a modem.

DSE   Data Switching Equipment.   The equipment used to route a call when there is no permanent link between two stations.

SERIAL PORT

The serial ports are detected at power up and their addresses stored in memory.   The normal base address for COM1 is 3F8h, COM2 is 2F8h, COM3 is 3E8h and COM4 is 2E8h. Prior to DOS v3.3, only two serial ports and 3 parallel ports were supported. Since v3.3, four serial and four parallel ports are supported, although some older BIOS routines only test for two serial ports. The port addresses in use on any particular computer can be found by using the MSDOS MSD utility.

The PC uses a standard known as RS232C and is implemented as COM1 and, if fitted, COM2. An updated version known as RS-232D meets CCITT V.24, V2.28 and ISO IS2110 standards.

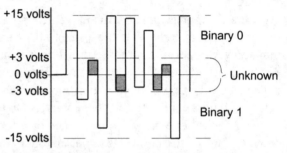

The letter 'T' being sent down a serial cable

PHYSICAL CHARACTERISTICS

The serial port is situated at the rear of most PCs. Some PCs, particularly portables, use 9-pin D-type connectors for the serial port. A large number of PCs use 25-pin D-type connectors. If the computer is 9-pin and the device is 25-pin - or vice versa - then a 9-pin to 25-pin adapter or a 9 to 25-way cable can be used to make the connection. The connector at the rear of the PC is male (ie has pins) while the cable end is female (ie has sockets).

The RS232 standard was designed to minimise interference on the wires carrying the data signals.

To aid this, the voltages carried are higher than the normal range for digital signals carried inside the PC.

The logic states inside the PC are either zero volts or five volts. With RS232, binary 0 is represented by a voltage of +3 to +15 volts and binary 1 is represented by a voltage of -3 to -15 volts. Ideally, the signals would be +15v and -15v but by specifying a positive and a negative range, allowance is made for signal losses along the line. Voltages between +3 volts and -3 volts cannot be converted to known values. These indeterminate values may be caused by interference spikes or may be the result of losses of signal on the line. They are shown shaded in the diagram. The transition from a bit 0 to bit 1 is represented by a change of voltage on the appropriate output pin.

SERIAL CONNECTORS

The connections for a 25-pin serial port are:

Pin	Purpose	Signal Direction	Signal Name
1	Frame Ground	-	FG
2	Transmit Data	Out	TXD
3	Receive Data	In	RXD
4	Request to Send	Out	RTS
5	Clear to Send	In	CTS
6	Data Set Ready	In	DSR
7	Signal Ground	-	SG
8	Data Carrier Detect	In	DCD
9	+ DC Test Voltage	In	+V
10	- DC Test Voltage	In	- V
11	Equaliser Mode	In	QM
12	Secondary DCD	In	DCD2
13	Secondary CTS	In	CTS2
14	Secondary TXD	Out	TXD2
15	Transmitter Clock	In	TC
16	Secondary RXD	In	RXD2
17	Receiver Clock	In	RC
18	Unused	-	NC
19	Secondary RTS	Out	RTS2
20	Data Terminal Ready	Out	DTR
21	Unused	In	NC
22	Ring Indicator	In	RI
23	Data Rate Selector	Out	DRS
24	Transmit Clock	Out	TC
25	Unused	-	NC

The connections for a 9-pin serial port are:

Pin	Purpose	Signal Direction	Signal Name
1	Carrier Detect	In	DCD
2	Receive Data	In	RXD
3	Transmit Data	Out	TXD
4	Data Terminal Ready	Out	DTR
5	Signal Ground	-	GND
6	Data Set Ready	In	DSR
7	Request to Send	Out	RTS
8	Clear to Send	In	CTS
9	Ring Indicator	In	RI

NOTE
The tables show all the pins for the RS232 standard. In practice, most equipment will use a smaller number of connections, as explained later.

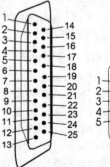

A summary of the signals is:

Voltage	Signal Name	Data Logic	Control Logic
+3 to +15	Space	0	True/High
-3 to -15	Mark	1	False/Low

Note that a positive voltage corresponds to a data bit logic of zero - but oddly also corresponds to a *'true'* logical statement.   Hence, a positive value on *'Transmit Data'* or *'Receive Data'* lines indicates the presence of a zero bit, while a control line such as DTR indicates that it is ready by placing a *'true'* condition (ie a positive voltage) on its line.   This is a source of confusion.   Some books and manuals refer to the *'enabling'* of a control pin as going high (in the sense of the voltage on the pin) while other describe enabling as going low (in the sense of the logic value).   Diagrams will show a bar over a signal to indicate that it is enabled by going low (eg $\overline{RD}$)

MODEMS

All data is held in binary format within the computer.   Ideally, computers would also wish to communicate in binary format.   However, due to the characteristics of long analogue telephone cables, there is too much loss on digital signals for this method to be used.   Telephone lines are designed to carry low frequency signals (from 300Hz to 3,500Hz).   To communicate, the binary data has to be converted into a signal in this audio range.   The device that allows these conversions is known as a MODEM, which stands for MODulator/DEModulator.

The diagram shows two computers being connected via a telephone line.   There is a modem at each end between the computer and the line.   The computer sending the data feeds the modem with a stream of binary zeros and ones.   The modem converts the 'zeros' into one audio tone and the binary 'ones' into a

different audio tone.   These audio tones can then be readily sent along a line.   At low transmission rates this can easily be a standard telephone line.   At the receiving end, the modem carries out the opposite function, converting one tone back to a logic 0 and the other tone back to a logic 1.   In this way, the modem reconstitutes the original digital data sent from the first computer.   This stream of digital information is then fed to the serial port of the receiving computer.

Essentially, the modem is a two-way device for connecting a computer to a telephone line.

The connection to the computer has to reflect the need to send data from the machine to the modem, and vice versa, including flow control of the data.   Modems differ from printers in that they have a range of error-checking methods and, if an error is detected, a request can be made for the re-transmission of the affected data.   Modems can be supplied as internal or external devices.   The internal modem is a card that plugs into an empty expansion slot on the motherboard.   It is generally supplied configured as a COM2 device, to avoid clashes with the existing COM1 port which most computers use as their main serial port at the rear of the computer.   It is likely that the modem will have DIP switches to allow it be configured as COM1 or COM2.   The link between the computer and the modem is via the normal address and data buses.   The communication protocols to the external cable would be set within the communications program, using the Hayes AT command set.

The external modem is supplied as a free-standing unit that sits outside the computer casing. This saves using up an expansion slot on the motherboard, but requires to be fitted to the computer via a serial port.   If the computer's serial port is already used for a printer or mouse, then an extra serial port will have to be added, using a serial card in an expansion slot.   The link between computer and modem is via the serial port and protocols between the computer and modem would require to be established.

MODEM WIRING

The diagram shows the basic RS232 cable connection between a computer and a modem.   Note that the computer's *'Transmit Data'* pin does not connect to the modem's *'Receive Data'* pin as may have been expected.   This is because all connections are described from the DTE (i.e. the computer) point of view.   This means that the pins on the DCE (i.e. the modem) describe their <u>service</u> to the computer rather than the <u>direction</u> of the signals entering or leaving the modem unit.
This could be expressed thus:

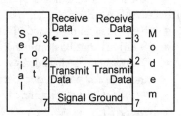

Simplified computer/modem link

Pin	Computer's point of view	Modem's point of view
Pin 2 (TXD)	Data that I wish to transmit	Data from the computer that I must transmit down the line
Pin 3 (RXD)	Data that I wish to receive	Data received from the line that I must pass on to the computer

Similarly, all other pins, such as RTS, CTS and DTR are wired directly to each other, i.e. pin 4 to pin 4, pin 5 to pin and so on.   The distinction between connecting DTE to other DTEs or to DCEs is important to avoid confusion and to prevent incorrect wiring of connections (see later).

NOTE
- This approach mainly applies to modems.   With most other devices, the wiring follows expected practice with the computer's *'transmit'* pin being wired to a device's *'receive'* pin and the computer's *'receive'* pin being connected to the device's *'transmit'* pin.

SYNCHRONISATION OF DEVICES

If two devices are to communicate, it is essential that the receiving device run at the same speed as the sending device. To maintain the synchronisation of the two devices, each has a clock.   The clock at the sending end tells the device when to transmit a bit of data on to the line.   The clock at the receiving end tells the device when it is time to check whether a 0 or a 1 has arrived.   It is vital that the two clocks be kept at the same speed.   If, for example, the transmitting clock sent 1,200 data bits every second and the receiving device checked the line at the rate of 1,300 times a second, the result would be the detection of 100 extra spurious bits of data which would completely disrupt the message.

SYNCHRONOUS MODE

The easiest way to synchronise the two clocks involves the sending clock keeping the receiving clock in step.   This would simplify matters, compared to alternative methods. The big drawbacks are that data has to be sent in a continuous synchronised stream, or in large blocks. This is not always possible or necessary, and it requires another wire between the devices.   It is, however, less prone to distortion than other methods and is therefore usable at higher transmission speeds.   It would not be found as a method for connecting computers to modems.

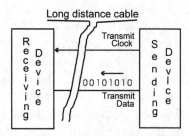

Simplified version of synchronous transmission

ASYNCHRONOUS MODE

The most common method of connecting PCs is the asynchronous method.   Here, there is no equal spacing between each character transmitted.   A character being sent in real time via a keyboard, for example, could be sent at any unknown moment.   For the system to be able to process a character, the hardware has to be told when a character is about to be received and when the transmission of the character has ceased. This involves enclosing the bits of the data with extra bits known as the START BITS

Asynchronous Transmission

1 1 1 1 1 0 0 1 0 0 1 0 1 0 1 0 1 1 1 1 1 . . . 1 0 0 1 1 0 1 0 1 0 1

idle   start   data   stop   idle   start   data
        bits   bit   bits

and STOP BITS.   As the names imply, the START BIT(s) take the signal off the idle state, so giving a kick to the clock.   Incoming bits can now be sampled at the clock rate. The STOP BIT returns the system back to the idle state.   In some systems, an additional PARITY BIT is employed as a means of error checking at the destination.   Conventionally, the least significant bit of the data (LSB) is transmitted first and the most significant bit (MSB) is transmitted last.   The idle state, also called the *'mark'* condition, is a logic 1 while the logic 0 is known as a *'space'* condition.

ADVANTAGES
- Requires less connection wires.
- Best for irregular date streams - e.g. keyboard entry transmissions

DISADVANTAGES
- Start bits can be missed. Data bits are then misread as start bits, producing errors.
- Spurious start bits can be generated by interference pulses on the line and non-existent bits are decoded.
- The system is slowed down, as a proportion of the data bits transmitted carry no useful information - they are for control purposes only.   For example, a system with 2 start bits and 1 stop bit will require 11 bits to transfer a single byte.

PARITY BIT

For the transmission of ASCII files, a 7-bit code is sufficient to cover the ASCII range and the extra bit can be used by the receiving device for error-checking.   The eighth bit is known as the parity bit and communication systems can use either even or odd parity - assuming that both devices know that they are checking by the same method.

EVEN PARITY

The sending device counts the number of 'one' bits in the character to be transmitted. If the number of these data bits is even, as in the top diagram, the parity bit is set to zero. If the number of 'one' bits is odd, as in the lower diagram, the parity bit is set to one.   Thus the total number of 'ones' in the byte should always be even, no matter how many 'ones' are in the character being transmitted. If any of the data bits or parity bits is accidentally altered during transmission, the receiving device can detect the problem by counting the number of bits. If the total is not an even number, there has been corruption of the data. This provides an elementary check for data errors.

Parity Bit

| 1 | 0 | 0 | 1 | 1 | 1 | 0 |

Parity Bit

| 0 | 1 | 0 | 0 | 1 | 0 | 1 |

ODD PARITY

Here, the sending device counts the number of 'one' bits in the byte to be transmitted. If the number of these data bits is even, as in the top diagram, the parity bit is set to one. If the number of 'one' bits is already odd, as in the lower diagram, the parity bit is set to zero.   In this way the total number of 'ones' in the group is always maintained at an odd value.

NOTE   Parity checking is a useful facility but it is not foolproof. For example, two bits in a byte both being altered from zero to one would produce a correct parity check although the data in the byte had been corrupted. In practice, larger blocks of data are examined for corruption (see section later on Error Detection).

FLOW CONTROL

In a half-duplex link, only one of the computers can transmit at any one time. If a modem detects an incoming signal from the remote modem, it must prevent its own computer from transmitting data to ensure that it stays in 'receive' mode.   When the incoming signal stops, the modem can then allow the computer to send its data.. Traffic on the link is regulated by having the modem control the flow of data out of the computer's serial port.   The process of control is known as *'handshaking'* and can be implemented in hardware or in software (XON/XOFF handshaking)

HARDWARE HANDSHAKING

In the diagram, the numbers on the side of the computer serial port and the modem port represent the pin numbers to be found in the device connectors.   When the computer and the modem are connected together and switched on, the computer's DTR (Data Terminal Ready) line on pin 4 on its serial port is enabled to inform the modem that is operational and wishes to establish a connection.   The computer DTR pin is wired to the modem's DTR pin.   The modem responds by enabling its DSR (Data Set Ready) line on pin 6 to inform the computer that it is switched on and ready for use. In effect, DSR means *'Modem Ready'*.   At this stage, both devices know that the other is connected and active so data transfer is

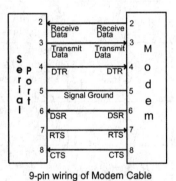

9-pin wiring of Modem Cable

possible.   This is done using the RTS and CTS lines to control the flow of information between the two devices.   A typical transmission sequence might be as below:

1. The computer wishes to send data to the modem.
2. The computer enables (ie high positive voltage) its RTS (Ready To Send) pin to inform the modem that it wishes to transmit. This signal is conveyed to the modem via its serial port's RTS line.
3. The modem has disabled its CTS (Clear To Send) pin (ie there must still be incoming data).
4. This condition is detected by the computer's CTS pin; no data is sent; the machine stays in receive mode.
5. The calling station stops transmitting and this is detected by the modem.
6. The modem enables its CTS line; this is detected by the computer's CTS pin and data is passed to the modem for transmission.
7. The computer sends a stream of text data out of its serial port TxD (Transmitted Data) pin.   This data stream is sent, via the wire, to the TxD pin of the modem.
8. The remote modem detects this incoming carrier and disables its CTS to ensure that the remote computer will read the data and not try to transit.

The CTS line is also used to prevent the computer sending data into the modem when the modem's memory buffer is full.   When the buffer is emptied, the CTS line is used to indicate that the modem is ready to receive more data.   Hardware handshaking is the preferred method for faster modems as there is no unnecessary data being passed around the system, occupying precious processing time.   The hardware handshaking method is also used with a serial printer interface.

XON/XOFF HANDSHAKING

DTR handshaking uses extra wires to carry the control signals; the handshaking is implemented via hardware. The other common method is to use a software handshake. This reduces the amount of connections to only three - one for data in each direction and one common line. While this simplifies the connections between the computer and the device, it leaves no obvious physical means for passing over handshake signals. Yet, the computer still needs to know when transmission can and cannot take place. In this system, specific ASCII numbers, outside the printable range, are used as codes to represent *'stop transmission'* and *'start transmission'*. This is where the Xon/Xoff method derives its name.

When the modem is switched on, it sends out an ASCII character known as DC1. This is the *'transmit enable'* code and is decimal 17 or 11 hex. This code is received by the computer, which knows that it is able to commence transmitting data to the modem. This is the Xon condition. If there is incoming traffic, the modem sends out an ASCII DC3 character. This is the Xoff condition and is 19 in decimal (13 in hex). The computer receives this code and stops transmitting data.

Notes:

- This method is be used with serial printers where the printer sends out an Xoff code when its internal buffer is full. As it prints, it reduces the amount of characters in its buffer. When the buffer has sufficient space, it sends out a DC1 code to the computer which resumes the transmission of data to the printer.
- The ASCII codes DC1 and DC3 stand for Device Control 1 and Device Control 3.
- This method can transmit and receive text files, since the printable ASCII set ranges from 32 to 127. Binary files (ie containing machine code) contain a full range of possible numeric values. This would include the values for the DC1 and DC3 signals, which means that Xon/Xoff is not suitable for transmitting and receiving binary files.

RS232 PINS

A summary of the uses of the main pins on a computer's serial port is shown in the following table.

DTR (Data Terminal Ready)	The computer informs the modem that it is powered up and ready to be active, by switching this pin to an 'ON' state. Most modems require to receive this signal before they will operate.
DSR (Data Set Ready)	The modem informs the computer that it is powered up and ready to be active, by switching this pin to an 'ON' state. Most computer ports require this signal before they will operate.
CTS (Clear to Send)	The modem informs the computer that it able to accept data for transmission, by switching this pin to an 'ON' state. The computer will not send out data while this pin is 'OFF'.
RTS (Ready to Send)	The computer informs the modem that it wishes to give it data for transmission, by switching this pin to an 'ON' state. The modem responds by switching its CTS line 'ON' - unless its memory buffer is full, or it is receiving incoming data..
TXD (Transmit Data)	Carries the data from the computer to the modem's RXD pin, to transmit data. Carries the data from the modem to the computer's RXD pin, to receive data.
RXD (Receive Data)	Receives the data from the modem's TXD pin, to receive incoming data. Receives the data from the computer's TXD pin, to send outgoing data.
DCD (Data Carrier Detect)	Used by the computer to determine whether the modem has an incoming carrier (i.e. whether the line is idle or not). Some communications packages must detect a DCD signal before they will carry on. This signal can be brought from the modem or can be provided locally by a *'wraparound'*. This connects the computer's DCD pin to the computer's DTR pin to simulate an idle condition.
RI (Ring Indicator)	This pin could be used by an auto-answer modem. Its value is raised high when the phone rings. The modem informs the DTE via this change in the RI line and the DTE responds by setting its DTR line high. The modem then answers the call and data is passed from the telephone line to the DTE.
SG (Signal Ground)	This pin is used as the reference for all other signal voltages. So, if a pin swing +15 volts, it means that the pin is 15 volts higher than the voltage on SG. This pin should not be confused with electric earth or Frame Ground (FG).

BREAKOUT BOX

Although the RS232 is an international standard. Every manufacturer uses the same pins to represent the same functions and all use the same voltage levels. However, different devices will use different combinations of these pins. Some devices will be wired as DTEs while others will be wired as DCEs. While all devices will use the TXD, RXD and GND connections, there is a wide variation in the usage of the other pins. This means that some devices will require the use of a certain pin while other devices ignore that pin.   In some cases, pins will required to be connected together before the device will operate; in other cases, the same wiring combination will prevent the device from operating.   Wherever possible, the device manual should be consulted.   The book *'RS-232 Made Easy'* by Martin Seyer, published by Prentice Hall shows the extent of the problem.   It devotes 271 pages to charts and wiring diagrams of different computers, printers, modems, multiplexors, etc.

Often, technicians will be working with equipment that has no documentation or with cables whose internal wiring is unknown.   In these cases, a device known as a *'breakout box'* is invaluable.   As the diagram overleaf shows, this is inserted in the cable between the computer and the device being connected. If the miniature switches are left in their *'on'* setting, every pin is connected straight through from computer to device.   If all the switches are thrown to their *'off'* setting, the computer is completely disconnected from the device.   In this disconnected mode, one row of the LEDs will display the signals that are coming from the computer while the other row of LEDs displays signals from the device.   These LEDs will be 'tri-state' the three states being *'off'* along with positive (green) and negative (red) polarities.

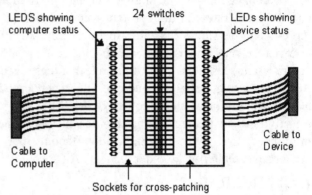

The breakout box is accompanied by a set of jumper leads that have a plug at each end.   When the switches are in their *'off'* state, jumper leads can be inserted into the sockets to connect computer pins to device pins.   For example, a lead may be plugged into socket 2 at the computer and socket 3 at the device end.   This ability to criss-cross leads allows the technician to quickly test various combinations.   When the working combination is determined, a cable can be wired up and soldered as a permanent replacement for the breakout box.

- Care must be taken when buying ready-made cables as some have pins strapped together (ie wired together) inside the plug.   It is common to find pins 4 and 5 strapped, or even 4,5,6 and 8 strapped.
- Serial printer connections are mostly wired as DTEs

READING/WRITING WITH RS232

As mentioned earlier, COM1's base address is 3F8h. This means that the memory location 3F8h is the start of a set of eight bytes that hold information and instructions to control the port's read and write operations.   Each byte is known as a *'register'* and these are numbered from 0 through to 7.   The register table for COM1 is:

Register Number	Memory Address	Status	Purpose
0	3F8h	R/W	Data Buffer - stores the byte to be transmitted or the byte received
1	3F9h	R/W	Interrupt Enable - sets what activities will generate a processor interrupt
2	3FAh	Read	Interrupt ID - for 8250 - holds the cause of any particular interrupt. Also a FIFO Register for the 16550 UART
3	3FBh	Write	Line Control - sets the baud rate, stop bits, parity and word length
4	3FCh	R/W	Modem Control - eg sets the RTS and DTR lines
5	3FDh	Read	Line Status - stores whether there was a parity error, the user sent a BREAK signal, etc.
6	3FEh	Read	Modem Status - stores the status of the DCD, RI, DSR and CTS lines
7	3FFh	R/W	The 'Scratch-pad' - a general one-byte memory store

Register 6 holds the status of the DCD, RI, DSR and CTS lines as single bits in the 3FEh memory location, in the 8th, 7th, 6th and 5th bits respectively.   The following Pascal program reads the Modem Status Register, recovers each required bit value, converts it to a binary value and displays it.

```
PROGRAM read_RS232_port;
USES crt;
VAR
    reading, dcd, ri, dsr, cts : BYTE;
BEGIN
    CLRSCR;   GOTOXY(18,10);
    WRITELN('pin 8    pin 22    pin 6    pin 5');
    WRITELN(' ':18,'DCD       RI       DSR       CTS');
    REPEAT
      reading := PORT[$3FE];
      dcd := (reading AND 128) SHR 7;
      ri  := (reading AND 64)  SHR 6;
```

```
          dsr := (reading AND 32)  SHR 5;
          cts := (reading AND 16)  SHR 4;
          GOTOXY(20,12);
          WRITE(dcd,'        ',ri,'        ',dsr,'        ',cts);
    UNTIL DCD = 99;
  END.
```

Similarly, the Modem Control Register can be written to by the command

```
                        port[$3FC] := outvalue;
```

TRANSMISSION SPEED

The speed of data transfer is measured in bits per second (bps).   The lowest rate of 75bps was used for Prestel connections and the highest current rate is 28.8kbps. Modem rates used to be measured in *'baud'* and the baud rate and the bps rate were identical.   This was only true when one signal on the line represented one single bit of information. Baud really measures the number of frequency changes on the line per second and ignores phase changes, amplitude changes and the fact that the data may be compressed (see later).   All of these techniques mean that more data can be passed down a cable while running at a relatively low baud rate. So, when a modem states that it has a certain transfer rate, it need not be actually producing frequency changes at that rate down the cable. The value given may be the effective rate of transfer taking into account the effect of these techniques. These schemes were only introduced on newer machines, above about 3000 bps, and 'baud' and 'bps' should only really be interchangeable terms for older models. All specifications are now usually given in bps.

UART UPGRADES

The notes on handshaking addressed the problem of the modem being slower than the serial interface. Increasingly, however, the problem is the reverse situation with serial interfaces being unable to transfer data at the rate required for the new fast breed of modems.   Early PCs were fitted with an 8250 type UART and more modern machines use 16450 models.   However, the likely top transfer rate of a 16450 is 19,200 bps while current modems can handle up to 38,400 bps or 56,000 bps.   To meet these greater demands, the computer's serial interface has to be upgraded.   Many top computers now sell their products with the new faster 16550 UART as standard. The 16550 is better as it has an internal 16-byte FIFO (first in first out) memory. The UART can then handle the bytes in the internal queue while more data is being fetched. This greatly speeds up transfer speeds compared to the earlier UARTs with their one byte memory.   The type of UART fitted in a machine can be determined by using the 'Com' option within the DOS MSD utility. This utility reports on the serial ports in use, the type of chip used and the speed and protocol settings for each port.

An upgrade can be achieved in two ways:

- Replacing the current UART chip with a 16550 chip.   This involves removing the old chip from its 40-pin holder and fitting the new chip.   The software then has to be 16550 compatible and has to be configured to accept the new chip. This option is not viable if the UART is embedded in motherboard or other component such as internal modem card.
- Fitting a new fast serial card that has one or more 16550 chips fitted.   Hayes, the leader in modem technology, has produced an 'Advanced Serial Port' card where DMA techniques are used to relieve the CPU of many of its data transfer activities thus further speeding up computer throughput.

MODULATION

The modem translates digital levels into differing tones on the telephone line. This can be achieved by altering the frequency of the tone according to whether each bit in the incoming data stream is a binary zero or a binary one.   This is called FSK (frequency shift keying) modulation.   A V21 system uses 1180Hz to represent a binary zero and 980Hz to represent a binary 1, while a V23 system uses 450Hz and 390Hz respectively.   Another method is to alter the phase of the tone dependent on the incoming data's binary state. Phase modulation would maintain the same frequency for a 1 and a 0 but would shift the waveform in time between the two states.   This is used with V22 systems.   It is also possible to combine both the alteration of the tone's phase and its amplitude (Quadrature Amplitude Modulation) so that a single baud can represent four bits.   So, a 2,400 baud modem can transfer at 9,600bps.

DATA COMPRESSION

Smaller files will be transmitted in a shorter time than larger files.   This saves both user time and telephone connect time.   This has led to the compression of files prior to their transmission.   The compressed file is later decompressed at the receiving end.   The most common ways to achieve data compression are V42bis and MNP levels, known as *'Classes'*.   It should be understood that modem compression systems have to achieve this compression at the point of transmission and this limits the degree of compression.   It is much better to compress a file using a normal file compression package such as PKZip and then transfer this file over the network.   Since packages such as PKZip do not have to analyse the entire file in real time they can arrive at the highest possible compression ratio.

MNP stands for *'Microcom Networking Protocol'* and covers both error detection and data compression. Each higher Class encompasses and expands on the features of the Class below.   Class 1 through to Class 4 provides increasingly sophisticated techniques to reduce time delays caused by transmission errors.   For example, MNP 3 acts like a synchronous modem, removing the need for start and stop bits and thereby increasing throughput.   Microcom's options now extend to MNP 10 which is targeted at noisy systems such as radiophones.   Its transmission speed slows down for noisy environments and returns to faster rates when the noise subsides, thus reducing losses.   Of the MNP range, MNP 5 is the most commonly used and has become a de facto industry 'standard'. Like other compression systems, it uses a pattern recognition algorithm to replace long or regularly occurring strings of data with shorter tokens that represent those strings.   At the receiving end, the communications software reverses the process and rebuilds the original data using the tokens.   Although popular, it only compresses in about a 2:1 ratio.   Consequently, the CCITT chose a different algorithm for its V42bis compression standard.   It uses a more efficient system based a British Telecom version of the famous Lempel-Ziv algorithm, known as BTLV.   With a V34 modem, this can produce an effective data transfer rate of 15,200bps.

ERROR DETECTION

Modem communication over the normal telephone network is always prone to losses due to poor line conditions.   As transmission rates become faster, the losses are increased.   If an interference pulse occurred on a line a 28800bps system it would be affected 24 times more badly than a 1200bps system, since 24 times more data will have been transferred during that time.   Serious attention has to be paid to detecting and correcting such errors.   The Parity bit system described earlier is only a rudimentary check and only applies to ASCII files.   Since most files are not plain ASCII, they will require to use all eight bits of the byte and there will be no parity bit.

CRC CHECKING

Data is transmitted in 'blocks' or 'packets' with a checksum created using the CRC (Cyclic Redundancy Check) method.   When the data is compiled into a block prior to transmission, a mathematical formula (using polynomial codes) is applied to the data to produce a check number that is unique to the data stream in the block.   These check digits are then transmitted along with the data. The receiver stores the incoming block of data in a buffer for examination. The same formula is applied to the data in the buffer and it should produce the same answer as that stored in the check bytes.   If the computed CRC figure accords with the stored CRC figure, the data in the buffer is fit to be passed on and an 'ACK' signal is returned to the transmitting end to acknowledge the receipt of a block in good condition.   If there has been any corruption of the data in the block, or even any corruption of the check bytes, then the formula will produce answers that do not match. In this case, the device will request that the block of data be re-transmitted.   This is done by returning a 'NAK' signal to the transmitting end.

A number of different block transmission techniques and error detection methods are in common use. These are referred to as *'File Transfer Protocols'* and include:

XMODEM

Xmodem sends a 128 byte block of data plus one checksum byte constituted from the sum of all the ASCII codes in the block. It then waits for an acknowledgement that it has been received. The waiting time reduces the data transfer average. All errors are given ten retries before abandoning the file transfer.   It also has a ten second timeout; it sends a NAK signal if has not received any incoming signal after a ten second wait.   A variation known as Xmodem/CRC sends the same 128 byte block but sends two CRC bytes.   This increases the redundant bytes to be transmitted but it improves the reliability of the system and is used in preference to Xmodem where it is available.

KERMIT

This is a long established system used with mini-computers and mainframes as well as PCs.   It also uses a 128 byte block and it provides a header with control information.   Although it is widely available and reliable, it is a slow method.   It is probably the best for noisy lines.

YMODEM

This method still uses 128 byte chunks but it sends eight of these chunks before sending a two byte CRC code that covers the entire 1024 data bytes. The method also pads out the data block until it is exactly 1024 bytes. This is fast since most of the transmission is made up of real data and there is only two bytes of redundant information. However, on a noisy line, corruption of a single bit results in the entire 1024+2 bytes being re-sent. YModem is faster than XModem on good lines but worse on noisy liens. It also allows multiple files to be transferred in the one operation. The user selects the group of files to be transferred and the system sends them all during the one long operation. This is sometimes referred to as Ymodem/Batch.

ZMODEM

The above systems send their block and then wait for an ACK or a NAK from the receiving end before sending another block. They are working in half-duplex mode and this results in wasted waiting time. Many modern methods do not wait for a response between sending blocks. Using a full duplex system, it is still able to receive the ACKs and NAKs when they arrive but further transmissions can be undertaken in the meantime. When an ACK arrives it knows that a particular block has been received successfully, while an incoming NAK indicates an unsuccessful transmission of a block. The system keeps track by using a *'windowing'* system. Each outgoing packet is given a packet number along with the transmission. The incoming ACK or NAK will also have a packet number attached. In the event of a NAK the system knows which packet to re-transmit. The difference between the packet currently being sent and the most recent incoming ACK or NAK is known as the *'window'*. Since a single byte can contain 256 different numbers, there is a limit to the range of available packet numbers and the older number will be reused after they have accomplished a successful transmission. This means that the 'window' covers a small range of the available numbers and is always changing. This gives the name *'sliding windows'* protocol; it is also implemented in the *'Sliding Windows Kermit'* and *'WXmodem'* systems.

Xmodem, Ymodem and Kermit are used at speeds below 9600bps. V42 is used at higher speeds and is implement in a ROM chip in the modem. The V42 standard encompasses the MNP 4 proprietary standard developed by Microcom. It is likely that future extensions of the V42 standard will move away from MNP 4 in favour of LAP-M (Link Access Protocol for Modems) scheme as already recommended by CCITT. The MNP 5 standard combines the MNP 4 error correction facilities with data compression. Like MNP 4 it is most commonly implemented in hardware although some communication packages implement it in software.

STANDARDS

Created by CCITT, The International Telegraph and Telephone Consultative Committee, working under the ITU (International Telecommunications Union) which is organised by the United Nations.

These standards are divided into a number of groups, including:
- the V-series, dealing with telephone circuits
- the X-series, dealing with data networks
- the G-series, dealing with digital networks (digital exchanges, multiplexing, PCM, etc.)
- the I-series, dealing with ISDN (see later)

V STANDARDS

There is a wide range of definitions and the most common ones are shown in the table. The V standards get their name from the first letter of the word *'vitesse'*, the French for speed although not all V standards are concerned with transmission rate. V24, for example, specifies the serial port standard and V42 and V42bis cover error correction. The *'bis'* added to a V number means that it is the second version of the standard. Dataflex, a large UK modem manufacturer, produces VFC models, also known V.Fast Class models, working at 28,800bps. These were introduced prior to the ratification of the V34 standard and there are some handshaking differences between their

V17	Fax 14,400 transmit/receive
V21	300bps transmit/receive. full duplex, dial-up
V22	1200bps transmit/receive. full duplex, dial-up
V22bis	2400bps transmit/receive. full duplex, dial-up
V23	1200bps transmit/75bps transmit, asymmetric duplex, dial-up
V24	The RS232 standard
V27	4800bps transmit/receive. full duplex, leased line
V27ter	4800bps transmit/2400bps receive, half duplex, Group III Fax
V29	9600bps transmit/receive. full duplex, leased line Also 9600bps half duplex Group III Fax
V32	9600bps transmit/receive, full duplex, dial-up
V32bis	14,4000bps transmit/receive, full duplex, dial-up
V34	28,800bps
V34bis	33,600bps - not yet ratified as a standard
V42	Error correction using CRC
V42bis	Data compression using Lempel Ziv

specifications. V.Fast modems can communicate with other VFC models at the top rate but with V35 models they can only communicate at 14,400bps in about 10% of cases.

56k TECHNOLOGY

ISDN lines, as explained later, have been the only mid-band communication links available for those who wish faster data rates than conventional modems, without the huge expense of fast links.   ISDN links provide 64k or 129k data rates.   Nevertheless the pricing policies for ISDN in the UK has led to a slow take-up rate.   Users require to have extra telephone lines installed in their premises, buy dedicated ISDN modems and pay large line fees.   The new cheaper alternative uses existing rented telephone lines and no extra standing charges beyond the normal telephone charges.   The existing modem is replaced with a faster types known as the 'X2' by US Robotics and as 'K56FLEX' by Rockwells.

British telephone exchanges work digitally and communications between parts of the telephone network are digital.   Likewise, Internet Service Providers (ISPs) now use digital links.   Only the cable between the exchange and the subscriber's premises uses analogue techniques.   The audio of a normal telephone conversation arrives at the exchange as an analogue signal and is converted into digital information for use in the main network.   The conversion techniques are covered in the chapter on multimedia.   The audio is converted into 8-bit resolution at an 8KHz sampling rate.   This provides a theoretical data rate of 64k but, according to Nyquist's theorem, the

Communication stages	Existing technology	56k technology
Data stores at ISP	Digital	Digital
ISP to Network	Digital	Digital
Network to Network	Digital	Digital
Network to local exchange	Digital	Digital
Exchange to subscriber	Analogue (tones)	Analogue (data)
Subscriber conversion	Analogue tones to digital	Analogue data to digital

reliable bandwidth of a signal is half its sampling rate.   So, the conversion supports around 32k which explains the previous upper limit of analogue modems.

ISDN adaptors, being digital devices in the first place, do not require analogue to digital conversion and vice versa, and can operate at the full 64k per channel.   56k modems use similar techniques of avoiding analogue/digital conversion losses.   With 56k modems the data, although arriving in analogue format, is viewed as digital data to be decoded.   Since Nyqusist's theorem does not apply (ie there is no audio reconstruction from a sampling rate) the full bandwidth of 64k is available.   In practice, figures up to 56k are achievable.   The modems of Internet Service Providers have to support 56k working before it can be used by subscribers 56k modems.   The 56k transfer rate is only between the ISP and the subscriber which comprises most Internet traffic.   Uploading of data to an ISP is at conventional rates.

ADSL

Asymmetric Digital Subscriber Line (ADSL) is an emerging technology which could become available to over 90% of BT customers if they choose to adopt it.   BT trials have concentrated on video-on-demand services and other interactive services but the technology can embrace the Internet and other communication mediums.   The ANSI working group has approved a standard of 6.1Mbps over standard copper telephone cables.

MODEM COMMANDS

The computer connects to the modem by a single serial connection.   The user will normally interface with the communications package software and will decide on actions by pressing menu options or by clicking on icons or buttons.   Basic user choices could include engaging the telephone line, dialling a number, downloading a file and eventually terminating the connection with the remote station.   A whole range of other options might be required.   For example, some telephone exchanges use the old rotary pulse dialling method while most exchanges use tone dialling.   The user might wish to have the modem's inbuilt loudspeaker turned off or a range of other refinements.   Although the user makes these choices via the software, the computer has to then inform the modem of these decisions.   Since there is only a single serial connection between them, the computer has to send this information in the form of messages along the serial cable.   The modem, in turn, will send messages ('result codes') back to the computer to indicate that it cannot get any dial tone, the dialled number is busy, etc.

As long as the modem and the computer understand and use the same set of messages, there is no communications difficulty with the system.   The most common way to use these strings is to save them with the communications software's setup information.   When the user runs the communications package, the desired command string is automatically associated with the package's corresponding menu and button options.   A default set of commands is offered by most packages and the user can alter them for local conditions (e.g. changing the string from a tone dial system to a pulse dial system).

HAYES AT COMMANDS

A commonly used modem command set is the Hayes AT set developed by Hayes Microcomputer Products.   Like other command sets, the Hayes commands are independent of the speed or performance of the modem.   An old slow modem and one of the latest models can both use the AT command set. Modems described as AT compatibles refer to their acceptance of this set of commands, or a superset or a subset.

THE COMMAND SET

All Hayes commands comprise of a string of characters, both alphabetic and numeric, that control modem functions.   Each individual command sent to the modem is preceded by the letters 'AT' which stands for ATtention.   So, for example, sending the string ATM0 would silence the modem's speaker. The chart shows the display for the default setting offered in the 'Telix' communications package:

```
┌─┤ Modem and dialing parameter setup ├──────────────────────────────┐
│                                                                     │
│   A - Init string ..........  ATZ^M~~~AT S7=45 S0=0 V1 X4^M~         │
│   B - Dialing prefix 1 : ...  ATDT                                  │
│   C - Dialing prefix 2 : ...  ATDT                                  │
│   D - Dialing prefix 3 : ...  ATDT                                  │
│   E - Dialing suffix .......  ^M                                    │
│   F - Connect string .......  CONNECT                               │
│   G - No connect strings ..   NO CARRIER            BUSY            │
│                               VOICE                 NO DIAL TONE    │
│   H - Hang-up string ......   ~~~+++~~~ATH0^M                       │
│   I - Auto answer string ::   ATS0=1^M                              │
│   J - Dial cancel string ..   ^M                                    │
│                                                                     │
│   K - Dial time ...........   30                                    │
│   L - Redial pause ........   1                                     │
│   M - Auto baud detect ....   Off                                   │
│   N - Drop DTR to hangup ..   On                                    │
│                                                                     │
│   Change which setting?        (Return or Esc to exit)              │
└─────────────────────────────────────────────────────────────────────┘
```

The initialisation string is the one that is sent to the modem when the package is first run.   The '^M' string is the equivalent of pressing the Enter key if the string was entered at the keyboard and the '~' characters are pauses.   A comma is also used as an alternative method of obtaining a pause.

The individual components of the initialisation string are explained in the following chart:

Command	Meaning
Z	Used to reset the modem to the factory default settings.
S7=45	Specifies that the modem will wait for 45 seconds after dialling. If there is no connection to the remote station within that time, the modem hangs up the line and sends a 'No Carrier' message to the computer. The range is 4 to 60 seconds.
S0=0	Used to set the number of rings before the modem auto-answers an incoming call. The permissible range is 0 to 255. A value of zero turns off the auto-answer.
V1	Specifies that result codes will be reported in text format. This is used when the communications session is under manual control. With automated systems, the results codes can be reported in numeric format, using 'V0', so that the numbers can be easier interpreted by the software.
X4	Used to enable the full range of result codes and supports both dial tone and engaged tone detection. Other permissible levels are X0, X1, X2 and X3 and are mainly available for backward compatibility with older models and some non-standard telephone systems.

DIALLING PREFIX

The dialling prefix in the example is 'ATDT'.   The 'D' is an instruction to commence dialling and the 'T' instructs the modem to use tone dialling.   If the string had been 'ATDP' it would instruct the modem to use pulse dialling.   Pulse dialling is the default and only has to be given as instruction to the modem if the modem had previously been ordered to use tone dialling.   The software would add the actual number to be dialled to the end of the string. So typical strings might be:

ATD 01292-470310   or   ATD 01292 470310   or   ATD 9,01292 470310

The first two strings are directly equivalent since any dashes or spaces between numbers are ignored.   The third example is for use in offices where the user has to dial '9' for an outside line.   The comma (or '~') is inserted to provide a time delay to allow the office exchange to engage an outside line.

HANG UP STRING

The hang up string is 'ATH0' which is the 'On Hook' condition, the equivalent of replacing a telephone on its rest.   The row of three plus signs switches the modem into 'Local Mode' also known as 'Command Mode'. Generally, the modem wishes to ignore the computer when it is getting on with its communications session.   If a long file transfer is underway it will not wish to be disturbed by the computer and will ignore most AT command strings.   However, there still has to be a way that the user can interrupt a session and this is achieved with the '+++' string.   To prevent accidental triggering (e.g. the data being sent happens to include three plus signs), this escape sequence is only recognised if it is prefaced and followed by a pause.   The default pause is 1 second and this is achieved by the '~~~' string that surrounds the three plus signs.

Other common AT commands are:

F	Sets the speed at which the modem will operate. F1 is for V21, F2 is for V23, F3 is for V22, F4 is for V22bis while F5 is for V32/4800bps and F6 is for V32/9600 working. If the command is set at F0, the modem is instructed to make the connection at the fastest rate available.
I	Instructs the modem to return details of its description and version number.
W	Instructs the modem to wait for secondary dial tone before proceeding to dial out. Used for modems connected to office exchanges (PABXs). This is an alternative to use the use of delays as shown earlier.
&K	Instructs the modem to use a specific flow control. AT&K0 inhibits all flow control, AT&K1 enables hardware (RTS/CTS) control and AT&K2 enables software (Xon/Xoff) control.
\C	Determines the level of data compression.. \C1 operates in MNP class 1 mode and the range extends up to \C5 for MNP class 5 mode.

The result codes returning from the modem to the computer include:

Number	Text equivalent	Meaning
0	OK	The last command executed without error.
1	CONNECT #	A connection is established at 300/300
2	RING	An incoming call has been detected.
3	NO CARRIER	Carrier cannot be detected or carrier has been lost.
4	ERROR	An invalid command has been given.
5	CONNECT 1200	A connection is established at 1200/1200
6	NO DIALTONE	No dial tone has been detected within the specified timeout period.
7	BUSY	An engaged tone or number unobtainable tone has been detected.

MODEM LIGHTS

Many modems have external lights to inform the user of their current state and to reassure the user of the success of the various activities.   When a communication session is

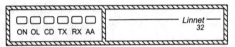

unsuccessful, the lights can be used to determine the likely problem.   The diagram shows the layout of a typical modem front panel although there is a wide variety both in the number of lights used and in the titles different manufacturers give to the same light function.   A normal sequence for sending a piece of data by modem would be:

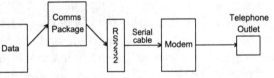

- ○ The communications package fetches the data (from memory or from a disc file) to be sent.
- ○ The data is sent out the computer's RS232 port.
- ○ The data is carried from the computer to the modem via a serial cable.
- ○ The data is converted to tones inside the modem.
- ○ The tones are sent to the telephone line via a plug connected to a standard telephone socket.

The receiving process is a mirror image of the transmitting process with the data coming in the telephone socket, converted to digital signals and being received by the application via the serial cable and the RS232 port.   The modem's lights can indicate which parts of the process are working allowing the user to determine the source of the problem.   An explanation of the each modem light is:

Light	Meaning	Purpose
ON	Power On	The modem is correctly powered up from its power supply. Also known as 'MR' - Modem Ready or DSR - Data Set Ready.
OL	On Line	The modem is holding the telephone connection. This is the equivalent of a telephone being off its hook. Also known as 'OH' - Off Hook.
CD	Carrier Detect	The modem is in touch with a remote station and is receiving its carrier tones. This means that someone has answered an outgoing call, or the user's modem has answered an incoming call. When this light goes out, the link has been broken. Also known as 'DCD' - Data Carrier Detect.
TX	Transmit Data	This light flickers when data is being transmitted out of the modem. Also known as 'SD' - Send Data.
RX	Receive Data	This light will flicker when it is receiving data in from the telephone line. Also known as 'RD'
AA	Auto Answer	This lights when the modem has been configured to automatically answer any incoming calls. This is used where a computer has to left unattended.
HS	High Speed	This light indicates that the modem is working at its highest speed. In some modems, the light flickers for several of the higher speeds.
TR	Terminal Ready	This light indicates that the modem is both powered and in communication with the modem. The computer has sent a DTR signal through the serial port to the modem to inform it that is running a communications package. The modem lights is TR light in response.
RI	Ring Indicate	Indicates the presence of an incoming call. The equivalent of the telephone ringing.
TST	Test	This light indicates that the modem is performing a self-test.
LB	Low Battery	Used with portable modems to indicate that their battery supply is running low.
SQ	Signal Quality	A steady light indicates a good connection; a flickering light indicates a poor quality connection.

DATA LINKS

A range of possible connection methods between communication stations is possible. These include:

SIMPLEX	Data is sent in one direction only. No longer in common use and is mostly now found as a means of driving older printers where no information is fed back to the computer from the device.
HALF-DUPLEX	The link can carry data in both directions but not simultaneously. It is analogous to a CB radio user who has to be either in talk or listen mode at any one time. A computer sends a packet of information and then switches into receive mode to wait for an acknowledgement from the other end. Once received, the computer can go back into transmit mode for the next packet. Used by Xmodem, Xmodem/CRC, Ymodem and Kermit protocols and common in domestic links to a host (eg CompuServe) and small businesses to a main link.
FULL-DUPLEX	The link can carry data in both directions simultaneously. It is analogous to a telephone user who can both talk and listen at the same time. Most modems work in this mode. It permits the use of sliding window protocols, as explained earlier, to speed up transmissions. Used by Zmodem, Sliding Windows Kermit, Sealink and the WXmodem file transfer protocols.

It should be noted that a simplex protocol can be used over a half-duplex channel and a half-duplex protocol can be used over a full-duplex channel.   In a half-duplex modem, the entire bandwidth is available to for use in the one direction. With a full-duplex system, the available bandwidth is divided into two sub-bands.   The two sub-bands comprise the *'originate carrier'* which carries data from the DTE to the DCE and the *'answer carrier'* which carries data from the DCE to the DTE.

BANDWIDTH

Every communications line is only capable of carrying data over a certain band of frequencies.   The range between the upper and lower limits are known as the *'bandwidth'*.   With audio, radio and television applications, the bandwidth is usually measured in Hertz - with one Hertz being a single cycle per second.   So, the bandwidth for transmitting voice may be less than 4KHz while music and colour TV signals may be 15KHz and 8MHz respectively.   With data communications, users wish to know the maximum data rates that a channel can handle and this is measured in bps - bits per second.

MULTIPLEXORS

Many computers or terminals may wish connection to a single computer at a remote location.   If each user was given a separate line to the remote computer, the cost would be unacceptable.   So, one communication channel is shared between different users. This sharing can be achieved in terms of time or of frequency space.   The device used at each end is known as a *'multiplexor'* or *'mux'*.   Its job is to provide a *'transparent'* connection for the user.   This means that neither the user nor the remote computer need know that a mux is in use; it requires no additional equipment or additional software. The local end *'multiplexes'* the channels while the remote end *'demultiplexes'* the channels.

TDM

The *'Time Division Multiplexing'* technique is used to transmit multiple digital signals and it gives each terminal a share of the available line time.   Four terminals are shown sharing the same communication line.   The two multiplexors are synchronised so that both connect to point *'A'* at the same time, followed by both connecting to point *'B'* and so on.   After *'D'*, connection *'A'* is returned to.

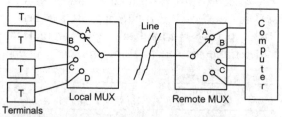

During the connection to each point, a piece of data is transferred over the line.   Each terminal has a series of timeslots when it has exclusive use of the channel.   In the example, each terminal only has one quarter of the line time.   With n terminals, each will have 1/n of the line time.   This needs a communications line with fast transfer rates, with its speed being the total of the combined speeds of the connected slow terminal connections. With a *'Statistical Multiplexor'*, a low speed channel is only given bandwidth on the high speed channel if it has data to send. The sum of the input speeds can now exceed that of the composite channel, since not all low speed channels are normally in use at any one time. To accommodate occasions of every channel wishing to transmit, buffering is used.   This makes most efficient use of the fast link but it cannot support synchronous data, due to the buffering.

FDM

The other technique, known as *'Frequency Division Mulitplexing'*, also conveys a number of different users' data along a single line.   In this case, all the users' data is transmitted simultaneously, with each terminal being transmitted at a different frequency.   This *'broadband'* approach is further explained in the chapter on Local Area Networks.   The communication line used must sufficient bandwidth to cope with the bandwidth of each channel, plus a margin between each channel, known as *'guard bands'*. This is the method used to transmit multiple analogue signals simultaneously.

ATTENUATION

As a signal moves along a communications wire line its amplitude diminishes with every metre. These losses are caused by:

- Heat dissipation. A copper conductor has a finite resistance to the passage of electric current. Thicker wires reduce line resistance but are very expensive.
- Frequency dependent losses. The capacitive effect between the elements of a pair of communication wires leaks the signal across the wires, reducing the signal that arrives at the end of the cable. Higher data rates produces increased change of signal on the line and increased capacitive losses .

Gain or loss is the ratio of the output voltage from a communications line or device (Vout), compared to the voltage fed into it (Vin). It is measured in units of *decibels* abbreviated to *dB*. This measurement is not linear - it follows a logarithmic scale. It is the ratio $20 \log_{10}$ (Vout/Vin).

NOISE

Noise is unwanted electrical signals that exist on the communication channel along with the desired data. As long as the noise stays at a low level there is no serious problem - but when the noise reaches the level where it will be regarded as a legitimate logic level, it will cause false triggering and corrupted messages. The main sources of noise are:

Component Noise - caused by random or unwanted electron fluctuations within both inactive devices (such as resistors) and active devices (such as integrated circuits).

External Interference - caused by everything from natural sources (such as cosmic radiation and electric thunderstorms) to manmade sources (such as radiation from electrical appliances).

Crosstalk - caused by signals from one communication line being picked up on another line. This occurs due to the effects of capacitive and inductive coupling between lines that run adjacently.

PRACTICAL LINKS

There are two main options for connecting to remote stations.

LEASED LINE

Here, BT or Mercury provides a permanent, dedicated cable link between two stations. Since no other person can use the line, there is no waiting; the line is never engaged even at peak times. In addition, the lines are of high quality, providing fewer errors and are usually faster. Of course, they are less flexible as they only connect to a single remote site but are very popular with business to connect different branches. Examples of leased lines are the BT Kilostream, Megastream and Satstream systems. These do not use modems as the connection is digital. Performances are:

Kilostream	2.4kbs up to 64kbps	Electronic mail, slow scan TV, fax, data, voice
Megastream	2Mbps up to 140Mbps	Often multiplexed (i.e. a group of connections share the bandwidth)
Satstream	2.4kbps up to 1.5Mbps	Satellite system used for short term links, remote site access and video conferencing

DIAL-UP LINE

Here, the user is sharing a network of cabling and switching apparatus. Lines are not exclusive but are cheaper due to the sharing of physical assets. Unlike a leased line, the user may often find a line is busy. Dial-up lines also suffer from poorer quality, producing a larger amount of errors. Increased errors require repeat transmissions and, since the user pays for the time used, error time costs money. Faster transmissions also usually result in more errors.

COMMUNICATION NETWORKS

A variety of services are available for data communications over a switched network system.

PSTN

The Public Switched Telephone Network is the normal network used for telephone connections. It is simple and cheap requiring modems to plugged into the system instead of telephones. It is used by a wide range of both private and company users and is the main medium for information providers such as CIX, CompuServe and a wide range of commercial and hobby bulletin boards.

The system is *'circuit switched'*. This means that the telephone exchanges set up a link between the calling and called ends. The switching will be physical with the older Strowger exchanges or will be electronic with modern exchanges. In both cases, once the connection is established, the originating caller has sole use of the cable between both ends. If the caller is in Aberdeen and the called end is in Truro, there will be a connection spanning the entire country that is dedicated to the one call. When the call is terminated, the channel can be used for other connections.

PSDN

The method of switching data traffic in the 1960's and 70's was *'Message Switching'* and this is still used with e-mail systems.   It is a 'store and forward' system, rather than today's real-time transmissions.   Traffic is temporarily stored on disc and is sent on when a link is free.   If there are three intermediate stations along the transmission route, the storing to disc and forwarding is repeated a further three times.   It uses data links inefficiently and allows queues to build up, thus producing bottlenecks.   Messages could take minutes or even hours to arrive.   The modern Public Switched Data Network is a parallel network to the telephone system but is dedicated to data communication.   This is a *'packet switched'* system which means that there is no permanent connection between the two stations during a session.   The data to be transmitted is broken up into smaller chunks called *'packets'* and these are sent to the called end by the best route available at that time.   The cabling between exchanges is used by all connections and the PSE (packet switched exchange)

NETWORK ROUTING

Most traffic travels long distances and passes through intermediate stations along the route.   These intermediate nodes clean up the signal and pass it on to the next chosen station on the route.   Since the data network is a collection of such stations, there are a number of alternative routes that a message could be sent.   For example, a message between Inverness and London may travel one of the following paths:

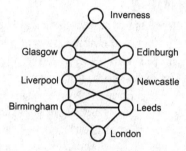

Inverness → Edinburgh → Newcastle → Leeds → London
Inverness → Glasgow → Liverpool → Birmingham → London
Inverness → Glasgow → Newcastle → Birmingham → Leeds → London

or any other permutation.   The performance of the network is determined by the way the links are used. One routing strategy, called *'non-adaptive routing'* or *'static switching'* provides each node on the network with a fixed table of routes.   So, for example, all traffic between Inverness and London must pass through Edinburgh, Liverpool and Leeds.   The Edinburgh node's table would store the information that all messages for London from Inverness should be passed on to Liverpool, while Liverpool table would know to pass that message on to Leeds.   So for every possible source and destination in the system there is a routing table that has been calculated and permanently used by each station.   If a station is added, deleted or altered, all the routing tables that are affected have to be manually updated.

AVAILABLILITY

Non-adaptive routing is an efficient system where traffic demands are relatively light and unchanging. However, it weakness lies in its inability to automatically react to faults in the system.   If the Leeds station broke down, then all traffic that was directed through it would be stopped until the fault was repaired.   This would introduce unacceptable delays, particularly when the lines between other nodes were working perfectly.   The *'availability'* of a station is simply the expected percentage of time that the station will work without problems.   So, a station with an availability factor of 0.9 can be expected to work 90% of the time.   However, the problem is magnified where a chain of stations are involved.   If Inverness, Edinburgh, Liverpool, Leeds and London all had 0.9 availability factors, the overall availability of the system is 0.9 x 0.9 x 0.9 x0.9 x 0.9 = 0.59.   Where stations are connected in parallel (eg Edinburgh and Liverpool are parallel stations between Glasgow and Newcastle) the availability calculation shows a much more efficient system. If one node completely ceases (eg Edinburgh) the other node (eg Liverpool) remains 100% functional.   This improvement cannot be utilised by non-adaptive methods, since the routing only directs traffic to a single node whether that node is functional or not.

CONGESTION CONTROL

Each node is connected to a number of incoming/outgoing connections (the example shows Newcastle connecting to five other nodes while Inverness connects to two).   Since each node only handles a defined amount of traffic at any one time, the system stops sending traffic to a busy node until the congestion eases.   Non-adaptive routing is a wasteful, since one node may congested while another node is quiet.

ADAPTIVE ROUTING

Adaptive routing responds to changes in the system (eg breakdowns, congestion) by automatically altering the traffic routes.   The tables held by each node are no longer fixed; their path information is altered to reflect the current state of the network.   There are two ways of implementing adaptive routing:

CENTRALISED ROUTING

One node on the network constantly collects information on the status of every other network node.   Each change in the system results in the centralised management system calculating the best new routes to maximise the efficient use of the system in its new state.   The new routing tables are then transmitted to each node for updating their routing activities.

DISTRIBUTED ROUTING

With this method, there is no central control and each node carries out its own monitoring, calculation and distribution of routing information.   So, for example, if the Newcastle/Leeds link failed or became congested, Leeds would inform Liverpool and Birmingham.   Each node responds to its own monitoring and to incoming status information by recalculating its own routing tables.

The calculation for routing tables, known as *'shortest path algorithms'*, would take into account the capacity of the alternate links (throughput in bps), the delays of each link, the cost of using each link and the error rate of each link.   The calculation produces the most efficient new route to adopt.

P.C. LINKS TO LARGE COMPUTERS

Data communications allow a P.C. to access the resources of mainframe and other large computer systems.   But mainframes were designed to connect to their own brand and design of *'terminals'*.   A terminal's main function is to transfer the user's keystrokes to the mainframe and to display the mainframe's output on the user's monitor.   The way this is achieved depends upon the design of the terminal and may range from simple ASCII screens to complex graphical screens.   Examples are the DEC VT100 ASCII systems and the IBM 3270 series which include colour graphics display stations. Terminals have no computational power other than that required to carry out their input and output functions - all the real program computation takes place inside the mainframe computer.

When a PC wishes to connect to the larger system, it has to communicate in exactly the same way as that expected by a terminal.   This is achieved by the communications software which allows the user to select a particular terminal *'emulation'*.   The software ensures that communication between the PC and mainframe works identically to that with a terminal.   The mainframe works normally, thinking its communicating with a standard terminal, and the software in the PC does all the conversion work.

P.C. TO P.C. LINKS

Users may also wish to link their P.C. to another P.C. so that communication can take place or so that resources can be shared.   This link can be either local or remote.

LOCAL CONNECTION

Where the PCs are in the same room or office.   This is commonly used for file transfers between a user's desktop computer in the workplace and the laptop computer that is carried around.   Typical users include salespersons downloading current prices and uploading the previous days orders and civil engineers bringing back information gathered on a site for analysis on the office machine.

In these cases, the PCs can be linked together using:

- A *'null modem'* serial cable connecting the two RS232 ports.   The speed of file transfers depends on the maximum data transfer rate of the slowest serial port of the two computers and this speed can be set up using the communications software.
- A parallel cable connecting the two parallel ports.   Data is transferred one byte at a time but the maximum transfer rate may be slowed by retransmissions to transmissions errors.
- Network cards fitted in each PC and linked together with LAN cabling.   This is common with laptops which have PCMCIA card LAN adaptors.   It is also growing in popularity as a means of games enthusiasts playing multi-player games.

Of course, each computer has to run appropriate software to manage the connection.   Examples are:

- Interlink which is provided with MSDOS v6 onwards.   This allows one of the PCs to control the other's resources - files, printers, etc.   This is explained more fully later.
- *'Direct Cable Connection'* provided with Windows 95.
- Laplink which is a stand-alone product where either PC can access the other's files.
- Peer-to-Peer software such as Windows for Workgroups or Lantastic which allow the sharing of each others file and peripheral resources.

Interlink and Laplink are designed for use with either serial or parallel connection between PCs, while network software expects the machines to be fitted with network interface cards and card driver software. Once connected, all the above systems allow file transfers from one machine's discs to the other's drives. With Interlink, the user is in command line mode and has to use normal DOS commands (eg COPY, XCOPY, wildcards, etc).   The other packages are more sophisticated and display the other PC's files on screen so that they can be highlighted, either singly or in groups, for copying.

NULL MODEM CABLE

A modem serial cable has no reversals in the cable wiring. Each pin on a plug is wired to the same plug pin number on the other end of the cable. This approach mainly applies to modems.   With most other devices, the wiring follows expected practice.   The diagram shows a basic connection without hardware handshaking.   The computer's *'transmit'* pin is wired to a device's *'receive'* pin and the computer's *'receive'* pin is connected to the device's

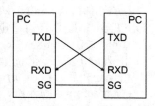

'transmit' pin.   With hardware handshaking, one computer's TXD pin would be wired to the other's RXD pin and vice versa.   Similarly, one computer's DTR pin would be wired to the other's DSR pin and vice versa and one computer's RTS line would connect to the other's CTS line.   Some communication software refuses to work unless its DCD line is set on.   In these case, the RTS and the CTS lines of the first PC should be wired together and taken to the DCD line of the second computer - and vice versa.

These are known as a *'null modem'* cables and they are widely used for transferring files across a serial port with packages such as Laplink and Interlink.

REMOTE CONNECTION

Where the PCs are at different sites, connection can be achieved over the public telephone network using modems at each end.   Again, each computer also requires remote connection software to be installed. The software can provide two separate functions:

REMOTE ACCESS

> Here the incoming PC has access to the remote (known as the *'host'* or *'server'*) PC's resources such as files and peripherals.   The user can download from the host system or can place data on the host system. Usually, either user can initiate the connection thereby making the called station the host.   Laplink is an example of remote access software which can provide file transfers over a modem, even connecting into a remote Local Area Network.   The data rates depend upon the speed of the serial ports, the modems and the quality of the transmission line.   Uses of remote access include:
> - Teleworking - This covers a range of work activities such as an employee working from home, working from another branch, working from a customers premises and even group working with other individuals who are similarly located remotely.
> - Distance learning - Enrolled students can access lessons, upload their course essays and e-mail enquiries to their tutor.   This is an area of much development and the quality of material varies.

REMOTE CONTROL

> Here the incoming PC takes control of the remote PC's activities.   The incoming machine's key and mouse activities control the remote machine and the incoming machine can see the same video output as that being displayed on the remote screen.   This provides opportunities for remote diagnostics and debugging; the problems at a remote machine can be solved without visiting the remote site.   Usually, one of the systems is permanently set up as the host while the other is used as the *'guest'* or *'client'*.   Examples of this software are pcANYWHERE, Carbon Copy and Reachout.   These products also allow remote control over a network so that a any user on the LAN can be directly in communication with, and receive support from, a remote user.

USING INTERLINK

Interlink first appeared with MSDOS version 6 and is a basic PC to PC resource sharing facility.   Consider the case of two PCs, each with an A: drive and a C: drive.   One of the PCs also has a printer attached.   The user without a printer would like to be able to print using the other machine's

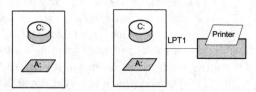

printer.   The user would also like to be able to access the disc drives on the other machine.

The first step would be to connect the two machines together.   This could be via a seven-wire null-modem cable or a bi-directional parallel cable.   The next step would be to run suitable software on both computers.   Interlink only allows one machine to be in control at any one time.   One machine must be set up as the *'client'* and the other must be set up as a *'server'*.   The machine set up as the client has

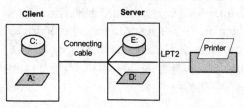

control over the server's drivers and ports, while the server remains unattended.   Machines often have both the client and the server software on their drives so that they can be configured to play either role. Once the software is run on both systems, the user will be able to access two floppy drives, two hard drives and the server's printer.   The exact drive letters allocated to the server's drives depends on those already installed on the client.

In the example, the client machine's last drive used drive letter was C: so the extra drives were allocated to D: and E:.   If the client machine already had two hard drives installed (C: and D:) then the extra drives would be allocated to E: and F:.   The user at the client machine can now treat the 'extra' drives as if they were local to the client machine.   Many of the usual commands will work (eg COPY, XCOPY, MD) but the following lower-level disc commands are not supported:

CHKDSK	DISKCOMP	DISKCOPY	DEFRAG	FDISK
FORMAT	MIRROR	SYS	UNDELETE	UNFORMAT

SETTING UP THE CLIENT

The client machine requires a device driver to be installed, to redirect user calls to its virtual local drives to the actual remote drives via the connecting cable.   It is achieved by adding the line

'DEVICE=C:\DOS\INTERLNK.EXE'   to CONFIG.SYS.

When the client machine is switched on, the driver is installed in memory and the machine automatically attempts a connection to the server.   The following switches allow variations on driver installation:

/NOSCAN   Installs the driver in memory but does not attempt to make a connection.

/AUTO   Only installs the driver into memory if client is able to establish a connection with the server.

In both cases, the user can run INTERLNK at any time from the DOS prompt.

The CONFIG.SYS file must also provide a LASTDRV command (see section on DOS) so that sufficient spare drive letters are available for allocation to the redirected (ie the server's) drives.

SETTING UP THE SERVER

If the command 'INTERSVR' is given at the service keyboard, the server machine automatically redirects all its drives to the client machine.   In the above example the hard disc (drive C:) was redirected as the client's E: drive while the floppy drive (drive A:) was redirected as the client's E: drive. The order of redirection can be altered by adding the drive letters in the initial command.   So,

INTERSVR C: A:

would set up the server's hard disc as the client's D: drive and the floppy as the client's E: drive.

Both INTERLNK and INTERSVR support a range of other switches as explained in the DOS help pages.

DIRECT CABLE CONNECTION

Windows 95 has built-in facilities to allow two computers to share files, using a serial or parallel cable. The fastest transfer rates are obtained with computers that have ECP parallel ports.

There are only four conditions to be met:

- Direct Cable Connection is installed.   If it is not installed, it can be added via the
  Start/Settings/Control Panel/Add-Remove Programs/Windows Setup/Communications/Components/Details
  menu options; the box beside *'Direct Cable Connection'* should be checked.
- NetBUI, TCP/IP or IPX is loaded. Check using the
  Start/Settings/Control Panel/Network
  menu options. The Configuration list should show one of these. If not, use the *'Add'* feature to install.
- The *'Client for Microsoft Networks'* is enabled.   The Configuration list should include this feature. If not, use the *'Add'* feature to install
- File and Printer Sharing is enabled.   The Configuration list should show sharing as enabled. If not, click the *'File and Print Sharing'* button and check both facilities.

The first, or 'host', computer is set up using the Start/Programs/Accessories/Direct Cable Connection menu options, to be the *'Host'* with a serial or parallel connection being chosen.   The second computer is similarly set up as the *'Guest'*.

Running

Start/Programs/Accessories/Direct Cable Connection/Listen

sets up the host computer, while

Start/Programs/Accessories/Direct Cable Connection/Connect

sets up the guest computer.   The two computers will now be able to share files.

OSI STANDARDS

Where data has to be transmitted from one location and received at another location, there has to be a set of protocols which ensure that both the transmitting and receiving devices handle data in the same way. These should cover issues such as packet size, the organisation of packet contents, speed of transmission, types of synchronisation and error correction; it must also cover the lowest level issue of how a single data bit is moved - e.g. voltage levels or current loop detection. As long as both sites use the same protocols, data movement is enabled. ˙ Where sites are numbered in millions internationally, as in the superhighway, there has to be an international set of standards. This prompted one description of OSI standards as *"the Esperanto of communications"*.

Networks, both LANs and WANs, were plagued by differing protocols for different proprietary products and this still inhibits the development of communications. The International Standards Organisation (*ISO*) addressed the problem and decided to introduce a model for the design of networks. This was known as the Open Systems Interconnection (*OSI*) model - mostly now known as the ISO/OSI model.

The model seeks to define the functions of the hardware and software involved in networks. It does this by creating seven levels of communication activity, known as *'layers'*. The seven layers, when interacting with each other, comprise the total system. The lowest layer performs the most basic hardware function. Each succeeding layer adds a greater level of sophistica-

Application Layer	- - - - - - - - - -	Application Layer
Presentation Layer	- - - - - - - - - -	Presentation Layer
Session Layer	- - - - - - - - - -	Session Layer
Transport Layer	- - - - - - - - - -	Transport Layer
Network Layer	- - - - - - - - - -	Network Layer
Data Link Layer	- - - - - - - - - -	Data Link Layer
Physical Layer	- - - - - - - - - -	Physical Layer

tion to the process and the interface between each layer is clearly defined. The ISO/OSI model is not in itself a standard - it is more a set of measures to be used in comparing current and new products. For a long time, few products emerged which used this model. This changed when the US and UK governments made OSI standards mandatory for most large government contracts. X.400 (Electronic messaging), X.500 and X.25 are some of the ISO/OSI standards.

THE SEVEN LAYERS

The chart shows the differing levels of complexity handled by each layer.   Layer 1 only works with single data bits while the upper layers handle entire messages. The highest layer is the layer seen by the user (eg e-mail or file transfer) while the rest should be hidden from the user.   The 'station' referred to in the description could be any communications equipment. At its simplest, it comprises a PC and modem. The 'medium' is any form of connection between the stations and covers from a telephone line to a vast switched network.

Layer Number	Layer Name	Information Handled
7	Application	Message
6	Presentation	Message
5	Session	Message
4	Transport	Message
3	Network	Packet
2	Data Link	Frame
1	Physical	Bit

LAYER 1 - PHYSICAL LAYER

The Physical Layer is concerned with moving data between the station and the medium that connects the stations.   It sets up, maintains and disconnects the physical link between the stations.   The layer defines the electrical (ie voltage levels) and mechanical (ie pin wiring) requirements for connecting the equipment to the medium.   Examples of the Physical Layer are RS-232, X.21 and V35.

LAYER 2 - DATA LINK LAYER

Layer 1 only accepts or sends a stream of data bits without paying any attention to the order or meaning of the bits.   So Layer 2 ensures that any corruption of the data stream is detected.   The data to be transmitted is fed into the Data Link Layer and it handles a block of data at a time, called a *'frame'*.   A checksum is added to the frame and the frame is then passed on to Layer 1 for transmission.   The receiving station's Layer 1 detects the incoming data stream and passes it on to Layer 2.   If there is no corruption of the data it can be passed on for further processing.   Layer 2 is also used for flow control and handles transmissions to and from the nearest DSE (data switching equipment).   Examples of the Data Link Layer are Ethernet's CSMA/CD and HDLC (High-Level Data Link Control).

LAYER 3 - NETWORK LAYER

Most communication sessions between computers are not directly wired but are routed through a switched network or even a series of network devices.   Layer 3 adds unique addressing information to packets so that they are routed to the correct receiving station.   The enlarged packet is sent to the Data Link Layer where the error checksum is added and the packet is sent out on to the transmission media (via the Physical Layer).   If a receiving station does not match the desired address the packet is ignored.   If it has the matching address, the data can be further processed.

Examples of this layer are X.25 used in wide area packet switched networks, Novell's IPX and the IP of Internet's TCP/IP.

LAYER 4 - TRANSPORT LAYER

The Transport Layer acts as the interface between the user's activities and the requirements of the data communications network (ie the lower three layers).   The message to be transmitted arrives at the Transport Layer and is often larger than the maximum size of data packet that can be handled by the lower system.   The Transport Layer splits the data into chunks that match the capacity of the network system in use (eg 4k blocks) and adds sequence numbers to each block before sending them to the Network Layer.   On a switched network, the various blocks may be sent via different routes.   The Transport Layer on the receiving end does not care what route the blocks took.   It is only concerned with passing on the incoming blocks in the correct sequence.   If a block arrives out of sequence (eg block 2 is delayed in the network and arrives after block 3) the Transport Layer places the blocks back into sequence.   If a duplicate block arrives (eg block 2 arrives twice) the Transport Layer detects the duplicate block and ignores it.

The Transport Layer, therefore, provides a pipe between systems to exchange data, operating independently of both higher layer application protocols and lower layer network protocols - effectively the link between user applications and the network.

Examples of the Transport Layer are Novell's SPX and the TCP of Internet's TCP/IP.

LAYER 5 - SESSION LAYER

The first four layers were *communications oriented*; they concentrated on the physical network and its rules.   Layers 5 to 7 are 'process oriented' layers.   These are high level protocols to allow two OSI-based models to exchange data - regardless of the physical connecting medium.   The Session Layer establishes, controls and terminates the dialogue between the two user application processes.   It treats the session as a single activity - even although the Transport Layer may have used a number of different connections to complete the data transfer.   The layer also controls the flow of information to match the system currently in use (ie simplex, duplex, half-duplex).   The layer also inserts *'checkpoints'* into the data.   This provides points from which to restart if the two ends get out of step (eg due to a connection failure).

Examples of this layer are Internet's TELNET and FTP and Novell's NETBIOS emulator.

LAYER 6 - PRESENTATION LAYER

The two computers in the dialogue may use different methods of representing numbers and graphical characters.   The Presentation Layer has to ensure that machines with different data representations (eg ASCII 7-bit, BCD, etc) can still pass the same meaning from one user to another.   The data supplied to the Presentation Layer is converted from its existing format into a universal OSI format (known as ASN.1) before being passed to the Session Layer.   When the data arrives at the receiving end's Presentation Layer, it is converted from the universal format into the format used by that particular machine (which may or may not differ from that of the sending machine).   The data, in its acceptable format, is then passed up.   The layer can also provide facilities such as compression/decompression, encryption/decryption and terminal emulation.

LAYER 7 - APPLICATION LAYER

The Application Layer is the link between the end user's application package and the communications system.   As such, it varies from program to program and from system to system.

Examples of this layer are X-Windows, the X400 standard for e-mail, Novell's DOS redirector and remote job entry functions.

OSI SUMMARY

The chart shows the basic functions of each layer when sending a message - each layer processing data and passing it down one layer.   The receive is the reverse process with incoming data being processed and passed up one layer.

Layer Number	Layer Name	Purpose
7	Application	Routes data from application packages into the communication system
6	Presentation	Ensures that machines with different data representations can still understand each other
5	Session	Handles simplex/duplex operations over an entire communications session
4	Transport	Divides data into a series of sequenced blocks for transmission
3	Network	Handles the routing of data to the required station
2	Data Link	Carries out flow control and error checking
1	Physical	Handles the physical and electrical characteristics of the communications network

TCP/IP

TCP/IP - *'Transmission Control Protocol over Internet Protocol'* - is now the most commonly used set of communication protocols.   It is used on the Internet, on Unix systems, on many local area networks, on wide area networks and as a means of connecting dissimilar systems (eg between minicomputers and mainframes).   IP is provided by Novell as an alternative to its own IPX in Netware 4.1 and it is also supported by Windows 95, OS/2 and NT.   As long as a system has TCP/IP it can communicate with any other TCP/IP-equipped system.   This means that a PC can talk to a Macintosh while an Amiga can talk to a mainframe.   Even better, the software is royalty-free - although many commercial products exist. TCP/IP was introduced in the 1970's as a protocol suite to support ARPAnet, the American defence network that developed into the Internet.

The TCP/IP protocols embodies four layers and these broadly compare with the OSI model as shown in the comparison chart.

The TCP component is concerned with the maintaining the dialogue between two computers and keeping data packets in order, detecting any corrupted or missing packets and requesting retransmission.   The

TCP/IP Layer	Corresponding OSI Layers
Application	5,6,7
Transport	4
Internet	3
Network Interface	1,2

IP component is concerned with the routing of packets to correct locations, from local organisations through to regions and then internationally.   The TCP components are a set of communications routines that applications can call upon.   The IP component is another set of routines that the TCP layer uses.   Some applications don't use the TCP and interface directly with the IP routines.

APPLICATION LAYER

The 'standard' set of TCP/IP applications include:

- TELNET - The PC acts like a terminal to a remote Unix machine and the user can access resources in the same manner as a user who was locally connected to the system.   With the growth of the World Wide Web, the use of Telnet has dwindled to use with universities, libraries and some bulletin boards.
- FTP - The *'File Transfer Protocol'* allows files to be copied from one computer to another over the Internet.   Users can directly use FTP as shown later.   In Web sites, the FTP facility may be hidden from the user who clicks on a *'Download File'* icon without realising that this invokes the FTP.
- E-MAIL - This allows for the transfer of messages between computers even if one of the two machines is switched off.   Instead of sending the message directly to the remote computer, it is sent to a *'mail server'* which stores it for future reading by the remote station.   The remote station can, at any time and from any location, log in to the mail server and check for any messages that have been left.   The two common protocols for e-mail are SMTP and POP (Post Office Protocol).
- NFS - The *'Network Filing System'* allows one computer to act as a file server to another remote computer. Since TCP/IP is machine-independent, a PC is able to use a remote Unix computer to save and recover files.
- REMOTE EXECUTION - A computer in one location initiates an activity on another remote computer.

These applications are under user control and consist of high-level activities (eg send this e-mail, fetch a copy of that file).   They pass down their needs to the lower layers which work how the tasks and operations will be achieved.

TRANSPORT LAYER

With TCP/IP, information is sent in blocks known as *'datagrams'*.   For most TCP/IP use, a packet and a datagram are the same size of 500 octets.   An octet is 8 bits - ie one byte; however, since some systems do not work on an 8-bit word, the octet is the preferred way to describe size.   A packet and a datagram are not always the same size.   For example, the X.25 interface creates data packets of 128 bytes and so several packets would be required to transport a single datagram.   On the Internet, there is no distinction between packets and datagrams and they are often used interchangeably.   Messages from the Application Layer are broken into datagrams and transmitted separately.   Since packets can get lost in the system or can arrive out of sequence, the task of maintaining the correct data flow rests with the Transport Layer .   This layer re-arranges out of order packets and ensures that lost packets are automatically re-sent.

INTERNET LAYER

All datagrams from the TCP are routed through the IP component of the system.   This means that datagrams from the Transport Layer are sent down to the Internet Layer for processing and sending on to the Network Interface for transmission.   The Internet Layer is concerned with getting the datagram to the correct location, as passed on to it from the Transport Layer along with the datagram.   The addressing system for each location is covered later.   The Internet Layer adds its own header to the datagram, works out the best route to take for delivering the packet (ie directly or via a gateway) and passes it on to the Network Interface.

NETWORK INTERFACE
This layer transmits and receives datagrams over a particular physical network and is specific to the characteristics of that network.   Datagrams could be sent via WANs, Ethernet LANs, Token Ring LANs, etc.

SLIP/PPP
IP is designed for routing in a large network.   Many home and small business users only own a single modem and dial up into the Internet via a normal telephone line. The server that they dial requires all the sophistication of IP for its connection to the Internet but only requires a simpler system to interface to the dial-up line.   The first protocol to allow telephone/modem connections to TCP/IP was SLIP (Serial Line Internet Protocol) and an improved version is PPP (Point to Point Protocol).   This consists of a driver to the computer's serial port and out to a SLIP or PPP server.

PORT NUMBERS
A server processes many different stations at any one time.   Each process has to be identified with a particular station to ensure that datagrams do not get hopelessly mixed.. Each process is identified by a 16-bit port number and this is generated by the application process initiating the contact. The more popular server applications are allocated their own port numbers eg FTP is port 21 while TELNET is port 23.   A computer wishing to initiate a file transfer would specify its own port number as, say, 2345, while requesting a remote port 21.

WINSOCK
The combination of address and port number is referred to as a *'socket'*. The TCP/IP software is known as the *'protocol stack'* and is implemented as either a DOS TSR, a Windows 3.1 DLL or a Windows 95 VxD.   The Trumpet Winsock package and Windows 95 both provide both SLIP and PPP drivers.   Winsock (Windows Socket Application Programming Interface) is the interface between a Windows version of a client application, such as FTP, and the TCP/IP protocol stack.   The application calls routines form the Winsock DLL and it calls routines from the TCP/IP drivers.   Each commercial implementation of a TCP/IP protocol stack will supply its own WINSOCK.DLL to work with its own proprietary brand of stack.   In this way, writers of applications do not need to know what stack is in use, since it will always communicate with the Winsock DLL and let it carry out the operations to the stack.   Applications that do not make use of Winsock have to write their own interface to the TCP/IP protocol stack.

DATACOMMS APPLICATIONS
World-wide data communications has opened up a wide variety of new applications for industry, commerce and domestic users.
These can be broadly described as:

- Remote Control   - remote monitoring, diagnostics, debugging, surveillance, process control.
- File Transfer   - the copying of files from a remote computer (see later).
- E-mail   - the sending/receiving/storing/categorising of messages between users.
- Information services - the availability of a mass of data, from test reports to train timetables.
- Consumer applications - multi-player games, home shopping, video-on-demand

The facilities also include:

User Groups	Company information	Press cuttings
Multi-user chat sessions	Government statistics	Electronic shopping
Hardware/Software News	Research papers	On line games
Software Fixes, updates	Consumer reports	Travel information
Latest drivers	Newswire services	Downloading of programs
Distance learning	Databases	Encyclopaedias
On-line magazines	Market information	Classified adverts

Access to these facilities can be provided in four ways.

INTERNAL ORGANISATION
Some of these services, such as remote control, file transfer and e-mail can be contained within an organisation; all activities are between the people and resources of that organisation.   The equipment used is exclusive to the organisation (eg internal networks, external leased private lines) and is not accessible by other users.

HOME BULLETIN BOARDS
Hundreds of non-commercial bulletin board systems (BBS) are established in the UK. Many are set up in the Sysop's (System Operator) bedroom where a telephone line is attached to an auto-answer modem.   The

computer has large hard discs and CD ROM players to provide a wide range of files for downloading. E-mail and specialist groups are supported by the linking up the facilities of various bulletin boards and real-time chat provisions are provided within a single BBS. These are run on a hobby basis with no charge or charges based on covering the cost of running the service. Some of these boards are of long standing but many spring up and close down again after a short time.

COMMERCIAL BULLETIN BOARDS

These are extended versions of home BBSs and charge users via '0891' telephone numbers. These allow new users to test whether they like such services before moving on to a permanent commercial contract. For regular users, they offer fewer services and usually are much more expensive than any other method.

COMMERCIAL PROVIDERS

These services are run for profit and offer a greater range of facilities than the non-commercial bulletin boards. The company allows access to the resources on the payment of fees which may include the following elements:

Standing charge	A monthly or quarterly charge, regardless of the amount of usage
Time charges	Charges based on each minute of connect time
Page charges	Charges for particular pages (eg financial information)

The three main commercial suppliers are:

COMPUSERVE

CompuServe is based in the USA and has around 4.5 million subscribers. Its strength lies in the breadth of its services. CompuServe offers the most comprehensive range of topics after the Internet, covering sports, health, travel, entertainment, news, weather, shopping, finance and computer support (with 800 of the main hardware and software suppliers enrolled). CompuServe's provides its own user conferences, known as *'Forums'* and a range of shareware programs, drivers and other files are available for downloading.

CompuServe files for downloading are stored under appropriate forums and can be located with the *'FIND'* icon. The search facility is not very sophisticated and it does not have the vast range of files available on the wider Internet. Internet search engines such as Alta Vista and Lycos provide more detailed searches which support complex logical syntax. The searches can also be for user e-mail addresses.

It also provides a range of e-mail services to other CompuServe members and, using gateways, to users of AOL, MSN and those with Internet connections via Internet Service Providers (ISPs). In common with most Internet software, it allows binary files (eg executable code) to be attached to e-mail text messages. This allows programs and text descriptions and messages to be contained in a single e-mail. CompuServe also provides access to the wider Internet. CompuServe customers can access all Internet facilities in addition to CompuServe's exclusive facilities. Internet users can access a limited range of CompuServe facilities.

Since the Internet is an international collection of networks, many of the sites are designed using languages other than English and even the English-speaking sites will have non-UK content (eg Australia, New Zealand, USA, Canada, Ireland, Hong Kong, etc). CompuServe users in the UK have the service tailored to local needs and the content includes UK newspapers, UK politics, UK news bulletins, UK weather and traffic information, UK shopping and UK entertainment. If CompuServe is used as a vehicle into the Internet, then foreign languages will only be encountered at that stage.

There is no connection charge, a flat rate monthly charge of £6.50 covering basic services and a connect time charge of £1.95 per hour (after the first 5 free hours per month). Certain services, such as newspapers and company information are classes as *'Premium Services'* and attract extra rates for their use. All charges are billed in American dollars, although paid in pounds sterling. The user pays all normal telephone charges but CompuServe has access numbers for most of the UK's cities and towns so that calls are at local rate. For users with no local connection, BT offers the use of its DialPlus network to connect from a wide range of localities into the CompuServe system. There is an additional separate charge for this service (£2.75 per hour) but this is still cheaper than making long distance calls. CompuServe can be contacted at 0800-000300.

AOL

America OnLine is marketed in the UK simply as 'AOL' and has over 100,000 UK subscribers and 5 million world-wide. Like CompuServe, it has its own services while being closely tied in with general Internet use. Its services include computing magazines online, computing forums and 120,000 files available for downloading. Files can be downloaded one at a time or can be marked for downloading as a batch.

File searches of AOL resources can be carried out using topic or filenames. Leaving AOL and entering the Internet allows AOL users to make more detailed searches of other Internet resources.

Its local content includes AA Roadwatch, the London Stock Market, and national newspapers.

It provides a range of e-mail services to other AOL subscribers and to all other Internet subscribers. It also allows binary files (eg graphics, sounds, video clips, spreadsheets) to be attached to e-mail text messages.

There is no connection charge, a flat rate monthly charge of £4.95 covering basic services and a connect time charge of £2.35 per hour (after the first 3 free hours per month). The entire country has local call rate access to the service. AOL can be contacted at 0800-376-5432.

MSN

The Microsoft Network continues the trend to integrate commercial systems with the Internet; it maintains its own internal resources while providing an easy access to the Internet. Its search facilities covers both MSN and Internet resources. Its local content includes information bases, online magazines and user forums. E-mail can be directed at other MSN subscribers or can be sent to any Internet address; messages can include binary attachments.

There is no connection charge and there is a flat rate of £14.95 a month, with no other charges apart from local telephone charges (all UK can access at local call rates).

THE INTERNET

The Internet is undoubtedly the largest computer resource on the planet. It provides all the facilities previously described for bulletin boards, AOL and CompuServe - but it is much more than the individual facilities. It is not a single entity; there is no Internet Ltd. At its simplest, it is a communications structure that links a huge number of independent PCs, networks and computer sites.

It began in the USA in the 70's as a Government sponsored interconnection of supercomputers for defence purposes and was called *'ARPAnet'* (Advanced Research Projects Agency). The drive for communication standards in the early years produced the TCP/IP protocol described earlier and the SMPT (Simple Mail Transfer Protocol). In the 80's, other academic network joined ARPAnet to produce a large publicly-funded university and research network. The defence areas split away in 1984, leaving ARAPnet to develop into our current Internet.

The original backbone has been extended throughout almost all countries of the world and is organised and run on a voluntary basis. It has been described as *"a network of networks"* and smaller localised clusters of networks are linked by fast-speed telephone cables, fibre optic cables, laser links and even satellite links. Each stage of these links is paid for from the subscriptions of those using the local service. The British network connects main centres, known as POPs *('Points of Presence')* and the entire network is connected to the rest of the world through links from London to America, Stockholm and Paris.

A Point of Presence is a server that remains continually connected to the Internet. Users connect to the Internet through their own POP, usually by simple dial-up modem or via digital ISDN links. A UK user may wish to talk to users in Germany or download a file from the USA, so the entire network has to be available to all the world's users. There is no centralised control of the traffic and data packets can travel a variety of routes between the sending and receiving locations. All packets contain their own source and destination information as well as the data to be sent.

INTERNET ADMINISTRATION

Although there is no control of the Internet's data providers and users, there are bodies who administer the development of the general structure. The Internet Society (ISOC) is the overall body that promotes Internet maintenance and evolution. It approves any new standards and protocols, ensuring that the whole structure remains compatible. The Society is a non-profit making body and is independent of any government control.

It has a President and a Board of 18 members and is located in Reston, USA.

A main component of the Internet Society is the Internet Engineering Task Force (IETF). ITEF is made up of professionals from the networking industry (eg designers, manufacturers and operators). Its main function is to maintain standards regarding the physical network (ie the wiring structure internationally) to ensure the most efficient use and expansion of the communications links. Its technical work is carried out in topic areas covering Applications, Operations and Management, Routing, Security, etc. Each topic area is covered by a large number of working groups which look in detail at specific aspects.

Another main body of the Internet Society is the Internet Architecture board (IAB). Its functions include reviewing the protocols and procedures used on the Internet and liasing with other national and international bodies that are concerned with communications standards. It also produces many papers to promote discussion and seek best experience and practice. These papers are known as RFCs (Request for Comment) and actively seek responses from interested parties.

The Internet Assigned Numbers Authority (IANA) co-ordinates the assignment of unique parameter values for Internet protocols and is chartered by the Internet Society.

GETTING ON THE NET

Connection to the Internet requires the following:

- A modem for telephone line access or a terminal adaptor for an ISDN link.
- A connection to a service provider. This is usually a dial-up connection or an ISDN link.
- An account with a service provider. All provide basic services such as WW, e-mail and newsgroups, while some also provide free web site space, faster speed lines (eg 33.6k, 56k or ISDN), technical support and additional private services. Costs vary substantially between different suppliers.
- Interface software (eg TCP/IP, Winsock) and application software (eg Netscape, Explorer).

Dial-up access via the public switched telephone network is available through hundreds of providers such as Demon, PIPEX, etc although this is a slow system due to the limitations of the medium. ISDN links are faster but more expensive. Larger organisations will provide Internet access via internal LAN or other corporate connections routed through a leased line to the Internet. Windows 95 and OS/2 Warp have Internet facilities built in, making access simple.

The modem should be installed according to the manufacturer's instructions. The *'Control Panel'* of Windows 95 has a *'Modems'* option that allows the modems to be installed, removed or re-configured. A similar modem configuration facility is available from the *'Communications'* option of the *'Settings'* icon in Windows 3.1. Typical concerns are ensuring that the modem's IRQ setting does not conflict with the IRQ used by the mouse or other devices and setting any modem jumpers that may be required. See the earlier material on IRQs for more advice.

The software has to be tailored to suit the user's account and will contain the following information:

- IP number (the unique number for the account)
- Subnet mask (required if used by gateways and supplied by the service provider)
- Host domain name (the name of the computer that the account works to - eg science)
- Your domain name (the name of the provider - eg lumchester)
- Service providers gateway computer IP number (supplied by provider)
- DNS address (supplied by provider)
- Communications details. These would include dial-up telephone number, transfer speed, timeout period (the amount of time that passes without network activity before the software hangs up).
- Account password (agreed between account holder and provider). Additional software can be added to

USER ADDRESSES

Each Internet user is allocated a different identification code so that the station can be uniquely identified for routing, e-mail and other purposes. Each user is registered through the Network Information Centre (NIC) which is run by the USA Department of Defence. The NIC allocates blocks of numbers, known as the IP (Internet Protocol) addresses, to organisations. These organisations, often called *'service providers'*, then allocate them to individual users or groups of users.

An IP address consists of four bytes and is written with a period separating them. So, a valid IP address might be   175.73.44.11

The NIC issues blocks of address in three ways. Class A addresses are issued with the first byte fixed by the NIC, allowing the provider to allocate over 16 million unique addresses. With Class B, the first two bytes are fixed, allowing the provider to allocate over 64,000 unique addressees. Since the demand for addresses is soaring, the NIC only issues Class C addresses. This has the first three bytes already allocated, allowing the provider a maximum of 254 unique addresses (the 0 and 255 address being used for other purposes). The rate of take-up of addresses means that there will soon be no spare numbers left to allocate and discussions are under way to expand the 32-bit IP address up to 128 bits.

Using numbers for the IP address is very confusing and users prefer to be identified by an agreed text substitute. The text is easier to understand and is composed of allocated *'domain'* and *'sub-domain'* names. Every user has both a domain name (eg dumbreck) and a unique IP address. When a user's account is set up, these details are stored in a DNS (domain name server) and all providers can access these servers to translate text names into the corresponding address for routing purposes.

These are general categories on the Internet. For example, the letters *'uk'* indicate that it is a British domain, with *'fr'* for France and so on. America is allocated *'us'* but it is rarely used; if no country is given, the country is assumed to be the USA. The domains in the table show organisational status. The American equivalents of *'co'* and *'ac'* are *'com'* and *'edu'*.

co	commercial organisation
org	non-profit making organisation
gov	government
mil	military
ac	educational establishment
net	networking organisation
int	international organisation

Organisations may expect more than one user to share a system and each user would use the @ symbol to show which IP address they were using.

So, the following address would be easy to remember:

sales@dumbreck.demon.co.uk

This is the Dumbreck Publishing account and shows the account's user name is *'dumbreck'*, the domain name is called *'Demon'* which is one of the largest commercial Internet service providers based in the UK.   If a number of computers were based at a site (as in universities), the full address might be:

eddie@science.lumchester.ac.uk

The computer's name, also called the *'hostname'* or *'nodename'*, is *'science'* and is one computer attached to the *'lumchester'* university in the UK.

INTERNET SERVICES

The Internet is so huge that it has not been fully catalogued. It is continually changing and growing, and sets of Internet software tools have been developed to help users find and exchange information.

E-MAIL

This is one of the most used Internet services.   Since millions of users are connected to the system, it is a cheap way for companies to exchange information, as there is no extra charge for this service.   Many believe that the Internet e-mail service will make the traditional fax services redundant.   It is faster than postal services and, unlike fax, does not depend upon the receiving end being switched on and ready.   It is also an improvement on some telephone conversations, as the contents are recorded and exact details (such as numeric values, post codes, spelling of names, etc) can be reviewed, preventing future errors.

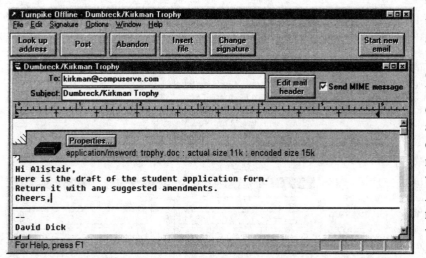

The Demon ISP recommends the use of *'Turnpike'* software and its e-mail facility is shown. Its facilities are typical of other e-mail applications.

When the ISP is dialled, the opening dialogue is displayed and the ISP's mail server is checked for any new mail or material from newsgroups to which the user is subscribed. Any new mail or newsgroup material is notified to the user who can then click the *'Mail/News'* button to view any messages received.   The *'Mailbox'* or *'Mailroom View'* icons allow the user to view any new incoming messages, review messages that the user has sent and delete messages.

The *'Start new e-mail'* button allows the user to send new e-mail and to reply to incoming messages. The example shows a reply being sent to incoming e-mail.   When the message is typed in, it is transmitted by clicking the *'Send'* button.   If the user is on-line, the e-mail message is sent immediately to the ISP mail server.   Most e-mail packages also provide *'cc'* (carbon copy) facilities, where the same message can be sent to more several addresses with a single posting. All recipients will know who received the message. Using *'bcc'* (blind carbon copy), all recipients will receive the e-mail and be unaware that it was also sent to others.

Turnpike also allows e-mail and newsgroup messages to be read 'off-line' - ie when the computer is not connected to the ISP.   This means that incoming messages can be downloaded during a connected session and read later at the user's leisure.   It also allows the user to write outgoing messages and mark them for posting.   When the user next logs into the Internet, the messages are sent to the ISP.   These both save telephone usage costs.

Messages can be saved or printed using the *'File'* menu and can be cut and pasted into other documents using the *'Edit'* menu.   There are options to view all outgoing messages and all incoming messages separately and multiple folders can be created for the default storage of messages.

MIME AND UUENCODE
Note that the main message in the example is in plain ASCII and that another file has been *'attached'* to the message. Where both the sending and receiving e-mail packages support MIME (Multipurpose Internet Mail Extensions) non-ASCII files can be transmitted along with the messages. These can be graphics, executables, spreadsheets - or any other form of binary file. This is because newsgroups were originally designed to carry 7-bit ASCII text. An older but still commonly used variant is UUencode (Unix-to-Unix encode) which converts 8-bit binary files into 7-bit versions for transmission. A UUdecoder at the receiving computer translates the file back into its original binary form.

E-MAIL ETIQUETTE
As in verbal or written communication, there are certain rules when using the Internet and its services. These are often referred to *'netiquette'*. General rules are covered later but the specific advice for those sending e-mail messages is:
- Treat other users with respect
- Avoid sexist, racist, culturally insensitive and judgmental language
- Keep sentences short; the recipient is paying the phone time
- Never forward a received e-mail to a third party without permission
- Don't type in upper case
- Use 'smileys' to convey emotions (see below)
- Learn and use e-mail acronyms (see below)

SMILEYS
Some of the more common smileys are shown below; they have to be viewed with a tilted head.

:-)	smiling	:-x	my lips are sealed
:-(	frowning	O:-)	angelic
:-D	laughing	:-I	indifferent
:'-(	crying	;-)	winking
:->	sarcastic	:-@	screaming
I-O	yawning	{{{()}}}	hugs

ACRONYMS
Acronyms are use to save time (and to show how smart a user is), common ones being:

IMHO	In My Humble Opinion	TYVM	Thank You Very Much
AAMOF	As A Matter Of Fact	WRT	With Respect To
CMIIW	Correct Me If I'm Wrong	FYA	For Your Amusement
BTW	By The Way	IKWYM	I Know What You Mean
OTOH	On The Other Hand	TIA	Thanks In Advance

FILE TRANSFER
Internet supports FTP (*'File Transfer Protocol'*) facilities. A user, known as a *'client'*, can access a remote site, known as a *'server'* site. The diagram shows a screen from WS_FTP, a popular Windows version. The left panel shows the drives, directories and files of the computer initiating the transfer. The right panel shows the directories and files of the remote system. Highlighting a file in the right panel and clicking the leftwards arrow, copies the file to the directory that is active in the left panel

Most FTP sites have a text file in each directory that describes the directory's contents; highlighting that file and clicking the *'View'* button allows the user to read descriptions of the files stored in that directory.

Some servers will request a password. By convention, the password *'anonymous'* allows the user to see those files that the remote site will allow public access. To see other files, the user requires a

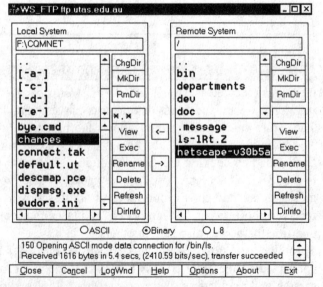

security password; this can be applied for and may be granted at the discretion of the site organisers.

Many Web browsers offer automatic FTP facilities. If a file is underlined for downloading, clicking the text switches the system into FTP mode and the only user involvement is in selecting the directory into which the file should be stored. This avoids the user having to learn how FTP operates, as the mechanisms are hidden by the browser's user interface.

To save on connect time, many files are stored in a compressed, usually ZIP, format.

DATA SEARCHES

The FTP service is very useful but it supposes that the user knows what files and information are available and what sites hold them.   Since the Internet is huge and continually growing, there are ways to get the system to search for information for the user.   The excellent search facilities within the World Wide Web has led to the rapid drop-off in the use of earlier utilities.   The most popular were:

ARCHIE   This utility uses public servers, called *'archie servers'* that will search for a known filename and will send a list back to the user of all Anonymous FTP sites that have hold that file. The list even includes the file's directory path for each site.   The search can be initiated by contacting any archie server (the British one being archie.doc.ic.ac.uk) and requesting a search.   If the user has an extra piece of software, called an *'archie client'* program the search is even easier and a typical command might be   archie coretest.zip

The command results in the user receiving a list of all sites storing the coretest.zip file with free access.

GOPHER   Archie finds a file and ftp downloads a file.   At its simplest, the Gopher utility combines both these facilities.   It is a menu driven system and it can be asked to find a file.   It can also be instructed to download the file or even send it on to someone else.   There are thousands of Gopher servers on the Internet.   While these are mostly set up to satisfy some local need, their contents are mostly open to public access.

Other search facilities were Veronica (a Gopher extension that searches all Gopher servers for a given menu item), Jughead (Jughead searches a specified area, rather than all Gopher servers to shorten the search time) and WAIS (*'Wide Area Information Service'*; a powerful tool that searches for files that contain keywords, making it a powerful tool for researchers to find a mass of reference material with little effort).

Web search facilities are much more powerful and are covered later.

USER GROUPS

Internet has over 25,000 user groups (also known as conferences or forums) operating on a wide variety of subjects.   These are extremely varied; some cover computer topics (programming, hardware, sales); some cover leisure (sports, music, hobbies); some are serious (politics, religion, support groups); some are frivolous

Hierarchy	Content
comp	computing hardware and software
news	network news
rec	recreations, hobbies, art and sport
sci	science
soc	social issues
talk	debate on controversial matters
misc	subjects that don't fit any of the other hierarchies

(jokes, games); a very small but highly publicised number of topics are unsavoury or illegal (pornography, hacking, pirate software).   There is no central control over newsgroups.   Each user group is organised and run by a volunteer.   Newsgroups are all categorised within Usenet's hierarchy as shown in the table.   Other hierarchies exist, such as *'biz'* (business) and the widely-used *'alt'* (alternative).

User groups are an extremely useful way to gain answers to technical or other queries since the correspondence for the most popular groups may be read by hundreds of thousands of users.   The service is called Usenet and the service is best approached with a piece of software called a *'newsreader'*. The newsreader can be set to view only the conferences that interest the user and it will filter these pages and show them to the user.   The user can then read the material and decide to move on, save the material to disc or send a reply.

This shows an example of a newsgroup for users of Macromedia Director, the multimedia authoring

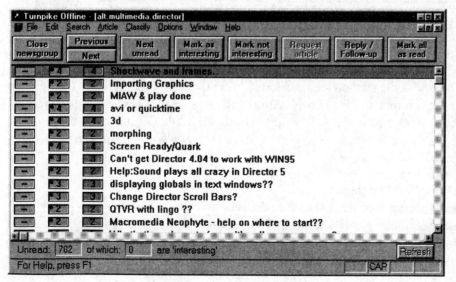

package. The dots indicate sub-divisions of the hierarchy - ie the *'alt'* hierarchy has a sub-group called *'multimedia'* and it has a sub-group called *'director'*.

Each subject is a *'thread'* that was begun by a user and added to by other participants. With controversial issues it is common to have up to several hundred contributions to a thread.

WORLD WIDE WEB

The World Wide Web, usually called the Web or WWW, is the current leader in Internet facilities with around of 70% of all Internet traffic..   It combines the features of Telnet, FTP, Gopher and WAIS in a modern graphical environment.   Its documents are read using WWW *'browsers'*.   A browser is a utility to assist the user through the Web.   A line-mode and full-screen browser can be used and although they produce results in a very much faster time than graphical browsers, they do not take full advantage of the graphical interface.   The Web's added features include:

- Hypertext browsing
- Screens can include graphics and animations
- Audio on Demand
- Running downloaded sub-programs via Java
- Videos, in MPEG or QuickTime format.
- VRML viewing
- Real-time voice Telephony

WEB BROWSERS

Hypertext takes the user away from navigating the Internet via menu textual options.   In the Web, the user is presented with an attractive graphical screen document.   The document may contain graphical images and the screen text may have words or phrases that are highlighted.   These highlighted areas are links that are created using HTML (the HyperText Markup Language) and they link information in one document with information in another part of the document - or an entirely different document.   The other documents may reside anywhere on the Internet.   So, clicking on a hyperlink area (the highlighted text or icon) takes the user to another retrieved document - the one pointed to by the hyperlink.   This other document may consist of further text with further links, or it may even contain a video clip, an audio clip, a small Java program, etc.   The hypertext features of the Web make it an ideal learning environment, where the user can explore paths that are of particular interest.

The most used utilities for graphical Web browsing are *'Microsoft Internet Explorer'* and *'Netscape Navigator'*.   They are in serious competition, having squeezed the other browsers, such as Mosaic and Cello, out of the race.   They strive to continually add new features (eg video, audio, VRML, Java) and many web sites demand that one, or either, of these browsers be used for best results, since their sites are optimised to use the latest Explorer and/or Navigator features.

URLs

Browsing requires a starting point and these are provided by URLs (Universal Resource Locations).   The diagram shows part of the screen of the Netscape browser.

The URL is a long single item of text without spaces and in the above example is
        http://home.netscape.com/
The part before the colon specifies the type of access.   In the example *'http'* is used; this is the *'Hypertext Transfer Protocol'* and is the method required to read HTML files.   Under HTTP, the browser sends the server requests in text format and the serves returns text files (HTML) which are interpreted and displayed on the screen.   Other possible access options include FTP, Gopher or Archie.   The remainder of the line specifies the server that is being accessed and may also optionally include a file name at the end.   Valid examples of URLs are:
        ftp://ftp.cdrom.com/pub/cdrom/photo_cd/writeablecd.txt
        http://rohan.sdsu.edu/home/llu/VRML.html
In both examples, file names are being specified along with the sub-directories on which they are stored.
The *'bookmarks'* menu manages a user's database of URLs, allowing URLs to be added, deleted and given user-defined titles (eg *"handy stuff about discs"*).   Web sites can then be easily fetched from the pull-down pick list instead of having to be sought and manually entered.

WEB SEARCHES

The Web is a vast area to explore and software tools, often described as *'search engines'*, are provided to aid users to locate the material that interests them.   Alta Vista, one of the most popular search engines claims to search through over one million host names, 31 million pages and 4 million newsgroup articles. Other engines include Excite and Lycos, claiming 50 million and 60 million pages respectively.

There are two methods of searching the web:

- Using a hierarchy of menus
- Typing in keywords to search for

The menu hierarchy system is very popular and most packages use this method.   The UK base search engine called Global On-Line Directory (GOD) offers the following list of main topics:

- Arts and Crafts
- Community and Education
- Environment
- Games
- Internet Resources
- Paranormal
- Technology and Computers

- Business
- Entertainment
- Financial Services
- Hot and Sexy
- Leisure and Pleasure
- Sports
- Travel

Clicking on a Computing option would display a further list of options.   Clicking on a 'Multimedia' option would display further options, and so on.   Eventually there would be no more menus and the user is offered a list of resources (such as reviews, shareware programs, academic papers, etc) that can be downloaded.   Clicking on a file will initiate an FTP downloading of the file to the local computer.

This is a very easy to use and is ideal for the casual user.

TEXT SEARCHES

Menu systems are created by search engine operators who make money from the advertising space they rent out.   They maintain their system to cover the most popular material on the web.   When a user wants a specific specialised item, it is unlikely to be available via menus.   In these cases the user enters the key word or words that describe the item and request that a search be made of the Internet for items that match the given description.   Searches can be made of the web sites or of the material stored in the usergroups' directories.   Most search engines provide user-entered search facilities in addition to their menu options.   The Alta Vista search engine specialises in text searches and has no menu hierarchy.   It is the fastest text search engine currently available.

There are a few golden rules of searching:

- Be as specific as possible.   Asking for a search on *'Computers'* will probably result in 100,000 matches. Searching through all of these matches would take months.   Searching for *"Compaq"*, for example, will narrow the search considerably and produce much less useless matches.
- If searching for a specific file, use the file extension in the search.   A search for *'winzip'* will probably produce matches that only contain comments such as *"winzip is great!"*.   Searching for *"winzip.exe"* will reduce the number of wasted matches.
- Learn and use the search syntax available for the search engines used.

Search allow for more than a single word to be entered and this produces a much more refined search. The common search syntax used by search engines is shown in the following examples:

Search text	Result
car engine car OR engine	Finds matches on 'car' (eg restaurant car) and other separate matches on 'engine' (eg steam engine)
"car engine" car AND engine car & engine car+engine	Finds matches on car and engine as a single entity; only references to car engines are displayed.
car NOT engine car-engine	Finds matches on all car references, except those containing the word 'engine'

Some search engines allow more complex searches to be built up, by combining various Boolean expressions.

Some search engines, such as Bigfoot, WhoWhere and Internet White Pages, specialise in searching for Internet users.   This is called X.500 and is based on searching a database that is maintained for the purpose. The database is comprised of users who have asked to be included or those have become public on the Internet for some reason (eg by posting to a newsgroup).

NETIQUETTE

While etiquette encourages good practice when using e-mail, there are a couple of ways in which the Internet in general could be used to the greater benefit of users.

- Switch off browser graphics when they are not essential; this reduces download time, saves phone costs and saves bandwidth for others.
- Use *'mirror'* sites where possible.   These are replicas of other busy sites.   By accessing mirror sites, congestion is reduced at the main site and overall use of the bandwidth is improved.   Since many sites being mirrored are American, European mirror sites reduce the strain on the Trans-Atlantic links.

HTML

The HyperText Markup Language is the language used for all web pages, although some other languages build round an HTML framework.   An HTML script is written in plain ASCII, using any plain text editor (eg Wordpad or EDIT) and can therefore be read by all types of computer on Internet.

It contains all the text that will be displayed on the screen.   It also contains *'tags'* which tell the browser how to display the various parts of the text (font size, underlining, etc).   Other tags instruct the browser to fetch an image and place it on a particular area of the screen.   It also contains hyperlinks which take the user to another HTML document.

The HTML language is too detailed to cover fully here.   The following is a shortened version of a typical web page to demonstrate some of the tags and links used.

Line of HTML script	Purpose
<HTML>	marks beginning of document
<HEAD><TITLE>Dumbreck Publishing</TITLE></HEAD>	places text in title bar
<BODY background="tilsnd.gif">	marks beginning of displayable section, selects a picture for the background
<p><FONT SIZE=5><B>Welcome to the Dumbreck Web Site</B></FONT>	select text face and font size, display text
<FONT FACE="ARIAL,HELVETICA" SIZE="3">	select text face and font size
<i>Best viewed with IE 3</i>	display text in italics
<p>	paragraph break
<a href="http://microsoft.com/ie/"><IMG src="ie_anim.gif" alt="Internet Explorer"></a>	hypertext link
<P>	paragraph break
<a href="bookdet.htm"><img src="book.gif" alt="Book Details"></A>	hypertext link
<P>	paragraph break
<a href="dumform.htm"><IMG src="e_btn.gif" alt="Send us an e-mail"></A>	hypertext link
<p>	paragraph break
<a href="contents.htm"><IMG src="c_btn.gif" alt="Book Contents"></A>	hypertext link
<p>	paragraph break
<a href="index.htm"><IMG src="i_btn.gif" alt="Book Index"></A>	hypertext link
<p>	paragraph break
<a href="links.htm">Links to useful sites</a>	hypertext link
<p>	paragraph break
<P>	paragraph break
</BODY>	marks end of displayable section
</HTML>	marks end of document

Consider the hypertext line:

<a href="links.htm">Links to useful sites</a>

This is constructed of the following elements:

Element	Purpose
<a	Anchor to link documents
href="links.htm">	The text after the =sign is the document to be read when the hyperlink is activated
Links to useful sites	This is the text that will be displayed as a hyperlink hotspot
</a>	Anchor to link documents

The following hyperlink is a little more complex:

<a href="contents.htm"><IMG src="c_btn.gif" alt="Book Contents"></A>

and is constructed thus:

Element	Purpose
<a	Anchor to link documents
href="contents.htm">	The text after the =sign is the document to be read when the hyperlink is activated
<IMG src="c_btn.gif"	This is the icon that will be displayed as a hyperlink hotspot
alt="Book Contents">	This is the text that will be displayed when the mouse is moved over the icon
</a>	Anchor to link documents

BROWSER ENHANCEMENTS

FRAMES

These are written in HTML and produce multiple windows on the screen, often used to maintain a web site's menu on screen while content is altered in the larger window.

ON-LINE FORMS

These provide a user screen requesting details to be typed into various fields.   The form could collect user information (eg preferred subjects), comments or product orders.   When completed, the user transmits the form's details to the web server.

GRAPHICS

This can be the display of a picture or icon as shown in the HTML example.   It also covers *'GIF89a'* or *animated GIFs'* which are single GIF graphics files which have a set of pictures embedded in them.   When the graphic is displayed, it cycles through the internal collection of pictures to provide a simple animation.   This is commonly used for animated logos and simple cartoons.

Macromedia *'Flash'* is a program that creates much more sophisticated animated text and graphics.   The animations are activated by standard HTML commands and can be viewed by anyone who has installed an add-on viewer to their browser; the plug-in is called *'Shockwave'* and is distributed free by Macromedia.   The program is downloaded and executed within the browser.   Even more impressive results, including sound and video, can be produced by creating multimedia products using *'Director'* and compressing them with *'Afterburner'*.   The resultant file is called by the HTML script and is played by Shockwave.

JAVA

Although users have a lot of control over the navigation of Net, the pages that are retrieved are identical for all users.   Java, which is essentially a subset of the C++ programming language, can be used to create *'applets'*.   These are small programs that can be downloaded along with HTML files and graphics files.   They are then run within the calling PC.   Applets range from simple animated icons and games through to database utilities.   They require that the browser support Java as in Netscape 2.0 onwards.

ACTIVE-X

A set of rules developed by Microsoft, it provides around 1,000 Windows controls. It is also designed to be downloaded and run within the local computer.   Whereas Java is capable of running all platforms (ie - on any type of computer) that are Java-enabled, Active-X is solely designed for Windows.   Its controls can be written in C, C++, Visual Basic and Java.

REAL AUDIO

Users with sound cards can listen, in real time, to radio programs from around the world.   There are already hundreds of stations to choose from and the quality is equivalent to a normal AM radio.   AudioNet provides indexing by content, source and theme.   Requires the computer to have *'Real Audio'*, *'Streamworks'* or *'TrueSpeech'* installed; these are free add-ons to the user's browser.

REAL TIME TELEPHONY

Users with a sound cards and a microphone can talk, in real time, to other similarly equipped users throughout the world - and at local call rates.   Products such as *'Web Talk'* and Intel's *'Internet Phone'* provide the software to call up one of a range of specially-created servers.   These list all users who are attached to the service and are currently on-line.   Both parties in the conversation should use the same software to ensure consistent results, as the technology has not yet evolved fully agreed standards.

VIDEO

The demand for video over the Internet stretches the capabilities of both the communications link and software.   RealVideo addresses the problem by optimising video for 28.8kbps and 56kbps transmission and uses streaming (see below) and the dynamic reduction of frame rates (number of pictures shown for each second of video) to overcome inconsistent data rates over the Internet link.   Other initiates are *'CuSeeMe'* which is free video-conferencing software and Intel's *'Video Phone'* software which provides video windows on a browser.   Both require a video or QuickCam camera to capture the user's video.

STREAMING

When downloading files over the Internet, the user is only concerned that the total file is fetched successfully.   Any delays in the network, due to congestion and re-routing of packets, only influence the time downloading time and have no affect on the quality of the file being downloaded.   This is not true of audio and video files that have to be presented to the user in <u>real time</u>.   Any delays in transmission would result in the break up of the sound or video continuity.   To overcome this, *'streaming'* is used.   This reads a number of data packets and stores them in a LIFO (Last In First Out) buffer in the computer.   The user will have a slight initial delay as the buffer is filled.   These data packets are then fed out from the head of the buffer, while incoming packets are fed into the tail of the buffer.   During periods of transmission delay, the user is fed information from the buffer, thus maintaining a constant audio or video stream.

VIRTUAL REALITY

VRML (Virtual Reality Modelling Language) is an ASCII description of a 3D scene such as a building, a human heart, a car engine, etc.   When VRML viewers are embedded in browsers, clicking an icon takes the user on a screen walk around the objects.

SURROUND VIDEO

This is also known as *'panoramic video'* since it provides an environment which completely surrounds the user. Special cameras capture an entire location as a 360^0 photograph and convert it to a graphics image.   The left and right edges of the image are aligned and the whole scene can be thought of comprising a cylinder in which the user is located.   At any stage, the use can view about one-tenth of the image.   Using the mouse or the keyboard moves the user round the image, giving the illusion that the user is situated in the middle of the scene. This is available as Apple's *'QuickTime VR'*, *'Surround Video'* and *'RealVR'*.   Development is being carried out to combine the panoramic background with the 3D objects available in Virtual Reality to produce ever more realistic presentations.

INTRANETS

Companies are developing systems that use Internet facilities within their own network structure.   These are called *'Intranets'* and they may have no physical connection with the Internet.   An intranet may be a self-contained system of company information, prices, projects, etc for employees to reference via browsers.   It may or may not be connected to the Internet but provides similar services such as WWW, e-mail and FTP, although these are all internally organised.   An intranet is not designed to replace the network's file servers for standard file activities.   It is likely to use its own internal IP addresses and these will probably not match external Internet assignments.   Much software, both freeware, shareware and commercial, is available for creating Web servers.   Commercial products offer 'off-the-shelf' solutions which combine easy setup with added facilities such as monitoring, virus detection, encryption and other security measures.

INTERNET PROBLEMS

Apart from the Internet's engineering problems such as bandwidth and the dwindling supply of unallocated user addresses, there are many legal and ethical problems facing Internet users.   Some of these can be tackled and solved within organisations, while others are of much broader concern and require political will and intervention.

SECURITY

Breaches of security on networks attached to the Internet receive wide publicity and hacking into systems from outside can be for reasons of industrial espionage, fraud or just to prove a point. The information held in networks should be protected by the terms of the Data Protection Act and it is the organisation's responsibility to ensure that the Act's terms are met.

FIREWALLS

The main current solution is to install a *'firewall'* - a hardware and software combination that surrounds the organisation's resources.   It is the route for all communication between the internal network and external networks.   Its purpose is to prevent unauthorised external access to the network without impeding the normal legitimate operations of the organisation.   The main policies of a firewall are:

- All traffic entering or leaving the local network must pass through the firewall.
- All firewall traffic must be examined.
- Only authorised traffic to be allow through.
- No passwords or internal address must pass out through the firewall.
- Any services that are allowed public access (eg product prices and specifications) must reside on a server which is outside the firewall.

Firewalls may include extra features such as monitoring the web sites accessed by network users and preventing access to non-approved sites.   It can also log traffic for audit or billing purposes and can incorporate virus checking.

ENCRYPTION

Normal traffic on the Internet is carried in plain ASCII format.   This is too insecure for organisations who wish to transmit confidential information over the Internet.   One answer is to encrypt the message - apply a mathematical algorithm to scramble the contents prior to transmission. The receiving end can unscramble the message and recover the information, assuming that it also uses the same algorithm. The use of encryption is a controversial issue between governments and their citizens and organisations.

ECONOMIC ISSUES

ELECTRONIC COMMERCE

Although the Internet began as a non-commercial communications link, the balance of net traffic is rapidly switching to commercial uses.   Marketing, selling, on-line publishing and commercial databases form the basis of the emerging dominance of financial interests over academic and hobby interests. The arrival of Internet shopping allows subscribers to view goods, specifications and prices and place orders using electronic transactions (ie using VISA or other credit cards). Banking and financial dealing is available and the range of Internet pay services will expand.

Information has become one of the most prized commodities in the world.   The creation, processing and marketing of financial, commercial and scientific information is a huge industry with enormous power. The possession of information is a driving force in the success of institutions and entire nations.   Those without knowledge and current information are destined to lag in an economic race.

This has led to the concept of the *'information rich'* and the *'information poor'*.   The rich can afford to buy the information that makes them rich(er); the poor cannot afford access to the information and remain poor.   Even within the developed countries, the majority of the population do not have Internet access. Within the system, premium services (financial newspapers, stock market information, company profiles, etc) are already only available by extra subscription.   The Internet is being used by the rich and powerful to maintain and extend their position.   The divide is even greater between the developed and developing countries of the world.   Many areas do not even have the telephone structure that would support the Internet.   Internet access is very restricted in many countries due to financial hardship. This may be worsened if future improvements in the Internet infrastructure are financed by big business, as they may demand priority in use of the bandwidth (possibly on payment basis).

GLOBILISATION OF WORLD ECONOMY

A group of 16 Internet-related companies, including BT and IBM, have formed GIP (the Global Internet Project).   GIP's main objectives are:
- an increase in global productivity
- the creation of new jobs and new markets
- improving education, manufacturing and healthcare

It promotes the need for a legal framework for international co-operation.   The increase in teleworking has begun to weaken the traditional work patterns and government control over work.   A programmer, for example, may work in Bombay and be paid by a UK software house.   Another programmer may work in UK and be paid through a tax haven country.   Teleworking can be a means to avoid national taxes and national labour and health and safety regulations.

LEGAL PROBLEMS

A range of legal problems show up the difficulties of obtaining a uniform enforceable framework for Internet use.

PRIVACY

The Data Protection Act (see chapter on Software) is a UK law guaranteeing individuals rights to privacy regarding information stored about them on computers in the UK.   Breaches of this Act within the UK are an offence but breaches committed from another country about a UK citizen would depend on whether that country had similar privacy protection.

COPYRIGHT

The international provisions on copyright apply to Internet material but is as difficult and expensive to pursue as other copyright wrangles.

LIBEL

The UK Defamation Act of 1996 holds that an ISP is not liable for libel if it acts solely as a transmitter of material which is libellous.   It is held to be secondarily responsible as it is not the actual author or editor of the material.   This is in recognition of the instantaneous nature of e-mail and newsgroup postings which make vetting almost impossible.   The mechanics of processing a libel action for an individual from country A against an ISP based in country B which has posted a libellous piece from an individual from country C is complex.

CENSORSHIP

With the Internet connecting a million web sites and 25,000 user groups, it is not all surprising that some material causes offence to some users. The Internet, like the Royal Mail, British Telecom, Parcel Force, Group 4, etc, is just a carrier - it distributes what it is given.   Crimes or outrages are not caused by the Internet any more than crimes or outrages are caused by the existence of the telephone or the mail service.   The public debate has centred on defining offensive material and deciding on the course of action, if any, that should be taken.

OFFENSIVE MATERIAL

Like all moral debates, there are problems producing a satisfactory definition. Some moral questions, such as murder and rape, have international agreement. Other issues vary with the traditions of that country.   Most Internet information is in English and most newsgroups promote English-speaking Christian culture and morality.   What is regarded as satisfactory conduct in that arena may be disgusting and/or illegal in another part of the world.   Each country has its own laws on a range of issues (eg outlawing racial hatred, pornography, political views, etc) but the Internet is international by its nature. If a user in country A is banned from viewing certain material in that country, the material is still available from country B by logging in to that web site.   The material can be sexual or political content. UK government reports that are 'classified' - ie banned from publication in the UK - are available freely in other countries who do not operate the same view of what is 'best' for British citizens.

Although Internet pornography generates much press and TV coverage, a recent survey found:

- 0.002% of newsgroups contained graphics with sexual content.
- Of these, most were of the 'soft' variety to be found on page 3 of most newspapers.
- The 'hard core' variety were mostly of sex between consenting adults.
- The remainder (ie a tiny proportion of the already minuscule 0.002%) displayed *unlawful sexual practice'*, thereby falling under the UK Obscene Publications Act (see below).
- Many of the sites that fell foul of the OPA are only accessible by credit card - not a commodity possessed by the children claimed to be corrupted by this material.

This is not to condone or condemn such sites, but to place the issue in perspective.

ACTIONS

The Internet remains a great source of knowledge, assistance, commerce and entertainment for the vast majority of its users.   It is one of the few areas that national governments have been unable to control. A large proportion of the Internet community, and the public at large, feel uneasy at some of the Internet's content but are totally against any censorship.   A powerful lobby, representing some religious and political interests, demand sweeping control over the Internet.   In the absence of a consensus, there remains the options of new legislation or accepting that the only laws to be enforced on Internet users and providers are the existing ones prevailing in each individual country.   The relevant UK laws are:

- The Obscene Publications Act of 1959 which makes the publication of an obscene article an offence. The definition of 'obscene' is its tendency to deprave and corrupt.
- The Criminal Justice and Police Order Act of 1994 which ensured that the OPA's provisions on pornography applied to the Internet in the UK.

Legal restrictions on the Internet have so far proven difficult to formulate and implement. In 1996, the American Communications Decency Act was overturned in their Supreme Court due to the Act's failure to adequately define offensive material.

There is now a trend for governments to pressurise Internet providers into acting as censors for all material that they provide to users. Since web sites and newsgroups are in permanent flux, the ability of ISPs to constantly monitor millions of pages every day is a totally impractical task.   For the same reason, governments do not expect postmen to open and read every letter before popping them in letterboxes.   Easier targets are the semi-permanent newsgroups whose titles are suspect and UK providers have evolved their own voluntary code on these.

Some newsgroups are already moderated by their organisers; any offensive or defamatory material received is not placed into the newsgroup. Another approach is self-regulation by the end-users. A variety of censoring software is available to prevent children, students or employees from gaining access to material that is deemed unsuitable by the person in control of the PC or local network. For example, Net Nanny allows a parent to maintain a dictionary of banned words - eg URLs and newsgroups, while WinWatch Home also allows children's on-line time to be restricted. Cyber Sentry and WebTrack are aimed at monitoring and controlling employees' access to the Internet.

THE INFORMATION SUPERHIGHWAY

Universal voice communication was achieved by an international network of telephone exchanges that allowed telephones in any location to be linked together via a series of switched connections.   This analogue system was exploited to allow slow speed data communication via modems; users could transfer files between locations or could connect to data providers (e.g. Prestel, Bulletin Boards, etc.). Thus, the normal switched telephone system already provides a slow and limited information highway.

A common definition of the Information Superhighway is a *'broadband network'*. Another definition of the Information Superhighway is given by a computer magazine as *"every piece of data held electronically anywhere is potentially accessible to people with the right technology"*.   Undoubtedly, wide area networks already now carry more data than voice information, a ratio that is continually increasing.   However, even the sweeping definition quoted is inadequate since it does not specifically include real-time activities such as videoconferencing, interactive systems, etc.

The information superhighway should meet the following requirements:

- The system should be fast.   Many modern activities require the movement of large amounts of data, often in real time.   This explains the broadband definition used by BT.
- The system should have easy general access.   Implicit in all definitions is the sharing of resources.   A dedicated high-speed line between branches of a company may pass all manner of data but still remains a closed system.   The Superhighway requires a more open access.   This may be through a network of ISDN users or through modem connection to the Internet.   It may also involve the use of ISDN to access the Internet at greatly increased transfer speeds, as with the BTnet service.

Many facilities are already widely available.   These vary from the simple downloading of a file from a dial-up bulletin board to the *'VC6000'* videoconferencing system from BT offering full-motion and full-colour over dial-up lines and their extended version *'Presence'*, working over ISDN2.   Other facilities, such as electronic newspapers and video on demand are still in their infancy.   High performance demands a network capable of handling digital information at fast speed.   This mean abandoning the conventional switched analogue network in favour of a dial-up network that allows users direct digital connection without the use of modems.   This currently is available through the use of the ISDN system.

ISDN

ISDN (Integrated Services Digital Network) is currently available to 97% of the UK market.   Other countries using the ISDN system are Australia, Belgium, Denmark, Finland, France, Germany, Holland, Hong Kong, Italy, Japan, New Zealand, Norway, Singapore, Spain, Sweden, Switzerland and the USA. The UK currently has 45,000 ISDN2 users and well over 100,000 ISDN30 users.   The USA, in comparison, has over one million ISDN users.   Overall, ISDN provides high speed communication over much of the developed world.   Key features of ISDN are:

- High bit-rate - an ISDN channel has a throughput of 64kbps (i.e. kilobits per second).   This compares very favourably with the average modem used on an analogue telephone system where speeds of 9.6kbps and 14.kbps are the norm and 28.8kbps models are starting to appear.
- All-digital interfaces - no need for modems.
- Very fast call setup time (800mS compared to up to 30sec for a dial up connection)
- Reduced noise.
- Supports both circuit switched and packet switched services
- Supports both digitised voice and digital data.   The human voice is sampled at 8000Hz and quantised to 8 bits giving a 64kbps data rate and getting the maximum quality from the bandwidth of a single channel.

ISDN SERVICES

There are two grades of service offered in the UK:

BTs Basic Rate Service - ISDN2

This service is only available from British Telecomms and it provides three digital channels into the user's premises.   Two of these, known as the *'B Channels'*, each provide a 64kbps digital data link.   The third channel, the *'D Channel'*, provides a 16kbps digital link which is used for signalling purposes. When not in use for signalling, the D channel can also be used to carry digital data

64kbps data channel
64kbps data channel
16kbps signalling channel

traffic.   Hence the maximum data capacity is 2 x 64k + 16k = 144Kbps.   This system is often called the 2B + D system.   ISDN2 installation costs are £199 per line, plus a rental charge of £133.75 per quarter.

Usage unit costs are the same as analogue telephone charges; if both B channels are used at the same time, then each is charged as a separate call.   A number of Internet points support ISDN access.

Primary Rate Service - ISDN30

This is currently the other commonly used service and is provided by both BT and Mercury.   It provides thirty B Channels, allowing for a bandwidth of up to about 2Mbps, depending on the number of channels in use at any one time.   As each extra channel is brought into use, the

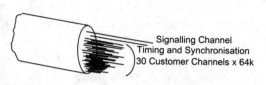

Signalling Channel
Timing and Synchronisation
30 Customer Channels x 64k

bandwidth - and the usage unit costs - is increased.   ISDN30 is an essential service where the highest data transfer rates are required.   Installation costs are £3,025 and there is a £3,854 annual rental.

GETTING CONNECTED

Connection to the ISDN system can be achieved in the ways described below:

ISDN2

This uses the existing copper wire phone lines into a user's premises. Instead of being connected to a phone, they are connected to a digital interface as described below. Of course, alterations are required at exchange end so that the line is connected to the ISDN network instead of the switched telephone network.   The cable comes into a user's premises as a normal twisted pair and is taken into an ISDN wall socket - called an NTE (Network Terminating Equipment).   Two connectors come out of the NTE (one pair of wires for the transmitting functions and one pair for the receiving functions).   The NTE looks similar to a twin telephone socket and connects to a terminal adapter or ISDN card on a PC.

ISDN CARDS

These cards plug into the expansion bus inside the PC and provide various levels of sophistication.   Some cards can handle aggregation (see below); some only handle a single B channel; some provide data compression and so on.   Card prices vary from £300 to £1,500 dependent upon the facilities offered.

TERMINAL ADAPTOR

Matches the NTE to the serial port of the PC. These are cheaper than ISDN cards but speed drops to 19.2kbps (the V.110 standard) or possibly 28.4kbps (with an extended proprietary version of V.110).   Since the ISDN line is capable of handling 64kbps, the bandwidth is padded out with the insertion of null data. These adaptors run at faster rates than the average serial port on a PC. To use these adaptors, the PC needs to have a fast 16550 UART inside, or have a high speed add-on serial card fitted.

ISDN cards and adaptors are expensive but they should drop in price with the increased uptake and sales. In addition, Intel is developing its own set of ISDN chips for its videoconferencing system.

ISDN30

The ISDN2 is not powerful enough for many needs and the ISDN30 system provides for multi-channel use.   Channels can be grouped in various ways known as 'aggregation' and 'bonding' - to increase user bandwidth. Aggregation allows two or more channels to used for a single call, effectively doubling the data transfer rate.   Bonding (Bandwidth On Demand Interoperability Group) is a dynamic equivalent of Aggregation.   A bandwidth manager monitors the users needs at any one point and maintains the requisite number of ISDN channels open.   These systems require that a channel aggregator is fitted at both ends of the link to maintain synchronisation. All 30 channels allow for 1.92Mbps although, in practice, about 8 channels is the maximum actually used.

Until recently, direct comparison of throughput on ISDN and modem linkups was muddied by the fact that compression techniques were commonplace on modems. Comparisons are now more meaningful with the arrival of compression on ISDN systems.

THE FUTURE

It is planned to use the ISDN D channel for more than simply call set up and routing. BT is to introduce a system using the D channel aimed at the credit card authorisation and the LAN interconnection markets.

Broadband ISDN (B-ISDN) is expected to be across Europe by end of the century. It will probably use optical fibre and ATM (Asynchronous Transfer Mode - a data transfer technique specially designed for use with wideband systems such as fibre optics), allowing end users 155Mbps and eventually 622Mbps data rates.   Siemens are currently developing a 135Mbps B-ISDN service.   Since wideband TV needs 140Mbps uncompressed, this can provide a viable multimedia link as well as high quality videoconferencing and home video-on-demand.

Local Area Networks

Local Area Networks, usually shortened to *'LANs'*, is a constantly growing area of computing.   The major players such as Intel and Xerox only published their specification for the Ethernet system in 1980, with real sales only developing in 1983/4.   IBM, the other major contender for the LAN market only appeared in 1985.   In the following years, there has been a dramatic growth in their popularity.   In 1987, around a tenth of all PCs were connected to a network. Now, the large majority of all non-domestic PCs are attached to LANs.   This growth is due to their great contribution to office and industrial automation. The linking of PCs has developed from a *'good idea'* to a powerful aid to industrial and commercial efficiency.   PC networks now carry out the tasks previously given to mainframe and mini systems.

The size of networks vary tremendously:
- 6 nodes in a typing pool.
- 10,000 users at IBM
- 4,500 users at Microsoft's headquarters.

There are many small networks in use and quite a few very large systems.   Around 70% of all commercial computers are networked.

WHAT ARE LANS

In non-networked organisations, the sharing of information and inter-personal communication is via *people* - in a networked organisation this is achieved via *computers*.   There are a number of definitions of a LAN, some trying to state the likely maximum distance covered, or the maximum speed used.   In the ever-changing technology of computing, a more useful general definition might be:

"A local area network is a communication system used to interconnect all of an organisation's computers, generally within a single building, or a single site".

In other words, a LAN would normally be owned and run within a single organisation, to link together the computers and peripherals found on a single location. This location could be a single office, or it could cover an entire commercial or production site.   In practice, the total distances covered range from a few yards (a typing pool) to over a mile (a shipyard or a university campus).   With Netware 4, all of the computers across the world owned by a single international company can be used as if they were all in the same building.   Although most computers on LANs would be PCs (with or without internal hard discs), the system could encompass minicomputers, mainframes and super computers and even dumb terminals.

WHY LINK USERS

80% of an organisation's communications is from within that organisation.   Less than 5% of a company's entire written/verbal communications involves direct interaction with people outside the company.   So, most communication is within the organisation's own boundaries.   Indeed, 90% of all information travels less than half a mile within the organisation - more than three-quarters travelling less than 600 ft. So, much of an organisation's activities is based on the internal sharing of information.   In a normal, paper-based company, (one whose data is held on cards and stationary files), the files can be held centrally.   Anyone wishing information can go to the appropriate cabinet and retrieve the desired data. However, in an office with many PCs, the information would be held on many different hard discs.   Of course,   the user of each PC could print out the machine's information and place it in the central filing area.   The problems with this are:
- wasted storage space
- wasted effort
- the information is never fully up-to-date
- only one person can look at the file at a time

The filing cabinets can be dispensed with, if the information from PCs is transferred to floppy discs. This can solve some of the above problems but can cause new problems - those of data integrity.   For example, if a word-processed file is given to a colleague and both versions are modified, then neither is now complete.   What is required is a central store of information, held in electronic form, which can be easily accessed from any PC in the system.   Since most departments are using their own computers, it makes sense that communication between individuals or departments should ignore memos/telephone conversations/central filing cabinets and directly link the computers. The savings that can be made are potentially vast - it is estimated that around 1.4 trillion dollars is spent on staffing of offices in America alone. Even a relatively small saving from the increased productivity is a huge amount of money. The proportion of UK information-related jobs is about 40% and increasing.

HOW

Each computer in the network has a special card installed which allows the machines to be connected together with cables. Each machine has its own software to handle the network's activities. These

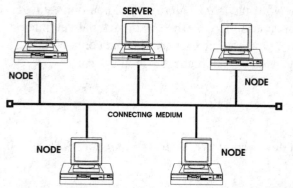

computer stations are referred to as *'nodes'*.

Connected to the cable is a special computer called the *'server'* (large installations will use several servers). A server will have a very large hard disc that holds all the application programs and data needed by the stations. The server will have particular software to allow it to play its role as the nerve centre of the system. The nodes send a message to the server, over the cable, requesting a copy of a particular program or item of data. The server responds by sending a copy of the program or data down the cable. This is then held in the node's memory for use. In fact, the node sees the server disc as if it was the nodes own local 'F' disc drive. All the usual COPY commands, etc. work as if the server hard disc was actually inside the node case. In this way, the activities of the network will be invisible to the user.

NOTES:
- To ensure that all users have fair access to the network, the data travelling between machines on the media is split into small *'packets'*. These packets will be interspersed on the cable.
- Very small LAN systems can use a similar method to the above, except that there is no special server for the system, as all the machines share each others' programs and data via the cable (this is known as a *'peer-to-peer'* system e.g. Windows for Workgroups)
- For long distance communication within an organisation, or between organisations, wide area networks (WANs) are employed, either using the public network or private rented lines.
- LANs can be connected to WANs, if required. This allows users of a LAN in the Glasgow office to contact LAN users in the London office and exchange messages/data.
- LANs can also connect to other LANs; this is known as *'internetworking'*.

LANs AND UNIX

Note that LANs are not really multi-user systems, in the same way as we understand mainframe and mini computer systems.
- A modern LAN is typically a collection of stand-alone PCs that are all capable of independent processing. They share the same files and resources from the common server. However, each user will run a copy of an application in his/her own node's memory. A user can load an application from the server and spend all day creating data. Apart from the initial download of the application, there need be no further communication between the node and the server. At the end of the day, the data from the node memory may be sent down the cable to be stored in the server disc. At its busiest, every user is attempting to move files between the server and the nodes at the same time; at its quietest, the server is sitting unused, while all the individual nodes are carrying out activities in their own machines.
- A mini computer, in comparison, would connect to a number of terminals and carry out all the processing, for all the users, within the UNIX box. Each station would be given a small share of the mini's CPU time on a *'time sharing'* basis. However, since the user's waiting time between bursts of activity is also small, the station activity appears continuous. All the users' data is held and updated centrally; no data is held in the memory of individual stations. This system is ideal for situations where many users are doing essentially the same job (e.g. simultaneous sales producing simultaneous stock-control updates). Normally, the mini computer is specially built for the job, with extra fast processing power. The normal PC MSDOS operating system would not be up to handling the task and the more powerful (but less friendly) UNIX operating system is the most common operating system for a mini.

Performance tests suggest that LANs outperform UNIX systems in most activities.

It is possible to connect a range of terminals (machines with I/O facilities and no processing power) to a network via a *'Terminal Server'* and special extra TCP/IP software.

ADVANTAGES OF A LOCAL AREA NETWORK

The main advantages are listed below (although there is a degree of overlap between them):

SHARED RESOURCES

Networks allow individual users to share the organisation's hardware and software resources.

SOFTWARE

Any file on the server hard disc can be available to every user.   Thus, only one copy of each program need be stored, rather than, say, 100 copies residing on 100 local hard discs.   When a program is upgraded, there is only a single copy to be tackled - not the 100 versions spread throughout the building.   This also ensures that every user is using the same, most modern, version of the software.

DATA

Similarly, any data in the organisation is available to every station in the entire building.   This advantage has led to the development of LAN applications such as multi-user databases, where the input at any terminal updates the records for access by any other node on the system.   Information is usually the most expensive item in an organisation - including its collection storage and maintenance.   It varies regularly and to keep it up-to-date and available is both onerous and expensive.   The distribution of the inputting and access to the database over the whole organisation provides the optimum use of the data.

HARDWARE:

Peripherals are often a small part of cost of running a large computer system.   However, specialised devices are often very expensive and are usually located in particular parts of the building.   Such items include:

Plotters	Phototypesetters	Colour lasers
Optical character readers	CD banks	ISDN lines
High capacity disc drives	Tape streamers	Internet links

On a network, access to these devices would be available to all nodes, in any part of the building.   This ensures the maximum use of these resources (e.g. most people only use a printer for less than 5% of the time they use a computer). It also allows connection of devices from different manufacturers.

Finally, the hardware is easily expanded, with little disruption to the existing system.

COST

Since all the data is stored on the server disc, the organisation need only buy discless workstations. Money can be saved - or spent on upgrading the rest of the node.   There is an increasing demand for node stations with a fast processor and a single floppy drive.

EFFICIENCY

On a non-networked office, the failure a machine meant that the programs and data in that machine could not be accessed until the machine was repaired.   This is not a problem on a computer network, since - in the event of a node going down, a user can carry on his/her normal work from another node. Of course, if the server was to fail, that it is very serious matter indeed, since it holds the entire programs/data for the whole company.   This can be overcome by rigorous backup facilities and the use of backup servers, which can take over in the event of a main server failure.   This is an expensive solution - but cheap in comparison to potential losses from the lack of computer facilities. In general then, a network organisation is more efficient than a collection of individual PCs.

Apart from the extra hardware efficiencies must be added all the benefits from file sharing and the flexible working possible on a network.   There is now a growing trend to not only sharing resources - but also sharing the actual processing power of the system.   The collective computing power of the many individual PCs is awesome - if it can be properly tapped.   If some of the processing tasks can be given to an idle CPU, then the overall processing will be speeded up.

SPEED

Ordinary telephone connections between computers, using modems, handle data at rates up to 56Kbps.   Special digital service lines can increase the rate to 64Kbps.   In comparison, a LAN can work at 10Mbps, 100Mbps or even 1Gbps. Since a single character requires 8 bits to represent it, a 10Mbps service could transfer the equivalent of the entire contents of a 3½" disc in a single second.

COMMUNICATION

Most companies have resources that are not connected to the humble desk PC. These include other networks, the company mainframe, other branches over public or leased lines (e.g. Kilostream), etc. Connecting these resources to a network means that they are then all available to every station in the network.

Other communication benefits are:
- Outside resources - via modems, fax machines, ISDN lines, other leased lines and the public packet switched network. This gives access to vast on-line databases containing scientific, commercial, and industrial information.
- Electronic mail - The simplest version sends a message. The sender is informed if the destination station is not connected, otherwise a message appears on destination screen. Mail servers will store a message if the destination not connected and will deliver the message when the station does connect.
- FAX gateway - This is a dedicated PC with fax board(s). Cheaper than single-user boards. Most allow faxing via the existing E-mail system. These computer systems use the same standards as normal fax therefore they can communicate with any other fax machine in the world.

FLEXIBLE WORKING
The integration of communications with networks allows for a much more flexible working environment:
- TELEWORKING
  Packages, such as Crosstalk, allow modem access to the computer network over the normal telephone line. Work can now be carried out remotely from the work place - known as *teleworking*. This work might be able to be carried out at a time and a place that suits the user, since the network will be available 24 hours a day. A salesperson can log in from his/her hotel in the evening and upload the days orders; a programmer can write software from home and be paid by results; a director can control the business from the comfort of Monte Carlo. Students can download the week's work, write the essays and send them back to their personal directories for marking; lecturers can stay at home and still mark and tutor students.
- DATA-LOGGING
  Data-logging (e.g. quantity measurement or salesmen's orders) on portable machines can be transferred via the telephone network to the office server for processing.

SECURITY
Although there is localised processing, control is centralised. The network supervisor can have a great degree of control over who can enter the network, what directories will be available to a particular user and what file activity will be allowed.

CURRENCY/INTEGRITY
In non-networked companies, copies of the same data may reside in many different station hard discs. When an item of data is altered, the data on every machine has to be updated. This is time-consuming and error-prone. If one station is not updated, then the 'facts' depend on the machine interrogated.

DISADVANTAGES
Network systems, while providing distinct advantages, also create possible problems:
- An 'error' in one node may propagate through the network, as in the 1987 Stock Market crash.
- More costly to manage - time - management rules - technical skills
- Always costs more than first thought.
- Less secure - more access points to the same data.
- More complex software
- Installation problems; at least 6 months to set up properly

It is generally believed that LANs will not replace mainframes/minis for payroll and general ledger applications. Nevertheless, the sales of LANs and mini computer systems will dominate most future applications, apart from the area of super-computers used in defence, national budgeting, etc.

FEATURES OF LANs
When viewing a LAN's characteristics, the following factors are a useful guide:
SIMPLICITY
  The system is relatively simple to configure and use. Working should be transparent to the novice user. Users can employ a large of facilities with minimal training.
EXPANDABILITY
  New nodes can be added to the system with little hardware and software disruption.
CONNECTIVITY
  Well over a hundred different LAN systems are currently on sale - with differences in hardware and software. Many hardware and software incompatibilities exist; this causes problems both with connecting together networks and running applications over them. There is a pressing need for agreed standards - to make applications independent of the media and the hardware. LANs often need to be connected to other systems (e.g. to other LANs, to WANs and to mainframes and mini computers).

RELIABILITY
Reliability is of great importance in a network; for the server it is absolutely vital.   LANs, once the initial settling down problems are overcome, are renowned for their reliability.

INTEGRITY / LOW ERROR RATE
WAN error rates can be up to 1:100,000. In comparison, LANs can be up to 1:100,000,000.

SPEED
Important, as this is the potential system bottleneck.   The measurement of data transfer speeds is difficult, since the actual speeds rarely correspond to the theoretical speeds.   The basic measure of data transfer speed is 'bits per second', being the number of binary digits that can be transferred between one machine and another in a second.   If it takes eight bits to represent each character and a 4Mbps system is in use, data should be transferred at the rate of 500,000 characters per second.   So, a 1/2Mb file should theoretically be transferred between nodes in a single second.   However, the system has to transfer other information - such as the source address, the destination address, etc., with each data packet. Also, the same medium has to be shared with other communicating nodes. Networks can be considered as grouped into four categories of speed:

LOW SPEED -	less then 1Mbps, used in small groups (less than 6) usually with low-cost systems.
MEDIUM SPEED -	between 1Mbps and 10Mbps - for larger groups up to 50 (as little as 20 if there is heavy traffic on the system).
HIGH SPEED -	greater than 10Mbps - for large groups or very heavy traffic.
TOP SPEED -	100Mbs up to 1000Mbps - for large organisations or video/multimedia

LAN TOPOLOGIES

'Topology' refers to the way in which the nodes are connected to the media, to form the complete network system.   Two systems dominate the LAN market - IBM's Token Ring system and the Ethernet system which uses a *'bus'* topology.

BUS

Half of the world's LANs are this type.   Invented by Xerox in the mid-70s, the Ethernet bus system is an international standard.   The original configuration has a common data-carrying coaxial cable that winds its way through the different areas of the building and individual stations connect at any point on this cable.

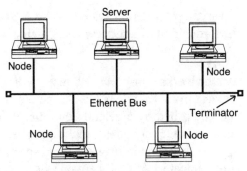

Each station has a *'tap'* on to the bus.   Data from a node is transmitted in *'packets'* and each node on the network receives the transmission.   Only a packet with the matching address is processed by the receiving node (i.e. station 17 will only respond to packets with a destination address of 17).   A failure in any one station affects only that station; the rest of the network functions normally.

Each end of an Ethernet coaxial cable has *'terminators'* fitted. These are special connectors that contain 50ohm resistors to absorb the signal thus preventing unwanted reflections of the transmission on the cable.   If the signal were allowed to reach the end of a cable and reflect back down to the cable, it would interfere with the fresh signal and cause loss of data integrity.   Ethernet runs at 10Mbps on either ThinNet or ThickNet. It can support 30 stations with ThinNet and 100 with ThickNet. The minimum distance between taps is 0.5m. Modern implementations use *'hubs'* to which the stations connect in a star-like layout. Since the cable is not run serially, there is no minimum distance between stations and the each station can be up to 100m distant from the hub.. Novell's various versions of NetWare, currently at v4, dominate the operating system market.

TOKEN-RING

Ring topologies were slow to develop, until the *'token ring'* system was adopted by IBM. This system has around a third of the market but is threatened by new faster technologies (see later). It is aimed at the larger end of the market, since it covers great distances and allows large amounts of users, through linking of individual rings.   The ring is a closed loop, with nodes connected via repeating elements, known as *'ring interface units'*.   These units boost the signal before passing it on, hence the greater

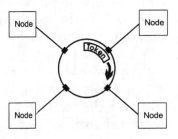

distances covered. There is no central controller. All devices on the ring have equal status.   The ring is a one-way system (e.g. all data going clockwise).   Data circulates round the loop as a series of point-to-point links between adjacent nodes. The right to send data passes from one node to another in an ordered sequenced determined by a token.

The token grants permission to send data. A node with a message/data to send waits for an empty token to arrive. It then accepts the token, inserts the message/data into it and sends it on.   This token passes the data in the form of a *'packet'*. This packet contains both the source and destination addresses, as well as the data itself.   Each node checks the incoming packet, to see whether the destination code is its own. When the data arrives at the destination node, it is copied into a local buffer.   The packet continues round the loop,   returning to the sending node specially marked to indicate its acceptance, to acknowledge to the sending node that the data was received.   Any node that is not the destination node, passes the token on unaltered. Token Ring systems use coaxial, twisted pair or fibre optic cable. Older versions operated at 4Mbps; newer versions run at 16Mbps; it can run at 100Mbps on fibre optic cable.

ADVANTAGES:
- Copes with heavy traffic better than bus systems (see later).
- Covers greater distances than bus systems, since the signal is re-generated at each node.

DISADVANTAGES:
- If one repeater fails, the entire system goes down.

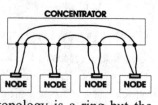

The network topology does not determine the cabling layout. Although the ring requires that nodes be connected in an electrical loop, the actual wiring need not be run round a building in a physical circle.   In fact, it is very common to connect a group of nodes to a network via a *'concentrator'*. The wiring of these nodes is brought to one location and they are then connected together in a ring within the concentrator.   As can be seen, the network topology is a ring but the cabling topology is that of a star.   Of course, an actual system would have a server in the ring!

A variation on IBM's system is the *'Cambridge Ring'* which circulates multiple tokens. This increases the throughput as nodes can use the first free circulating token.

STAR

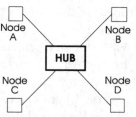

Star networks constitute less than 10% of the market. The wiring to each node radiates from a single point - hence the *'star'* description   All traffic is switched and controlled by a central controller - the *'hub'*.   A node wishing to transmit data to another node must make a request to the central controller, which will set up a dedicated path between the respective nodes. Once established, the nodes communicate as if they were on a dedicated point-to-point system.

ADVANTAGES:
- Protocol may be simple - only the two stations involved in a link need to be involved.
- Because information transmission does not involve all parts of the network, the overall speed of the network may be higher than the maximum transmission rate allowed.   For example, station A can transmit to station B, at the same time as station C transmits to station D.
- All data transmitted passes through the Central Hub, so the network can be easily monitored.
- Additional stations are easily and cheaply added, for the cost of the station plus the cabling.

DISADVANTAGES:
- The initial cost of installing the network is high because the expensive Central Hub is required, no matter whether a couple of nodes are added or many nodes.
- Problems at the hub close the whole system down.

NOTE

Most networks using twisted pair cabling connect the computers to the network via hubs. These are different from the hubs mentioned in the star network. In a <u>star</u> network, the hub is the main server processor.   Hubs in a <u>bus</u> system are only a means of station connection.   The server is wired to the hub and stations connect to one of the hub's 8, 16 or more ports on the basis of one socket per UTP lead. Although wired like a star, it remains a bus systems since all stations receive all transmissions. UTP hubs are mains operated, to supply the internal electronics used to balance the signals. A managed hub has more electronics to accept even more PCs and create sub-networks inside the hub. It programs connections between ports and can manage other hubs (eg for monitoring and diagnosis purposes).

LANs AND COLLISIONS

The benefits of a LAN flow from the fact that many stations share the same transmission medium. However, this is also a potential source of problems. If two or more stations attempt to transmit simultaneously, then the signals interfere with each other. The result is that no useful intelligence is received by any station. This happening is known as a *'collision'*. All LANs, then, have to use a method of preventing or limiting this effect.

COLLISION DETECTION

This method is used by BUS networks, such as Ethernet. It is described as a Carrier Sense Multiple Access- Collision Detection system (CSMA-CD) and uses the principle of *'listen before speaking'*. Here, a station which wishes to send a message will listen on the medium and only start to transmit when the medium is free. It is still possible, however, that two stations could sense the medium as free and begin to transmit simultaneously. An Ethernet station, therefore, listens to its own broadcast, to see whether it is being interfered with. If a collision is detected, the station immediately ceases transmission. The stations then wait for a while before making another attempt at transmission. This is a random delay, to prevent the same machine making their second attempt at the same time.

This is an efficient method, since it greatly reduces wasted transmission time. Where many stations are trying to use the medium (during peak spells) there will be a great deal of wasted time, as the number of collisions will rise. The rise in collisions and the subsequent decline in throughput develop at an alarming rate.

COLLISION AVOIDANCE

Collision detection is an effective system and is the most common system.   However, it has a serious flaw - the very act of detecting a collision means that the collision has already taken place!   The node can take measures to overcome the problem, but the damage (in terms of time wastage) has still occurred.   An improved method would be to prevent the collision taking place in the first instance.   By its design, a token-passing system can only have a single user packet on the system at any one time - therefore the possibility of a collision is nil. This saves wasting time and increases throughput.

NOTE:

As the traffic on a collision-detection system increases, the system performance deteriorates. Useful working is no more than 30-40% of the potential maximum of the system. The traffic on a token-passing system will maintain a steady rate over a wide range of traffic demands.   A 10Mbps token ring system can provide as much usable bandwidth as a 10Mpbs Ethernet segment. A 16Mbps system can run at over 80% capacity without problems.

COMPONENTS OF A NETWORK

COMPUTERS

At the simplest, the computers attached to a network can be normal run-of-the-mill PCs. The existing PCs in an organisation can have a network interface card fitted in one of the expansion sockets of the machine and a few files added to the hard disc; the result is a network node.

In Novell NetWare, each node has two files:

- IPX.COM which is used to energise the interface card and connect the node to the media
- NETX.COM   which routes user requests to the normal MSDOS command interpreter, or sends any appropriate user request on to the interface card.

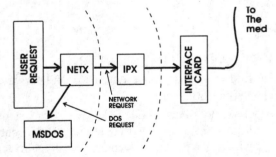

Where Novell shares the Ethernet with other software (TCP/IP, AppleTalk), a driver called ODI is installed.

There is a growing market for LAN *'workstations'*.

These can be specially built PCs with Ethernet hardware already built on to the board.   This opens up a new market for PCs. Since most, or all, of the users processing will take place at the local node, it would be efficient to have as fast a processor as possible in the local station. However, since all, or most, of the user's data will be held centrally, there is no need for a local hard disc. This allows manufacturers to offer high-performance machines for the LAN market - where the cost savings on the disc is spent on faster processors and/or higher resolution monitors.

Manufacturers provide a range of machines that are completely discless - sometimes called a *'LANstation'*. This offers advantages as far as security is concerned. It greatly reduces the ability of users to purloin copies of data from the organisation, since it is impossible to download data from the network. It also eliminates virus problems on the network, since users cannot bring in and use their favourite games. In such systems, the station is fitted with a remote boot ROM system, which allows the node to be booted directly from the server; the node retrieves the files from the server that it needs to boot. Also available are stations that only have a floppy drive fitted, to allow the transfer of data (where this is required), while retaining major cost benefits.

NETWORK COMPUTERS

Network computers, NCs, are computer that have been designed as *'network centric computing'* systems. Earlier workstations were really cut-down PCs that were sold for connection to a network. Network Computers have been specially designed as LAN stations. They are housed in cases about the size of this book and have no discs, no software and not even an operating system. A flash ROM in the NC contains a program that locates the server and downloads all its software from it. The server requires additional software to handle NCs.

NETWORK INTERFACE CARDS

The network interface card (NIC) is a device to connect the computer on to the network cabling. In most cases, it is a card which fits into the expansion bus of the computer motherboard. In other cases, it is separate unit which attaches to the computer's serial or parallel port. External units are particularly useful for portable and notebook computers, where there no space for internal expansion (these units are often referred to as *'lan adapters'*). Interface units come in a range of types, sizes and speeds. Performance of interface units is a key factor in network performance.

The interface card takes the data from the node computer and puts into the appropriate format before sending it on the cable to another interface card. When the card receives data it puts into a form that can be recognised by the computer. To achieve this, the card must perform many operations - e.g. buffers must be checked, requests must be acknowledged, sessions must be established, perhaps tokens are sent, collisions may be detected, etc. The list of activities can be categorised thus:

- host-card communications
- packet formation
- encoding/decoding
- handshaking

- buffering
- parallel-serial conversion
- cable access
- transmission/reception

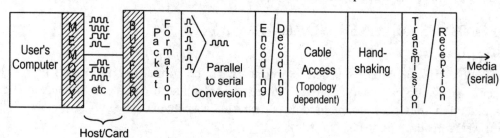

HOST-CARD COMMUNICATIONS

The first need is to move data back and forward between the PC and the interface unit. This can be achieved in three ways:

Direct Memory Access (DMA)

All Intel-based computers come with a DMA controller which handles the transfer of data from an input/output device to the PC's main memory, thereby relieving the PC's main processor. The controller informs the main CPU that it needs to perform DMA. The CPU then gives up control of the computer bus to the DMA controller. The DMA controller can then take data from the card and place it directly into memory. When all the data is in memory, the DMA controller passes control of the bus back to the computer CPU and informs it of the amount of data placed in memory.

I/O Mapping

The most common version is a 'memory-mapped' system. The computer CPU allocates some of the 640k main memory space to the interface unit (around 12k). Data is read from the card straight into this memory area.

There are no extra instructions required to get data from the card, since it is already sitting in the computer memory. All that is required is the movement of data from one part of the memory to another, using standard memory movement instructions. The Western Digital token ring cards use the memory mapped method.

Shared Memory

This is similar to I/O mapping in that the CPU memory is shared with the card's processor. However, both the card and the CPU do their work on the data in the same area, eliminating any subsequent transfers.

Comparisons

- ❍ The shared Memory method is the fastest but is the least used for various cost and execution reasons.
- ❍ The DMA method allows the computer CPU to perform other tasks while it is transferring data (as long as these tasks don't involve memory access).
- ❍ I/O mapping takes up main memory and doesn't relieve the CPU from any work; but it is still usually faster than the DMA method.

BUS SIZES

Interface cards were originally 8-bit but now have 16-bit or 32-bit connections to the computer data bus. The wider the data bus, the more data can be transferred in a single operation - i.e. the wider bus cards have a faster performance. The wider bus cards are, naturally, more expensive than more basic models. The older 8-bit models are generally said to be *'NE1000 compatible'* with 16-bit cards being termed *'NE2000 compatible'* and 32-bit cards being *'NE3000 compatible'.*. A 16-bit MCA or ISA card handles around 3Mbps while a 32-bit PCI card handles 7Mbps.

BUFFERING

The interface units are mostly fitted with buffer chips to store data as it moves between the media and the computer. This temporary storage is provided to compensate for the differing speeds of different parts of the process. Data is received into the interface at a faster rate than it can be processed (e.g. being converted to/from a packet, being converted from serial or parallel). The interface holds the data while it is processed. It is possible to use the PC's RAM as a buffer area, although this takes up main memory and can be slow.

PACKET FORMATION

Part of the responsibility of a network is to give each user a fair proportion of media time. So, if a user wishes to download a giant file from the server, other users do not require to patiently wait until this is transmitted. Instead, all traffic between nodes is composed of subsections of files that can then be interspersed on the media. In this way, a user requiring a small file from the server can have that need served during the time a larger file is being transferred.

A *'packet'* is the smallest independent unit of data that will be sent on the media. The Interface Card has the responsibility of breaking a file into packets before sending them onto the media; conversely, it will assemble the incoming packets into a coherent file for the computer. The packet's size and layout are dependent on the networks' access method. Each packet has three sections:

- The header will include information on the packet's source address and destination address.

- The data section contains the data being sent (e.g. word-processing or spreadsheet files - or could be a program file). The data section can be as large as 12k but is usually between 1k and 4k (Ethernet, for example has a data section size of 4kbytes).
- The trailer section contains information that is used for checking whether the data has arrived without any corruption. The information is subjected to a mathematical calculation which aims to produce a unique number for each different packet (for the mathematically minded, a constant is derived from a polynomial expression). This is called the 'cyclic redundancy check - CRC' and the resultant value is sent in the trailer section. When the packet is received by a node, the same calculation is applied to the information. If it produces the same value as in the trailer, then no corruption has taken place - any corrupted data will result in a different calculated CRC value.

PARALLEL-SERIAL CONVERSION

The data that comes from the computer to the interface card is in parallel format. However, the media that carries the transmission is only capable of handling serial transmission. The interface card has the task of converting the data from parallel to serial form. Serial transmission is slower than parallel transmission, hence the need for buffering previously mentioned.

ENCODING/DECODING

When data is made up into a packet and converted to serial format, it can be sent down the transmission medium, as a series of offs and ons.

At its simplest, the interface card could transmit a binary 1 as a positive voltage and a binary 0 as a negative voltage.   At the other end, the card would translate the series of voltages as a stream of binary 0s and 1s.   However, most interface cards use a less error-prone method known as *'Manchester Coding'*.   This is a *'polar code'* - which means that it does not have positive and negative swings.   A logic high - i.e. a bit 1 - is represented by 0v and a logic low - i.e. bit 0 - is represented by -2.05v.   The serial data uses a *'50% duty cycle'* - which means that the time allocated to each bit of the data stream is divided into two periods.   The first time period holds the actual bit representation.   The second period provides a signal that is always the opposite of the first period.   In this way, a constant change is guaranteed and this is used to ensure that the received signal is accurately synchronised, so that no false decoding occurs.

MEDIA ACCESS

The interface card also has the task of gaining access to the media (e.g. the cable).   This is no simple matter, since only one card can effectively communicate with the media at the one time.   Access is gained to the media in different ways, dependent on the network protocol in use.

HANDSHAKING

For successful transmission of a packet from one card to another, both cards have to be using the same parameters.   Typical parameters might be maximum packet size, buffer sizes, how many packets before an answer, acknowledge time-outs (how long to wait for an answer), etc.   Before the data packets are sent, the originating card transmits its parameters; the receiving card responds with its parameters.   The most sophisticated card then lowers its specification to match the other.

TRANSMISSION/RECEPTION

The lowest level of card activity is to interface all this activity to the media itself.

The transmitting card translates the data stream into a signal of sufficient power to be successfully transmitted down the media.   At the other end, the receiving card has to take the varying signal and convert it back into the data stream for decoding, serial/parallel conversion and depacketing.

SERVERS

Most networks are based on a *'client/server'* architecture, where there is a single computer at the operational heart of the system; this handles all the other machines' disc storage requirements and acts as a data exchange - routing data to any machine that requires it.   This central machine is called the *'server'* and generally is not used for any other purpose than controlling the network; this is called a *'dedicated server'*.   A *'non-dedicated server'* is a machine that carries out the functions of a file server, while also being able to be used as normal PC machine.   This is OK in small systems but would slow things down on a larger system, since the processor would have to share its time between network activities and the activities of the user at the server machine.   There are two types of server -

Utility servers -
These servers carry out the routine roles or the specialist roles in the network, where required (in a small organisation there may be no need of specialist utility servers).
    Examples of this type are:
        STANDARD :   file servers, print servers.
        SPECIALIST :   fax, mail, Internet and CD servers, modem pool servers, micro-to-mainframe gateways.
Application servers -
These servers perform computational tasks for network users
    (see client/server software later)
Large systems will have a number of servers on the one network system.

CHARACTERISTICS OF SERVERS

In the earliest days of networking, manufacturers marketed their own specially made machines as LAN servers.   These were overpriced and users realised that a standard PC could be used as a server, if it was powerful and reliable enough.   As a consequence, high-performance PCs now capture 90% of server sales.   Dedicated servers are still produced.   Often, they come as dedicated boxes (of various shapes and sizes) with no monitor or keyboard.   Since most network activities can be organised from any node, the lack of add-ons is not a disadvantage.   In fact, it is even claimed as an advantage, since it provides an extra level of security.   Some of the advertised benefits of dedicated servers over PCs are hype; however, dedicated servers can have advantages.

The following criteria may act as a yardstick for choosing a server:

SPEED

The raw processing speed of the server CPU is not as vitally important as it may appear at first glance. Buying the fastest 266MHz Pentium chip server may not produce a very significant improvement over a machine with a slower, older chip.   This is because the speed of the processor is generally less a bottleneck than the speed of the server's disc drives and NICs.

Consider the following:

- A file server activity does not require much in the way of computing time, in comparison to the disc access time.
- If a NIC is unable to transfer the data quickly, then there is no benefit in having the server process that data at a vastly faster rate.
- Consequently, faster computers do not necessarily produce faster server throughput; a basic Pentium is often regarded as being sufficiently powerful for a single-segment Ethernet.

The above is not true in every case. The CPU speed is important in the following situations:

- Where the server acts as an SQL server.   In this case, the server has to perform considerable computational tasks in addition to a normal server role.
- Where the server runs particular NLMs (Network Loadable Module) which have considerable computational roles.
- Where the server Interface Card is not of the 'bus master' type.   Here, the NIC circuitry does not relieve the server CPU of data transfer tasks - i.e. biggest part of server's work.

MULTI-PROCESSING

Some servers employ two CPUs - one for I/O activities and one for processing.   This is particularly useful in client/server operations (see later).   Examples of such servers are the Compaq SystemPro, the Apricot FT and the Olivetti Netframe.

BUS SIZE

The data bus of the node machine is connected to the data bus of the NIC when the card is plugged into the node's expansion slot.   A wide data bus would speed up the transfer of data from the node's memory into the NIC's buffer area (e.g. a 32-bit bus could transfer 32-bit binary data in a single operation, while a 16-bit bus would require to transfer the same 32-bit data as two separate 16-bit operations). In general, a wider data bus speeds up node/NIC communications and reduces bottlenecks.   The AT series, and its clones, used a 16-bit ISA bus and this proved too slow for network I/O tasks.

In response, IBM introduced MCA (Micro Channel Architecture). This is a 'bus mastering' system and it supports 32-bit cards.   However, it hit a number of problems:

- The cards for MCA won't fit ISA slot and MCA slots don't support ISA hardware.
- Users are concerned that they may end up tied in to IBM as a sole supplier.

As a result, the MCA system has not been taken up by other manufacturers.

To produce a viable alternative, a consortium led by Compaq introduced the EISA system.   This is also a bus mastering system with a 32-bit data transfer rate.   However, it remains AT-bus compatible. Most network systems use EISA-based servers. A big feature of networks is expandability - connecting the server to other systems.   Two, or often more, separate networks (or network segments) can meet at a single server.   That server will have a NIC which connects it to each network.   To provide this ability, servers will often have 8 - 11 expansion slots.   The Compaq System Pro, for example, handles six 32-bit controllers.   All current servers have moved over to PCI buses.

STORAGE

The server disc drive(s) store all application programs and data for the whole organisation.   This demands that the drives be the largest, fastest and most reliable that money can buy.

DISC ACCESS TIME

The old disc drive technology is being replaced on PCs with the more efficient EIDE system.   On servers, and high specification PCs, the new drive technology is SCSI (Small Computer Systems Interface).   This is the most popular server disc choice and has an access time of around 10mS.

DISC FAULT TOLERANCE

Due to the vital role of data in any organisation, it is not acceptable to have only a single copy on a single server drive.   Although organisations have rigorous and systematic backup procedures, this is insufficient for situations where data is rapidly changing. To ensure that data is always available, networks make use of multiple storage techniques such as disk shadowing and disk mirroring. The objective is to keep two copies of the data on different drives, in case one copy is corrupted. Of course, there is still a problem if the two drives are in the same server - and that server breaks down! In *'mission critical'* applications (those where it is essential that processing must continue), users employ a system of *'server mirroring'*. Here, if a server goes down, a duplicate server kicks in immediately, with the same applications and data. So, every update to the current server is also made to the shadow server.

RAID TECHNOLOGY

In large installations with multiple disc drives, access can be speeded up with a process known as *'striping'*. The data is written/read in parallel fashion over different drives. An extension of this principle is *'RAID'* technology. This is a *'Redundant Array of Inexpensive (or Independent) Discs'* and uses the following features:

- A set of discs is configured to perform like a single large drive.
- Redundancy is built in; extra discs are used, not to store data, but to protect the data.
- Discs are *'hot swappable'*; they can be removed and replaced while the network remains operational; the network carries on without loss of data.

The table shows the levels of protection available.

RAID Level	Method	Advantages	Disadvantages
0	Basic disc striping	Improves performance	No protection. Any disc failing collapses the system.
1	Discs are mirrored	Improves performance. Easily implemented.	Expensive as it requires all data discs to be duplicated (mirrored).
0+1	Data striping on mirrored drives	Improves performance. High level of data protection.	Expense. Slower writes.
2	2 or 3 check discs for every 4 data discs.	Improves performance. High level of data protection.	Expensive. Rarely implemented.
3	One additional disc stores parity bits.	Common, low-cost choice, requiring only one additional disc.	Slows when many disc write requests are implemented.
4	One additional disc stores ECC data.	Improves performance. Can handle multiple read requests.	Only handles one write operation at a time.
5	ECC data spread over all array's discs	Can handle read and write requests simultaneously.	Slow to rebuild after a disc crash.
6	ECC data written to two separate discs.	Good data security, as two discs can fail and data can be rebuilt.	Slower performance than Level 5.

MEMORY

The memory of the server is used for a wide range of caching, buffering and other activities. The minimum RAM for reasonable performance is around 16Mb. The system will run with less memory but the performance will degrade (e.g. a small disc cache allocation means more disc accesses, a small buffer allocation may result in lost packets).

RELIABILITY

Possibly the most important of all the factors when purchasing a server is the issue of reliability. A reliable network of average speed is much more productive than a faster system that is always breaking down.

Influencing factors are:

- Ordinary PCs that are pressed into service as servers may have hardware interrupt calls which will, on occasion, clash with the calls required by the network hardware. PCs that take this into account are called 'Network Compatible'.
- Whether servers have SETUP and diagnostics built in (e.g. Compaq).
- The use of an 'Uninterrupted Power Supply' - (UPS). This smoothes out mains spikes and fluctuations and - in the event of a complete power failure - provides a temporary supply to allow the data to be saved to disc. Servers, such as the Apricot FT, Keen MS range have a built-in UPS.
- The use of a standby CPU, in case of the failure of the main chip. This is a bit extreme but might be regarded as important in mission-critical work. A stand-by processor is standard in the Keen MS range.
- The replacement of NICs and disc controllers with built-in controllers and interfaces on the server main printed circuit board (PCB). This provides an increased MTBF (mean time between failure) rate. In other words, this area of the system does not break down so often!

PEER-TO-PEER LANs

Most medium and large systems use a dedicated server to control the network. There is a trend, in smaller organisation of say less than 10 users, to adopt a network system that has no main server. Instead, all the facilities of a node (i.e. local disc, local printer, etc.) are available to all others on the network. This is known as *'peer-to-peer'* working since there is no master PC. It is simple to implement but provides less facilities than a full network operating system. It is also slower, since all PCs also carry out some server activities.

PRINT SERVERS

Many users will be connected to a particular printer on the network. It is likely that several stations will send text files to the printer over the same period. A printer server will maintain a queue of such files. This appears to be similar to the PRINT command in MS-DOS in that 'spooling' is taking place. In fact, the print server handles the activity differently from MS-DOS. Each incoming print file is copied on to the disc of the print server. The file is then placed in the print queue to wait its turn. When the file is printed, it is deleted from the print server disc. It is also possible, in most networks, to place priorities on a file when it enters the queue, to change the order in which files are printed. A high priority file will be allowed to 'jump the queue'.

This system is perfectly acceptable in small, compact systems. The fact that all the documents end up in the one laser printer tray in the one location is not necessarily a problem. However, if the organisation is spread over a wide area, or many floors, then there could be a considerable inconvenience in collecting the printed material. In addition, there could be a problem of security, if sensitive documents are routed to a general pickup point (possibly breaching commercial or personal secrecy, not to mention the Data Protection Act).

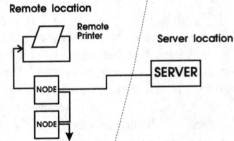

One solution lies in re-directing the de-spooled files from the server to a node on the network. This workstation has a TSR (terminate-and-stay-resident) program in its memory which routes the print file to its local printer. However, this local node will be used by ordinary users. As such it is liable to be switched off or crashed by the users, making the print process vulnerable.

Note that the term *'remote printing'* means remote from the server, not necessarily remote from the user.

Alternatively, a node on the network could be dedicated to handling an office's printing. The machine will not be used by staff, who will have their own workstations. The file server directs the user requests for printing to this print server which then handles all the associated file and print activities. This relieves the file server from much of its work and improves the overall efficiency of the system.

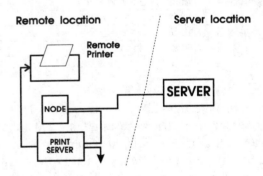

LAN MEDIA

The topology of a network describes how one device connects to another. It does not take into account the data transfer speed achievable on the media between the devices. It is analogous to connecting two towns on a map. The route may exist but the pathway could be anything from a country road to a motorway. In other words, the speed of a network is as fast as its slowest link.

There are two main performance factors when considering media:
- Transfer speed (easy to measure)
- Signal reliability

The three most common media types in networks are:
- Coaxial cable
- Twisted pair cable
- Fibre optic cable

Other transmission methods include wireless, infrared, satellite and microwave techniques. Many systems use coaxial cable but most new installations are using twisted pair cabling.

WIRE SYSTEMS

By far the most common method of data transmission is to send a simple electrical pulse along a length of wire. This is the basis of both the co-axial cable and twisted-pair systems.

ADVANTAGES:
- Cable and its connectors are relatively cheap.
- The cabling is easily installed.
- The ends of the cables are easily connected.

DISADVANTAGES:
- The electrical pulses on the cable are easily upset by electrical and magnetic disturbances.
- The pulses are also upset by temperature and humidity changes.
- The above necessitates careful routing of the network cables (e.g. if cable goes outside to connect to office blocks, it is best to use a pair of modems at either end, rather than use a simple cable link).
- Limited bandwidth compared to fibre optic systems.
- Segment length is short compared to fibre optic systems. Cat3 cable works up to 100m with cat4 and cat5 at 150m.

TWISTED PAIR

This type was initially used in IBM token-rings and Cambridge ring systems. It was also used on StarLan networks (AT&T) and 3Com's Ethernet. The LAN standards of Ethernet, Arcnet and token-ring have been modified to allow them to run on twisted-pair and fibre-optic.   Although previously only common in small offices of 10-12 nodes, the faster speeds of the system and the associated electronics has led to a rapid expansion in twisted pair's use as the main medium for larger installations.

Twisted-pair cable is available in both shielded (STP) and unshielded (UTP) varieties.

UNSHIELDED

The basic twisted pair system uses a cable, similar to telephone cable; made up of two insulated copper wires twisted together (usually a total of two pairs). They often use telephone-style jack sockets to connect PCs to the cabling system. The wires are twisted to minimise crosstalk with other cables and to reduce the effects of external interference.   It is the cheapest of the media types and, due to its construction, is the easiest to install. Unshielded twisted-pair cabling is used in 4Mbps token-ring systems. Although unshielded pair cable is used for Ethernet systems, additional apparatus such as bridges, equalisers and transceivers can result in the system being significantly more expensive than coaxial cable systems. Nevertheless, unshielded pair is the most common medium for low-cost, short-distance LANs. UTP cables follow the specifications in the chart.

Category	Usage
Cat 1	up to 20Kbps
Cat 2	up to 4Mbps
Cat 3	up to 16MHz
Cat 4	up to 20MHz
Cat 5	up to and beyond 100MHz

SHIELDED

To limit interference problems, the twisted pair can be covered in a metal braid that is grounded. This is known as 'shielded' cable and makes the cable vastly less prone to interference (around 1000 times better). The braid also provides great extra physical strength to the cable.   It is this cable that is used for the IBM token-ring (16Mbps) and Cambridge ring system, which runs at 10Mbps.   IBM offers both shielded and unshielded versions. The IBM shielded cable is rather more expensive. It consists of two pairs of twisted cable, each wrapped in plastic, then wrapped in aluminium file and copper braid; both pairs being enclosed in a final plastic sheath.

The diagram shows the wiring for the standard RJ-45 plug - the type that is used with twisted pair plugs.

Token ring systems use pairs 1 and 3.

10Base-T uses pairs 2 and 3.

100Base-T4 uses all four pairs of wires.

100Base-VG uses all four pairs of wires.

Where two nodes require to be connected to connected to each other for PC to PC transfers, the transmit and receive pins in the cable have to be reversed to create a *'nul modem'* cable.

Pin	Function	Data Direction	Function	Pin
1	[TX+]	→	[RX+]	3
2	[TX-]	→	[RX-]	6
3	[RX+]	←	[TX+]	1
6	[RX-]	←	[TX-]	2

COAXIAL CABLE

This cable is similar to the type used to connect TV aerials.   This was the most popular choice of media, since it offered high speeds, greater bandwidth, fair distances and reasonable costs.

Coaxial cable is designed to minimise the *'skin effect'* problem that affects all wire carriers.   As the data transfer rate in a wire is increased, the current in that wire tends to flow along its outer skin.   Since there is now less surface to carry the current, there is greater cable resistance, hence greater signal losses. Therefore, twisted pair is less efficient at higher speeds. To help overcome this skin effect, coaxial cable was introduced.   Its outer conductor is in the shape of a tube. The copper in its construction is all effectively used.   As a result, practically all network operating system software includes drivers for Ethernet cards.

There are two Ethernet standards - thin and thick co-axial cable. Both transmit at 10Mbps. These are called 10Base-2 and 10Base-5.

The 10 indicates the maximum system speed in Mbps, the 'Base' indicates the system runs in baseband mode (see later) and the final number indicates the maximum length allowed for a single cable segment (in hundreds of metres).

ETHERNET THIN

Ethernet thin is also known as CheaperNet, ThinNet or 10BASE2.   Coaxial cable has two conductors.

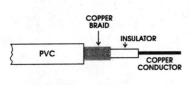

ETHERNET THIN CABLE

The inner conductor is a solid copper core. The outer copper braid acts as the second conductor. The two conductors are held apart by plastic insulation.   The cable is enclosed in a PVC casing.   The bus cable has to visit every station that is used on the network, where it connects to the node with a BNC connector. ThinNet environments are designed for 30 nodes per segment and a maximum segment length of 185m (extending to 925m with repeaters).   It uses a 50 ohm cable (type RG58) which supports up to 10Mbps baseband working with an error rate of only 1 in 10^7.

ETHERNET THICK

Also known as Standard, ThickNet or 10BASE5.   Its construction is similar to ThinNet, with an added layer of aluminised tape and an extra layer of copper braid. It is also a 50 ohm baseband cable and uses a coaxial n-type connector.

Due to its more complex construction, Standard Ethernet is somewhat more expensive than ThinNet.

The size of ThickNet (10.3mm thick) also makes it expensive to install - as it is difficult to thread through existing cable runs. However, due its increased size, it suffers fewer losses than ThinNet. Consequently, it covers greater distances (up to 500m, extending to 2,500m with repeaters) and handles up to 100 users. Taps off the cable must be at least 2.5m apart. It is often used as a cabling *'spine'* - i.e. a main backbone from which ThinNet spurs can attach. The use of coaxial cable is declining, in favour of twisted-pair.

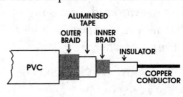

ETHERNET THICK CABLE

TRANSCEIVERS

Notice that, with both thin and thick cable, the station can be situated remotely from the bus cable. To route a cable to the remote site and another cable returning from the site would greatly add to the overall

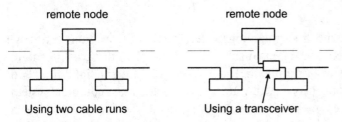

Using two cable runs   Using a transceiver

length of the segment.   This in turn, limits the remaining area that can be covered by the cable.

An alternative strategy is to tap a transceiver on to the bus cable.   The node can then be connected to the transceiver by a single cable. The bus cable is tapped into by connecting a transceiver. The special cable from the transceiver to the station can be up to 50m in length.   These are expensive cables (costing more than ThickNet cable) and connect to the transceiver with an N series plug.   The other end of the cable connects to the PC card with a 15-pin or 9-pin D connector. Transceivers have to be at least 2.5m apart and a maximum of 100 transceivers is allowed on a single bus.

FIBRE OPTIC

All electrical conductors suffer from electrical resistance, poor insulation and electrical disturbance, due to unwanted electrical signals. These effects can be greatly overcome by the use of optical fibre cables. This system uses light instead of electrical pulses. The cable consists of a thin, flexible strand of glass,

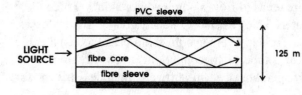

only slightly larger than a human hair. Plastic-clad silica or all-plastic versions are also available, but they are not as efficient or as easy to use. Most systems are made from a very pure silica, covered with a glass clad. A light source (either LED or laser) is fed into one end of the cable and the light travels along the cable core, reflecting off the cable's walls (the *'clad'*). There is total internal reflection within the cable, occurring at the core/cladding interface. Total internal reflection occurs because the core has a higher refractive index compared to the cladding.

LED or laser light sources can be used. LED light sources are much lower powered and are used for shorter distances (a few kilometres) at speeds of around 200 Mbps. Laser sources are much more expensive but can handle longer distances and higher transmission speeds (around 1000 Mbps).

DISADVANTAGES:
- Held back by lack of standards.
- Held back by lack of knowledge.
- Most expensive of the media types.
- Difficult to install.

ADVANTAGES:
- Handles much greater speeds (10-100 times faster than coax)
- Greater distances than coaxial cable (less attenuation)
- Performs faultlessly at 100Mbps. It has the lowest error rate, at one faulty bit in every 10,000,000,000.
- It is immune from electromagnetic interference. Ideal for 'noisy' environments e.g. lift shafts, shop floor
- Safe in most conditions. The cable carries only light, so there is no electrical energy to cause a spark in a hazardous or explosive environment (e.g. mines/oil plants/ gas plant).
- Greater security (very hard to tap into; no radiation allowing remote monitoring)
- Electrical isolation - no crosstalk

Most networks do not support fibre optics as standard. It is available for token-ring and Ethernet systems and is expected to increase its share of use. Its main use is seen where there are a large volume of traffic or where very large files are used (eg video, multimedia, etc)

There are two kinds of optical cable - mono-mode (or single-mode) and multi-mode.

MONO MODE

Mono-mode fibre cable is only about 8 micro-metres in diameter and is used mostly in long-distance communications. Here, the diameter of the core is only a few times greater than the wavelength of the transmitted light and only a single ray will be propagated, in almost a straight line. A large part of the power is propagated in the cladding near the core. The cable is difficult to connect to transmitters and receivers, since precise alignment is required. It supports a greater data rate than multi-mode, with a bandwidth of 1GHz over 1km being not uncommon.

MULTI-MODE

Multi-mode fibre consists of a thicker core, with a surrounding fibre sleeve with different refractive qualities. Most of the power travels in the core. The core is many times greater than that used in single-mode. This allows WDM (Wavelength Division Multiplexing) since several different light signals at different frequencies can be transmitted simultaneously. Multi-mode cable is the most common system, since it requires a lower manufacturing tolerance, making it cheaper to produce. They are also easier to attach to hardware.

However, there is no agreement amongst manufacturers as to the dimension of multi-mode cable. All makes use an outer diameter of 125 micro-metres, with the exception of IBM who promote 140 micro-metres. Additionally, different manufacturers promote different inner core diameters (50 to 100 microns).

LIGHT EMITTERS

The problems of getting the light into the fibre are often the greatest cause of loss in the system.   As the surface area of the light emitter and the end of the cable are so small, even a small misalignment can mean that the light does not even enter the cable.   Alignment is very critical and needs expertise and the proper equipment.   LEDs (Light Emitting Diode) deliver up to 100 microwatts into the cable.   They are cheap, have long lives and work up to 100MHz.   ILDs (Injection Laser Diodes) deliver a couple of milliwatts into the cable.   They are expensive and require complex circuitry (not to mention coolers!) to maintain a stable output.   They have bandwidths of over several hundred MegaHertz.

BYTE-WIDE

Since an individual fibre is so small, it is common to have more than a single fibre in a cable.   Normally, they would carry separate data information for different users.   In ultra-high performance systems, a single user can use eight separate channels on the cable, one for each bit of a byte.   In effect, the user is able to make parallel transmissions at eight times the normal rate.

FDDI

In an attempt at standardisation, ANSI (the American National Standards Institute) has issued the FDDI (Fibre Distributed Data Interface) standard, covering data only.   This promotes a 100 Mbps ring topology LAN with 125 micro-metre outer and a range of inner diameters (from 50 to 85 micro-metres) to suit different manufacturers.   The system has two rings, the second being a backup (built-in redundancy).   Its characteristics are:

- supports 500 nodes
- nodes can be up to 2km apart
- maximum ring circumference of 100km
- does not require amplifiers or signal conditioning apparatus

A successor, FDDI II, which includes digitised live voice and video, is being developed.

The main uses for FDDI are seen as being:

- backbone connecting low-speed LAN systems together
- use for high-performance workstations/image processing
- LANs to mainframes, minis and high-speed devices
- future need to integrate voice/video on LAN (bandwidth)
- increase of nodes on networks

Token-ring LANs are more easily supported by fibre-optic cabling than Ethernet.

WIRELESS NETWORKS

In this system, there is no cable connecting the various nodes.   The transmission between the node and the server is carried by either:

Infrared	Line-of-sight only. Cheap to implement. Supported by newer motherboards and by Windows 95. No requirement for a licence. IrDA standards are version 1 (115.2Kbps) and version 2 (115.2Kbps and 4Mbps).
Microwave	Line-of-sight only. Costly but wide bandwidth. Requires a licence. Used by large private and public systems with heavy data throughput requirements.
Radio wave	Implemented as wireless LANs (for small defined areas) or as mobile LANS (see below).

With Wireless LANs, the computer is connected to a radio transmitter/receiver, similar to the kind found in a CB radio.   This provides easy communication to the server (e.g. from a remote area of a building). The system requires no cabling and is ideal for setting up temporary networks.

MOBILE LANs

Cellular radio has brought mobile phones to a large section of the business community.   Many of these users also own small handheld computers.   Mobile LANs are ways of integrating the two products so that handhelds, such as the Psion 3C, Apple Newton Message Pad 130 and Hewlett Packard 700LX, can link to the office network system from any location.   This technology is still in its infancy and data rates are only 9,600bps which is similar to an older modem.   It can handle e-mail, file transfers and slow Internet access.

MAINS WIRING

A cheap alternative media is the use of the existing mains cabling, since it already spans every room in a building. To avoid problems with mains fluctuations, a form of frequency modulation is used.   These are normally small systems running at relatively slow speeds.

TRANSMISSION METHODS

There are two main methods of transmitting over a network:

BASEBAND

This is the most common method for LANs.   It is essentially a digital technique, with the node's signal being applied directly to the media, in a similar fashion to TTL or RS232 levels (i.e. +15v represents 0 and -15v represents 1).   There is no signal processing and the entire medium bandwidth is used for a single transmission at any one time.   Since only one transmission can be handled, high transmission rates are necessary.   It is also necessary to share the medium between nodes on a time-sharing basis known as TDM (time division multiplexing).

Digital signals are transmitted as a sequence of 0s and 1s. A negative voltage on the line represents a '0' condition, while a positive signal represents a '1' condition.   Changes of signal voltage cannot be used as a means of detecting '0' and '1' states, since a series of 0s or 1s could be sent - producing no voltage change.   It is necessary, therefore, to time each pulse to detect whether there are multiple occurrences of the same pulse.   This requires that the transmitting and receiving nodes be synchronised.   This is achieved by sending the data in a form known as *'Manchester coding'* which uses the codes themselves to maintain the necessary synchronisation.

BROADBAND

Where an organisation has large/complex communication demands, a broadband system will normally be in operation. The advantages of the broadband system include:

- The ability to carry multiple channels
- The ability to carry analogue signals, e.g. voice and TV
- The ability to cover long distances. Analogue signals do not suffer from degradation to the same extent as digital signals and are easier to boost using analogue amplifiers.
- The ability to interface different baseband systems, using the broadband system as the network 'backbone'.

The disadvantages are:

- High initial cost; the equipment is expensive to buy and to set up. The operation also takes careful planning.
- Each network adapter needs its own modem
- Needs regular testing and adjustment (as with a radio, mistuning leads to loss of the information).
- Difficult to insert new stations

A better name for this system would be 'multi-band' since the cable carries more than one data channel, using 'frequency division multiplexing'.   The channels are separated by using each data source to modulate a different radio frequency, called the 'carrier' frequency. These carriers are then placed on the media, where they occupy different parts of the radio spectrum. The channels are separated out at the receiving end into the required channels.   This is the same technique as used by cable TV firms to place several TV channels on the one TV cable.   Each data channel can then effectively be considered as a separate baseband channel, from an access and sharing point of view.

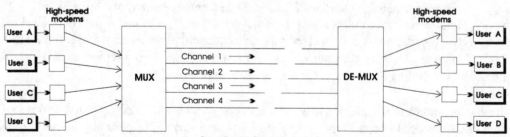

Broadband Transmission

Each channel operates independently of the others and can therefore run at different speeds using different access methods. For example, one channel could be dedicated to networking PCs while another connects IBM 3270 terminals to a mainframe computer. A node will usually be allocated to a particular channel (e.g. a node running AUTOCAD would be attached to the channel allocated to the transfer of the image files). A node could be allowed to choose which channel to connect to.

The width of a broadband channel depends on the data being carried. For data channels, the required bandwidth will increase with increasing data transfer rates. Ethernet, for example, will require 18MHz of bandwidth. LocalNet, on the other hand, opts for 120 slow-speed channels (only 128Kbps) each channel requiring 300KHz of bandwidth. Broadband systems are currently in use to carry multiple data channels and video for LAN applications, although it appears likely that it will be overtaken by fibre-optic systems.   The only PC network to use broadband is the IBM token ring system, which transmits on 50.75MHz and receives on 219MHz.

NOTES:

> The system uses cable TV equipment - i.e. one way only - and is therefore usually a twin cable system. An alternative is to split the bandwidth into transmit and receive bands.

> The system uses expensive, high-speed, modems at each node. Modems can be a single pair of frequencies (1 for transmit, 1 for receive) or can be 'frequency agile' - can access several channels.

ETHERNET AND IEEE STANDARDS

In the ideal world, all computer devices would easily connect together, using the same electronic methods and the same communication protocols.   However, due to the historical development of networks via competing manufacturers, many differences exist between the brand names - even where the products are supposed to conform to the same standard.   The chart shows the most common systems in use

Ethernet Specification	IEEE Standard	Band	Usage
1Base5	802.3	Baseband	1Mbps using UTP, STP cable
10Base2	802.3	Baseband	10Mpbs using thin coax cable
10Base5	802.3	Baseband	10Mpbs using thick coax cable
10BaseF	802.3	Baseband	10Mbps using fibre optic cable
10BaseT	802.3	Baseband	10Mbps using UTP cable
10Broad36	802.3	Broadband	10Mpps using broadband cable
100BaseT	802.3u	Baseband	100Mbps using UTP, fibre optic cable
100VG-AnyLAN	802.12	Baseband	100Mbps using UTP cable

The IEEE Local Networks Standards Committee has developed the series of LAN standards listed below:
- IEEE 802.3 Covers the carrier sense multiple access and collision detection (CSMA/CD) access method and physical layer specification.
- Ethernet, mainly developed by Xerox, Intel and DEC, introduced in 1980.
- IEEE 802.5 Covers the token passing ring access method and physical layer specification mainly developed by IBM, introduced in 1985.
- 802.1 Covers the system overview, architecture, addressing, internetworking and network management.
- 802.4 Covers the token passing bus access method. Usually found in factory environments, where MAP (Manufacturing Automation Protocol) is its most popular implementation.
- 802.6 Covers the Metropolitan network access method.

PRACTICAL CABLING

The simplest network cable configuration is a single segment of cable on which the server and all nodes are located.   This is a perfectly satisfactory layout for a small network but many networks gradually grow both in the number of stations connected and the distance the network has to cover.   Greater usage and greater distances normally leads to additions to the system and these have to be planned.

EFFECT OF SEGMENT LENGTH ON COLLISIONS

Consider three nodes on a network, one attached at each extreme end and one in the middle of the segment length. The left-most node transmits a packet and needs to detect if it has collided with another packet on the cable, say one being sent by the right-most node. A user's packet, being in serial format, takes a finite time to place on the cable. It also takes a finite time to travel to the ends of the cable.   The distance between the two furthest nodes must be short enough for one node's packet to travel to all other nodes (the other end of the cable being the furthest cases) during the lifetime of the other's transmission. If this is the case, then the packets will corrupt each other and the collision will be detected.   However, if the segment length is too great, the left node's packet will be completely sent before the right node's transmission arrives. A collision has still occurred but has not now been detected. Both packets still collide in the middle of the cable and both are corrupted.   This explains why a limit is placed on the length of a network segment.

EXTENDING A NETWORK

A range of hardware is available to allow a single segment to join with another segment, or several segments, to form a larger network.

REPEATERS

Individual segments of a LAN bus can be connected with *'repeaters'*.   A repeater receives the transmission from one segment, amplifies and cleans up the signal and re-transmits it to the other segment.   In this way, the maximum cable length and number of stations can be increased from the previous limits.   Repeaters do not have any control over addressing or forwarding and therefore do not ease congestion and collision on the system.   They operate at the OSI physical layer 1.

A multiport repeater has many outlet sockets and copies the transmission over multiple segments.

BRIDGES

A bridge connects two segments and passes traffic between them. It is used to extend the network size

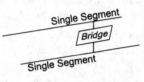

without breaking the limit on any segment size, attached device count, or number of repeaters per segment.   It is very popular with small networks.   A bridge can be a standalone piece of equipment but is often a PC with two NICs, one connecting to each segment. A learning bridge builds up a picture of what addresses are on each side of the bridge and decides whether packets are allowed to cross the bridge.   For this purpose, it operates at the Data Link Layer level 2 and uses the MAC (Media Access Control) sub-layer to check addresses.   The only traffic allowed on a segment is

traffic destined for a node on that segment. Since there is reduced traffic, there are also less collisions and less wasted traffic. However, when a bridge becomes busy, it places traffic in memory buffers and when these buffers become full, user's frames are discarded.

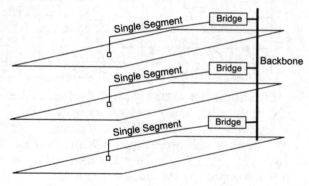

A bridge is also used as a connection between the building's main data backbone and separate segments for each floor.   So, packets addressed to a node on the ground floor will not be sent on to the segments on the other floors; they will not pass through the first floor and second floor bridges.

ROUTERS

A router is like a bridge except that it works on OSI Network Layer level 3 protocols.   Messages are transmitted to other segments dependent upon their protocol level address (eg TCP/IP address) rather than the MAC addresses.   So they can bridge an Ethernet with token ring, translating and passing packets between them. They are slower than bridges but are used for larger networks, since they are better at handling collisions and bandwidth utilisation.   Routers can communicate with other routers on the network to which route of possible options is most efficient.

GATEWAYS

A gateway is used to connect two networks whose communications protocols are different.   So, a gateway device might connect an Ethernet segment to a Unix system, a mainframe computer or an ISDN or X.25 communications line. Gateways handle a larger range of protocols than a router The gateway device carries out the translation of information between the systems.

DESIGN RESTRICTIONS

There is a *'5-4-3'* rule for connecting unbridged systems.

    The system must not have more than 5 repeated segments

    The system must not have more 4 repeaters/hubs between any 2 stations

    The system must have no more than 3 of the segments populated

The layout of the network structure must follow these rules to ensure consistent network operation.

In addition, a maximum of 7 bridges is allowed in a system.

STRUCTURED CABLING

The above additions can, and often do, develop in a piecemeal way, as the organisation gradually expands.   They keep the network operating but a large collection of such segments and components may eventually not produce the efficient working that is required.   For systems that need reorganised, and particularly for new networks, the principle of structured cabling is important.

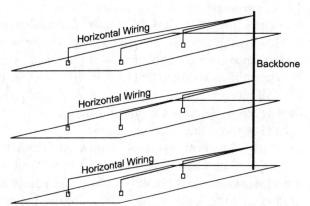

With structured cabling, the total system comprises simple wiring structures that are repeated in various locations, or various floors of the building and then combined.

The diagram shows a 3 floor building with the outline of a structured cabling layout.   The type of cabling and type of hardware components offer a range of options to suit an organisation's operational needs as well as the building layout.

The main features should be:

- A fast cabling type for the building's data backbone.   This vertical cabling carries the heavy data needs throughout the building.   The backbone could be fibre optic, Thicknet or cat5 UTP depending upon the implementation decided upon.
- Floors are *'flood wired'*.   Cables are not only routed to where computers currently sit; cables are taken to all places where a computer may be located in the future.   This is usually a ratio of connections per square metre of floor space.
- Cabling provides enough spare capacity for future use (eg running two cables to each workspace).
- All cables on a particular floor are taken to a *'wiring closet'*.   This is a small cupboard or room with a patch panel with connections for each cable.
- All further connections to equipment is carried out in the wiring closet, providing flexibility.
- Fast systems must provide slower speed ports for connecting to printers, routers and bridges that are not designed for fast speeds.
- Data hungry workstations, such as those used for CAD, Multimedia, video and DTP, can be linked to the main system using a fast network card.

FAST SYSTEMS

A number of competing technologies exist for fast 100Mbps and above operation.   FDDI has the best performance but is very expensive.   The other options are:

- 100Base-T
- 100Base-VG
- Ethernet switches
- ATM

100Base-T

Also known as Fast Ethernet, this remains a CSMA/CD Ethernet system.   It offers three options:

- 100Base-TX, which uses 2 pairs of the cat5 cable
- 100Base-T4, which uses 4 pairs of cat3, cat4 or cat5 cable
- 100Base-FX, which uses 2 strands of optical fibre

100BaseTX and 100BaseT4 have a 100m maximum length between node and hub.   The two furthest nodes cannot be greater than 200m apart (including 2 repeaters or hubs which cannot be more than 5m apart in between. Longer distances are achieved using switches or switching hubs.

Fast Ethernet requires new switched hubs and NICs. Existing 10Mbps hubs and NICs can be retained for average users while power users have direct 100Mbps connections as shown in the diagram.   The server has a 100Mbps switched NIC and feeds 100Mbps to the Fast Ethernet switch.   Power users with heavy bandwidth needs are connected directly to this switch to maximise their bandwidth.   The switch also

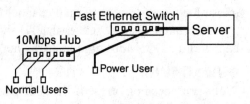

feeds 100Mbps to normal 10Mbps hubs which each feed a number of normally loaded PCs.   The Fast switch could feed 100Mbps to another 100Mbps switch in a 'cascade' of high speed connections.

It is a simpler and cheaper system than 100VG but is less efficient at handling time-dependent data.

100VG-AnyLAN

100VG supports token ring frames but is mainly used with Ethernet .   It doesn't use the standard Ethernet CSMA/CD.   Instead, it uses *'Demand Priority Protocol'* which has a normal and high priority level.   High priority transmissions are given precedence over lower priority activities to ensure adequate performance for time-critical applications such as process control, multimedia and live video.   It is a high performance system that uses up to 95% of its maximum theoretical capacity.

Like all modern wiring systems, it uses twisted pair connected to hubs and the hubs can be cascaded to three levels of depth as shown in the diagram.

100VG supports the following options

- 4 pairs of cat3, cat4 - with a 100m limit between node and hub and also between hubs
- 2 or 4 pairs for cat5 - with a 150m limit between node and hub and also between hubs

Since the system does not have to listen for collisions, the signalling pair used by 10Base-T is no longer used and all four pairs in the UTP can be used to carry data.   So, the multi-core cable designed to carry 10Mbps now carries 40Mbps.   There is also much redundant data sent in a normal Manchester coded (see page 406) packet.   Two bits of data are transmitted for every bit of actual data.   100Base-VG uses a method called 5B6B NRZ which uses 6 bits to represent every 5 bits instead of the 10 bits required by Manchester encoding.

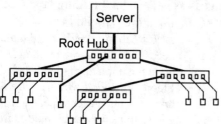

The system uses round robin access (ie token ring access) inside the hub.   The hub checks each node in turn looking for traffic. So, all ports get a fair share of the bandwidth, apart from any changed priorities imposed by the Demand Priority protocol.

With 100VG, packets are sent to the destination node only, not transmitted to all nodes as in a single bus segment.   It requires new hubs and NICs, since it is no longer based on the collision detection mechanism of layer 2.   The network can retain the existing cabling but a translation bridge is required between the 100VG and 10Base-T components.

SWITCHED ETHERNET .

While 100Base-T retained CSMA/CD for its high-speed system, Switched Ethernet abandons shared access methods in favour of a point-to-point connection set up by switched components for the duration of the communication.   By eliminating collisions, the existing bandwidth is used much more effectively. As the diagram shows, the server, power users and normal hubs all connect to the switch.   The users then have 'bandwidth on demand' - a guaranteed 10Mbps allocation.

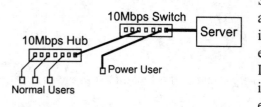

Switched Ethernet uses the existing servers, nodes, cabling and NICs but requires changes and additions to the cabling infrastructure (ie the addition of an Ethernet Switch and existing nodes reconfigured through extra hubs).

It is a cheap option and is easily set up.   It is a great improvement over standard Ethernet but is not powerful enough for large throughput demands.

ATM

Asynchronous Transfer Mode is available in two options:

- 25Mbps for cat5, with a 150m limit between switch and node.
- 155Mbps for multi-mode fibre, with a 2km limit

It uses switching hubs and 'cells' (packets of only 48 data bytes and 5 header bytes).   Cells are transmitted over 'pipes' (virtual channels) between a node, a switch and another node. The bandwidth for each channel can be set separately, allowing heavy users such as multimedia to run with a guaranteed bandwidth of 155Mbps right up to the node. At the moment it is used largely for fast backbones.

THE FUTURE

Work is proceeding on the IEEE 802.3z standard which provides for Gigabit Ethernet. Versions for Fast Ethernet and 100VG are being developed. UTP and fibre optic in both single mode and multi-mode are the likely carriers of this technology. With Fast Ethernet working at 70% and 100VG working at 96% of maximum throughput, Gigabit technology promises actual performances os700Mbps and 960Mbps respectively.

SOFTWARE ON THE NETWORK

Most modern software is capable of being run on a stand-alone PC or over a network. An application is loaded from the hard disc of the file server into the memory of the calling node. The program is then run in the machine memory. This means that the program can be downloaded to as many nodes as require it. This has encouraged the purchase of single copies of applications, rather than the multi- licence network versions. The lack of network facilities in the applications could sometimes be overcome by the network utilities of the operating system. To prevent this, many single-user applications (e.g. SuperCalc) now test to see whether it is being used in a machine with a network operating system. If it detects such a system, it refuses to run. Some applications, such as dBase and Paradox, operate on a network as standard. Others, such as DataEase, require that network versions be purchased.

FILE PROBLEMS

The main difference between stand-alone and network use is in the ability to share files. The application program can be easily copied into the memory of several stations; the problems arise from stations trying to use the same data files. Consider the case of two station users running Wordstar which is on the file server in single-user mode. Both users decide to load the same monthly report to make their own amendments/additions. The first user will successfully load the original file and begin working on it. While this is happening, the second user can also successfully load the original file and make other changes. The problem arises when the users save their files, since only a single copy of a unique file-name can be exist on the disc. Both users amended versions will be saved - but whoever saves second overwrites the file of the first user to save. In other words, the amendments of the first user are lost - and the user will not even know it has happened. An even worse situation exists if both users try to save simultaneously. At best, a new file will be created which has elements of both files. At worst, the disc file organisation may be affected, causing other files to be irretrievable.

There are other occasions when the user would wish an entire file to be used exclusively by a single user. For example, when packing a database (to remove records marked as deleted), no other user should have access to that file. These problems are overcome by a system of 'file locking'.

FILE LOCKING

This is enacted either by automatic or manual means.

AUTOMATIC LOCKING

When MS-DOS version 3 was issued, it introduced new facilities for 'file locking'. These additions were designed specifically to support multi-user networks and are were called the NOS (Network Operating System). In MS-DOS v3 onwards, when a file is opened (for reading or writing), access to that file is denied to any user. Thus, the file is only available to one user at any one time. This eliminates the file problems previously mentioned. MS-DOS, from version 3.3 onwards, contains a utility called SHARE.EXE, which maintains a table of all open files. This utility is used by MSDOS (version 3.3 on) compatible network operating systems. Nowadays the vendors of most Network Operating Systems use the file-locking and record-locking interrupts of DOS 3.1 and above, to allow applications to control access to the files. Thus, spreadsheets, databases and word processors can run happily on the network. The default locking mechanism of MS-DOS overcomes the simultaneous update clashes by stopping file sharing completely. However, most application files are never updated and could therefore be shared by many simultaneous users. To provide this flexibility, MS-DOS won't lock a file that is set to be Read Only. It would seem to make sense, therefore, to set all shareable programs to be Read Only. Unfortunately some applications, usually for reasons of copy protection, write to their own program and overlay files and this makes them effectively unshareable.

In Novell, the supervisor of the network can ensure that certain files are only able to be read but cannot be amended (i.e. written to). This allows multiple users to download and run system files, review product information, etc. from databases and read text files.

When a file is allowed to be written to, it will be marked accordingly (by changing a file attribute bit). When one of these files is opened by a user, the file is automatically 'locked' by the network operating system. When another user attempts to open the same file, either a 'file locked' message will be presented, or the user may be allowed to open the file on a read-only basis (dependent on the application being used). If a non-LAN version of an application is in use, other miscellaneous error messages are liable to be generated.

MANUAL LOCKING

The use of SHARE.EXE works well in those situations where the file is kept open (therefore kept locked) during the entire time that the file is being worked on by a user. However, a number of applications (such as spreadsheets and word processors) only open the file, read the contents into computer memory, then close the file again. The user works on the data within memory, the file being closed - and therefore free to be opened by other users. When the user is finished working on the data, the file is re-opened to write away the new details. This presents most of the original problems, since the file is only locked during the actual process of reading and writing the data. Apart from the short time needed for disc operations, the file is free to be opened by anyone.

Because of this, many network applications ensure that the file is kept open for the entire period between opening and closing the file. A more flexible approach is give the user control over whether the file should be locked. After all, the user may only load in a spreadsheet to view it - with no intention of making any alterations. In that situation, this first user might be quite happy that a second user can load and alter the worksheet file.

EXAMPLE

Users of Lotus 123 can lock a file by using the command:

/F(ile)A(dmin)R(eservation)G(et)

A reservation is another description for file locking. The above command ensures that only the user can now save that file, since only one user at a time can make the reservation.

The file can be unlocked by giving the command:

/F(ile)A(dmin)R(eservation)R(elease)

Similar facilities exist for SuperCalc 5, Quattro, Wordstar, WordPerfect, etc.

DEADLY EMBRACE

Also known as deadlock, this is an ever-present threat for application programmers.

Consider the example shown in the diagram.

> Stations A and B both require files A and B to be simultaneously open for their activities.
> Station A uses file A followed by file B, then ends its program.
> Station B uses file B followed by file A, then ends its program.

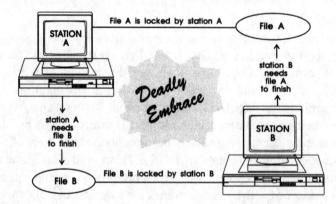

Consider the following sequence:
- Station A accesses file A, locking the file to other users.
- Station B accesses file B, locking it.
- Station A tries to open file B but is locked out. It cannot continue, so file A is not closed.
- Station B tries to open file A but is similarly locked out. It cannot continue either, so file B is not closed.

Both stations now wait for the other to release the file they need to complete their program. This is an endless situation called 'deadlock' or 'deadly embrace'. The only solution is to terminate one of the programs, with any consequences that may produce. The simplest way to prevent this problem is to write the software such that an application will acquire all its required resources before continuing.   This prevents deadlock but may result in valuable resources lying unused until the application is ready for it.

RECORD LOCKING

File locking is the most appropriate method for preventing possible concurrent updates but is unsuitable for databases, particularly large databases. A database is composed of a collection on individual records.

A user is often only concerned with viewing/updating a single record in the file.   It would be very inefficient if all other users had to wait for consecutive access to the file.   A better method would be to lock at a record level, rather than file level. If a user wished access to a particular record, that record would be locked. This would allow the user to modify and save that record; all other users would only have read access to that record during that time. Of course, all the other records could be handled similarly, allowing many users concurrent access to the database - while only one user at a time could have write access to a particular record.   In practice, it is usually more practical to lock a portion of the file, rather than individual records.

The above works well for modifying records but causes problems when a user wishes to add a new record to the file. Adding a record changes the file structure and many databases require that the entire file be locked during this alteration.   Since the file can only be locked when there is only a single user and since the database is likely to be in continuous use by multiple users, additions to a file could be a time-consuming business. The general solution is to design the database so that spare blank records are added to a database each time the system is used.   This allows users to modify the blank records into new records - without the problems mentioned above.

OTHER SINGLE-USER PROBLEMS

Apart from the file-sharing problems already mentioned, there are other difficulties with using single-user software on networks:

TEMPORARY FILES:

When running, a number of applications produce temporary files.   During this period, a second user is effectively locked out.   The solution is to direct the temporary output to different directories, using the applications configuration setups. Creating specific directories for different users overcomes the problem.

CONFIGURATION FILES:

Configuration files are used to determine the specific hardware, directories, etc. that an application will use. Since different nodes may have different hardware and directory requirements, the same copy of a program may not run on all stations.   Dependent on the program, it is usually possible to overcome this by the use of individual batch files for each node.

WORD PROCESSING:

Nowadays, most word processors have an in-built spell-checker. There is no problem in simultaneous use of this dictionary, when users wish only to read the file. However, there is not control over users wishing to add new words to the dictionary.   Since different nodes may well have different needs (e.g. to add financial, scientific or legal words to the dictionary) the file could soon become very large and contain many words never likely to be used by a particular node.

If the network application allows it, users could be granted personal extensions to the main dictionary - which would not be accessed by any other nodes' search.   Of course, this option does not exist on single-user versions.

COPY PROTECTION:

Apart from the built-in check which certain applications make for their single-user version being used on a network, many programs have a general copy protection method built in.   This prevents unauthorised copying of the program's master discs and often works by the timing of a disc operation or a direct read or write of the disc drive. Since this is impossible over a network, the program is treated as a pirate copy and will not function.

PURCHASING SOFTWARE

Most stand-alone applications are sold on a single-user basis; this requires that the application be used by a single user on a single machine at a single site.

Borland (of Paradox, Turbo C, Turbo Pascal and Delphi fame) have no objection to the user and the site being varied, as long as only a single copy is being used at any one time. From a network point of view, a single copy can be downloaded to any one node at any one time.   The responsibility of preventing concurrent use rests with the user.   Clearly, using single-user applications on a network can be difficult - not to mention illegal.   On the other hand, users don't wish to buy a complete package (discs, manuals, etc.) for every user on the network.   To meet this situation, an organisation can purchase a licence for a set number of concurrent users. For example, a 10-user licence would allow up to 10 users to run the application at the same time, from any of the stations on the network. When an 11th user attempts to use the application, access is denied until of the previous 10 users ceases running the application. Packages such as dBase and SuperCalc provide this method of licensing.

LANGUAGES

Networked application packages are very useful but do not meet everyone's needs. Consequently, there is a role for programming languages on a network. This means that the language has to have additional commands to make it operate a network - commands to implement the MS-DOS locking facilities.

CLIENT/SERVER SOFTWARE

Up to recently, networks consisted simply of a collection of PCs which all processed independently. The linking of the stations was only used as a means of resource sharing and communications. As a consequence, many stations could be sitting idle while others were working flat out. The ideal world would have the idle stations carrying out some of the functions of the busy stations. Unfortunately, this is still some way off.   However, there are steps in this direction with the new 'client/server' systems. In such a system, the user machine (the 'client' or 'front end') concerns itself with the user interface/editing tasks, while the core data remains on the server end (or 'back-end'). The backend could, of course, be a mainframe, mini or high-end PC.   Not only does the data to be processed stay in the server, the actual processing of the data can now be done in the server end.

ADVANTAGES:

- Improves performance, due to reducing traffic on the network - since part of the processing coding remains on the server and the core data remains on the server. Since this is no longer required to be sent down the network, the normally heavy traffic can thereby be substantially reduced. With applications being ever more complex (thereby ever larger), the traffic reduction savings will become more and more significant.
- Makes savings on hardware upgrades.   With the increasing complexity of applications, came the demand for increased power from workstations. If the main tasks of the workstation are reduced to user interface activities then the node system can be relatively simple (therefore cheaper), while the high performance server carries out the more demanding activities such as searching, sorting, producing statistics, etc. For example, why have a Pentium 133MHz processor in each station. If calculations only account for 10% of the workload, then the station is being underused for 90% of the time.

DISADVANTAGES:

- High initial software costs, due to having to buy both server software and client application software.
- The client database software (the software in each node) has to have SQL (Structured Query Language) capability and the database server software is more complex than normal server software.

The most common example of an application server is the SQL database server. Consider an earlier, non client-server type, network database package.   A node would require to carry out all its processing in the node PC. So, to find out a count of all records matching search criteria (e.g. how many Glasgow-based customers in a file), the entire file would have to be copied along the network from the server to the node. The processing of the records would then take place within the node PC. This involves a substantial amount of network traffic.   If the network is a large user of databases, then the system would soon slow down to a snail's pace.

This is where SQL and client/server software come in.   Structured Query Language provides a common database language, allowing the splitting of functions over different machines (of course, it can also be used on a single-user machine).   It is rapidly gaining acceptance as a standard and will provide some further compatibility between database applications.   Eventually, a single database server using SQL could be used to service requests from stations using different database packages.   The client (sometimes called the *'Front End'*) is the node PC running the database package.   The client's job is to provide the user with the user interface - menus, output screens, query tools. The database server (sometimes called the *'Back End'*) carries out all the database functions such as storage allocation, indexing, record selection, file statistics, etc.   The user formulates a request in SQL which is sent to the database server for implementation. Thus, for a function such as narrowing a search to a subset of records, only the matching records are sent over the network. If the user requests a count of those records matching a set of criteria, then only the final figure is transmitted over the network. This has the following benefits:

- Substantial reductions in network traffic, greatly enhancing overall network performance.
- More nodes can process the same file simultaneously; database servers are designed to be multi-tasking.

Implementations of the above techniques are now becoming available; the DataEase, dBase IV and Excel SQL packages for networks being good examples.

Multimedia

The term *'multimedia'* requires some explanation.   It is most often spoken of in the same breath as CD-ROM.   However the CD-ROM is not always used for multimedia purposes, and multimedia does not necessarily require the use of a CD-ROM.   The Novell 4 network operating system, for instance, has a facility to automatically archive files to writeable CD-ROM but no-one would describe this as multimedia.   On the other hand, a multimedia production can be stored on a large hard disc or fetched from the Internet.   Although multimedia can be stored on any storage device, the often huge capacities required are best met by the storage space offered by CD-ROM.   This is the main reason why the two are so often associated.   Although it is feasible to store an audio-visual multimedia presentation on a hard disc, high-quality audio or visuals can easily consume most of that hard disc.   A 256-colour digitised animation, even in low-resolution MCGA mode on a PC, takes up to 500k of storage space for each second of action. Digitised sound can also consume lots of disc space.

In its simplest definition, multimedia is the use of several types of output to more effectively communicate with the user or viewer.   Multimedia elements consist of the following:

- still graphic images
- digitised sound/music
- plain text
- animated graphics
- synthesised sound/music
- digitised photographs
- moving video images composed of user-recorded material on disc (hard disc or CD)
- moving video images from pre-recorded material on disc (hard disc or CD)
- moving video images from normal videotape players

A distinguishing feature of multimedia is the ability of the user to interact with the media. This may be through choosing menu options or clicking the mouse on icons.   The vast amounts of data are usually linked through hypertext systems or authoring packages.

COMMERCIAL USES OF MULTIMEDIA

There has been a general association of multimedia with computer games and standalone machines. However, there is also wide scope for multimedia in a commercial setting.   In the short term this is commonly used for sophisticated training systems and promotional material.   This is inevitably going to grow into new areas.   Current and future commercial developments of multimedia include:

- Multimedia over local area networks and wide area networks
- Integration of sound and/or video into application packages
- Integration of sound and/or video into data produced by applications

This provides new facilities such as:

- Easy access to centrally stored video training.
- Huge databases of material such as research results, specifications, legal documents, etc.; these may include diagrams, personal signatures, scanned documents and voiceprints.
- Electronic publishing - News, books, technical manuals, public information, promotional brochures.
- Applications with greatly enhanced help through video and sound assistance.
- Entertainment such as games, films and music.

APPLICATIONS FOR MULTIMEDIA

New uses are constantly being found for multimedia and these can be generally categorised as:
TRAINING
Training is concerned with the acquisition of specific skills, of the mind or the hand.   Examples are learning a foreign language or playing the guitar.   Boeing use multimedia material to train their ground personnel.
EDUCATION
Education is *'knowledge based'*; specific skills may not flow from the absorption of this knowledge.   The theories of evolution, politics, religion, pure science, mathematics, etc may be learned for their own sake rather than to be practised. The Educational Software & CD-ROM Yearbook by REM is jam-packed with details of 1,000 different educational CD ROMs on subjects such as history, science, geography, art and architecture, economics and media studies, etc.
DISTANCE LEARNING
Distance learning assumes that the student is remote from the educational establishment. This could be for any of a variety of reasons, such as disability, family commitments, working abroad, shift working, etc.   Those undertaking study communicate via downloading material, uploading exercises and carrying on e-mail

dialogues with support lecturers. Educational CDs are often used by students where a teacher/lecturer is present to answer specific questions or to clear up any vagueness in the application's presentation. This immediate help is less available with distance learning students and the multimedia material has to reflect this. It must anticipate possible student problems, provide adequate help and guided support. The package should have facilities for student self-assessment, to reinforce students in their learning. Many establishments have, or are preparing, distance learning multimedia-based courses.

EDUTAINMENT

Edutainment combines elements of education and entertainment in a manner that imparts knowledge to a user while wrapping the material up as an entertaining experience. Packages featuring the adventures of Peter Rabbit or Barney Bear provide children with animated stories; the text of the story is displayed on screen and each word is highlighted as the story is read out. Children can activate parts of the screen and can control the flow of the story by mouse clicks. Serious learning is taking place in conjunction with the attractive *activities*. Adult edutainment equivalents are CD with conducted tours of *'The Louvre'*, investigating *'Great Artists'* and exploring *'The Ultimate Human Body'*.

ENTERTAINMENT

These are solely aimed at providing fun with no attempt at any serious education, although in some packages a little general knowledge may be picked up along the way. Applications include the *'Cinemania'* and *'Music Central'* multimedia databases on films and music, interactive music CDs such as *'Explora'* by Peter Gabriel and *'Jump'* by David Bowie, and the guide to *'Wines, Spirits and Beers'*. Other well-known applications of multimedia are the effects produced in films such as *'Toy Story'*, *'The Mask'* and *'Jurassic Park'* and the huge range of games that now exists on CD ROM.

SIMULATION

Simulation provides a computer replica of a living or supposed situation and there are applications for use in both entertainment and industry. Leisure applications cover both the real world (eg flight simulators) and the imagined world (eg fighting the aliens on the planet Zog). Industry has many serious uses for simulations in situations where training staff can be hazardous both to the trainees and to real equipment. Typical applications are training French train drivers using simulations of railway routes and British firefighters learning to handle dangerous situations. Users can learn from their mistakes without any harm being done.

MARKETING

Marketing covers the promotion of both opinions and products; it is aimed at altering the views and preferences of those who use the application. After viewing the application, users are hoped to desire certain products, holiday at a particular location, study at a particular university, etc. Example marketing applications are the *'virtual kitchens'* demonstrated by Matsushita, unattended public information displays (known as kiosks) promoting clothes or holidays, and CD ROM travel guides covering from the *'AA Days Out in Britain and Ireland'* to *'Travel Mexico'* and *'Voyage in Spain'*. Multimedia marketing has a large growth potential, both in CR ROM format and over the Internet.

HOME SHOPPING

This overlaps with marketing activities. While marketing promotes the demand for the product, home shopping provides the convenience to place the order. A growing number of product catalogues are provided on CD or many more are available on the World Wide Web. Users can log into a company's web site and use the search facilities to bring up details of desired products. The user can read the text descriptions and view the images. The product range is huge covering from computers to books and clothes. In the case of music CDs, the user is also allowed to hear short clips from albums. The user can instantly place an order and can pay with a credit card. Tesco is running a pilot scheme at their Ealing branch, where users can browse and purchase from a range of 4,000 items.

REFERENCE

Reference material is readily available in book format but multimedia versions provide many extra facilities such as very quick subject searching and cross-referencing, the use of animations to aid explanations and sound and video clips of famous people and events. Examples of reference material are BOOKBANK(British books in print), specifications, dictionaries (eg the Oxford Compendium), the Guinness Book of Records and a range of impressive annually-updated multimedia encyclopaedias (eg Compton's, Grolier, Hutchinson, Microsoft and Britannica).

ELECTRONIC PUBLISHING

Electronic publishing is an area with anticipated rapid growth. Its contents can be electronic 'books', sales literature, or information banks. The contents of many daily papers are posted to the Internet and CDs containing a year's contents can be purchased. CD versions involve a single payment, whereas on-line versions may involve paying for connect time compared to hard copy subscription charges. On-line versions provide constantly updated information while CD versions provide archive reference material. As in all publishing, copyright problems presents a legal framework that has to be adopted.

PIONEERING SYSTEMS

Current multimedia systems have their roots in the development of interactive video, CBT (computer based training) and hypertext systems.

INTERACTIVE VIDEO

The system was comprised of the following components:

- A TV monitor
- A videodisc player (usually the Philips laservision player which used larger versions of our current CD-ROM discs). The player had a normal TV output.
- A computer or microprocessor built into a special video player

The discs were larger than modern CD discs and contained previously recorded video sequences which could be viewed by choosing options from the keyboard. Examples of use are Lloyds Bank's training staff in till, cash and cheque transactions; McDonell Douglas staff training manuals on aircraft maintenance and repair. Some used an actions/consequences approach, where a video displayed an activity and the play was suspend while the user (often in groups) considered and choose from a selection of responses. The chosen response ran another video clip which displayed the consequences resulting from the selection. This method was also adopted for early arcade video games. These were radical applications in the early 1980's and the programmes were very expensive to produce. The user content was mostly video sequences linked together by text and user responses, reflecting the state of technology at that stage. Nevertheless, these elements are in common use in modern multimedia applications.

CBT/CAL

With the growing popularity of desktop PCs, the drive towards interactive systems moved to centre round the computer and its programs. This removed the requirement for specialist apparatus and early CAL/CBT was distributed on ordinary floppy discs. The system provided new levels of user support. Computer Based Training (CBT) developed specific skills (eg typing tutors) while Computer Aided Learning (CAL) explored ideas (eg science and philosophy). Both applications provided user options and stored user responses in variables. In this way, a user's progress was monitored and appropriate advice given. Users could be given assessments and told their scores. Users could be given a certain number of attempts at a multi-choice question. The support given for a wrong answer could depend on what incorrect choice was entered and the previous experience of the user as judged by previous responses.

CBT/CAL provided an 'intelligent' system which users enjoyed as they had more control over the learning experience. They could work at their own pace, reviewing a page, changing direction and stopping for a break. Early applications tended to have a linear format within each lesson and they lacked the visual impact of interactive video. Again, most of the elements of CBT can be found in current multimedia systems.

HYPERTEXT

Both interactive video and CBT tended to require the user to follow a fixed training pattern with clear end objectives. Options were allowed but they were temporary detours from the main path to be tread by the user. Although this had distinct advantages in certain situations, and is still implemented in some packages today, it did not follow the way humans think and approach issues. Few people learn a subject by systematically working through a linear path of material. Only fiction is read linearly. People learn by association; having grasped a concept it leads them to one or more linked concepts. For example, reading a car repair manual on fixing carburettors may inspire a reader to find out more about how the ignition systems works, what a catalytic converter is, or how to use a double-grommeted nut wrench. Hypertext builds a system that supports that way of thinking. Users can leave a particular subject area and explore something linked - or completely different; they can choose to return to the previous theme or can more onwards or sideways if they wish. Each person will use the system in a different way.

Users move from one subject to another by selecting menu options or by clicking the mouse on a highlighted word (a hypertext link) or on a particular area of the screen (a hotspot). Early systems were solely text based and graphical interfaces followed later.

The best definition of hypertext is that it:

> *"produces large, complex, richly connected*
> *and cross-referenced bodies of information"*

Hypertext is widely implemented in Windows applications' help systems and this *'navigation'* process is one of the cornerstones of multimedia packages. The largest example of hypertext is the World Wide Web.

Hypertext's benefits include good browsing abilities, rapid navigation, the ability to annotate results and the ability to save results and queries for later use.

Reported problems with hypertext are disorientation (it is much easier to get lost than when page-hopping with a printed book) and *'cognitive overhead'* (the large variety of options stuns the brain's ability to easily consider alternatives).

MULTIMEDIA HARDWARE

The common aspects of multimedia usually require little or no specialised hardware.   It is possible to create a simple multimedia presentation, involving text, graphics and sounds, on a basic computer without any extra add-ons.   Of course, the more sophisticated presentations require a high performance machine and special equipment.   One range of add-ons is required for the production of multimedia applications, while other hardware is required for the delivery of such applications.

HARDWARE FOR CREATION

The list below is the minimum for a home-quality production facility.   The sound and video hardware would be upgraded for professional quality results.

- Video Capture Card
- Sound Card (with hand microphone, tie-clip microphone or headset system)
- Graphics card with MPEG support
- MIDI interface with Synthesiser/Keyboard
- VCR
- Video Camera (tape or digital)
- Digital Still Camera
- Scanner
- CD-ROM player/writer
- Large, fast hard discs

HARDWARE FOR DELIVERY

Completed multimedia products can either be distributed on CD ROMs or via the Internet.

CD ROM

- CD ROM player
- Graphics card with MPEG support
- Sound Card with speakers
- MIDI interface with Synthesiser/Keyboard

This has the advantage of using a known performance standard and quality is predictable.   However, content can become outdated quickly and there is no contact between the manufacturer and the users. As it only offers single-user access and provides the most security, it is the obvious choice when the CD is itself the product designed for sale.

INTERNET

- Graphics card with MPEG support
- MIDI interface with Synthesiser/Keyboard
- Sound Card with speakers
- Modem or ISDN link

This has the advantage that material can be easily updated and reaches a potentially larger market. Orders and queries can be dealt with on-line.   However, the transfer of large graphics and video files is still a major obstacle on the Internet.   Since data on the Internet can easily be accessed, it is the obvious choice for general promotional material for a product that can be ordered and supplied outwith the Internet.

Newer CD applications have Internet links to provide the best features of both methods. The core content (text descriptions, pictures, etc) reside on the CD ROM while constantly changing information (eg prices) is downloaded as the application is viewed.

MULTIMEDIA STANDARDS

There is a wide range of multimedia products, some requiring greater resources than others if they are to operate efficiently.   This has led to the creation of a set of minimum standards by manufacturers and companies such as Microsoft.   The Multimedia PC Working Group of the Software Publishers Association have, to date, produced three standards (Levels) of system, as shown:

	MPC Level 1	MPC Level 2	MPC Level 3
CPU	386SX, 16MHz	486SX, 25MHz	75MHz Pentium or equivalent
RAM	2Mb	4Mb	8Mb
CD-ROM	150kbs data transfer rate, access time 1second	300kbs data transfer rate, multi-session, XA, access time 400ms	600kbps data transfer rate, multi-session, XA, access time 250ms
Hard Disc	30Mb	160Mb	540Mb
Audio Card	SoundBlaster compatible with 8-bit sound, synthesiser and MIDI facilities	SoundBlaster compatible with 16-bit sound, synthesiser and MIDI facilities	SoundBlaster compatible with 16-bit sound, wavetable and MIDI facilities
Graphics Card	16-colour VGA	65,536 colour VGA	Scaling capability, direct access to frame buffer for video-enabled graphics
Video Playback	n/a	n/a	MPEG1 capability, 352x240 at 30fps without dropping frames
External ports	MIDI interface, Joystick	MIDI interface, Joystick	MIDI interface, joystick

A future version 4, being worked on, will include telephony and videoconferencing.

THE ELEMENTS OF MULTI-MEDIA

The following pages consider the main components of a multimedia presentation, outlining how they operate and considering the main factors affecting performance.

TEXT

The display of multimedia text requires only a standard PC monitor and a main concern is how the text is accessed. The user requires to access specific subjects from a huge range of material. The text-handling software should be capable of detecting and displaying all stored material on the user's chosen subject. The user also requires the ability to explore cross-references in the material, to look at an item in further detail before returning to the main theme. These are the *'hypertext'* elements previously described. These may require the user to type in the data to be searched for or to select from a menu. Another method is to click the mouse on a key word or phrase within the displayed text. These elements can be seen in use in various Windows Help systems.

TEXT CREATION

All multimedia applications employ text and the attributes used should reflect the nature of the application. The attributes to choose from are text face (what the basic face looks like), font (its size), style (normal, bold, italics, underlined), justification (left, right, centred) and colour. A psychedelic or bizarre collection of text faces and colours may fit the mood of some music applications but would be entirely inappropriate for a training package for funeral undertakers. Too much text on the screen repels viewers while text that is too small or too large makes the viewer uncomfortable. The number of words on any one line should be no more than 8 or 10 and each line should make a single point. Text should be presented with a mix of upper and lower case characters. Any one screen should not have text of many different colours; however, colours used to highlight titles or hypertext links are effective.

Similarly the choice of words used in the text is important; the grammar should suit the intended audience. Young children should not be bamboozled with complex words and older users should not be patronised. Jargon, abbreviations and acronyms should also be avoided.

The authoring packages which create multimedia projects all have the normal cut, paste and copy facilities to improve the screen layout.

TEXT IMPORTATION

Multimedia authoring packages do not generally have spell-checking or grammar-checking features and the author has to be very careful that misspelled words do not slip through and mar an otherwise professional project. All packages allow text to be imported into the project and this is the safest way to protect against typing or grammatical errors. Text can be entered into a word processed file which can be checked before being imported into the authoring package's project. The file types allowed by the authoring package should be checked and the text file should be saved in one of the acceptable formats. In some cases, this may mean converting a Word 7 file, for instance, into an older Word 2 format to be acceptable by the authoring package.

TEXT MANIPULATION

Once the basic text is entered into the authoring screen, it can be manipulated to provide the desired effects. The facilities include:

LOCATION

Placing headings, sub-headings and body text in the most attractive layout.

ALIGNMENT

Placing text on a horizontal or a vertical plane.

LAYERING

Note that the first two letters of 'Dumbreck' are layered over the upper case 'P' to produce a pleasing effect.

EFFECTS

The effects of applying shadows and extrusions to text can be seen in the examples.

TRANSITIONS

The author can choose to place all the text on the screen at the one time, or to make the text appear on the screen gradually to a pre-set pattern. These are called *'transitions'* and include dissolves, fades, various wipes and other effects. Transitions can be used to good effect but when overdone can be very annoying to viewers.

AUDIO

THE NATURE OF AUDIO

Sound from a natural source such as the human voice or a musical instrument is analogue This means that it alters in a continuous way as shown in the example diagram.

If a number of people were to sing exactly the same musical note, their voices would remain unique and identifiable.   This is because of the harmonic content of each person's voice.   Apart from sounding the correct frequency of the note, the human voice will introduce an individual collection of other sounds that are mixed with the basic frequency.   These other sounds are multiples of the original frequency and it is the quantity and relative volumes of each of these harmonics that makes each person's voice different.   In the same way, a piano is very rich in harmonics while a tin flute is devoid of harmonics.   The extra components give the piano its 'richness' of tone in comparison to the purer sound of the flute.   A sound that is rich in harmonics contains much more detailed information than a pure sound and this causes problems for their storage on computer, as explained below.

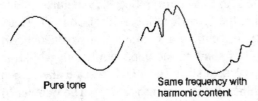

Pure tone   Same frequency with harmonic content

Computer sound is one half of an audio/visual display, and proper sound effects can make a simple, predictable slide show or an animated display much more memorable. The final audio waveform is fed to the loudspeakers, vibrating the internal cones of the speakers in sympathy with the amplitude of the wave.   The vibrating cones vibrate the surrounding air, causing the sound to travel to the human ear.

Digitised Sound

Digitised sound is used in multimedia to accompany animations and graphics, giving a more convincing presentation. It can also be used to link sounds to events in Windows.   Sound is fed into a sound card in analogue format, from a microphone or other audio source.   As explained, the computer is only capable of storing data in digital format.   So the card has to convert analogue sounds into a digital equivalent. This is achieved by a chip in the sound card called the *'ADC'* - the *'Analogue-to-Digital-Converter'*. The ADC converts a sample of sound into a series of numbers that can be stored to disc for later replay. The numbers store the amplitude of the sound waveform at different points during the time of the sound sample.   In most formats, the waveform swings above and below a reference point of zero.   This means that low amplitude levels have a negative integer representing them while high amplitude levels are represented by positive integer numbers. Two factors determine the quality of digitised sound:

- The dynamic range (i.e. the accuracy in terms of absolute amplitudes)
- The sampling rate (i.e. the accuracy of the amplitude at any one instant)

Dynamic Range

The more complex the waveform to be stored, the greater total of different numbers required to store the sound.   The span from the lowest amplitude to the greatest amplitude is known as the *'dynamic range'*. This is sometimes also described as *'resolution'* or *'bit-range'*. In the left diagram, only a small number of bits are allocated to store the waveform so it is incapable of handling the small amplitude variations in the waveform and these details are averaged away.   In that case, the ADC produces a series of numbers that approximate to the overall waveform but the harmonics that make a piano sound different from a guitar are lost as are the harmonics that differentiate between different human voices.   The right-hand diagram shows a greater dynamic range allowing the same analogue signal to be converted into a greater number of digital levels.

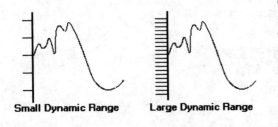

Small Dynamic Range   Large Dynamic Range

This allows for a greater clarity of reproduction as the replayed sound is closer to the original sound.

The earlier standard 8-bit sound card had 8 bits to store sound data.   Eight bits allows a range of 256 different levels.   This is sufficient for many purposes but does not provide a high quality sound system.

Newer 16-bit sound cards handle a range of 65,536 different sound levels, giving a quality expected from a domestic audio CD system. This is not a professional quality, since each of the 65,536 levels is a linear step while the human ear responds to amplitude variations in a logarithmic way. This means that many of the discrete stored levels do not store changes that can be detected by the ear and so are wasted. This is not a problem since only a few professionals use PCs for their audio work. Given these limitations, the 16-bit sound card has obvious quality advantages over an 8-bit card. It does, of course, require twice as much disc storage space as an equivalent 8-bit sound sample.

Sampling Rate

The dynamic range determines the accuracy of the amplitude reading at any one point in time. Of equal importance is the frequency of taking these readings. If the readings are too infrequent, an amplitude change will pass undetected. If the readings are too frequent, the conversion will produce a giant series of amplitude readings. The timing of the conversions is known as the *'sampling rate'* and is measured in kilohertz (i.e. how many thousand amplitude conversions are carried out each second).

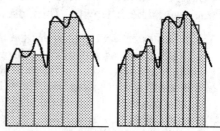

Low Sampling Rate   High Sampling Rate

The left diagram shows the effects of a low sampling rate. The sound sample is converted into six samples with varying amplitude levels. When the sample is replayed, the sound card's DAC (Digital-to-Analogue Converter) uses the six levels to reconstruct the sound wave. This sound wave is then amplified and sent to the loudspeakers. As the diagram shows, the final output is an approximation of the original sound with a considerable loss of detail. The inertia in the loudspeaker cones acts to smooth the transitions between different output voltage levels from the DAC. The right-hand diagram shows the same sound sample with twice the sampling rate. The audio is now stored in twelve different samples and this is much more representative of the original sound source. In practice, the sampling rate must be at least double the frequency of the highest frequency to be sampled. Since the average human ear can only hear frequencies up to about 20KHz, a sampling rate of 44KHz is adequate for most uses. Indeed, the human voice itself does not produce sounds above much more than 3KHz.

The original Sound Blaster card was first introduced with a sampling rate of 11KHz. Most cards now usually operate as high as 44.1KHz, the same rate as audio CD, and sampling rates are adjustable down to as low as 4KHz.

Storage Overheads

Most current sound cards have stereo channels, allowing each channel to process independent contents. This improves the quality of the reproduced sound but requires double the disc space. The table shows the amount of disc space required for even short digitised samples, with the top quality 44.1KHz sampling rate.

	bytes per sec	bytes per min
8-bit mono	44,100	2,646,000
8-bit stereo	88,200	5,292,000
16-bit mono	88,200	5,292,000
16-bit stereo	176,400	10,584,000

A four minute snatch of song in stereo would require a staggering 42Mb of disc space!

MINIMISING STORAGE OVERHEADS

A number of techniques are employed to minimise the use of disc space and these include:
- Forcing the system down to a 22.05KHz sampling rate when recording in stereo.
- Replacing periods of silence in the audio with a token that describes how long the silence lasted.
- Compressing the file on recording and decompressing again on playback. This can use a CODEC chip (compression/decompression) to carry out these tasks in hardware to speed the process. Implementing the system in software is a problem as the higher sampling rates require a very fast response from the processing software (which explains why some boards can only compress while at low sampling frequencies). Some systems offer a range of possible compression ratios, ranging from low-compression lossless samples to high-compression samples with loss of some detail. Software CODECS such as ADPCM (see below) are available as alternatives to hardware implementations.

All sound boards use ADCs and DACs. Most cards have a DSP (*'Digital Signal Processing'*) chip to carry out these tasks, combined with handling MIDI and sound file compression /decompression.

AUDIO FILE FORMATS

One of the first things a user notices is the bewildering array of file formats and acronyms. All elements of multimedia, even simple text, have several different formats, each with its own benefits and restrictions. Dredging through the morass of standards to find the one that is best suited may seem a huge task, but many of the file formats are either very specialised or just too old and inefficient to be of use. For instance, sound samples may come with extensions like VOC, WAV, SND, SOU, AU, IFF, SAM, RAW, ULW; some may even have no extension at all. There are also many samples out there which are *'raw'* samples, and have extensions given completely arbitrarily, such that they may appear to be separate file formats. But really there are only a few ways to store digitised sound, and the rest is just dressing. All the file formats below may be used to store the same audio content; only the manner of storage would be different. The most important sound file formats are:

RAW : This extension indicates that the file's contents consist solely of the string of numeric data, with no special processing or headers. Although raw sound samples may be stored with the extension .RAW, more often they have a less obvious name, or sometimes no extension at all. SOU and some SND files are raw files with a short header to tell the playback software information as what sampling speed to use for the playback. If the raw sample has no header that stores the frequency of the sample, then the user has to calculate, or estimate, the sampling frequency (number of samples per second of digitised sound). It should be obvious when the user hears the sound whether the frequency is correct.

VOC : Arguably the most common digitised sound format on PCs is the VOC format, created for the Sound Blaster card. Other than the sampled data itself, a VOC file can contain other 'blocks', such as a loop, end-of-loop, or silence block. A silence block allows any length of silence in a sound sample without the comparatively data-hungry sampling of that silence. VOC files also allow compression of the sound sample, albeit usually with some noticeable loss of quality. The Sound Blaster software includes utilities to convert VOC files to the Windows-compatible WAV files, and vice versa.

WAV : Introduced along with Windows, the WAV file format is a simple sound sample with a short file header. The benefit of WAV files is that many Windows programs can use them with a single Windows sound driver. Of course, the Windows sound driver is not limited to WAV files, but Windows programs themselves tend to prefer WAV files since they are the native format for Windows sound.

MOD : Introduced by the Amiga, MOD files are more compact than their WAV counterparts and many are freely available for downloading from bulletin boards or the Internet.

IFF : The Amiga's IFF format is used for many other things apart from sound samples. The Interchange File Format stores sound samples in unsigned format - ie the wave is sampled from zero upwards, rather than from zero in either direction. The end result is the same, but this small peculiarity means that PC sample files will have to be converted to play on an Amiga, and vice versa. Some other digitised samples use the unsigned format but are not IFF files, bearing the extension .SMP or .SAM.
This should not be confused with the AIFF (Audio Interchange File Format) format from Apple. The Amiga file extensions are .iff while the Apple extensions are .aif.

ULAW : This format is comparatively unusual on PCs, being more accustomed to use on SUN stations and NeXT computers. These files are generally found with the extension .AU or .SND.

ADPCM : The *'Adaptive Delta Pulse Code Modulation'* system takes standard audio which has been encoded into its normal PCM values and compresses the data so that it requires less space than its .WAV equivalent. By only storing the deltas (ie changes between samples) it requires about a quarter of the normal disc space. This method is offered in Windows 95 (and is also the technique employed by Sony for its Mini Disc recorder/players).

RECORDING A SOUND

Although a wide range of digitised sound samples exists, there will be many occasions when a specific message is required. The audio input can come from a microphone or can be from the *'line in'* socket of sound card to allow the sampling of music or voice from a variety of sources such as CD, cassette tape, video tape, etc. The provisions of copyright will apply to such samples. Sound cards provide their own software to create audio samples and Windows has its own simple utility called *'Sound Recorder'* as shown in the diagram. The right hand button has a

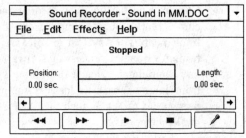

microphone icon and clicking on this icon starts a recording process. The time of the sample is shown on screen as the recording is made.   When the recording is finished, the user clicks on the button to the right of the microphone.   The final sample length is displayed.   Clicking the middle button will cause the sample to be replayed.   This system is adequate for day-to-day use but the more sophisticated software of the sound card utilities allows the selection of sampling rates.   With Windows 95, the Sound Recorder is found in the *'Multimedia'* option of the *'Accessories'* menu within the *'Programs'* menu.

EDITING A SOUND

A user-created sound sample may not be immediately usable.   It may contain unwanted pauses or require augmenting by special effects before it is used.   The *'Sound Recorder'* utility has some basic tools.   Clicking the arrow key icons moves the sample through different time stages of the waveform and the wave shape can be seen in a window while this is being adjusted.   Facilities include deleting all silences or unwanted sounds before the chosen time point or after the chosen time point.   This allows unwanted sections to removed and results in a smaller sample file.   Other facilities include introducing echo effects, reversing the sound sample and mixing in other sound samples. The final file can be saved as a WAV file for later use.   The software included with most sound cards, such as Sound Blaster's VOC Editor, provides further facilities.   These include the gradual fading up or down of sounds, the panning of sounds between stereo channels (ie the volume of the sound in the left channel is decreased while the volume in the right channel is increased),cut and paste operations and other waveform editing. The DSP - Digital Signal Processing - facility can provide a range of additional effects.   So, for example, the effect of a sound being played in a football stadium or a church can be imposed on any audio being reproduced.

SOUND CARDS

Early PCs used the internal speaker to provide a limited audio facility.   This is still used to *'beep'* for a user's attention but the size of the single internal speaker still restricts the quality of the sound generated. The solution rests in add-on cards that are dedicated to providing high quality stereo sound from a PC. These are now inexpensive and many machines are supplied equipped with a basic sound card.

The leader in the field of PC sound is the Sound Blaster card from Creative Labs. It was not the first nor, arguably, the best sound card on the market, but it balanced quality and effectiveness with a reasonable price tag.   It handles input from many sources, through a variety of physical connections. The

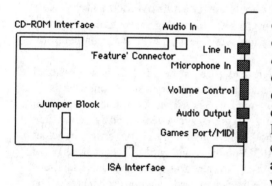

'Microphone Input' captures live sounds so that the sound card can store them in a digital fashion.   The *'Line Input'* captures any other audio source such as that from the *'audio out'* sockets of a cassette player, an audio CD player or a domestic video recorder.   The *'Audio In'* allows the direct entry of an audio source into the card.   This is most commonly connected to the *'Audio Out'* socket on a CD-ROM thus allowing normal audio CDs to be played on the computer's CD player (with the appropriate software).   It also has an interface connector to a CD-ROM through which data on the CD can be used to sent to the sound card for translation into audio.   The *'Games Port'* allows the connection of a joystick or of a MIDI interface. The MIDI input allows the real-time capture of a musician's work.   This is stored in the MIDI format as explained later.   The MIDI output connects to a MIDI-compatible device such as an electronic music keyboard, synthesiser or drum machine.   Finally, it can receive input via the normal bus connections to the computer.   This allows programs to directly send data to the sound card through the data bus.

The card is capable of controlling a CD-ROM and allows a CD-ROM to be fitted without the need for its own controller card.   The cable between the card and the CD-ROM takes the control signals to the CD-ROM that carry out the usual drive functions such as moving the head, etc.   The cable also takes the audio data from the CD-ROM down into the sound card.

The sound card's outputs are the Audio output and the MIDI output.   The card has an inbuilt amplifier capable of around 4 Watts of audio output power.   Alternatively, the connection can be taken to the input of another amplifier for greater output.   Connecting to a domestic hi-fi will boost the audio output to the maximum afforded by the hi-fi amplifier.   Manufacturers also produce a set of external speakers for sound cards and one of these speakers usually has an in-built amplifier.

The sound card can, therefore, perform the following output functions :
- Playback of audio CD.
- Recording of audio.   A real audio source, such a human speech or music is processed into digitised data for later re-processing (see later)
- Playback of digitised audio.   The data is translated from data into audio.
- FM synthesis.   The sound card contains synthesiser chips that are capable of generating a sound that is broadly similar to that produced in the real world.   For example, the chips can produce the sound of a piano or guitar even although no musical instrument was involved in its creation.   The chips can also produce sounds that are intended to have no human equivalent - e.g. the electronic organ.   The most commonly used chips are the OPL2 and OPL3 from Yamaha and they use a frequency modulation technique to produce a sound with the desired harmonic mix.   Each different synthetic sound is known as a *'voice'* and most cards have 20 voices, with other models ranging from 11 to 32.
- MIDI equipment interfacing.   The sound card is able to communicate with an external MIDI device, such as a musician's electronic keyboard.   The sound card carries out the processing of the musical score but the MIDI device produces the actual sound from its own synthesiser chips.

The Sound Blaster card also offered compatibility with the older Adlib sound standard.   Other sound cards have appeared since, including new and improved Sound Blaster cards. However, the extra functions generally have less software support than the basic Sound Blaster.   Many sound cards will be, or claim to be, Sound Blaster compatible, meaning that software designed for use with the Sound Blaster can be used with these cards.   Some sound cards offer compatibility with many standards. For example, the Gravis Ultrasound card is Adlib and SoundBlaster compatible, as well as being compatible with the Sound Source card.   These types of sound cards generally offer better performance than the basic Sound Blaster as well as backward compatibility, but quite often little software other than that supplied with the card will use these extra functions.

With the arrival of Windows 3.1 and 95, it is possible for any Windows application to utilise a sound card's benefits through the use of a single sound driver.   Stereo cards are now standard and produce a sound that the human ear detects on a two-dimensional plane - i.e. between left and right of the listener. Some current cards now also include *'surround sound'* similar to that available on current hi-fi systems. This simulates a three-dimensional effect where the sound has 'depth' added to the 'width'.

CURRENT DEVELOPMENTS
The quality of the output from the budget sound cards is limited and current improvements are:
- 8-bit cards have quality limitations and are mostly replaced by 16-bit cards with greater quality output.
- The MIDI interface is non-standard on most cards but many are available with MPU-401 compatibility (a music industry standard).
- Roland, the electronic keyboard manufacturer, produces high quality sound boards for the professional musician; these are the MT-32 and the LAPC-10.   MT-32 emulation is available in some sound cards.
- Synthesised sound output is not comparable with a natural sound.   The richer the sound source is in harmonics, the more difficult it is to reproduce synthetically.   That is why even expensive electronic keyboards have had difficulty in emulating the humble piano.   The solution lay in converting an actual sound into a set of digitised data and storing the sample in ROM on the sound card. This is called Wave Table Synthesis and produces greatly improved sound quality.   Some cards now have these facilities built-in while others provide a *'daughter board'* that plugs into the sound card's *'feature'* connector.   The new Yamaha OPL4 chip combines wavetable and FM.   The Sound Blaster AWE-32 is able to reproduce 128 instruments and 6 drum kits, with up to 32 of these sounds being played at the same time. Wavetable cards normally also provide on-board RAM so that users can use their own captured samples.
- Improving on the background noise produced in cards.   The Digital Audio Labs 'CardD Plus' has a signal to noise ratio of 90db compared to the average of 60db.

MUSIC
There are two distinct categories of music reproduction with the PC:
- Replaying pre-recorded music to liven up a presentation, or for personal pleasure.
- The creation of musical pieces.

The first category requires no knowledge of music theory as the *'artistic'* work has already been done. The user only requires to connect the correct equipment and to install and use the correct software. The latter category is outside the book's scope, being an area normally for the professional musician.

A basic musical piece will, in general, contain a table of musical notes, played in sequence much like a musical score.

Each note has a number of characteristics:

FREQUENCY

The table shows a range of musical notes and their corresponding frequencies.   All instruments would produce the same frequency for a given note, even though the sound of the notes may be widely different. A saxophone and a piano, for example would both produce exactly the same frequency for Middle C on the musical scale.

The notes are often referred to as having 'pitch' rather than frequency. A note may have a 'vibrato' effect superimposed upon it, with the note being swung above and below the original frequency. In such a case the frequency is always slightly altering but there remains a base frequency - the pitch.

Note	Frequency	Note	Frequency	Note	Frequency	Note	Frequency
C	65.41	C	130.81	C	261.63	C	523.25
C#	69.30	C#	138.59	C#	277.18	C#	554.37
D	73.42	D	146.83	D	293.66	D	587.33
D#	77.78	D#	155.56	D#	311.13	D#	622.25
E	82.41	E	164.81	E	329.63	E	659.26
F	87.31	F	174.61	F	349.23	F	698.46
F#	92.50	F#	185.00	F#	369.99	F#	739.99
G	98.00	G	196.00	G	392.00	G	783..99
G#	103.83	G#	207.65	G#	415.30	G#	830.61
A	110.00	A	220.00	A	440.00	A	880.00
A#	116.54	A#	233.08	A#	466.16	A#	932.33
B	123.47	B	246.94	B	493.88	B	987.77

TIMBRE

The difference between musical instruments lies in their different harmonic mixes, as explained earlier. The mix of harmonics and their relative strengths is referred to as the instrument's timbre.   Sound cards may refer to the 'voices' they support.   These are usually the number of different instruments that the card's synthesiser is capable of playing concurrently.   Each of these voices will corresponding instrument timbre but it is likely that the card will handle more instruments (timbres) than it is capable of playing concurrently.

DURATION

Each note's length is considered relative to the other notes in the musical piece, since a musical work can be played at differing paces. The diagram shows the relative lengths of the commonly used durations.   So, a Semi-Breve lasts 32 longer than a Demi-Semi-Quaver, regardless of the tempo of the piece being played. The note

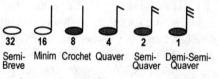

lengths would be supplemented by 'rests' of various durations. These are short periods of silence. A rest may be used as part of the overall composition or may be inserted between notes to make note distinct to the listener. This is more important where there is a long run of notes of the same frequency as the listener must discern different notes rather than a continuous longer note.

OTHER ATTRIBUTES

The sound is often described in terms of its 'envelope' and this encompasses four different features - often called the ADSR.

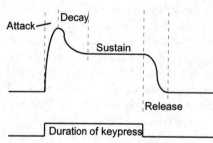

ATTACK   Describes the speed at which the note's initial volume increases

DECAY   Describes the speed at which the volume fades away

SUSTAIN   Describes the main amplitude that will be maintained during the note (e.g. if a synthesiser keyboard key is held down)

RELEASE   Describes the time it takes for the sound to completely stop.

MUSIC FORMATS

Music formats vary with the following being the most common:

CMF : The Creative Music Format was introduced with the Sound Blaster card. It uses instruments defined in the file, or in .SBI Sound Blaster Instrument files, along with a note sequence, to play the music. CMF music is generally not as good as some other formats, but produces compact files.

ROL : Similar in basic idea to the CMF file, the ROL musical format was introduced with the Roland sound card. Again, it generally means small files, but slightly lesser quality.

MOD : Designed on the Amiga, the MODule format uses digitised instruments played at different sampling frequencies. Since each instrument is digitised, MOD files have a much more convincing, realistic feel, but are usually slightly larger files. MOD files are prolific on BBS services, and other than MIDI, it is probably the most used music format on PCs.

MIDI

The *'Musical Instrument Digital Interface'* was developed as a standard interface between different pieces of musical apparatus such as electronic keyboards, synthesisers, sequencers, drum machines, etc. These were initially produced by different manufacturers with different interfaces and were notoriously difficult to connect together.   As a response, the first MIDI standard was introduced in 1983 as an agreement between manufacturers.   This standard (The MIDI 1.0 Specification) specifically mentioned the use of home computers but MIDI-compatible items can be connected and used together without the need for a computer.   However, there are many benefits from using a computer in a MIDI music system. When music is played directly at a music keyboard, the keystrokes can be saved and manipulated.   The computer can be used to synchronise the notes more accurately, allow cut and paste of passages of music, etc.   The completed piece can be saved for later playing through a MIDI music device.   MIDI music can be played through computer sound cards, but is much better when used in conjunction with MIDI connected instruments such as keyboards. This allows the computer to read a .MID file and thereby tell the MIDI instrument which notes to play. The result is that the sound comes from a dedicated musical instrument rather than a simple wave modulator.   This usually provides a superior and more versatile result.   However, sound cards are available which incorporate the quality waveforms associated with external instruments.   GM (General MIDI) compatibility allows the playing of commercially produced MIDI music files. It is an extension of the MIDI specification, such that specific channels and voices are linked to specific pre-defined sounds (e.g. 26 is always an electric guitar).

THE MIDI INTERFACE

External connections to MIDI instruments require a dedicated MIDI port on the computer. This is either directly available from a sound card or is supplied as an add-on to a sound card.   The MIDI standard specifies both the hardware and software requirements for the interface.

HARDWARE   The computer's MIDI connection will have both an input and an output socket. The input connector (marked as 'MIDI IN') can be used to receive input from an electronic keyboard.   The output connector (marked as 'MIDI OUT') takes the messages from the computer to the external synthesisers, etc.   Many MIDI devices also support a MIDI THRU connector and this reproduces whatever appears on the device's MIDI IN socket.   This allows

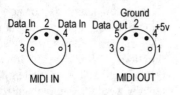

multiple MIDI devices to be connected together.   The connectors are of 180 degree 5-pin DIN type and pins 1 and 3 are not used and have no wired connections.   The connecting cable is twisted-pair wires with a protective shielding to prevent electrical interference to the signal.   It is important that this shield is only connected at the one end, to provide interference protection while maintaining the electrical isolation of both devices.

The messages are passed in serial format comprising byte-sized packets as shown in the diagram.   The signal is very similar to that used in the RS232 serial interface. The signals are asynchronous and have a start bit, eight data bits and a stop bit.   The start and stop bits are used to ensure the proper synchronisation of the data (i.e. the receiving device is able to properly decode the status of each data bit at any one point in time.   No parity bit is used. The ten bits require a time of 320 microseconds.   This means that the MIDI messaging system runs at a 31.25Kbaud rate.   This is a relatively slow interface but it is a simple serial device saving the use of

| Start | D0 | D1 | D2 | D3 | D4 | D5 | D6 | D7 | Stop |

320μs

multicore cable or multi-wire ribbon cable to connect devices.   Cables must be a maximum of 50ft in length.

MESSAGES   Note the MIDI message does not contain any actual sounds embedded in it.   The message contains a description of each note in terms of its frequency, timing and timbre (which musical instrument).   Each message is spread over several bytes and typical information includes:

Message	Meaning
Note on	indicates the start of information on a note.
Channel number	indicates which of the 16 available channels to use. This is allocated to a particular instrument and acts like a single recording track on a conventional recording studio system. However, different devices may use a particular channel number for different instruments. So, a note intended for a guitar may be reproduced as a piccolo. Windows includes a 'MIDI Mapper' utility to map the correct instruments for particular MIDI devices.
Key	indicates the pitch of the note.
Duration	indicates the note's length.
Volume	indicates the note's amplitude.
Velocity	indicates how hard a key was struck
Note off	indicates the end of the note information.

These explanations simplify the process and interested readers are advised to read up on the more detailed issues of Omni Mode, Poly Mode, Channel and System Messages and the detailed content of the Data Bytes. The use of sophisticated software for music score writing and printing is also beyond the scope of this chapter.

GRAPHIC IMAGES

A graphic can be stored as a bitmap, or as a vector image. For multimedia purposes, the majority of uses are filled by bitmap images.

BITMAPS

A bitmapped image is one in which every pixel on the screen or in the image is *mapped* to a *bit* of data. With a monochrome picture there is a direct correlation between the number of screen pixels and the number of bits to store the picture. Each bit only stores whether the pixel is white or black. With colour pictures, each pixel is represented by a group of bits which determine the pixel's colour.

A simple bitmap   A vector image

VECTORS

A vector image is one where the data represents not pixels, but *objects*. These objects could be text, circles, squares or such. The two example images display an extremely simplified image, shown in each type of format. Note, however, that the bitmap has been rendered very crudely at small scale to show the basic idea; bitmaps are generally much more complex, and far more graphically impressive. Depending on the image, either form could be more efficient. Bitmapping is far easier to use on complex coloured images such as digitised pictures, whereas a simple piece of computer-drawn clip-art would be much more efficiently stored as a vector oriented image. In the example above, the digitised picture would take up far less disc space. However, if a large bitmapped graphic could be easily converted to a vector image without loss of quality (which is not often the case) then the vector image would most likely be smaller in size. As far as bitmapped images go, the only difference between one file format and another is the way the data is compressed, and how much extra information is needed, such as height and width of the picture, number of colours, etc. This information is normally stored in a portion of the file called a *'header'*.

Picture Scaling

The benefits of vector files lie in their *'scalability'*. The user may wish to expand or shrink a picture so that it fits into a particular space in a document. This should be achieved with no loss of detail or picture distortion. The top diagram shows the result of scaling up a picture that contains a straight line to twice its height and width. Where there was a single pixel there is now a group of four pixels. Scaling the picture to four times its original size results in a group of 16 pixels for

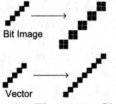

Bit Image

Vector

every original single picture. The result is a very *'blocky'* image known as *'pixellation'*. The vector file on the other hand represents the line as *'draw a row of pixels between point A and point B'*. Scaling the picture up still produces a single row of pixels, maintaining the fine detail.

FILE FORMATS

The most common graphic file formats on a PC are:

GIF : The acronym *'GIF'* is meant to be pronounced as *'jiff'*, but is usually pronounced *'giff'*. GIF was designed for fast transfer of graphics data over modems, and stands for <u>G</u>raphics <u>I</u>nterchange <u>F</u>ormat.. It uses a technique called LZW or String-table compression to compress graphic images, making them smaller for faster transfer over the CompuServe network. Now a very common file format, GIF files can be found on bulletin boards and graphics packages everywhere. GIF files can have a colour range of any power of 2 - up to 2 to the power of 8. This means it could have 2, 4, 8, 16, etc. up to 256 colours. This doesn't mean that all those colours must be used, however.

PNG : Unisys own the patent for the LZW compression used in GIF files and this produced a demand for royalties for the use of GIF files. In response, the Portable Network Graphics standard was produced for transferring bitmap graphics files over CompuServe and the Internet. It improves on GIFs by offering 24-bit colour and its own 'zlib' compression system.

PCX : Nobody seems to know what PCX stands for, other than that the first two letters are for *'Personal Computer'*. PCX files use run-length encoding RLE), which means that simple computer-generated pictures are stored fairly efficiently. It is comparatively inefficient at storing digitised or complicated pictures. Nonetheless, it has been around for some time and is now fairly common. PCX pictures may be found in monochrome (2 colours), 16 colours, 256 colours, 24-bit true colour, or even, rarely, in 4 colours. PCC files are PCX files by another name though they are usually smaller, intended for clipart.

TIFF : The Tagged Image File Format originated on the Mac computer, and was designed for use with desktop publishing. It is a complicated standard, so much so that some alleged TIFF-using packages may not import TIFFs from other packages. It can use a variety of compression schemes, and can have any number of colours, as well as a huge array of options, used by putting *'tags'* in the file header. The more exotic *'tags'* cause TIFF readers to occasionally *'screw up'* on TIFF files. TIFF files tend to be used more for DTP than multimedia.

BMP : BMP most probably stands for Bit-Mapped Picture and is the Windows standard bitmap graphics file. BMP files are used for the background wallpaper in Windows. It is uncompressed, meaning that simple pictures will occupy much more space than is strictly necessary. It also means that complicated, true colour pictures will not require a sophisticated decoder to display. Also, a damaged BMP file will mean image distortion may occur, while corruption to most compressed files means complete unusability. There is also another format called the RLE format, which is a compressed version of BMP, but this is little used. Finally, a BMP file may be found with the extension DIB, for Device Independent Bitmap, but is basically the same as a BMP file.

JPEG : When the Joint Photographic Experts Group was appointed by the CCITT to design a graphic compression and storage scheme, the JPEG file format was eventually created. It uses *'lossy'* compression, which means that slight detail will be lost during compression. The level of detail loss is controllable, and a substantial space saving can be made even with very little detail loss. The JPEG compression standard is a complicated process involving several levels, and at first specialised hardware was needed to perform the process. There is a lossless version of JPEG, but this may require the extra hardware. JPEG files are stored in true 24-bit colour, and the JPEG scheme is much less efficient in storing images of any lower colour range.

WMF : The Windows Meta-File format is a comparatively simple vector oriented format born through the Windows interface. It is very effective for DTP. Like most vector formats, is little used for multimedia.

CH3 : Harvard Graphics 3 uses files stored in .CH3 format. Harvard Graphics is a vector-based image format, but it is also very good at simple graphic demonstrations for multimedia. It is generally used when high-quality photorealistic graphics take a back seat to abstract designs.

EPS : Encapsulated PostScript. This file format uses the standard PostScript language to talk to PostScript printers and is used for high-quality output. It is independent of the make of printer as all Postscript printers produce exactly the same text and graphic images when given the same PostScript commands. Most video cards are not equipped to display files in the PostScript language and it is common to embed pre-prepared EPS images into other applications such as DTP documents.

CDR : The vector file saved by the Corel Draw application package with a .CDR extension. Corel Draw is also capable of saving its files in a variety of formats such as EPS, PCX, etc.

CLP : The file saved in the Windows Clipboard when the user uses cut and paste operations or presses the PrintScreen button. The Windows Clipboard viewer allows the image to be saved away as a .CLP file. This file can be recovered from disc and placed back in the clipboard at any time.

TGA : The bit-mapped file format used by Fantavision's Targa systems. It is most commonly found in 24-bit colour, though it may also be 8-bit colour, or even monochrome. Targa files can be run-length compressed, which works well with monochrome and some 8-bit files, or uncompressed, which is most useful with 24-bit files.

HPGL : The Hewlett Packard Graphics Language is most common format for use with plotters.

ANIMATION

Animation may seem uncomplicated at first. It is simply a succession of graphic images displayed on the screen one after the other in quick succession. The eye possesses a persistence of vision such that, if the images are images are updated quickly enough, the viewer will not detect the sequence as a set of different pictures. In this way, animation creates the illusion of movement. This is the technique used to show movies in the film theatre. Of course, it's not as simple as all that. Vector animations can be hideously complex, although fortunately this is fairly rare on PCs. Bitmapped animations tend to use complex frame compression schemes such as delta compression, predictive compression and such, in order to keep the final file sizes down to a manageable level. This responds to the problem of the amount of data that has to be stored, read and displayed.

Ideally, an animation should display at 30 frames per second. Even the MCGA standard common to FLI files uses a 320x200 screen resolution and 256 different available colours at any one time. This would require 64Kbits to store a single frame. At 30 frames/sec, this requires 1.875Mb for every second of animation - and a staggering 112Mb for a single minute's animation. The production of a five-minute computer animation would require around a half of a Gigabyte of storage! If the animation was to improve on the limited 320x200 format to 1024x768 and the 256 colours was to be raised to full 24-bit colour, the requirements would be beyond any feasible storage abilities (67.5Mb per second!).

This explains the use of the low-resolution MCGA screens and the colour range restrictions. It also explains why some systems work at less than the desired 30 frames per second, although anything below 10fps is regarded as too slow to maintain the illusion of continuous movement.

Solutions to these problems lie in:

- The use of CDs to store the large amounts of data required.
- The use of ever higher data-transfer rate CDs.
- The use of compression techniques to minimise storage and speed up file access. The time taken to uncompress a file is much less than that need to read a larger uncompressed version of the file.
- The use of improved animation techniques. Delta compression is one of these improvements. Instead of storing each picture successively after each other in its entirety, only the changes from each picture to the next are stored. This works well because quite often there is little change between each frame, requiring little data to be stored.
- Using extended memory to store the images, where there is sufficient memory in the computer. This ensures that the images are fetched at the fastest possible speed.

Improving the rate at which the data is fetched overcomes one of the bottlenecks in the animation process. However, the manipulation of such vast amounts of data places a great strain on the computer's CPU. Animations will obviously run better on a faster CPU but animation software will detect whether a CPU is being overstretched and automatically compensate by lowering the frame rate. The alternative is to maintain the same rate but *'drop'* (ignore) frames along the way.

SOFTWARE

Animation creation software ranges from simple programs such as Disney's Animation Studio to top-of-the-range professional products such as Autodesk Animator Pro. There are a greater variety of animation display programs around. Depending on whether DOS or Windows is running, it is more likely to be using either FLI or AVI files respectively. The AAPLAY utility is also available. This is a shareware program that comes with Autodesk's Animator to play FLI animation files. The program MMPLAY, which comes with the Sound Blaster Pro, allows the playing of FLI files synchronised with CMF music and VOC sound samples. In Windows, AVI files allow the playing of animations along with sound effects. However, the Windows environment is currently less than ideal for photorealistic bitmapped animations. Nonetheless, the result should still get the message across much more effectively than plain text.

ANIMATION FORMATS

FLI : FLI, and its successor FLC, are both short for *Flick*, a file format used by Autodesk Animator, the market leader in animation software. It is without doubt the most common animation format currently used on PCs, and uses a (comparatively) simple delta compression scheme. There are several programs other than Animator that will read and display FLI files. The FLC format is similar to FLI, but is not limited to 320 x 200 resolution. It also has better control over the animation speed.

ANI : The Amiga uses animations in files called ANI or sometimes ANM. These are basically a collection of IFF images. They are somewhat rare on PCs.

AVI : The Windows-born AVI, (Audio-VIsual or Audio Video Interleave) animation format, is a true multimedia format. It stores animations along with, optionally, a simultaneous digitised soundtrack. Files can be produced with packages such as PhotoMorph. Players and other utilities for AVI files can currently only be found for the Windows environment. AVI is also a major format for video files as explained next. Supports compressed and uncompressed files.

GIF89a : One variety of this file type is really a collection of graphics images that are embedded into a single file. Each file is a single frame in an animation. The file header contains specific playback information. If the viewing software cannot handle animated GIFs, it still reads and displays the first picture in the sequence. Otherwise, it plays back the file as a sequence of pictures at a pre-determined rate. This technique is used extensively on Internet web pages.

GRAPHICS CREATION

Graphics creation software is available in *'painting'* format (for handling bitmapped images) and *'drawing'* format (for handling line art).

The main options when creating graphics are:

FORMAT TYPE   Bitmaps can store photographic images while vector graphics are comprised of many drawn components.   Bitmaps provide a range of manipulation options that are not available to vector images but lose much of their quality when scaled (see below).   Vector images are scaleable with no loss of quality and would be the likely choice for creating symbols, line drawings.

ELEMENTS   Unless the image is from a real-world source (ie scanned photograph, picture from a digital camera, etc), it will be constructed from a collection of squares, rectangles, circles, polygons, lines, arcs or bezier curves.

CONTENT   The elements have certain properties which can be altered for the maximum impact. These are element size (ie circle diameter, line width, rectangle dimensions) and appearance (eg box or circle colour, line type (plain, dotted).

LOCATION   Where the graphics appear on the screen and what proportion of the screen they occupy will depend on the nature of the final application.   Large graphics are suitable where they have a crucial role in the presentation (eg a car repair program would use large and clear diagrams).   Small graphics should be used where they should not distract the viewer from the main presentation.   Similarly, graphics backgrounds should not overpower the foreground message.

PERSPECTIVE   The monitor screen is two-dimension; all screen content has only width and height.   To provide the illusion of depth, images can be made to appear as if they recede into the background. The left box in the diagram has a front panel and rear panel of the same size.   The rear panel in the right-hand box is smaller, which is perceived by the viewer as depth.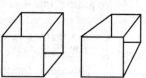

LAYER As in the example shown for text, graphics layering allows one item to partially obscure another.   In the boxes above, the front square is layered over the other lines and partially hides them from view.

GRAPHICS IMPORTATION

Multimedia authoring packages do not generally provide more than elementary painting features which are sufficient for basic boxes and lines.   For all other purposes, images are created in dedicated fully-featured graphics packages and the finished item is imported into the authoring project.   The file types allowed by the authoring package should be checked as it is unlikely that every file format is supported by the authoring package. This may require, for example, exporting a Corel Draw image as a BMP file to be acceptable by the authoring package.

GRAPHICS MANIPULATION

The facilities offered by graphics packages vary and the most common manipulations are:

SCALING   The sides of the image can be pulled or squeezed so that it shrinks or expands to fill a given area. While this poses no problems for vector images, bitmaps will lose detail on shrinking and will become *'blocky'* when expanded.

FILLING   The diagram shows a number of squares that have been filled with either a plain solid colour, a fountain file (eg linear, radial or conical gradations) or a pre-determined pattern (eg bricks, curtains, granite).

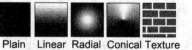

Plain   Linear   Radial   Conical   Texture

TRANSITIONS   As with text transitions, the graphic can be written to the screen in a pre-defined way such as being drawn form the left or filling in from the centre outwards.

CLIPPING/CROPPING Images often contain more detail than is required.   This distracts the viewer from the essential detail and occupies more disc space than is necessary.   The image can be clipped or cropped.   This brings the picture in from the top or bottom, or left and right borders.   The example shows the continent of Africa being taken from a map of the globe.

Cropping

ROTATING   The text can be rotated from its normal horizontal axis to any degree and in any direction.   This can be used for visual effect or can be used to align the text along the outline of an object.

Rotating

REFLECTIONS   A mirror image of an object can be in either the vertical plane, as in the example, or in the horizontal plane.   It is used for visual effect, or to save drawing time by drawing half of a symmetrical shape and creating an identical mirror image of the other half.

Reflections
Reflections

MORPHING   This takes two images and creates a set of intermediate images, showing the stages of transformation from one to the other. Morphing can be applied to objects (eg swords are turned into ploughshares) or photographs (eg Tony Blair turns into Margaret Thatcher).

VIDEO

The field of video cards is complex. Graphics cards are discussed elsewhere in this book, but of special note to multimedia users is the extension port on many graphics cards. This is a pin-out on the internal circuitry of the card called the *'feature'* connector, which can be attached by a ribbon cable to other cards such as video capture cards, full-motion video cards and genlocking equipment.   Now many cards provide these features internally, ie a card functions both as a normal graphics card and as a player/recorder of full-motion video.   Video cards can be purchased simply to play back video or can be used, in conjunction with a video source such as a camcorder, to capture video information.   Capture can be of individual still photographs or can be a full motion sequence.

VIDEO STILLS

The diagram shows the operation of a frame grabber card.   The card takes input from the computer's existing video card and also accepts any other standard video source as its input.   This may be the output from a domestic video recorder or the output straight from a video camera.   Cards may accept video from either the PAL system (for UK sources) or NTSC (for US sources).   Some cards may also support SECAM (the French system). The image is stored in RAM chips within the video capture card before being fed to the monitor

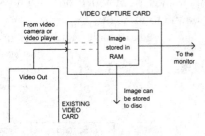

for display.   The video RAM in the existing video card has its contents automatically updated and the user has no control over this process.   However, the software supplied with the video capture card allows the user to prevent its video RAM from being updated, thereby *'freezing'* the current stored picture. Typically, the input from the video source is shown in a resizable window.   The user presses a particular keyboard key and the captured picture is displayed on the monitor screen window.   If the picture is not to the user's satisfaction, a keypress recommences the updating process.   If the captured frame is satisfactory the user can store the image as a graphics file, in formats such as TIFF, BMP and PCX. This often means that the graphic image will be stored as a *'true colour'* image - a 24-bit picture capable of over 16 million shades of colour, reckoned to be the best colour range distinguishable by the human eye.   All full-motion video capture cards will capture single frames; typical products are the VideoBlaster, the Vidi PC and the Win/TV card.   Another product is the *'Video Snapshot'* which is an external model that connects to the parallel port.

FULL-MOTION VIDEO

Where a continuous sequence of movement is to be recorded, a full-motion video card is required.   These cards, sometimes called FMV cards, capture complete moving video sequences. The chart shows the number of frames displayed per second in various systems, to maintain the illusion of continual movement.

Typical frame rates and their uses	
0fps	Still frame
15fps	Minimum acceptable for motion
24fps	Motion pictures
25fps	British television
30fps	American television

The capturing of a sequence is done as a single operation and, due to their added complexity, FMV cards are considerably more expensive than simple frame capture cards.

FILE FORMATS

There are three main formats for storing video files:

AVI :   The Audio Video Interleave format is the Windows standard and is so-called because it stores the audio and video information as a single file, with the video data and audio being divided into blocks and interleaved in the file.   Since both streams of data are stored next to each other in time, it aids the synchronisation process. Where video and audio files are held separately, the delays in reading both sets of data from disc and interpreting the separate streams leads to severe problems of keep the sound synchronised to the picture. AVI files can be in compressed or uncompressed format depending whether one of the compression algorithms (see later) has been applied them.

QuickTime : The *'Macintosh'* range of computers made by Apple have long led the field in innovation and are still the most popular system for use with art, design and DTP. The *'Mac'* range was introduced in 1984 and Apple were the first to use a Graphical User Interface (in their 1983 *'Lisa'* computer), colour monitors (in their 1977 Apple II model), built-in sound and eventually video (in their own QuickTime format). The Windows-type environment was embedded in the Mac operating system form its introduction; users never had to struggle with a command-line environment like DOS.

Unfortunately, the Mac computer range are not compatible with PCs as they use a different processor range which uses different machine code instructions. The QuickTime video format was originally produced by Apple for their range of Macintosh machines. This format also interleaves audio and video information. The QuickTime and AVI formats are incompatible but the files can be converted between the two standards.

MPEG : The Motion Picture Experts Group standard MPEG compression forms the core of VideoCD as used in CD-I players, etc. and can store about 70 minutes of video on a single CD. It is explained more fully later.

VIDEO STORAGE

Like animations, full-motion video captured this way can easily occupy huge amounts of hard disc space. The chapter on video covered the storage requirements for a single picture frame at different resolutions. Video has to store and play back between 15 and 30 individual screens per second. The highest demands from video on currently-available CDs is a 800x600 screen at 256 colours, although this is bound to increase.

The storage capacity per second of video can be calculated thus:

File Size = Bit Depth x Screen Resolution x Frames/Sec

This is divided by 8 to get the answer in bytes and divided again by 1,048,576 to get the answer in Mbs. A 256-colour (ie 8bits) VGA (ie 640x480) at a 15fps screen update would require

640 x 480 x 8 x 15 / 8 / 1048576 = 4.39Mb

Number of colours	Screen Resolution	Frame Rate	Storage/Sec
256	640 x 480	15	4.39Mb
256	800 x 600	15	6.86Mb
256	1024 x 768	15	11.25Mb
256	640 x 480	25	7.32Mb
256	800 x 600	25	11.44Mb
256	1024 x 768	25	18.75Mb
16.78m	1024 x 768	30	67.5Mb
16.78m	1600 x 1200	30	164.79Mb
256	352 x 288	25	2.41Mb
16.78m	352 x 288	25	7.25Mb

The chart shows the amount of storage required for a range of popular displays.

The smallest figure for a full screen image is 4.39Mb, while the professional performance figure is around 165Mb per second! The two bottom chart entries describe the resolution of MPEG-1 in its uncompressed form. The saving and playing back of live video involves not only the storage but the transfer of huge amounts of data; this requires a fast hard disc, a fast CPU and a fast video system.

These storage figures are not practical and a number of methods are introduced to reduce this size:

- Using only a portion of the screen to display the video; if the video occupies a quarter of the screen area, it only needs a quarter of the storage space. This is commonly used on CDs to accommodate the low performance of most discs/CPUs/video cards.
- Reducing the colour palette to 256 colours would mean a barely noticeable loss of colour gradation, but would mean that the video clip is a third of the size of a 16.78m colour clip.
- Lower the frame rate at which the picture is displayed. This makes savings but the picture is jerkier.
- Compressing the files for storage and decompressing them when they are to be played. Unlike the other three methods, compression need not produce any deterioration in picture quality. The user has the option to make even bigger savings at the expense of some picture quality.

COMPRESSION

Data compression schemes are mostly based on the following techniques:

INTRAFRAME   This considers each individual frame and discards any trivial data. This is the method used by both JPEG and MJPEG compression systems.

INTERFRAME   This considers the differences between successive frames, removes the unchanged parts of the information and applies JPEG type compression on whats left. This is also called 'difference compression' and is used by the MPEG system.

Other, less well used methods involve converting 24-bit colour down to 16-bit colour and using dithering to represent the lost colours. This reduces file sizes at the expense of introducing a *'grainy'* effect to the clip when played back.

CODECS

The CODEC (compressor/decompressor) is an engine that shrinks the files on saving and expands them again when they are to be used. CODECs can be implemented in either hardware or software. Hardware CODECs are more expensive but, because they use dedicated chips instead ot the computer's CPU time, they are significantly more efficient. No CODECs were supplied with Windows 3.1 and these had to be installed by the user.

Windows 95 comes with four CODECs pre-installed:

CINEPAK : Developed by Apple for their SuperMac computers and now licensed to Microsoft, it supports 320x240 at 15fps and both the compression and decompression are implemented in software. Only works for 24-bit colour.

INDEO : This system was developed by Intel and the compression process requires capture cards that are based on the Intel i750 video processor chip. This results in an AVI file with Indeo compression. Indeo uses both interframe compression and run length encoding techniques (see below). The playback process can be implemented in software at 320x240 with 15fps and 24-bit colour; this does not require the use of any special hardware. Playback is 'scaleable' - the faster the CPU, the greater will be the screen size and frame rates used. Where a i750 card is also used for playback, a full-screen at 30fps is supported.

MSVC : The Microsoft Video Compressor, also known as Video 1. Developed to use algorithms that place less pressure on the CPU. Although supported by cards such as the Black Widow Media Master Plus, it has not found a place in general use. This is probably because it only supports 256 or 32k colours.

RLE : Run Length Encoding takes a horizontal area of a colour and stores the length of the band rather than the individual pixels. This is very effective in animations where backgrounds are plain but produces poor results as a video CODEC.

Apart from the four CODECs supplied with Windows 95, there are some other very significant drivers that can be installed. These include:

QuickTime

This is produced in Mac and PC Windows versions and mixes sound and vision into the one file, similar to the AVI format, with added MIDI tracks. It is a software CODEC and therefore needs some of the CPU's time. It also has 'scalable performance' which means that it automatically adjusts to the capabilities of the machine in use. It handles AVI files and will provide 15fps, 20fps or 30fps depending on the machine speed. Similarly, it will produce from one-tenth screen up to full screen images depending upon the abilities of the system on which it is run. The 3.2 version is intended for use with Pentiums and provides full screen graphics.

MPEG

The <u>M</u>oving <u>P</u>ictures <u>E</u>xperts <u>G</u>roup format uses a complicated set of compression methods including spatial compression, Huffman coding and predictive compression - based on only saving the <u>differences</u> (or 'deltas') between successive frames. It produces a result similar to television's VHS quality. Depending on the quality and speed required, it may sometimes require expensive hardware, but can achieve surprising compression rates. These rates vary depending on the quality of the stored image, because MPEG compression is a type known as 'lossy' - i.e. the final image has lost small, less noticeable details in order to effect greater compression. Compression ratios up to 50:1 can be achieved before the picture quality deteriorates noticeably.

Current systems are designed around MPEG-1 with data rates of around 1.4Mbps and frame rates up 30fps. MPEG-2 is being finalised as a standard for higher quality with a resultant increase in data rates. The increased demands of MPEG-2 will lead to further improvements in component specifications. It provides the lowest common formats as it can produce 340x240 at 30fps for American NTSC TV (or 352x288 at 25fps for European PAL TV) from a standard CD-ROM player; this is sometimes referred to as SIF - the Standard Interchange Format. Many video clips on CDs are designed for this format and don't therefore take advantage of the significant hardware improvements that modern PCs contain. It is also a common multimedia format.

M-JPEG

Motion-JPEG, called M-JPEG, is similar in basis to the JPEG graphic format. Each individual frame is compressed using JPEG techniques and each frame is stored individually and separately. By concentrating on individual frame compression, it produces less spectacular compression ratios (around 8:1) but provides 24-bit depth, higher quality and easier manipulation. Its increased data rate meant that it could not be supported by the slow speeds of early CD players and is the choice of the professional user. (eg video production, video editing).

Since an AVI file may have been encoded using one of a variety of CODECS, Windows 95 provides a method to get a report on a file's configuration. If an AVI file is highlighted in *'Explorer'* and the mouse right-hand button is clicked, the *'Properties'* option of the resulting menu produces the screen shown.

There are three main options:
- The *'General'* option shows file dates, size, etc.
- The *'Preview'* option runs the clip in miniature.
- The *'Details'* option shows that the file called 'Beatles' is designed to be run in a quarter of a VGA screen at 15fps using a Cinepak CODEC.   Its data rate is only 146kbps, allowing it to be run directly from even the slowest CD-ROM drive.   This is a good example of how early AVI files were produced to match the lowest possible hardware performance.

Since even compressed video clips tend to be enormous, most clips found in the public domain are low resolution with a low frame rate. The result is below TV quality, but gets the message across effectively, which is the intention of multimedia in the first place.   The clips that are found in many magazine's 'free' CDs are of larger size but they still have to be tailored to the lowest standards, to be compatible with the largest numbers of user machines.

CAPTURE METHODS
There are two ways that live video can be captured and saved:
TWO-STEP DIGITISER
This is the older system and the video input is saved directly to disc in uncompressed form.   The package's CODEC (compression/decompression) system then creates an improved version by compressing the saved file.   The CODEC can be implemented as a dedicated chip or can be a software program.   This two-step system is useful for less-powerful computers that cannot cope with simultaneous reading and compression of data.   It is a more laborious method and requires more free disc space.   An example of this type is the VideoSpigot.   It can handle a top rate of 30fps with a window size of 192x144 and a window size of 384x288 with a very low rate of 8fps or so.

SINGLE-STEP DIGITISER
Single-step digitisers convert the video input into a digitised form, compress it and save it - all in a single stage.   There is no need to first store it in uncompressed form.   An even more efficient system results from using hardware for single-step compression.   The chip on the capture board does all the compression processing and relieves the computer's CPU of that work.   An example of this type is the Intel Smart Video Recorder which uses an Intel i750 compression chip.   It can handle 30fps at 160x120 or 15fps at 320x240. The VideoBlaster RT300 also uses the i750 chip and handles up to 30fps at 320x240.

At the professional end, the Miro DC20 and the FAST Electronic AV Master support full screen PAL (ie 768x576, the resolution of a UK TV screen) at 50fps, using M-JPEG compression of about 5:1.

Single-step compression is also known as 'On-the-Fly' compression since it occurs in real time.

Some cards offer the addition of an MPEG daughterboard to provide MPEG compression, while cards such as the Vitec Video NT and the REALmagic Producer are designed as MPEG encoder cards.

NB   Even compressed files demand high data transfer rates from the disc system.   This has led to the production of discs with guaranteed uninterrupted data rates, such as the Micropolis AV range of drives.

PLAYBACK SYSTEMS
All video files require to be played back using some type of driver routines.   These routines are usually implemented in software although hardware implementations are also available and are more efficient.
SOFTWARE CODECS
All AVI files compressed by a particular CODEC should be decompressed with that same CODEC.   So, an AVI file with Cinepack compression should be run using Cinepack decompression software.
HARDWARE CODECS
These use dedicated chipsets to produce full screen playback of AVI files.   Typical is the VideoLogic 928Movie card.   It uses an enhanced S3 928 video card to play AVI Indeo and Cinepak files full screen. It uses a *'digital movie accelerator chipset'* which means that it uses an interpolated algorithm to estimate the extra pixels required to fill the full screen.   This prevents *'blockiness'* and *'jagged edges'* on the image but tends to soften the picture.   The smaller the original AVI file, the more marked will be this loss of contrast. Other examples are the Matrox Millenium and the Miro 12PD.

PLAYING BACK MPEG
Clips that were created and saved using MPEG compression require to be decompressed before the video information can be sent to the monitor.   The machine to show these clips requires to be fitted with an MPEG playback card or have MPEG decoding software routines.   The hardware implementation is potentially faster as the card contains chip that are dedicated to MPEG decoding.   This saves much of the computer's CPU time.

MPEG cards are available in the following varieties:
- An add-on to an existing graphics card, usually via a plug-in daughterboard, such as offered by the VideoLogic 928 Movie card.
- An MPEG decoder card that plugs into the VESA *'feature connector'* of existing graphics card. An example is the Aztech Galaxy Oscar.
- Cards that do not connect to feature connectors (handy for older cards without feature connectors or for cards that are not fully VESA compliant). An example is the Black Widow MoviePlus 1100.
- Cards that completely replace existing graphics cards. They act both as a standard graphics card and as an MPEG decoder. Examples are the RealMagic Rave for the VL-Bus and the PCI Marvel II.

Software CODECs are becoming more popular. The speed of CPUs and the general data transfer rates of computer systems have increased to a point where software MPEG decoding is possible, dispensing with the need for a dedicated decoder card. This is not a serious option for anything below a 120MHz Pentium, as the added load on the CPU results in dropping of frames. Software CODECs are supplied with cards such as the VideoLogic, Miro and Matrox ranges. Microsoft are negotiating a licensing agreement that will provide a MPEG CODEC to be bundled with Windows 95 in the future.

M-JPEG cards won't handle MPEG files and only play back M-JPEG files. Convertors are available which take the higher specification M-JPEG files and convert them into MPEG files for general use.

MPEG AND CD-I

Dedicated CD-I players are microprocessor-controlled CD playback systems that are intended to run dedicated interactive video CDs for training, educational and entertainment purposes. They have no keyboard and use only a controller with mouse, joystick or rollerball to control simple on-screen menus. Their output is to a TV set or a colour monitor. They have no hard disc and therefore cannot save any information. They have their own internal operating system (RTOS) which is different from any used in PCs. They are produced to the 'Green Book' CD specification (see the chapter on discs and drives). CDs that are made to the 'White Book' specification use MPEG compression. If a DV (digital video) cartridge is fitted to a CD-I player, the machine can also play back those White Book full-motion video CDs. A range of films, music concerts, etc is now available in CD-I format and these can be viewed on a PC as long as it is fitted with a CD ROM that reads the CD-I format and an MPEG decoder.

NSP

Digital Signal Processors, DSPs, are used in sound cards, video cards and other devices. These are chips dedicated to tasks such as analogue to digital signal processing and vice versa, along with a range of other data processing functions. These chips are fitted on the boards of sound and video cards. With the coming of higher performance PCs, there is an attempt to have these specialist processing tasks carried out by the CPU. This is known as *'Native Signal Processing'* and, if successful would require less add-on cards making the computer system cheaper.

DATA TRANSFER RATES

Users constantly demand improvements in multimedia performance - more colours, higher resolutions, bigger and smoother video clips. The space required to store one minute of video is becoming ever larger. But buying a larger disc drive doesn't solve the problem. The playback system still has only one minute to move around this larger set of data. This places great demands on all

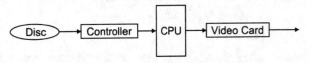

components in the system. As the diagram shows, the playback process moves the data from the disc through a chain of components to the monitor. The system is only as powerful as its weakest link.

So, the CD player or disc drive must have a fast access time and a fast data transfer rate. For video recording and CD writing the flow in and out of the disc drive must be continuous. Temporary slowdowns in the DTR would result in lost frames while recording and potential loss of the entire gold disc while CD writing. On way to guarantee uninterrupted data transfer is to use the new AV disc drives. The disc controller interface has to high performance with IDE being replaced by EIDE or SCSI-2 or even SCSI-UW. The CPU must be at least a Pentium, with preference to high speed MMX, Pro or Pentium II chips. Finally, the video card specification should include a wide internal bus (eg 128-bit), sufficient memory to cope with high screen resolutions and a large colour palette, and a chipset that copes with required demands (eg high-speed DAC, 3D playing, MPEG decoding).

CURRENT DEVELOPMENTS

A number of major developments affecting multimedia have appeared. These affect the computer's hardware, the packaging of video and audio, multimedia over the Internet and virtual reality.

COMPUTER

The main aims have been to achieve improvements in both raw speed and in consistent performance. The arrival of the MMX chip, with 57 new internal instructions and a larger internal cache, produces a machine that is capable, with MMX-aware software, of processing up to 8 data bytes processed in a single instruction cycle. But video handling is not concerned with the maximum burst rate; it has to process data at a continual guaranteed rate. The normal computer's CPU has to carry out housekeeping tasks (eg keyboard and mouse handling, video handling, etc) as well as video handling. This could produce dropped frames when top performance is demanded. Newer machine now offer dual or even quad processors on the motherboard. This will produce some further speed improvement but its main effect is to even out the load on the system.

VM-CHANNEL

The Video Media Channel is a fairly new VESA standard for connecting the heavy data demands of multimedia devices. The system takes all video traffic off the PC's data bus and moves it around on an extra, parallel, high-speed bus system. This lowers the demands on the data bus and relieves much of the CPU time. This VM-C system is <u>additional</u> to the PC's normal data movements. So, program code, etc. will still transfer over the normal ISA, VL, PCI or whatever bus. This means that VM-Channel can be implemented on all existing machines so long as they are fitted with a VM-Channel graphics card. The channel can be used to connect the video card to other media devices such as compression cards, 3D graphics engines, TV cards and digitisers. Devices are connect by a 68-wire ribbon cable capable of connecting 15 devices in a daisy chain. The channel works on a 'token ring' packet scheduling model (see LAN chapter) and runs at up to 132Mbps. Although the cable is a 32-bit bus, it will happily work with 8-bit and 16-bit VMC devices.

The 'feature' connector on current video cards is an <u>output</u> device to feed video to other devices. The VMC-equipped video card's feature connector is known as a VAFC (VESA Advanced Feature Connector). Unlike the normal output-only connector, the VAFC is also a main <u>input</u> device capable of displaying the output of the other video devices on the cable. For example, with sufficient equipment, the system could support a 15-person videoconference with each participant appearing in a separate real-time updating window. VideoLogic's 928Movie card, and the VideoLogic Gráfix Star series of cards support VMC and there is a great deal of development going on with major players such as Novell planning VMC products.

VIDEO

The main developments in video are the increased storage capacities offered by the DVD (*'Digital Versatile Disk'*) which can store 4.7Gb on a single surface due to the higher wavelength of the laser beams. The future promises both double sided and multi-layer versions with ever greater capacity.
Support for MPEG-1 (ie 352x 240 at 30 fps) is now widespread and MPEG-2 (ie 720x480 at 60 fps) will make an appearance soon.

AUDIO

Audio arrived at CD-quality performance some time ago and the main development have been in producing quality audio over the Internet. This include initiates such as *'RealAudio'* which can pipe recorded audio to users; even better, it allows users to listen to real time audio (eg US radio stations).
The audio that is stored on a normal audio CD is the plain digitised version with no compression is applied to it. The CD is filled after 10 or 12 tracks. Audio MPEG promises file sizes that are 6-12 times smaller than the standard digitised version. This allows many more tracks to be placed on an audio CD. It also allows audio data to transmitted over the Internet much more efficiently. Net phones are now gathering momentum. Users who have the software can make international calls at local rates using the Internet.

COMMUNICATIONS

Raw speed has been improved with the advent of the 56k modem and a range of new facilities are appearing. These include the use of Java applets and the introduction of Surround Video.

VIRTUAL REALITY

Virtual reality (VR) has received much publicity and is still in the development stage. Crude versions have appeared in amusement arcades and much work has been carried out in the areas of staff training and work simulation.

VR produces an artificial world that is generated by computer. It uses four elements:

- Database (to store the elements of the scenario - eg buildings, trees, roads, etc. These are not stored as graphics images; they are stored in descriptive format.)
- Graphics engine (to convert object data in graphics shapes, implementing 3D shading and texture mapping)
- Input (to sense activities in the real world)
- Output (to stimulate human senses)

VR is produced in two ways:

Fully-immersive

The user wears a head-mounted display that contains LCD screens for each eye, along with motion detectors. This is the most realistic method, as the user can only view the scene presented by the computer and there are no outside distractions. The helmet's sensors track head movements, such that turning the head to the left generates a picture which pans to the left. However, it is still expensive, uncomfortable and renders the user prone to motion sickness.

Partially-immersive

The user views the artificial world through a window (ie the monitor) and is already popular for games use. It is less effective than fully-immersive systems as the surrounding environment distracts from the effect of the simulation.

The main outputs are to the users sight and hearing. The main inputs are from helmet sensors, joystick, keyboard and foot levers. Future outputs will include smell, touch, heat and taste. Input and output will use data gloves and data suits.

GATHERING DATA

This chapter does not attempt to discuss the planning and content of a multimedia presentation. This is a bigger issue than can be usefully covered here. This chapter concentrates on the practical tasks in multimedia production. Once the presentation's content is formulated, the user has an idea of the material that is required to put across the required concepts. The designer than has to decide on the source of any graphics and animations, special sound effects or musical accompaniment.

There are many varied ways to gather data for a multimedia presentation.

BULLETIN BOARDS/INTERNET

A very useful source is wide access to bulletin boards and on-line services with a modem. This will ensure access to the latest freely distributable imaging and audio software, as well as plenty of raw data for use in multimedia, and even communication with people who can explain how it can be used. However, this can be an expensive proposition in terms of telephone costs.

CD-ROM SOURCES

An alternative is CD-ROM. Although CD-ROM at first looks expensive, the amount of data it can store compared with magnetic discs or especially downloading time through modems, means that it will become economical after buying only a few CD-ROM discs. Many CD-ROMs are dedicated to multimedia, as it is well suited to carrying the huge amounts of data needed for multimedia purposes. CD ROMs are available with clip art, digitised pictures, sound samples, and music clips. Some of these files are public domain and some are copyrighted.

CREATING GRAPHICS FILES

Many packages are available to view, edit and create graphics and more are appearing all the time. In addition to the drawing/painting tools described earlier, there are other specialised tools:

RAY TRACING

For the more mathematically inclined, there are many public domain ray-tracing programs, where even a few simple spheres, planes and cubes can be surprisingly effective when used properly. Perhaps the best-known PC raytracer is Persistence Of Vision, which is available from almost any shareware vendor. Professional packages range up to the industry standard 3D Studio package.

FRACTALS

There are programs that create images with little or no input from the user. Although a Mandelbrot fractal may be too abstract for use in most multimedia presentations, it can make a very effective background to other graphics, and can also be used in conjunction with a raytracer to produce complex, realistic landscapes.

FLY-THROUGHS

Another program, a shareware program called *Vistapro*, can create extremely realistic landscapes, and fly-through animations of those landscapes, with little effort on the part of the designer. Although this may be of limited application to, for instance a CAL (Computer Aided Learning) programme to teach Excel, it is very eye-catching and therefore very suitable for commercial multimedia shows.

SCREEN CAPTURE

Material for multimedia can be culled from almost anywhere, to do almost anything. For example, to create a Computer Aided Learning demonstration to teach people a certain technique in Microsoft Word for Windows, the *Alt+PrtScr* keystrokes can be used to capture the screen in the midst of using the technique. This can be pasted into Paintbrush and saved as a PCX file for later use in a multimedia show.

SCANNERS

Existing graphic material can be easily be incorporated into presentations with the use of scanners. These capture the graphics contents from any sheet of paper and convert them into a graphics file. Most devices are able to save the data in a variety of formats such as TIFF, BMP, PCX, TGA, or even EPS or JPEG. The scanner is able to handle line drawings, text and full photographs. Models are available to handle monochrome and colour input. Any material that is captured has to be within the laws of copyright. This means that pictures from newspapers and magazines cannot be used without permission. Similarly, the law covers the illegal copying of company logos, company letterheads, £20 notes, etc. Nevertheless, the device is very convenient for converting pen sketches, users' signatures and any authorised photographs.

The most convenient scanner is the flatbed model. This is usually an A4 size device, where the sheet to be scanned is placed on a glass plate. In this respect, the scanner is similar to a photocopier. However, the data read is saved straight to a disc file rather than being used to

directly produce a replica sheet. Some models allow multiple sheets to be scanned . Flatbeds come with either interface cards or with SCSI interfaces.

Flatbed Scanner

Where items to be scanned are small, or there are budget restrictions, handheld models are available. These are smaller and can only scan around 10cm width and users may be forced to scan a document in several strips. The software finds the area of overlap, and aligns the images to create a single larger file. Handheld scanner resolutions are switchable from 100-400dpi, with flatbeds working up to 9600dpi. The specification should be checked as the *'optical scan resolution'* may differ from the *'output resolution'*. The image may be scanned at a

Hand Scanner

lower resolution (say 800dpi) and enhanced in software to produce a file with greater resolution (say 1600dpi). 300dpi is generally considered as minimum standard for DTP work but screen-based multimedia requires much lower scanning rates. Dependent upon the monitor size and the screen mode (VGA or SVGA), only around 60 to 90 pixels are displayed for each screen inch. Any scanning at a higher dpi rate produces no improvement in quality, while consuming much more disc storage space. Monochrome scanners with 256 grey level are now less common as 24-bit colour scanner prices have fallen. Modern scanners are *'Twain'* compatible. This is the Windows interface agreed by major manufacturers such as Hewlett Packard and Logitech.

STILL CAPTURE

There are professional imaging centres that can digitise pictures for use on computers, or users can create their own using a video capture card and a video camera. Of course, a digitised picture can rarely be used *'as is'*. Generally, a digitised picture has to be manually re-touched, to remove such things as movement artefacts, (generated when a moving image is being digitised) dithering patterns, (visible when a full-colour digitised is reduced to a paletted image for viewing on a PC screen) and so on. Photo retouch packages, such as Photofinish, provide facilities such spot removal, brightness and contrast adjustment, diffusing; it also provides special effects such as motion blur, mosaic and emboss effects, etc. Users may also want to edit the image to include some extra details such as superimposing a logo on a picture, or drawing an arrow pointing out an important feature.

DIGITAL CAMERAS

An alternative is to use a digital camera. These have all the features of normal cameras (eg zoom, focus, shutter speed, etc) but the image is digitised and saved to memory or to mini-disc inside the camera. The images can then be transferred to a PC using a serial or other link. The number of pictures that can be stored depends upon the size of the flash memory or mini-disc, the picture resolution and the compression ratio.

Typical models are the Casio QV-10a which takes 320x240 pictures and the Kodak DC50 which takes 765x504 pictures but costs twice as much. Kodak DCS-420 works at 1012x1524 resolution (less than half the resolution of a 35mm slide) while the Sharp MD-PS1 can capture up to 2,000 images on its 140Mb mini-disc.

None of these models are as effective as using a real camera and scanning in the developed photographs; this results in a much higher resolution graphics file.

VIDEO CLIPS

These are available from the Internet but are normally poor quality or of short duration.

Using the video capture cards described earlier, video clips of all types become available. These can range from clips set up by the user (eg how to repair a car) to live coverage of events (although the laws of privacy, copyright, etc still apply here). Although the capture card provides the technology, there is still a lot to learnt to get the best from a camcorder. Issues such as lighting, sound, placing of subject, developing a storyboard beforehand, etc should be addressed and there are many books and magazines for home movie makers.

SOUND

Sound samples and music files can generally be found in the same places as graphics and animations, but creating sound samples is a relatively inexpensive business. Assuming the use of a sound card such as a Sound Blaster or compatible, a simple microphone can be used to record sounds. Most sound cards capable of sampling come with sample editing software, to allow the addition of special effects such as echo, fade, or mix.

COPYRIGHT

While professionals rarely react to their work being adopted for personal use, they will take action when their photographs, film clips, audio tracks, etc are re-used in a commercial product. Great care should be taken to protect against legal action. The Copyright Licensing Agency run a *'Copywatch'* scheme to detect illegal copying and advice can be sought from them at 90 Tottenham Court Rd, London W1P 0LP (Tel 0171-436-5931). If in doubt, seek permission or stick to using copyright-free sound, pictures and clip-art collections.

MULTIMEDIA SOFTWARE

The range of software to support the creation of multimedia products includes:

	Typical Example	Purpose
Audio Editing	Blaster Master, Software Audio Workshop, Wave for Windows	WAV files can be manipulated in many ways to create the final clip to be included in a production. These include cut and paste, mixing, merging, filtering out frequencies, adding echo effects, looping, muting, reversing, pitch altering, volume altering, panning, fading and waveform editing.
Video Editing and effects	Premiere, Elastic Reality, Morph2, Digital Video Producer	*'Linear editing'* as offered by Video Director copies snatches of recordings from the camcorder directly to the VCR; no capture card is used but it lacks precision and control. The other packages use *'Non-Linear Editing'* where the video clip is digitised and individual frames can easily be accessed for editing and the application of effects. Typical facilities are cut and paste, adding filters, transitions between scenes such as fades and wipes, titling, warping and morphing (gradually transforming one object into another object).
Graphic Creation	Paintbrush, Corel Draw, Freehand	To create drawings, charts, cartoons, etc from graphic elements such as lines, boxes, circles and polygons. The line widths, styles (eg dotted, arrowed) and colour are alterable and a variety of fill patterns are provided. Text of various sizes, types styles and colours can be added. Packages such as Paintbrush produce bitmap files while upmarket products produce vector images (although these can be converted to bitmaps).
Graphic Effects	3D Studio, Visual Reality, Ray Dream Studio	The most common effects are 3D objects using wireframes and rendered fills and animations. Many authoring packages provide animation facilities but these are not as sophisticated as dedicated animation packages.
Image Editing	Photoshop, Picture Publisher, PhotoStudio	Used to manipulate a photographic image. This includes altering the colours, altering contrast and brightness, and zooming, scaling and cropping of the image. It may also include special effects such as quantizing (producing an oil painting effect) and altering the data masks (producing a pop video effect).
Authoring Packages	Director, Authorware, Icon Author, MasterClass, Toolbook	This is the key piece of software that integrates all the sound, video, graphic and text components into a meaningful order to achieve a set purpose.

SOFTWARE FOR DELIVERY

The software requirements for the delivery of multimedia are small. Windows 95 users will already have the capability of playing WAV and AVI files. Additional software drivers and CODECs are required to support a full range playback devices. For example, MPEG and QuickTime files both require to have their own CODECs installed. Sound cards require that their software be configured and if the user is downloading multimedia from the Internet, then communications and browser software is required.

DESIGNING A MULTIMEDIA PROJECT

The main steps in designing projects for multimedia are similar to those for any software project, although there are extra considerations. The main phases are:

ANALYSIS

It is vital that a clear understanding of the project is achieved before any other work is undertaken; this will prevent many wasted hours and potential disputes with the client commissioning the project. The client will provide a project brief, which is a short summary of the aims of the project. The aim of systems analysis is to convert the project brief into a project plan that can be implemented.

A thorough set of discussions clarifies the detailed aims of the project. This would include issues such as the general content (eg education, training, entertainment), the target audience (the likely age, sex, previous knowledge/experience of those using the multimedia) and the mood (serious, light-hearted).

This will lead to the production of a project specification. This is essentially a requirements list covering educational requirement and technical requirements such as the proposed delivery system, screen resolution and colours, screen layout and project navigation).

PROTOTYPING

Prototyping is an excellent, although time-consuming, way to develop an understanding and a client agreement on a project. A prototype is a partial implementation of a project, showing the key structural and layout details. This is shown to the client and used as a means of sharpening up the definition of their needs. Misunderstandings and extra features can be picked up and settled at this stage, before a great deal of expensive and possibly wasted effort has been expended.

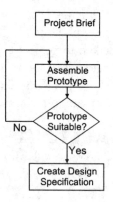

The aim of the analysis phase is to produce precise statements which can act as a checklist in the later testing phase. Example statements might be that all menus will be in a bottom panel, or that every page should provide help and exit options.

DESIGN

The design phase lays out how the project will work in detail. A number of methods are used by different developers, but a top-down approach (where the main functions are outlined followed by subsidiary functions, continuing to the end of the outline) and flowcharts (showing the links between screen pages) are common development methods. The design phase produces all the content details. This will cover all internal resources (ie the company's own talent, hardware and raw material) and requirements for buying in skills (eg commissioning photographers, video camera teams, sound studios, graphics artists, animators, voice-over artists, etc). Details of copyright would also be addressed at this stage. The two main guides that are produced from the design phase are:

- STORYBOARD   This is a set of sketches and notes that describe each scene, video clip, audio clip, text, navigation icon, and the mood to be set.   It provides snapshots of the intended sequence to convey the impression of the final result. Storyboards can be hand-drawn or can be created using storyboard software.   They can be finely detailed, listing every sound, colour, etc; this is slower to produce but leaves less margin for error.   Storyboards that are more of a rough guide sometimes require more versions to be produced to adequately define the project.

- NAVIGATION MAP   This is required for all but the very simplest of projects. It details every connection between one part of the project and another. Users navigate (ie move round) the application by choosing menu options, clicking on icons, buttons or hypertext entries, or clicking on 'hotspots' (active areas of the screen - eg a county on a map).   The map shows where the user is taken on activating one of the navigation tools.

IMPLEMENTATION

The implementation phase is concerned with the production of the components (ie creating the graphics and animation, recording the interviews and voiceovers, filming/digitising/editing the video clips, writing the text copy) and integrating them into a project with an authoring package. Large projects would benefit from the use of project management software, to ensure that the most efficient use is made of resources and to achieve a working product in the shortest possible time.   A video crew might require a long advance booking, the well-known personality for the presenter/voice-over may only be in the country over a short time period, etc. and the activities have to be planned to prevent hold-ups.

TESTING

The testing stage is vital to ensure that the product meets the client's needs and to maintain the reputation of the company.   Testing can be of two types:

VALIDATION   These tests ensure that the project has been built to the original specification and has not moved away from the client's original intention.   These tests are on content, presentation and style, testing whether it addresses the agreed client group, and such issues.

VERIFICATION - These tests ensure that the project functions work correctly.   This tests that all buttons work correctly, all navigation tools take the user to the intended destination, self-assessed tests provide correct marks, all video and audio clips play correctly, etc.

MAINTENANCE

The maintenance phase looks at making program changes after the completion and distribution of project. This is a potentially costly business if the changes are due to programming.   Other changes may be made at the client's request, as an additional chargeable contract.   It also involve adding new features for future updates (eg internet linking, client databases).

AUTHORING SOFTWARE

Multimedia authoring packages range from hobbyist products to those with full-blown commercial purposes.   The generally price reflects the facilities provided by the packages and they use a number of different production methods:

Method	Example Packages	Explanation
Icon/Flow Control	AuthorWare, Authority, IconAuthor	A flow chart plots the possible routes between activities; this is the 'navigation map'. An activity is represented by an icon which could be a decision to be made, a user entry to be requested, a new screen of graphics to be shown, a video or sound clip to be run and so on. At the design and implementation stages, groups of icons can be grouped together under a single icon - implementing a top-down down design of sub-modules. The example shows the second level of a package which displays a top menu with four choices (eg Memory Types, Organisation). Each choice produces a drop-down menu with other choices (eg Error Detection, Cache Memory).
Cast/Score/Script	Director	Uses a 'timeline' as in the example, where each vertical frame stores all the objects that will be used during that particular timeslot. Objects can be graphics, video clips, user entry buttons or dialogue boxes, screen effects, etc. Each object can therefore be controlled down to the precision of a single frame (for a 25fps production, this means control down to 1/25th of a second).
Card/Script	Toolbook	Uses a book as its presentation format. Users can flick through the pages of the book and pages can contain text, graphics, video or user input.

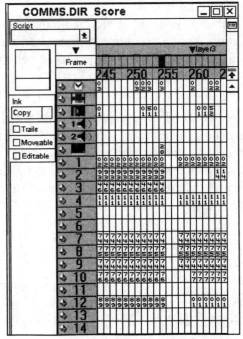

Part of a Director score

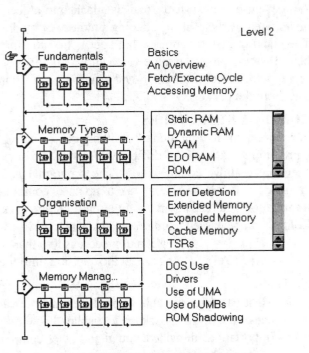

Part of an Authorware design screen

SCRIPTING

Some packages provide very simple navigation links but for greater control of navigation and to support internal logic decisions, the author has to learn the programming language behind the package.   The examples show the minimum scripts used by the leading *'Director'* and *'Toolbook'* packages.

```
      Director's Lingo              Toolbook
      on mouseup                    TO HANDLE buttonClick
            go frame "quiz"              go to next page
      end                           END buttonClick
```

PRESENTATION FACILITIES

In all multimedia presentations, the user approaches the application in an interactive way, expecting to be given control over the package.

The three most important elements are:

BUTTONS

The user has to control the flow of information in a package.   This will normally be achieved by the user clicking the mouse on on-screen *'buttons'* that represent a particular choice.   The choice may be from a selection of menu options (ie where to go next) or might be from a selection of possible data entries (eg choosing a correct answer or saving or loading a set of data).   Buttons can be the default grey variety provide in most authoring packages or can be user-defined such as pictures or shapes.

Alternatives to buttons are using dialogue boxes, where the user is asked to enter data (eg user name or age) and the *'hot spot'* where an area of the screen is designated as a large button.   Clicking a hot spot has the same effect as clicking a button but a hot spot can be an irregular shape.   This allows the user to, for example, click anywhere on the Isle of Wight in a screen map of the UK to see more information about that island.

Other on-screen system control are

- radio buttons (ie only one option can be active at a time)
- check boxes (ie more than option can be active at the same time)
- scroll bars
- file/directory selection

EVENTS

Normal conventional programs are written to be mainly sequential; the program starts at the beginning of the code and finishes at the end of the code.   Multimedia products are explored in a different manner. With event-driven systems, code is attached to objects and remains inactive until it is called.   Calls can be initiated by the user (eg clicking a mouse) or by the system (eg a timeout).

The clicking of the button or hot spot is tied to a particular action.   So clicking the *'Show Interview'* button always plays the same video clip.   Clicking a *'More Details'* button may produce an entirely new screen with more information and a further set of buttons.   Clicking the *'Quit'* button should exit the user from the package.

CONTROL STRUCTURES

For more control, conditional branching can be carried out.   So, a user when presented with six buttons representing six levels of difficulty may only be allowed to pursue a higher level if the lower level has been successfully completed.   The program has kept the user's previous performance in a set of variables and the branching taken up is a combination of what button the user pressed and what information is already stored.   In a multi-choice question, the user may only be allowed three attempts. Control can be passed to internal code using constructs such as:

```
      IF ..          eg if a user score is less than 50% ....
      REPEAT ...     eg repeat the question until the user chooses the correct answer.
```

NOTES

- Most packages are able to produce run-time versions - executable files that do not require the use of the original package to display them.
- Important as the video, sound and other components are, the final presentation is only as good as the skill of the designer - an issue beyond the scope of this chapter.

INDEX

A

Abort/Retry/Ignore	52, 159, 246
Accelerator cards	144, 147
Access Time (Discs)	151, 157, 163, 408
Access Time (Memory)	67, 68, 109, 143, 198, 203, 205, 209-11
Adaptive Routing	374
AND (logic)	76, 101, 389
ADPCM	430
Additive Mixing	125
Address Bus	67-8, 72,78-82, 90, 198, 203-4, 212, 215, 243
Address Clashes	313, 320, 324, 332, 335
'AIDS' virus	295, 305
Aliases using Doskey	168
ALU	67, 79, 80, 85, 86
Amphenol plug	117
Analogue screen drive	133
Animations	423, 436-37
Anti-Virus Software	300-303
ANSI	10, 153, 156, 164, 201
Anti-Aliasing	132
Anton Pillar order	24
AOL	382
APPEND command	162
Appending Virus	295
Archie	387
Archive attribute	41, 49, 50, 271, 282, 283
ASCII	10, 165, 386
Aspect ratio (monitors)	124, 131
Assembly Language	91-107
Asterisk as a wildcard	48
Asynchronous	210, 362, 434
AT command set	370-71
AT model PC	88, 90, 109, 251, 259, 261, 334, 337
ATAPI	260, 288
Attenuation	373
ATTRIB command	41, 49, 50, 193
Audio file formats	435-36
Audio on Demand	388
Audio Theory	428-29
AUTOEXEC.commands	161-168
AVI files	437, 439, 441, 442
AZERTY keyboard	162

B

Backache	136, 330
Backup	181, 183-4, 281-3, 309, 399
Bandwidth	85, 124, 142, 369, 272, 396
Bandwidth On Demand	396, 418
Baseband transmissions	411, 414, 415
Baud rate	165-166, 224, 240, 349, 366
Baudot	71
BCD	71
BCS	24
BEDO	113, 207, 211
Bi-directional	9, 119, 120, 239, 334, 376
Binary Numbering	68, 73-75
BIOS	31, 67, 82, 83,84, 90, 114, 129, 150, 199, 200, 204, 208, 227, 246, 252, 253, 259, 261, 267, 278-9, 297, 300, 342

BIOS extensions	114, 144, 148, 174
Bit	71
Bitmap (BMP) images	227, 229, 435, 436
Blue Book CD	289, 290
Boot Failure	327-28
Boot Record	268-69
Boot Sector Virus	297-98, 305
Bootstrapping	150
Branching (batch files)	183
BREAK	159
Breakout Box	364-65
Bridges	416
Broadband transmissions	414-15
BSA	24
Buffers	116
- Disc	151-52, 157, 169, 171
- DOSKEY	167-68
- Keyboard	53
- Pre-fetch	86, 89
- Printer	13, 216
- Video frame	142-43
- XCOPY	49
Bulletin Boards	284, 306, 318, 381-82, 445
Burst Mode	86, 89, 206, 211, 261, 444
Bus architectures	108-113
Byte	3, 4, 72

C

Cache controllers	264
Caching of discs	154-57, 216, 240-1, 265-66, 288, 322-3
Cache memory	87, 89-90, 205-207, 324
CALL in batch files	189
'Cascade' virus	295, 296, 305
CAV/ZCAV	287, 291, 292-3
CBT/CAL	425
CCITT	120, 360, 367, 368, 436
CD-I	443
CD command	43-44
CD ROM	16, 286-291, 426, 445
CD XA	289
CD-Bridge	290
CDFS	288, 290
CDR files	436
CD-R	287
Centronics	116, 117-9, 164, 165
CGA	17, 124, 129, 131, 133, 134, 141, 148, 310
CHKDSK command	273, 275-7, 309, 320
CHOICE in batch files	191-2
CH3 files	436
Cinepak	441, 442
CISC	89, 90
CIX	318
Client/Server systems	406
Client/Server software	422
Clipboard	59-60, 63, 436
Clipping level	248
Clock Multiplying	85, 87
Clock Speeds	72, 90
CLP files	60, 436
CLS	37

Cluster Virus   295
Clusters   246, 267-77, 320
CMF files   433, 437, 451
CMOS   207, 214, 261-2, 279, 329
CMYK   11, 125
Coaxial cable   401, 411
CODECs   440-43
Coercivity (Oersteds)   248, 252
Colour monitors   See 'Monitors'
Colour purity   127
COM   17, 18, 38, 120, 165-6, 224,
                             239, 334, 348, 359-61, 365
Command Calls, Order   177
Command recall   53, 167-8
COMMAND.COM   52, 151, 200-201, 305
Composite drive   133
Command line editing   53
Compression of files   283-4, 366-7, 379, 429, 430,
                             435-6, 440-42
Compression of discs   283, 285-6
COMPSPEC   159,166
Compuserve   318, 382
Computer Misuse Act   29
CON device   153, 164, 166
CONFIG.SYS   151-161, 175-6
Control Bus   67, 78-9
CONTROL.INI   233-34
Convergence   127, 138
Co-processors   87-8
Copying files   46-7, 48, 49, 54, 58, 59, 65
Copyright   23, 446, 447
CoreTest   323-24
Costing equipment   356-58
Country information   153, 162, 221, 223, 238, 240
CPI (chars per inch)   12
CPU - Introduction   3, 67, 78-81
   - Range of types   88-90
   - Clock Multiplying   85, 87
   - Fetch-Execute Cycle   81-2
   - Maths co-processors   5, 87-8
   - Pipelining   86
   - Pre-fetching   86, 89
   - Registers   79-80
   - Superscalar   86
CRC checks   246, 300, 367-8, 405
Creating DOS directories   44-5
Ctrl-Break keys   7, 159, 180
Cylinders   250-51, 253-4, 261-2, 267

D

'Dark Avenger' virus   296, 305
Data Bus   67-8, 78-82, 143, 198, 212-3,
                             335, 336
Data Protection Act   27, 31-3, 392, 393
Data Transfer Rate   108-13, 165, 256, 261, 288,
                             323-4, 366, 395-6, 401, 410-13,
                             415, 426, 443
DCE   359, 361-2, 364-5, 372
DDC1, DDC2   133
Deadlock   420
DEFRAG, defragmenters   274-5
Degaussing   127
DEL command   46, 48, 309
Deleting files   37, 45-6, 54, 58, 64, 234, 236,
                             272, 309

DELTREE command   45, 309
Density of discs   8-9, 245, 247-9, 250, 252, 253,
                             259, 290-1
Desktop settings   229, 237
Device drivers   15, 115, 163, 171-5, 201, 321,
                             349
Device Manager   119, 240, 243, 324, 333, 334,
                             345, 348, 349
DEVICEHIGH   172-3
Diagnostic Tools
   - MSD   117, 120, 174, 200, 319-20,
                             334, 335, 360, 366
   - CHKDSK   273, 275-7, 309, 320
   - Coretest   323-4
   - Checkit/WinCheckit   309, 318, 320, 324, 333, 334,
                             345
   - SmartMon   322-3
   - Device Manager   119, 240, 243, 324, 333, 334,
                             345, 348, 349
Dial-up lines   368, 373, 384
Digital Signal Processing   429, 431, 443
Digitised Sound   428-9
DIMMs   113, 213, 337
DIR command   40-41, 48, 168,
DIRCMD   163
DIrect Cable Connection   377
Directory structures   42-43
   - Changing Directory   43-4
   - Comparing Directories   188
   - Creating Directories   44-5, 58, 65
   - Path to directories   43
   - Removing Directories   45, 58, 64
   - Viewing structures   45-6, 53-4, 57, 64
Discs and Drives
   - Access Time   151, 157, 163, 408
   - Backup   181, 183-4, 281-3, 309, 399
   - Basics   8-9, 217
   - Cache controllers   264
   - Caching of discs   154-57, 216, 240-1, 265-66,
                             288, 322-3
   - Care of discs   9, 250
   - Clusters   246, 267-77, 320
   - Coercivity (Oersteds)   248, 252
   - Compression   283, 285-86
   - Controller cards   227, 256-63, 278-9, 327, 329
   - Density   8-9, 245, 247-9, 250, 252,
                             253, 259, 290-1
   - Directory Area   270-1, 273-4
   - DOS Boot Record   268-9
   - DOS organisation   266-74
   - DTR   See 'Data Transfer Rate'
   - Drives and the BIOS   See 'BIOS'
   - Encoding methods   257-8
   - Entry 47   262
   - FAT   252, 272-6, 320
   - Floppy discs   8-9, 245-50, 329, 343
   - Formatting   50-51, 58, 65-6, 246, 278-80
   - Fragmentation   274
   - Hard discs   250-64
   - Interleave   256-7
   - Interfaces   258-63
   - LBA   254
   - Long Filenames   278
   - Low level format   278
   - Master Boot Record   268
   - Magnetoresistive   253

- Partitioning   253-4, 268-9, 279-80
- PRML   253
- Recording terms   9
- RECOVER command   277
- SCANDISK   277, 309
- Sectors   9, 246-48, 251-4, 266-8
- Stepper motors   254
- Voice coils   254
- Write precompensation   262, 263-4
Disc Copying   49, 59, 297, 375-77
DLLs   234, 235
DMA   119, 243, 261, 324, 334, 366, 404-5
DNS   384
DOS   - What it is   36, 149
- Error messages   52, 150
- Filters   193-5
- Installation   178
- Pipes   195-6
- DOS from Windows   55, 66, 230
- Redirection   196-7
- Shell   53-4
- Upgrading   178
DOSKEY   167-8
Dot Pitch in monitors   130
Double Buffering   155
Down Time   312
DPMS power saving   128-9
DRAM   207, 209
Drivers   See 'Device Drivers'
DSE   359
DRIVER.SYS   158
DTE   359, 361-2, 364-5, 372
DVD   290-1
Dynamic Range   428-9

E

ECHO in batch files   166, 179-80, 197
EBCDIC numbering   71
ECC   214
EDO RAM   207, 208, 211
EEPROM   208-9
EGA   129, 131, 133, 134, 141
EIDE   260-61, 263, 342
EISA bus   110, 113
Elevator Seeking   251, 258, 265
ELSPA   24
E-Mail   374, 380, 384-6
EMS (Expanded)   170, 207, 215-7
Emulations   13, 375, 379
Energy Star Programme   113, 128
Enhanced Mode   218
Environment area   159, 166
Entry 47   262
EPP   119
EPROM   208-9
EPS files, Postscript   228, 436
Errorlevel   184, 190-91, 282
Error Detection (datacomms)   367-8
ESDI   259
EVGA   129,131
EXCLUDE command   174
Expanded Memory   170, 207, 215-7
Explorer   64-6
Extended Memory   169-77, 207, 215-6, 340

F

Fantavision   436
FASTOPEN command   162-3, 220
FAT   252, 272-6, 320
FAT32   277
Fault Finding   325-9
Fault Reports   319
FCBS   161, 163
FDDI   413, 417
FDISK   253-4, 268-9, 279-80
FDM   372
Feature connector   146, 439, 443, 444
Fetch-Decode-Execute   81-2
Fibre Optic cable   412-3
File attributes   41, 49, 50, 193, 271
File extensions   38-40
File Locking   419-20
File Manager   57-9
File names in DOS   38-9
FILES command   152
Filters in DOS   193-5
FIND   193-5
Fingerprinting   300
Firewire   121
Firewall   392
FLI files   437
Floppy discs   8-9, 245-50, 329, 343
Floptical Drives   293
Flow Control   118, 363-4
Fonts   13, 225, 227-8, 237, 239, 241
FOR IN DO (batch files)   187-9
Formatting discs   50-51, 58, 65-6, 246, 278-80
Fragmentation   274
Frame refresh speeds   123, 134, 143
Freeware   22
FTP   379, 380, 381, 386
Full-Duplex Data Links   372
Full-Motion Video (FMV)   290, 439-43

G

GIF files   435
Graphic File formats   435-6
Generic Virus Scanners   299-300
Glare from monitors   128, 136
Gopher   387
GOTO in batch files   176, 183-5
Graphics cards
- Connections   17, 141, 339
- Accelerator   144, 147
- Bandwidth   124, 142
- Chip Set   144
- Co-processor   144, 147
- RAM Size   141
- RAM Type   142
- RAMDACs   146
Green Book CD   289, 443

H

Hacking   29
Half-Duplex Data Links   368, 372
Handshaking   118, 363-4
Hayes AT commands   370-1
Heads   251, 252-3
Help Desk - Aims   315
- Aids   317
- Record Keeping   315-6

- Resources | 298
Help in DOS | 37
Help in Windows | 55, 51, 63
Hercules | 131, 134
Health & Safety - Acts | 27, 330-1
- Monitors | 135-7
- Safe Practices | 313-5
Hidden files | 41, 50, 271
HIMEM.SYS | 171-2
HMA | 171, 175, 207
HPGL files | 436
HTML | 390
Hypertext | 425, 427, 448

I

IDE | 251, 253, 357, 259-60, 261, 263, 279
IF EXIST in batch files | 185
IF in batch files | 184
IFF files | 430
INCLUDE command | 174
Indeo | 441, 442
Information Superhighway | 395-6
Information Processing | 20-21, 26-28
INI Files | 231-4, 241, 244
Installing DOS | 178
Interactive Video | 425, 443
Interfacing methods | 116
Interlaced monitors | 124
Interleave for discs | 256-7
Interleave for memory | 210
Interleave for video | 437, 439, 440
Interlink | 376-7
Intermittent Problems | 328
Internet | 318, 383-394
- Administration | 383
- Audio | 444
- Browsers | 388, 391
- E-Mail | 385-6
- File Transfer | 386
- Firewalls | 392
- HTML | 390
- Phones | 444
- TCP/IP | 380
- User Addresses | 384
- User Groups | 387
- URLs | 388
- World Wide Web | 388
Interrupts (IRQs) | 82-4, 95, 324, 333-4, 348
Intranets | 392
IO.SYS | 150, 200
IP addresses | 384-5
ISA bus | 109
ISDN | 395-6
ISO/OSI 7-Layer Model | 378
ISO 9002 | 356
ISO 9241 | 135-6
ISO 9660 | 285
ISO IS2110 | 120, 360

J

JAVA | 444
'Jerusalem' virus | 295, 296, 305
'Joshi' virus | 295, 305
JPEG/MJPEG files | 284, 436, 440, 441, 442, 443
Jughead | 382

K

KERMIT | 367, 368, 372
KEYB command | 162
Keyboard - Key groups | 6-7
- Cleaning | 308
- Failure | 327
- In Windows | 221-2, 238
- RSI | 331
- Settings | 166
Kerr Effect | 292
KiloStream | 373
Kodak Photo CD | 290

L

LABEL command | 50
Labels in batch files | 183-4
Local Area Networks | 21, 397
- LANs and Unix | 398
- Advantages/Features | 399-401
- Topologies | 401-3
- Collisions | 403
- Interface cards | 404-6
- Servers | 406
- Print Servers | 409
- Media | 409-13
- Cabling | 415-6
- Software | 419-22
- Client/Server | 422
- RAID | 408
- Peer-to-peer | 409
- LAN standards | 415
- 100Base-T | 417
- 100VG | 418
- Switched Ethernet | 418
LASTDRIVE command | 156
Latency period | 255
LBA | 254
Liquid Crystal Display | 139, 222, 238
Library for media storage | 34
Licensing agreements | 22-3
Line refresh speeds | 123, 134
LOADHIGH | 172
Local bus systems | 111-2
- VESA bus | 112
- PCI bus | 112-3
- PCMCIA | 114-5
Logic operators | 76
Long Filenames | 278
Low level format | 260, 278-9
LRU algorithm | 265
LZW (Lempel-Ziv-Welch) | 284, 435

M

Macros with DOSKEY | 168
Macros in Windows | 60
Macros virus | 294, 298
Magneto-Optical Drives | 292-3
Maintenance programme | 307-311
Maintenance contracts | 306-7
Main Group in Windows | 56
Maths co-processors | 5, 87-8
Master Boot Record (MBR) | 268-69
MCA bus | 110, 113
MCGA | 131
MD command | 44-5
MDA | 131, 134

MDRAM   207, 211
Media Change Line   250
MegaHertz   5, 72
MegaStream   373
MEM command   169-70
MemMaker   173-4
Memory - Basics   3-4
    - Access   198, 203-4
    - Bus   111
    - Burst Mode   86, 89, 206, 211
    - Cache   87, 89-90, 205-207, 324
    - CMOS   207, 214, 261-2, 279, 329
    - DIMMs   113, 213, 337
    - DIPs   211
    - DRAM   207, 209
    - ECC   214
    - EDO   207, 211, 212
    - EEPROM   209
    - EMS (Expanded)   170, 207, 215-7
    - Environment   159, 166
    - EPROM   208-9
    - FPM   210
    - HMA   171, 175, 207
    - Interleaving   210
    - Management   169-77, 215-7
    - Parity   213-4
    - PROM   208
    - ROM   3, 67, 150, 204, 208
    - SIMMs   212-3
    - SRAM   207, 210
    - Synchronous   210
    - UMB   170, 172-3
    - User area   170, 199, 201, 207
    - VRAM   142-3, 207
    - WRAM   207, 211
    - XMS (Extended)   169-77, 207, 215-6, 340
Merging files   47
MFLOPs   4, 85
MFM   257-8, 279
MIME   386
MIRROR command   168, 297
MNP   337, 339, 341
Modems
    - Definition   16, 361
    - Error Detection   367
    - Handshaking   363
    - Hayes AT Commands   369-71
    - Modem Lights   371
    - Modulation   366
    - Parity   362-3
    - Synchronisation   362
    - 'V' standards   368
    - 56k Modems   369
    - Wiring   361
Monitor - Adjustments   94, 111-2, 293-4
    - Aspect ratio   124
    - Bandwidth   124, 142
    - Basics   5
    - Checks   327
    - Cleaning   308
    - Colour principles   125
    - Colour purity   127
    - Connections   141
    - Convergence   127, 138
    - DDC1/2   133
    - Degaussing   127
    - Dot Pitch   130
    - Energy saving   128-9
    - Frame/Line refresh speeds 123
    - Health & Safety   135-7
    - Interlacing   124
    - Modulation   123
    - Resolution   129
    - Scanning   122
    - Screen drives   133
    - Screen sizes   132
    - Shadow Mask tube   126-7
    - Synchronisation   124, 134
    - Trinitron tubes   128
    - VESA video modes   148
    - Video standards   130-2, 148
MIDI   434, 441
MIME   386
MODE command   164-5
MORE   193
Motherboard   3, 337, 352
Mouse   2, 14-5, 56, 163-4, 222, 238
MOVE command   47, 54, 58, 65
MPC1, MPC2, MPC3   426
MPEG, MPEG2   147, 441, 443
MSVC   441
MSD   See 'Diagnostic Tools'
MSDOS.SYS   150, 200
MSN   383
MTBF   255, 356
Multi-configuration   175-6
Multimedia
    - Basics   423
    - Applications   423-4
    - Animations   436-7
    - Audio File Formats   430
    - Audio Theory   428-9
    - Project Design   448-50
    - Forerunners   425
    - Full-Motion Video   439-261, 355, 391-2, 395
    - Graphic Files   435-6, 438
    - MIDI   434, 441
    - Music Basics   432-3
    - Music File Formats   433
    - Recording/Editing   430-31
    - Standards   426
    - Sound Cards   345, 431-2
    - Software   447
Multiplexors   **372, 414**
Multi-tasking systems   55, 114, 203, 218-9

N

Navigation Map   448
Native Signal Processing   443
Network Computers   404
Network interface cards   404-6
Network routing   374
Nibble   71
Noise   373
'Nomenclatura' virus   305
NOT logic   77, 389
NTSC   439, 441
Null Modem Cable   375, 376, 377, 410
Numbering Systems
    - Decimal   68
    - ASCII   10, 70
    - Baudot   71

- BCD	71
- Binary	68
- EBCDIC	71
- Hexadecimal	69-70, 75
- Octal	71
NUMLOCK command	160

O

Octal Numbering	71
Oersteds	248, 252
OR logic	77
Orange Book CD	290
OSI standards	See 'ISO'
Overdrive chips	336
Over-writing Virus	295
Overlays	203

P

P-Rating	85
PAL	133, 439, 441, 442
Parallel Port	116, 117-9, 164, 165
Parity for memory	213-4
Parity bit (datacomms)	362-3
Partitioning	253-4, 268-9, 279-80
Passwords	31, 304, 384, 386, 392
PATHs	43, 161
PAUSE in batch files	179, 180
PCMCIA	114-5
PCI Chipsets	113
PCX files	435-6
Peer-to-Peer	409
Pentium/Pro CPU	86-7, 89-90, 336
Photo CD	290
Partition Sector Virus	297-8
Phase Change CD	293
Pipelining	86
Pipes in DOS	195-6
Piracy	23-5
Platters	250-52
Plotters	16
Plug And Play	61, 114, 115, 120
Pointing Devices	See 'Mouse'
POP (Net connection)	383
POP (e-mail)	380
POST	150, 213, 326-7
PPP	381
Pre-fetching	86, 89
Pre-pending Virus	295
PRINT command	37-8
Print Servers	409
Printer	2, 9-14
- Connection	116, 117-9, 164, 165
- Adding Paper	14
- Buffers	13, 216
- Types	9-12
- Emulations	13
- Fonts	13, 227-8, 241
- In Windows	223-5, 239-40
- Postscript	13
- Print quality	12
- Printer characters	10-11, 70
- Printer drivers	13, 201
- Proportional spacing	12
- With DOS	37-8,164-6
PRML	253
PRN device	37-8, 153, 164

Processing Systems	20-1
PROGMAN.INI	234
Program Groups/Items	56, 229-30
Program Manager	55-6, 226,
PROM	208
PROMPT command	162
PrtScrn	7, 18, 37
Protocol Stack	381
PSTN	373
PSDN	374
Public Domain software	22
Purity	127

Q

QuickTime	439, 441
Quad density discs	8, 9, 247-8

R

Radiation from monitors	135
RAID	408
RAMDACs	146
RAMDRIVE	156-7
RAW files	430
RD command	45, 58, 64
RDRAM	207, 211
Read Attribute	50, 271
Real-time systems	21
Recorder in Windows	60
Record Locking	420-21
Recordable CD	287
Recording/Editing a sound	430-31
RECOVER command	277
Red Book CDs	289
Redirection	196
Registry	244
Renaming files	47, 58, 65
Repeaters	416
Replaceable parameters	182
Resolution of monitors	129
Restoring from a backup	282
RGB drive	126, 133, 134
RLE	435, 436, 441
RISC	89-90
RLL	257
ROL files	433
ROM	3, 67, 150, 204, 208
ROM Shadowing	204
RS232	See 'Serial Port'
RSI	331

S

Sampling rate for audio	429
SatStream	373
SCANDISK	277, 309
Scanners	16, 345, 446
Screen sizes	132
SCSI	254, 257, 261, 262-3, 342
SDRAM	207, 211
SECAM	439
Sectors of discs	9, 246-48, 251-4, 266-8
Security	29-31
Seek Time	227, 263-4, 286, 313
Serial Port	17, 120, 165-6, 224, 240, 348, 365-6
Servers	406-9
SETVER command	160

SGRAM	207, 211
Shadow Mask tube	126-7
SHARE command	163, 419
Shareware	23
SHELL command	158
SHIFT in batch files	189
SIF	441
Signature Scanning	299
SIMD	89
SIMMs	212-3
Simplex Data Link	372, 379
Single-tasking systems	20-21
SIPs	210, 211
Sleuth/Winsleuth	333-5, 345, 348
SLIP	381
SMARTDRV	154-7, 216, 264-6
SmartMon	322-3
Socket	381
Software - Application	20
- Freeware	22
- Installation	25-6
- Licensing agreements	22
- Piracy	23-4
- PD/Shareware	22-3
- System	19
Software Audits	24-5
SORT	192, 195-6
Sound Cards	345, 431-2
SPAudit	25
SRAM	207, 210
ST412	258
ST506	258
STACKS command	160
Standard Mode (Windows)	218
Star Networks	402
Start Menu	62-3, 242
Stealth Virus	295, 298, 302
Stepper motors	254
'Stoned' Virus	297, 305
STP	410
SUBST command	159
Subtractive mixing	125
Superscalar architecture	86
SVGA	129, 131, 134, 339
Swap Files in Windows	225-6, 241
SYSEDIT	233
System Area of memory	199
System floppy discs	51, 58, 178
SYSTEM.INI	231

T

TaskBar	62, 63, 242
Task Manager in Windows	59
TCO-92	129, 136
TCP/IP	380-81
'Telefonica' virus	298, 305
'Tequila' virus	296, 298, 301, 305
Teleworking	376, 393
TELNET	379, 380, 381
TFT	140
TGA files	436
ThinNet / Thicknet	411
TIFF files	436
Time Bomb	294, 297
Token-Ring	401-2
Trackerball	14, 16

Tracks on discs	245-7, 250
Transceivers	411
Trees	42-6
Trinitron	127, 128
Trojan Horse	294, 297
TrueType Fonts	227
TSRs	202-3
TTL	123, 124
Twain	446
Twisted Pair cable	410

U

UART	348, 359, 366
ULAW files	430
Undeleting files	46, 61, 65, 272
Uninstalling Windows components	234, 236
Upgrading DOS	178
Upgrading a PC	
- Adding memory	340
- Connecting a mouse	343
- Fitting a CD ROM	346
- Fitting a CPU upgrade	336
- Fitting a floppy drive	343
- Fitting a network card	347
- Fitting a second IDE	341-2
- Fitting a serial port	348
- Fitting a sound card	345
- Fitting a scanner	345
- Fitting a ZIP drive	349
- Fitting a UPS	344
- Upgrading a motherboard	337
- Upgrading to an IDE drive	341
- Upgrading to an EIDE drive	342
- Upgrading to a SCSI drive	342
- Upgrading video	338-9
Unified Memory Architecture (UMA)	204
Upper Memory Area	199, 207
Upper Memory Blocks	172-5, 207
UPS	328, 344
URLs	388
USB	204
UTP	410

V

'V' standards for modems	368
Variables in batch files	197
Vcache	156, 240-41, 264, 266, 277
Vector images	435
VERIFY command	49
VESA	112, 113, 148, 204, 444
VGA	129, 131, 134, 339
Video Accelerators	144, 147
Virtual memory	225-6, 241
Viruses	
- Definitions/Methods	294-7
- Anti-Virus products	300-302
- Boot Sector Problems	297
- Common Viruses	305
- File Viruses	298
- Fingerprinting	300
- Macro	298
- Scanning Techniques	298
- Virus Activity	296
- Virus Elimination	302
- Virus Prevention	303-4
VM-Channel	146, 444

VOC files   430, 431
VOL command   37
Von Neuman architecture   86, 198
VRAM   142-3, 207, 211
Virtual Reality   392, 445
VTOC   287
VxD   302

_____W_____

WAIS   396
Wait states   121, 205
WAV files   430
Wavetable   432
White Book CD   289, 290, 443
Wildcards   48
WIN.INI   232
Windows 3.1
  - Basics   55-6
  - Accessories Group   57
  - Altering options   220-234
  - Clipboard   59
  - Custom Objects   230
  - Desktop   229, 237
  - DOS Prompt   55, 66, 230
  - Enhanced Mode   218
  - File Manager   57-9
  - Fonts   227-8
  - INI files   231-4
  - Installation   219-20
  - Main Group   56
  - Printers   223-5
  - Program Groups/Items   56, 229-30
  - Program Manager   55
  - Recorder   60
  - Standard Mode   218
  - Task Manager   59
  - Virtual memory   225-6
  - Wallpaper   229, 232
Windows 95
  - Accessories Menu   63
  - Adding Hardware   349
  - Basics   61

  - Device Manager   243
  - Diagnostics   324
  - Display   237
  - Explorer   64-6
  - Fonts   241
  - Hardware Requirements 61
  - Installing   235-6
  - Keyboard   238
  - Mouse   238
  - OSR2   236
  - Printers   239-40
  - Registry   244
  - Start Menu   62-3, 242
  - TaskBar   66
  - Uninstalling   236
  - Virtual memory   241
  - Viruses   302
Winsock   381
WMF files   436
Worm drive   286, 293
WRAM   143, 207, 211
Write Precompensation   263
WWW (World Wide Web)   388-92
WYSIWYG   129, 227

_____X_____

XCOPY command   49
XGA   141, 144, 147
XModem   367, 368
XMS (Extended Memory)   169-77, 207, 215-6, 340
XOn/XOff   364, 371
XOR logic   77
XT model PC   108, 113

_____Y_____

Yellow Book CD   289
YModem   368

_____Z_____

ZIF socket   336
ZModem   368
Zoo compression   283